**W9-CNV-299**

# TEST ITEMS
*AND*
# INTERACTIVE ELECTRONIC STUDY GUIDE QUESTIONS

FOR STARR'S
# B I O L O G Y
*Concepts and Applications*
*Third Edition*

LARRY G. SELLERS
Louisiana Tech University

DAVID J. COTTER
Georgia College

KENDALL CORBIN
University of Minnesota

JOHN D. JACKSON
North Hennepin Community College

ALLEN REICH
Harvard University

JANE B. TAYLOR
Northern Virginia Community College

TOMMY E. WYNN
North Carolina State University

**Wadsworth Publishing Company**
I(T)P® An International Thomson Publishing Company

Belmont, CA • Albany, NY • Bonn • Boston • Cincinnati • Detroit • Johannesburg
London • Madrid • Melbourne • Mexico City • New York • Paris • San Francisco
Singapore • Tokyo • Toronto • Washington

# Preface

This book contains over 4,000 test items and interactive electronic study guide questions to accompany Starr's *Biology: Concepts and Applications*, Third Edition. The test items and electronic study guide questions are available on disk.

We hope you find these questions useful, and we welcome any comments that will help to improve them.

## Test Items

Several instructors contributed to the test bank, including three who have extensive experience writing questions for the Educational Testing Service. Eight reviewers also have contributed valuable suggestions to help eliminate inadvertent ambiguity and to check for possible errors. The test bank represents a consensus of the kind of questions that are most suitable for students.

All questions are ranked according to level of difficulty (E = Easy, M = Moderate, and D = Difficult). (On the disk version of the test bank, because of the requirements of the test-generator program, 1 = Easy, 3 = Moderate, and 5 = Difficult.) Each rank is represented by about a third of the total questions. The Test Items section of this book includes the following categories:

1. Multiple-choice questions
2. Matching questions
3. Classification questions, which use the same group of answers for a series of questions.
4. Select the Exception questions, which require the student to select the exception from four or five given answers.
5. Problems, which appear only in two of the genetics chapters.

## Interactive Electronic Study Guide Questions

When students take multiple-choice exams they are often not told why a particular answer is correct and are almost never told why a choice is wrong. The Interactive Electronic Study Guide includes this feedback, thus improving the ability of students to learn the material. In addition to being used as a learning tool by students, the electronic study guide questions can be used as test items.

The Electronic Study Guide is interactive because students choosing the wrong answer are told the answer is incorrect and why. Students choosing the correct answer are told they are right and information is given to justify the correct choice. On the electronic disk the answers also identify the text reference and topic so that students can refer back to the text for review. The level of understanding necessary to answer the questions varies as does the level of detail being covered. This approach encourages students to completely cover the test and to read the tables, figure legends, and commentaries.

# Test Items

# Table of Contents

1    Methods and Concepts in Biology......................................................................1

2    Chemical Foundations for Cells ....................................................................6

3    Cell Structure and Function .........................................................................15

4    Ground Rules of Metabolism .......................................................................21

5    Energy-Acquiring Pathways .........................................................................26

6    Energy-Releasing Pathways .........................................................................30

7    Cell Division and Mitosis .............................................................................35

8    Meiosis .........................................................................................................39

9    Observable Patterns of Inheritance .............................................................43

10    Chromosomes and Human Genetics ............................................................57

11    DNA Structure and Function........................................................................66

12    From DNA to Proteins..................................................................................70

13    Recombinant DNA and Genetic Engineering..............................................76

14    Microevolution ............................................................................................80

15    Speciation ....................................................................................................86

16    The Macroevolutionary Puzzle ...................................................................92

17    The Origin and Evolution of Life ...............................................................97

18    Bacteria, Viruses, and Protistans ................................................................104

19    Plants and Fungi...........................................................................................114

20    Animals: The Invertebrates..........................................................................122

21    Animals: The Vertebrates ............................................................................130

22    Plant Tissue .................................................................................................140

23    Plant Nutrition and Transport .....................................................................145

24    Plant Reproduction and Development .........................................................150

25    Tissues, Organ Systems, and Homeostasis..................................................158

26    Protection, Support, and Movement............................................................163

27    Circulation ...................................................................................................168

28    Immunity......................................................................................................174

29    Respiration...................................................................................................180

30    Digestion and Human Nutrition ..................................................................184

31    The Internal Environment............................................................................191

32    Neural Control and the Senses.....................................................................197

33    Integration and Control: Endocrine Systems...............................................213

**34**      Reproduction and Development ................................................220

**35**      Population Ecology ................................................230

**36**      Community Interactions ................................................236

**37**      Ecosystems ................................................243

**38**      The Biosphere ................................................249

**39**      Human Impact on the Biosphere ................................................257

**40**      Animal Behavior ................................................262

# CHAPTER 1
# METHODS AND CONCEPTS IN BIOLOGY

## Multiple-Choice Questions

### ORGANIZATION IN NATURE

E    **1.** Which is the smallest unit of life that can exist as a separate entity?
*    a   a cell
   b.   a molecule
   c.   an organ
   d.   a population
   e.   an ecosystem

E    **2.** Which of the following is defined as "all of the various species living in the same area?"
   a   ecosystem
*    b.   community
   c.   biosphere
   d.   organism
   e.   population

E    **3.** The chemical processes in the living cell are collectively called
   a   adaptation.
   b.   homeostasis.
   c.   evolution.
   d.   respiration.
*    e.   metabolism.

E    **4.** During metabolism, ATP (adenosine triphosphate) is an energy source for the following processes:
   a   reproduction and growth
   b.   reproduction and maintenance
   c.   growth
   d.   growth and maintenance
*    e.   reproduction, growth, and maintenance

E    **5.** The ability to acquire, store, transfer, or utilize energy is called
   a   biochemistry.
   b.   photosynthesis.
*    c.   metabolism.
   d.   respiration.
   e.   phosphorylation.

E    **6.** Organisms designated producers obtain their energy from
   a   other producers.
   b.   dead consumers.
   c.   decomposers.
*    d.   the sun.
   e.   all of the above.

### SENSING AND RESPONDING TO THE ENVIRONMENT

E    **7.** The ability to maintain a constant internal environment is
   a   metabolism.
*    b.   homeostasis.
   c.   development.
   d.   physiology.
   e.   thermoregulation.

E    **8.** Homeostasis provides what kind of environment?
   a   positive
*    b.   constant
   c.   limiting
   d.   changing
   e.   chemical and physical

M    **9.** The adjective that best describes homeostasis in living organisms is
   a   rigid.
   b.   biological.
*    c.   dynamic.
   d.   chemical.
   e.   physical.

E    **10.** Each cell is able to maintain a constant internal environment. This is called
   a   metabolism.
*    b.   homeostasis.
   c.   physiology.
   d.   adaptation.
   e.   evolution.

M    **11.** About 12 to 24 hours after the last meal, a person's blood sugar level normally varies from 60 to 90 milligrams per 100 milliliters of blood, although it may rise to 130 mg/100 ml after meals high in carbohydrates. That the blood sugar level is maintained within a fairly narrow range despite uneven intake of sugar is due to the body's ability to carry out
   a   adaptation.
   b.   inheritance.
   c.   metabolism.
*    d.   homeostasis.
   e.   all of the above

### CONTINUITY AND CHANGE—THE NATURE OF INHERITANCE

M    **12.** A fertilized moth egg passes through which stages of development before becoming an adult?
   a   larval
   b.   pupal
*    c.   larval and pupal
   d.   larval and reproductive
   e.   pupal and reproductive

E 13. Hereditary instructions must
    a be unchanging most of the time.
    b. pass from one generation to the next.
    c. control a large number of different characteristics.
    d. provide for the rare change in instructions.
  * e. all of the above

E 14. A mutation is a change in
    a homeostasis.
    b. the developmental pattern in an organism.
    c. metabolism.
  * d. hereditary instructions.
    e. the life cycle of an organism.

## SO MUCH UNITY, YET SO MANY SPECIES

M 15. All organisms are alike in
    a their requirements for energy.
    b. their participation in one or more nutrient cycles.
    c. their ultimate dependence on the sun.
    d. their interaction with other forms of life.
  * e. all of the above

E 16. The genus portion of a scientific name when written by hand is
    a never capitalized; never underlined.
  * b. always underlined; always capitalized.
    c. always capitalized; never underlined.
    d. never capitalized; always underlined.
    e. connected with the species names to form one word.

E 17. The plural for genus is
    a genus.
    b. geni.
  * c. genera.
    d. genuses.
    e. genae.

E 18. Which group includes all of the other groups?
  * a phylum
    b. order
    c. family
    d. genus
    e. species

E 19. A scientific name consists of which of the following?
    a family name
    b. genus name
    c. species
    d. both a and b
  * e. both b and c

M 20. The least inclusive of the taxonomic categories listed here is
    a family.
    b. phylum.
    c. class.
    d. order.
  * e. genus.

E 21. Members of what kingdom are single cells of considerable internal complexity?
    a Animalia
  * b. Protista
    c. Fungi
    d. Plantae
    e. Monera

E 22. Members of what kingdom are multicellular producers?
    a Animalia
    b. Protista
    c. Fungi
  * d. Plantae
    e. Monera

## AN EVOLUTIONARY VIEW OF LIFE'S DIVERSITY

E 23. The animals used by Darwin to show variation in domesticated forms were
  * a pigeons.
    b. chickens.
    c. pigs.
    d. dogs.
    e. cats.

M 24. The principal point of the Darwin theory of evolution by natural selection was that
    a long-term heritable changes in organisms are caused by use and disuse.
    b. those mutations that adapt an organism to a given environment somehow always arise in the greatest frequency in the organisms that occupy that environment.
    c. mutations are caused by all sorts of environmental influences.
  * d. survival of characteristics in a population depends on competition between organisms, especially between members of the same species.
    e. all of the above

M 25. Which premise used by Darwin in his theory is incorrectly stated?
    a More offspring are produced than can survive to reproduce.
    b. Members of populations show heritable variation.
    c. Some varieties have a better chance to survive and reproduce.
  * d. Organisms that possess advantageous traits have a decreased chance of producing offspring.
    e. Some traits become more common because their bearers contribute more offspring to the next generation.

## THE NATURE OF BIOLOGICAL INQUIRY

M 26. A scientific principle is a(n)
    a  observable fact of nature.
  * b.  synthesis of several explanations of many observations.
    c.  scientific statement.
    d.  testable hypothesis.
    e.  experimental procedure.

M 27. Of the following, which is the first explanation of a problem? It is sometimes called an "educated guess."
    a.  principle
    b.  law
    c.  theory
    d.  fact
  * e.  hypothesis

E 28. Hypotheses are
    a.  often in the form of a statement.
    b.  often expressed negatively.
    c.  sometimes crude attempts to offer a possible explanation for observations.
    d.  testable predictions.
  * e.  all of the above

E 29. Which statement is true about observations in the scientific process?
    a.  They are made directly.
    b.  They are made indirectly.
    c.  Special equipment may be necessary.
    d.  They may be made with an instrument such as a microscope.
  * e.  all of the above

E 30. Who first stated that the Earth circled the sun?
    a.  Galileo Galilei
  * b.  Nicolaus Copernicus
    c.  Sir Isaac Newton
    d.  Cecie Starr
    e.  Johannes Kepler

E 31. In a scientific experiment, conditions that could affect the outcome of the experiment, but do not because they are held constant, are called
    a.  independent variables.
    b.  dependent variables.
  * c.  controlled variables.
    d.  statistical variables.
    e.  data set.

M 32. To eliminate the influence of uncontrolled variables during experimentation, one should
    a.  increase the sampling error as much as possible and suspend judgment.
  * b.  establish a control group identical to the experimental group except for the variable being tested.
    c.  use inductive reasoning to construct a hypothesis.
    e.  all of the above

E 33. Which represents the lowest degree of certainty?
  * a.  hypothesis
    b.  conclusion
    c.  fact
    d.  principle
    e.  theory

E 34. In order to arrive at a solution to a problem, a scientist usually proposes and tests
    a.  laws.
    b.  theories.
  * c.  hypotheses.
    d.  principles.
    e.  facts.

D 35. Which statement could be considered a scientific principle?
    a.  Beauty pageant contestants are becoming increasingly more beautiful.
    b.  Chemistry and physics are more exact sciences than biology.
  * c.  Radioactive isotopes can be used as tracers because radioactive isotopes behave the same as other isotopes.
    d.  The growth of a plant is faster in a growth chamber than in a greenhouse.
    e.  Leaves bend toward the light because they know light is needed to grow.

M 36. The control in an experiment
    a.  makes the experiment valid.
    b.  is an additional replicate for statistical purposes.
    c.  reduces the experimental errors.
    d.  minimizes experimental inaccuracy.
  * e.  allows a standard of comparison for the experimental group.

D 37. Which statement is false?
    a.  It is easier to prove something false than true.
    b.  Scientific experiments have limited applications.
    c.  Experimental data are valid if they can be repeatedly obtained by the same experiment.
  * d.  Scientific conclusions are invalid if any step in the scientific method is omitted.
    e.  Good science often uses experimentation.

M 38. An experimenter does all but which of the following?
    a.  revises a hypothesis as a result of data collected
  * b.  manipulates dependent variables
    c.  reviews other research results obtained by other scientists
    d.  examines the effects of independent variables
    e.  draws conclusions based only on appropriate experimental data

M   39.   As a result of experimentation
          a   more hypotheses may be developed.
          b.  more questions may be asked.
          c.  a new biological principle could emerge.
          d.  entire theories may be modified or
              discarded.
       *  e.  all of the above

M   40.   In an experiment, the control group
          a   is not subjected to experimental error.
          b.  is exposed to experimental treatments.
       *  c.  is maintained under strict laboratory
              conditions.
          d.  is treated exactly the same as the
              experimental group, except for the one
              independent variable.
          e.  is statistically the most important part of the
              experiment.

E   41.   The choice of whether a particular organism
          belongs to the experimental group or the control
          group should be based on
          a   age.
          b.  size.
       *  c.  chance.
          d.  designation by the experimenter.
          e.  sex.

## THE LIMITS OF SCIENCE

E   42.   The validity of scientific discoveries should be
          based on
          a   morality.
          b.  aesthetics.
          c.  philosophy.
          d.  economics.
       *  e.  none of the above

E   43.   Science is based on
          a   faith.
          b.  authority.
       *  c.  evidence.
          d.  force.
          e.  consensus.

M   44.   After an experiment is completed and the results
          are collected, the next step is to
          a   resample the data.
          b.  generalize from the conclusion.
          c.  randomize the results.
       *  d.  organize the data.
          e.  manipulate the results.

## Classification Questions

Answer questions 45–48 by matching the statement to the most appropriate function, process, or trait listed below.
          a   metabolism
          b.  reproduction
          c.  photosynthesis
          d.  growth
          e.  homeostasis

M   45.   A process found only in plants and some bacteria

E   46.   Most organisms exhibit this characteristic that
          tends to buffer the effects of
          environmental change

M   47.   The capacity to acquire, store, and use energy

E   48.   Process in which one generation replaces another

*Answers:*   45.  c      46.  e      47.  a
             48.  b

Answer questions 49–56 by matching the statement with the most appropriate kingdom listed below.
          a   Monera
          b.  Protista
          c.  Plantae
          d.  Fungi
          e.  Animalia

E   49.   Multicellular producers

E   50.   Bacteria

M   51.   Unicellular organisms of considerable internal
          complexity

M   52.   Multicellular consumers

E   53.   First living organisms

M   54.   One-celled producers

D   55.   Multicelled producers

M   56.   Multicelled decomposers

*Answers:*   49.  c      50.  a      51.  b
             52.  e      53.  a      54.  b
             55.  c      56.  d

## Selecting the Exception

E    **57.**  Four of the five answers listed below are
            necessary characteristics to the life of an
            individual.  Select the exception.
            a   metabolism
            b.  homeostasis
            c.  development
            d.  heredity
          * e.  diversity

E    **58.**  Four of the five answers listed below are aspects
            of the scientific method. Select the exception.
            a   observation
            b.  hypothesis
            c.  experimentation
          * d.  philosophy
            e.  conclusion

M    **59.**  Four of the five answers listed below are terms
            associated with the scientific method.  Select the
            exception.
          * a   fact
            b.  theory
            c.  principle
            d.  law
            e.  hypothesis

M    **60.**  Four of the five answers listed below are
            taxonomic categories.  Select the exception.
            a   family
          * b.  kind
            c.  species
            d.  order
            e.  genus

D    **61.**  Four of the five answers listed below are
            deductions made by Charles Darwin. Select
            the exception.
            a   natural selection is a result of differential
                reproduction
            b.  much of biological variation is heritable
            c.  more offspring are produced than can
                survive
          * d.  mutations produce changes in inheritance
            e.  some variations of heritable traits improve
                chances of survival

M    **62.**  Four of the five answers listed below are
            characteristics of life.  Select the exception.
          * a   ionization
            b.  metabolism
            c.  reproduction
            d.  growth
            e.  cellular organization

M    **63.**  Four of the five answers listed below are names
            of kingdoms. Select the exception.
            a   Animalia
            b.  Protista
          * c.  Bacteria
            d.  Fungi
            e.  Plantae

# CHAPTER 2
# CHEMICAL FOUNDATIONS FOR CELLS

## Multiple-Choice Questions

**REGARDING THE ATOMS**

M    **1.** Which is the smallest portion of a substance that retains the properties of an element?
    *   a. atom
      b. compound
      c. ion
      d. molecule
      e. mixture

E    **2.** The atom that represents the greatest weight in the human body is
      a. hydrogen.
      b. carbon.
      c. nitrogen.
    *   d. oxygen.
      e. phosphorus.

E    **3.** The negative subatomic particle is the
      a. neutron.
      b. proton.
    *   c. electron.
      d. both a and b
      e. b and c

E    **4.** The positive subatomic particle is the
      a. neutron.
    *   b. proton.
      c. electron.
      d. both a and b
      e. b and c

E    **5.** The neutral subatomic particle is the
    *   a. neutron.
      b. proton.
      c. electron.
      d. both a and b
      e. none of the above

E    **6.** Which components of an atom do not have a charge?
      a. electrons
      b. protons
    *   c. neutrons
      d. both a and b
      e. both b and c

E    **7.** The atomic number refers to the
      a. mass of an atom.
    *   b. number of protons in an atom.
      c. number of both protons and neutrons in an atom.
      d. number of neutrons in an atom.
      e. number of electrons in an atom.

M    **8.** The atomic number is determined by the number of
      a. neutrons and protons.
      b. neutrons and electrons.
      c. protons and electrons.
    *   d. protons only.
      e. neutrons only.

E    **9.** All atoms of an element have the same number of
      a. ions.
    *   b. protons.
      c. neutrons.
      d. electrons.
      e. protons and neutrons.

E    **10.** The nucleus of an atom contains
    *   a. neutrons and protons.
      b. neutrons and electrons.
      c. protons and electrons.
      d. protons only.
      e. neutrons only.

M    **11.** The atomic weight (or mass) of an atom is determined by the weight of
    *   a. neutrons and protons.
      b. neutrons and electrons.
      c. protons and electrons.
      d. protons only.
      e. neutrons only.

D    **12.** If the atomic weight of carbon is 12 and the atomic weight of oxygen is 16, the molecular weight of glucose $C_6H_{12}O_6$ expressed in grams is
      a. 24 grams.
      b. 28 grams.
      c. 52 grams.
      d. 168 grams.
    *   e. 180 grams.

M    **13.** Radioactive isotopes
      a. are electrically unbalanced.
      b. behave the same chemically and physically but differ biologically from other isotopes.
      c. are the same physically and biologically but differ from other isotopes chemically.
    *   d. have an excess number of neutrons.
      e. are produced when substances are exposed to radiation.

M    **14.** Radioactive isotopes have
      a. excess electrons.
      b. excess protons.
    *   c. excess neutrons.
      d. insufficient neutrons.
      e. insufficient protons.

M 15. Radioactive iodine tends to concentrate in the
    a  heart.
    b.  lungs.
    c.  gonads.
    d.  bones.
*     e.  thyroid glands.

## WHAT IS A CHEMICAL BOND?

E 16. Which components of an atom are negatively charged?
*     a  electrons
    b.  protons
    c.  neutrons
    d.  both a and b
    e.  both b and c

M 17. Magnesium has 12 protons. How many electrons are in its third energy level?
*     a  2
    b.  4
    c.  6
    d.  8
    e.  10

M 18. Magnesium has 12 protons. How many electrons are in its first energy level?
*     a  2
    b.  4
    c.  6
    d.  8
    e.  10

M 19. Magnesium has 12 protons. How many electrons are in its second energy level?
    a  2
    b.  4
    c.  6
*     d.  8
    e.  10

M 20. Which statement is NOT true?
    a  Electrons closest to the nucleus are at the lowest energy level.
    b.  No more than two electrons can occupy a single orbital.
*     c.  Electrons are unable to move out of the assigned orbital space.
    d.  The innermost orbital holds two electrons.
    e.  At the second energy level there are four possible orbitals with a total of eight electrons.

D 21. When a molecule is excited by heat or light
    a  it may lose an electron.
    b.  it may gain an electron.
*     c.  an electron from an inner energy level may move to another level.
    d.  an electron from an outer energy level may move to an inner level.
    e.  an electron may be ejected from the nucleus of the atom.

E 22. Water is an example of a(n)
    a  atom.
    b.  ion.
*     c.  compound.
    d.  mixture.
    e.  element.

M 23. Which includes the other four?
    a  atoms
*     b.  molecules
    c.  electrons
    d.  elements
    e.  protons

M 24. Which is NOT an element?
*     a  water
    b.  oxygen
    c.  carbon
    d.  chlorine
    e.  hydrogen

E 25. Which is NOT a compound?
    a  salt
    b.  a carbohydrate
*     c.  carbon
    d.  a nucleotide
    e.  methane

M 26. A molecule is
*     a  a combination of two or more atoms.
    b.  less stable than its constituent atoms separated.
    c.  electrically charged.
    d.  a carrier of one or more extra neutrons.
    e.  none of the above

## IMPORTANT BONDS IN BIOLOGICAL MOLECULES

E 27. What is formed when an atom loses or gains an electron?
    a  mole
*     b.  ion
    c.  molecule
    d.  bond
    e.  reaction

E 28. The bond in table salt (NaCl) is
    a  polar.
*     b.  ionic.
    c.  covalent.
    d.  double.
    e.  nonpolar.

M 29. How do hydrophobic molecules react with water?
    a  attracted to
    b.  absorbed by
*     c.  repelled by
    d.  mixed with
    e.  polarized by

D  30. The shape (or tertiary form) of large molecules is often controlled by what kind of bonds?
   * a hydrogen
     b. ionic
     c. covalent
     d. inert
     e. single

D  31. A hydrogen bond is
     a a sharing of a pair of electrons between a hydrogen and an oxygen nucleus.
     b. a sharing of a pair of electrons between a hydrogen nucleus and either an oxygen or a nitrogen nucleus.
   * c. an attractive force that involves a hydrogen atom and an oxygen or a nitrogen atom that are either in two different molecules or within the same molecule.
     d. none of the above
     e. all of the above

## PROPERTIES OF WATER

D  32. Water is an excellent solvent because
     a it forms spheres of hydration around charged substances and can form hydrogen bonds with many nonpolar substances.
     b. it has a high heat of fusion.
     c. of its cohesive properties.
     d. it is a liquid at room temperature.
   * e. all of the above

D  33. In a lipid bilayer, _____ tails point inward and form a region that excludes water.
     a acidic
     b. basic
     c. hydrophilic
   * d. hydrophobic
     e. none of the above

D  34. Glucose dissolves in water because it
     a ionizes.
     b. is a polysaccharide.
   * c. is polar and forms many hydrogen bonds with the water molecules.
     d. has a very reactive primary structure.
     e. none of the above

## WATER, DISSOLVED IONS, AND THE WORLD OF CELLS

M  35. Which of the following is a naked proton?
   * a hydrogen ion
     b. acid
     c. base
     d. hydroxyl ion
     e. acceptor

M  36. A pH of 10 is how many times as basic as a pH of 7?
     a 2
     b. 3
     c. 10
     d. 100
   * e. 1,000

M  37. A solution with a pH of 8 has how many times fewer hydrogen ions than a solution with a pH of 6?
     a 2
     b. 4
     c. 10
   * d. 100
     e. 1,000

D  38. Sodium chloride (NaCl) in water could be described by any of the following EXCEPT:
     a $Na^+$ and $Cl^-$ form
     b. a solute
     c. ionized
   * d. forms spheres of hydration
     e. dissolved

M  39. A salt will dissolve in water to form
     a acids.
     b. gases.
   * c. ions.
     d. bases.
     e. polar solvents.

M  40. A reaction of an acid and a base will produce water and
     a a buffer.
   * b. a salt.
     c. gas.
     d. solid precipitate.
     e. solute.

M  41. Which of the following would NOT be used in connection with the word *acid*?
     a excess hydrogen ions
     b. contents of the stomach
   * c. magnesium hydroxide
     d. HCl
     e. pH less than 7

M  42. Cellular pH is kept near a value of 7 because of
     a salts.
   * b. buffers.
     c. acids.
     d. bases.
     e. water.

## PROPERTIES OF ORGANIC COMPOUNDS

E  43. The three most common atoms in your body are
   * a hydrogen, oxygen, and carbon.
     b. carbon, hydrogen, and nitrogen.
     c. carbon, nitrogen, and oxygen.
     d. nitrogen, hydrogen, and oxygen.
     e. carbon, oxygen, and sulfur.

E 44. Carbon usually forms how many bonds with other atoms?
a. 2
b. 3
* c. 4
d. 5
e. 6

E 45. The atom diagnostically associated with organic compounds is
* a. carbon.
b. oxygen
c. nitrogen.
d. sulfur.
e. hydrogen.

M 46. Which are NOT macromolecules?
a. proteins
b. starches
* c. nucleotides
d. lipids
e. nucleic acids

D 47. Which compound is hydrophobic?
a. ethyl alcohol
b. simple sugar
* c. hydrocarbon
d. glycerol
e. amino acid

M 48. An —OH group is a(n) _____ group.
a. carboxyl
* b. hydroxyl
c. amino
d. methyl
e. ketone

M 49. A —CH$_3$ group is a(n) _____ group.
a. carboxyl
b. hydroxyl
c. amino
* d. methyl
e. ketone

M 50. An —NH$_2$ group is a(n) _____ group.
a. carboxyl
b. hydroxyl
* c. amino
d. methyl
e. ketone

M 51. A —COOH group is a(n) _____ group.
* a. carboxyl
b. hydroxyl
c. amino
d. methyl
e. ketone

E 52. Amino acids are the building blocks for
* a. proteins.
b. steroids.
c. lipids.
d. nucleic acids.
e. carbohydrates.

M 53. Nucleotides are the building blocks for
a. proteins.
b. steroids.
c. lipids.
* d. ATP, NAD$^+$, and FAD.
e. carbohydrates.

M 54. The formation of large molecules from small repeating units is known as what kind of reaction?
a. oxidation
b. reduction
* c. condensation
d. hydrolysis
e. decarboxylation

M 55. The breakdown of large molecules by the enzymatic addition of water is an example of what kind of reaction?
a. oxidation
b. reduction
c. condensation
* d. hydrolysis
e. decarboxylation

M 56. Which reaction results in the breakdown of a chemical into simpler substances?
a. synthesis
* b. hydrolysis
c. condensation
d. polymerization
e. both b and c, but not a or d

E 57. Which is a "building block" of carbohydrates?
a. glycerol
b. nucleotide
c. simple sugar
d. monosaccharide
* e. c and d above

E 58. Which substance is the most common in cells?
a. carbohydrates
b. salts and minerals
c. proteins
d. fats
* e. water

M 59. Which of the following includes all the others?
a. sucrose
b. glucose
c. cellulose
d. glycogen
* e. carbohydrate

**CARBOHYDRATES**

M 60. Which of the following is composed of a 1:2:1 ratio of carbon to hydrogen to oxygen?
* a. carbohydrate
b. protein
c. lipid
d. nucleic acid
e. steroid

M 61. Which is NOT a monosaccharide?
    a. glucose
    b. fructose
    c. deoxyribose
*   d. starch
    e. ribose

M 62. Cellulose is
*   a. a material found in cell walls.
    b. a component of cell membranes.
    c. a plant protein.
    d. formed by photosynthesis.
    e. the most complex of the organic compounds.

D 63. Monosaccharides are characterized by all EXCEPT which of the following?
    a. a carboxyl group
    b. carbon, hydrogen, and oxygen in a 1:2:1 ratio
    c. a molecule of three to seven carbon atoms
    d. possession of one or more hydroxyl groups
*   e. the presence of glycerol and fatty acids

M 64. Fructose and glucose are
    a. isotopes.
    b. monosaccharides.
    c. disaccharides.
    d. six-carbon sugars.
*   e. both b and d, but not a or c

M 65. Fructose and glucose are
    a. hexoses.
    b. structurally different.
    c. monosaccharides.
    d. simple sugars.
*   e. all of the above

M 66. Glucose and ribose
    a. have the same number of carbon atoms.
    b. have the same structural formulas.
    c. are the two components of sucrose.
*   d. are monosaccharides.
    e. are molecules whose atoms are arranged the same way.

M 67. Sucrose is composed of
    a. two molecules of fructose.
    b. two molecules of glucose.
*   c. a molecule of fructose and a molecule of glucose.
    d. a molecule of fructose and a molecule of galactose.
    e. two molecules of fructose.

M 68. The combination of glucose and galactose forms
    a. fructose.
    b. maltose.
*   c. lactose.
    d. sucrose.
    e. mannose.

E 69. Plants store their excess carbohydrates in the form of
*   a. starch.
    b. glycogen.
    c. glucose.
    d. cellulose.
    e. fats.

M 70. Glycogen is a polysaccharide used for energy storage by
*   a. animals.
    b. plants.
    c. protistans.
    d. monera.
    e. both a and c, but not b or d

**LIPIDS**

M 71. Triglycerides are
    a. carbohydrates.
    b. nucleotides.
    c. proteins.
*   d. fats.
    e. amino acids.

M 72. Oils are
    a. liquid at room temperatures.
    b. unsaturated fats.
    c. found only in animals.
    d. complex carbohydrates.
*   e. both a and b, but not c or d

E 73. Which of the following are lipids?
    a. steroids
    b. triglycerides
    c. oils
    d. waxes
*   e. all of the above

M 74. An example of a saturated fat is
    a. olive oil.
    b. corn oil.
*   c. butter.
    d. oleo.
    e. soybean oil.

M 75. Lipids
*   a. serve as food reserves in many organisms.
    b. include cartilage and chitin.
    c. include fats that consist of one fatty acid molecule and three glycerol molecules.
    d. are composed of monosaccharides.
    e. none of the above

M 76. Plasma membranes are characterized by the presence of
    a. triglycerides.
*   b. phospholipids.
    c. unsaturated fats.
    d. steroid hormones.
    e. fatty acids.

M 77. All steroids have
   a. the same number of double bonds.
   b. the same position of double bonds.
 * c. four rings of carbon to which are attached other atoms.
   d. the same functional groups.
   e. both a and b, but not c or d

M 78. Steroids are
   a. compounds that are related to lipids.
   b. sex hormones.
   c. components of membranes.
   d. troublesome on walls of arteries.
 * e. all of the above

## AMINO ACIDS AND PROTEINS

D 79. Which element is NOT characteristic of the primary structure of proteins?
   a. sulfur
   b. carbon
 * c. phosphorus
   d. oxygen
   e. nitrogen

M 80. Proteins may function as
   a. structural units.
   b. hormones.
   c. storage molecules.
   d. transport molecules.
 * e. all of the above

E 81. What kind of bond exists between two amino acids in a protein?
 * a. peptide
   b. ionic
   c. hydrogen
   d. amino
   e. sulfhydroxyl

E 82. The sequence of amino acids is the _____ structure of proteins.
 * a. primary
   b. secondary
   c. tertiary
   d. quaternary
   e. stereo

E 83. Amino acids are linked by what kind of bonds to form the primary structure of a protein?
   a. disulfide
   b. hydrogen
   c. ionic
 * d. peptide
   e. none of the above

M 84. The secondary structure of proteins is
   a. helical.
   b. sheetlike.
   c. globular.
   d. the sequence of amino acids.
 * e. both a and b

## SOME EXAMPLES OF FINAL PROTEIN STRUCTURE

E 85. A fully functional molecules of hemoglobin is a good example of _____ protein structure.
   a. primary
   b. secondary
   c. tertiary
 * d. quaternary
   e. none of these

M 86. Cholesterol freely circulating in human blood is mostly likely
   a. complexed with carbohydrates.
   b. unattached to any other molecule.
 * c. in the form of a lipoprotein.
   d. attached to a fatty acid.
   e. a glycoprotein.

E 87. When a hen's egg is cooked for breakfast, which of the following statements does not apply?
   a. High temperature breaks the hydrogen bonds.
 * b. Gentle cooling will reverse the denaturation that has occurred.
   c. The covalent bonds are not broken.
   d. Denaturation has resulted in a change from "runny" to "semi-solid."

## NUCLEOTIDES AND NUCLEIC ACIDS

M 88. Which of the following is NOT found in every nucleic acid?
 * a. ribose
   b. phosphate group
   c. purine
   d. pyrimidine
   e. all of the above are characteristic of every nucleotide

M 89. The nucleotide most closely associated with energy is
   a. cyclic AMP.
   b. FAD.
   c. NAD.
 * d. ATP.
   e. all of the above

M 90. Nucleotides contain what kind of sugars?
   a. three-carbon
   b. four-carbon
 * c. five-carbon
   d. six-carbon
   e. seven-carbon

M 91. DNA
   a. is one of the adenosine phosphates.
   b. is one of the nucleotide coenzymes.
 * c. contains protein-building instructions.
   d. all of the above
   e. none of the above

## Matching Questions

M    92.    Choose the one most appropriate answer for each.

1 _____ enzymes

2 _____ glucose

3 _____ nucleotide coenzymes

4 _____ phospholipids

    A.  a six-carbon sugar

    B.  energy carrier such as NAD and FAD

    C.  principal components of cell membranes

    D.  speed up metabolic reactions

    E.  DNA and RNA

*Answers:*    1.  D        2.  A        3.  B
                4.  C

## Classification Questions

The various energy levels in an atom of magnesium have different numbers of electrons. Use the following numbers to answer questions 93–95.

    a    1
    b.   2
    c.   3
    d.   6
    e.   8

D    93.    Number of electrons in the first energy level

D    94.    Number of electrons in the second energy level

D    95.    Number of electrons in the third energy level

*Answers:*    93.  b        94.  e        95.  b

The following are types of chemical bonds. Answer questions 96–100 by matching the statement with the most appropriate bond type.

    a    hydrogen
    b.   ionic
    c.   covalent
    d.   disulfide
    e.   peptide

M    96.    The bond between the atoms of table salt

M    97.    The bond type holding several molecules of water together

M    98.    The bond between the oxygen atoms of gaseous oxygen

M    99.    The bond that breaks when salts dissolve in water

M    100.   Atoms connected by this kind of bond share electrons

*Answers:*    96.  b        97.  a        98.  c
               99.  b        100.  c

The following are chemical functional groups that may be part of a biologically active molecule. Answer questions 101–111 by matching the statement with the most appropriate group.

    a —COOH
    b.—$CH_3$
    c.—$NH_2$
    d.—OH
    e.  $>C=O$
    f.

$$-\overset{\overset{\textstyle O}{\|}}{\underset{\underset{\textstyle O}{|}}{P}}-O$$

    g.—CHO

E    101.   The amino group

E    102.   The carboxyl group

M    103.   The group that is acidic

M    104.   The group that occurs repeatedly in sugars; composed of two elements

E    105.   The methyl group

E    106.   The hydroxyl group

E    107.   The ketone group

M    108.   The group on the amino-terminal end of proteins

M    109.   The group on the carboxy-terminal end of proteins

D    110.   A group composed of three different elements; found in sugars

M    111.   The group typical of energy carriers such as ATP

*Answers:*    101.  c        102.  a        103.  a
               104.  d        105.  b        106.  d
               107.  e        108.  c        109.  a
               110.  g        111.  f

The following are basic building blocks of biopolymers. Answer questions 112–119 by matching the statement with the most appropriate building block.

    a  amino acids
    b.  glucose
    c.  glycerol
    d.  fatty acids
    e.  nucleotides

E   112.  The basic unit of proteins

E   113.  The basic unit of DNA

E   114.  The basic unit of messenger RNA

E   115.  The basic unit of cellulose

E   116.  The basic unit of glycogen

E   117.  The basic unit of starch

M   118.  The "building block" unit of a polypeptide chain

M   119.  Which two units combine in various ways to form lipids?
    a  amino acids and glucose
    b.  amino acids and glycerol
    c.  glucose and glycerol
    d.  glucose and fatty acids
    e.  glycerol and fatty acids

*Answers*:     112.  a        113.  e        114.  e
               115.  b        116.  b.       117.  b.
               118.  a        119.  e

## Selecting the Exception

D   120.  Four of the five answers listed below possess electrons in the third energy level. Select the exception.
    a  sodium
    b.  magnesium
    c.  chlorine
    * d.  nitrogen
    e.  sulfur

D   121.  Four of the five answers listed below are related by a unifying characteristic. Select the exception.
    a  ionic bond
    b.  covalent bond
    c.  polar bond
    d.  hydrogen bond
    * e.  cluster of nonpolar groups

D   122.  Four of the five answers listed below are alkaline (pH above 7). Select the exception.
    a  milk of magnesia
    b.  household ammonia
    c.  Tums
    d.  phosphate detergent
    * e.  wine

D   123.  Four of the five answers listed below are acidic (pH below 7). Select the exception.
    a  vinegar
    b.  soft drink
    * c.  soap
    d.  lemon juice
    e.  beer

M   124.  Four of the five answers listed below are positively charged ions. Select the exception.
    a  potassium ion
    b.  hydrogen ion
    c.  calcium ion
    d.  magnesium ion
    * e.  chlorine ion

M   125.  Four of the five answers listed below are characteristics of water. Select the exception.
    a  stabilizes temperature
    b.  common solvent
    c.  cohesion and surface tension
    * d.  produces salts
    e.  changes shape of hydrophilic and hydrophobic substances

D   126.  Four of the five answers listed below are related by a common chemical similarity. Select the exception.
    a  cellulose
    * b.  hydrochloric acid
    c.  amino acid
    d.  protein
    e.  nucleic acid

M   127.  Four of the five answers listed below are related as members of the same group. Select the exception.
    a  glucose
    b.  fructose
    * c.  cellulose
    d.  ribose
    e.  deoxyribose

D   128.  Four of the five answers listed below are related as members of the same group. Select the exception.
    a  lactose
    b.  sucrose
    c.  maltose
    d.  table sugar
    * e.  fructose

D   129.  Four of the five answers listed below are carbohydrates. Select the exception.
    * a  glycerol
    b.  cellulose
    c.  starch
    d.  sucrose
    e.  glycogen

D     **130.** Four of the five answers listed below are lipids. Select the exception.
- a   triglyceride
- b.   wax
- c.   cutin
- \*   d.   insulin
- e.   steroid

M     **131.** Three of the four answers listed below are saturated fats. Select the exception.
- a   butter
- b.   bacon
- \*   c.   peanut oil
- d.   animal fat

D     **132.** Four of the five answers listed below are amino acids. Select the exception.
- a   glycine
- \*   b.   adenine
- c.   phenylalanine
- d.   valine
- e.   tyrosine

# CHAPTER 3
# CELL STRUCTURE AND FUNCTION

## Multiple-Choice Questions

### BASIC ASPECTS OF CELL STRUCTURE AND FUNCTION

E **1.** The first cell that was seen under a microscope was a
* a   cork cell.
  b.  blood cell.
  c.  sperm cell.
  d.  skin cell.
  e.  root tip cell.

E **2.** One portion of the cell theory states that
  a   all cells have a nucleus.
  b.  all cells divide by meiosis.
* c.  all living organisms are made up of cells.
  d.  cells arise through spontaneous generation.
  e.  growth is solely the result of cell division.

E **3.** The cell theory was proposed by
  a   Robert Hooke.
  b.  Robert Brown.
* c.  Theodor Schwann and Matthias Schleiden.
  d.  Rudolf Virchow.
  e.  Antony van Leeuwenhoek.

E **4.** The idea that all living cells come from preexisting living cells was proposed by
  a   Robert Hooke.
  b.  Robert Brown.
  c.  Theodor Schwann.
* d.  Rudolf Virchow.
  e.  Antony van Leeuwenhoek.

M **5.** The phospholipid molecules of most membranes have
  a   a hydrophobic head and a hydrophilic tail.
  b.  a hydrophobic head and a hydrophobic tail.
  c.  a hydrophobic head and two hydrophobic tails.
* d.  a hydrophilic head and two hydrophobic tails.
  e.  none of the above

E **6.** Hydrophobic reactions of phospholipids may produce clusters of their fatty acid tails, which form
* a   a lipid bilayer.
  b.  hydrolysis of the fatty acids.
  c.  a protein membrane.
  d.  a cytoskeleton.
  e.  a nonpolar membrane.

M **7.** Unsaturated tails of lipids
  a   are hydrophilic.
  b.  are unstable and tend to break apart.
* c.  have kinks in them and lessen the interaction between adjacent fat
  d.  will break whenever exposed to phosphate ions.
  e.  all of the above

M **8.** The relative impermeability of membranes to water-soluble molecules is a result of the
  a   nonpolar nature of water molecules.
  b.  presence of large proteins that extend through both sides of membranes.
  c.  presence of inorganic salt crystals scattered through some membranes.
  d.  presence of cellulose and chemicals such as cutin, lignin, pectin, and suberin in the membranes.
* e.  presence of phospholipids in the lipid bilayer.

D **9.** Which statement is NOT true?
  a   Membranes are often perforated by proteins that extend through both sides of the membrane.
  b.  Some membranes have proteins with channels or pores that allow for the passage of hydrophilic substances.
* c.  Hydrophilic substances have an easier time passing through membranes than hydrophobic substances do.
  d.  The current concept of a membrane can be best summarized by the fluid mosaic model.
  e.  The lipid bilayer serves as a hydrophobic barrier between two fluid regions.

M **10.** Which of the following membrane proteins is responsible for binding hormones that can switch on a cell?
  a   recognition proteins
* b.  receptor proteins
  c.  transport proteins
  d.  adhesion proteins

### CELL SIZE AND CELL SHAPE

M **11.** There are how many nanometers in a meter?
  a   1,000
  b.  100,000
  c.  1,000,000
* d.  1,000,000,000
  e.  1,000,000,000,000

E    12. The maximum power of magnification of a light
         microscope is
         a  500.
         b. 1,000.
      *  c. 2,000.
         d. 4,000.
         e. 10,000.

E    13. The highest magnification generally used to
         study cells is provided by the
      *  a  transmission electron microscope.
         b. compound light microscope.
         c. phase contrast microscope.
         d. scanning electron microscope.
         e. binocular dissecting microscope.

M    14. Which microscope has the highest
         magnification?
         a  compound light
      *  b. transmission electron
         c. scanning electron
         d. phase contrast
         e. dissecting

## EUKARYOTIC CELLS

M    15. Which of the following are made of two subunits
         and are composed of RNA and protein?
         a  Golgi
         b. mitochondria
         c. chloroplasts
      *  d. ribosomes
         e. endoplasmic reticula

E    16. Organelles composed of a system of canals,
         tubes, and sacs that transport molecules inside
         the cytoplasm are
         a  Golgi bodies.
         b. ribosomes.
         c. mitochondria.
         d. lysosomes.
      *  e. endoplasmic reticula.

M    17. These are the primary cellular sites for the
         recapture of energy from carbohydrates.
         a  Golgi bodies
         b. ribosomes
      *  c. mitochondria
         d. lysosomes
         e. endoplasmic reticula

M    18. These are the primary structures for the
         packaging of cellular secretions for export from
         the cell.
      *  a  Golgi bodies
         b. ribosomes
         c. mitochondria
         d. lysosomes
         e. endoplasmic reticula

E    19. Cell part responsible for maintaining cell shape,
         internal organization, and cell movements is the
         a  vesicle.
         b. nucleus.
         c. endoplasmic reticulum.
      *  d. cytoskeleton.
         e. ribosome.

E    20. What cell organelle is found in plant cells but
         NOT in animal cells?
         a  nucleoplasm
      *  b. cell wall
         c. plasma membrane
         d. Golgi body
         e. microtubules

E    21. An organelle found in the nucleus is a
         a  plastid.
         b. vacuole.
         c. microvillus.
      *  d. nucleolus.
         e. basal body.

M    22. Which of the following is NOT true concerning
         the nuclear envelope?
         a  It has two lipid bilayers.
         b. There are pores in the membrane.
         c. Ribosomal subunits can pass out of the
            nucleus.
      *  d. DNA molecules are transported out through
            the pores.
         e. Protein filaments are attached to the inner
            surface.

M    23. Scientists use the word "chromosome" to
         describe
      *  a  an individual DNA molecule.
         b. any hereditary material in the nucleus.
         c. the total collection of DNA in a cell.
         d. hereditary material that is not duplicated.
         e. all of the above

## THE CYTOMEMBRANE SYSTEM

E    24. These are sometimes referred to as rough or
         smooth, depending on the structure.
         a  Golgi bodies
         b. ribosomes
         c. mitochondria
         d. lysosomes
      *  e. endoplasmic reticula

M    25. These are the primary cellular sites for the
         production of proteins.
         a  Golgi bodies
      *  b. ribosomes
         c. mitochondria
         d. lysosomes
         e. smooth endoplasmic reticula

E 26. This organelle's appearance has been likened to a stack of pancakes.
* a Golgi body
b. ribosome
c. mitochondria
d. lysosome
e. vesicle

M 27. These contain enzymes and are the main organelles of intracellular digestion.
a Golgi bodies
b. ribosomes
c. mitochondria
* d. lysosomes
e. endoplasmic reticula

a nucleoli.
* b. peroxisomes.
c. lysosomes.
d. endoplasmic reticula.
e. Golgi bodies.

D 29. Animal cells dismantle and dispose of waste materials by
a using centrally located vacuoles.
* b. several lysosomes fusing with a sac that encloses the wastes.
c. microvilli packaging and exporting the wastes.
d. mitochondrial breakdown of the wastes.
e. all of the above

## VESICLES THAT MOVE SUBSTANCES OUT OF AND INTO CELLS

M 30. White blood cells use _____ to get rid of foreign particles in the blood.
a simple diffusion
b. bulk flow
c. osmosis
* d. phagocytosis
e. facilitated diffusion

M 31. All of the following are associated with the process of endocytosis except
* a secretion of cell products.
b. endocytic vesicles.
c. "coated pits."
d. surface receptors.
e. phagocytosis.

## MITOCHONDRIA

M 32. These contain enzymes used in the breakdown of glucose and generation of ATP.
a Golgi bodies
b. ribosomes
* c. mitochondria
d. lysosomes
e. endoplasmic reticula

D 33. Energy stored in which of the following molecules is converted by mitochondria to a form usable by the cell?
a water
* b. carbon compounds
c. NAD
d. ATP
e. carbon dioxide

E 34. The number of membranes surrounding a mitochondrion is
a one.
* b. two.
c. three.
d. four.
e. unknown.

a filaments.
b. cilia.
c. chromatin.
* d. cristae.
e. centrioles.

## SPECIALIZED PLANT ORGANELLES

M 36. Fluid-filled sacs that may store food or water in cells are called
a plastids.
* b. vacuoles.
c. microvilli.
d. nucleoli.
e. Golgi.

E 37. Organelles in plant cells that function in photosynthesis or storage are called
a stroma.
b. grana.
* c. plastids.
d. vacuoles.
e. mitochondria.

E 38. Stroma and grana are portions of
* a chloroplasts.
b. mitochondria.
c. ribosomes.
d. chromosomes.
e. Golgi bodies.

## CELL SURFACE SPECIALIZATIONS

M 39. Which is NOT found as a part of all cells?
a cell membrane
* b. cell wall
c. ribosomes
d. DNA
e. RNA

M  40. Which of the following statements concerning cell walls is NOT true?
a  The cell wall is located outside the plasma membrane.
*  b.  Water cannot move through a cell wall.
c.  The cell wall is more rigid than the plasma membrane.
d.  Cell walls cannot form connections to one another.

D  41. Plasmodesmata are
a  used in energy transformations within the cell.
b.  typical of animal cells more than plant cells.
*  c.  cross connections between cell walls.
d.  both a and b
e.  both b and c
a  gap junctions
b.  plasmodesmata
*  c.  tight junctions
d.  adhering junctions
e.  blocking proteins

**THE CYTOSKELETON**

M  43. Structural features that contain the protein actin and help to control the shapes of cells are
a  plastids.
b.  vacuoles.
c.  microvilli.
d.  nucleoli.
*  e.  microfilaments.

M  44. Organelles used to move chromosomes are the
a  cilia.
b.  flagella.
*  c.  microtubules.
d.  microfilaments.
e.  Golgi apparatuses.

M  45. Organelles that dramatically increase the cell size and surface area are
a  plastids.
*  b.  vacuoles.
c.  chloroplasts.
d.  nucleoli.
e.  microfilaments.

E  46. The organelle that is compared to a whip is a
a  microfilament.
b.  cilium.
c.  microvillus.
*  d.  flagellum.
e.  microtubule.

E  47. A 9+2 array refers to
a  microtubules.
b.  Golgi bodies.
c.  ribosomes.
d.  cilia.
*  e.  both a and d, but not b or c

M  48. MTOCs are most closely associated with
a  chromosomes.
*  b.  centrioles.
c.  central vacuoles.
d.  chloroplasts.
e.  cytoskeletons.

E  49. Which are examples of prokaryotes?
a  Protozoa
*  b.  Bacteria
c.  Algae
d.  Fungi
e.  Mosses

M  50. Prokaryotic cells do NOT have
a  nucleoid regions.
*  b.  membrane bound nuclei.
c.  cytoplasm.
d.  plasma membrane.
e.  a and b

E  51. Prokaryotes
a  have DNA regions.
b.  are unicellular.
c.  have cell walls.
d.  are monera.
*  e.  all of the above

## Matching Questions

M    **52.**    Choose the one most appropriate answer for each.

1 _____ microtubules

2 _____ chloroplasts

3 _____ Golgi bodies

4 _____ DNA molecules

5 _____ RNA molecules

6 _____ central vacuoles

7 _____ lysosomes

8 _____ mitochondria

9 _____ nucleoli

10 _____ ribosomes

    A.  contain enzymes for intracellular digestion

    B.  primary cellular organelles where proteins are assembled

    C.  package cellular secretions for export

    D.  extract energy stored in carbohydrates; synthesize ATP; produce water and $CO_2$

    E.  synthesize subunits that will be assembled into two-part ribosomes in the cytoplasm

    F.  transcription, translation of hereditary instructions into specific proteins

    G.  increase cell surface area; store substances

    H.  encoding hereditary information

    I.  help distribute chromosomes to the new cells during cell division

    J.  convert light energy to chemical energy stored in the chemical bonds of glucose or starch

*Answers:*

| 1. I | 2. J | 3. C |
|------|------|------|
| 4. H | 5. F | 6. G |
| 7. A | 8. D | 9. E |
| 10. B | | |

---

The following items a–e are organelles found in animal cells. Answer questions 53–61 with reference to these organelles.

    a.  ribosomes

    b.  mitochondria

    c.  lysosomes

    d.  Golgi bodies

    e.  endoplasmic reticula

E    **53.**    These are th structures upon which proteins are assembled.

M    **54.**    The cellular digestion and disposal of biological molecules occurs inside this organelle.

M    **55.**    Aerobic respiration occurs in this organelle.

M    **56.**    RNA carries out the genetic code translation process in association with ribosomes on this organelle.

M    **57.**    The packaging of secretory proteins occurs in association with this structure.

M    **58.**    This organelle is involved in lipid production and protein transport.

D    **59.**    The hemoglobin of mammals and birds is synthesized on these tiny, two-part organelles.

E    **60.**    Sugar metabolism occurs in association with this organelle.

D    **61.**    DNA synthesis occurs in the nucleus. Its breakdown can occur in this organelle.

*Answers:*

| 53. a | 54. c | 55. b |
|-------|-------|-------|
| 56. e | 57. d | 58. e |
| 59. a | 60. b | 61. c |

## Selecting the Exception

D    **62.**    Four of the five answers listed below are related by a common observation. Select the exception.

    a.  Hooke

\*    b.  Galileo

    c.  Schwann

    d.  Schleiden

    e.  Virchow

M    **63.**    Four of the five answers listed below are portions of a well-known theory. Select the exception.

    a.  Cells are the structural and functional components of living things.

    b.  Cells arise from preexisting cells.

    c.  All organisms are composed of cells.

    d.  Cells are the basic living unit or organization of living things.

\*    e.  All cells have a nucleus.

M     **64.**   Four of the five answers listed below are familiar organelles in the cytoplasm. Select the exception.
*     a   nucleolus
      b.   mitochondria
      c.   ribosome
      d.   Golgi apparatus
      e.   chloroplast

M     **65.**   Four of the five answers listed below are features of plasma membrane extensions. Select the exception.
*     a   amyloplast
      b.   centriole
      c.   microtubule
      d.   basal body
      e.   9+2 array

M     **66.**   Four of the five answers listed below are bound by membranes. Select the exception.
      a   mitochondria
*     b.   ribosome
      c.   chloroplast
      d.   vacuole
      e.   lysosome

M     **67.**   Four of the five answers listed below are characteristics of the plasma membrane. Select the exception.
      a.   phospholipid
      b.   fluid mosaic
      c.   lipid bilayer
*     d.   inert and impermeable
      e.   hydrophobic tails

# CHAPTER 4
# GROUND RULES OF METABOLISM

## Multiple-Choice Questions

### ENERGY AND LIFE

D    **1.** According to the first law of thermodynamics
- a   although energy in the universe is constant, energy in an earthly system may accumulate.
- b.   the amount of energy in the universe is constant.
- c.   chemical reactions do not create or destroy energy.
- d.   energy can change from one form to another.
- \*   e.   all of the above

D    **2.** The second law of thermodynamics holds that
- a   matter can neither be created nor destroyed.
- b.   energy can neither be created nor destroyed.
- \*   c.   energy of one form is converted to a less concentrated form whenever energy is transformed or transferred.
- d.   entropy decreases with time.
- e.   none of the above

M    **3.** The second law of thermodynamics states that
- a   energy can be transformed into matter and, because of this, we can get something for nothing.
- b.   energy can only be destroyed during nuclear reactions, such as those that occur inside the sun.
- c.   if energy is gained by one region of the universe, another place in the universe also must gain energy in order to maintain the balance of nature.
- \*   d.   energy tends to become increasingly more disorganized.
- e.   none of the above

E    **4.** Essentially, the first law of thermodynamics says that
- a   one form of energy cannot be converted into another.
- b.   entropy is increasing in the universe.
- \*   c.   energy can be neither created nor destroyed.
- d.   energy cannot be converted into matter or matter into energy.
- e.   all of the above

### DIFFUSION IN THE CELLULAR WORLD

D    **5.** Which affects the rate of diffusion through a semipermeable membrane?
- I    steeper concentration gradients
- II.   higher temperatures
- III.   membrane pore size
- a   I only
- b.   II only
- c.   I and II
- d.   II and III
- \*   e.   I, II, and III

D    **6.** The rate of diffusion through a semipermeable membrane will be lowest when which of the following are true?
- I    Concentration gradients are steep.
- II.   Temperatures are low.
- III.   Solutes are small molecules.
- a   I only
- \*   b.   II only
- c.   I and III
- d.   II and III
- e.   I, II, and III

M    **7.** In simple diffusion
- a   the rate of movement of molecules is controlled by temperature and pressure.
- b.   the movement of individual molecules is random.
- c.   the movement of molecules of one substance is independent of the movement of any other substance.
- d.   the net movement is away from the region of highest concentration.
- \*   e.   all of the above

M    **8.** A single-celled freshwater organism, such as a protistan, is transferred to salt water. Which of the following is likely to happen?
- a   The cell bursts.
- b.   Salt is pumped out of the cell.
- \*   c.   The cell shrinks.
- d.   Enzymes flow out of the cell.
- e.   all of the above

M    **9.** Which statement is true?
- a   A cell placed in an isotonic solution will swell.
- \*   b.   A cell placed in a hypotonic solution will swell.
- c.   A cell placed in a hypotonic solution will shrink.
- d.   A cell placed in a hypertonic solution will remain the same size.
- e.   A cell placed in a hypotonic solution will remain the same size.

M 10. A red blood cell will swell and burst when placed in which of the following kinds of solution?
* a hypotonic
b. hypertonic
c. isotonic
d. any of the above
e. none of the above

M 11. If a plant cell is placed in a hypotonic solution
a the entire cell will not swell or shrink.
b. the entire cell will shrink.
c. the turgor pressure will increase.
d. the cell wall prevents the cell from exploding.
* e. c and d above

M 12. Wilting of a plant occurs
a if the plant is placed in an isotonic solution.
b. if there is a rise in turgor pressure.
c. as a result of facilitated diffusion.
* d. when a plant with flexible cell walls is placed in a hypertonic solution.
e. any of the above

M 13. Which of the following is NOT a form of active transport?
a sodium–potassium pump
b. endocytosis
c. exocytosis
* d. diffusion
e. none of the above

E 14. Movement of a molecule against a concentration gradient is
a simple diffusion.
b. facilitated diffusion.
c. osmosis.
* d. active transport.
e. passive transport.

M 15. The method of movement that requires the expenditure of ATP molecules is
a simple diffusion.
b. facilitated diffusion.
c. osmosis.
* d. active transport.
e. passive transport.

E 16. The sodium-potassium pump is an example of
a simple diffusion.
b. facilitated diffusion.
c. osmosis.
* d. active transport.
e. passive transport.

M 17. The carrier molecules used in active transport are
a calcium ions in the calcium pump.
* b. proteins.
c. ATP molecules.
d. carbohydrates.
e. lipids.

## CHARACTERISTICS OF METABOLIC REACTIONS

M 18. Which reaction is NOT an exergonic reaction?
* a protein synthesis
b. digestion
c. fire
d. respiration
e. movement

M 19. Reactions will reach a chemical equilibrium under which of the following conditions?
a There is enough time.
b. The reactions are reversible.
c. A product remains after it is formed.
d. There are sufficient reactants.
* e. all of the above

M 20. A chemical equilibrium
a means the concentration of reactants and products is the same.
* b. means the rate of opposing reactions is equal.
c. means highly spontaneous reactions are less likely to occur than when the system is not at equilibrium.
d. means that both reactions are typically proceeding against concentration gradients.
e. occurs only in endergonic reactions.

## ENZYMES

M 21. Although it its too simple an explanation, the concept of a key fitting into a lock is descriptive of the
a inhibition of enzymes by small molecules.
b. fit of coenzymes to enzymes.
* c. matching of enzyme with substrate.
d. regeneration of ATP from ADP.
e. stepwise cascade of electrons in the oxidation–reduction reactions.

M 22. During enzyme-catalyzed reactions, *substrate* is a synonym for
a end products.
b. byproducts.
c. enzymes.
* d. reactants.
e. none of the above

D 23. Which of the following may show enzymatic activity?
a lipids
* b. proteins
c. DNA
d. a and b
e. b and c

M   **24.** Which of the following is NOT true of enzyme behavior?
- a   Enzyme shape may change during catalysis.
- b.   The active site of an enzyme orients its substrate molecules, thereby promoting interaction of their reactive parts.
- c.   All enzymes have an active site where substrates are temporarily bound.
- *   d.   Each enzyme can catalyze a wide variety of different reactions.
- e.   none of the above

E   **25.** Enzymes
- a   are very specific.
- b.   act as catalysts.
- c.   are organic molecules.
- d.   have special shapes that control their activities.
- *   e.   all of the above

M   **26.** Enzymes
- a   control the speed of a reaction.
- b.   change shapes to facilitate certain reactions.
- c.   may place physical stress on the bonds of the substrate.
- d.   may require cofactors.
- *   e.   all of the above

M   **27.** The active site of an enzyme
- a   is where the coenzyme is located.
- b.   is a specific bulge or protuberance on an enzyme.
- *   c.   is a groove or crevice in the structure of the enzyme.
- d.   will react with only one substrate no matter how many molecules may resemble the shape of the substrate.
- e.   rigidly resists any alteration of its shape.

M   **28.** Enzymes increase the rate of a given reaction by lowering what kind of energy?
- a   combination
- *   b.   activation
- c.   thermal
- d.   electrical
- e.   solar

M   **29.** Enzymatic reactions can be controlled by
- a   the amount of substrates available.
- b.   the concentration of products.
- c.   temperature.
- d.   modification of reactive sites by substances that fit into the enzyme and, later, their reactive site.
- *   e.   all of the above

## MEDIATORS OF ENZYME FUNCTION

D   **30.** Which of the following substances would be unlikely to function as a coenzyme?
- a   a water-soluble vitamin
- b.   an iron ion
- *   c.   glucose
- d.   $NAD^+$
- e.   a magnesium ion

M   **31.** Allosteric inhibition is generally a result of
- a   excess substrates.
- *   b.   binding regulatory molecules at another site.
- c.   a change in the temperature of the system.
- d.   a lack of coenzymes.
- e.   pH inhibition.

D   **32.** An allosteric enzyme
- *   a   has an active site where substrate molecules bind and another site that binds with intermediate or end-product molecules.
- b.   is an important energy-carrying nucleotide.
- c.   carries out either oxidation reactions or reduction reactions but not both.
- d.   raises the activation energy of the chemical reaction it catalyzes.
- e.   all of the above

## ATP—THE MAIN ENERGY CARRIER

M   **33.** ATP acts as what type of agent in almost all metabolic pathways?
- *   a   transfer
- b.   feedback
- c.   catalytic
- d.   allosteric
- e.   enzymatic

E   **34.** ATP contains
- a   alanine.
- b.   arginine.
- *   c.   ribose.
- d.   tyrosine.
- e.   glucose.

E   **35.** ATP contains
- *   a   adenine.
- b.   cytosine.
- c.   uracil.
- d.   thymine.
- e.   guanine.

## ENERGY AND THE FLOW OF ELECTRONS

M   **36.** A molecule that gives up an electron becomes
- a   ionized
- b.   oxidized
- c.   reduced
- *   d.   a and b
- e.   b and c

M    37.    The removal of electrons from a compound is
            known as
            a    dehydration.
    *       b.    oxidation.
            c.    reduction.
            d.    phosphorylation.
            e.    a nonreversible chemical reaction.

M    38.    When NAD$^+$ combines with hydrogen, the
            NAD$^+$ becomes
    *       a    reduced.
            b.    oxidized.
            c.    phosphorylated.
            d.    denatured.
            e.    none of the above

## Matching Questions

M    39.    Choose the one most appropriate answer for
            each.
            1  _____    active site
            2  _____    allosteric enzyme
            3  _____    adenosine triphosphate
            4  _____    catalyst
            5  _____    denaturation
            6  _____    equilibrium
            7  _____    feedback inhibition
            8  _____    phosphorylation
                  A.    rate of forward reaction equals rate
                        of reverse reaction
                  B.    attaching a phosphate group by a
                        high-energy bond
                  C.    an excess of end-product molecules
                        alters the shape of the first enzyme
                        in the pathway and shuts off that
                        metabolic pathway
                  D.    part of an enzyme that binds to the
                        substrate
                  E.    by binding a regulatory molecule, it
                        changes the activity of a metabolic
                        pathway
                  F.    lowers the activation energy of a
                        reaction
                  G.    universal energy currency
                  H.    a permanent loss of protein
                        structure

*Answers:*      1.  D        2.  E        3.  G
                4.  F        5.  H        6.  A
                7.  C        8.  B

## Classification Questions

Items a–c below are processes that occur during different stages
of photosynthesis. Answer questions 40–43 by selecting one of
these three processes.
            a    oxidation
            b.    reduction
            c.    phosphorylation

E    40.    This process leads to the formation of ATP from
            ADP plus inorganic phosphate.

M    41.    When an electron is passed to an electron
            acceptor molecule, such as NADP, this process
            occurs to the NADP.

D    42.    When a photon of light energy causes an electron
            to leave the chlorophyll molecule, this process is
            involved.

M    43.    When an electron transport molecule, such as
            ferrodoxin, gives up an electron, this process
            occurs in the ferrodoxin.

*Answers:*      40.  c        41.  b        42.  a
                43.  a

Questions 44-47 ask about membrane permeability. Answer them
in reference to the four processes below:
            a    simple diffusion
            b.    facilitated diffusion
            c.    osmosis
            d.    active transport

E    44.    This process specifically moves water molecules
            across a differentially permeable membrane.

E    45.    This phenomenon explains the movement of any
            kind of molecule from areas of higher
            concentration to ones of lower concentration.

E    46.    This is the process whereby a protein assists in
            simple diffusion.

M    47.    This explains the movement of molecules against
            a concentration gradient.

*Answers:*      44.  c        45.  a        46.  b
                47.  d

## Selecting the Exception

E    48.    Four of the five answers listed below are related
            to the second law of thermodynamics. Select the
            exception.
            a    entropy
    *       b.    energy can neither be created nor destroyed
            c.    the amount of available energy in a closed
                  system declines with time
            d.    energy is lost as it is transferred or
                  transformed to another form
            e.    energy flows spontaneously from high- to
                  low-quality forms

M  **49.** Four of the five answers listed below apply to conditions where energy is released. Select the exception.

   * a  endergonic reaction

      b.  respiration

      c.  entropy

      d.  second law of thermodynamics

      e.  exergonic reaction

M  **50.** Four of the five answers listed below are related by their description of enzyme properties. Select the exception.

      a  cofactors

      b.  active sites

      c.  activation energy

   * d.  substrate

      e.  catalyst

D  **51.** Four of the five answers listed below are cofactors or coenzymes. Select the exception.

      a  mineral

      b.  water-soluble vitamin

      c.  metallic ions

      d.  $NAD^+$

   * e.  protein

D  **52.** Four of the five answers listed below affect the rate of an enzymatic reaction. Select the exception.

      a  pH

      b.  temperature

      c.  concentration

      d.  built-up product

   * e.  presence of hormones

D  **53.** Three of the four answers listed below are parts of a common molecule. Select the exception.

      a  phosphate group

      b.  adenine

   * c.  deoxyribose

      d.  ribose

M  **54.** Four of the five answers listed below result when a cell is placed in a hypertonic solution. Select the exception.

      a  wilting

      b.  plasmolysis

   * c.  turgid

      d.  limp

      e.  shriveled

D  **55.** Four of the five answers listed below are related by energy requirements. Select the exception.

      a  active transport

      b.  endocytosis

   * c.  facilitated diffusion

      d.  exocytosis

      e.  sodium–potassium pump

# CHAPTER 5
# ENERGY-ACQUIRING PATHWAYS

## Multiple-Choice Questions

### SUN, RAIN, AND SURVIVAL

E    1.  Plants need which of the following to carry on photosynthesis?
         a   $H_2O$
         b.  $CO_2$
         c.  $O_2$
         d.  lipid
    *    e.  a and b

D    2.  Chemosynthetic bacteria may use which element as a hydrogen donor instead of water?
         a   potassium dihydrogen phosphate
    *    b.  sulfur
         c.  hydrogen sulfate
         d.  hydrogen chloride
         e.  hydrogen peroxide

M    3.  Chemosynthetic bacteria (autotrophs) obtain energy from
         a   sunlight.
         b.  sugar.
         c.  water.
    *    d.  inorganic ions.
         e.  chlorophyll.

E    4.  Organisms that derive their chemical energy either from the process of chemosynthesis or photosynthesis are classified as
    *    a   autotrophs.
         b.  parasites.
         c.  heterotrophs.
         d.  saprophytes.
         e.  mutualists.

### PHOTOSYNTHESIS: AN OVERVIEW

E    5.  The carbon source for organisms that derive their energy from photosynthesis is
         a   carbon monoxide.
    *    b.  carbon dioxide.
         c.  hydrocarbons.
         d.  methane.
         e.  glucose.

M    6.  Most carbon enters the web of life through
         a   chemosynthesis.
         b.  aerobic respiration.
         c.  anaerobic respiration.
    *    d.  photosynthesis.
         e.  both a and b, but not c or d

M    7.  The oxygen released in photosynthesis comes from
         a   carbon dioxide.
         b.  glucose.
         c.  ribulose bisphosphate.
    *    d.  water.
         e.  atmospheric oxygen.

M    8.  The internal membrane system of the chloroplast is called a
    *    a   thylakoid.
         b.  stroma.
         c.  lamella.
         d.  mitochondrion.
         e.  tracheid.

E    9.  Thylakoid disks are stacked in groups called
    *    a   grana.
         b.  stroma.
         c.  lamellae.
         d.  cristae.
         e.  none of the above

E    10. Plants need which of the following to carry on photosynthesis?
    *    a   carbon dioxide and water
         b.  nitrogen and hydrogen
         c.  oxygen and carbon dioxide
         d.  water and oxygen
         e.  ribose and carbon dioxide

### LIGHT-TRAPPING PIGMENTS

M    11. All of the following statements are true EXCEPT:
         a   photons are packages of solar energy.
    *    b.  the longer the wavelength of light, the more energy it has.
         c.  chlorophyll absorbs energy from light.
         d.  photons with different energy levels produce different colors.
         e.  visible light is a very small portion of the electromagnetic spectrum.

M    12. Chlorophyll reflects (does not absorb) which color of light?
         a   red
         b.  yellow
         c.  orange
    *    d.  green
         e.  blue

M **13.** Where in a plant cell is chlorophyll found?
 a   on the outer chloroplast membrane
 b.  inside the mitochondria
 c.  in the stroma
* d.  in the thylakoids
 e.  none of the above

E **14.** Which of the following are the pigments characteristic of the red algae and cyanobacteria?
 a   chlorophyll a
 b.  photons
* c.  phycobilins
 d.  carotenoids
 e.  thylakoids

## LIGHT-DEPENDENT REACTIONS

M **15** When light excites chlorophyll, the chlorophyll molecule
 a   changes to carotene.
 b.  becomes agitated and moves rapidly.
 c.  becomes radioactive.
* d.  absorbs the energy and moves an electron to a higher energy state.
 e.  becomes ionized.

M **16.** The first event in photosynthesis is the
 a   formation of phosphoglyceric acid.
* b.  donation of an electron from the photosystem to an acceptor.
 c.  fixation of carbon dioxide.
 d.  breakdown of the thylakoid membrane.
 e.  formation of phosphoglyceraldehyde.

E **17.** The final hydrogen acceptor in the noncyclic pathway of ATP formation is
 a   FAD.
 b.  PGA.
* c.  $NADP^+$.
 d.  FMN.
 e.  PEP.

E **18.** The cyclic pathway of ATP formation functions mainly to
 a   fix $CO_2$.
 b.  produce $O_2$.
* c.  make ATP.
 d.  reduce NADP.
 e.  split $H_2O$.

M **19.** Photolysis involves
 a   the cyclic pathway of ATP formation.
 b.  photosystem I.
 c.  carotenoid pigments.
* d.  the noncyclic pathway of ATP formation.
 e.  both a and b, but not c or d

M **20.** The electrons that are passed to $NADP^+$ during noncyclic pathways were obtained from
* a   chlorophyll.
 b.  $CO_2$.
 c.  glucose.
 d.  sunlight.
 e.  ATP.

M **21.** Plant cells produce one molecule of $O_2$
 a   by splitting carbon dioxide.
 b.  during respiration.
 c.  by splitting ribulose bisphosphate.
* d.  by splitting two molecules of water.
 e.  by breaking down glucose.

E **22.** An important electron and hydrogen acceptor in noncyclic pathways of ATP formation is
* a   $NADP^+$.
 b.  ADP.
 c.  $O_2$.
 d.  $H_2O$.
 e.  none of the above

## A CLOSER LOOK AT ATP FORMATION IN CHLOROPLASTS

M **23.** The concept that concentration differences in $H^+$ and electric gradients across a membrane are responsible for ATP formation is known as the
* a   chemiosmotic theory.
 b.  photosystem mechanism.
 c.  process of photolysis.
 d.  electron transfer system.
 e.  cyclic pathway.

D **24.** Hydrogen ion flow in the thylakoid compartments
 a   occurs between photosystems I and II.
 b.  is called the hydrogen transfer system.
* c.  provides energy to produce ATP molecules.
 d.  causes excitation of chlorophyll molecules.
 e.  requires the intermediary action of acceptor molecules.

D **25.** In the noncyclic pathways
 a   there is a one-way flow of electrons from photosystem I to photosystem II.
 b.  ATP alone is produced.
* c.  hydrogen ions accumulate in the thylakoid compartments.
 d.  only electrons are transferred to hydrogen acceptors.
 e.  water is not involved in any of the reactions.

## LIGHT-INDEPENDENT REACTIONS

E **26.** All but which condition must be present for light-independent reactions to occur?
 a   Carbon dioxide is present.
* b.  The plant is exposed to light.
 c.  Ribulose bisphosphate is present.
 d.  ATP and NADPH are present.
 e.  Required enzymes are present.

E **27.** The light-independent reactions were discovered by
 a   M. D. Hatch.
 b.  Andrew Benson.
 c.  Melvin Calvin.
 d.  Robert Hill.
* e.  both b and c

M **28.** The first stable compound produced from $CO_2$ in the light-independent reactions is
  * a phosphoglycerate (PGA).
  b. ribulose bisphosphate (RuBP).
  c. phosphoglyceraldehyde (PGAL).
  d. glucose.
  e. oxaloacetate.

M **29.** The carbon dioxide acceptor in the Calvin–Benson cycle is
  a phosphoglycerate (PGA).
  * b. ribulose bisphosphate (RuBP).
  c. phosphoglyceraldehyde (PGAL).
  d. glucose.
  e. oxaloacetate.

M **30.** Which of the following chemicals has five carbon atoms?
  a phosphoglycerate (PGA)
  * b. ribulose bisphosphate (RuBP)
  c. phosphoglyceraldehyde (PGAL)
  d. glucose
  e. oxaloacetate

D **31.** For each six atoms of carbon dioxide fixed in the light-independent reactions, how many molecules of PGAL (phosphoglyceraldehyde) are produced?
  a 2
  b. 3
  c. 6
  * d. 12
  e. 15

D **32.** How many molecules of PGAL (phosphoglyceraldehyde) are used to regenerate the six molecules of RuBP (ribulose bisphosphate)?
  a 3
  b. 6
  * c. 10
  d. 12
  e. 18

M **33.** The joining of carbon dioxide to RuBP occurs in the
  a thylakoids.
  * b. stroma.
  c. mitochondria.
  d. cytoplasm.
  e. P700.

M **34.** Which chemical has six carbon atoms?
  a phosphoglycerate (PGA)
  b. ribulose bisphosphate (RuBP)
  c. phosphoglyceraldehyde (PGAL)
  * d. glucose
  e. oxaloacetate

M **35.** Which chemical has the most energy?
  a phosphoglycerate (PGA)
  b. ribulose bisphosphate (RuBP)
  c. phosphoglyceraldehyde (PGAL)
  * d. glucose
  e. oxaloacetate

**FIXING CARBON—SO NEAR, YET SO FAR**

M **36.** Which chemical has four carbon atoms?
  a phosphoglycerate (PGA)
  b. ribulose bisphosphate (RuBP)
  c. phosphoglyceraldehyde (PGAL)
  d. glucose
  * e. oxaloacetate

M **37.** Which is a $C_4$ plant?
  a corn
  b. pine
  c. sugarcane
  d. crabgrass
  * e. all except b

M **38.** The $C_4$ pathway involves
  a RuBP.
  b. FAD.
  * c. oxaloacetate.
  d. ATP.
  e. water.

## Matching Questions

M **39.** Choose the one most appropriate answer for each.

  1 _____ cyclic pathway
  2 _____ noncyclic pathway
  3 _____ carbon dioxide fixation
  4 _____ the PGA to PGAL conversion
  5 _____ the formation of glucose

  A. uses ribulose bisphosphate; produces PGA
  B. uses ATP and NADPH
  C. detaches two phosphate groups
  D. produces ATP and NADPH
  E. uses an electron transport system to produce ATP

*Answers:*   1. E    2. D    3. A
            4. B.    5. C

## Classification Questions

The processes listed below represent major chemical pathways in the photosynthetic process. Answer questions 40–44 with reference to these five processes.

    a.  light-dependent reactions
    b.  chemosynthetic reactions
    c.  carbon dioxide fixation
    d.  Calvin–Benson cycle
    e.  $C_4$ pathway

D   **40.** Glucose-6-phosphate (sugar phosphate) is formed from two molecules of phosphoglyceraldehyde.

M   **41.** Carbon dioxide is incorporated first into an unstable intermediate compound and then into phosphoglycerate.

E   **42.** This process yields NADPH as well as ATP.

M   **43.** This is a carbon-fixing system that precedes the Calvin–Benson cycle in some plants.

M   **44.** PGAL molecules are formed from the reaction of PGA molecules with ATP and NADPH.

*Answers:*    40.  d     41.  c     42.  a
            43.  e     44.  d

The five reactions listed below occur during noncyclic pathways of ATP formation. Use them to answer questions 45–49.

    a.  reduction of NADP
    b.  phosphorylation of ADP
    c.  photolysis of water
    d.  oxidation of chlorophyll
    e.  reduction of chlorophyll

D   **45.** This process releases electrons to fill "holes" in chlorophyll in noncyclic pathways.

D   **46.** When light energy is absorbed by a leaf, this will be the first result.

D   **47.** This is the final step that occurs during noncyclic pathways of ATP formation.

M   **48.** High energy phosphate bonds are formed during this process.

D   **49.** Oxygen is produced by this process.

*Answers:*    45.  c     46.  d     47.  a
            48.  b     49.  c

## Selecting the Exception

E   **50.** Four of the five answers listed below are heterotrophs. Select the exception.
    a.  fungus
*   b.  carrot
    c.  earthworm
    d.  lobster
    e.  parasite

M   **51.** Four of the five answers listed below are autotrophic. Select the exception.
    a.  self-nourishing
    b.  carbon source is $CO_2$
    c.  chemosynthetic organisms
*   d.  most bacteria
    e.  sulfur bacteria

D   **52.** Four of the five answers listed below are part of the light-independent reactions. Select the exception.
*   a.  water
    b.  carbon dioxide
    c.  ribulose bisphosphate
    d.  phosphoglyceraldehyde
    e.  phosphoglycerate

M   **53.** Four of the five answers listed below are participants in photosynthesis. Select the exception.
    a.  photosystem
    b.  grana
*   c.  mitochondrion
    d.  chloroplast
    e.  thylakoid

D   **54.** Four of the five answers listed below are processes associated with light-dependent reactions. Select the exception.
    a.  photolysis
    b.  chemiosmosis
*   c.  fixing carbon dioxide
    d.  photosystem I and II
    e.  noncyclic pathways of ATP formation

D   **55.** Four of the five answers listed below are processes associated with light-independent reactions. Select the exception.
    a.  uses ATP and NADPH
    b.  involves RuBP
    c.  produces PGA
    d.  is called the Calvin–Benson pathway
*   e.  requires light

M   **56.** Three of the four answers listed below are $C_4$ plants. Select the exception.
    a.  corn
*   b.  spinach
    c.  sugarcane
    d.  crabgrass

M   **57.** Three of the four answers listed below are sources of energy for chemosynthesis. Select the exception.
    a.  ammonium ions
    b.  iron compounds
*   c.  sunlight
    d.  sulfur compounds

# CHAPTER 6
# ENERGY-RELEASING PATHWAYS

## Multiple-Choice Questions

### HOW CELLS MAKE ATP

E | 1. The ultimate source of energy for living things is the
  - a. Krebs cycle.
  - b. fossil fuels.
  - * c. sun.
  - d. glycolysis.
  - e. aerobic respiration.

M | 2. When molecules are broken apart in respiration
  - a. the heat produced is used to drive biological reactions.
  - b. the oxygen in the compounds that are broken apart is used as an energy source.
  - * c. the energy released in respiration is channeled into molecules of ATP.
  - d. ATP is converted into ADP.
  - e. ADP is released as a waste product.

M | 3. Which of the following has the most energy?
  - a. cAMP
  - b. ADP
  - c. ATP
  - * d. glucose
  - e. NADPH

E | 4. The main source of energy for humans is
  - a. fats.
  - * b. carbohydrates.
  - c. proteins.
  - d. nucleotides.
  - e. steroids.

E | 5. ATP is
  - * a. the energy currency of a cell.
  - b. produced by the destruction of ADP.
  - c. expended in the process of photosynthesis.
  - d. produced during the phosphorylation of any organic compound.
  - e. none of the above

M | 6. ATP
  - a. can be produced by photosynthesis.
  - b. is produced in the degradation of organic compounds such as glucose.
  - c. is generated in anaerobic respiration.
  - d. is released in aerobic respiration.
  - * e. all of the above

D | 7. The amount of energy released from a glucose molecule is dependent on what happens to
  - a. carbon atoms.
  - b. oxygen atoms.
  - * c. hydrogen atoms.
  - d. phosphorus atoms.
  - e. water molecules.

E | 8. Which liberates the most energy in the form of ATP?
  - * a. aerobic respiration
  - b. anaerobic respiration
  - c. alcoholic fermentation
  - d. lactate fermentation
  - e. All liberate the same amount, but through different means.

M | 9. Aerobes use _____ as the final electron acceptor in electron transport phosphorylation.
  - a. hydrogen
  - b. carbon
  - * c. oxygen
  - d. $H_2O$
  - e. NAD$^+$

M | 10. The correct operational sequence of the three processes listed below is:
  - I.   glycolysis
  - II.  ETP
  - III. Krebs
  - a. I —> II —> III
  - b. II —> I —> III
  - c. III —> I —> II
  - d. II —> III —> I
  - * e. I —> III —> II

M | 11. The greatest number of ATP molecules is produced in
  - a. glycolysis.
  - b. alcoholic fermentation.
  - c. anaerobic electron transport.
  - * d. electron transport phosphorylation.
  - e. the Krebs cycle.

### GLYCOLYSIS: FIRST STAGE OF THE ENERGY-RELEASING PATHWAY

D | 12. Before a glucose molecule can be broken down to release energy
  - a. one ATP molecule must be added to glucose.
  - * b. two phosphate groups must be attached to glucose.
  - c. three ATP molecules must be added to glucose.
  - d. one ATP molecule must be taken away from glucose.
  - e. two ATP molecules must be taken away from glucose.

D | 13. Glycolysis depends on a continuous supply of
  - a. NADP.
  - b. pyruvate.
  - * c. NAD$^+$.
  - d. NADH.
  - e. $H_2O$.

E 14. Glycolysis
   a  occurs in the mitochondria.
   b. happens to glucose only.
   c. results in the production of pyruvate.
   d. occurs in the cytoplasm.
 * e. c and d

M 15. The end product of glycolysis is
   a  acetyl CoA.
   b. oxaloacetate.
 * c. pyruvate.
   d. citrate.
   e. a and b

M 16. How many ATP molecules (net yield) are produced per molecule of glucose degraded during glycolysis?
   a  1
 * b. 2
   c. 4
   d. 36
   e. 38

D 17. The conversion of PGAL to pyruvate involves
   a  anaerobic respiration.
   b. photophosphorylation.
   c. the electron transport chain.
 * d. substrate-level phosphorylation.
   e. the Krebs cycle.

M 18. In the breakdown of glucose, the compound formed after two phosphorylation reactions is split into two three-carbon compounds. The three-carbon compound is named
 * a  phosphoglyceraldehyde (PGAL).
   b. pyruvate.
   c. acetyl CoA.
   d. lactate.
   e. acetaldehyde.

E 19. Pyruvate can be regarded as the end product of
 * a  glycolysis.
   b. acetyl CoA formation.
   c. fermentation.
   d. the Krebs cycle.
   e. electron transport.

**SECOND STAGE OF THE AEROBIC PATHWAY**

M 20. Which is capable of being reduced during both glycolysis and the Krebs cycle?
 * a  NAD$^+$
   b. FAD$^+$
   c. ADP
   d. NADH
   e. NADP$^+$

E 21. The Krebs cycle takes place in the
   a  ribosomes.
   b. cytoplasm.
   c. nucleus.
 * d. mitochondria.
   e. chloroplasts.

M 22. The breakdown of pyruvate in the Krebs cycle results in the release of
   a  energy.
   b. carbon dioxide.
   c. oxygen.
   d. hydrogen.
 * e. all except c

D 23. To break down a glucose molecule completely requires how many passes through the Krebs cycle?
 * a  2
   b. 3
   c. 4
   d. 6
   e. 12

M 24. The first intermediate produced in the Krebs cycle is
   a  pyruvate.
   b. acetyl CoA.
   c. fructose bisphosphate.
   d. oxaloacetate.
 * e. citrate.

M 25. The last intermediate produced in the Krebs cycle is
   a  pyruvate.
   b. acetyl CoA.
   c. fructose bisphosphate.
 * d. oxaloacetate.
   e. citrate.

D 26. During which phase of aerobic respiration is ATP produced directly by substrate-level phosphorylation?
   a  glucose formation
   b. ethanol production
   c. acetyl CoA formation
 * d. the Krebs cycle
   e. all of the above

M 27. Which is a transition from glycolysis to the Krebs cycle?
 * a  acetyl CoA formation
   b. conversion of PGAL to PGA
   c. regeneration of reduced NAD$^+$
   d. oxidative phosphorylation
   e. substrate-level phosphorylation

**THIRD STAGE OF THE AEROBIC PATHWAY**

E 28. When glucose is used as the energy source, the largest amount of ATP is produced in
   a  glycolysis.
   b. acetyl CoA formation.
   c. the Krebs cycle.
   d. substrate-level phosphorylation.
 * e. electron transport phosphorylation.

M    **29.** What is the name of the process by which reduced NAD$^+$ transfers electrons to oxygen?
     a   glycolysis
     b.   acetyl CoA formation
     c.   the Krebs cycle
 *   d.   electron transport phosphorylation
     e.   substrate-level phosphorylation

E    **30.** During electron transport phosphorylation, which ions accumulate in the outer compartment of the mitochondria?
     a   calcium
 *   b.   hydrogen
     c.   oxygen
     d.   phosphorus
     e.   sodium

M    **31.** The ultimate electron acceptor in aerobic respiration is
     a   NAD$^+$
     b.   $CO_2$
     c.   ADP
     d.   NADP$^+$
 *   e.   $O_2$

D    **32.** Which is NOT ordinarily capable of being reduced at any time?
     a   NAD$^+$
     b.   FAD
     c.   oxygen, $O_2$
 *   d.   water
     e.   all of the above

M    **33.** The energy used to generate most of the ATP formed in aerobic respiration is released when electrons ultimately are passed from NADH to which of the following?
 *   a   oxygen
     b.   acetyl CoA
     c.   FADH
     d.   $CO_2$
     e.   NADPH

M    **34.** The generation of concentration gradients across the membranes of mitochondria is known as which theory of ATP production?
     a   glycolytic
     b.   negative ion generator
     c.   phosphate pump
 *   d.   chemiosmotic
     e.   none of the above

## ANAEROBIC ROUTES

M    **35.** The first forms of life that produced ATP probably used pathways similar to
     a   photosynthesis.
     b.   photophosphorylation.
 *   c.   glycolysis and fermentation.
     d.   the Krebs cycle.
     e.   aerobic respiration.

D    **36.** The bacteria that live in hot springs use _____ as their final hydrogen acceptor.
     a   oxygen
 *   b.   sulfate
     c.   nitrogen
     d.   magnesium
     e.   phosphorus

E    **37.** Under anaerobic conditions muscle cells produce
     a   ethyl alcohol.
     b.   acetaldehyde.
     c.   pyruvate.
 *   d.   lactate.
     e.   citrate.

E    **38.** Sour cream and sour milk are produced by bacteria that form
     a   ethyl alcohol.
     b.   acetaldehyde.
     c.   pyruvate.
 *   d.   lactate.
     e.   citrate.

D    **39.** If fermentation follows glycolysis,
     a   $CO_2$ will be one of the products as pyruvate is converted to lactate.
 *   b.   the two NADH molecules produced during glycolysis will (depending on the organism) be used to reduce pyruvate to either lactate or ethanol and $CO_2$.
     c.   ATP will be required to convert pyruvate to either lactate or ethanol and $CO_2$.
     d.   oxidative phosphorylation occurs either on the plasma membrane or on derivatives of the plasma membrane.

D    **40.** Fermentation
 *   a   may occur in a muscle under anaerobic conditions.
     b.   produces more ATP than is liberated in the hydrogen transfer series.
     c.   breaks down glucose in reaction with oxygen.
     d.   is restricted to yeasts.
     e.   none of the above

D    **41.** If you were searching for anaerobic bacteria, you would NOT look for them in
     a   the guts of farm animals.
     b.   swamps.
 *   c.   mountain streams.
     d.   sediments of lakes and oceans.
     e.   sealed canned goods.

M    **42.** Lactate production in muscle cells is
     a   temporary.
     b.   due to oxygen deficiency.
     c.   an NAD regenerator.
     d.   a and b only
 *   e.   a, b, and c

## ALTERNATIVE ENERGY SOURCES IN THE HUMAN BODY

D 43. Which statement is false?
- a High concentrations of ATP inhibit the formation of more ATP.
- b. When cells need large supplies of energy, the ATP concentration in these cells actually decreases at first.
- * c. When ATP concentration declines, enzymatic activity that produces ATP declines.
- d. Cells constantly adjust their metabolic reactions to provide energy whenever it is needed.
- e. The activity of many different enzymes influences the supply of ATP in cells.

D 44. In glycolysis, approximately what percent of the total energy in glucose is released?
- * a 2
- b. 6
- c. 10
- d. 15
- e. 20

M 45. Molecules associated with glycolysis and the Krebs cycle provide
- a sources of energy for ATP formation.
- b. intermediates in the formation of carbohydrates.
- c. intermediates in the formation of lipids.
- d. intermediates in the formation of proteins.
- * e. all of the above

Ṁ 46. When blood glucose levels decrease (as between meals), what reserves are tapped?
- * a glycogen
- b. fats
- c. proteins
- d. steroids
- e. amino acids

M 47. When proteins and fats are used as energy sources, their breakdown subunits enter
- a glycolysis.
- b. electron transport.
- * c. Krebs cycle.
- d. chemiosmosis.
- e. fermentation.

E 48. What is the waste product of amino acid metabolism?
- a ATP
- b. pyruvate
- c. NADH
- d. glycerol
- * e. urea

## Matching Questions

M 49. Matching. Choose the one most appropriate answer for each.

1 _____ glycolysis
2 _____ fermentation
3 _____ acetyl-CoA formation
4 _____ the Krebs cycle
5 _____ electron transport phosphorylation

- A. produces NADH and $CO_2$; changes pyruvate
- B. produces ATP, NADH, and $CO_2$
- C. splits glucose into two pyruvate molecules
- D. regenerates $NAD^+$ as pyruvate is converted to ethanol or lactate
- E. uses a membrane-bound system that contains cytochromes to produce ATP

*Answers*:  1. C     2. D     3. A
4. B     5. E

## Classification Questions

Use the five processes listed below to answer questions 50–54.
- a glycolysis
- b. aerobic respiration
- c. anaerobic electron transport
- d. alcoholic fermentation
- e. lactate fermentation

E 50. This process yields two molecules of ATP and the final product ethanol.

E 51. This process yields a final product called lactate.

M 52. This process yields the most energy.

D 53. This process involves electron transport phosphorylation.

E 54. This process precedes the Krebs cycle.

*Answers*:  50. d     51. e     52. b
53. b     54. a

Use the five compounds listed below to answer questions 55–59.

    a  ethanol
    b.  pyruvate
    c.  lactate
    d.  citrate
    e.  acetaldehyde

M    **55.**  This compound is utilized in alcoholic fermentation and lactate fermentation.

M    **56.**  This compound is the most likely end-product of a human runner experiencing an oxygen debt.

D    **57.**  This compound is an intermediate product of alcoholic fermentation, but not lactate fermentation.

M    **58.**  This compound is the end product of glycolysis.

E    **59.**  This compound is an end-product of anaerobic respiration in exercising muscle.

*Answers:*    55.  b    56.  c    57.  e
               58.  b    59.  c

## Selecting the Exception

D    **60.**  Four of the five answers listed below are hydrogen acceptors. Select the exception.
        a  oxygen
        b.  cytochrome
    *  c.  ATP
        d.  $NAD^+$
        e.  FAD

D    **61.**  Four of the five answers listed below are compounds associated with anaerobic respiration. Select the exception.
        a  pyruvate
        b.  lactic acid
        c.  ethanol
    *  d.  oxaloacetic acid
        e.  phosphoglyceraldehyde

D    **62.**  Four of the five answers listed below are compounds in the glycolysis reactions. Select the exception.
        a  fructose-1,6-bisphosphate
        b.  3-phosphoglycerate (3 = PGA)
        c.  pyruvate
        d.  phosphoenol pyruvate (PEP)
    *  e.  isocitrate

D    **63.**  Four of the five answers listed below are intermediates in the Krebs cycle. Select the exception.
        a  succinate
        b.  citrate
        c.  malate
        d.  fumarate
    *  e.  acetyl CoA

D    **64.**  Four of the five answers listed below are compounds in the Krebs reactions. Select the exception.
        a  oxaloacetate
        b.  isocitrate
        c.  alpha-ketoglutarate
    *  d.  pyruvate
        e.  succinyl CoA

D    **65.**  Four of the five answers listed below are molecules that donate hydrogens to $NAD^+$. Select the exception.
        a  pyruvate
        b.  alpha-ketoglutarate
        c.  isocitrate
    *  d.  succinate
        e.  malate

D    **66.**  Four of the five answers listed below are degradation processes for carbon compounds. Select the exception.
    *  a  Calvin–Benson cycle
        b.  Krebs cycle
        c.  fermentation
        d.  respiration
        e.  glycolysis

# CHAPTER 7
# CELL DIVISION AND MITOSIS

## Multiple-Choice Questions

### DIVIDING CELLS: THE BRIDGE BETWEEN GENERATIONS

M    **1.** When a cell undergoes mitosis
      a   the daughter cells have identical genes.
      b.   the daughter cell has genes identical to those of the mother cell that produced it.
      c.   the amount of cytoplasm in the mother cell and in each of the daughter cells is equal.
      d.   there is an exact duplication and division of all of the organelles between daughter cells.
  *    e.   both a and b, but not c or d

D    **2.** When a eukaryotic cell divides, the daughter cells
      a   manufacture all the organelles from material in the cytoplasm.
  *    b.   receive enough of the organelles to start up the new cells and produce additional organelles as needed.
      c.   produce individual organelles that attach to the spindle fibers and are distributed just like chromosomes.
      d.   produce an equal number of organelles distributed to each cell.
      e.   get cellular organelles by an unknown process.

E    **3.** In mitosis, if a parent cell has 16 chromosomes, each daughter cell will have how many chromosomes?
      a   64
      b.   32
  *    c.   16
      d.   8
      e.   4

E    **4.** Chromatids that are attached at the centromere are called what kind of chromatids?
      a   mother
      b.   daughter
  *    c.   sister
      d.   programmed
      e.   either a or b, but not c or d

E    **5.** Cells two sets of genetic information are described by the term
      a   polyploid.
  *    b.   diploid.
      c.   triploid.
      d.   haploid.
      e.   tetraploid.

### MITOSIS AND THE CELL CYCLE

M    **6.** DNA replication occurs
  *    a   between the gap phases of interphase.
      b.   immediately before prophase of mitosis.
      c.   during prophase of mitosis.
      d.   during prophase of meiosis.
      e.   at any time during cell division.

E    **7.** Chromosomes are duplicated during which period?
      a   M
      b.   D
      c.   $G_1$
      d.   $G_2$
  *    e.   S

E    **8.** The chromosomes and genes are actually replicated during
      a   anaphase.
      b.   metaphase.
  *    c.   interphase.
      d.   prophase.
      e.   telophase.

### STAGES OF MITOSIS

E    **9.** The spindle apparatus is made of
      a   Golgi bodies.
  *    b.   microtubules.
      c.   endoplasmic reticulum.
      d.   nucleoprotein.
      e.   chromatids.

M    **10.** Mitosis comes from the Greek word *mitos* , which means
      a   divide.
      b.   grow.
      c.   swell.
  *    d.   thread.
      e.   shrink.

M    **11.** In eukaryotic cells, which can occur during mitosis?
      a   the duplication of chromatids
      b.   the replication of DNA
      c.   pairing of homologous chromosomes
  *    d.   fragmentation and disappearance of nuclear envelope and nucleolus
      e.   all of the above

E **12.** The chromosomes are aligned at the spindle equator during
  a anaphase.
  * b. metaphase.
  c interphase.
  d prophase.
  e telophase.

E **13.** The spindle apparatus becomes visible during
  a anaphase.
  b. metaphase.
  c interphase.
  * d. prophase.
  e telophase.

M **14.** The chromosomes detach from one another and become visibly separated during
  * a anaphase.
  b. metaphase.
  c interphase.
  d prophase.
  e telophase.

E **15.** The chromosomes are moving to opposite poles during
  * a anaphase.
  b. metaphase.
  c interphase.
  d prophase.
  e telophase.

E **16.** The chromosomes have arrived at opposite poles during
  a anaphase.
  b. metaphase.
  c interphase.
  d prophase.
  * e telophase.

E **17.** The nuclear membrane reforms during
  a anaphase.
  b. metaphase.
  c interphase.
  d prophase.
  * e telophase.

M **18.** Strictly speaking, mitosis and meiosis are divisions of the
  a nucleus.
  b. cytoplasm.
  c chromosomes.
  * d only a and c
  e a, b, and c

D **19.** Which of the following is the proper sequence for mitosis?
  **I.** **metaphase**  **II.** **telophase**
  **III.** **prophase**  **IV.** **anaphase**
  a I, III, IV, II
  b. I, II, III, IV
  * c III, I, IV, II
  d IV, I, III, II
  e III, IV, I, II

D **20.** In which of the stages below does the chromosome consist of two DNA molecules?
  **I.** **metaphase**  **II.** **telophase**
  **III.** **prophase**  **IV.** **anaphase**
  a III and IV
  b. I, III, and IV
  * c I and III
  d I, II, and III
  e I, II, III, and IV

## DIVISION OF THE CYTOPLASM

M **21.** Cytokinesis (cytoplasmic division)
  a in animal cells begins with various deposits of material associated with groups of microtubules at each pole of the nucleus.
  b. in animal cells occurs when the plasma membrane is pulled inward by a ring of microtubules that has become attached to the cell plate.
  * c usually accompanies nuclear division.
  d in plant cells begins with the deposition of a very rigid lipid bilayer, which is the major constituent of the cell wall.
  e all of the above

M **22.** The distribution of cytoplasm to daughter cells is accomplished during
  a prokaryotic fission.
  b. mitosis.
  c meiosis.
  * d cytokinesis (cytoplasmic division).
  e karyokinesis.

## Matching Questions

E 23. Matching. Choose the one most appropriate answer for each.

1 _____ centriole
2 _____ centromere
3 _____ chromatid
4 _____ cytokinesis
5 _____ metaphase
6 _____ microtubules
7 _____ prophase
8 _____ telophase

A. cytoplasm apportioned between the two daughter cells

B. final phase of mitosis; daughter nuclei re-form

C. two sister chromatids are joined here

D. chromosomes condense and mitotic spindle begins to form

E. chromosomes line up at spindle equator

F. sister chromatids separate; move to opposite spindle poles now

G. about 25 mm in diameter; form mitotic spindle

H. half of a chromosome in prophase

I. in pairs in some eukaryotic cells; move to poles during spindle formation

*Answers:*

| 1. I | 2. C | 3. H |
|------|------|------|
| 4. A | 5. E | 6. G |
| 7. D | 8. B | |

## Classification Questions

Answer questions 24–33 in reference to the eukaryotic cell cycle. Each question has only one BEST answer.

a $G_2$
b. mitosis
c. S
d. $G_1$
e. cytokinesis

E 24. Period when DNA is duplicated

E 25. Period when interphase ends in the parent cell

M 26. Event that forms two daughter cytoplasmic masses

M 27. Period of cell growth before DNA duplication

M 28. Period after DNA is duplicated

E 29. Period of nuclear division

M 30. Period when interphase begins in a daughter cell

E 31. Period commonly followed by cytokinesis

E 32. Period in which metaphase occurs

D 33. Period prior to mitosis

*Answers:*

| 24. c | 25. a | 26. e |
|-------|-------|-------|
| 27. d | 28. a | 29. b |
| 30. d | 31. b | 32. b |
| 33. a | | |

Answer questions 34–44 with reference to these phases of the cell cycle:

a. interphase
b. prophase
c. metaphase
d. anaphase
e. telophase

E 34. During this stage homologous pairs of chromosomes are lined up on the equatorial plate.

M 35. Chromosomes replicate during this phase

M 36. Genes replicate during this phase

E 37. DNA replicates during this phase

E 38. Condensation and shortening of chromosomes occurs during this phase.

E 39. Spindle fibers first appear during this stage.

M 40. During this phase the centromeres break apart as the separated sister chromatids begin to move to opposite poles.

E 41. The microtubular spindle develops during this phase.

E 42. Sister chromatids joined at their centromeres are attached to spindle fibers during this phase.

M 43. Cytokinesis occurs as this phase of mitosis proceeds.

E 44. New daughter nuclear membranes form during this phase.

*Answers:*

| 34. c | 35. a | 36. a |
|-------|-------|-------|
| 37. a | 38. b | 39. b |
| 40. d | 41. b | 42. c |
| 43. e | 44. e | |

## Selecting the Exception

E  **45.** Four of the five answers listed below are stages of actual nuclear division. Select the exception.
- a  anaphase
- b  prophase
- *  c  interphase
- d  telophase
- e  metaphase

D  **46.** Four of the five answers listed below are related by a common phase of mitosis. Select the exception.
- a  microtubules start to assemble outside the nucleus
- *  b  division of centromere
- c  disappearance of nucleolus
- d  disappearance of nuclear membrane
- e  shortening and condensation of a visible chromosome

M  **47.** Four of the five answers listed below are periods of the same cycle. Select the exception.
- a  $G_1$
- b  M
- *  c  R
- d  S
- e  $G_2$

D  **48.** Four of the five answers listed below are related by a common phase of mitosis. Select the exception.
- a  chromosomes decondense
- b  spindle microtubules disappear
- c  nucleolus reappears
- *  d  chromosomes separate
- e  nuclear envelope reforms

M  **49.** Four of the five answers listed below are events occurring during mitosis. Select the exception.
- *  a  chromosome replication
- b  division of centromere
- c  lining chromosomes up at the cellular equator
- d  spindle microtubules attach to centromeres
- e  chromosomes migrate to opposite ends of the cell

D  **50.** Four of the five answers listed below assist in chromosome movement. Select the exception.
- a  microtubule
- b  spindle microtubules
- c  centromeres
- d  centriole
- *  e  nuclear envelope

D  **51.** Four of the five answers listed below are related by a common phase of mitosis. Select the exception.
- *  a  chromosomes align at the spindle equator
- b  sister chromatids become individual chromosomes
- c  centromeres divide
- d  the chromosomes move apart
- e  spindle microtubules shorten, pulling chromosomes toward the poles

D  **52.** Four of the five answers listed below are related by a common division association. Select the exception.
- a  mitochondria
- *  b  chromosomes
- c  ribosomes
- d  plastids
- e  microbodies

# CHAPTER 8

# MEIOSIS

## Multiple-Choice Questions

### COMPARISON OF ASEXUAL AND SEXUAL REPRODUCTION

M    **1.** The essence of meiosis is that
- a   gametes are formed that receive one copy of *each* member of *each* pair of homologous chromosomes.
- b.   gametes are formed that are diploid.
- c.   each gamete receives one member of *each* pair of homologous chromosomes.
- d.   gametes are formed that are haploid.
- *   e.   c and d are correct

M    **2.** Through meiosis
- a   alternate forms of genes are shuffled.
- b.   parental DNA is divided and distributed to forming gametes.
- c.   the diploid chromosome number is reduced to haploid.
- d.   offspring are provided with new gene combinations.
- *   e.   all of the above

M    **3.** Asexually produced daughter cells are
- a   identical to each other.
- b.   identical to mother cell.
- c.   different from mother cell.
- d.   different from each other.
- *   e.   a and b

M    **4.** Sexual reproduction
- a   leads to uniform characteristics in a population.
- *   b.   results in new combinations of genetic traits.
- c.   produces genetic clones.
- d.   requires less tissue differentiation than asexual reproduction.
- e.   c and d

D    **5.** Which process is absolutely necessary for sexual reproduction to occur in a life cycle, but is not necessarily required for organisms that only reproduce asexually?
- a   prokaryotic fission
- b.   mitosis
- *   c.   meiosis
- d.   cytokinesis
- e.   karyokinesis

E    **6.** If a parent cell has 16 chromosomes and undergoes meiosis, the resulting cells will have how many chromosomes?
- a   64
- b.   32
- c.   16
- *   d.   8
- e.   4

M    **7.** The number of chromosomes found in a eukaryotic cell
- a   indicates the phylogenetic position of the organism.
- b.   is constant during the life cycle.
- c.   is haploid among asexually reproducing forms and diploid if they reproduce sexually.
- *   d.   is doubled by fertilization and cut in half by meiosis.
- e.   is dependent on the age of the tissue.

### MEIOSIS AND THE CHROMOSOME NUMBER

E    **8.** Chromatids are
- a   attached at the centriole.
- b.   a pair of chromosomes, one from the mother and one from the father.
- c.   attached at their centromeres.
- d.   identical until crossing over occurs.
- *   e.   both c and d, but not a or b

M    **9.** Homologous chromosomes
- a   may exchange parts during meiosis.
- b.   have alleles for the same characteristics even though the gene expression may not be the same.
- c.   are in pairs, one chromosome of each pair from the father and one from the mother.
- d.   pair up during meiosis.
- *   e.   all of the above

E    **10.** Copies of chromosomes linked together at their centromeres at the beginning of meiosis are appropriately called what kind of chromatids?
- a   mother
- b.   daughter
- *   c.   sister
- d.   homologous
- e.   none of the above

M    11. Chromosomes of a pair of homologous chromosomes may differ from other chromosomes in terms of
     a   size.
     b.   shape.
     c.   alleles they carry.
     d.   position of the centromere.
*     e.   all of the above

## A VISUAL TOUR OF THE STAGES OF MEIOSIS

M    12. Meiosis typically results in the production of
     a   2 diploid cells.
     b.   4 diploid cells.
*     c.   4 haploid cells.
     d.   2 haploid cells.
     e.   1 triploid cell.

D    13. During meiosis II
     a   cytokinesis results in the formation of a total of two cells.
*     b.   sister chromatids of each chromosome are separated from each other.
     c.   homologous chromosomes pair up.
     d.   homologous chromosomes separate.
     e.   sister chromatids exchange parts.

E    14. The chromosomal DNA is duplicate in _____ of meiosis.
     a   prophase I
     b.   metaphase I
*     c.   interphase
     d.   prophase II
     e.   anaphase II

E    15. The sister chromatids become separated during _____ of meiosis.
     a   metaphase I
     b.   anaphase I
     c.   telophase I
*     d.   anaphase II
     e.   prophase II

D    16. Each of the cells formed during telophase I is
     a   diploid.
     b.   tetraploid.
     c.   in synapsis.
     d.   ready to be fertilized.
*     e.   haploid.

M    17. Sister chromatids remain joined at the centromere in all of the stages of meiosis listed below except
     a   metaphase II.
*     b.   anaphase II.
     c.   telophase I.
     d.   metaphase I.
     e.   prophase II.

M    18. Crossing over could be detected in all of the following stages of meiosis except
     a   prophase II.
*     b.   interphase.
     c.   anaphase II.
     d.   metaphase I.
     e.   telophase II.

## KEY EVENTS OF MEIOSIS I

D    19. Crossing over
     a   generally results in binary fission.
     b.   involves nucleoli.
     c.   involves breakages and exchanges being made between sister chromatids.
*     d.   alters the composition of chromosomes and results in new combinations of alleles being channeled into the daughter cells.
     e.   all of the above

E    20. Pairing of homologues and crossing over occur during
     a   anaphase I.
     b.   metaphase II.
*     c.   prophase I.
     d.   prophase II.
     e.   telophase II.

E    21. Under favorable conditions, during which phase of meiosis will the chromosomes appear as packets of four chromatids?
     a   anaphase I
     b.   telophase II
     c.   anaphase II
*     d.   prophase I
     e.   metaphase II

M    22. Which does NOT occur in prophase I of meiosis?
*     a   cytokinesis
     b.   formation of groups of four chromatids
     c.   homologue pairing
     d.   crossing over
     e.   condensation of chromatin

M    23. Which is NOT true of human chromosomes?
     a   The haploid number is 23.
     b.   The diploid number is 46.
     c.   There are 23 pairs of chromosomes.
*     d.   Human gametes end up with two of each type of 23 chromosomes.
     e.   Human gametes end up one of each type of 23 chromosomes.

D       24.     Crossing over is one of the most important events in meiosis because
*       a.      it produces new arrays of alleles on chromosomes.
        b.      homologous chromosomes must be separated into different daughter cells.
        c.      the number of chromosomes allotted to each daughter cell must be halved.
        d.      homologous chromatids must be separated into different daughter cells.
        e.      all of the above

**FROM GAMETES TO OFFSPRING**

M       25.     Gamete formation is
        a.      the result of the process of mitosis.
        b.      the pairing of homologous chromosomes.
*       c.      the formation of sex cells.
        d.      the fusion of gametes.
        e.      a process that occurs only in asexually reproducing forms.

M       26.     Sperm are formed directly from the maturation of
        a.      sperm mother cells.
*       b.      spermatids.
        c.      spermatagonial cells.
        d.      primary spermatocytes.
        e.      secondary spermatocytes.

M       27.     The mature ovum is produced by maturation of the
        a.      oogonium.
        b.      primary oocyte.
        c.      secondary polar body.
        d.      polar body I.
*       e.      none of the above

M       28.     Which does NOT produce variation?
        a.      crossing over
        b.      random alignment of chromosomes during meiosis
*       c.      asexual reproduction
        d.      genetic recombination of alleles
        e.      sexual reproduction

**MEIOSIS AND MITOSIS COMPARED**

M       29.     Maternal and paternal chromosomes are shuffled most during
        a.      anaphase II.
*       b.      metaphase I.
        c.      prophase I.
        d.      telophase II.
        e.      interphase.

D       30.     In comparing mitosis and meiosis, which of the following statements is true?
        a.      Meiosis I is more like mitosis than is meiosis II.
        b.      Both processes result in four cells.
        c.      Synapsis occurs in both.
        d.      Chromatids are present only in mitosis.
*       e.      Meiosis II resembles mitosis.

## Classification Questions

With reference to the mammalian reproductive system, answer questions 31-33 by using the five items listed below.

    I.      sperm
    II.     mature ova
    III.    primary oocytes
    IV.     primary spermatocytes
    V.      zygotes

E       31.     During fertilization, which two items combine to form a fertilized egg?
*       a.      I and II
        b.      I and III
        c.      I and IV
        d.      II and IV
        e.      III and IV

M       32.     Which item or items are the same as fertilized eggs?
        a.      II only
        b.      III only
*       c.      V only
        d.      II and III
        e.      III and V

D       33.     Which is a normal sequence of development?
        a.      I $\longrightarrow$ II $\longrightarrow$ III
        b.      I $\longrightarrow$ IV $\longrightarrow$ V
        c.      II $\longrightarrow$ III $\longrightarrow$ V
*       d.      III $\longrightarrow$ II + I $\longrightarrow$ V
        e.      I $\longrightarrow$ IV + II $\longrightarrow$ V

Answer questions 34–37 by using the five numbers below.

        a.      10
        b.      20
        c.      40
        d.      60
        e.      80

M       34.     How many sperm would eventually be produced from 20 spermatids?

M       35.     How many sperm would eventually be produced from 20 primary spermatocytes?

M       36.     How many ova (eggs) would eventually result from 20 secondary oocytes?

M       37.     How many ova (eggs) would eventually result from 20 primary oocytes?

*Answers*:      34.     b       35.     e       361.    b
                37.     b

Some of the stages of meiosis are listed under a–e below. Answer questions 38–45 with reference to these phases of meiosis.

    a   prophase I
    b.  prophase II
    c.  anaphase II
    d.  anaphase I
    e.  telophase I

E    **38.**   The formation of groups of four chromatids occurs during this stage.

E    **39.**   Recombination via crossing over occurs during this stage.

D    **40.**   The number of homologous chromosomes is reduced by half at the end of this phase.

M    **41.**   During this stage the sister chromatids separate.

D    **42.**   Following this phase, each individual *cell* is haploid.

M    **43.**   Chiasmata are present during this stage?

D    **44.**   During this phase the centromeres separate.

D    **45.**   New genetic combinations, upon which natural selection can act, are present after this stage.

*Answers*:

| 38. | a | 39. | a | 40. | d |
|-----|---|-----|---|-----|---|
| 41. | c | 42. | e | 43. | a |
| 44. | c | 45. | a |   |   |

# Selecting the Exception

M    **46.**   Three of the four answers listed below concern cells with two chromosome sets. Select the exception.
       a   zygote
       b.  somatic cells
  *   c.  gamete
       d.  diploid

D    **47.**   Four of the five answers listed below are characteristic of meiosis. Select the exception.
       a   involves two divisions
       b.  reduces the number of chromosomes
  *   c.  results in producing genetically identical cells
       d.  produces haploid cells
       e.  occurs in the gonads

M    **48.**   Four of the five answers listed below are terms describing haploid cells. Select the exception.
       a   ovum
  *   b.  primary spermatocyte
       c.  spermatid
       d.  polar body
       e.  secondary spermatocyte

# CHAPTER 9
# OBSERVABLE PATTERNS OF INHERITANCE

## Multiple-Choice Questions

### MENDEL'S INSIGHT INTO PATTERNS OF INHERITANCE

E    **1.** In Mendel's time, most people believed that
     a   all genetic traits bred true.
     b.   only certain forms of domesticated plants and animals bred true.
     \*   c.   the characteristics of parents were blended in the offspring.
     d.   acquired characteristics were inherited.
     e.   the inheritance of traits was controlled by blood.

M    **2.** Which of the following statements is true?
     \*   a   Darwin did not know which mechanisms were responsible for the variation he saw.
     b.   The blending theory of inheritance provides excellent support for evolution.
     c.   Darwin received Mendel's paper but did not understand its significance.
     d.   The explanation for genetics had no implications for evolution.
     e.   both a and b

M    **3.** In his experiments with plants, Mendel removed which part of the plant to prevent unwanted fertilizations?
     a   flowers
     b.   petals
     c.   pistils
     \*   d.   stamens
     e.   stigmas

E    **4.** A locus is
     a   a recessive gene.
     b.   an unmatched allele.
     c.   a sex chromosome.
     \*   d.   the location of an allele on a chromosome.
     e.   a dominant gene.

M    **5.** Mendel's study of genetics differed from those of his contemporaries because he
     a   used only pure-breeding parents.
     b.   examined several different traits at the same time.
     \*   c.   kept careful records and analyzed the data statistically.
     d.   worked on plants rather than animals.
     e.   confirmed the blending theory of inheritance.

E    **6.** Which of the following descriptions of Mendel is incorrect?
     \*   a   He was simply lucky to work out the laws of genetics.
     b.   He focused on contrasting phenotypic characteristics.
     c.   He demonstrated that the blending theory of inheritance was wrong.
     d.   He kept exact mathematical data and was the first scientist to utilize numerical analysis of results.
     e.   He was a monk, a science teacher, and a gardener.

E    **7.** Which organism did Mendel use to work out the laws of segregation and independent assortment?
     a   the fruit fly
     b.   *Neurospora*
     \*   c.   the garden pea
     d.   the chicken
     e.   *E. coli*

E    **8.** Various forms of a gene at a given locus are called
     a   chiasmata.
     \*   b.   alleles.
     c.   autosomes.
     d.   loci.
     e.   chromatids.

M    **9.** Diploid organisms
     a   have corresponding alleles on homologous chromosomes.
     b.   are usually the result of the fusion of two haploid gametes.
     c.   have two sets of chromosomes.
     d.   have pairs of homologous chromosomes.
     \*   e.   all of the above

### MENDEL'S THEORY OF SEGREGATION

M    **10.** If *R* is dominant to *r*, the offspring of the cross of *RR* with *rr* will
     a   be homozygous.
     \*   b.   display the same phenotype as the *RR* parent.
     c.   display the same phenotype as the *rr* parent.
     d.   have the same genotype as the *RR* parent.
     e.   have the same genotype as the *rr* parent.

M  **11.** Mendel found that pea plants expressing a recessive trait

   \* a   were pure-breeding.

   b.   appeared only in the first generation of a cross between two pure-breeding plants expressing contrasting forms of a trait.

   c.   disappeared after the second generation.

   d.   could be produced only if one of the parents expressed the recessive trait.

   e.   none of the above

E  **12.** Hybrid organisms produced from a cross between two pure-breeding organisms belong to which generation?

   a   $P_1$

   b.   $H_1$

   c.   $A_1$

   \* d.   $F_1$

   e.   $F_2$

E  **13.** If short hair ($L$) is dominant to long hair ($l$), animals $LL$ and $Ll$ have the same

   a   parents.

   b.   genotypes.

   \* c.   phenotypes.

   d.   alleles.

   e.   genes.

M  **14.** According to Mendel, what kind of genes "disappear" in $F_1$ pea plants?

   a   sex-linked

   b.   dominant

   \* c.   recessive

   d.   codominant

   e.   lethal

M  **15.** If tall ($D$) is dominant to dwarf ($d$), and two homozygous varieties $DD$ and $dd$ are crossed, then what kind of offspring will be produced?

   a   all intermediate forms

   \* b.   all tall

   c.   all dwarf

   d.   1/2 tall, 1/2 dwarf

   e.   3/4 tall, 1/4 dwarf

E  **16.** The $F_2$ phenotypic ratio of a monohybrid cross is

   a   1:1.

   b.   2:1.

   c.   9:3:3:1.

   d.   1:2:1.

   \* e.   3:1.

M  **17.** If all offspring of a cross have the genotype $Aa$, the parents of the crosses would most likely be

   \* a   $AA$ x $aa$.

   b.   $Aa$ x $Aa$.

   c.   $Aa$ x $aa$.

   d.   $AA$ x $Aa$.

   e.   none of the above

D  **18.** Short hair ($L$) is dominant to long hair ($l$). If a short-haired animal of unknown origin is crossed with a long-haired animal and they produce one long-haired and one short-haired offspring, this would indicate that

   a   the short-haired animal was pure-breeding.

   \* b.   the short-haired animal was not pure-breeding.

   c.   the long-haired animal was not pure-breeding.

   d.   the long-haired animal was pure-breeding.

   e.   none of the above can be determined with two offspring

M  **19.** For Mendel's explanation of inheritance to be correct,

   a   the genes for the traits he studied had to be located on the same chromosome.

   \* b.   which gametes combine at fertilization had to be due to chance.

   c.   genes could not be transmitted independently of each other.

   d.   only diploid organisms would demonstrate inheritance patterns.

   e.   none of the above

M  **20.** The results of a testcross reveal that all offspring resemble the parent being tested. That parent necessarily is

   a   heterozygous.

   b.   polygenic.

   \* c.   homozygous.

   d.   recessive.

D  **21.** Some dogs have erect ears; others have drooping ears. Some dogs bark when following a scent; others are silent. Erect ears and barking are due to dominant alleles located on different chromosomes. A dog homozygous for both dominant traits is mated to a droopy-eared, silent follower. The phenotypic ratio expected in the $F_1$ generation is

   a   9:3:3:1.

   \* b.   100 percent of one phenotype.

   c.   1:1.

   d.   1:2:1.

   e.   none of the above

D  **22.** Some dogs have erect ears; others have drooping ears. Some dogs bark when following a scent; others are silent. Erect ears and barking are due to dominant alleles located on different chromosomes. If two dihybrids are crossed

   a   the most common phenotype is drooping ears and barking.

   \* b.   all droopy-eared silent dogs are pure-breeding.

   c.   the least common phenotype is drooping ears and barking.

   d.   there will be no phenotypes or genotypes that resemble the original parents.

   e.   there will be no offspring that resemble the $F_1$ generation.

D 23. A testcross involves
   a. two $F_1$ hybrids.
   b. an $F_1$ hybrid and an $F_2$ offspring.
   c. two parental organisms.
   d. an $F_1$ hybrid and the homozygous dominant parent.
   * e. an $F_1$ hybrid and an organism that is homozygous recessive for that trait.

M 24. For monohybrid experiments, a testcross could result in which of the following ratios?
   * a. 1:1
   b. 2:1
   c. 9:3:3:1
   d. 1:2:1
   e. 3:1

M 25. If all the offspring of a testcross are alike and resemble the organism being tested, then that parent is
   * a. homozygous dominant.
   b. homozygous recessive.
   c. heterozygous.
   d. recessive.
   e. incompletely dominant.

E 26. The theory of segregation
   a. deals with the alleles governing two different traits.
   b. applies only to linked genes.
   c. applies only to sex-linked genes.
   * d. explains the behavior of a pair of alleles during meiosis.
   e. none of the above

E 27. If short hair ($L$) is dominant to long hair ($l$), then what fraction of the offspring produced by a cross of $Ll$ x $ll$ will be homozygous dominant?
   a. 1/2
   b. 1/4
   c. 1/3
   * d. none (no chance of this offspring)
   e. none of the above is correct

M 28. If short hair ($L$) is dominant to long hair ($l$), then to determine the genotype of a short-haired animal it should be crossed with
   a. $LL$.
   b. $Ll$.
   * c. $ll$.
   d. all of the above
   e. none of the above

**INDEPENDENT ASSORTMENT**

M 29. Mendel's principle of independent assortment states that
   a. one allele is always dominant to another.
   b. hereditary units from the male and female parents are blended in the offspring.
   c. the two hereditary units that influence a certain trait segregate during gamete formation.
   * d. each hereditary unit is inherited separately from other hereditary units.
   e. all of the above

E 30. An individual with a genetic makeup of $aa BB$ is said to be
   * a. pure-breeding.
   b. recessive.
   c. hybrid.
   d. dihybrid.
   e. heterozygous.

M 31. A dihybrid cross of two contrasting pure-breeding organisms
   a. produces homozygous offspring.
   b. must produce a phenotype different from either pure-breeding parent.
   * c. results in the disappearance of the recessive traits for the first generation.
   d. takes place only in the laboratory under precisely controlled conditions.
   e. will result in the immediate formation of another pure-breeding variety.

D 32. Individuals with the genotype $Gg\ Hh\ Ii\ Jj$ will produce how many different kinds of gametes?
   a. 2
   b. 4
   c. 6
   d. 8
   * e. 16

M 33. An individual with a genotype of $Aa\ Bb\ CC$ is able to produce how many different kinds of gametes?
   a. 2
   b. 3
   * c. 4
   d. 7
   e. 8

D 34. In cocker spaniels, black coat color ($B$) is dominant over red ($b$), and solid color ($S$) is dominant over spotted ($s$). If a red male was crossed with a black female to produce a red spotted puppy, the genotypes of the parents (with male genotype first) would be
   a. $Bb\ Ss$ x $Bb\ Ss$.
   * b. $bb\ Ss$ x $Bb\ Ss$.
   c. $bb\ ss$ x $Bb\ Ss$.
   d. $bb\ Ss$ x $Bb\ ss$.
   e. $Bb\ ss$ x $Bb\ ss$.

D  35. In cocker spaniels, black coat color (B) is dominant over red (b), and solid color (S) is dominant over spotted (s). If a red spotted male was crossed with a black solid female and all the offspring from several crosses expressed only the dominant traits, the genotype of the female would be
*   a   BB SS.
    b.  Bb SS.
    c.  Bb Ss.
    d.  BB Ss.
    e.  none of the above

D  36. In cocker spaniels, black coat color (B) is dominant over red (b), and solid color (S) is dominant over spotted (s). If two black solid dogs were crossed several times and the total offspring were eighteen black solid and five black spotted puppies, the genotypes of the parents would most likely be
    a   Bb Ss x Bb Ss.
    b.  Bb Ss x Bb SS.
    c.  BB Ss x Bb ss.
*   d.  BB Ss x Bb Ss.
    e.  Bb ss x Bb SS.

M  37. In cocker spaniels, black coat color (B) is dominant over red (b), and solid color (S) is dominant over spotted (s). If two dihybrids (Bb Ss) were crossed, the most common phenotype would be
*   a   black and solid.
    b.  black and spotted.
    c.  red and solid.
    d.  red and spotted.
    e.  none of the above

M  38. In cocker spaniels, black coat color (B) is dominant over red (b), and solid color (S) is dominant over spotted (s). If two dihybrids (Bb Ss) were crossed, which would be produced?
    a   black and spotted pure-breeding forms
    b.  black and solid pure-breeding forms
    c.  red and solid pure-breeding forms
    d.  red and spotted pure-breeding forms
*   e.  all of the above

D  39. In cocker spaniels, black coat color (B) is dominant over red (b), and solid color (S) is dominant over spotted (s). If two dihybrids (Bb Ss) were crossed, what fraction of the black solid offspring would be homozygous?
    a   4/16
    b.  9/16
*   c.  1/9
    d.  3/16
    e.  3/4

D  40. In cocker spaniels, black coat color (B) is dominant over red (b), and solid color (S) is dominant over spotted (s). In the $F_2$ generation of a cross between BB ss with bb SS, what fraction of the offspring would be expected to be black and spotted?
    a   1/16
    b.  9/16
    c.  1/9
*   d.  3/16
    e.  3/4

M  41. In cocker spaniels, black coat color (B) is dominant over red (b), and solid color (S) is dominant over spotted (s). A cross of Bb Ss with bb ss would produce the phenotypic ratio
    a   9:3:3:1.
*   b.  1:1:1:1.
    c.  1:2:1.
    d.  3:1.
    e.  none of the above

D  42. In cocker spaniels, black coat color (B) is dominant over red (b), and solid color (S) is dominant over spotted (s). If Bb Ss were crossed with Bb ss, the chance that a black solid individual would be produced is
    a   3/16.
    b.  1/3.
    c.  9/16.
*   d.  3/8.
    e.  1/16.

M  43. Assume short hair (L) is dominant to long hair (l) and black hair (B) is dominant to brown (b). If you found a black short-haired animal, you could determine its genotype by crossing it to an animal with a genotype of
    a   LL BB.
    b.  ll BB.
    c.  ll Bb.
*   d.  ll bb.
    e.  LL bb.

D  44. In the second generation of a cross of DD RR with dd rr, the most common genotype would be
    a   DD RR.
    b.  Dd RR.
*   c.  Dd Rr.
    d.  dd RR.
    e.  dd Rr.

E  45. The usual $F_2$ phenotypic ratio of a dihybrid cross is
    a   1:1.
    b.  2:1.
*   c.  9:3:3:1.
    d.  1:2:1.
    e.  3:1.

M  46. The theory of independent assortment
   * a. cannot be demonstrated in a monohybrid cross.
   b. is illustrated by the behavior of linked genes.
   c. indicates that the expression of one gene is independent of the action of another gene.
   d. states that alleles for the same characteristic separate during meiosis.
   e. is negated by the phenomenon of epistasis.

M  47. If all the offspring of a cross had the genotype *Aa Bb*, the parents of the cross would most likely be
   a. *AA BB* x *aa bb*.
   b. *AA bb* x *aa BB*.
   c. *Aa Bb* x *Aa Bb*.
   d. *Aa bb* x *aa Bb*.
   * e. both a or b, but not c or d

E  48. What fraction of the time will the cross of *Aa Bb Cc* with *Aa Bb Cc* produce an offspring of genotype *aa bb cc*?
   * a. 1/64
   b. 1/32
   c. 3/64
   d. 1/16
   e. 9/64

M  49. What fraction of the time will the cross of *Aa Bb Cc* with *Aa Bb Cc* produce an offspring of genotype *Aa bb CC*?
   a. 1/64
   * b. 1/32
   c. 3/64
   d. 1/16
   e. 9/64

D  50. What fraction of the time will the cross of *Aa Bb Cc* with *Aa Bb Cc* produce an offspring that expresses the dominant traits *A* and *B* and *cc* (*A_ B_ cc*)?
   a. 1/32
   b. 3/64
   c. 1/16
   * d. 9/64
   e. 27/64

D  51. What fraction of the time will the cross of *Aa Bb Cc* with *Aa Bb Cc* produce an offspring that expresses the phenotype represented by the dominant gene *C* (*aa bb C_*)?
   a. 1/32
   * b. 3/64
   c. 1/16
   d. 9/64
   e. 27/64

D  52. What fraction of the time will the cross of *Aa Bb Cc* with *Aa Bb Cc* produce an offspring that expresses all three dominant genes?
   a. 3/64
   b. 1/16
   c. 1/8
   d. 9/64
   * e. 27/64

D  53. What fraction of the time will the cross of *Aa Bb Cc* with *Aa Bb Cc* produce an offspring that is pure-breeding?
   a. 3/64
   b. 1/16
   * c. 1/8
   d. 9/64
   e. 27/64

D  54. The chance of producing an offspring of genotype *Aa BB cc* from a cross of *Aa Bb Cc* with *Aa Bb Cc* is
   a. 1/64.
   * b. 1/32.
   c. 3/64.
   d. 1/16.
   e. 3/32.

D  55. The chance of producing an offspring of genotype *Aa Bb cc* from a cross of *Aa BB Cc* with *Aa BB Cc* is
   a. 1/32.
   b. 1/16.
   c. 3/32.
   d. 1/8.
   * e. none (no chance of this offspring)

D  56. What fraction of the time will a cross of *Aa Bb Cc* with *Aa BB cc* produce an offspring of genotype *Aa Bb Cc*?
   a. 1/32
   b. 1/16
   c. 3/32
   * d. 1/8
   e. none (no chance of this offspring)

D  57. What fraction of the time will a cross of *Aa BB cc* with *Aa Bb CC* produce an offspring of genotype *Aa Bb CC*?
   a. 1/32
   b. 1/16
   c. 3/32
   d. 1/8
   * e. none (no chance of this offspring)

M **58.** Mendel's dihybrid crosses, but not his monohybrid crosses, showed that
   a   some genes were linked together.
   b.  the two alleles controlling a trait were divided equally among the gametes.
*  c.  alleles for different traits were inherited independently.
   d.  one of the pair of alleles is dominant to the other.
   e.  the crossing of two different homozygous forms will not produce any offspring in the first generation that will look like either of the parents.

## DOMINANCE RELATIONS

D **59.** Coat color in one breed of mice is controlled by incompletely dominant alleles so that yellow and white are homozygous, while cream is heterozygous. The cross of two cream individuals will produce
   a   all cream offspring.
   b.  equal numbers of white and yellow mice, but no cream.
   c.  equal numbers of white and cream mice.
   d.  equal numbers of yellow and cream mice.
*  e.  equal numbers of white and yellow mice, with twice as many creams as the other two colors.

D **60.** An incompletely dominant gene controls the color of chickens so that *BB* produces black, *Bb* produces a slate-gray color called blue, and *bb* produces splashed white. A second gene controls comb shape, with the dominant gene *R* producing a rose comb and *r* producing a single comb. If a pure-breeding black chicken with a rose comb is mated to a splashed white chicken with a single comb in the $F_2$ generation, what fraction of the offspring will be black with rose comb?
   a   9/16
   b.  3/8
*  c.  3/16
   d.  1/8
   e.  1/16

D **61.** An incompletely dominant gene controls the color of chickens so that *BB* produces black, *Bb* produces a slate-gray color called blue, and *bb* produces splashed white. A second gene controls comb shape, with the dominant gene *R* producing a rose comb and *r* producing a single comb. If a pure-breeding black chicken with rose comb is mated to a splashed white chicken with a single comb in the $F_2$ generation, what fraction of the offspring will be black with a single comb?
   a   9/16
   b.  3/8
   c.  3/16
   d.  1/8
*  e.  1/16

D **62.** An incompletely dominant gene controls the color of chickens so that *BB* produces black, *Bb* produces a slate-gray color called blue, and *bb* produces splashed white. A second gene controls comb shape, with the dominant gene *R* producing a rose comb and *r* producing a single comb. If a pure-breeding black chicken with a rose comb is mated to a splashed white chicken with a single comb in the $F_2$ generation, what fraction of the offspring will be blue with single comb?
   a   9/16
   b.  3/8
   c.  3/16
*  d.  1/8
   e.  1/16

D **63.** An incompletely dominant gene controls the color of chickens so that *BB* produces black, *Bb* produces a slate-gray color called blue, and *bb* produces splashed white. A second gene controls comb shape, with the dominant gene *R* producing a rose comb and *r* producing a single comb. If a pure-breeding black chicken with a rose comb is mated to a splashed white chicken with a single comb in the $F_2$ generation, what fraction of the offspring will be blue with rose comb?
   a   9/16
*  b.  3/8
   c.  3/16
   d.  1/8
   e.  1/16

M **64.** If red (*RR*) is crossed with white (*rr*) and produces a pink flower (*Rr*), and tall (*D*) is dominant to dwarf (*d*), the $F_2$ phenotypic ratio from a cross of *RR dd* with *rr DD* would be
   a   9:3:3:1.
   b.  1:1:1:1.
   c.  1:2:2:4:1:2:1:2:1.
*  d.  3:6:3:1:2:1.
   e.  none of the above

M **65.** The $F_2$ phenotypic ratio of a monohybrid cross involving a gene with incompletely dominant alleles is
   a   1:1.
   b.  2:1.
   c.  9:3:3:1.
*  d.  1:2:1.
   e.  3:1.

D **66.** If shape and color of radishes are due to incompletely dominant genes, crossing two dihybrid heterozygotes will produce how many different phenotypes?
   a   2
   b.  3
   c.  4
   d.  5
*  e.  9

M  **67.** In radishes, red and white are the pure-breeding colors and long and round are the pure-breeding shapes, while the hybrids are purple and oval. The cross of a red long radish and a white round radish will produce an $F_1$ generation of what phenotype?
   a.  all long red radishes
   b.  all long white radishes
   c.  all long purple radishes
   d.  all round purple radishes
   *  e.  none of the above

D  **68.** In radishes, red and white are the pure-breeding colors and long and round are the pure-breeding shapes, while the hybrids are purple and oval. The cross of a red long radish and a white round radish will produce an $F_2$ generation in which
   a.  the most common phenotype will be oval and purple.
   b.  the purple color will occur with all three shapes of radish.
   c.  the red color will occur with all three shapes of radish.
   d.  all white long forms produced will be pure-breeding.
   *  e.  all of the above

D  **69.** In radishes, red and white are the pure-breeding colors and long and round are the pure-breeding shapes, while the hybrids are purple and oval. The cross of a red oval with a purple oval will produce all but which of the following phenotypes?
   *  a.  white and long
   b.  purple and oval
   c.  red and oval
   d.  purple and long
   e.  red and long

D  **70.** In radishes, red and white are the pure-breeding colors and long and round are the pure-breeding shapes, while the hybrids are purple and oval. The cross of a white oval and a purple oval will produce more
   a.  red long than white long.
   b.  purple round than white long.
   *  c.  purple oval than purple long.
   d.  purple long than purple round.
   e.  purple round than white oval.

D  **71.** In radishes, red and white are the pure-breeding colors and long and round are the pure-breeding shapes, while the hybrids are purple and oval. The cross of a purple oval with a purple oval
   a.  is a cross between two pure-breeding forms.
   b.  is an example of a testcross.
   c.  produces only homozygous pure-breeding forms.
   d.  produces only heterozygous offspring.
   *  e.  none of the above

D  **72.** In radishes, red and white are the pure-breeding colors and long and round are the pure-breeding shapes, while the hybrids are purple and oval. The $F_2$ generation of a cross between long and white and red and round will produce
   a.  offspring that will all express dominant traits.
   b.  offspring that will all be phenotypically identical.
   c.  offspring that will all be genotypically identical.
   *  d.  purple round, purple long, white oval, and red oval offspring in equal numbers, as well as other phenotypes.
   e.  both b and c, but not a or d

E  **73.** In incomplete dominance
   a.  one allele is not dominant to another allele.
   b.  the genotype can be determined by the phenotype.
   c.  the heterozygote is somewhat intermediate to the two homozygotes.
   d.  the intermediate phenotype may be the result of enzyme insufficiency.
   *  e.  all of the above

M  **74.** If a pure-breeding long-tail cat ($LL$) is crossed with a pure-breeding cat with no tail (rumpy, $ll$), and a cat with a short tail (stumpy) is produced, the simplest explanation is
   a.  a mutation.
   b.  an X-linked gene.
   *  c.  an incompletely dominant gene.
   d.  a lethal gene.
   e.  chromosomal aberration.

M  **75.** If a child belonged to blood type O, he or she could not have been produced by which set of parents?
   a.  Type A mother and type B father
   b.  Type A mother and type O father
   *  c.  Type AB mother and type O father
   d.  Type O mother and type O father
   e.  a and c could not, but both b and d could produce a type O child

D  **76.** Susan, a mother with type B blood, has a child with type O blood. She claims that Craig, who has type A blood, is the father. He claims that he cannot possibly be the father. Further blood tests ordered by the judge reveal that Craig is AA. The judge rules that
   a.  Susan is right and Craig must pay child support.
   *  b.  Craig is right and doesn't have to pay child support.
   c.  Susan cannot be the real mother of the child; there must have been an error made at the hospital.
   d.  it is impossible to reach a decision based on the limited data available.
   e.  none of the above

M    **77.** If a child has an AB blood type, the parents
   a   must both have different blood types.
   b.   must be A and B, but not AB.
   c.   must both be AB.
   d.   can be any blood type.
   *   e.   can have different blood types, but neither can be blood type O.

## MULTIPLE EFFECTS OF SINGLE GENES

E    **78.** A gene that produces multiple effects is called
   a   a multiple allele.
   b.   an autosome.
   c.   an epistatic gene.
   *   d.   a pleiotropic gene.
   e.   an incompletely dominant gene.

E    **79.** Multiple effects of a single gene is known as
   a   expressivity.
   b.   penetrance.
   c.   codominance.
   *   d.   pleiotropy.
   e.   multiple alleles.

E    **80.** Pleiotropic genes
   a   act on secondary sexual characteristics.
   *   b.   influence more than one aspect of phenotype.
   c.   are additive.
   d.   produce lethal effects when homozygous.
   e.   none of the above

E    **81.** Which of the following is not a known factor in the expression of sickle-cell anemia?
   a   loss of shape of red blood cells with insufficient oxygen
   b.   rheumatism
   c.   overactive bone marrow
   *   d.   excessive absorption of oxygen causing the cell to swell
   e.   enlarged spleen

## INTERACTIONS BETWEEN GENE PAIRS

E    **82.** Genes at one locus that affect the expression of genes at a different locus are said to be
   *   a   epistatic.
   b.   linked.
   c.   codominant.
   d.   penetrant.
   e.   alleles.

D    **83.** If the cross of two guinea pig hybrids produces 9 black, 3 brown, and 4 white, when the hybrid is testcrossed the results will be
   a   1 black, 1 brown, 1 white.
   *   b.   1 black, 1 brown, 2 white.
   c.   2 black, 1 brown, 1 white.
   d.   1 black, 2 brown, 1 white.
   e.   none of the above

M    **84.** An $F_2$ phenotypic ratio of 13:3 is the result of
   a   single recessive epistasis.
   b.   double or duplicate recessive epistasis.
   c.   single dominant epistasis.
   d.   double or duplicate dominant epistasis.
   *   e.   one dominant and one recessive gene epistasis.

M    **85.** An $F_2$ phenotypic ratio of 9:7 is the result of
   a   single recessive epistasis.
   *   b.   double or duplicate recessive epistasis.
   c.   single dominant epistasis.
   d.   double or duplicate dominant epistasis.
   e.   one dominant and one recessive gene epistasis.

D    **86.** An $F_2$ phenotypic ratio of 9:3:4 is the result of
   *   a   single recessive epistasis.
   b.   double or duplicate recessive epistasis.
   c.   single dominant epistasis.
   d.   double or duplicate dominant epistasis.
   e.   one dominant and one recessive gene epistasis.

## LESS PREDICTABLE VARIATIONS IN TRAITS

E    **87.** A bell-shaped curve of phenotypic variation is a representation of
   a   incomplete dominance.
   *   b.   continuous variation.
   c.   multiple alleles.
   d.   epistasis.
   e.   environmental variables on phenotypes.

## EXAMPLES OF ENVIRONMENTAL EFFECTS ON PHENOTYPE

E    **88.** The color of Siamese cats is controlled by
   a   multiple alleles.
   b.   quantitative inheritance.
   c.   incompletely dominant genes.
   d.   nondisjunction.
   *   e.   variation in temperature, with cold temperature producing dark fur.

E    **89.** The variation of the color in Siamese cats is due to
   a   incomplete codominance.
   b.   inactive X chromosomes.
   *   c.   environmental effects on phenotypes.
   d.   quantitative inheritance.
   e.   multiple alleles.

M    **90.** The reason for the darker fur on the tail, ears, nose, and legs of a Siamese cat is
   a   incomplete dominance.
   *   b.   the interaction of the environment with gene expression.
   c.   quantitative inheritance.
   d.   epistasis.
   e.   none of the above

## Problems

**M** **91.** In a certain plant, when individuals with blue flowers are crossed with individuals with blue flowers, only blue flowers are produced. Plants with red flowers crossed with plants with red flowers sometimes produce only red flowers, while other times they produce either red or blue flowers. When plants with red flowers are crossed with plants with blue flowers, sometimes only red flowers are produced; other times either red or blue flowers are produced. Which gene is dominant?

**M** **92.** Which is easier to establish in a pure-breeding population, a dominant or a recessive gene?

**M** **93.** Tall ($D$) is dominant to dwarf ($d$). Give the $F_2$ genotypic and phenotypic ratios of a cross between a pure-breeding tall plant and a pure-breeding dwarf plant.

**M** **94.** If wire hair ($W$) is dominant to smooth hair ($w$) and you find a wire-haired puppy, how would you determine its genotype by a genetic breeding experiment? Give both the genotype and phenotype involved with the cross with the unknown.

**M** **95.** In poultry, rose comb is controlled by a dominant allele and its recessive allele controls single comb.
  (a) Give the genotype and phenotype produced from crossing a pure-breeding rose comb chicken with a pure-breeding single comb chicken.
  (b) Give the results of the backcross of the $F_1$ hybrid with both pure-breeding parents.

**M** **96.** If black fur color is controlled by a dominant allele ($B$) and brown by its recessive allele ($b$), give the genotypes of the parents and offspring of a cross of a black male with a brown female that produces 1/2 black offspring and 1/2 brown offspring.

**D** **97.** If 2 spot ($S$) is dominant to 4 spot ($s$), give the genotypes for the parents in the following crosses:
  (a) 2 spot x 2 spot yields 2 spot and 4 spot
  (b) 2 spot x 4 spot yields only 2 spot
  (c) 2 spot x 4 spot yields 2 spot and 4 spot
  (d) 2 spot x 2 spot yields only 2 spot
  (e) 4 spot x 4 spot yields only 4 spot

**D** **98.** In humans, normal skin pigmentation is influenced by a dominant gene ($C$), which allows pigmentation to develop. All individuals who are homozygous for the recessive allele ($c$) are unable to produce an enzyme needed for melanin formation and are therefore referred to as albino. Two normal parents produce an albino child. What are the chances that the next child will be an albino?

**D** **99.** The allele for albinism ($c$) is recessive to the allele for normal pigmentation ($C$). A normally pigmented woman whose father is an albino marries an albino man whose parents are normal. They have three children, two normal and one albino. Give the genotypes for each person listed.

**D** **100.** In garden peas, one pair of alleles controls the height of the plant and a second pair of alleles controls flower color. The allele for tall ($D$) is dominant to the allele for dwarf ($d$), and the allele for purple ($P$) is dominant to the allele for white ($p$). A tall plant with purple flowers crossed with a dwarf plant with white flowers produces 1/2 tall with purple flowers and 1/2 tall with white flowers. What is the genotype of the parents?

**D** **101.** In garden peas, one pair of alleles controls the height of the plant and a second pair of alleles controls flower color. The allele for tall ($D$) is dominant to the allele for dwarf ($d$), and the allele for purple ($P$) is dominant to the allele for white ($p$). A tall plant with white flowers crossed with a dwarf plant with purple flowers produces all tall offspring with purple flowers. What is the genotype of the parents?

**D** **102.** In garden peas, one pair of alleles controls the height of the plant and a second pair of alleles controls flower color. The allele for tall ($D$) is dominant to the allele for dwarf ($d$), and the allele for purple ($P$) is dominant to the allele for white ($p$). A tall plant with purple flowers crossed with a dwarf plant with white flowers produces 1/4 tall purple, 1/4 tall white, 1/4 dwarf purple, and 1/4 dwarf white. What is the genotype of the parents?

**D** **103.** In garden peas, one pair of alleles controls the height of the plant and a second pair of alleles controls flower color. The allele for tall ($D$) is dominant to the allele for dwarf ($d$), and the allele for purple ($P$) is dominant to the allele for white ($p$). A tall plant with white flowers crossed with a dwarf plant with purple flowers produces 1/4 tall purple, 1/4 tall white, 1/4 dwarf purple, and 1/4 dwarf white. What is the genotype of the parents?

**D** **104.** In garden peas, one pair of alleles controls the height of the plant and a second pair of alleles controls flower color. The allele for tall ($D$) is dominant to the allele for dwarf ($d$), and the allele for purple ($P$) is dominant to the allele for white ($p$). A tall plant with purple flowers crossed with a tall plant with white flowers produces 3/8 tall purple, 1/8 tall white, 3/8 dwarf purple, and 1/8 dwarf white. What is the genotype of the parents?

D 105. In garden peas, one pair of alleles controls the height of the plant and a second pair of alleles controls flower color. The allele for tall ($D$) is dominant to the allele for dwarf ($d$), and the allele for purple ($P$) is dominant to the allele for white ($p$). A tall purple crossed with a tall purple produces 3/4 tall purple and 1/4 tall white. What is the genotype of the parents?

D 106. In horses, black coat color is influenced by the dominant allele ($B$), and chestnut coat color is influenced by the recessive allele ($b$). Trotting gait is due to a dominant gene ($T$), pacing gait to the recessive allele ($t$). If a homozygous black trotter is crossed to a chestnut pacer,
  (a) what will be the appearance of the $F_1$ and $F_2$ generations?
  (b) which phenotype will be the most common?
  (c) which genotype will be the most common?
  (d) which of the potential offspring will be certain to breed true?

D 107. In horses, black coat color is influenced by the dominant allele ($B$) and chestnut coat color by the recessive allele ($b$). Trotting gait is due to a dominant gene ($T$), pacing gait to the recessive allele ($t$). What color horse would you use to find out the genotype of a black trotter? Give the genotype and phenotype.

D 108. Crosses between a yellow rat and a yellow rat always produce yellow. Crosses between a white rat and a white rat always produce white. The alleles affect the same aspect of coat color. The crosses of a white with a yellow produce a cream. What happens if you cross two creams?

D 109. Assume red plants crossed with white plants give rise to pink plants. Explain how to eliminate red plants if you start with two pinks.

D 110. If long or round are homozygous forms of an incompletely dominant gene and oval is the phenotype of the heterozygote, give the $F_2$ ratio of the cross between long and round (both genotype and phenotype).

D 111. A breeder of cattle has a herd of white cows and a roan bull. Hair color in this breed is controlled by an incompletely dominant gene. The two homozygous forms are either red or white, and the heterozygous is roan.
  (a) What color of calves are expected and in what proportions?
  (b) Outline a procedure to develop an all-red herd.

D 112. In radishes, two incompletely dominant genes control color and shape. Red and white radishes are homozygous, while the hybrid is purple. Long and round are homozygous and, if crossed, will produce an oval hybrid. Give the $F_2$ genotypic and phenotypic ratio produced by crossing pure-breed red long radishes with white round varieties.

D 113. In a certain breed of chicken an incompletely dominant gene controls color. The homozygous black, when crossed with the homozygous splashed-white, produces an intermediate gray color pattern referred to as blue. A second gene controls the shape of the comb. The dominant allele ($R$) produces rose, while the recessive allele ($r$) produces single. Give the $F_1$ and $F_2$ genotypic and phenotypic ratios of a cross between a pure-breeding black single and a pure-breeding splashed-white rose.

D 114. There are three alleles controlling the ABO blood types. $I^A$ and $I^B$ are codominant genes so that the combination $I^A I^B$ produces the AB blood type. The third allele $I^O$ is recessive to the other two alleles. Indicate which of these parents could produce the given child:

| Parents | Child | Yes or No |
|---------|-------|-----------|
| (a) A x AB | B | |
| (b) A x O | A | |
| (c) A x B | O | |
| (d) A x AB | O | |
| (e) A x AB | B | |
| (f) B x B | O | |
| (g) AB x AB | A | |

D 115. In horses there are four alleles at the $A$ locus. Arranged in dominance sequence they are:

$A$ (wild) $a^b$ (bay) $a^c$ (brown) $a^d$ (black)

If you bred several bay mares whose sires were brown to a brown stallion whose sire was black, what type of offspring would be produced and in what proportion?

D 116. In rabbits there are four alleles at the $c$ locus. Arranged in dominance sequence they are:

$C$ (agouti) $c^{ch}$ (chinchilla) $c^h$ (Himalayan) and $c$ (albino)
  (a) Is it possible to cross two agouti rabbits and produce both chinchilla and Himalayan offspring?
  (b) Is it possible to cross two chinchillas and produce 1/2 chinchilla and 1/2 Himalayan?

D 117. Gray is homozygous while blue is a heterozygous form of a semilethal gene. Give the ratio of the offspring produced in the cross of two blues.

D **118.** A cross of two Kerry horses always produces Kerry. A cross of a Kerry with a Dexter produces half and half. Crosses of two Dexters produce two Dexters for every Kerry. Explain.

D **119.** In the late 1920s, a mutation occurred in many silver fox farms around the world. The fox farms that sold expensive furs were proud of the quality of their furs, and each advertised that it had the best, most pure breed of all the fox farms. The new mutations produced a "platinum" coat pattern that was commercially desirable, so the farms crossed them to get more. The results of their breeding experiments were as follows: (1) silver x silver ——> all silver offspring; (2) silver x platinum ——> equal numbers of silver and platinum; (3) platinum x platinum ——> 2 platinum for each silver offspring. Explain.

D **120.** There is a color pattern inherited in certain mice in which agouti (gray) is homozygous and yellow is heterozygous. A cross of two yellows produces two yellows for each agouti. A second gene, $C/c$, controls the expression of the color genes: $C$ is the dominant allele that allows color to be expressed, and the recessive gene in the homozygous condition ($cc$) prevents any color from being expressed.
 (a) Give the genotypes of a white parent crossed with a yellow parent that produces 1/2 white, 1/3 yellow, 1/6 agouti offspring.
 (b) Give the results of the cross of two forms heterozygous for each gene.
 (c) Can you develop a pure-breed population for any of the colors?

D **121.** In poultry, the genes for rose comb ($R$) and pea comb ($P$) produce walnut whenever they occur together ($R\_ P\_$); single-combed individuals have the homozygous condition for both genes ($rr\ pp$).
 (a) Give the $F_1$ and $F_2$ phenotypic results of a cross of a pure-breeding rose comb ($RR\ pp$) with a pure-breeding pea comb ($rr\ PP$).
 (b) Give the phenotypic results of a cross of $Rr\ Pp$ x $rr\ Pp$.
 (c) Give the phenotypic results of a cross of $RR\ Pp$ x $rr\ Pp$.
 (d) Give the phenotypic results of a cross of $Rr\ pp$ x $rr\ Pp$.
 (e) Give the phenotypic results of a cross of $Rr\ Pp$ x $rr\ pp$.

D **122.** Congenital deafness in humans is due to the homozygous condition of either or both of the recessive genes $d$ or $e$. Both dominant $D$ and $E$ are necessary for normal hearing. Gene $D/d$ affects the middle ear, while gene $E/e$ affects the inner ear. It does not matter how good the normal inner ear (as indicated by $E\_$) is; if there is something wrong in the middle ear, the individual is unable to hear. The same applies for the other gene. Give the phenotypic results of the following crosses:
 (a) $Dd\ EE$ x $Dd\ EE$
 (b) $Dd\ Ee$ x $Dd\ Ee$
 (c) $dd\ EE$ x $DD\ ee$
 (d) $Dd\ EE$ x $Dd\ ee$
 (e) $Dd\ EE$ x $DD\ Ee$

D **123.** White fruit color in summer squash is influenced by a dominant allele $W$, while colored fruit must be $ww$. In the presence of $ww$, a dominant gene $G$ results in yellow fruit, and if the individual had both recessive genes in the homozygous condition, it would be green. Give the $F_2$ phenotypic ratios resulting from a cross of a pure-breeding white of genotype $WW\ GG$ with a green.

D **124.** In cultivated stocks, the cross of a variety of white-flower plants produced all red flowers in the $F_1$ generation, but the $F_2$ generation produced 87 red, 31 cream, and 39 white. Explain these results by giving the genotypes possible for each phenotype.

D **125.** In summer squash, spherical-shaped fruit has been shown to be dominant to elongated fruit. On one occasion two different spherical varieties were crossed and produced all disk-shaped fruits. When these hybrid disk-shaped fruits were crossed they produced 75 disk-shaped fruits, 48 spherical fruits, and 9 elongated fruits. Explain these results.

D **126.** In sweet peas, genes $C$ and $P$ are necessary for colored flowers. In the absence of either ($\_\ pp$ or $cc\ \_$), or both ($cc\ pp$), the flowers are white. What will be the color of the offspring of the crosses in what proportions for the following?
 (a) $Cc\ Pp$ x $cc\ pp$
 (b) $Cc\ Pp$ x $Cc\ Pp$
 (c) $Cc\ PP$ x $Cc\ pp$
 (d) $Cc\ pp$ x $cc\ Pp$

D **127.** In sweet peas, genes $C$ and $P$ are necessary for colored flowers. In the absence of either ($\_\ pp$ or $cc\ \_$), or both ($cc\ pp$), the flowers are white. Give the probable genotype of a plant with colored flowers and a plant with white flowers that produced 38 plants with colored flowers and 42 plants with white flowers.

D **128.** In a certain variety of plants a cross between a red-flowered plant and a white-flowered plant produced an all-red flower $F_1$. In the $F_2$ there were 140 red, 50 cream, and 65 white.
   (a) Offer an explanation for this $F_2$ ratio.
   (b) What ratio would be produced in a testcross of the $F_1$ hybrid?
   (c) What ratio would be produced if all the white $F_2$ plants were crossed among themselves?

D **129.** In a certain breed of chicken two genes control color. A dominant allele ($I$) inhibits the expression of any color gene ($C$). A second recessive gene ($c$) results in albinism when homozygous ($cc$). Give the $F_2$ phenotypic ratio of a colored chicken $ii\,CC$ with a white $II\,cc$.

D **130.** In mice the allele for colored fur ($C$) is dominant to the allele for albinism ($c$). The allele ($W$) for normal behavior is dominant to that for waltzing movement ($w$). Give the probable genotypes of the parents if they produced the offspring listed after the following crosses:
   (a) Colored normal $x$ white waltzer produced 10 colored normal, 8 colored waltzers, 2 white waltzers, 11 white normal.
   (b) Colored normal $x$ white normal produced 35 colored normal, 13 colored waltzers.
   (c) Colored normal $x$ colored normal produced 37 colored normal, 14 colored waltzers, 9 white normal, and 5 white waltzers.

D **131.** Pure-breeding yellow guinea pigs crossed with pure-breeding white ones produce only cream-colored offspring. This pattern indicates incomplete dominance. Rough hair is found to be dominant to smooth hair. Give the $F_1$ and $F_2$ genotypic and phenotypic ratios of a cross of a smooth white guinea pig with a homozygous rough yellow guinea pig.

D **132.** There are nine coat colors known in foxes. If a red fox were crossed with a double-black fox, all the hybrids would be red above and black below in a pattern known as blended cross. If two blended crosses were mated, the $F_2$ ratio would be as follows: 1 red, 2 smokey red, 2 cross red, 4 blended cross, 1 standard silver, 2 substandard silver, 1 Alaskan silver, 2 sub-Alaskan silver, and 1 double black.
   (a) Using the letters $A/a$ and $B/b$ to serve as the genes for these animals, develop a genotype for each variety listed.
   (b) Two crosses will produce all blended-cross offspring. One is used above (red fox x double black); what is the other?
   (c) List the genotype and phenotype of all the pure-breeding foxes.
   (d) Give the genotypic and phenotypic ratio of a cross between two substandard silvers.
   (e) Give the genotype and phenotype of the offspring produced in a cross of 1 sub-Alaskan silver and a cross red.

D **133.** In the garden pea Mendel found that tall ($D$) green pods ($G$) and inflated pods ($C$) were dominant to their alleles, dwarf ($d$) yellow pods ($g$) and constricted pods ($c$). Given the following genotypes, determine the chances of producing the offspring shown.
   (a) $DD\,Gg\,Cc$ x $Dd\,Gg\,cc$ $\longrightarrow$ $DD\,gg\,Cc$
   (b) $DD\,Gg\,Cc$ x $Dd\,Gg\,Cc$ $\longrightarrow$ tall green pod, constricted pod
   (c) $Dd\,Gg\,Cc$ x $Dd\,GG\,cc$ $\longrightarrow$ tall green pod, inflated pod
   (d) $Dd\,Gg\,Cc$ x $Dd\,Gg\,Cc$ $\longrightarrow$ $D\_\,G\_\,cc$
   (e) $Dd\,Gg\,Cc$ x $Dd\,gg\,CC$ $\longrightarrow$ $D\_\,G\_\,C\_$
   (f) $Dd\,gg\,cc$ x $DD\,Gg\,cc$ $\longrightarrow$ tall green pod, inflated pod
   (g) $Dd\,Gg\,Cc$ x $Dd\,Gg\,Cc$ $\longrightarrow$ $Dd\,Gg\,Cc$
   (h) $Dd\,Gg\,Cc$ x $Dd\,Gg\,Cc$ $\longrightarrow$ $dd\,gg\,cc$

D **134.** In tomatoes red ($R$) is dominant to yellow ($r$), tall ($D$) is dominant to dwarf ($d$), and smooth ($H$) is dominant to peach or hairy ($h$).
   (a) How many different genotypes are there in relationship to these three characteristics?
   (b) How many different phenotypes are there in relationship to these three characteristics?
   (c) How many different homozygous pure-breeding forms can be produced?

D **135.** If you were following the inheritance patterns of two different sets of multiple alleles located on different chromosomes, how many different possible gametes could be produced if locus 1 had five possible alleles and locus 2 had six alleles?

## Classification Questions

Answer questions 136–140 using the group of answers below.

    a  4
    b.  6
    c.  8
    d.  12
    e.  24

D    **136.** In a dihybrid cross between a parent that is a double heterozygote (*Aa Bb*) and a parent that is homozygous dominant for one gene and heterozygous for the other (*AA Bb*), how many unique genotypes potentially will be present in their offspring?

D    **137.** In a dihybrid cross between a parent that is a double heterozygote (*Aa Bb*) and a parent that is homozygous recessive for one gene and heterozygous for the other (*aa Bb*), how many unique phenotypes potentially will be present in their offspring?

D    **138.** In a dihybrid cross between a parent that is a double heterozygote (*Aa Bb*) and a parent that is a double homozygous recessive (*aa bb*), how many unique phenotypes potentially will be present in their offspring?

D    **139.** Plant species X is diploid ($2n = 24$) and has a quantitative trait, the expression of which is controlled by gene loci on each of its chromosomes. What is the maximum number of alleles for this trait that any one individual of species X could have?

D    **140.** Animal species X is tetraploid ($4n = 12$). Following gene duplication and translocation, a given gene is found on each chromosome. How many alleles for this gene can be present in an individual of this species?

*Answers*:    136.  b    137.  a    138.  a
                139.  e    140.  d

## Selecting the Exception

D    **141.** Four of the five answers listed below are dominant traits. Select the exception.
    a  green pod
    b.  purple flower
    c.  yellow seed coat
  *  d.  dwarf plant
    e.  axial flower position

E    **142.** Four of the five answers listed below describe the heterozygous condition. Select the exception.
  *  a  homozygous
    b.  carrier
    c.  heterozygotes
    d.  hybrid
    e.  *Aa*

M    **143.** Four of the five answers listed below describe the gene makeup. Select the exception.
    a  pure breeding
    b.  homozygous
    c.  heterozygous
    d.  carrier
  *  e.  phenotype

M    **144.** Four of the five answers listed below are accepted as valid explanations of genetic behavior. Select the exception.
  *  a  blending
    b.  dominance
    c.  segregation
    d.  independent assortment
    e.  probability

E    **145.** Four of the five answers listed below are pure breeding. Select the exception.
    a  *AA BB*
  *  b.  *Aa BB*
    c.  *AA bb*
    d.  *aa BB*
    e.  *aa bb*

## Answers to problems in Chapter 9

91.  Red
92.  Recessive
93.  1 *DD*, 2 *Dd*, 1 *dd*; 3 tall, 1 dwarf
94.  Smooth hair, *ww*
95.  (a) *Rr*, rose
     (b) *Rr* x *RR* Æ all rose, *Rr* x *rr* Æ 1/2 rose, 1/2 single
96.  Black male (*Bb*) x brown female (*bb*) offspring: black (*Bb*) brown (*bb*)
97.  (a) *Ss* x *Ss* ——> *S_* + *ss*
     (b) *Ss* x *ss* ——> *Ss*
     (c) *Ss* x *ss* ——> *Ss* + *ss*
     (d) *SS* x *S_* ——> *S_*
     (e) *ss* x *ss* ——> *ss*
98.  1/4 chance
99.  Normal pigmented woman, *Cc*; albino father, *cc*; albino man, *cc*; normal parents, *Cc* + *Cc*; 3 children, 2 normal *Cc*, 1 albino *cc*
100.  *DD Pp* x *dd pp*
101.  *DD pp* x *dd PP*
102.  *Dd Pp* x *dd pp*
103.  *Dd pp* x *dd Pp*
104.  *Dd Pp* x *Dd pp*
105.  *Dd Pp* x *DD Pp*
106.  (a) F$_1$: black trotters; F$_2$: 9 black trotters, 3 black pacers, 3 chestnut trotters, 1 chestnut pacer
     (b) Black pacer
     (c) *Bb Tt*
     (d) *bb tt,* chestnut pacers
107.  *bb tt*, chestnut pacer
108.  1 yellow, 2 cream, 2 white

109. Cross until you get white, and use white in crosses until you cross two whites, then all subsequent plants will be white.

110. 1 *LL*, 2 *Ll*, 1 *ll*; 1 long, 2 oval, 1 round

111. (a) 1/2 white, 1/2 roan
(b) Roan with white ——→ roan,
roan x roan ——→ red,
roan x red ——→ red, red x red ——→ red

112. 1 *LL RR* long red, 2 *LL Rr* long purple,
2 *Ll RR* oval red,
4 *Ll RR* oval purple, 1 *ll RR* round red,
1 *ll Rr* round oval,
1 *Ll rr* long white, 2 *Ll rr* oval white,
1 *ll rr* round white

113. $F_1$. *Bb Rr* blue rose; $F_2$: 3 *BB R_* black rose,
6 *Bb R_* blue rose, 3 *bb R_* splashed-white rose,
1 *BB rr* black single, 2 *Bb rr* blue single,
1 *bb rr* splashed-white single

114. (a) yes; (b) yes; (c) yes; (d) no; (e) yes;
(f) yes; (g) yes

115. $a^b a^c$ x $a^c a^d$; 1/2 bay, 1/2 brown

116. (a) no; (b) not likely but possible—would expect a 3:1

117. 1 gray, 2 blues (1 lethal)

118. Kerry is homozygous (*DD*), Exter is heterozygous (*Dd*), *dd* is lethal.

119. *PP* (silver), *Pp* (platinum), *pp* (lethal)

120. (a) *Yy Cc* x *Yy cc*
(b) *Yy Cc* x *Yy Cc* Æ 3/12 *YY C_* agouti,
6/12 *Yy C_* yellow, 3/12 *_ cc* albino
(c) white and agouti

121. (a) $F_1$: *Rr Pp* walnut; $F_2$: 9 *R_ P_* walnut,
3 *R_ pp* rose,
3 *rr P_* pea, 1 *rr pp* single
(b) 3/8 walnut, 3/8 pea, 1/8 rose, 1/8 single
(c) 3/4 walnut, 1/4 rose
(d) 1/4 walnut, 1/4 rose, 1/4 pea, 1/4 single
(e) 1/4 walnut, 1/4 rose, 1/4 pea, 1/4 single

122. (a) 3/4 normal, 1/4 deaf
(b) 9/16 normal, 7/16 deaf
(c) all normal
(d) 3/4 normal, 1/4 deaf
(e) all normal

123. 12/16 *W_ _ _* white, 3/16 *ww G_* yellow,
1/16 *ww gg* green

124. *R*-red, *r*-cream, *A*-pigment, *a*-albino
9 *R_ A_* red, 3 *rr A_* cream, 4 *_ aa* white

125. 9 *D_ S_* disk, 3 *D_ ss* spherical, 3 *dd S_* spherical,
1 *dd ss* elongated; presence of both dominant genes produces disk, while the presence of either one of the genes as homozygous recessive produces spherical, and both recessive produces elongated fruit.

126. (a) 1/4 color, 3/4 white
(b) 9/16 color, 7/16 white
(c) 3/4 color, 1/4 white
(d) 1/4 color, 3/4 white

127. *Cc Pp* x *CC pp*

128. (a) *R*-red, *r*-cream, *A*-color, a-albino;
9 *R_ A_* red, 3 *rr A_* cream, 4 *_ aa* white
(b) 1/4 red, 1/4 cream, 1/2 white
(c) all offspring would be white because all would be *_ aa*

129. 9 *I_ C_* + 3 *I_ cc* + 1 *ii cc* = 13 white +
3 *ii C_* = 3 color

130. (a) *Cc Ww* x *cc ww*
(b) *CC Ww* x *cc Ww*
(c) *Cc Ww* x *Cc Ww*

131. $F_1$: rough cream *Yy Rr*; $F_2$: 3 *YY R_* yellow rough,
6 *Yy R_* cream rough, 3 *yy R_* white rough,
1 *YY rr* yellow smooth, 2 *Yy rr* cream smooth,
1 *yy rr* white smooth

132. (a) 1 *AA BB* red
2 *AA Bb* smokey red
2 *Aa BB* cross red
4 *Aa Bb* blended cross
1 *aa BB* standard silver
2 *aa Bb* substandard silver
1 *AA bb* Alaskan silver
2 *Aa bb* sub-Alaskan silver
1 *aa bb* double black
(b) *aa BB* standard silver x *AA bb* Alaskan silver
(c) *AA BB* red, *AA bb* Alaskan silver,
*aa BB* standard silver, *aa bb* double black
(d) 1 standard silver *aa BB*
2 substandard silver *aa Bb*,
1 double black *aa bb*
(e) 1 smokey red *AA Bb*,
2 blended cross *Aa Bb*,
1 substandard silver *aa Bb*

133. (a) (1/2) (1/4) (1/2) = 1/16
(b) (1) (3/4) (1/4) = 3/16
(c) (3/4) (1) (1/2) = 3/8
(d) (3/4) (3/4) (1/4) = 9/64
(e) (3/4) (1/2) (1) = 3/8
(f) (1) (1/2) 0 = 0
(g) (2/4) (2/4) (2/4) = 8/64
(h) (1/4) (1/4) (1/4) = 1/64

134. (a) 27  (b) 8  (c) 8

135. 30 possibilities

# CHAPTER 10
# CHROMOSOMES AND HUMAN GENETICS

## Multiple-Choice Questions

E **1.** Who discovered chromosomes?
  - a Morgan
  - b. Mendel
  - c. Sturtevant
  - d. Weismann
  - * e. Flemming

E **2.** Who discovered the process of meiosis?
  - a Morgan
  - b. Mendel
  - c. Sturtevant
  - * d. Weismann
  - e. Flemming

E **3.** Who was the first to use fruit flies in genetics experiments?
  - * a Morgan
  - b. Mendel
  - c. Sturtevant
  - d. Weismann
  - e. Flemming

M **4.** Weismann proposed that
  - a the number of chromosomes is cut in half in the sex cells.
  - b. the number of chromosomes is doubled by mitosis.
  - c. half the chromosomes in a diploid cell come from the father and the other half from the mother.
  - d. fertilization restores the number of chromosomes.
  - * e. all except b

### THE CHROMOSOMAL BASIS OF INHERITANCE—AN OVERVIEW

E **5.** Genes are
  - a located on chromosomes.
  - b. inherited in the same way as chromosomes.
  - c. arranged in linear sequence on chromosomes.
  - d. assorted independently during meiosis.
  - * e. all of the above

E **6.** Chromosomes other than those involved in sex determination are known as
  - a nucleosomes.
  - b. heterosomes.
  - c. alleles.
  - * d. autosomes.
  - e. liposomes.

M **7.** DNA coding regions that affect the same trait are called
  - a homologues.
  - * b. alleles.
  - c. autosomes.
  - d. loci.
  - e. gametes.

E **8.** The location of a gene on a chromosome is its
  - a centromere.
  - * b. locus.
  - c. autosome.
  - d. allele.
  - e. none of the above

E **9.** A karyotype
  - a compares one set of chromosomes to another.
  - * b. is a visual display of chromosomes arranged according to size.
  - c. is a photograph of cells undergoing mitosis during anaphase.
  - d. of a normal human cell shows 48 chromosomes.
  - e. cannot be used to identify individual chromosomes beyond the fact that two chromosomes are homologues.

E **10.** In karyotyping, individual chromosomes may be distinguished from others by
  - a a comparison of chromosome lengths.
  - b. bands produced on chromosomes by differential staining.
  - c. the position of centromeres.
  - * d. all of the above
  - e. none of the above

M **11.** Karyotyping is usually done using what kind of cells?
  - a muscle
  - * b. blood
  - c. cartilage
  - d. sex
  - e. epidermal

M **12.** Which chemical is used to keep chromosomes from separating during metaphase?
  - a Giemsa stain
  - b. acetone
  - * c. colchicine
  - d. alcohol
  - e. formaldehyde

M 13. Karyotyping involves taking pictures of chromosomes during
    a. prophase.
    b. telophase.
*  c. metaphase.
    d. interphase.
    e. anaphase.

M 14. Karyotype analysis
    a. is a means of detecting and reducing mutagenic agents.
    b. is a surgical technique that separates chromosomes that have failed to segregate properly during meiosis II.
*  c. is used to detect chromosomal mutations and metabolic disorders in embryos.
    d. substitutes defective alleles with normal ones.
    e. all of the above

## SEX DETERMINATION IN HUMANS

E 15. Sex chromosomes
    a. determine sex.
    b. vary from one sex to another.
    c. carry some genes that have nothing to do with sex.
    d. were unknown to Mendel.
*  e. all of the above

E 16. Which of the following designates a normal human female?
    a. XXY
    b. XY
*  c. XX
    d. XYY
    e. XO

E 17. Which of the following designates a normal human male?
    a. YY
    b. XX
*  c. XY
    d. XO
    e. XYY

## EARLY QUESTIONS ABOUT GENE LOCATIONS

D 18. In his experiments with *Drosophila melanogaster*, Morgan demonstrated that
    a. fertilized eggs have two sets of chromosomes, but eggs and sperms have only one set in each gamete.
    b. aneuploidy exists in karyotypes that have undergone deletions and inversions in specific chromosomes.
    c. colchicine is effective in producing polyploidy in $F_2$ generations.
*  d. certain genes are located only on an X chromosome and have no corresponding alleles on the Y chromosome.
    e. all of the above

M 19. All of the genes located on a given chromosome comprise a
    a. karyotype.
    b. bridging cross.
    c. wild-type allele.
*  d. linkage group.
    e. none of the above

E 20. If two genes are on the same chromosome,
    a. crossing over occurs frequently.
    b. they assort independently.
*  c. they are in the same linkage group.
    d. they are segregated during meiosis.
    e. an inversion will usually occur.

M 21. If two genes are almost always found in the same gamete,
*  a. they are located close together on the same chromosome.
    b. they are located on nonhomologous chromosomes.
    c. they are located far apart on the same chromosome.
    d. they are found on the sex chromosome.
    e. all except c

M 22. Genes that are located on the same chromosome
    a. tend to be inherited together.
    b. will appear together in the gamete.
    c. are said to be linked.
    d. may be separated during crossing over.
*  e. all of the above

D 23. If alleles $L$, $M$, and $N$ are on the maternal chromosome and $l$, $m$, and $n$ are on the paternal chromosome, the only way that a gamete from a heterozygote will produce a gamete with alleles $l$, $m$, and $N$ is through
    a. nondisjunction.
    b. the laws of segregation.
    c. the law of independent assortment.
*  d. crossing over.
    e. chromosome aberration.

D 24. If the paternal chromosome has alleles $L$, $M$, and $n$ and the maternal chromosomes have $l$, $m$, and $N$, then the chromosome that cannot be produced by crossing over is
    a. *LMN*
*  b. *LMn*
    c. *LmN*
    d. *Lmn*
    e. *lmn*

M 25. Genetic recombination as a result of crossing over occurs more readily in genes that
    a. are on the sex chromosomes.
    b. are on the autosomes.
    c. are located close together on the same chromosome.
*  d. are located far apart on the same chromosome.
    e. are located on different chromosomes.

M  26. Which is NOT a chromosomal aberration?
      a  deletion
      b.  extra chromosomes
      c.  translocation (exchange of parts between nonhomologues)
  *   d.  crossing over
      e.  inversion

## HUMAN GENETIC ANALYSIS

E  27. Which of the following would be the least satisfactory organism for genetic research?
  *   a  humans
      b.  bacteria
      c.  corn
      d.  fruit flies
      e.  peas

E  28. In a pedigree chart a male showing the specific trait being studied is indicated by a
  *   a  darkened square.
      b.  clear square.
      c.  darkened diamond.
      d.  clear triangle.
      e.  darkened circle.

E  29. In a pedigree chart a female who does not demonstrate the trait being studied is represented by a
      a  darkened square.
      b.  clear diamond.
  *   c.  clear circle.
      d.  darkened triangle.
      e.  darkened oval.

M  30. All of the following would be classified as genetic disorders except
      a  galactosemia
  *   b.  polydactyly.
      c.  progeria.
      d.  hemophilia.
      e.  Turner syndrome.

## PATTERNS OF INHERITANCE

M  31. Galactosemia
      a  is an X-linked recessive trait expressed more commonly in males.
      b.  occurs more frequently in some ethnic groups than others.
      c.  is an autosomal recessive inheritance.
      d.  must be homozygous to be expressed.
  *   e.  both c and d

D  32. A colorblind man and a woman with normal vision whose father was colorblind have a son. Colorblindness, in this case, is caused by an X-linked recessive gene. If only the male offspring are considered, the probability that their son is colorblind is
      a  .25 (or 25 percent).
  *   b.  .50 (or 50 percent).
      c.  .75 (or 75 percent).
      d.  1.00 (or 100 percent).
      e.  none of the above

M  33. Red–green colorblindness is an X-linked recessive trait in humans. A colorblind woman and a man with normal vision have a son. What is the probability that the son is colorblind?
  *   a  100 percent
      b.  75 percent
      c.  50 percent
      d.  25 percent
      e.  0 percent

M  34. Red–green colorblindness is an X-linked recessive trait in humans. What is the probability that a colorblind woman and a man with normal vision will have a colorblind daughter?
      a  100 percent
      b.  75 percent
      c.  50 percent
      d.  25 percent
  *   e.  0 percent

M  35. If a daughter expresses an X-linked recessive gene, she inherited the trait from
      a  her mother.
      b.  her father.
  *   c.  both parents.
      d.  neither parent.
      e.  her grandmother.

M  36. A human X-linked recessive gene may be
      a  found on the Y chromosome.
      b.  passed to daughters from their fathers.
      c.  passed to sons from their mothers.
      d.  expressed more commonly among females.
  *   e.  both b and c

M  37. An X-linked carrier is a
      a  homozygous dominant female.
  *   b.  heterozygous female.
      c.  homozygous recessive female.
      d.  homozygous male.
      e.  heterozygous male.

M  38. A human X-linked gene is
      a  found only in males.
      b.  more frequently expressed in females.
      c.  found on the Y chromosome.
      d.  transmitted from father to son.
  *   e.  found on the X chromosome.

D  39. Colorblindness is an X-linked trait in humans. If a colorblind woman marries a man with normal vision,
      a  only their daughters will be colorblind.
  *   b.  their sons will be colorblind; daughters will be carriers.
      c.  their sons will have normal vision; their daughters will be carriers.
      d.  all their children will be colorblind.
      e.  all their children will have normal vision.

M 40. A woman heterozygous for colorblindness (an X-linked recessive allele) marries a man with normal color vision. What is the probability that their first child will be colorblind?
* a 25 percent
b. 50 percent
c 75 percent
d. 100 percent
e. none of the above

E 41. Queen Victoria
* a was a carrier of hemophilia.
b. had a hemophilic parent.
c had hemophilia.
d. married a man with hemophilia.
e. both b and d

M 42. Hemophilia
a is rare in the human population.
b. is more common among men.
c was common in English royalty.
d. is an X-linked recessive trait.
* e. all of the above

**CHANGES IN CHROMOSOME NUMBER**

M 43. The condition occurring when an organism has a 2n + 1 chromosome composition is known as
a monosomy.
* b. trisomy.
c diploid.
d. haploid.
e. both b and d

E 44. Down syndrome involves trisomy
a 3.
b. 5.
c 15.
d. 19.
* e. 21.

E 45. Syndrome means
a a chromosome disorder.
b. a simple genetic disease.
* c a set of symptoms that occur together.
d. an incurable disease.
e. a rare inborn defect.

M 46. In Down syndrome
* a as the age of the mother increases, the chance of the defect occurring in the unborn children increases.
b. the father has very little influence on the defect.
c most embryos abort before complete term.
d. a person with the defect cannot have a normal child.
e. none of the above

E 47. The sex chromosome composition of a person with Turner syndrome is
a XXX.
* b. XO.
c XXY.
d. XYY.
e. none of the above

E 48. The sex chromosome composition of a person with Klinefelter syndrome is
a XXX.
b. XO.
* c XXY.
d. XYY.
e. none of the above

D 49. Suppose a hemophilic male (X-linked recessive allele) and a female carrier for the hemophilic trait have a nonhemophilic daughter with Turner syndrome. Nondisjunction could have occurred in
a both parents.
b. neither parent.
* c the father only.
d. the mother only.
e. none of the above

M 50. A genetic abnormality that may result in sterile males with mental retardation or breast enlargement is
* a XXY.
b. XYY.
c Turner syndrome.
d. Down syndrome.
e. none of the above

M 51. Males who tend to be taller than average and show mild mental retardation may be designated
a XXY.
* b. XYY.
c Turner syndrome.
d. Down syndrome.
e. none of the above

D 52. Nondisjunction involving the X chromosomes may occur during oogenesis and produce two kinds of eggs. If normal sperm fertilize these two types, which of the following pairs of genotypes are possible?
a XX and XY
* b. XXY and XO
c XYY and XO
d. XYY and YO
e. none of the above

**CHANGES IN CHROMOSOME STRUCTURE**

M 53. A chromosome's gene sequence that was ABCDEFG before modification and ABCDLMNOP afterward is an example of
a inversion.
b. deletion.
c duplication.
* d. translocation.
e. crossing over.

M    54.  A chromosome's gene sequence that was
          ABCDEFG before modification and
          ABCDCDEFG afterward is an example of
          a   inversion.
          b.  deletion.
      *   c.  duplication.
          d.  translocation.
          e.  crossing over.

E    55.  A chromosome that has been broken and rejoined
          in a reversal sequence has undergone
      *   a   inversion.
          b.  deletion.
          c.  duplication.
          d.  translocation.
          e.  crossing over.

E    56.  A chromosome's gene sequence that was
          ABCDEFG before damage and ABCFG after is
          an example of
          a   inversion.
      *   b.  deletion.
          c.  duplication.
          d.  translocation.
          e.  crossing over.

E    57.  A chromosome's gene sequence that was
          ABCDEFG before damage and ABFEDCG after
          is an  example of
      *   a   inversion.
          b.  deletion.
          c.  duplication.
          d.  translocation.
          e.  crossing over.

M    58.  Certain human cancer cells may demonstrate
          which of the following?
          a   deletion
          b.  inversion
      *   c.  translocation
          d.  duplication
          e.  none of the above

## FOCUS ON BIOETHICS: PROSPECTS IN HUMAN GENETICS

M    59.  Routine treatments for genetic disorders
          currently involve
          a   substituting normal for defective parents.
          b.  substituting normal for defective genes.
          c.  supplying a missing gene.
      *   d.  supplying missing enzymes or gene
              products.
          e.  all of the above

M    60.  Phenotypic treatments for genetic disorders
          include
          a   preventing the disorders in the carriers.
          b.  elimination of the defective gene.
          c.  preventing a disorder from being passed on.
      *   d.  preventing a disorder from being expressed.
          e.  all of the above

M    61.  Phenotypic treatments
      *   a   may increase the number of defective genes
              in a population.
          b.  do not affect the number of defective genes
              in a population.
          c.  decrease the number of defective genes in a
              population.
          d.  are the ultimate cures for genetic disorder.
          e.  have no biological value for either the
              individual or the population.

E    62.  Symptoms of phenylketonuria (PKU) may be
          minimized or suppressed by a diet low in
          a   serine.
          b.  glycine.
      *   c.  phenylalanine.
          d.  proline.
          e.  glutamic acid.

E    63.  Galactose buildup in galactosemia can be
          detected by
          a   karyotyping.
          b.  urine analysis.
          c.  blood tests.
          d.  saliva tests.
      *   e.  both b and c

M    64.  Preimplantation diagnosis
          a   usually requires abortion.
      *   b.  relies on in-vitro fertilization.
          c.  is a form of amniocentesis.
          d.  is a phenotypic treatment.
          e.  occurs about midway  through a pregnancy.

M    65.  Amniocentesis involves sampling
          a   the fetus directly.
      *   b.  the fetal cells floating in the amniotic fluid.
          c.  sperm.
          d.  blood cells.
          e.  placental cells.

M    66.  Amniocentesis is
          a   a surgical means of repairing deformities.
          b.  a form of chemotherapy that modifies or
              inhibits gene expression or the function of
              gene products.
      *   c.  used in prenatal diagnosis to detect
              chromosomal mutations and metabolic
              disorders in embryos.
          d.  a form of gene replacement therapy.
          e.  all of the above

M    67.  The most recent technique for analyzing the
          genetics of the unborn child involves the
          sampling of
          a   the fetus directly.
          b.  cells in the amniotic fluid.
          c.  material from the allantois.
      *   d.  the chorionic villi.
          e.  yolk sac material.

## Matching Questions

**68.** Matching I

1 _____ colchicine

2 _____ deletion

3 _____ duplication

4 _____ inversion

5 _____ monosomy

6 _____ translocation

7 _____ trisomy

A. a chromosome segment is permanently transferred to a nonhomologous chromosome

B. $(2n - 1)$; a gamete deprived of a chromosome

C. a repeat of a particular DNA sequence in the same chromosome or in nonhomologous ones

D. $(2n + 1)$; three chromosomes of the same kind are present in a set of chromosomes

E. a piece of the chromosome is inadvertently left out during the repair process

F. inhibits microtubule assembly; prevents chromosome movement

G. a chromosome segment that has been cut out and rejoined at the same place, but backward

*Answers:*   1. F      2. E      3. C
            4. G      5. B      6. A
            7. D

E  **69.** Matching II. Match the cause of the disorder with the disorder.

1 _____ Down syndrome

2 _____ galactosemia

3 _____ hemophilia

4 _____ Turner syndrome

A. autosomal recessive inheritance; lactose metabolism is blocked

B. nondisjunction of the twenty-first chromosomal pair

C. X-linked recessive inheritance

D. nondisjunction of the sex chromosomes

*Answers:*   1. B      2. A      3. C
            4. D

M  **70.** Matching III. Match each of the following phenotypic defects with its most used method of treatment.

1 _____ diabetes

2 _____ cleft lip

3 _____ phenylketonuria, PKU

4 _____ sickle-cell anemia

5 _____ albinism

A. chemotherapy

B. diet modification

C. environmental adjustments

D. surgical correction

*Answers:*   1. B      2. D      3. B
            4. C      5. A

## Problems

D  **71.** In cats the allele $B$ produces black, while $b$ produces yellow. Neither gene is dominant, and in the heterozygous state the phenotype is a combination of yellow and black spots called tortoiseshell. The alleles $B$ and $b$ are X-linked. If a tortoiseshell cat has three tortoiseshell kittens and two black kittens, give the genotype and phenotype of the tomcat that produced them, and give the sex of the kittens.

D  **72.** An X-linked recessive gene ($c$) produces red–green colorblindness. A woman with normal vision whose father was colorblind marries a colorblind man.

a. What are the possible genotypes for the mother of the colorblind man?

b. What are the possible genotypes for the father of the colorblind man?

c. What are the chances that the first son will be colorblind?

d. What are the chances that the first daughter will be colorblind?

D    **73.** In cats an X-linked pair of alleles, *B* and *b*, controls color of fur. The alleles are incompletely dominant: *B* produces black, *b* produces yellow, and *Bb* produces tortoiseshell.

     a   A yellow cat had a litter of two tortoiseshell kittens and one yellow. What is the sex of the yellow kitten?

     b.   A tortoiseshell cat brings home a litter of black, yellow, and tortoiseshell kittens. The color of which sex would tell you the color of the tomcat that produced them?

     c.   A yellow male is crossed with a tortoiseshell female. If the female has all male kittens in her litter of four, what color(s) would they be?

     d.   A tortoiseshell cat brings home her litter of black, yellow, and tortoiseshell kittens. By what method could you possibly decide whether the male parent was the black tomcat next door?

D    **74.** If a father and a son are both colorblind and the mother has normal vision, is it likely that the son inherited colorblindness from his father?

D    **75.** If a human recessive X-linked characteristic occurred with a 10 percent frequency, what would its frequency be in males and females?

D    **76.** In humans an X-linked disorder called coloboma iridia (a fissure in the iris) is a recessive trait. A normal couple has an afflicted daughter. The husband sues the wife for divorce on the grounds of infidelity. Would you find in his favor?

D    **77.** In *Drosophila* a narrow reduced eye is called a bar-eye. It is due to a dominant X-linked allele (*B*), while the full wild-type is due to the recessive gene (*B+*). Give the $F_1$ and $F_2$ genotypic and phenotypic expectations of a cross of a homozygous wild-type female with a bar-eyed male.

D    **78.** If the gene for yellow body color (*y*) is an X-linked recessive and its dominant counterpart (*y+*) produces wild body colors, give the expected phenotypes and frequencies for these four crosses:

     a   yellow female x wild male

     b.   wild carrier female x wild male

     c.   wild carrier female x yellow male

     d.   homozygous wild female x yellow male

D    **79.** Two *Drosophila* are crossed several times, with a total number of offspring of 106 females and 48 males. There is too great a deviation from the expected 1:1 ratio for chance alone to account for the difference. What other factor could account for this difference?

D    **80.** White eyes in *Drosophila* is a mutation that turned out to be an X-linked recessive. Would you expect that the first time the white eye was discovered it was in a male or female?

D    **81.** Hemophilia is an X-linked recessive gene. A normal woman whose father had hemophilia marries a normal man. What are the chances of hemophilia in their children?

D    **82.** Colorblindness is an X-linked recessive gene. Two normal-visioned parents produce a color-blind child.

     a   Is this child male or female?

     b.   What are the genotypes of the parents?

     c.   What are the chances that their next child will be a colorblind daughter?

D    **83.** If an X-linked recessive gene is expressed in 4 percent of the men, what proportion of women would express the recessive trait?

D    **84.** Red–green color blindness is an X-linked recessive trait. Two normal-visioned parents have a colorblind son. Indicate the genotype and phenotype of each parent and the son.

D    **85.** There is an autosomal gene that controls baldness, and its expression is sex influenced, so that the gene for baldness (*B*) is dominant in males but recessive in females. In females the allele $B^1$ for nonbaldness is dominant over the gene for baldness. If a heterozygous nonbald woman marries a nonbald man, what will be the appearance of their children? Work out the possibilities for each sex.

D    **86.** Short index fingers (shorter than ring finger) are dominant in males and recessive in females, while long index fingers (as long or longer than ring fingers) are dominant in females and recessive in males. Give the $F_2$ genotype and phenotype resulting from the cross of a male with long fingers with a female with short fingers.

## Classification Questions

Answer questions 87–91 in reference to the five items listed below.

     a   12

     b.   23

     c.   24

     d.   46

     e.   47

D    **87.** How many chromosomes does each somatic cell have in a human male who has two X chromosomes?

D    **88.** Following a gene duplication event involving only five loci, how many chromosomes will a human female have?

D    **89.** How many chromosomes are present in the somatic cells of a child born with Down syndrome (trisomy 21)?

D  **90.** How many chromosomes are present in each cell of the germ cell line for a tetraploid species where its normal complement of chromosomes is 48?

D  **91.** The normal sperm cell of a particular species carries 11 chromosomes. Following nondisjunction in the formation of secondary spermatocytes and their subsequent fertilization of normal ova, some of the zygotes will have 21 chromosomes, others will have 22, and the remainder will have how many chromosomes?

*Answers*:  87. e  88. d  89. e
  90. c  91. b

Answer questions 92–96 in reference to the five processes listed below. To answer these questions, you need to remember that the sequence of amino acids directly reflects the sequence of genes that coded for their placement.

    a.  an inversion
    b.  a deletion
    c.  a gene duplication
    d.  a translocation
    e.  an addition

D  **92.** Homologous sets of genes ABCDEF and aBCdEF are located on nonhomologous chromosomes. Crossing over between them is suppressed because their locations are the result of ____.

D  **93.** Homologous sets of genes ABCDEF and AEDCBF are located on homologous chromosomes. Crossing over between them is suppressed because of ____.

D  **94.** A small region of a protein from three species is sequenced and found to be as follows:

    species X is alanine, glycine, glycine, threonine, alanine
    species Y is alanine, glycine, threonine, alanine
    species Z is alanine, valine, glycine, threonine, alanine

The difference in the amino acid sequence of species Y is most likely due to ____.

D  **95.** A small region of a protein from three species is sequenced and found to be as follows:

    species X is alanine, valine, threonine, alanine
    species Y is alanine, glycine, threonine, alanine
    species Z is alanine, valine, glycine, threonine, alanine

The differences in the amino acid sequence of species Z is most likely due to ____.

D  **96.** The nucleotide sequences of homologous regions of DNA of two species is AATGCCCCGTTA and AATGCCCCGCTTA. If this is not the result of a nucleotide base-pair addition, then it is most likely the result of ____.

*Answers*:  92. d  93. a  94. b
  95. e  96. b

Answer questions 97–101 in reference to the five disorders listed below:

    a.  galactosemia
    b.  Turner syndrome
    c.  AIDS
    d.  hemophilia
    e.  Down syndrome

D  **97.** For this disorder both a phenotypic and a genotypic cure are *potentially* possible.

D  **98.** This disorder is an autosomal recessive disorder.

M  **99.** This disorder is the result of an X-linked recessive trait.

E  **100.** This disorder is also known as trisomy 21.

D  **101.** This disorder is due to a sex chromosome abnormality probably caused by nondisjunction of sex chromosomes at meiosis.

*Answers*:  97. a  98. a  99. d
  100. e  101. b

Answer questions 102–106 in reference to the five items listed below:
    a.  surgical correction
    b.  chemotherapy
    d.  genetic counseling
    e.  gene therapy

M  **102.** Familial hypercholesterolemia can be treated by this method.

M  **103.** This method is most often used to provide a phenotypic cure for a genetic disorder.

M  **104.** Once the risks have been determined, this method is an effective way of dealing with a genetic disorder prior to its occurrence in a child.

M  **105.** Radiation treatment of a cancer victim is an example of this method.

M  **106.** The substitution of a normal allele for a defective allele via genetic engineering would be an example of this method.

*Answers*:  102. b  103. a  104. d
  105. b  106. e

## Selecting the Exception

D    **107.** Four of the five answers listed below provide
evidence that genes are located on chromosomes.
Select the exception.
   a.   the chromosome number is cut in half by
meiosis
   b.   original chromosome number is restored by
fertilization
   c.   some genes tend to be inherited together
*  d.   environmental factors may influence gene
expression
   e.   there are two sets of chromosomes, one
maternal, one paternal in diploid forms

M    **108.** Four of the five answers listed below are related
conditions in which abnormal numbers of
chromosomes are present. Select the exception.
   a.   monosomy
   b.   Down syndrome
   c.   nondisjunction
*  d.   complete chromosome set
   e.   trisomy

E    **109.** Four of the five answers listed below are
organisms widely used in genetic research. Select
the exception.
   a.   peas
   b.   fruit flies
   c.   *Neurospora*
*  d.   dogfish shark
   e.   *E. coli*

M    **110.** Four of the five answers listed below are
conditions caused by chromosomal
nondisjunction. Select the exception.
   a.   Down syndrome
*  b.   Huntington disorder
   c.   Turner syndrome
   d.   Klinefelter syndrome
   e.   trisomy 21

M    **111.** Four of the five answers listed below are
methods of current or potential use in reducing
the number of defective genes in a population.
Select the exception.
   a.   genetic counseling
   b.   gene replacement
   c.   mutagen reduction
*  d.   diet modification
   e.   genetic screening

D    **112.** Four of the five answers listed below are caused
by recessive genes. Select the exception.
*  a.   Huntington disorder
   b.   phenylketonuria
   c.   colorblindness
   d.   hemophilia
   e.   albinism

71.   $BY$ black, tortoiseshell female, black males
72.   a.   $Cc$ or $cc$          b.   $CY$ or $cY$
      c.   1/2                d.   1/2
73.   a.   male               b.   female
      c.   1/2 yellow 1/2 black
      d.   black female kitten
74.   No, males inherit all sex-linked traits from the
mother.
75.   Males 10 percent, females 1 percent
76.   Yes, the daughter would have to inherit the
recessive trait from both parents.
77.   $B+B+$ x $BY$ ———> $F_1$: $B+B$ wild female $B+Y$
wild male $F_2$: 1/4 $BY$ bar male
1/4 $B+Y$ wild male 1/4 $B+B+$ wild female
1/4 $B+B$ wild female
78.   a.   yellow male wild female
      b.   1/4 wild male 1/4 yellow male
           1/4 wild female 1/4 wild carrier female
      c.   1/4 wild male 1/4 yellow male
           1/4 yellow female 1/4 wild carrier female
      d.   1/2 wild carrier female 1/2 wild male
79.   a sex-linked recessive lethal gene expressed in the
males, who received it from their mothers
80.   Male
81.   All females would be normal but 1/2 of them
would be carriers; 1/2 of the males would have
hemophilia, the other 1/2 normal.
82.   a.   male               b.   $Cc$ x $CY$
      c.   no chance to produce a color-blind daughter
83.   4/100 x 4/100 = 16/10,000, or 4 out of 2,500
84.   father $CY$, mother $Cc$, son $cY$
85.   $BB^1$ x $B^1B^1$ Æ $BB^1$ + $B^1B^1$; all daughters nonbald,
1/2 sons bald, 1/2 sons nonbald
86.   $F_2$: 3/4 males with short fingers,
1/4 males with long fingers
$F_2$: 3/4 females with long fingers,
1/4 females with short fingers

# CHAPTER 11
# DNA STRUCTURE AND FUNCTION

## Multiple-Choice Questions

### DISCOVERY OF DNA FUNCTION

M    **1.** The significance of Fred Griffith's experiment in which he used two strains of *Streptococcus pneumoniae* is that
     a   the semiconservative nature of DNA replication was finally demonstrated.
   *   b.   it demonstrated that harmless cells had become permanently transformed through a change in the bacterial hereditary system.
     c.   it established that pure DNA extracted from disease-causing bacteria transformed harmless strains into killer strains.
     d.   it demonstrated that radioactively labeled bacteriophages transfer their DNA but not their protein coats to their host bacteria.
     e.   all of the above

M    **2.** Which statement is NOT true about Fred Griffith's experiments?
     a   Mice injected with S bacteria die.
   *   b.   Mice injected with heat-killed S bacteria die.
     c.   Mice injected with heat-killed S bacteria and live R bacteria die.
     d.   Mice injected with R bacteria live.
     e.   S bacteria are transformed into harmless R bacteria.

E    **3.** Which scientist(s) identified the transforming substance involved in changing R bacteria to S?
   *   a   Avery
     b.   Griffith
     c.   Chargaff
     d.   Hershey and Chase
     e.   Pauling

E    **4.** Bacteriophages are
     a   large bacteria.
     b.   pathogens (disease-producing bacteria).
   *   c.   viruses.
     d.   cellular components.
     e.   protistans.

M    **5.** The significance of the experiments in which $^{32}P$ and $^{35}S$ were used is that
     a   the semiconservative nature of DNA replication was finally demonstrated.
     b.   it demonstrated that harmless bacterial cells had become permanently transformed through a change in the bacterial hereditary system.
     c.   it established that pure DNA extracted from disease-causing bacteria transformed harmless strains into killer strains.
   *   d.   it demonstrated that radioactively labeled bacteriophages transfer their DNA but not their protein coats to their host bacteria.
     e.   none of the above

D    **6.** If a mixture of viruses labeled with radioactive sulfur and phosphorus is placed in a bacterial culture,
     a   the bacteria will absorb radioactive sulfur.
   *   b.   the bacteria will absorb radioactive phosphorus.
     c.   the bacteria will absorb both radioactive sulfur and phosphorus.
     d.   the bacteria will not absorb either sulfur or phosphorus.
     e.   the viruses will not attach to the bacteria.

E    **7.** Nucleic acid contains
     a   sulfur.
   *   b.   phosphorus.
     c.   potassium.
     d.   iron.
     e.   manganese.

M    **8.** Which statement is false?
     a   Protein molecules contain no phosphorus.
   *   b.   Hershey and Chase discovered that $^{35}S$ and not $^{32}P$ had been incorporated into the hereditary system of the bacteria.
     c.   Bacteriophages are viruses that inject their nucleic acid genetic code into bacteria and use the bacterial genetic apparatus to make viral proteins.
     d.   Each nucleotide is composed of a five-carbon sugar, a phosphate group, and either a purine or a pyrimidine.
     e.   Viruses are particles of nucleic acid encased in protein.

M 9. Sulfur is
* a found in proteins but not nucleic acids.
   b. found in bacteria.
   c. found in nucleic acid but not proteins.
   d. needed for bacteriophages to attach to bacteria.
   e. needed for the enzyme that splits the wall of bacteria.

## DNA STRUCTURE

M 10. In the pairing of two nucleotides within the double helix
   a hydrogen bonds are used.
   b. adenine and thymine bind together.
   c. purines bind with pyrimidines.
   d. double-ring nitrogenous bases connect to single-ring bases.
* e. all of the above

E 11. A nucleotide may contain a
   a purine.
   b. pentose.
   c. phosphate group.
   d. pyrimidine.
* e. all of the above

M 12. From X-ray diffraction data, which of the following was determined about DNA?
   a The molecule had uniform diameter.
   b. The molecule was long and narrow.
   c. Part of the molecule repeated itself often.
   d. The shape of the molecule could be spiral.
* e. all of the above

M 13. Rosalind Franklin's research contribution was essential in
   a establishing the double-stranded nature of DNA.
   b. establishing the principle of base pairing.
* c. establishing most of the principal structural features of DNA.
   d. sequencing DNA molecules.
   e. determining the bonding energy of DNA molecules.

M 14. James Watson and Francis Crick
   a established the double-stranded nature of DNA.
   b. established the principle of base pairing.
   c. explained how DNA's structure permitted it to be replicated.
   d. proposed the concept of the double-helix.
* e. all of the above

E 15. In the bonding of nitrogenous bases
   a adenine is paired with cytosine.
   b. adenine is paired with guanine.
   c. cytosine is paired with thymine.
* d. guanine is paired with cytosine.
   e. two of the above

E 16. The DNA molecule could be compared to a
   a hairpin.
* b. ladder.
   c. key.
   d. globular mass.
   e. flat plate.

E 17. In DNA, complementary base pairing occurs between
   a cytosine and uracil.
   b. adenine and guanine.
   c. adenine and uracil.
* d. adenine and thymine.
   e. all of the above

M 18. Adenine and guanine are
* a double-ringed purines.
   b. single-ringed purines.
   c. double-ringed pyrimidines.
   d. single-ringed pyrimidines.
   e. amino acids.

M 19. Rosalind Franklin used which technique to determine many of the physical characteristics of DNA?
   a transformation
   b. transmission electron microscopy
   c. density-gradient centrifugation
* d. X-ray diffraction
   e. all of the above

E 20. In DNA molecules
* a the nucleotides are arranged in a linear, unbranched pattern.
   b. the nitrogenous bases are found on the outside of the molecule.
   c. the pentose–phosphate pattern runs the same way on each DNA strand.
   d. all of the above
   e. none of the above

M 21. Which statement is true?
* a The hydrogen bonding of cytosine to guanine is an example of complementary base pairing.
   b. Adenine always pairs up with guanine in DNA, and cytosine always teams up with thymine.
   c. Each of the four nucleotides in a DNA molecule has the same nitrogen-containing base.
   d. When adenine base pairs with thymine, they are linked by three hydrogen bonds.
   e. In the DNA of all species, the amount of purines never equals the amount of pyrimidines.

E 22. Each DNA strand has a backbone that consists of alternating
   a purines and pyrimidines.
   b. nitrogen-containing bases.
   c. hydrogen bonds.
* d. sugar and phosphate molecules.
   e. amines and purines.

## A CLOSER LOOK AT DNA

M 23. The appropriate adjective to describe DNA replication is
   a. nondisruptive.
   * b. semiconservative.
   c. progressive.
   d. natural.
   e. lytic.

E 24. Replication of DNA
   a. produces RNA molecules.
   b. produces only new DNA.
   * c. produces two molecules, each of which is half-new and half-old DNA joined lengthwise to each other.
   d. generates excessive DNA, which eventually causes the nucleus to divide.
   e. is too complex to characterize.

M 25. DNA polymerase
   a. is an enzyme.
   b. adds new nucleotides to a strand.
   c. proofreads DNA strands to see that they are correct.
   d. derives energy from ATP for synthesis of DNA strands.
   * e. all of the above

E 26. Proteins associated with DNA in eukaryotes are
   a. repressors.
   b. tryptophans.
   * c. histones.
   d. nucleosomes.
   e. operons.

E 27. Histone–DNA units are called
   a. polysomes.
   b. ribosomes.
   * c. nucleosomes.
   d. chromocenters.
   e. vesicles.

M 28. The DNA molecule is associated with histone in
   * a. looped series.
   b. scattered introns.
   c. hairpin lattices.
   d. tightly coiled complexes.
   e. lampbrushes.

## Matching Questions

D 29. Matching. Choose the one most appropriate answer for each.

   1 _____ Avery and colleagues
   2 _____ Rosalind Franklin
   3 _____ Fred Griffith
   4 _____ Hershey and Chase
   5 _____ Friedrich Miescher
   6 _____ Watson and Crick

   A. discovered that the hereditary system of one strain of bacteria could be transformed by materials from another strain of bacteria

   B. first to discover DNA and isolate it from fish sperm

   C. in 1944, reported that DNA was the "transforming principle"

   D. the first to build a scale model of DNA and to describe it explicitly in a publication

   E. the first to demonstrate, through the use of radioactive isotopes, that DNA, not protein, was the substance transmitted through generations of cells

   F. obtained excellent X-ray diffraction photographs that suggested that DNA was a long, thin molecule with regularly repeating structures; also said that DNA had to be helical like a circular stairway

*Answers:*

| 1. C | 2. F | 3. A |
|------|------|------|
| 4. E | 5. B | 6. D |

## Classification Questions

Answer questions 30–34 in reference to the five nucleotides listed below:

    a.  guanine
    b.  cytosine
    c.  pyrimidine
    d.  thymine
    e.  uracil

E    **30.** Early data indicated that within a species the amount of this was always equal to the amount of adenine.

E    **31.** This nucleotide is not incorporated into the structure of the DNA helix.

D    **32.** This nucleotide is a double-ringed molecule.

M    **33.** If one chain of a DNA molecule had a purine at a given position, this would be its complement on the other chain.

M    **34.** Two hydrogen bonds connect adenine to this in the DNA molecule.

*Answers*:    30.  d    31.  e    32.  a
                33.  c    34.  d

## Selecting the Exception

M    **35.** Four of the five answers listed below are bases used to construct nucleic acids. Select the exception.
    a.  cytosine
    b.  adenine
    c.  thymine
    d.  guanine
    *  e.  phenylalanine

D    **36.** Four of the five answers listed below are correctly paired. Select the exception.
    *  a.  A – C
    b.  C – G
    c.  A – T
    d.  T – A
    e.  purine – pyrimidine

# CHAPTER 12

# FROM DNA TO PROTEINS

## Multiple-Choice Questions

### TRANSCRIPTION OF DNA INTO RNA

E    **1.** The DNA molecule is usually made up of how many strands?
- a   1
- \*   b.   2
- c.   3
- d.   6
- e.   12

E    **2.** The RNA molecule is made up of how many strands?
- \*   a.   1
- b.   2
- c.   3
- d.   6
- e.   12

E    **3.** In terms of their nitrogenous base component, how many different kinds of RNA molecules are there?
- a   3
- \*   b.   4
- c.   5
- d.   6
- e.   12

E    **4.** What is the form of RNA that carries the code from the DNA to the site where the protein is assembled?
- \*   a.   messenger RNA
- b.   nuclear RNA
- c.   ribosomal RNA
- d.   transfer RNA
- e.   structural RNA

M    **5.** Which of the following carries amino acids to ribosomes, where amino acids are linked into the primary structure of a polypeptide?
- a   mRNA
- \*   b.   tRNA
- c.   hnRNA
- d.   rRNA
- e.   all of the above

M    **6.** Transfer RNA differs from other types of RNA because it
- a   transfers genetic instructions from cell nucleus to cytoplasm.
- b.   specifies the amino acid sequence of a particular protein.
- \*   c.   carries an amino acid at one end.
- d.   contains codons.
- e.   none of the above

E    **7.** The nitrogenous base found in DNA but not in RNA is
- a   adenine.
- b.   cytosine.
- c.   guanine.
- d.   uracil.
- \*   e.   thymine.

E    **8.** Which substance is found in RNA but not in DNA?
- a   thymine
- b.   deoxyribose
- \*   c.   ribose
- d.   guanine
- e.   cytosine

E    **9.** The nitrogenous base found in RNA but not in DNA is
- a   adenine.
- b.   cytosine.
- c.   guanine.
- \*   d.   uracil.
- e.   thymine.

E    **10.** Uracil will pair with
- a   ribose.
- \*   b.   adenine.
- c.   cytosine.
- d.   thymine.
- e.   guanine.

M    **11.** The synthesis of an RNA molecule from a DNA template strand is
- a   replication.
- b.   translation.
- \*   c.   transcription.
- d.   DNA synthesis.
- e.   metabolism.

E    **12.** The relationship between strands of RNA and DNA is
- a   antagonistic.
- b.   opposite.
- \*   c.   complementary.
- d.   an exact duplicate.
- e.   unrelated.

M    **13.** Transcription
- a   occurs on the surface of the ribosome.
- b.   is the final process in the assembly of a protein.
- \*   c.   occurs during the synthesis of any type of RNA from a DNA template.
- d.   is catalyzed by DNA polymerase.
- e.   all of the above

M   14. Which of the following dominates in the process of transcription?
    *   a   RNA polymerase
        c.  phenylketonuria
        d.  transfer RNA
        e.  all of the above

M   15. In transcription
        a   several RNA molecules are made from the same DNA molecule.
        b.  promoters are needed so that RNA polymerase can bind to DNA.
        c.  DNA produces messenger RNA.
        d.  a specific enzyme called RNA polymerase is required.
    *   e.  all of the above

M   16. The portion of the DNA molecule that is translated is composed of
        a   introns.
        b.  anticodons.
    *   c.  exons.
        d.  transcriptons.
        e.  both c and d, but not a or b

M   17. The portion of the DNA molecule that is not translated and is a noncoding portion of DNA is composed of
    *   a   introns.
        b.  anticodons.
        c.  exons.
        d.  transcriptons.
        e.  both c and d, but not a or b

M   18. In transcription
        a   several amino acids are assembled by the messenger RNA molecules at one time.
    *   b.  a special sequence called a promoter is necessary for transcription to begin.
        c.  certain polypeptide sequences are governed by one ribosome, while other sequences are produced by other ribosomes.
        d.  the transfer RNA molecules arrange the messenger RNA codons into the appropriate sequence.
        e.  none of the above

M   19. When a gene transcription occurs, which of the following is produced?
        a   more DNA
        b.  protein or polypeptide sequences
    *   c.  messenger RNA
        d.  enzymes
        e.  genetic defects

## DECIPHERING mRNA TRANSCRIPTS

E   20. The genetic code is made up of units consisting of how many nucleotides?
        a   2
    *   b.  3
        c.  5
        d.  6
        e.  12

E   21. There are how many different kinds of amino acids in proteins?
        a   3
        b.  6
        c.  12
    *   d.  20
        e.  28

M   22. There are how many different kinds of RNA codons?
        a   3
        b.  12
        c.  28
    *   d.  64
        e.  120

M   23. If the codon consisted of only two nucleotides, there would be how many different kinds of codons?
        a   4
        b.  8
    *   c.  16
        d.  32
        e.  64

M   24. The concept that a set of three nucleotides specifies a particular amino acid provides the basis for
        a   the one gene, one enzyme hypothesis.
        b.  the one gene, one polypeptide hypothesis.
    *   c.  the genetic code.
        d.  biochemical reactions among nucleic acids.
        e.  all of the above

M   25. Of all the different codons that exist, three of them
        a   are involved in mutations.
        b.  do not specify a particular amino acid.
        c.  cannot be copied.
        d.  provide punctuation or instructions such as "stop."
    *   e.  both b and d

E   26. Each "word" in the mRNA language consists of how many letters?
    *   a   three
        b.  four
        c.  five
        d.  more than five
        e.  none of the above

D   27. If each nucleotide coded for a single amino acid, how many different types of amino acids could be combined to form proteins?
    *   a   4
        b.  16
        c.  20
        d.  64
        e.  none of the above

M    28.  If the DNA triplets were ATG–CGT, the mRNA codons would be
       a    AUGCGU.
       b.   ATGCGT.
    *  c    UACGCA.
       d.   UAGCGU.
       e.   none of the above

M    29.  If the DNA triplets were ATG–CGT, the tRNA anticodons would be
    *  a    AUGCGU.
       b.   ATGCGT.
       c    UACGCA.
       d.   UAGCGU.
       e.   none of the above

## STAGES OF TRANSLATION

E    30.  Ribosomes function as
       a    a single unit.
    *  b.   two-part units.
       c    three-part units.
       d.   four-part units.
       e.   a multidivisional unit.

E    31.  The "start" codon is
       a    UUU.
       b.   CUC.
       c    GUC.
    *  d.   AUG.
       e.   AUA.

E    32.  Amino acids are joined together in proteins by
       a    hydrogen bonds.
    *  b.   peptide bonds.
       c    anticodons.
       d.   wobble effects.
       e.   codon bonds.

M    33.  Termination of protein translation is due to
       a    lack of amino acids.
       b.   wobble effects.
       c    the AUG codon.
       d.   lack of messenger RNA.
    *  e.   a stop

## HOW MUTATIONS AFFECT PROTEIN SYNTHESIS

E    34.  The difference between normal hemoglobin and sickle-cell hemoglobin is in the
       a    heme portion of the molecules.
       b.   number of chains of amino acids.
    *  c    substitution of a specific amino acid for another specific amino acid.
       d.   addition of one amino acid to the normal hemoglobin molecule.
       e.   loss of only one amino acid from the normal hemoglobin molecule.

M    35.  A gene mutation
       a    is a change in the nucleotide sequence of DNA.
       b.   may be caused by environmental agents.
       c    may arise spontaneously.
       d.   can occur in all organisms.
    *  e.   all of the above

E    36.  Mutations can be
       a    random.
       b.   beneficial.
       c    harmful.
       d.   heritable.
    *  e.   all of the above

## THE NATURE OF CONTROLS OVER GENE EXPRESSION

M    37.  A regulator gene produces which of the following?
    *  a    repressor protein
       b.   regulatory enzyme
       c    promoter
       d.   operator
       e.   transcriber

D    38.  In a negative control system over gene espression
       a    iniation of transcription is promoted by a regulatory protein binding to DNA.
    *  b.   an inducer promotes transcription.
       c    inhibitor proteins unblock the promoter.
       d.   the promoter is missing.

## EXAMPLES OF GENE CONTROL IN PROKARYOTIC CELLS

D    39.  During the early part of a young mammal's life, the *E. coli* in the young offspring's intestinal tract are exposed to high levels of which of the following that later generations of *E. coli* will never be exposed to?
       a    glucose
       b.   ribose
       c    cellulose
    *  d.   lactose
       e.   fructose

M    40.  A repressor protein binds with
       a    messenger RNA.
    *  b.   the operator.
       c    the regulator.
       d.   a product.
       e.   a substrate.

M    41.  The region that determines the rate at which a certain mRNA chain is to be synthesized.
       a    heterogeneous nuclear DNA
       b.   repressor gene
    *  c    promoter sequence
       d.   operator sequence
       e.   all of the above

## GENE CONTROL IN EUKARYOTIC CELLS

M   42. Genes located in different regions of the body during embryonic development may be
  a   turned on and off.
  b.  never turned on.
  c.  turned on and left on.
  d.  activated for only a short time in one cell and a long time in another cell.
  * e. all of the above

E   43. Cells of all multicellular organisms arise during mitosis from a single cell known as a(n)
  a.  gamete.
  * b. zygote.
  c.  embryo.
  d.  clone.
  e.  fetus.

E   44. Which term refers to the processes by which cells with identical genotypes become structurally and functionally distinct from one another?
  a.  metamorphosis
  b.  metastasis
  c.  cleavage
  * d. differentiation
  e.  induction

M   45. The mosaic effect in human females can be observed in
  a.  skin color.
  b.  hair color.
  c.  distribution of fat cells.
  * d. distribution of sweat glands.
  e.  all of the above

M   46. Phytochrome
  a.  inhibits plant development.
  b.  amounts increase after sunset.
  c.  is a protein,
  * d. becomes more active after sunrise.
  e.  is more sensitive to blue light waves.

## FOCUS ON SCIENCE: GENES, PROTEINS, AND CANCER

M   47. Cancer cells
  a.  have altered plasma membranes.
  b.  are unable to attach to other cells.
  c.  divide to produce high densities of cells.
  d.  have a different metabolism, using glycolysis even when oxygen is available.
  * e. all of the above

D   48. Which characteristic seems to be most uniquely correlated with metastasis?
  a.  loss of nuclear–cytoplasmic controls governing cell growth and division
  * b. changes in recognition factors on membrane surfaces
  c.  "puffing" in the polytene chromosomes
  d.  the massive production of cyclic adenosine monophosphate and its secretion into the environment
  e.  none of the above

M   49. The spread of a cancer from one site to others in the body is known as
  a.  benign tumor.
  * b. metastasis.
  c.  malignant tumor.
  d.  remission.
  e.  both a and c, but not b or d

E   50. The specific name given to a cancer-producing chemical is
  a.  pathogen.
  * b. carcinogen.
  c.  teratogen.
  d.  mutagen.
  e.  oncogene.

## Matching Questions

D   51. Matching. Choose the best matching element.
  1  _____   anticodon
  2  _____   codon
  3  _____   messenger RNA
  4  _____   promoters
  5  _____   transcription
  6  _____   translation

  A. RNA-directed synthesis of polypeptide chains
  B. sites at which RNA polymerases can bind and initiate transcription
  C. binds to small subunit platform of a ribosome
  D. guided and catalyzed by RNA polymerases
  E. a tRNA triplet opposite an amino acid
  F. a set of three nucleotides

*Answers:*

| 1. E | 2. F | 3. C |
|------|------|------|
| 4. B | 5. D | 6. A |

## Classification Questions

Answer questions 52- 56 in reference to the five RNA codons listed below:

    a   AUG
    b.  UAA
    c.  UUU
    d.  UUA
    e.  AAA

D    **52.**  This codon terminates a coding region.

D    **53.**  The anticodon AAA would pair with this codon.

M    **54.**  A single mutation involving the second letter of codon AUA would convert it to this codon.

M    **55.**  A DNA codon of ATT would be complementary to this RNA codon.

M    **56.**  This codon specifies an amino acid and indicates the beginning of a coding region.

*Answers*:    52.  b      53.  c      54.  e
                55.  b      56.  a


Answer questions 57-61 in reference to the five items of gene regulation listed below:

    a.  operon
    b.  operator
    c.  promoter
    d.  lactose
    e.  regulator gene

M    **57.**  This item contains regulator, promoter, and operator regions.

D    **58.**  A repressor protein can shut down transcription by binding to this item.

M    **59.**  This item codes for the production of repressor.

D    **60.**  When the repressor is inactivated, RNA polymerase can bind to this item and allow transcription to occur.

M    **61.**  The molecule that can activate the operon is represented by this item.

*Answers*:    57.  a      58.  b      59.  e
                60.  c      61.  d


## Selecting the Exception

E    **62.**  Three of the four answers listed below are different forms of a class of nucleic acids. Select the exception.
    *    a  template
          b.  ribosomal
          c.  messenger
          d.  transfer

M    **63.**  Three of the four answers listed below are involved in gene action. Select the exception.
          a  replication
          b.  transcription
          c.  translation
    *    d.  polymerization

D    **64.**  Four of the five answers listed below are related pairings. Select the exception.
          a  double-stranded DNA–messenger RNA
          b.  purine–pyrimidine
          c.  codon–anticodon
          d.  small subunit–large subunit
    *    e.  promoter–terminator

D    **65.**  Four of the five answers listed below describe changes at the chromosomal level. Select the exception.
    *    a  base substitution
          b.  duplication
          c.  translocation
          d.  deletion
          e.  inversion

M    **66.**  Four of the five answers listed below are sources of genetic variation. Select the exception.
          a  crossing over
          b.  mutation
    *    c.  asexual reproduction
          d.  chromosome aberration
          e.  sexual reproduction

D    **67.**  Four of the five answers listed below are components of a nucleotide. Select the exception.
          a  pentose sugar
    *    b.  amino acid
          c.  pyrimidine
          d.  phosphate group
          e.  purine

D    **68.**  Four of the five answers listed below are related by a common number. Select the exception.
          a  number of nucleotides in a codon
          b.  number of building blocks (parts) in a nucleotide
          c.  number of stop codons
    *    d.  number of types of DNA
          e.  number of types of RNA

D    **69.**  Three of the four answers listed below are steps in translation. Select the exception.
          a  initiation
    *    b.  replication
          c.  chain elongation
          d.  termination

D    **70.**  Four of the five answers listed below are features of the lactose operon. Select the exception.
          a  regulator
    *    b.  terminator
          c.  operator
          d.  promoter
          e.  structural gene

D  71. Four of the five answers listed below are
       descriptions of cancer cells. Select the exception.
    *    a   abnormal shaped nucleus
         b.  decline in ability to adhere to substrates
         c.  changes in the plasma membrane
         d.  abnormal growth and division
         e.  cytoplasm shrinks and becomes
             disorganized

E  72. Four of the five answers listed below are
       carcinogens. Select the exception.
    *    a   egg white
         b.  asbestos
         c.  radiation with X-ray
         d.  components in cigarette smoke
         e.  ultraviolet radiation

# CHAPTER 13

# RECOMBINANT DNA AND GENETIC ENGINEERING

## Multiple-Choice Questions

### RECOMBINATION IN NATURE—AND IN THE LABORATORY

M **1.** Recombinant DNA
   a   has occurred in sexually reproducing forms.
   b.  can be produced with new biological techniques.
   c.  occurs with viral infections of various forms of life.
   d.  has produced changes that resulted in evolution.
 * e.  all of the above

E **2.** New genetic combinations result from
   a   crossing over.
   b.  sexual reproduction.
   c.  mutations.
   d.  exchange of genes between different species.
 * e.  all of the above

E **3.** A tangelo is a combination
   a   orange and lemon.
   b.  orange and tangerine.
   c.  navel orange and tangerine.
   d.  tangerine and cantaloupe.
 * e.  tangerine and grapefruit.

M **4.** The process by which one bacterial cell transfers DNA to another is
   a   fission.
   b.  gametic fusion.
 * c.  conjugation.
   d.  lysis.
   e.  none of the above

E **5.** Small circular molecules of DNA in bacteria are called
 * a   plasmids.
   b.  desmids.
   c.  pili.
   d.  F particles.
   e.  transferrins.

E **6.** Enzymes used to cut DNA molecules in recombinant DNA research are
   a   ligases.
 * b.  restriction enzymes.
   c.  transcriptases.
   d.  DNA polymerases.
   e.  replicases.

M **7.** The fragments of chromosomes split by restriction enzymes
   a   have fused ends.
   b.  have specific sequences of nucleotides.
   c.  have sticky ends.
   d.  form a circle.
 * e.  both b and c

D **8.** Plasmids
   a   are self-reproducing circular molecules of DNA.
   b.  are sites for inserting genes for amplification.
   c.  may be transferred between different species of bacteria.
   d.  may confer the ability to donate genetic material when bacteria conjugate.
 * e.  all of the above

M **9.** The "natural" use of restriction enzymes by bacteria is to
   a   integrate viral DNA.
 * b.  destroy viral DNA.
   c.  repair "sticky ends."
   d.  copy the bacterial genes.
   e.  clone DNA.

M **10.** Restriction enzymes
   a   often produce staggered cuts in DNA that are useful in splicing genes.
   b.  are like most enzymes in being very specific in their action.
   c.  are natural defense mechanisms evolved in bacteria to guard against or counteract bacteriophages.
   d.  are used along with ligase and plasmids to produce a DNA library.
 * e.  all of the above

M **11.** Which of the following enzymes joins the paired sticky ends of DNA fragments?
   a   reverse transcriptase
   b.  restriction enzymes
 * c.  DNA ligase
   d.  DNA polymerase
   e.  transferase

M **12.** A collection of DNA fragments produced by restriction enzymes and incorporated into plasmids is called
   a   copied DNA.
   b.  transcribed DNA.
   c.  DNA amplification.
 * d.  a DNA library.
   e.  plasmid DNA.

## WORKING WITH DNA FRAGMENTS

D     **13.** For polymerase chain reaction to occur,
- a   isolated DNA molecules must be primed.
- b.   all DNA fragments must be identical.
- c   the DNA must be separated into single strands.
- d.   a sticky end must be available for the ligase enzyme to function.
- \*   e.   a and c are correct, but b and d are not

E     **14.** The enzyme used in the polymerase chain reaction is
- a   a restriction enzyme.
- b.   reverse transcriptase.
- \*   c.   DNA polymerase.
- d.   RNA replicase
- e.   all of these

M     **15.** The laboratory technique used to separate the DNA fragments produced by restriction enzymes is
- a   the polymerase chain reaction.
- \*   b.   gel electrophoresis.
- c.   ultracentrifugation.
- d.   electron microscopy.
- e.   fluorescence microscopy.

D     **16.** The use of RFLPs for "genetic fingerprinting" is based on
- a   the type of gel used in electrophoresis.
- b.   identical alleles at loci.
- \*   c.   differences of locations where enzymes make their cuts.
- d.   differences between blood and semen DNA.
- e.   bonding of DNA to RNA.

D     **17.** Which of the following statements about restriction fragment length polymorphism is false?
- a   RFLPs can be used as a genetic fingerprint.
- b.   RFLPs are based on variations in alleles at the same locus.
- c.   RFLPs reflect the fact that molecular differences in alleles alter the site where restriction enzymes function.
- \*   d.   RFLPs can be used to distinguish between identical twins.
- e.   RFLPs have greatly increased the number of sites involved in mapping the human genome.

## MODIFIED HOST CELLS

D     **18.** Probes for cloned genes use
- \*   a   complementary nucleotide sequences labeled with radioactive isotopes.
- b.   certain media with specific antibodies.
- c.   specific enzymes.
- d.   certain bacteria sensitive to the genes.
- e.   all of the above

D     **19.** Because it has no introns, researchers prefer to use _____ when working with human genes.
- \*   a   cDNA
- b.   cloned DNA
- c.   hybridized DNA
- d.   RFLPs
- e.   viral DNA

M     **20.** RNA can manufacture DNA via the action of
- a   DNA polymerase.
- b.   RNA polymerase.
- \*   c.   reverse transcriptase.
- d.   ligase.
- e.   restriction endonuclease.

D     **21.** Multiple copies of DNA can be produced by
- a   cloning a DNA library.
- b.   genetic amplification.
- c.   the use of reverse transcriptase.
- d.   the action of DNA polymerase.
- \*   e.   all of the above

## BACTERIA, PLANTS, AND THE NEW TECHNOLOGY

M     **22.** Which statement is true?
- a   There is no danger involved in recombinant DNA research in humans.
- b.   There is no danger involved in recombinant DNA research in bacteria.
- c.   There is no danger in releasing recombinant organisms into the environment.
- \*   d.   Stringent safety rules make the use of recombinant DNA research possible.
- e.   It is safe to conduct recombinant DNA research in plants.

E     **23.** Which of the following has NOT been produced commercially by genetically altered bacteria?
- \*   a   AIDS vaccine
- b.   human insulin
- c.   growth hormone
- d.   bacterial capable of cleaning oil spills
- e.   bacteria that retard ice crystals during freezing weather

M     **24.** Ice-minus bacteria
- a   were released into the environment.
- b.   have been genetically engineered to delete a harmful gene.
- c.   will reduce the chance of ice forming on commercial plants such as strawberries.
- d.   field trials generated protests by environmental activists.
- \*   e.   all of the above

E    25.    Which of the following statements is NOT true?
      a    Plant geneticists are searching for wild
           ancestors of modern crop plants.
      b.   Botanists have grown whole plants from
           cultured cells.
 *    c.   Modern crop strains are more resistant than
           ancient ones.
      d.   Researchers have introduced DNA
           fragments directly into cells using bullets.
      e.   Plants can be engineered to produce human
           proteins.

## GENETIC ENGINEERING OF ANIMALS

E    26.    Which of the following statements is true?
 *    a    Goats have been used to produce CFTR, a
           protein used in the treatment of cystic
           fibrosis.
      b.   Scientists have actually changed mice to
           rats by genetic engineering.
      c.   Scientists tried unsuccessfully to get a bull
           to produce a milk protein.
      d.   The attempt to map the human genome has
           failed.
      e.   Gene therapy has not yet been attempted in
           humans.

M    27.    Gene therapy
      a    has not yet been used successfully with
           mammals.
      b.   is a surgical technique that separates
           chromosomes that have failed to segregate
           properly during meiosis II.
      c.   has been used successfully to treat victims
           of Huntington disorder by removing the
           dominant damaging autosomal allele and
           replacing it with a harmless one.
 *    d.   offers the possibility of replacing defective
           alleles with normal ones.
      e.   all of the above

## Classification Questions

Answer questions 28–32 in reference to the five items listed
below:
      a    restriction enzymes
      b.   recombinants
      c.   plasmids
      d.   clones
      e.   restriction sites

M    28.    These are bacterial populations containing
           thousands or millions of identical copies of one
           to several genes.

D    29.    When one uses the techniques of genetic
           engineering to move a novel or foreign piece of
           DNA into the DNA of an organism, these new
           DNA regions are known by this name.

M    30.    When pieces of DNA are moved by a genetic
           engineer from one organism to another, they are
           first incorporated into these entities.

E    31.    The sole function of these is to cut apart foreign
           DNA molecules.

D    32.    These may incorporate all of the entities listed
           above.

*Answers:*    28.  d        29.  b        30.  c
             31.  a        32.  d


Answer questions 33–37 in reference to the four items listed
below:
      a    cDNA
      b.   a restriction enzyme
      c.   reverse transcriptase
      d.   a DNA library

M    33.    This is from a viral source and catalyzes
           reactions to construct DNA strands from mRNA.

E    34.    Any DNA copied from mRNA transcripts is
           known by this name.

E    35.    This is the name of a nuclease whose only
           function is to cut apart foreign DNA entering a
           cell.

M    36.    Collections of DNA fragments produced by
           restriction enzymes and incorporated into cloning
           vectors are known by this name.

D    37.    This is a type of probe constructed of
           radioactively labeled DNA subunits.

*Answers*:    33.  c        34.  a        35.  b
             36.  d        37.  a

## Selecting the Exception

M     **38.**   Four of the five answers listed below are aspects of the process known as gene splicing. Select the exception.
- a   cloning vector
- b.   restriction enzymes
- c.   sticky ends
- d.   exposed base pairs
- \*   e.   crossing over

M     **39.**   Four of the five enzymes below are used in genetic engineering. Select the exception.
- a   ligase
- b.   reverse transcriptase
- c.   restriction
- \*   d.   replicase
- e.   DNA polymerase

M     **40.**   Four of the five statements below are true of cloned DNA. Select the exception.
- a   The plasmid used is the cloning vector.
- b.   Identical copies are produced.
- \*   c.   Cloned DNA is produced by reverse transcriptase.
- d.   Multiple copies are produced.
- e.   Cloned DNA is manufactured in bacteria cells.

# CHAPTER 14
# MICROEVOLUTION

## Multiple-Choice Questions

### EARLY BELIEFS, CONFOUNDING DISCOVERIES

M  **1.** The forelimbs of early mammals were similar in all features except
   a  embryonic origin.
   b.  position on the body.
   c.  number.
*  d.  function.
   e.  composition.

E  **2.** The pelvic girdle is
   a  part of the backbone of vertebrates.
   b.  a place where the forelimbs are attached.
*  c.  a place where the hindlimbs are attached.
   d.  completely absent in snakes, which do not have legs.
   e.  found only during embryonic development and is not present in many mature vertebrates.

E  **3.** Fossils found in the lowest geological strata are generally the most
   a  advanced.
   b.  complex.
*  c.  primitive.
   d.  widespread.
   e.  specialized.

E  **4.** In the early 1800s, creationist thinking would have included all of the following EXCEPT
   a  All species are links in a great chain.
   b.  The key to understanding nature is to discover all the links in the great chain.
   c.  All species originated in one place and at approximately the same time.
*  d.  Species become modified over time.
   e.  Nature was perfect in the original creation.

### A FLURRY OF NEW THEORIES

E  **5.** Darwin's mentor, who obtained Darwin's position on H.M.S. *Beagle*, was
   a  Alfred Wallace.
*  b.  John Henslow.
   c.  Jean-Baptiste Lamarck.
   d.  Georges Cuvier.
   e.  Charles Lyell.

M  **6.** The place Darwin visited on his trip around the world that had the greatest impact on his thinking was
   a  the Canary Islands.
   b.  Africa.
   c.  the Hawaiian Islands.
*  d.  the Galápagos Islands.
   e.  Brazil.

E  **7.** Georges Cuvier was a strong proponent of the theory of
   a  uniformity.
   b.  relativity.
*  c.  catastrophism.
   d.  natural selection.
   e.  acquired characteristics.

D  **8.** Which of the following statements is NOT true concerning Lamarck's theory of inheritance of acquired characteristics?
*  a  Nature selects the best adapted individuals to survive and reproduce.
   b.  Environmental pressures cause changes that are inherited.
   c.  Life forms gradually proceeded toward perfection.
   d.  A great pianist would likely beget a great pianist.
   e.  The drive for improvement was in the "fluida" of the nerves.

E  **9.** Darwin was influenced by which of the following concepts attributable to Charles Lyell?
   a  The geological history of the earth is a series of catastrophes.
   b.  Acquired characteristics can be inherited.
   c.  Natural selection operates on the tremendous variation found in nature.
   d.  All life forms a part of a great Chain of Being.
*  e.  The geologic forces in earth's history show predictable uniformity.

### DARWIN'S THEORY TAKES FORM

M  **10.** In Argentina, Darwin noted the similarity of fossils of glyptodonts to modern
   a  rodents.
   b.  finches.
   c.  turtles,
*  d.  armadillos.
   e.  ostriches.

M  **11.** The development of Darwin's theory of evolution by natural selection was based largely on his study of which of the following organisms?
   a  butterflies
   b.  butterflies and Galápagos finches
   c.  domestic animals
   d.  domestic animals and Galápagos finches
   e.  all three organisms

M  12. According to Darwin, natural selection is based on the _____ found in populations.
   a   acquired characters
 * b   variations
   c   weakest members
   d   noncompetitors
   e   similarities

E  13. Artificial selection occurs when
   a   the environment controls which organisms will survive.
 * b   humans determine which organisms will survive.
   c   the extremes of the population have a lesser chance to survive.
   d   the extremes of the population have a better chance to survive.
   e   the organisms on one extreme of the population have a better chance to survive than those on the other extreme.

E  14. Thomas Malthus proposed that
   a   the food supply multiplied faster than the population.
 * b   the population multiplied faster than the food supply.
   c   the food supply and populations multiplied at the same rate.
   d   artificial selection was the key to evolution.
   e   natural selection was the key to evolution.

E  15. The person credited with being the codiscoverer of the theory of natural selection was
 * a   Alfred Wallace.
   b   Charles Lyell.
   c   Thomas Malthus.
   d   James Hutton.
   e   John Henslow.

E  16. *Archaeopteryx* was a transitional form between
   a   birds and mammals.
   b   reptiles and mammals.
 * c   birds and reptiles.
   d   fish and amphibians.
   e   amphibians and reptiles.

## INDIVIDUALS DON'T EVOLVE, POPULATIONS DO

M  17. For which group of individuals of the same species are there no restrictions to random mating among its members?
   a   individual
   b   species
 * c   population
   d   polyploid
   e   all of the above

E  18. Which of the following evolve?
 * a   populations
   b   genera
   c   kingdoms
   d   a and b

E  19. New alleles arise by
 * a   mutation.
   b   migration.
   c   genetic drift.
   d   random mating.
   e   independent assortment.

E  20. New variations of genes may be produced by
   a   immigration.
   b   mutation.
   c   crossing over.
   d   sexual reproduction.
 * e   all of the above

M  21. New alleles that appear by mutation
   a   are inherently disadvantageous to their bearers.
   b   are seldom advantageous or disadvantageous in themselves.
   c   either have or lack survival value only in the context of their environment.
 * d   both b and c
   e   both a and b

E  22. Which are sources of new alleles within a population?
   a   genetic recombination
   b   meiosis
 * c   mutation
   d   genetic drift
   e   mitosis

M  23. The Hardy–Weinberg formula
 * a   is useful in determining the extent to which a sexually reproducing population is evolving.
   b   is used to predict when genetic drift will occur in a sexually reproducing population.
   c   is useful in determining the extent to which polyploidy is occurring in specific plant populations.
   d   is used to predict when specific groups of organisms will become extinct.
   e   all of the above

M  24. The maintenance of Hardy–Weinberg equilibrium is encouraged
   a   when sexual selection occurs.
   b   when mutations occur.
   c   in small populations.
 * d   when there is no gene flow between different populations.
   e   all of the above

M 25. Which statement is NOT true?
   a. Migration leads to genetic variation.
 * b. Dominant genes always occur more frequently in a population than recessive genes do.
   c. Nonrandom mating may result in changes in gene frequency.
   d. The Hardy–Weinberg law applies to large, stable populations.
   e. Crossing over increases variation.

E 26. Of the following, which does NOT characterize a population in Hardy–Weinberg equilibrium?
   a. large population size
   b. no mutation
 * c. differential reproduction
   d. absence of gene flow

*FOCUS ON SCIENCE*: **WHEN IS A POPULATION NOT EVOLVING?**

D 27. If the frequency of expression of a recessive trait in a population is 16 percent, the frequency of the recessive allele would be what percent?
   a. 16
   b. 25
 * c. 40
   d. 50
   e. 67

M 28. If the frequency of a recessive allele is 36 percent, the frequency of the dominant allele would be what percent?
   a. 5
   b. 8
   c. 25
   d. 48
 * e. 64

D 29. In the Hardy–Weinberg equation, the term $q^2$ refers to the frequency of
   a. a recessive allele of a given locus.
 * b. the homozygous recessive genotype at a given locus.
   c. recessive alleles in a population.
   d. heterozygotes in a population.

M 30. If the frequency of the recessive allele is 30 percent, the frequency of the heterozygous carrier would be what percent?
 * a. 42
   b. 9
   c. 27
   d. 60
   e. 80

D 31. In a population that is in Hardy–Weinberg equilibrium, the frequency of the recessive homozygous genotype is 0.49. The percentage of the population that is heterozygous is
   a. 51.
   b. 49.
 * c. 42.
   d. 7.
   e. 3.

D 32. Suppose you have a population of guinea pigs in which two-thirds of the alleles for coat color specify black and one-third specify white. According to the Hardy–Weinberg rule, what will be the ratio of these alleles in the gene pool in future generations, provided all the guinea pigs reproduce?
   a. 1:1
 * b. 2:1
   c. 3:1
   d. 0.67: 0.11

D 33. Of 400 people who dwell on a Pacific island, 16 are homozygous recessive for a trait that has only two different types of alleles in the population. The number of heterozygous people is
   a. 256.
   b. 32.
   c. 64.
 * d. 128.
   e. 384.

**A CLOSER LOOK AT NATURAL SELECTION**

E 34. Which of the following is NOT a components of Darwin's principle of natural selection?
 * a. New alleles are constantly produced through mutation.
   b. Populations exhibit great variation.
   c. Organisms produce more offspring than can be sustained by the environment.
   d. Over time, adaptive phenotypes increase in frequency within a population.

E 35. Which of the following is NOT a components of Darwin's principle of natural selection?
   a. Populations exhibit great variation.
   b. Organisms produce more offspring than can be sustained by the environment.
   c. Over time, adaptive phenotypes increase in frequency within a population.
 * d. The least competitive individuals have the greatest survival chances.

M 36. According to Darwin, adaptive traits will increase in frequency
   a. as the mutation rate increases due to environmental pressures.
 * b. if they promote survival and reproduction.
   c. if the alleles that control them decrease competitiveness.
   d. as populations grow smaller.

## DIRECTIONAL CHANGE IN THE RANGE OF VARIATION

M **37.** A color mutation in a moth from light to dark
    a  is an advantage in industrial environments.
    b.  may be beneficial under changing environmental conditions.
    c.  produces a form of moth that will have a better chance for survival in some environments.
    d.  may be easily spotted by predators in some environments.
  *  e.  all of the above

M **38.** Directional selection occurs when
    a.  the environment controls which organisms will survive.
    b.  humans determine which organisms will survive.
    c.  the extremes of the population have a lesser chance to survive.
    d.  the extremes of the population have a better chance to survive.
  *  e.  the organisms on one extreme of the population have a better chance to survive than do those on the other extreme.

E **39.** An insect that exhibits resistance to a pesticide
    a.  developed the resistance in response to the pesticide.
    b.  mutated when exposed to the pesticide.
  *  c.  inherited genes that made it resistant to the pesticide.
    d.  none of the above

## SELECTION AGAINST OR IN FAVOR OF EXTREME PHENOTYPES

M **40.** Stabilizing selection occurs when
    a.  the environment controls which organisms will survive.
    b.  humans determine which organisms will survive.
  *  c.  the extremes of the population have a lesser chance to survive.
    d.  the extremes of the population have a better chance to survive.
    e.  the organisms on one extreme of the population have a better chance to survive than those on the other extreme.

D **41.** The fact that the average human birthweight remains at about seven pounds is due to
    a.  modern prenatal care.
  *  b.  the forces of stabilizing selection.
    c.  conscious effort on the part of mothers.
    d.  limitations of the size of the human womb.
    e.  selection tendencies moving in the direction of increasing birthweight.

M **42.** In an unchanging environment, selection in a well-adapted population is
    a.  directional.
    b.  disruptive.
  *  c.  stabilizing.
    d.  absent.

E **43.** In a certain bird species, clutch size (the number of eggs laid by a female in one breeding season) ranges from four to eight and the most frequent clutch size is six. This phenomenon is an example of
    a.  sexual selection.
  *  b.  stabilizing selection.
    c.  disruptive selection.
    d.  directional selection.

M **44.** Disruptive selection favors
    a.  the intermediate forms.
    b.  average human birthweights of seven pounds.
  *  c.  the extremes of a range of variation.
    d.  a greater number of individuals in the center of the bell-shaped curve.
    e.  a shift toward higher and higher academic grades.

## SPECIAL OUTCOMES OF SELECTION

E **45.** Male northern sea lions are nearly twice the size of females because
    a.  males live longer than females.
    b.  predators of the sea lions favor males.
  *  c.  males compete to mate with females.
    d.  each male must protect the one female with which he mates.

M **46.** The HbS allele (sickle cell) occurs at a higher frequency in Africa than it does in the United States because
    a.  it is a dominant allele in Africa and a recessive one in the United States.
    b.  genetic recombination occurs at different rates in different human populations.
  *  c.  natural selection favors heterozygotes in Africa, but favors homozygous normal individuals in the United States.
    d.  the U.S. population is descended from a small group of individuals who possessed the allele at a high frequency.

## GENE FLOW

M 47. What accounts for the fact that polydactylism is prevalent and Tay-Sachs disease virtually absent in one human population in the United States while Tay-Sachs disease is prevalent and polydactylism virtually absent in another?
- a  Natural selection has promoted these differences since humans live in many different environments.
- b. Mutation rates differ between different loci.
- * c. There is little gene flow between the two populations.
- d. The populations are small, and therefore genetic drift is a major factor in the determination of allele frequencies.

D 48. Immigration of individuals to a population in Hardy–Weinberg equilibrium will NOT upset the equilibrium if
- * a  they are beyond the age of reproduction.
- b. females and males are in equal proportions.
- c. they mate randomly in the new population.
- d. they arrive in large numbers.

## GENETIC DRIFT

M 49. The introduction of a small population onto an island that results in a limited gene pool for a population best describes
- a  the Hardy–Weinberg law.
- b. genetic drift.
- c. the bottleneck effect.
- * d. the founder principle.
- e. the effect of genetic isolation.

M 50. The sharp reduction of the gene pool and the numbers of a population through a severe epidemic is an example of
- a  natural selection.
- b. genetic isolation.
- * c. the bottleneck effect.
- d. the founder principle.
- e. all of the above

E 51. The influence of genetic drift on allele frequencies increases as
- a  gene flow increases.
- * b. population size decreases.
- c. mutation rate decreases.
- d. the number of heterozygous loci increases.

M 52. When a population goes through a bottleneck,
- * a  genetic drift is likely to occur.
- b. mutation rates increase.
- c. extinction rates decrease.
- d. natural selection decreases in intensity.

D 53. Although there are as many starlings in North America as there are in Europe, genetic variability in the North American population is reduced relative to that in Europe because
- a  there are more environments in Europe.
- * b. the North American population is derived from a small founder population.
- c. there is more gene flow in Europe.
- d. there is less mutation in North America.

## Classification Questions

Answer questions 54–57 in reference to the four evolutionary processes listed below:
- a  mutation
- b. gene flow
- c. genetic drift
- d. natural selection

M 54. Which is most likely to lead to the loss of genetic variation in a small population?

E 55. Which process produces new genetic variation within a species?

M 56. Which process can rapidly offset the effects of genetic isolation when two populations come into secondary contact?

D 57. The reduced contribution of one phenotype in comparison to another in the next generation is an example of what?

*Answers*:  54. c    55. a    56. b
57. d

## Selecting the Exception

M 58. Four of the five answers listed below are sources of variation in a population. Select the exception.
- a  mutation
- b. sexual reproduction
- c. crossing over
- d. independent assortment
- * e. law of dominance

D 59. Four of the five answers listed below are characteristics of an unchanging, nonevolving population. Select the exception.
- a  random mating
- b. no mutation
- * c. differential survival
- d. no migration or gene flow
- e. infinitely large population

E 60. Four of the five answers listed below are characteristics of mutations. Select the exception.
    * a. predictable
    b. lethal or beneficial
    c. random
    d. effects depend on environment
    e. heritable

M 61. Four of the five answers listed below are portions of the theory of natural selection. Select the exception.
    a. Variation is heritable.
    b. Heritable traits vary in adaptability.
    c. More organisms are produced than can survive.
    * d. The largest and strongest always contribute more genes to the next generation.
    e. Natural selection is the result of differential reproduction.

E 62. Four of the five answers listed below are types of selection exhibited by nature. Select the exception.
    * a. artificial
    b. disruptive
    c. stabilizing
    d. directional
    e. sexual

M 63. Four of the five answers listed below are examples of disruptive selection. Select the exception.
    * a. pesticide resistance
    b. sexual dimorphism
    c. sickle cell anemia
    d. balanced polymorphism
    e. differential mortality

D 64. Four of the five answers listed below can upset genetic equilibrium. Select the exception.
    * a. interbreeding
    b. genetic drift
    c. mutation
    d. natural selection
    e. gene flow

# CHAPTER 15
# SPECIATION

## Multiple-Choice Questions

M **1.** The genes of snails would probably not be dispersed as widely as ducks because
   a   snails are lower on the evolutionary scale.
   b.  ducks eat snails.
   c   snails are hermits in their protective shells.
   d.  ducks can swim.
   * e   snails cannot move as rapidly as ducks.

M **2.** Speciation is most precisely determined
   a   by careful observation of anatomical traits.
   b.  at the moment of conception.
   c   by mutation.
   * d.  when interbreeding is not longer possible.
   e   at the time of birth or in early postnatal development.

### ON THE ROAD TO SPECIATION

E **3.** The word "species" could be translated
   a   group.
   * b.  kind.
   c   portion.
   d   type.
   e   section.

E **4.** The word "phenotype" designates the
   a   portion of the genes that are not expressed.
   b.  type of genes an organism possesses.
   c   amount of change seen from one generation to the next.
   * d.  observable aspects of any individual organism.
   e   extent of mutation.

E **5.** In the biological species concept of Ernst Mayer, what aspect of a population is critical to determining a species?
   a   physical appearance
   b.  similar behavior patterns
   * c   interbreeding capabilities
   d.  polyploidy
   e   similar genotypes

M **6.** Members of the same species would be expected to
   a   look alike.
   b.  be reproductively isolated from one another.
   * c   share the same gene pool.
   d.  have the same phenotype.
   e   resist evolution.

M **7.** A species is composed of
   a   related organisms.
   b.  a group of reproductive females.
   * c   populations that have the potential to interbreed and produce fertile offspring.
   d.  organisms located in the same habitat.
   e   all males and females in the same geographical range with the same ecological requirements.

D **8.** Which of the following is a characteristic feature that would NOT distinguish two different species?
   a   They have different gene pools.
   b.  If hybrids are produced as a result of mating, the offspring are sterile.
   c   Their ranges do not overlap.
   * d   Their courtship patterns are different so that they do not attempt to interbreed.

M **9.** Two individuals are members of the same species if they
   a   possess the same number of chromosomes.
   b.  breed at the same time.
   c   are phenotypically indistinguishable.
   * d   can mate and produce fertile offspring.

E **10.** Complete reproductive isolation is evidence that what has occurred?
   a   extinction
   * b.  speciation
   c   polyploidy
   d   hybridization
   e   gene flow

E **11.** The term "reproductive isolation mechanism" refers to
   a   specific areas where males compete or display for females.
   b.  the process by which sexual selection evolves within a population.
   * c   a blockage of gene flow between populations.
   d   the inability of a species to continue reproduction.

M **12.** Which of the following is NOT an example of an isolating mechanism?
   a   species-specific courtship rituals
   * b.  Hardy-Weinberg equilibrium
   c   incompatible reproductive structures
   d   earthquakes and floods
   e   all of the above

M | **13.** | Incompatibilities between the developing embryo and the maternal organism that cause the embryo to abort spontaneously may prevent individuals of different populations from producing fertile offspring. Such differences may be which of the following?

* a isolating mechanisms
    b. allele frequencies
    c. mutations
    d. founder effects
    e. gene flow

M | **14.** | The primary reason for hybrid sterility is
    a the inability of the hybrid to attract a mate.
    b. the difficulty in finding a suitable habitat in which to survive.
    c. that the hybrids are usually weak and have difficulty surviving to reproductive maturity.
* d. the difficulty in the pairing of homologous chromosomes.
    e. the inability of the hybrid to develop an appropriate courtship pattern.

D | **15.** | Which of the following will NOT promote speciation?
    a gamete differences
* b. gene flow
    c. season of fertility
    d. natural selection
    e. genetic drift

D | **16.** | Speciation occurs
* a after populations become reproductively isolated and diverge.
    b. when mutations generate observable differences.
    c. when transitional forms develop between different populations.
    d. when natural selection pressures reach their maximum.
    e. when humans intervene and establish new breeds.

D | **17.** | Divergence may lead to
    a genetic drift.
* b. speciation.
    c. balanced polymorphism.
    d. gene flow.
    e. genetic equilibrium.

E | **18.** | Isolating mechanisms that take effect before or during fertilization are termed
    a hybridizing.
* b. prezygotic.
    c. genetically divergent.
    d. postzygotic.
    e. persistent.

E | **19.** | The 13-year and 17-year cicadas are isolated by
    a space.
    b. behavior.
    c. incompatibility of reproductive body parts.
* d. time.
    e. gamete incompatibility.

E | **20.** | "Seasonal", "daily", "monthly" all describe isolation that can be termed
    a behavioral.
* b. temporal.
    c. mechanical.
    d. gametic.
    e. ecological.

M | **21.** | The fact that the courtship song of the offspring is not recognized by either of the pareents is an example of
    a speciation.
    b. balanced polymorphism.
* c. behavioral isolation.
    d. sexual selection.
    e. ecological isolation.

M | **22.** | Suppose you witness the mating of a cat and a dog, obviously two different species, but realize that there will be no viable offspring due to isolating mechanisms that are
    a mechanical.
* b. gametic.
    c. behavioral.
    d. temporal.
    e. ecological.

M | **23.** | During a study of two closely related animals it did not appear as though they were reproductively isolated until the possibility that their different niches could result in __?__ isolation was noted.
* a ecological
    b. gametic
    c. temporal
    d. behavioral
    e. mechanical

E | **24.** | Hybrid inviability is an example of what kind of isolation?
    a gametic
    b. prezygotic
    c. divergent
    d. mechanical
* e. postzygotic

M | **25.** | Mules are an exceptional hybrids because
    a they are weak.
    b. their survival rate is low.
* c. they are sturdy and strong.
    d. they are sterile.
    e. their offspring are sterile.

## MODELS OF SPECIATION

E **26.** Allopatric speciation requires
    a   gradual evolutionary changes.
*   b.   geographic isolation.
    c.   polyploidy.
    d.   adaptive radiation.

E **27.** In allopatric speciation, daughter species form
    a   abruptly.
    b.   in proportion to the parental stock.
    c.   rapidly but are then reduced by environmental factors.
*   d.   gradually over rather long periods of time.
    e.   in the same homeland.

M **28.** The greatest contributor(s) to allopatric isolation is (are)
*   a   geographical barriers.
    b.   differences in reproductive timing.
    c.   gametic incompatibility.
    d.   hybrid inviability.
    e.   behavioral peculiarities.

M **29.** The effectiveness of geographical barriers in promoting speciation is related to the
    a   size of the barrier.
*   b.   ability of the organisms to overcome the barrier.
    c.   speed at which the barrier forms.
    d.   duration of the barrier before it is torn down.
    e.   size of the population it separates.

E **30.** Changes in the Mississippi River caused by earthquakes are thought to have caused speciation by
    a   divergence.
    b.   parapatry.
*   c.   allopatry.
    d.   gene flow.
    e.   sympatry.

M **31.** Speciation caused by the break of the continents would be by
    a   divergence.
    b.   parapatry.
    c.   gene flow.
*   d.   allopatry.
    e.   sympatry.

E **32.** The construction of the Panama Canal led to the development of _____ isolation in fish.
    a   morphological
    b.   behavioral
    c.   genetic
*   d.   geographical
    e.   chronological

M **33.** Sympatric speciation occurs
    a   gradually.
    b.   rapidly.
    c.   in the same homeland.
    d.   a and c
*   e.   b and c

E **34.** Which is NOT necessary for sympatric speciation?
    a   organisms living together in same location
    b.   "same homeland"
*   c.   geographical barriers
    d.   existing interbreeding population
    e.   reproductively mature individuals

M **35.** The cichlids of the African crater lakes are an example of
    a   divergence.
    b.   parapatry.
    c.   gene flow.
    d.   allopatry.
*   e.   sympatry.

E **36.** Sympatric speciation through polyploidy has been a frequent phenomenon in the evolution of
    a   insects.
    b.   mammals.
    c.   bacteria.
*   d.   plants.

M **37.** Which of the following can result in instant speciation?
    a   development of a physical barrier
*   b   polyploidy
    c.   increase in physical size
    d.   change in environmental conditions
    e.   the introduction of a new predator into an area

D **38.** Which of the following is accurate concerning polyploidy?
    a   It is more common in animals than plants.
    b.   It is the result of mitotic irregularities.
    c.   It cannot be passed on to offspring.
*   d.   It often arises due to nondisjunction.
    e.   It is limited to no more than three sets of chromosomes.

E **39.** Parapatric speciation would be expected to occur most often
    a   in the same homeland.
*   b.   near a common border between two populations.
    c.   within a group of interbreeding populations.
    d.   across obvious geographical barriers.
    e.   by divergence from a common interbreeding population.

E    **40.** The border across which genes can flow between two populations is called the
*    a   hybrid zone.
     b   parapatric zone.
     c   zone of speciation.
     d   demilitarized zone.
     e   zone of polyploidy.

## PATTERNS OF SPECIATION

E    **41.** A speciation pattern which exhibits branching of populations is termed
     a   allopatric.
     b   anagenesis.
     c   nondivergent.
     d   hybridizing.
*    e   cladogenesis.

M    **42.** Evolutionists use the term anagenesis
     a   to describe a divergence of one species into several.
     b   to indicate branching speciation patterns.
*    c   for speciation from a single, unbranched line of descent.
     d   for both a and b

E    **43.** Scientists have traditionally drawn evolutionary diagrams in the form of
     a   interlocking circles.
     b   pyramids.
     c   a set of parallel lines.
*    d   a tree.
     e   nested squares or boxes.

E    **44.** The gradual model of evolutionary change proposes that most morphological change occurs
     a   gradually but without development of new species.
     b   rapidly but without speciation.
*    c   gradually during speciation.
     d   rapidly leading to new species.

E    **45.** The punctuation model of evolutionary change proposes that most morphological change occurs
     a   gradually but without development of new species.
     b   rapidly but without speciation.
     c   gradually during speciation.
*    d   rapidly leading to new species.

M    **46.** According to the punctuation model of speciation, an evolutionary diagram descent would be characterized by
*    a   vertical lines with horizontal branchings.
     b   vertical lines with branchings at narrow angles.
     c   broad-angled lines with horizontal branches.
     d   broad-angled lines with branching at narrow angles.

D    **47.** The lack of transitional forms of organisms would be
     a   more expected in the gradual model than in the punctuation model.
*    b   more expected in the punctuation model than in the gradual model.
     c   equally expected in both models.
     d   expected in neither model.

D    **48.** Which of the following contributes to adaptive radiation within a lineage?
     a   extinction of competitors
     b   new phenotypic characteristics
     c   genetic uniformity
*    d   a and b
     e   a, b, and c

D    **49.** Which of the following adaptations would be most important for an animal that is to live on land?
     a   three germ layers
     b   a moist skin without scales
*    c   internal fertilization
     d   external gills with major sense organs concentrated in the head region

D    **50.** An advantage of the evolution of the penis is that it
     a   increased the efficiency of the reproductive act.
     b   reduced the threat of predation of the fertilized eggs.
     c   removed the requirement to return to the water to breed.
*    d   all of the above

E    **51.** The acquisition of a key evolutionary innovation by a species gives evidence for the concept of
     a   uniformitarianism.
     b   gradualism.
     c   convergence.
*    d   adaptive radiation.
     e   special creation.

E    **52.** Background extinction is a measure of
     a   the rate of species turnover at the end of geologic eras.
     b   the number of species that suffer extinction at the beginning of geologic eras.
*    c   the steady rate of species turnover within a lineage throughout most of their evolutionary history.
     d   the lowest rate of species turnover within a lineage observed within a geologic era.

M    **53.** Which of the following is NOT an explanation for mass extinction?
     a   collisions between the earth and other bodies in the solar system
     b   continental movements
*    c   adaptive radiation of new predator species in many lineages
     d   alterations in sea level

M  54. Mass extinctions are usually followed by
  a. periods of recovery.
  b. adaptive radiations.
  c. smaller extinctions.
  * d. both a and b
  e. a, b, and c

## Matching Questions

D  55. Matching. Choose the most appropriate letter for each.

  1. ___ cladogenesis
  2. ___ species
  3. ___ isolating mechanism
  4. ___ sympatric speciation
  5. ___ polyploidy
  6. ___ punctuation model
  7. ___ mass extinction
  8. ___ allopatric speciation
  9. ___ adaptive radiation

  A. geographic separation of two populations accompanied by gradual divergent evolution between them; reproductive isolation
  B. encompasses all of those actually or potentially interbreeding populations that are reproductively isolated from other such groups
  C. a population occupying the same distribution range undergoes reproductive isolation
  D. morphological changes compressed into brief periods followed by speciation
  E. branching pattern of speciation
  F. catastrophic, global loss of species
  G. a burst of microevolution within a lineage
  H. inheritance of three or more of each type of chromosome
  I. prevents gene flow between populations

*Answers:*

| 1. E | 2. B | 3. I |
|------|------|------|
| 4. C | 5. H | 6. D |
| 7. F | 8. A | 9. G |

## Classification Questions

Answer questions 56-60 in reference to the four microevolutionary processes listed below:
  a. mutation
  b. gene flow
  c. genetic drift
  d. natural selection

M  56. This process erodes species cohesion.

E  57. This is the original source of new alleles.

M  58. This preserves species cohesion.

M  59. This can preserve or erode species cohesion depending on environmental pressures.

M  60. This results from differential survival and reproduction.

*Answers*  56. c    57. a    58. b
           59. d    60. d

## Selecting the Exception

M  61. Four of the five answers listed below are used in describing a species. Select the exception.
  a. interbreeding
  b. sexual reproduction
  c. natural
  d. populations
  * e. appearance

D  62. Three of the four answers listed below promote evolution. Select the exception.
  a. genetic drift
  b. mutation
  * c. gene flow
  d. natural selection

E  63. Four of the five answers listed below are types of prezygotic isolating mechanisms. Select the exception.
  a. temporal
  * b. hybrid inviability
  c. mechanical
  d. ecological
  e. gametic

M  64. Four of the five answers listed below are portions of the theory of natural selection. Select the exception.
  a. Variation is heritable.
  b. Heritable traits vary in adaptability.
  c. More organisms are produced than can survive.
  * d. The largest and strongest always contribute more genes to the next generation.
  e. Natural selection is the result of differential reproduction.

M   **65.** Four of the five answers listed below are types of
speciation. Select the exception.
* a   postzygotic
b.   allopatric
d.   parapatric
e.   punctuation
c.   sympatric

E   **66.** Four of the five answers listed below can
function to isolate populations. Select the
exception.
a   geography
b.   behavior
c.   time
d.   gametes
* e   external fertilization

# CHAPTER 16
# THE MACROEVOLUTIONARY PUZZLE

## Multiple-Choice Questions

### FOSSILS—EVIDENCE OF ANCIENT LIFE

M **1.** The idea that fossils were the remnants of ancient forms of life was developed because
    a  fossils were found throughout the world.
    b.  unique fossils are found in specific layers of stratified rocks.
    c.  fossils resembled living organisms.
    d.  fossils could be used to study past geologic events.
    \* e.  all of the above

M **2.** Macroevolution refers to changes in all but which one of the following?
    a  phyla
    b.  classes
    \* c.  species
    d.  genera
    e.  divisions

E **3.** The fossil record is incomplete because
    a  very few organisms were preserved as fossils.
    b.  organisms tend to decay before becoming a fossil.
    c.  animals with hard parts are preserved more easily.
    d.  geological processes may destroy fossils.
    \* e.  all of the above

E **4.** Fossils would include
    a  skeletons.
    b.  shells.
    c.  seeds.
    d.  tracks.
    \* e.  all of the above

M **5.** Which of the following organisms would you expect to find preserved as a fossil?
    a  a jellyfish
    \* b.  a shelled arthropod such as a trilobite
    c.  an earthworm
    d.  a nematode
    e.  a protistan such as an amoeba.

M **6.** Which of the following habitats is most likely to be rich in fossils?
    a  eroding hillsides
    b.  deserts
    c.  polar ice caps
    \* d.  bed of former shallow sea
    e.  rocky plateau

E **7.** The geologic time scale is subdivided on the basis of
    a  the appearance of different radioactive isotopes in different strata.
    b.  levels of background extinction.
    \* c.  periods of mass extinction.
    d.  both a and b
    e.  a, b, and c

### EVIDENCE FROM COMPARATIVE EMBRYOLOGY

M **8.** The study of comparative morphology has revealed the conservative nature of the genes responsible for
    a  food procurement.
    b.  reproductive behavior.
    \* c.  embryonic development.
    d.  size.
    e.  intelligence.

D **9.** The fact that many vertebrate embryos are more similar to one another than their respective adult stages are to one another may ultimately be due to
    a  environment.
    b.  hormones.
    c.  microevolution.
    \* d.  genes.
    e.  speciation.

M **10.** The variation in the forms of adult vertebrates probably arose through mutations in _____ genes.
    a  dominant
    \* b.  regulatory
    c.  oncogenic
    d.  promoter
    e.  operator

### EVIDENCE OF MORPHOLOGICAL DIVERGENCE

M **11.** The convergence in external morphology of sharks, penguins, and porpoises is attributed to
    a  reduced genetic variability in these groups.
    \* b.  selection pressures that are common to these groups.
    c.  reproductive isolation of these groups.
    d.  identical genes in all three groups.

M **12.** Which of the following serve as examples of morphological convergence?
    \* a  sharks, penguins and porpoises
    b.  panthers and tigers
    c.  apes and monkeys
    d.  sharks, skates, and rays
    e.  mice, rats, and gerbils

M 13. Phylogenetic relationships, when determined solely by the study of comparative morphology, may be incorrect due to
   a. morphological divergence.
 * b. morphological convergence.
   c. adaptive radiation.
   d. extinction.
   e. homology

D 14. The wings of a bird and the wings of a butterfly are _____ and show morphological _____.
   a. homologous; convergence
 * b. analogous; convergence
   c. homologous; divergence
   d. analogous; divergence

D 15. Which of the following would be considered more primitive based upon the structure of their limbs?
   a. bats
 * b. early reptiles
   c. porpoises
   d. penguins
   e. birds

M 16. The bones in the forelimbs of a mammal
 * a. can often be traced to a common ancestor.
   b. offer no evidence to support the theory of evolution.
   c. perform the same function no matter which species they are in.
   d. may exhibit either analogy or homology but not both when compared to the forelimb of another animal.
   e. show convergence with some invertebrate structures.

D 17. Which of the following structures are analogous but not homologous to each other?
 * a. wing of a bird and the wing of a butterfly
   b. wing of a bird and the wing of a bat
   c. the dew claw of a dog and the little toe of a human
   d. the flipper of an aquatic animal and the arm of a human

M 18. Sharks, penguins, and porpoises together exhibit
   a. morphological divergence.
   b. parallel evolution.
 * c. morphological convergence.
   d. regression.
   e. coevolution.

## EVIDENCE FROM COMPARATIVE BIOCHEMISTRY

E 19. Which mutations are NOT subject to natural selection?
   a. lethal
   b. physiological
 * c. neutral
   d. morphological
   e. beneficial

M 20. Neutral mutations
 * a. are not subjected to selection.
   b. occur at different rates at different times during evolution.
   c. confer a disadvantage.
   d. do not occur; either a gene enhances survival or it does not.
   e. account for the difference between hemoglobin in normal blood and that found in sickle-cell anemia.

D 21. Neutral mutations
   a. code for different proteins.
 * b. allow the time of divergence between different forms to be pinpointed.
   c. can be used to accurately establish the relationship between widely differing animals.
   d. are responsible for the variation in the various hemoglobin molecules found in mammals.
   e. cannot give us any indication of the rates and degrees of evolutionary change.

M 22. The concept of a molecular clock is based on the idea that
 * a. neutral mutations occur at regular rates.
   b. genetic relatedness can be determined by timing antibody–antigen reactions.
   c. radioactive isotopes decay at a constant rate.
   d. speciation is a rapid event.
   e. cytochrome c is very similar in primates.

M 23. Which of the following is NOT a useful indicator of phylogenetic relatedness?
   a. base sequences in DNA
   b. amino acid sequences in a protein
 * c. similar ecological requirements
   d. similar embryonic development
   e. morphological divergence

D 24. Comparisons of protein similarity between species can reveal the degree of genetic kinship because
   a. the number of protein variations is limited.
 * b. specific amino acids are dictated by known nucleotide sequences.
   c. gel electrophoresis converts proteins to nucleotides.
   d. protein can be hybridized with DNA.
   e. DNA is made by directions stored in proteins.

D 25. Which of the following statements about proteins is true?
- a Neutral mutations may produce changes in the primary structure of proteins without affecting their function.
- b. It is possible to distinguish among proteins by subjecting them to electrophoresis.
- c. Humans, chimpanzees, and Rhesus monkeys have all been placed in the order Primates based upon the similarity in cytochrome c.
- d. The more closely related two forms are, the greater similarity there is in cytochrome c.
- \* e. all of the above

D 26. DNA-DNA hybridization studies
- a depend upon determining the exact sequence of nucleotides in a gene.
- b. can be done using a simple tissue homogenizer and computer-assisted analysis.
- c. involve generating new nucleotide sequences by using ultracentrifugation.
- \* d. measure the amount of heat necessary to separate two single strands of DNA that have been allowed to fuse together.
- e. give little clue as to how genes mutate.

M 27. The most conclusive evidence used in establishing the relationship of closely related species is
- a fossil remains.
- b. taxonomy.
- \* c. DNA-DNA hybridization.
- d. homologous structures.
- e. analogous structures.

## ORGANIZING THE EVIDENCE—CLASSIFICATION SCHEMES

E 28. Which of the following includes all the others?
- a family
- \* b. phylum
- c. species
- d. class
- e. order

E 29. Which includes all related genera?
- \* a. family
- b. phylum
- c. species
- d. class
- e. order

E 30. The higher taxa are groupings of
- a species.
- b. genera.
- c. families.
- d. phyla.
- \* e. all of the above

E 31. The organizing units of classification schemes are
- a binominal systems.
- \* b. higher taxa.
- c. taxonomies.
- d. systematics.
- e. links of the Chain of Being.

E 32. Linnaeus may have used all but which of the following to assign names and categories to organisms?
- a anatomy
- b. behavior
- \* c. DNA-DNA hybridization
- d. physiology
- e. ecology

M 33. Which of the following groups represents the most closely related organisms?
- a kingdoms
- \* b. species
- c. orders
- d. genera
- e. taxa

M 34. Organisms "X" and "Y" are suspected to be the same species. Which of the following will provide the ultimate proof?
- \* a interbreeding
- b. anatomy
- c. physiology
- d. ecology
- e. behavior

E 35. Scientific names of organisms are written in
- a French.
- b. English.
- \* c. Latin.
- d. German.
- e. Swedish.

E 36. Which of the following is written correctly?
- a *Felis* domestica
- b. Felis Domestica
- c. *felis domestica*
- \* d. *Felis domestica*
- e. *felis Domestica*

M 37. Which of the following is NOT correct?
- \* a The specific name can be used alone.
- b. The generic name can be used alone.
- c. The specific name must be preceded by a generic name.
- d. A family includes related genera.
- e. The kingdom is the most inclusive category.

E 38. "House fly" is the _____ applied to a small, pestiferous insect that is often an uninvited guest at dinner.
- a scientific name
- b. genus and species
- c. universal name
- \* d. English common name
- e. Latin name

M **39.** Which of the following is the least inclusive category?
    a. family
    b. order
\*   c. species
    d. kingdom
    e. genus

M **40.** The only taxonomic category in which microevolution can occur is the
    a. genus.
\*   b. species.
    c. kingdom.
    d. family.
    e. class.

M **41.** Phylogeny refers to what aspects of individuals?
    a. morphological traits
\*   b. evolutionary relationships
    c. physiological characteristics
    d. behavioral features
    e. all of the above

E **42.** The most widely accepted classification system in use today was proposed by
    a. Charles Darwin.
    b. James Hutton.
    c. Jean-Baptiste Lamarck.
\*   d. Robert Whittaker.
    e. Alfred Russel Wallace.

D **43.** Fungi were removed from the Kingdom Plantae in Whittaker's system because
    a. they grow underground.
    b. of unicellularity.
    c. they are prokaryotes.
\*   d. they are heterotrophs.
    e. they are multicellular.

M **44.** All prokaryotes belong to the kingdom
\*   a. Monera.
    b. Protista.
    c. Fungi.
    d. a and b
    e. b and c

D **45.** The only kingdom NOT characterized by heterotrophy is
    a. Monera.
    b. Protista.
    c. Animalia.
    d. Fungi.
\*   e. Plantae.

M **46.** Which kingdom includes single-celled organisms with a true nucleus?
    a. Monera.
\*   b. Protista.
    c. Animalia.
    d. Fungi.
    e. Plantae.

M **47.** Which kingdom is exclusively heterotrophic including many predators and parasites?
    a. Monera.
    b. Protista.
\*   c. Animalia.
    d. Fungi.
    e. Plantae.

## Matching Questions

D **48.** Matching. Choose the most appropriate letter for each blank.

1. ___ analogous
2. ___ binomial system
3. ___ coprolites
4. ___ DNA-DNA hybridization
5. ___ fossil
6. ___ Fungi
7. ___ molecular clock
8. ___ Monera
9. ___ morphological divergence
10. ___ phylogeny
11. ___ Plantae
12. ___ stratification

A. schemes that reflect evolutionary relationships among species
B. fossilized feces
C. body structures similar in function but of distant lineage
D. multicelled eukaryotes; nearly all photoautotrophs
E. recognizable evidence of the past
F. bacteria; prokaryotic
G. heterotrophs with extracellular digestion and absorption
H. sediment layering
I. two-part Latin name
J. most exact method of determining evolutionary relationship
K. modification of body structures from a common ancestor
L. use of accumulated neutral mutations to determine past evolutionary events

*Answers:*

| 1. C | 2. I | 3. B |
|------|------|------|
| 4. J | 5. E | 6. G |
| 7. L | 8. F | 9. K |
| 10. A | 11. D | 12. H |

## Classification Questions

Answer questions 49–52 in reference to the five taxonomic categories listed below:

a. genus
b. species
c. order
d. family
e. phylum

E 49. This category is not included in any of the other listed categories.

E 50. This category is included in each of the other categories.

M 51. The term *Hominidae* is an example of this.

E 52. Humans belong to the taxon *Homo*. This category denotes the taxonomic category of *Homo*.

*Answers:*  49. e   50. b   51. d
52. a

## Selecting the Exception

D 53. Four of the five answers are habitats favoring fossil preservation. Select the exception.
* a. deserts
b. swamp
c. tar pits
d. seafloor
e. caves

D 54. Four of the five answers listed below have a common relationship. Select the exception.
a. Protista
b. Plantae
c. Animalia
* d. Monera
e. Fungi

E 55. Four of the five answers below are taxonomic categories. Select the exception.
a. species
b. class
* c. taxon
d. order
e. phylum

E 56. Four of the five answers below are related to investigations into evolutionary evidence from comparative biochemistry. Select the exception.
a. neutral mutations
* b. homologous structures
c. molecular clock
d. protein comparisons
e. DNA-DNA hybridizations

D 57. Four of the five answers below are members of the same group. Select the exception.
a. tulips
b. mosses
c. conifers
d. ferns
* e. protozoans

# CHAPTER 17
# THE ORIGIN AND EVOLUTION OF LIFE

## Multiple-Choice Questions

M    1. According to astronomers, the universe is
- a contracting.
- b. getting warmer.
- c. the same as it was on the day of creation.
- d. getting smaller.
- * e. expanding.

E    2. The "big bang" refers to
- * a an event marking the beginning of the universe.
- b. the appearance of life on earth.
- c. the impending end of the universe.
- d. both a and b

### CONDITIONS ON THE EARLY EARTH

E    3. The solar system is approximately how many years old?
- a 10–12 billion
- * b. 4.6–5 billion
- c. 750 million
- d. 400 million
- e. 200 million

E    4. Fossil evidence of the earliest living organisms now dates back
- a 570 million years.
- b. 1.4 billion years.
- * c. about 3.8 billion years.
- d. more than 5 billion years.
- e. to 4004 B.C.

M    5. Life on earth began how many years ago?
- a 6,000
- b. 350,000
- c. 35,000,000
- d. 350,000,000
- * e. 3,800,000,000

E    6. The primitive earth's atmosphere did NOT contain
- a water vapor.
- b. free nitrogen.
- c. free hydrogen.
- * d. free oxygen.
- e. inert gases.

E    7. It is doubtful that many of the organic compounds essential for life, such as amino acids and nucleotides, would be able to assemble spontaneously in the presence of
- a hydrogen.
- * b. free oxygen.
- c. carbon dioxide.
- d. nitrogen.
- e. argon.

M    8. The earth is able to maintain water in a liquid state on the surface by virtue of
- a insufficient life to use up the available water.
- b. the distance of the earth from the sun.
- c. the availability of oxygen in the atmosphere.
- d. the size of the earth.
- * e. both b and d

M    9. The early atmosphere of the earth
- * a originated when gases from beneath the slowly solidifying crust were vented by vulcanism.
- b. did not exist before 1 billion years ago.
- c. probably consisted of hydrogen, methane, nitrogen, ammonia, and hydrogen sulfide, but no water vapor.
- d. all of the above

E    10. Organic compounds break down spontaneously in the presence of _____; hence, life probably never would have emerged if the ancient atmosphere had been the same as the present one.
- a carbon dioxide
- b. hydrogen
- * c. oxygen
- d. nitrogen
- e. silica

E    11. Experiments like those first performed by Stanley Miller in 1953 demonstrated that
- a DNA forms readily and reproduces itself.
- * b. many of the lipids, carbohydrates, proteins, and nucleotides required for life can form under abiotic conditions.
- c. complete, functioning prokaryotic cells are formed after approximately three months.
- d. a lipid–protein film will eventually be formed by thermal convection.
- e. all of the above

E 12. Which of the following was NOT included in Miller's reaction chamber, which contained substances intended to duplicate the atmosphere of ancient earth?
* a. carbon dioxide
  b. methane
  c. ammonia
  d. water vapor
  e. both b and c

E 13. Who demonstrated the possibility of producing organic compounds from gases and water if the mixture is bombarded with a continuous spark discharge?
* a. Miller
  b. Starr
  c. Thompsen
  d. Pauling
  e. Platt

E 14. The Miller experiment designed to study the early synthesis of organic compounds included all of the following molecules EXCEPT
  a. methane.
  b. ammonia.
  c. water.
* d. oxygen.

E 15. In several experiments in which energy is supplied to a sealed chamber containing a mixture of gases simulating the primitive earth's atmosphere, what will be formed?
  a. amino acids
  b. sugars
  c. nucleotides
  d. adenine
* e. all of the above

M 16. The primitive template that was thought to be used for protein synthesis was
  a. stratified mica crystals.
* b. clay crystals.
  c. the bottoms of tidal pools.
  d. dried-out mud flats.
  e. pockets in lava beds.

M 17. Clay crystals were thought to be original sites for the formation of
  a. amino acids.
  b. sugars.
  c. polysaccharides.
* d. protein chains.
  e. lipid molecules.

## EMERGENCE OF THE FIRST LIVING CELLS

M 18. Protein synthesis on the primordial earth may have been catalyzed by _____ before the evolution of enzymes.
  a. DNA
  b. carbohydrates
  c. amino acids
* d. RNA
  e. lightning

M 19. The formation of polypeptide chains under abiotic conditions was important because they served as
  a. a supply of structural units.
  b. enzymes to catalyze reactions.
  c. subunits in the formation of DNA.
  d. subunits in the formation of RNA.
* e. both a and b

E 20. The first templates for protein synthesis were
  a. complex carbohydrates.
  b. mineral crystals.
* c. layers of clay.
  d. sheets of layered minerals such as mica.
  e. multiple oil liposomes or micelles.

M 21. The most likely molecules to serve as a replacement for clay as a template for protein synthesis are
  a. coenzymes.
* b. RNA.
  c. DNA.
  d. other proteins.
  e. complex carbohydrates.

M 22. What step occurred first in the evolution of life?
  a. formation of lipid spheres
  b. formation of protein-RNA systems
  c. formation of membrane-bound protocells
* d. spontaneous formation of lipids, proteins, carbohydrates, and nucleotides under abiotic conditions
  e. formation of ATP

M 23. Which step in the evolution of life is the most complex and occurred last?
  a. formation of lipid spheres
  b. formation of protein-RNA systems
* c. formation of membrane-bound protocells
  d. spontaneous formation of lipids, proteins, carbohydrates, and nucleotides under abiotic conditions
  e. formation of ATP

M 24. Sidney Fox found that if heated protein chains were allowed to cool in water, they would
  a. form nitrogen, which would escape as a gas.
  b. form proteinoids.
* c. form small, stable spheres or microspheres.
  d. clot and form a complex latticework frame for chemical reactions.
  e. break down into the original amino acids from which the protein chain was made.

D 25. Contemporary hypotheses concerned with the origin of life focus on what two characteristics of living systems?
  a. energy conversion and development of a nucleus
  b. self-replication and utilization of oxygen
* c. plasma membranes and self-replication
  d. growth and transcription

## LIFE ON A CHANGING GEOLOGIC STAGE

E   26. The large land mass that contained all the continents was called
    a Laurasia.
    * b. Pangea.
    c. Gondwana.
    d. Atlantis.
    e. all of the above

D   27. Plate tectonic theory is based on
    a. a thermal convection model, in which cool material in the earth's mantle rises and spreads laterally beneath the crustal plates.
    b. the idea that the earth's crust is fragmented into rigid crusts that are sinking slowly beneath crustal plates.
    c. the idea that coacervate formation causes continents to drift apart slowly on their crustal plates.
    * d. observations that the sea floor is slowly spreading away from oceanic ridges due to thermal convection in the mantle.
    e. all of the above

E   28. Which geological era is the most recent?
    * a. Cenozoic
    b. Mesozoic
    c. Proterozoic
    d. Archean
    e. Paleozoic

E   29. Which geological era is the most ancient?
    a. Cenozoic
    b. Mesozoic
    c. Proterozoic
    * d. Archean
    e. Paleozoic

E   30. Geological time is divided into major divisions known as
    * a. eras.
    b. epochs.
    c. periods.
    d. all of the above

E   31. The geologic time scale is subdivided on the basis of
    a. the appearance of different radioactive isotopes in different strata.
    b. levels of background extinction.
    * c. periods of mass extinction.
    d. a and b

## ORIGIN OF PROKARYOTIC AND EUKARYOTIC CELLS

E   32. The first organisms
    a. had to be autotrophic.
    b. were parasitic.
    * c. were heterotrophic.
    d. were aerobes.
    e. all of the above

M   33. The first organisms
    a. absorbed their food supplies from the organic molecules that surrounded them.
    b. were eukaryotes.
    c. utilized fermentation for energy production.
    d. utilized ATP.
    * e. all of the above except b

M   34. The first organisms were most probably
    a. autotrophic.
    b. multicellular.
    c. protozoans.
    * d. prokaryotic.

M   35. The earliest organisms were probably unicellular
    a. autotrophs.
    b. aerobes.
    * c. heterotrophs.
    d. eukaryotes.

D   36. During the Archean era, divergence of the prokaryotes led to all but which of the following?
    a. archaebacteria
    b. eukaryotes
    * c. multicelled organisms
    d. eubacteria
    e. additional prokaryotes

M   37. The early atmosphere
    a. was essentially the same as occurs now.
    * b. was changed drastically by the liberation of oxygen following the evolution of photosynthesis.
    c. was characterized by high concentrations of oxygen and ozone.
    d. was characterized by high concentrations of inert gases before the evolution of living organisms.

M   38. The presence of free oxygen in the atmosphere
    a. was a result of the accumulation of the byproducts of photosynthesis.
    b. prevented the further spontaneous generation of life.
    c. provided the opportunity to extract more energy through aerobic respiration.
    d. did not occur immediately after the earth was formed.
    * e. all of the above

M   39. When free oxygen ($O_2$) became available in the atmosphere,
    a. some organisms changed their metabolism.
    b. oxygen was used as a dumping place for hydrogen ions and electrons.
    c. some cells and forms of life became extinct.
    d. aerobic respiration emerged.
    * e. all of the above

## FOCUS ON SCIENCE: WHERE DID ORGANELLES COME FROM?

D **40.** Mitochondrial DNA
- a  is replicated independently from nuclear DNA.
- b.  transcribes some RNA and protein used by the mitochondrion.
- c.  has some codons that have a different meaning from those of nuclear DNA.
- d.  may have been the genetic instructions for an organism that lived symbiotically within a predatory form.
- * e.  all of the above

D **41.** Chloroplasts
- * a  resemble photosynthetic bacteria.
- b.  utilize the same pigments regardless of what organism they inhabit.
- c.  apparently evolved mitochondria.
- d.  utilize DNA derived from the nucleus.
- e.  all of the above

D **42.** Which of the following is the strongest evidence for the hypothesis that present-day eukaryotic aerobes are the descendants of the successful symbiotic association of anaerobes and mitochondria?
- a  Mitochondria can produce ATP.
- b.  A mitochondrion can survive indefinitely when removed from a eukaryotic cell.
- * c.  A mitochondrion has its own set of DNA molecules.
- d.  Fossilized mitochondria are older than the oldest fossilized eukaryotes.

D **43.** Mitochondrial DNA
- * a  contains a few codons that specify amino acids other than those specified by codons of nuclear DNA.
- b.  uses the same assortment of codons as does the DNA in the nucleus.
- c.  can never replicate itself because DNA polymerases are not present in mitochondria.
- d.  can never be transcribed or translated because RNA polymerases are not in mitochondria.
- e.  can never replicate itself because there are no promoter sequences to initiate transcription.

D **44.** The mitochondrion
- a  has its own DNA.
- b.  transcribes its own DNA.
- c.  has DNA that functions independently of nuclear DNA.
- d.  has DNA that is somewhat different from nuclear DNA.
- * e.  all of the above

M **45.** Lynn Margulis and other biologists believe that
- a  the mitochondrial DNA code was a parallel but more ancient code than nuclear DNA.
- b.  mitochondria were at one time separate, free-living organisms similar to bacteria, rather than organelles.
- c.  mitochondria were obligate symbionts, with both the mitochondrion and the cell it inhabited benefiting from the relationship.
- * d.  all of the above
- e.  none of the above

## LIFE IN THE PALEOZOIC ERA

E **46.** Which Paleozoic geological period is the most recent?
- a  Carboniferous
- * b.  Permian
- c.  Cambrian
- d.  Devonian
- e.  Ordovician

E **47.** Which Paleozoic geological period is the most ancient?
- a  Carboniferous
- b.  Permian
- * c.  Cambrian
- d.  Devonian
- e.  Ordovician

M **48.** What mud-crawling, mud-burrowing crustaceans eventually had 600 genera living during the Cambrian Period?
- a  jawless fishes
- b.  cephalopods
- c.  brachiopods
- * d.  trilobites
- e.  isopods

D **49.** Which characterizes the earth during the Cambrian period?
- * a  trilobites abundant, extensive shallow seas at tropical latitudes
- b.  active predators, land masses at the poles
- c.  adaptive radiation of fish, land masses at the poles
- d.  first eukaryotes, Pangea land mass

M **50.** What was the most abundant and conspicuous animal during the Cambrian?
- a  primates
- * b.  trilobites
- c.  fish
- d.  cephalopods
- e.  sea scorpions

M **51.** Insects became abundant during which period?
- * a  Carboniferous
- b.  Devonian
- c.  Silurian
- d.  Ordovician
- e.  Cambrian

E  52. Fossil fuels were formed in which period?
* a  Carboniferous
   b. Devonian
   c. Silurian
   d. Ordovician
   e. Cambrian

D  53. The great burst of diversification in metazoan families, especially those with marine representatives, occurred during which geological period?
   a  Silurian
   b. Devonian
* c. Ordovician
   d. Carboniferous

M  54. Much of the fossil fuel used by humans today represents the organic remains of organisms that lived during which geological era?
* a  Carboniferous
   b. Devonian
   c. Silurian
   d. Permian

M  55. All earth's land mass was located in a single continent, Pangea, during which period?
   a  Cretaceous
   b. Permian
   c. Triassic
   d. Jurassic
* e. both b and c

M  56. The largest extinction the world has ever known occurred at the end of which period?
   a  Cretaceous
* b. Permian
   c. Triassic
   d. Jurassic
   e. Tertiary

## LIFE IN THE MESOZOIC ERA

D  57. Which of the following events did not take place during the Mesozoic?
   a  an asteroid impact and the extinction of the dinosaurs
   b. origination of mammals and gymnosperms as the dominant plants
   c. breakup of Pangea and evolution of angiosperms
* d. first land vertebrates, the amphibians, arise
   e. the Age of the Dinosaurs

D  58. Which of the following plants are the most complex and evolved last?
   a  conifers
   b. cycads
* c. angiosperms
   d. ginkgos
   e. gymnosperms

E  59. During which geologic era did Pangea break up?
   a  Archean
   b. Paleozoic
   c. Cenozoic
   d. Proterozoic
* e. Mesozoic

M  60. The greatest mass extinction in the history of life on earth occurred between which two geological periods?
   a  Devonian and Carboniferous
   b. Silurian and Devonian
* c. Triassic and Permian
   d. Cretaceous and Tertiary

## LIFE IN THE CENOZOIC ERA

E  61. Which epoch is the most recent?
   a  Eocene
* b. Pleistocene
   c. Paleocene
   d. Miocene
   e. Pliocene

M  62. The disappearance of dinosaurs is correlated with the transition between which two periods?
   a  Devonian, Carboniferous
   b. Silurian, Devonian
   c. Carboniferous, Permian
* d. Cretaceous, Tertiary

E  63. The extensive adaptive radiation of the mammals occurred during which geological era?
   a  Paleozoic
   b. Cretaceous
* c. Cenozoic
   d. Mesozoic

M  64. Compared to later epochs of the Cenozoic, climates in the Paleocene tended to be
   a  colder .
   b. drier.
* c. warmer.
   d.  both a and b
   e. both b and c

## Matching Questions

D     **65.** Matching. Choose the most appropriate letter for each.

1. ___ geologic time scale
2. ___ Archean
3. ___ Cenozoic
4. ___ plate tectonic theory
5. ___ Mesozoic
6. ___ Paleozoic
7. ___ Proterozoic

A. Mammals, birds, and flowering plants evolved mostly during this era.

B. an era that harbored the oldest definite fossils known

C. movement of slabs of earth's crust

D. an era that ended with the great Permian extinction about 240 million years ago

E. an era during which free oxygen became abundant in Earth's atmosphere, and the first forms of life evolved into more complex, multicellular types 2.5 billion years ago until 570 million years ago

F. an era that ended with the massive Cretaceous extinction that wiped out the dinosaurs

G. time spans of the different eras

*Answers:*

| 1. | G | 2. | B | 3. | A |
|---|---|---|---|---|---|
| 4. | C | 5. | F | 6. | D |
| 7. | E | | | | |

## Classification Questions

Answer questions 66- 70 in reference to the five geologic periods listed below:

a. Cambrian
b. Ordovician
c. Silurian
d. Devonian
e. Carboniferous

M     **66.** Vertebrates, represented by the jawless fishes, first arose during this period.

E     **67.** Most of the invertebrate phyla are present in the fossil record as early as this period.

D     **68.** The cephalopods underwent a major radiation during this period.

D     **69.** The ancestors of modern conifers first arose during this period.

D     **70.** The most primitive fossil reptiles are associated with this geologic period.

*Answers*

| 66. | b | 67. | a | 68. | b |
|---|---|---|---|---|---|
| 69. | d | 70. | e | | |

Answer questions 71- 80 in reference to the five geologic periods listed below:

a. Permian
b. Triassic
c. Jurassic
d. Cretaceous
e. Tertiary

D     **71.** Birds evolved from reptiles during this period.

M     **72.** Mammals evolved from reptiles during this period.

M     **73.** This period is referred to as the Age of Reptiles.

M     **74.** The mass extinction of the dinosaurs occurred at the end of this period.

M     **75.** The evolution of hominids occurred during this period.

D     **76.** Flowering plants began their radiation during this period.

M     **77.** During this period, all land masses began to combine into a single continent called Pangea.

M     **78.** This geologic period falls at the beginning of the Mesozoic Era.

D     **79.** Major extinctions of marine organisms occurred at the beginning of this period.

D     **80.** The first flying vertebrate evolved during this period.

*Answers*

| 71. | c | 72. | b | 73. | d |
|---|---|---|---|---|---|
| 74. | d | 75. | e | 76. | d |
| 77. | a | 78. | b | 79. | a |
| 80. | b | | | | |

## Selecting the Exception

D     **81.** Four of the five answers listed below are related by a common era. Select the exception.
a. Permian
b. Ordovician
c. Carboniferous
\*   d. Cretaceous
e. Cambrian

D     **82.** Four of the five answers listed below are related by a similar relationship. Select the exception.
a. Mesozoic
\*   b. Tertiary
c. Cenozoic
d. Proterozoic
e. Archean

D     **83.** Four of the five answers listed below are related by a common period. Select the exception.
\*   a. Pleistocene
b. Miocene
c. Oligocene
d. Pliocene
e. Paleocene

D     **84.** Four of the five answers listed below are periods of mass extinctions. Select the exception.

        a   Ordovician
*    b.   Silurian
        c.   Cretaceous
        d.   Permian
        e.   Triassic

M     **85.** Four of the five answers listed below are components of the mixture used in Miller's experiment. Select the exception.

        a   hydrogen
*    b.   oxygen
        c.   methane
        d.   ammonia
        e.   water

# CHAPTER 18
# BACTERIA, VIRUSES, AND PROTISTANS

## Multiple-Choice Questions

M **1.** Which of the following are of the smallest size?
* a viruses
b. bacteria
c. fungi
d. protistans
e. plants

M **2.** The reproduction of microorganisms is self-limiting because
a the accumulation of waste products can be toxic.
b. the supply of nutrients may run out.
c. other organisms may prey on them.
d. both a and b
* e. a, b, and c

E **3.** Which of the following could be called "pathogens"?
a viruses
b. bacteria
c. protozoans
d. b and c only, because they are alive
* e. a, b, and c

## CHARACTERISTICS OF BACTERIA

E **4.** Which of the following can bacteria use as an energy source?
a hydrogen sulfide
b. nitrites
c. sunlight
d. ammonia
* e. all of the above

E **5.** Bacteria can obtain their nutrition by
a photosynthesis.
b. chemosynthesis.
c. heterotrophy.
d. both a and b
* e. all of the above

E **6.** Spherical bacteria are called
a bacilli.
b. spirilla.
* c. cocci.
d. bacteriophages.
e. all of the above

M **7.** A rod shaped bacterium is called a
a spirillum.
* b. bacillus.
c. coccus.
d. both b and c

E **8.** Spherical bacteria are called
a bacilli.
b. spirilla.
* c. cocci.
d. bacteriophages.
e. all of the above

M **9.** Peptidoglycan is
a found in the chromosomes of most bacteria.
* b. composed of polysaccharides crosslinked with proteins.
c. composed of long polypeptides held together by disulfide bridges.
d. a unique combination of protein lipid and fat.
e. both a and c

D **10.** Gram-positive bacteria react to which of the following, whereas Gram-negative bacteria do NOT?
a presence of oxygen
* b. presence of a chemical stain
c. presence of light
d. absence of carbohydrates
e. presence of magnetic fields

D **11.** Which of the following distinguishes the bacterial flagellum from those of eukaryotes?
a quantity per cell
b. general appearance
c. function
* d. mechanism of movement
e. all of the above

E **12.** Which of the following allow the bacteria to join together to transfer genes?
a flagella
b. pores
c. connecting channels
* d. pili
e. stylets

M **13.** Which statement is NOT characteristic of bacteria?
* a Some may be completely naked.
b. Some may have hairlike structures called pili.
c. Some may have rigid cell walls.
d. Some may have flagella and move about.
e. Some may have a thin polysaccharide covering.

E  14. All of the following are characteristics of at least some of the Monera EXCEPT
   a  photosynthesis.
   b. heterotrophy.
   c. chemosynthesis.
   *  d. multicellularity.

M  15. Which statement about bacteria is true?
   a  They are diploid organisms.
   b. They produce gametes.
   *  c. They possess circular DNA molecules.
   d. They are eukaryotic.

E  16. In bacteria, DNA is found
   a  in the nucleus alone.
   b. in organelles alone.
   c. in both the nucleus and organelles.
   *  d. as a single circular thread, and possibly as additional pieces.
   e. as particles scattered throughout the entire bacterial cell.

M  17. Bacteria
   a  have cell walls composed of cellulose.
   b. reproduce primarily by conjugation.
   *  c. have a single chromosome.
   d. are eukaryotic.
   e. that stain Gram-negative have thick peptidoglycan cell walls.

D  18. Some bacteria resemble viruses in that they
   a  perform photosynthesis.
   *  b. are obligate intracellular parasites.
   c. are aerobic.
   d. employ RNA as the genetic material.

## BACTERIAL REPRODUCTION

D  19. Which of the following statements is false?
   a  Pili enable bacteria to attach to another bacterium or to the surface membranes of their hosts.
   b. Some plasmids confer resistance to various antibiotics.
   c. Plasmids can act in a way that allows a bacterium to donate DNA during conjugation.
   d. In bacterial photosynthesis, oxygen is not a by-product.
   *  e. Plasmids permit bacteria to carry on autotrophic reactions such as chemosynthesis.

E  20. All but which one of the following bacterial structures are external to the cell?
   a  flagellum
   b. pilus
   *  c. plasmid
   d. capsule
   e. peptidoglycan

D  21. In what way does bacterial binary fission resemble eukaryotic mitosis?
   a  movement of chromosomes
   *  b. genetically identical daughter cells
   c. intracellular mechanisms
   d. b and c only
   e. a, b, and c

E  22. Small circular molecules of DNA in bacteria are called
   *  a  plasmids.
   b. desmids.
   c. pili.
   d. F particles.
   e. transferins.

D  23. Plasmids
   a  are self-reproducing circular molecules of DNA.
   b. are sites for inserting genes for amplification.
   c. may be transferred between different species of bacteria.
   d. may confer the ability to donate genetic material when bacteria conjugate.
   *  e. all of the above

M  24. The process by which one bacterial cell transfers DNA to another is
   a  fission.
   b. gametic fusion.
   *  c. conjugation.
   d. lysis.
   e. none of the above

M  25. During conjugation between two *E. coli* cells, which of the following would most likely occur?
   a  transfer of an antibiotic
   b. transfer of a plasmid
   c. transfer of viral genes
   d. lysogeny
   *  e. b and c above but not a and d

## BACTERIAL CLASSIFICATION

E  26. One of the newest techniques used to identify bacteria is to determine their
   a  diseases.
   b. reproductive types.
   c. metabolic processes.
   *  d. nucleotide sequences.
   e. metabolic by-products.

M  27. Traditionally, bacteria have been grouped on the basis of all but which one of the following?
   a  mode of nutrition
   *  b. evolutionary relationships
   c. response to staining techniques
   d. energy source
   e. pathogenicity or nonpathogenicity

## MAJOR GROUPS OF BACTERIA

E 28. Which is a swamp gas?
- a carbon monoxide
- b carbon dioxide
- c ammonia sulfide
- * d methane
- e hydrogen sulfide

E 29. The type of bacterium most likely to be found in a swamp is
- a thermophilic.
- b halophilic.
- c cyanobacteria.
- * d methanogens.
- e *E. coli.*

M 30. Which type of bacterium is restricted to the waste piles of coal mines?
- * a extreme thermophiles
- b halophiles
- c cyanobacteria
- d methanogens
- e *E. coli*

D 31. Which of the following makes archaebacteria different from other monerans?
- * a absence of peptidoglycan
- b two chromosomes
- c existence of organelles
- d aerobic

M 32. The methane-producing bacteria (methanogens) belong to the
- * a archaebacteria.
- b prokaryotes.
- c eukaryotes.
- d urkaryotes.
- e eubacteria.

M 33. Which terms accurately describe the archaebacteria?
- a extinct, aerobic
- b extinct, anaerobic
- c present, aerobic
- * d present, anaerobic

M 34. The archaebacteria can be described by all but which one of the following?
- a anaerobic
- b chemosynthetic
- * c pathogenic
- d halophilic
- e heterotrophic

D 35. Which of the following bacteria are the least related to the others?
- a archaebacteria
- b extreme halophiles
- * c chemosynthetic eubacteria
- d extreme thermophiles
- e methanogens

M 36. Heterocysts are regions in filamentous cyanobacteria
- a that can break and allow for reproduction by fragmentation.
- b where endospores are formed.
- c where the filament is attached to its substrates.
- * d where nitrogen fixation occurs.
- e where photosynthesis occurs.

D 37. The following human disorders can be caused by bacteria EXCEPT
- a diarrhea.
- b Lyme disease.
- * c malaria.
- d botulism.

D 38. Endospores are produced by
- a Chrysophytes.
- * b bacteria.
- c protozoans.
- d viruses.

M 39. Which statement is true of all autotrophic bacteria?
- a They produce molecular oxygen.
- b They synthesize sugar.
- c They are anaerobic.
- * d They synthesize ATP.

M 40. When nutrients are scarce, some bacteria
- a engage in conjugation.
- b switch to photosynthesis.
- * c form endospores.
- d become pathogenic.
- e die.

M 41. Endospores
- a are resistant bodies.
- b enable some bacteria to survive for long periods of time.
- c may contain concentrated poisons.
- * d all of the above

E 42. The strongest poison known to humans is produced by
- * a *Clostridium botulinum.*
- b *Clostridium tetani.*
- c fer-de-lance snakes.
- d certain nettles in Java.
- e curare.

M 43. The bacterium *E. coli*
- a is a normal inhabitant of the human intestinal tract.
- b produces conditions that prevent invasion by other bacteria.
- c enhances digestion, particularly the digestion of fats.
- d produces vitamin K.
- * e all of the above

D  44. Which of the following statements concerning the bacterium *E. coli* is NOT true?
   a  It synthesizes vitamins that are essential to its mammalian host.
   b.  It can act as a pathogen.
   c.  It can prevent colonization of the gut by pathogens.
   *  d.  It is capable of photosynthesis.

M  45. *E. coli*
   a  is rarely found in the intestinal tract of people who live in industrially developed countries.
   *  b.  may cause high infant mortality by producing severe diarrhea.
   c.  is photosynthetic and autotrophic.
   d.  causes fecal material to move through the colon at a slow rate and frequently causes constipation.
   e.  all of the above

M  46. The bacterium *E. coli*
   a  is a normal inhabitant of human intestinal tracts.
   b.  has some strains that produce toxins and cause disease.
   c.  may be the leading cause of infant mortality in developing countries.
   d.  produces vitamin K and compounds used in fat digestion.
   *  e.  all of the above

M  47. *Borrelia burgdorferi* is the cause of
   a  tetanus.
   b.  syphilus.
   *  c.  Lyme disease.
   d.  legionnaires disease.
   e.  severe diarrhea.

M  48. Bacteria are able to make responses to
   a  chemicals.
   b.  light.
   c.  gravity.
   d.  oxygen concentration.
   *  e.  all of the above

M  49. In many aspects, bacteria are more "advanced" in their _____ than in their _____.
   a  reproduction; structure
   b.  metabolism; genetic composition
   c.  chemical composition; classification
   *  d.  behavior; structure

**THE VIRUSES**

E  50. Which statement is NOT true?
   a  Viruses are not able to move by themselves.
   b.  Viruses are not able to reproduce by themselves.
   *  c.  Viruses are not structurally organized.
   d.  Some biologists consider that viruses are forms of life and other biologists consider them to be nonlife.
   e.  Viruses contain instructions to manufacture themselves.

M  51. Most scientists do not consider viruses to be "alive" because
   a  they have no genes.
   *  b.  their metabolic machinery is borrowed from the host cell.
   c.  they are unable to reproduce.
   d.  no definite structural features are seen under the microscope.
   e.  all of the above

M  52. Which disease is NOT caused by a virus?
   a  smallpox
   b.  polio
   c.  influenza
   *  d.  syphilis
   e.  herpes

D  53. Which virus is an RNA virus?
   a  adenovirus
   *  b.  retrovirus
   c.  parvovirus
   d.  Herpes virus
   e.  papovavirus

M  54. A virus is characterized by all of the following EXCEPT
   *  a  enzymes of respiration.
   b.  nucleic acid core.
   c.  noncellular organization.
   d.  protein coat.

E  55. Plant viruses are transmitted primarily by
   a  wind.
   b.  water.
   c.  bacteria.
   *  d.  animals.

D  56. Which of the following is correct regarding plant viruses?
   a  They are mostly DNA viruses.
   b.  Most of them cause little outward change in plant appearance.
   c.  The capsid is spiral-shaped.
   d.  All plant viruses cause disease.
   *  e.  RNA viruses cause the most plant diseases.

M 57. Which statement about viruses is true?
a They were the first forms of life to evolve.
b. They do not attack plants.
c They are able to reproduce without using other organisms.
d They are made of protein only.
* e They include some forms that are able to attack bacteria.

E 58. Viroids differ from viruses in that the former lack
a a nucleic acid core.
* b. a protein coat.
c the ability to reproduce.
d a and b

M 59. Flu pandemics are caused by the spread of
a pathogenic bacteria.
* b. RNA viruses.
c DNA viruses.
d parasitic protozoans.

D 60. Infective proteins are known as
a retroviruses.
b. vivoids.
c viruses.
* d prions.
e none of the above, because nucleic acids are needed for infections

## VIRAL MULTIPLICATION CYCLES

E 61. When a virus takes over the machinery of a cell, it forces the cell to manufacture
a more mitochondria for energy for the virus.
b. more liposomes to isolate themselves from water.
c more food particles.
* d more viral particles.
e more Golgi bodies so that the cell will secrete the excess viruses.

M 62. The lysogenic pathway is characterized by
* a passive replication of viral DNA.
b. extensive transcription of viral DNA.
c destruction of the bacterial host.
d a and b
e a, b, and c

M 63. Retroviruses are characterized by
a an RNA core.
b. temperate pathways of replication.
c the enzyme reverse transcriptase.
d being the causative agent for AIDS.
* e all of the above

M 64. Lengthy periods of latency are most often associated with viruses that infect
* a animal cells.
b. plant cells.
c bacteria.
d other viruses.
e viroids.

## PROTISTAN CLASSIFICATION

E 65. Which of the following does NOT belong to the protistans?
* a bacteria
b. protozoans
c chrysophytes
d dinoflagellates
e euglenids

D 66. All of the following are members of the same kingdom EXCEPT
a *Amoeba*.
* b. *Clostridium*.
c *Euglena*.
d *Paramecium*.

E 67. The simplest of the eukaryotes are the
* a protistans.
b. plants.
c fungi.
d animals.
e both a and c

E 68. Most protistans are
a autotrophic.
b. heterotrophic.
* c unicellular.
d multicellular.

## PREDATORY AND PARASITIC MOLDS

M 69. The group characterized by its use of rhizoids when feeding on plants in muddy habitats is
a water molds.
* b. chytrids.
c oomycetes.
d sac fungi.
e club fungi.

M 70. The failure of the potato crop and the subsequent Irish famine was due mainly to a fungus belonging to which group?
a chytrids
b. imperfect fungi
c club fungi
d ascomycetes
* e water molds

M 71. Slime molds are classified as
* a protistans.
b. fungi.
c protozoans.
d a and c only
e a, b, and c

M 72. The signal for aggregation and communal activity by cellular slime molds is
a a pheromone.
* b. cyclic AMP.
c glycoprotein slime.
d RNA.
e unidentified as yet.

D **73.** Cellular slime molds can be distinguished from plasmodial slime molds on the basis of
    a  reproductive structures.
    b.  spore formation.
  \*  c.  nuclei per cell.
    d.  slime trails.
    e.  food requirements.

## ANIMAL-LIKE PROTISTANS

E **74.** Protozoans are classified on the basis of their
    a  photosynthetic nature.
    b.  life cycle.
    c.  unique structures.
  \*  d.  type of motility.
    e.  feeding habitats.

E **75.** Protozoans are placed into four groups on the basis of
    a  cell membrane and cell wall components.
    b.  heterotrophic or autotrophic mode of nutrition.
  \*  c.  means of locomotion.
    d.  characteristics of the nucleus.

E **76.** Pseudopodia are characteristic of which of the following groups of protozoans?
    a  ciliated
    b.  flagellated
  \*  c.  amoeboid
    d.  sporozoan

D **77.** Which of the following specialized structures is NOT correctly paired with a function?
    a  gullet–ingestion
    b.  cilia–food gathering
  \*  c.  contractile vacuole–digestion
    d.  anal pore–waste elimination
    e.  ribosome–protein synthesis

M **78.** The sporozoan parasite *Plasmodium* infects cells of which of the following?
    a  blood
    b.  liver
    c.  brain
  \*  d.  a and b
    e.  a, b, and c

E **79.** Structurally, the most complex unicellular organisms are
    a  viruses.
    b.  bacteria.
    c.  dinoflagellates.
  \*  d.  ciliates.

D **80.** Which of the following are NOT able to carry on photosynthesis?
    a  cyanobacteria
    b.  euglenids
    c.  chrysophyta
  \*  d.  protozoans
    e.  dinoflagellates

E **81.** *Paramecium* is a representative of the
    a  sporozoans.
    b.  amoebas.
    c.  flagellates.
    d.  euglenoids.
  \*  e.  ciliates.

M **82.** Which of the following has a simple sort of sexual reproduction called conjugation?
  \*  a  ciliates
    b.  flagellates
    c.  sporozoans
    d.  amoebas
    e.  euglenoids

D **83.** Which of the following diseases is NOT caused by a flagellated protozoan?
  \*  a  malaria
    b.  sleeping sickness
    c.  Chagas disease
    d.  vaginal trichomonas
    e.  intestinal giardiasis

M **84.** The least mobile protistans include
    a  euglenoids.
    b.  ciliates.
  \*  c.  sporozoans.
    d.  dinoflagellates.
    e.  flagellates.

D **85.** Protozoans cause all of the following diseases EXCEPT
    a  dysentery.
    b.  African sleeping sickness.
    c.  malaria.
  \*  d.  elephantiasis.
    e.  trichomonal infections of the reproductive tract.

## THE (MOSTLY) PHOTOSYNTHETIC SINGLE-CELLED PROTISTANS

M **86.** Certain euglenids are unique among the Protista in that they
    a  possess flagella.
    b.  reproduce by longitudinal fission.
  \*  c.  are heterotrophic and autotrophic.
    d.  are multicellular.

M **87.** Which of the following is NOT true of *Euglena*?
  \*  a  It moves by pseudopodia.
    b.  It contains chloroplasts.
    c.  It can detect light sources by using an eyespot.
    d.  Its cell body is not surrounded by a cell wall.
    e.  none of the above; all statements are true

D 88. All but which of the following are protozoan parasites of humans?
a. *Trypanosoma*
b. *Trichomonas*
* c. *Euglena*
d. *Entamoeba*

E 89. A pellicle is
a. a defensive organ.
* b. the covering of a euglenoid.
c. an organelle of motion.
d. a storage organ.
e. a component of the nucleus.

M 90. Diatoms are characterized by all but which of the following?
a. overlapping shells
b. classification as chrysophytes
c. silica composition
* d. flagella
e. perforations in the shell

M 91. The gritty substance you may feel on your teeth after using toothpaste is actually
a. small deposits of sand.
* b. diatomaceous earth.
c. cellulose from dinoflagellates.
d. a synthetic abrasive.

D 92. The pigment that makes chrysophytes golden-brown is
a. phycobilin.
b. chlorophyll.
c. algin.
* d. fucoxanthin.
e. carrageenan.

M 93. "Red tides" and extensive fish kills are caused by population "blooms" of
a. *Euglena*.
* b. specific dinoflagellates.
c. diatoms.
d. *Plasmodium*.
e. fish.

M 94. "Red tide" neurotoxins are produced by members of which phylum?
a. Chrysophyta
* b. Pyrrophyta
c. Sarcomastigophora
d. Ciliophora

M 95. Dinoflagellates are characterized by all of the following EXCEPT:
a. they secrete neurotoxins that can kill fish.
b. they possess flagella that fit in grooves.
c. they kill shellfish such as clams, oysters, scallops, and mussels.
* d. they have two shells that fit together like petri plates.
e. they are photosynthetic.

## THE (MOSTLY) MULTICELLED PHOTOSYNTHETIC PROTISTANS

E 96. The red algae are classified as
* a. Rhodophyta.
b. Chlorophyta.
c. Phaeophyta.
d. Bryophyta.
e. Pterophyta.

M 97. Red algae
* a. are primarily marine organisms.
b. are thought to have developed from green algae.
c. contain xanthophylls as their main accessory pigments.
d. all of the above

D 98. Red algae can live in deeper water because of
* a. phycobilins.
b. holdfasts.
c. chlorophyll *a*.
d. stonelike cell walls.
e. their preference for freshwater habitats.

M 99. Agar is produced by
a. brown algae.
* b. red algae.
c. phycobilins.
d. a and c only
e. b and c only

M 100. Kelp, and *Sargassum* are examples of
a. Rhodophyta.
b. Chlorophyta.
* c. Phaeophyta.
d. Bryophyta.
e. Pterophyta.

M 101. Holdfasts, gas-filled floats, and a thick leathery surface are found in species of
a. red algae.
* b. brown algae.
c. bryophytes.
d. green algae.
e. blue-green algae.

M 102. Which of the following parts of a brown alga does not have a counterpart in land plants?
a. blade
b. stipe
* c. float
d. holdfast

M 103. A source for a thickening, emulsifying agent found in ice cream, salad dressing, beer, toothpaste, cough syrup, and floor polish is the
a. seed plants.
b. ferns.
* c. brown algae.
d. red algae.
e. green algae.

E   104. The largest algae would be included in which of the following groups?
* a   brown algae
b.   red algae
c.   green algae
d.   blue-green algae

E   105. Most freshwater algae belong to which phylum?
a   Rhodophyta
* b.   Chlorophyta
c.   Phaeophyta
d.   Bryophyta
e.   Pterophyta

M   106. The unicellular alga *Chlamydomonas*
a   lacks an asexual stage.
b.   lacks a sexual stage.
c.   lacks a haploid and a diploid phase.
* d.   possesses both a haploid and a diploid phase.

## Matching Questions

D   107. Matching. Choose the most appropriate letter for each.
1 _____   *Amoeba proteus*
2 _____   *Anabaena*
3 _____   *Clostridium botulinum*
4 _____   diatoms
5 _____   *Escherichia coli*
6 _____   foraminifera
7 _____   golden algae
8 _____   Herpes virus
9 _____   methanogens
10 _____   *Paramecium*
11 _____   *Plasmodium*
12 _____   thermophiles
13 _____   *Volvox*

A.   cyanobacteria
B.   produce swamp gas
C.   colonial flagellate
D.   moves by pseudopodia
E.   produce deadly toxin
F.   normal inhabitant of human intestine
G.   chrysophytes
H.   live in "glass" houses
I.   thrive in thermal vents
J.   causes malaria
K.   live in hardened shells that have thousands of tiny holes
L.   a single-celled ciliate
M.   cause cold sores and a type of venereal disease

*Answers*:   1. D   2. A   3. E
4. H   5. F   6. K
7. G   8. M   9. B
10. L   11. J   12. I
13. C

## Classification Questions

Answer questions 108- 112 in reference to the five groups of organisms listed below:
a   eubacteria
b.   archaebacteria
c.   euglenids
d.   dinoflagellates
e.   protozoans

D   108. Modern, blue-green algae belong to this group

M   109. This is the only group represented by modern bacteria.

D   110. Methanogenic bacteria, common in the shallow seas of the Carboniferous Period, belonged to this group.

M   111. Organisms responsible for the red tides along ocean coasts belong to this group.

M   112. Chagas Disease, or American Trypanosomiasis, which eventually killed Charles Darwin, is caused by a species in this group.

*Answers*:   108. a   109. a   110. a
111. d   112. e

Answer questions 113- 117 using the five groups listed below:
a   halophiles
b.   cyanobacteria
c.   thermophiles
d.   actinomycetes
e.   methanogens

D   113. These bacteria live in temperatures that are not ususally conducive to life.

M   114. These produce "swamp gas.".

D   115. These bacteria can live in water of very high salt concentration.

M   116. These can form heterocysts, valuable in nitrogen fixation.

M   117. These can serve as a source of antibiotics.

*Answers*   113. c   114. e   115. a
116. b   117. d

Answer questions 118-122 in reference to the four groups of protozoans listed below:

    a  Mastigophora
    b.  Sarcodina
    c.  Sporozoa
    d.  Ciliophora

E    **118.**  The common amoeba, *Amoeba proteus*, is a member of this group.

M    **119.**  The radiolarians, which produce glass shells, are members of this group.

M    **120.**  The malarial parasite *Plasmodium* is a member of this group.

M    **121.**  This group derives its motility from the presence of a flagellum.

M    **122.**  An organism commonly used in competition experiments is the *Paramecium*, which belongs to this group.

*Answers*:    118.  b    119.  b    120.  c
    121.  a    122.  d

Answer questions 123-127 using the five groups listed below:

    a  sporozoans
    b.  amoebas
    c.  euglenoids
    d.  dinoflagellates
    e.  trypanosomes

D    **123.**  This group of protozoans has no locomotor organelles.

M    **124.**  These possesses an eyespot for detecting light needed for photosynthesis.

D    **125.**  These move by means of pseudopodia.

M    **126.**  Neurotoxin from this group can kill humans.

M    **127.**  Chagas disease and African sleeping sickness are caused by members of this group.

*Answers*    123.  a    124.  c    125.  b
    126.  d    127.  e

## Selecting the Exception

E    **128.**  Three of the four answers listed below are descriptions of bacterial shape. Select the exception.
    a  coccus
    b.  bacillus
*    c.  pili
    d.  spirillum

M    **129.**  Four of the five answers listed below are members of the same kingdom. Select the exception.
*    a  archaebacteria
    b.  protozoa
    c.  chrysophyte
    d.  dinoflagellate
    e.  euglenoid

M    **130.**  Four of the five answers listed below are bacterial structures. Select the exception.
    a  endospore
    b.  pilus
    c.  capsule
*    d.  eyespot
    e.  heterocyst

M    **131.**  Four of the five answers listed below are found in viruses. Select the exception.
    a  coat
*    b.  prions
    c.  DNA
    d.  tail fibers
    e.  envelope

D    **132.**  Four of the five answers listed below are related by a similar category. Select the exception.
    a  rhinoviruses
*    b.  poxviruses
    c.  togaviruses
    d.  retrovirus
    e.  enteroviruses

D    **133.**  Four of the five answers listed below are related by a similar category. Select the exception.
    a  Herpes viruses
    b.  papovaviruses
    c.  parvoviruses
*    d.  paramyxoviruses
    e.  adenoviruses

D    **134.**  Four of the five answers listed below are protozoans. Select the exception.
    a  amoeboids
*    b.  dinoflagellates
    c.  ciliates
    d.  sporozoans
    e.  flagellates

D    **135.**  Four of the five answers listed below are cellular. Select the exception.
*    a  viroid
    b.  diatom
    c.  trypanosome
    d.  trichosome
    e.  dinoflagellate

M    **136.**  Four of the five answers listed below are protistan structures. Select the exception.
    a  cell membrane
*    b.  pili
    c.  mitochondrion
    d.  eyespot
    e.  food vacuole

D    137.  Four of the five answers listed below are related
           by a similar category. Select the exception.
           a    amoebas
       *   b.   euglenas
           c.   foraminiferans
           d.   radiolarians
           e.   heliozoans

D    138.  Four of the five answers listed below are related
           by a similar category. Select the exception.
           a    golden algae
           b.   red algae
           c.   green algae
       *   d.   blue-green algae
           e.   brown algae

D    139.  Four of the five answers listed below are
           amoeboid protozoans. Select the exception.
           a    amoebae
           b.   foraminiferans
           c.   heliozoans
           d.   radiolarians
       *   e.   diatoms

# CHAPTER 19
# PLANTS AND FUNGI

## Multiple-Choice Questions

### EVOLUTIONARY TRENDS AMONG PLANTS

E 1. Which are seed plants?
   - a cycads and ginkgos
   - b. conifers
   - c. angiosperms
   - * d. all of the above

E 2. The first group with flowers were
   - a algae.
   - b. fern allies.
   - c. ferns.
   - * d. angiosperms.
   - e. gymnosperms.

M 3. All are Bryophytes EXCEPT
   - a hornworts.
   - b. liverworts.
   - * c. lycopods.
   - d. mosses.

M 4. Which of the following produces no seeds?
   - a cycads
   - b. conifers
   - * c. horsetails
   - d. ginkgos
   - e. tomato

M 5. All but which of the following would be associated with vascular plants?
   - a root systems
   - * b. bryophytes
   - c. angiosperms
   - d. gymnosperms
   - e. shoot systems

E 6. Green plants need which of the following?
   - a sunlight energy
   - b. water
   - c. carbon dioxide
   - d. minerals
   - * e. all of the above

M 7. Which of the following is true of xylem?
   - a conducts water downward in the plant
   - b. transports food upward in the plant
   - * c. transports water and minerals
   - d. transfers materials from stem to leaf

M 8. The cuticle of a plant is primarily for
   - * a retention of water.
   - b. conduction of fluids.
   - c. absorption of carbon dioxide.
   - d. protection from strong sunlight.
   - e. all of the above

M 9. Stomata are responsible for
   - a water escape from the leaves.
   - b. carbon dioxide entry.
   - c. mineral absorption.
   - * d. a and b only
   - e. a, b, and c

M 10. In the life cycle of primitive plants, which of the following predominates?
   - * a haploid stage
   - b. diploid stage
   - c. large sporophyte body
   - d. both b and c
   - e. both a and c

M 11. Which of the following is NOT a major trend in terrestrial autotroph evolution?
   - a development of vascular tissue.
   - b. adaptation to environmental stress.
   - c. nonmotile gametes.
   - d. fertilization by biotic vectors.
   - * e. reduction of the sporophyte phase.

M 12. Gametophytes are
   - a haploid plants that produce spores.
   - b. diploid plants that produce spores.
   - * c. haploid plants that produce gametes.
   - d. diploid plants that produce gametes.
   - e. diploid or haploid plants that produce gametes.

M 13. In complex land plants the diploid stage is resistant to adverse environmental conditions, such as dwindling water supplies and cold weather. The diploid stage progresses through which sequence?
   - a gametophyte Æ male and female gametes
   - b. spores Æ sporophyte
   - * c. zygote Æ sporophyte
   - d. zygote Æ gametophyte

M 14. The increased complexity among the different divisions of land plants is paralleled by increased complexity of which of the following?
   - a male gamete
   - b. female gamete
   - c. gametophyte
   - * d. sporophyte
   - e. all of the above

M 15. A gametophyte is
   - a a gamete-producing plant.
   - b. haploid.
   - c. the plant produced by the fusion of gametes.
   - d. the dominant generation in the higher plants.
   - * e. both a and b

D    16.    All but which of the following describe trends in plant evolution?
      a    nonvascular to vascular
   *  b.    spores of two types to spores of one type
      c.    motile gametes
      d.    seedless to seeds
      e.    haploid to diploid dominance

D    17.    Which of the following is NOT a trend evident in plant evolution?
      a    increasing independence from water
      b.    development of vascular tissue
   *  c.    increasing dominance of the gametophyte generation
      d.    evolution from homospory (one type of spore) to heterospory (two types of spores)
      e.    development of the importance of the diploid phase of the life cycle

M    18.    The first haploid cell in the life cycle of a plant is the
      a    zygote.
      b.    gamete.
      c.    gametophyte plant.
   *  d.    spore.
      e.    spore mother cell.

D    19.    In the life cycle of vascular plants, meiosis occurs
      a    immediately before fertilization.
      b.    during the production of gametes.
      c.    as a way of reducing the number of chromosomes in a zygote.
   *  d.    in the process of spore formation.
      e.    in the gametangia.

D    20.    Which of the following is true concerning the male gametophyte?
      a    The male gametophyte develops from the pollen grain.
   *  b.    The pollen grain is the male gametophyte.
      c.    The pollen grain develops from the male gametophyte.
      d.    The male gametophyte is the pollen tube.

D    21.    Which of the following is true concerning seeds?
      a    Ferns produce seeds.
   *  b.    Seeds form from the female gametophyte.
      c.    Pollen grains mature into seeds.
      d.    Most seeds are heterosporous.
      e.    All of the above are true.

D    22.    The heterosporous condition led to evolution of
      a    gymnosperms and angiosperms.
      b.    pollen grains and seeds.
      c.    male and female plant parts.
      d.    b and c only
   *  e.    a, b, and c

**BRYOPHYTES**

E    23.    The mosses and liverworts are members of which division?
      a    Psilophyta
      b.    Lycophyta
      c.    Sphenophyta
   *  d.    Bryophyta
      e.    Pterophyta

D    24.    Bryophytes differ from all other land plants in that they
      a    possess swimming sperm.
   *  b.    have independent gametophytes and dependent sporophytes.
      c.    were the first forms to successfully invade land.
      d.    exhibit alternation of generations.
      e.    possess gametangia that produce sperm and eggs.

D    25.    Which statement about Bryophyta is NOT true?
   *  a    The sporophyte is haploid.
      b.    The sporangium produces spores.
      c.    The sporophyte is parasitic and attached to the gametophyte.
      d.    Meiosis precedes spore formation.
      e.    Bryophytes require water for sexual reproduction.

M    26.    Which of the following do not possess vascular tissue?
      a    angiosperms
   *  b.    bryophytes
      c.    conifers
      d.    ferns
      e.    ginkgoes

M    27.    All but which of the following are bryophytes?
      a    hornworts
      b.    liverworts
   *  c.    lycophytes
      d.    mosses

E    28.    Mosses are
      a    algae.
   *  b.    bryophytes.
      c.    vascular plants.
      d.    gymnosperms.
      e.    extinct.

M    29.    Which statement is false?
      a    Mosses do not have xylem and phloem.
      b.    Mosses do not have true leaves.
      c.    Mosses do not have true stems.
      d.    Mosses use rhizoids, not roots, for attachment and absorption.
   *  e.    Mosses are different from all other plants in that they have an independent sporophyte generation and a dependent gametophyte generation.

## EXISTING SEEDLESS VASCULAR PLANTS

M **30.** In horsetails, lycophytes, and ferns,
* 
    a spores give rise to gametophytes.
    b. the main plant body is a gametophyte.
    c. the sporophyte bears sperm- and egg-producing organs.
    d. all of the above

D **31.** Which of the following is NOT true of seedless vascular plants?
    a Sporophytes are independent of gametophytes.
*   b. Water is not needed for gamete transport.
    c. Sporophytes have vascular tissue.
    d. Seeds are not produced.
    e. Living members still exist.

M **32.** Rhizomes in the whisk ferns serve the same function as _____ in more advanced land plants.
    a leaves
    b. stems
*   c. roots
    d. seeds
    e. flowers

M **33.** Strobili are
    a gametangia.
*   b. cones.
    c. homospores.
    d. accessory stems.
    e. horizontal stems.

E **34.** The feature of horsetails that was useful to pioneers of the American West was
    a rhizomes.
*   b. silica in the stems.
    c. photosynthetic cells.
    d. cones at the tips.

D **35.** Which statement concerning fertilization in ferns is true?
    a It occurs within an archegonium.
    b. It requires water.
    c. The fertilization product is a seed.
*   d. a and b
    e. a, b, and c

M **36.** Ferns are more advanced than mosses because mosses lack which structure found in ferns?
    a spores
    b. cuticle
*   c. xylem
    d. sporophytes
    e. pollen

E **37.** What is the name given to the "leaves" of a fern?
    a rhizome
    b. rhizoid
*   c. frond
    d. sorus
    e. bronchus

M **38.** Which of the following statements is false?
    a The ferns differ from the other vascular plants because they lack seeds.
    b. The ferns differ from other vascular plants by having an independent sporophyte generation.
    c. The ferns are restricted to wet environments because of the requirements of the gametophytes.
*   d. Ferns have true roots, stems, and leaves.
    e. Ferns possess both xylem and phloem.

M **39.** A sorus is
    a a collection of rust-colored disease spots on a fern.
    b. the fern gametophyte.
    c. an egg-producing structure.
    d. where the sperm are produced.
*   e. a collection of sporangia.

## GYMNOSPERMS—PLANTS WITH NAKED SEEDS

E **40.** The seed develops from the
    a gametophyte.
    b. ovary.
*   c. ovule.
    d. pollen grain.
    e. zygote.

M **41.** Gymnosperms
*   a were the first plants not to have swimming sperm and were therefore freed from the need for water to reproduce.
    b. are divided into two groups, the monocots and dicots.
    c. were the first plants to develop vascular tissues.
    d. were the first plants to develop flowers to attract insects.

M **42.** The first organisms that did not require water for reproduction were the
    a ferns.
    b. lycophytes.
    c. cycads.
    d. flowering plants.
*   e. gymnosperms.

E **43.** Which of the following is NOT a conifer?
    a pine
    b. fir
    c. cedar
*   d. ginkgo
    e. cypress

E **44.** The conifers, such as pines and junipers, are examples of the
*   a gymnosperms.
    b. angiosperms.
    c. bryophytes.
    d. filicinae.
    e. none of the above

E    45. A pine tree is
     a   an angiosperm.
     b.  a haploid plant body.
  *  c.  a sporophyte.
     d.  a living fossil.
     e.  all of the above

E    46. What are major sources of pulp, lumber, and
         numerous industrial products?
     a   cycads
     b.  ginkgos
  *  c.  conifers
     d.  hardwoods
     e.  all of the above

M    47. What is the most appropriate term for a mature
         pollen grain?
     a   megaspore
     b.  microsporangium
  *  c.  microgametophyte
     d.  microgamete
     e.  all of the above

M    48. Microspores mature into
     a   ovules.
     b.  seeds.
  *  c.  pollen grains.
     d.  anthers.

## ANGIOSPERMS—FLOWERING, SEED-BEARING PLANTS

M    49. Angiosperms are more advanced than
         gymnosperms because gymnosperms lack which
         structure found in angiosperms?
     a   independent gametophytes
     b.  pollen grains
  *  c.  fruits
     d.  roots

M    50. The vast majority of plant species are
     a   algae.
     b.  bryophytes.
     c.  gymnosperms.
  *  d.  angiosperms.

E    51. The first group with flowers was the
     a   algae.
     b.  fern allies.
     c.  ferns.
  *  d.  angiosperms.
     e.  gymnosperms.

M    52. The flowering plants and gymnosperms differ
         from other plants by
     a   the possession of vascular tissue.
     b.  the presence of nonmotile gametes.
     c.  the presence of two types of spores.
     d.  dominance by the diploid generation.
  *  e.  both ⅓ and d
         b
         c

M    53. The rapid expansion of angiosperms late in the
         Mesozoic era appears to be related to their
         coevolution with
     a   dinosaurs.
     b.  gymnosperms.
  *  c.  insects.
     d.  mammals.
     e.  birds.

E    54. The group of plants that has the most species is
     a   mosses.
     b.  ferns.
     c.  gymnosperms.
  *  d.  dicots.
     e.  monocots.

M    55. Dependence on animal vectors for fertilization
         and dispersal is characteristic of many species of
     a   ferns.
  *  b.  angiosperms.
     c.  mosses.
     d.  conifers.

## CHARACTERISTICS OF FUNGI

E    56. The life cycles are known for how many major
         groups of fungi?
     a   one
     b.  two
  *  c.  three
     d.  four
     e.  none

M    57. The major groups of fungi are assigned names on
         the basis of
     a   feeding structures.
     b.  mode of nutrition.
     c.  ecological role.
  *  d.  reproductive structures.
     e.  when they appear in the fossil record.

M    58. In fungi, food materials are digested
     a   within food vacuoles.
  *  b.  outside the body.
     c.  intracellularly.
     d.  by the mitochondria.
     e.  by the host organism.

D    59. The value of fungi in the scheme of nature is
         described by which of the following statements?
     a   Fungi "fix" nitrogen from the air for use by
         plants.
     b.  Fungi trap sunlight energy in carbohydrates.
  *  c.  Fungi release elements from organic matter.
     d.  Fungi suppress population explosions by
         parasitizing overproductive animals.
     e.  Fungi can do any of the above, depending
         on the species and environment.

E    60.  Saprobes are
          a.  cytoplasmic organelles.
          b.  metabolic by-products.
      *   c.  organisms that feed on dead material.
          d.  parasites of plants.
          e.  an evolutionary dead end.

E    61.  Fungi
          a.  are producers.
      *   b.  are generally saprobes.
          c.  usually have life cycles in which the diploid
              phase dominates.
          d.  include *Fucus* and liverworts.
          e.  are typically marine forms.

M    62.  Which fungus relies on extracellular digestion
          and absorption of energy-rich substances found
          in living organisms?
          a.  slime molds
          b.  saprobic
      *   c.  parasitic
          d.  plasmodial
          e.  autotrophic

E    63.  All fungi are
          a.  unicellular.
          b.  multicellular.
          c.  autotrophic.
      *   d.  heterotrophic.

M    64.  All fungi
          a.  are saprobes.
      *   b.  perform extracellular digestion.
          c.  are parasites.
          d.  a and b
          e.  a, b, and c

M    65.  Which of the following could NOT be used to
          describe any fungus?
          a.  saprophytic
          b.  decomposer
          c.  parasitic
      *   d.  autotrophic
          e.  heterotrophic

D    66.  The chief advantage of the growth habit of the
          mycelium is
      *   a.  a large surface-to-volume ratio.
          b.  the ability to penetrate organic material.
          c.  that it allows for more rapid growth than
              any other approach.
          d.  that it enables the organism to spread
              through the soil.
          e.  that it allows growth in many directions at
              the same time.

M    67.  The walls of fungi contain
          a.  cellulose.
          b.  lignin.
      *   c.  chitin.
          d.  pectin.
          e.  protein.

E    68.  In most true fungi the individual cellular
          filaments of the body are called
          a.  mycelia.
      *   b.  hyphae.
          c.  mycorrhizae.
          d.  asci.
          e.  gills.

**CONSIDER THE CLUB FUNGI**

E    69.  Mushrooms are members of which of the
          following?
          a.  sac fungi
      *   b.  club fungi
          c.  imperfect fungi
          d.  water molds
          e.  zygospore-forming fungi

M    70.  The most reliable way to distinguish edible
          mushrooms from poisonous ones is to
          a.  look for basidiospores.
          b.  distinguish their colors.
          c.  reject any with a brownish tint.
      *   d.  rely on mycologists—fungus experts.

D    71.  Which of the following reproductive structures is
          incorrectly matched with the group in which it is
          found?
          a.  zygospore – zygomycetes
          b.  ascus – sac fungi
      *   c.  conidia – club fungi
          d.  basidiospores – mushrooms
          e.  spores – imperfect fungi

D    72.  Members of the club fungi include all but which
          of the following?
          a.  shelf fungi
          b.  mushrooms
      *   c.  black bread mold
          d.  puffballs
          e.  toadstools and poisonous mushrooms

M    73.  Which of the following is a diploid stage in the
          life cycle of fungi?
          a.  spores
          b.  vegetative growth of hyphae
      *   c.  zygote
          d.  gametes
          e.  cells produced by budding or fragmentation

**SPORES AND MORE SPORES**

M    74.  In what way do fungi reproduce?
          a.  asexually, through spores
          b.  budding of the parent body
          c.  sexually, through gametes
          d.  a and b
      *   e.  a, b, and c

D 75. The major difference between a mature zygospore and a spore produced in the zygomycete sporangium is that the mature zygospore
    a. produces gametes.
    b. is metabolically active.
  * c. is diploid.
    d. is produced asexually.

M 76. Which organism is a member of zygospore-forming fungi?
    a. water mold
    b. smut or rust
  * c. bread mold
    d. mushroom

D 77. The life cycle of a zygomycete differs markedly from that of animals because in this fungus,
    a. there is no sexual stage.
  * b. mitosis occurs in the haploid stage.
    c. there is no fusion of nuclei.
    d. meiosis never occurs.
    e. a diploid stage is unknown.

M 78. Rhizoids are
    a. vegetative hyphae.
  * b. rootlike absorbing filaments.
    c. fruiting bodies.
    d. sexually reproductive organs.
    e. fragments of a mycelium.

E 79. Yeasts are members of which of the following?
  * a. sac fungi
    b. club fungi
    c. imperfect fungi
    d. water molds
    e. zygospore-forming fungi

E 80. Baking bread and making wine are dependent on
    a. yeasts.
    b. sac fungi.
    c. zygospores.
  * d. a and b only
    e. a, b, and c

M 81. Edible fungi belong mainly to
    a. ascomycota.
    b. basidiomycota.
    c. imperfect fungi.
  * d. a and b only
    e. b and c only

D 82. Which of the following are NOT members of the sac fungi?
    a. yeast
  * b. smuts and rusts
    c. truffles and morels
    d. *Neurospora*
    e. *Penicillium*

D 83. Imperfect fungi are those that lack (or do not show)
    a. spores.
  * b. sexual reproduction.
    c. cross walls within hyphae.
    d. rhizoids.

## BENEFICIAL ASSOCIATIONS BETWEEN FUNGI AND PLANTS

M 84. Which factor is the most important algal contribution to the fungal component of a lichen?
    a. improved water conservation
    b. mechanical protection from being blown away
  * c. photosynthetically derived food
    d. less overlap between individual algal cells
    e. pigment for camouflage

M 85. A lichen is a composite organism made up of
    a. two different fungi.
  * b. a fungus and an alga.
    c. a fungus and a gymnosperm.
    d. a fungus and a bryophyte.

D 86. In a lichen, the more "independent" member is the
  * a. alga.
    b. fungus.
    c. mycorrhiza.
    d. imperfect fungus.
    e. water mold.

D 87. Which of the following is NOT one of the species found in lichens?
    a. sac fungi
    b. green algae
    c. club fungi
    d. cyanobacteria
  * e. imperfect fungi

E 88. Lichens are unable to grow
    a. on bare rocks.
    b. on tree trunks.
  * c. in polluted areas.
    d. in cold temperatures, such as in the tundra.
    e. none of the above

M 89. Despite their tolerance for harsh climates, lichens are particularly intolerant of
    a. drought.
    b. cold.
    c. sunlight.
  * d. airborne toxic materials.
    e. shade.

M 90. Mycorrhizae and plants exhibit
  * a. mutualism.
    b. parasitism.
    c. commensalism.
    d. competition.
    e. all of the above

E    91.  Mycorrhizae are
         a.  roots.
         b.  bacteria.
    *    c.  fungus roots.
         d.  isolated plants.
         e.  small animals found in agricultural soils.

M    92.  Mycorrhizae
         a.  increase plant growth.
         b.  are symbionts.
         c.  allow a plant to absorb more water.
         d.  increase the surface area for absorption of
             water and minerals.
    *    e.  all of the above

M    93.  Algae are to lichens as _____ are to
         mycorrhizae.
         a.  club fungi
    *    b.  tree roots
         c.  water molds
         d.  plant leaves
         e.  mosses

## Matching Question

D    94.  Matching. Choose the most appropriate answer
         for each.
         1.  ___  dicots
         2.  ___  conifers
         3.  ___  club mosses
         4.  ___  cycads
         5.  ___  ferns
         6.  ___  flowering plants
         7.  ___  ginkgos
         8.  ___  horsetails
         9.  ___  mosses, liverworts
         10. ___  angiosperm
         A.  have rhizoids, cuticle, and protected
             embryo sporophyte
         B.  "vessel seed"
         C.  non-seed-bearing, heart-shaped
             gametophytes; spore-bearing leaves with
             sori
         D.  *Lycopodium;* cone-bearing sporophyte;
             free-living gametophyte
         E.  only one species left
         F.  cypress and redwood; heterosporous;
             mostly evergreen
         G.  confined to tropics or warm, temperate
             zones; resemble squat cone-bearing palm
             trees
         H.  two seed leaves
         I.  *Equisetum;* homosporous; rhizomes
             present; aerial stems jointed
         J.  have coevolved with pollinating vectors

*Answers:*
| | | | | | |
|---|---|---|---|---|---|
| 1. | H | 2. | F | 3. | D |
| 4. | G | 5. | C | 6. | J |
| 7. | E | 8. | I | 9. | A |
| 10. | B | | | | |

## Classification Questions

Answer questions 95- 99 in reference to the five divisions of
vascular plants listed below:
         a.  Lycophyta
         b.  Sphenophyta
         c.  Pterophyta
         d.  Coniferophyta
         e.  Dicots and Monocots

E    95   The tree ferns that are common in today's
         tropical forests are members of this division.

D    96.  The giant ground pines of the Carboniferous
         Period often reached heights of 50–100 feet.
         They were members of this division.

M    97.  Flowering plants are members of this grouping.

D    98.  This is heterosporous with well-developed seed
         and pollen-bearing cones.

M    99.  This seed is enclosed in an ovary, which, when
         ripened, may form a fruit.

*Answers*
| | | | | | |
|---|---|---|---|---|---|
| 95. | c | 96. | a | 97. | e |
| 98. | d | 99. | e | | |

Answer questions 100- 104 in reference to the five groups of
fungi listed below:
         a.  Zygomycetes
         b.  Sac fungi
         c.  Club fungi
         d.  Imperfect fungi

M    100. The common mushroom bought in the average
         supermarket is most likely a member of this
         group.

D    101. *Penicillium,* the source of antibiotics, is a
         FORMER member of this group

M    102. The yeast used in the fermentation of grape juice
         to produce the wines of the world is a member of
         this group.

D    103. The common black bread mold is a member of
         this group.

M    104. The delicious, edible morel is a member of this
         group.

*Answers*
| | | | | | |
|---|---|---|---|---|---|
| 100. | c | 101. | d | 102. | b |
| 103. | a | 104. | c | | |

## Selecting the Exception

M 105. Four of the five answers listed below are related by the quantity of chromosomes present. Select the exception.
  a. spores
  * b. sporophyte
  c. egg
  d. sperm
  e. gametophyte

D 106. Three of the four answers listed below do not have vascular tissue. Select the exception.
  * a. ferns
  b. liverworts
  c. mosses
  d. hornworts

D 107. Four of the five answers listed below exhibit a dominant sporophyte. Select the exception.
  * a. Bryophyta
  b. Lycophyta
  c. Dicotyledonae
  d. Gnetophyta
  e. Sphenophyta

M 108 Four of the five answers listed below are seed producers. Select the exception.
  * a. Pterophyta
  b. Coniferophyta
  c. Dicotyledonae
  d. Ginkgophyta
  e. Monocotyledonae

D 109. Four of the five answers below possess vascular tissue. Select the exception.
  a. whisk ferns
  * b. mosses
  c. pine trees
  d. flowering plants
  e. horsetails

E 110. Four of the five answers listed below are conifers. Select the exception.
  a. hemlock
  b. spruce
  c. fir
  * d. palm
  e. pine

D 111. Four of the five answers listed below are of the gametophyte generation. Select the exception.
  a. pollen grains
  b. megaspore
  * c. ovule
  d. pollen tube
  e. male gametophyte

M 112. Four of the five answers listed below are terms used in describing fungi. Select the exception.
  a. hyphae
  * b. peptidoglycan
  c. saprobic
  d. spore
  e. mycelium

E 113. Four of the five answers below can be used to describe fungal life. Select the exception.
  a. heterotrophic
  b. saprobic
  c. parasitic
  d. decomposer
  * e. autotrophic

# CHAPTER 20
# ANIMALS: THE INVERTEBRATES

## Multiple-Choice Questions

### OVERVIEW OF THE ANIMAL KINGDOM

M   1. All but which of the following statements are true?
   a   Mammals are vertebrates.
   b.   Invertebrates have no backbone.
   *   c.   There are more vertebrate species than invertebrates.
   d.   The phylogenetic tree of animals begins with the sponges.
   e.   All of the above statements are true.

M   2. Which of the following characteristics is NOT true of most animal phyla?
   a   multicellular
   *   b.   organ systems
   c.   heterotrophic
   d.   diploid
   e.   sexual reproduction

M   3. Major trends in the evolution of animals include
   a   cephalization, the development of a definite head region.
   b.   the development of types of symmetry.
   c.   variation in coelomic cavities.
   d.   the development of segments.
   *   e.   all of the above

E   4. The most successful of the invertebrate phyla with respect to the numbers of species is
   a   Annelida.
   *   b.   Arthropoda.
   c.   Mollusca.
   d.   Echinodermata.
   e.   Nematoda.

M   5. The second greatest number of species in an animal phylum is found in
   a   nematodes.
   *   b.   mollusks.
   c.   platyhelminths.
   d.   echinoderms.
   e.   cnidarians.

D   6. An animal with bilateral symmetry
   a   has left and right sides.
   b.   usually displays cephalization.
   c.   produces mirror images regardless of the number of "cuts" through the central axis.
   *   d.   a and b only
   e.   a, b, and c

M   7. Which insulates various internal organs from the stresses of body-wall movement and bathes them in a liquid through which nutrients and waste products can diffuse?
   *   a   a coelom
   b.   mesoderm
   c.   a mantle
   d.   a water-vascular system
   e.   all of the above

M   8. All animals are
   *   a   multicellular, heterotrophic, and diploid.
   b.   multicellular, heterotrophic, and haploid.
   c.   multicellular, autotrophic, and diploid.
   d.   multicellular, autotrophic, and haploid.

M   9. A digestive tract is said to be complete if it at least
   a   possesses specialized regions for different digestive tasks.
   b.   produces acids and contains enzymes.
   *   c.   is a one-way tube with a mouth and an anus.
   d.   is surrounded by muscle.

M   10. Creeping behavior and a mouth located toward the head end of the body may have led, in some evolutionary lines, to
   a   development of a circulatory system with blood.
   b.   sexual reproduction.
   c.   feeding on nutrients suspended in the water (filter feeding).
   *   d.   concentration of sense organs in the head region.
   e.   radial symmetry.

### PUZZLES ABOUT ORIGINS

M   11. Which of the following statements concerning the origin of multicelled animals is NOT true?
   a   Maybe the forerunner was a ciliate.
   b.   Perhaps a colony like *Volvox* was the ancestor.
   *   c.   Sponges are good candidates for consideration as the earliest ancestor.
   d.   The first multicellular animals may been like *Trichoplax.*

E   12. *Trichoplax* is a
   a   sponge.
   b.   cnidarian.
   *   c.   placozoan.
   d.   roundworm.
   e.   flatworm.

## SPONGES—SUCCESS IN SIMPLICITY

E 13. Sponges are
    a herbivores.
  * b. filter feeders.
    c. scavengers.
    d. predators.
    e. carnivores.

D 14. Unlike most other animals, sponges lack
    a. a digestive tract.
    b. a symmetrical body plan.
    c. nerve cells.
    d. a and b only
  * e. a, b, and c

D 15 Cells of the outer surface of a sponge obtain nutrients by
    a. absorbing food that diffuses from the central cavity.
    b. capturing food in their microvilli.
  * c. absorbing food distributed by amoeboid cells.
    d. phagocytosing bacteria and other small food items.

M 16. Sponges have only which one of the following?
    a. symmetry
    b. organs
    c. anus
  * d. skeleton
    e. appendages

M 17. Feeding in sponges is dependent on
    a. collar cells.
    b. pores.
    c. water flow.
    d. b and c only
  * e. a, b, and c

D 18. Which of the following groups does NOT have tissues?
    a. nematodes
  * b. sponges
    c. echinoderms
    d. flatworms
    e. cnidarians

M 19. Gemmules
    a. are used in respiration.
    b. capture food.
    c. function in excretion.
    d. serve in digestion.
  * e. are reproductive agents.

## CNIDARIANS—TISSUES EMERGE

E 20. Nematocysts are
    a. reproductive cells.
    b. excretory organs.
    c. sets of muscle cells.
    d. circulatory cells.
  * e. defensive cells.

M 21. In the life cycle of a typical cnidarian, which of the following would likely be free-swimming?
    a. medusa
    b. polyp
    c. planula
  * d. a and c only
    e. a, b, or c depending on the season

E 22. "Nerve net" describes the nervous system of
    a. flatworms.
  * b. cnidarians.
    c. annelids.
    d. sponges.
    e. none of the above

E 23. The bulk of a jellyfish consists of
    a. mesoderm.
    b. mesohyl.
    c. mesophyll.
  * d. mesoglea.
    e. mesogel.

M 24. Which of the following phyla is characterized by radially symmetrical members?
    a. Arthropoda
  * b. Cnidaria
    c. Platyhelminthes
    d. Mollusca
    e. Annelida

D 25. Members of a colony would be described best by which of the following words?
    a. dependent
    b. independent
  * c. interdependent
    d. nondependent

M 26. Which is a stage in the life cycle of *Obelia*, a cnidarian?
    a. medusa
    b. planula
    c. polyp
  * d. all of the above

M 27. Mesoglea is found in which group?
    a. sponges
  * b. cnidarians
    c. nematodes
    d. annelids
    e. mollusks

M 28. A planula is
    a. a sedentary, attached, tree-shaped form found in corals.
  * b. a swimming larval form with an outer ciliated epidermis.
    c. a kind of parasitic worm.
    d. a fleshy lobe that extends laterally from the body wall of a marine worm.
    e. a rasplike tongue.

M  29. Nematocysts are found only in
*  a. cnidarians.
   b. nematodes.
   c. crustaceans.
   d. echinoderms.

## FLATWORMS, ROUNDWORMS, ROTIFERS—AND SIMPLE ORGAN SYSTEMS

M  30. Which body plan is characterized by simple gas exchange mechanisms, two-way traffic through a highly branched, saclike gut, and a thin, flat body with all cells fairly close to the gut?
   a. cnidarian
   b. nematode
   c. echinoderm
*  d. flatworm

M  31. Bilateral symmetry is characteristic of
   a. cnidarians.
   b. sponges.
   c. jellyfish.
*  d. flatworms.

M  32. The organs of excretion in flatworms are
   a. nephridia.
   b. contractile vacuoles.
   c. Malpighian tubules.
*  d. protonephridia.
   e. book lungs.

M  33. Animals that are hermaphroditic usually
   a. fertilize their own eggs.
*  b. cross-fertilize.
   c. donate eggs to other individuals.
   d. none of the above
   e. all of the above

D  34. An organism that possesses a scolex and proglottids lacks
   a. bilateral symmetry.
*  b. a coelom.
   c. mesodermal tissue.
   d. a and b
   e. a, b, and c

M  35. A scolex is
*  a. the anterior attachment organ of a tapeworm.
   b. the feeding organ of a fluke.
   c. an appendage of a sandworm.
   d. the egg of a sea star.
   e. the larva of an aquatic insect.

D  36. The tapeworm might be called the "ultimate" parasite because it
   a. has no need of a host.
   b. can fertilize itself indefinitely.
   c. is immortal.
*  d. has no digestive tract.
   e. is flat.

M  37. Which have a tough cuticle, a false coelom, and a complete digestive system and are facultative anaerobes?
*  a. roundworms
   b. cnidarians
   c. flatworms
   d. echinoderms
   e. porifera

M  38. A segmented body plan is common to each group EXCEPT
   a. arthropods.
   b. chordates.
   c. annelids.
*  d. roundworms.

D  39. For roundworms living in the intestine of a vertebrate, the cuticle would most probably serve in what capacity?
   a. water retention
   b. nutrient absorption
*  c. protection from digestive enzymes
   d. excretion of metabolic wastes
   e. sensory detection

M  40. In size, rotifers would be most comparable to which of the following?
   a. flukes
   b. roundworms
*  c. protistans
   d. jellyfishes
   e. sponges

M  41. Rotifers take their name from
   a. their tumbling movements through the water.
*  b. actions of anterior cilia.
   c. their radial symmetry.
   d. rotational action around the central body axis.

E  42. Rotifers possess
   a. cilia.
   b. stomach.
   c. protonephridia.
   d. nerve cells.
*  e. all of the above

## A MAJOR DIVERGENCE

D  43. Which are deuterostomes?
   a. annelids
*  b. chordates
   c. arthropods
   d. mollusks
   e. all of the above

M  44. Which of the following is NOT a protostome?
   a. earthworm
   b. crayfish
*  c. sea star
   d. squid
   e. clam

D    **45.** Which of the following is applicable in describing a deuterostome?
 - a   spiral cleavage
 - b.   first embryonic indentation becomes mouth
 - \*   c.   coelom develops from gut outpouchings
 - d.   mollusca

D    **46.** Which of the following is true of deuterostomes?
 - \*   a.   Radial cleavage occurs.
 - b.   The first opening that develops becomes the anus.
 - c.   The coelom arises from tissues at the side of the blastopore (opening of gut).
 - d.   a and b, but not c
 - e.   a, b, and c

## MOLLUSKS—A WINNING BODY PLAN

D    **47.** Bivalves lack which of the following molluskan features?
 - a   foot
 - \*   b.   head
 - c.   mantle
 - d.   shells
 - e.   visceral mass

D    **48.** Which of the following features do bivalves share with sponges?
 - a   lack of symmetry
 - b.   flagellated collar cells
 - \*   c.   suspension feeding
 - d.   siphons
 - e.   none of the above

D    **49.** Cephalopods are the only mollusks that possess
 - a   a mantle.
 - b.   gills.
 - \*   c.   closed circulation.
 - d.   jet propulsion.
 - e.   both c and d

D    **50.** Which of the following is NOT a characteristic of mollusks?
 - a   radula
 - b.   mantle
 - c.   ctenidia
 - \*   d.   radial cleavage
 - e.   shell

M    **51.** A radula is which of the following?
 - a   foot
 - \*   b.   feeding organ
 - c.   ear
 - d.   sensitive hair
 - e.   balance organ

D    **52.** Which of the following is in the phylum characterized by a mantle and a radula?
 - a   lobster
 - b.   rotifer
 - \*   c.   octopus
 - d.   sand dollar

M    **53.** A mantle is found only among the
 - a   arthropods.
 - b.   annelids.
 - c.   echinoderms.
 - \*   d.   mollusks.
 - e.   chordates.

D    **54.** The mollusks with the most complex nervous systems are
 - a   chitons.
 - \*   b.   cephalopods.
 - c.   gastropods.
 - d.   bivalves.

## ANNELIDS—SEGMENTS GALORE

M    **55.** Which annelid structure may resemble the ancestral structure from which the vertebrate kidney evolved?
 - a   trachea
 - \*   b.   nephridium
 - c.   mantle
 - d.   parapods
 - e.   none of the above

D    **56.** Which of the following is most closely related to an organism that possesses setae and nephridia and exhibits coordinated movements of circular and longitudinal muscle?
 - a   millipede
 - b.   tapeworm
 - \*   c.   polychaete
 - d.   hookworm
 - e.   flatworm

E    **57.** Nephridia are
 - a   circulatory organs.
 - b.   respiratory organs.
 - \*   c.   urinary organs.
 - d.   endocrine organs.
 - e.   part of the nervous system.

D    **58.** Earthworms can perform all but which of the following?
 - \*   a   chewing of food
 - b.   respiration
 - c.   tillage of the soil
 - d.   movement using setae
 - e.   excretion of water

D    **59.** Polychaetes are the only annelids that possess
 - a   setae.
 - b.   jaws or teeth.
 - \*   c.   parapods.
 - d.   ganglia.
 - e.   a complete digestive tract.

M 60. Which annelid structure may resemble the ancestral structure from which the vertebrate kidney evolved?
   a. trachea
* b. nephridium
   c. mantle
   d. parapods
   e. none of the above

M 61. The movement of earthworms is dependent on
   a. circular muscles.
   b. longitudinal muscles.
   c. hydrostatic skeleton.
   d. setae.
* e. all of the above

E 62. Which of the following is NOT related to the other three?
   a. free-living flatworms
* b. earthworms
   c. flukes
   d. tapeworms

M 63. Which of the following has a gut with two openings, a mouth and an anus?
   a. Cnidaria
* b. Annelida
   c. Platyhelminthes
   d. Porifera

## ARTHROPODS—THE MOST SUCCESSFUL ORGANISMS ON EARTH

E 64. The animal group that contains the greatest number of named species is
   a. mollusks.
* b. arthropods.
   c. nematodes.
   d. chordates.

M 65. Which adaptation has contributed to the success of the insects?
   a. specialized sensory organs
   b. wings
   c. high reproductive capacity
   d. a and b
* e. a, b, and c

M 66. Exoskeletons are most characteristic of which of the following?
   a. mollusks
* b. arthropods
   c. echinoderms
   d. chordates
   e. annelids

E 67. The unique tissue adaptation for respiration used by many arthropods, including insects, is
   a. gills.
   b. lunglike chambers.
* c. tracheae.
   d. mantle.
   e. pedipalps.

E 68. Molting in arthropods involves primarily a change in
   a. body form and maturity.
   b. sex.
* c. body size.
   d. eating habits.
   e. sensory structures.

M 69. Which of the following is a disadvantage of an exoskeleton?
* a. It must be shed for its owner to grow.
   b. It does not provide as efficient a muscle anchorage as an endoskeleton.
   c. It allows for excess water loss.
   d. It is not flexible enough to allow a full range of movement.
   e. It is not able to absorb pigments for sufficient camouflage.

M 70. The appendages of members of several phyla share common functions; however, only certain appendages of arthropods are capable of
   a. walking.
* b. flight.
   c. feeding.
   d. copulation.
   e. swimming.

E 71. The most successful forms of life that have ever evolved are the
   a. vertebrates.
* b. insects.
   c. humans.
   d. protozoans.
   e. mollusks

## A LOOK AT SPIDERS AND THEIR KIN

D 72. Which is NOT a chelicerate?
   a. tick
* b. mosquito
   c. spider
   d. scorpion
   e. horseshoe crab

E 73. Spiders use which of the following mouthparts for subduing prey?
   a. mandibles
   b. pedipalps
* c. chelicerae
   d. maxillae
   e. labial palps

M 74. An unidentified arthropod has no antennae and eight pairs of legs. It is probably most closely related to
   a. grasshoppers.
* b. ticks.
   c. crayfish.
   d. millipedes.
   e. trilobites.

## A LOOK AT THE CRUSTACEANS

D **75.** Which animal belongs to a subphylum different from that of the other four?
    a  tick
*   b.  shrimp
    c.  mite
    d.  spider
    e.  scorpion

M **76.** Which of the following groups can be distinguished from the other arthropods by its possession of two pairs of antennae?
    a  insects
    b.  millipedes
    c.  chelicerates
*   d.  crustaceans
    e.  trilobites

E **77.** What is the crustacean appendage that is used for chewing food?
    a  antenna
    b.  pedipalp
*   c.  mandible
    d.  maxilla
    e.  carapace

## VARIABLE NUMBERS OF MANY LEGS

M **78.** Based on the criterion of segmentation, which organism most closely resembles the earliest ancestral arthropod?
    a  dragonfly
*   b.  millipede
    c.  tick
    d.  crab

M **79.** A wormlike arthropod with a flattened body and carnivorous eating habits would be identified as a
    a  crustacean.
    b.  millipede.
    c.  spider.
    d.  trilobite.
*   e.  centipede.

## A LOOK AT INSECT DIVERSITY

M **80.** In the course of evolution, the thorax of an insect has become specialized for
    a  digestion.
    b.  reproduction.
*   c.  locomotion.
    d.  excretion.
    e.  sensation

M **81.** Which of the following adaptations has contributed to the success of the insects?
    a  specialized sensory organs
    b.  wings
    c.  high reproductive capacity
    d.  a and b only
*   e.  a, b, and c

D **82.** Which of the following is NOT an organ for excreting excess water from the body?
    a  nephridium
    b.  flame cell
*   c.  trachea
    d.  Malpighian tubule
    e.  siphon

## THE PUZZLING ECHINODERMS

E **83.** A water-vascular system is characteristic of the
    a  arthropods.
    b.  annelids.
    c.  chordates.
    d.  mollusks.
*   e.  echinoderms.

D **84.** Which phylum is strictly marine, with no freshwater or terrestrial forms?
*   a  Echinodermata
    b.  Platyhelminthes
    c.  Cnidaria
    d.  Mollusca
    e.  Annelida

M **85.** The water-vascular system is used primarily for
    a  excretion of excess water.
*   b.  locomotion.
    c.  respiration.
    d.  circulation.
    e.  sensation.

E **86.** A feature found only in echinoderms is the
    a  radula.
*   b.  water-vascular system.
    c.  nephridium.
    d.  nematocyst.
    e.  mandible.

E **87.** The most unusual feature of the echinoderms is
    a  a motile larval form.
    b.  the presence of a radula.
    c.  radial symmetry.
*   d.  a water-vascular system.
    e.  the protonephridial network.

## Matching Question

**88.**  Matching. Choose the most appropriate answer for each.

1. ___  placozoa
2. ___  annelids
3. ___  arthropods
4. ___  chordates
5. ___  cnidarians
6. ___  echinoderms
7. ___  flatworms
8. ___  rotifers
9. ___  mollusks
10. ___  roundworms
11. ___  sponges

A.  *Trichoplax*
B.  vertebrates
C.  planarians, flukes, tapeworms
D.  nematodes
E.  snails, squids, clams
F.  wheel animals
G.  collar cells present
H.  jellyfish and corals
I.  crustaceans, ticks, and insects
J.  polychaetes, earthworms, leeches
K.  sea urchins, sea stars

*Answers:*

| | | | | | | |
|---|---|---|---|---|---|
| 1. | A | 2. | J | 3. | I |
| 4. | B | 5. | H | 6. | K |
| 7. | C | 8. | F | 9. | E |
| 10. | D | 11. | G | | |

## Classification Questions

Answer questions 89- 93 in reference to the five animal phyla listed below:

a   Porifera
b.  Cnidaria
c.  Platyhelminthes
d.  Nematoda
e.  Annelida

D   **89.**  Members of this phylum have a pseudocoelomic cavity.

D   **90.**  Members of this group have a brain with nerve cords, a saclike or branched gut, and lack a circulatory system.

M   **91.**  Members of this phylum have a brain with a ventral nerve cord, a complete gut, and a circulatory system that is usually closed.

E   **92.**  This phylum contains the most primitive species of the animal kingdom.

M   **93.**  This phylum includes jellyfish and sea anemones.

*Answers*   89.  d   90.  c   91.  e
            92.  a   93.  b

Answer questions 94- 98 in reference to the five animal phyla listed below:

a   Annelida
b.  Arthropoda
c.  Mollusca
d.  Echinodermata
e.  Rotifera

D   **94.**  Members of this phylum display obvious, uniform segmentation from anterior to posterior.

M   **95.**  The larval stage in this phylum has bilateral symmetry, whereas the adult stage exhibits radial symmetry.

M   **96**  Although most are enclosed by hardened shells, this phylum name literally means "soft body."

E   **97**  This phylum has the greatest number of species.

D   **98.**  Wheel animals are in this phylum.

*Answers*   94.  b   95.  d   96.  c
            97.  b   98.  e

## Selecting the Exception

D    99.   Four of the five answers listed below are true of a majority of animals. Select the exception.
      a   multicellular
   *  b.  exhibits alternation of generations
      c.  usually motile at least during part of their life cycle
      d.  usually diploid sexually reproducing forms of life
      e.  usually heterotrophic

D    100.  Four of the five answers listed below are members of a common group. Select the exception.
      a   jellyfish
      b.  hydra
   *  c.  sea squirts
      d.  corals
      e.  sea anemones

D    101.  Four of the five answers listed below are members of a common group. Select the exception.
      a   sea star
   *  b.  sea anemone
      c.  sea urchin
      d.  sea lily
      e.  sea cucumber

D    102.  Four of the five answers listed below possess some type of coelom. Select the exception.
      a   nematodes
      b.  annelids
      c.  arthropods
      d.  mollusks
   *  e.  flatworms

M    103.  Four of the five answers listed below are characteristics of cnidarians. Select the exception.
      a   planula larvae
      b.  polyp form
      c.  mesoglea
      d.  nematocyst
   *  e.  pharynx

M    104.  Four of the five answers listed below are found in flatworms. Select the exception.
      a   proglottid
   *  b.  setae
      c.  scolex
      d.  flame cell
      e.  first form to develop a mesoderm

M    105.  Four of the five answers listed below are parasites. Select the exception.
   *  a   planaria
      b.  fluke
      c.  nematodes
      d.  leech
      e.  tapeworm

M    106.  Four of the five answers listed below are descriptive of annelids. Select the exception.
      a   first segmented form
      b.  possess nephridia
   *  c.  jointed appendages
      d.  setae
      e.  complete gut with closed circulatory system and coelom

E    107.  Four of the five answers listed below are crustaceans. Select the exception.
      a   crabs
      b.  shrimps
      c.  lobsters
   *  d.  centipedes
      e.  barnacles

M    108.  Four of the five answers listed below are grasshopper mouthparts. Select the exception.
   *  a   proboscis
      b.  maxilla
      c.  palps
      d.  mandible
      e.  labrum

M    109.  Four of the five answers listed below are molluscan body features. Select the exception.
      a   gills
      b.  head and foot
      c.  mantle
   *  d.  carapace
      e.  radula

M    110.  Four of the five answers listed below are characteristics of adult sea stars. Select the exception.
      a   spiny skin
      b.  tube foot
      c.  water-vascular system
   *  d.  bilateral symmetry
      e.  ampulla

# CHAPTER 21

# ANIMALS: THE VERTEBRATES

## Multiple-Choice Questions

### THE CHORDATE HERITAGE

M    **1.** Which statement is NOT true?
- a   All chordates have notochords.
- b.   All chordates have pharyngeal pouches or slits.
- c.   All chordates have dorsal tubular nerve cords.
- *   d.   All chordates are vertebrates.
- e.   Chordates are found in all major types of environments.

E    **2.** The notochord is most closely associated with the
- a   nervous system.
- b.   spinal cord.
- *   c.   skeletal system.
- d.   skin system.
- e.   a and b only

E    **3.** The only chordate feature still present in the human adult is
- a   pharyngeal gill slits.
- *   b.   nerve cord.
- c.   notochord.
- d.   tail.
- e.   all of the above

E    **4.** Which of the following statements is false?
- *   a.   All vertebrates have a ventral tubular nervous system.
- b.   All vertebrates have a tail at some stage in their life cycle.
- c.   All vertebrates have a notochord at some stage in their life cycle.
- d.   All vertebrates have pharyngeal gill slits at some stage in their life cycle.

M    **5.** Which of the following is NOT a feature that is found exclusively among all vertebrates?
- a   notochord
- b.   pharyngeal gill slits
- *   c.   four legs
- d.   post-anal tail
- e.   dorsal nerve cord

E    **6.** Which of the following is NOT a subphylum of Chordata?
- a   Urochordata
- *   b.   Hemichordata
- c.   Cephalochordata
- d.   Vertebrata

### INVERTEBRATE CHORDATES

M    **7.** In filter-feeding chordates, which structure has cilia that create water currents and mucous sheets that capture nutrients suspended in the water?
- a   notochord
- b.   differentially permeable membrane
- c.   filiform tongue
- *   d.   gill slit
- e.   jaw

M    **8.** The invertebrate chordates are
- *   a   filter feeders.
- b.   scavengers.
- c.   herbivores.
- d.   predators.
- e.   parasites.

M    **9.** A form of metamorphosis is found in
- a   tunicates.
- b.   insects.
- c.   amphibians.
- d.   a and c only
- *   e.   a, b, and c

M    **10.** Which of the following is a diagnostic feature of the sea squirts that forms the basis for its classification?
- a   metamorphosis from a motile larva to a sessile adult
- b.   a heart that allows circulation of blood
- *   c.   a notochord located in the tail of the larva
- d.   sexual reproduction during the larval stage
- e.   the presence of a tunic or coat over the body of the adult

M    **11.** During the life of a tunicate, the notochord
- a   is present throughout life.
- *   b.   appears in the larva only.
- c.   develops during adulthood.
- d.   is completely absent.
- e.   changes into the nerve cord.

E    **12.** The "tunic" of tunicate refers to
- *   a   a body covering.
- b.   the type of food-gathering mechanism.
- c.   muscle arrangements in the larva.
- d.   the immature stage of a true fish.

M    **13.** Lancelets possess which of the following all their lives?
- a   notochord
- b.   gill slits
- c.   nerve cord
- d.   a and c only
- *   e.   a, b, and c

E **14.** Lancelets are
    a  predators.
\*   b.  filter feeders.
    c.  scavengers.
    d.  parasites.
    e.  scrapers that feed on the ocean bottom.

## EVOLUTIONARY TRENDS AMONG THE VERTEBRATES

M **15.** Which phylum is most closely related phylogenetically to the first vertebrates?
\*   a  Echinodermata
    b.  Arthropoda
    c.  Mollusca
    d.  Annelida
    e.  none of the above

M **16.** The most primitive vertebrates are members of the group of
\*   a  jawless fishes.
    b.  amphibians.
    c.  cartilaginous fish.
    d.  birds.
    e.  bony fish.

M **17.** The vertebrate jaw first appeared in which organism?
\*   a  fishes
    b.  amphibians
    c.  reptiles
    d.  birds
    e.  mammals

M **18.** Which of the following is NOT one of the trends of vertebrate evolution?
    a  conversion of the support for locomotion from the notochord to the vertebral column
    b.  expansion of the nerve cord to form the brain and spinal cord
    c.  changes in the respiratory system from gills to lungs with accompanying changes in the circulatory system
\*   d.  increases in size, speed, strength, and physical processes
    e.  modification of limbs for more efficient movement

D **19.** The evolution of vertebrates
    a  is believed to have proceeded from cephalochordates.
    b.  is most closely tied to urochordates.
\*   c.  is probably in a lineage apart from present-day invertebrate chordates.
    d.  possibly proceeded from cephalochordates to hemichordates.

D **20.** In vertebrate evolution, the appearance of the vertebral column led most directly to development of
    a  limbs such as arms and legs.
\*   b.  jaws.
    c.  sense organs and the nervous system.
    d.  more efficient breathing systems.
    e.  greater speed of locomotion.

M **21.** In fishes ancestral to land vertebrates, pouches in the gut wall developed into
    a  heart chambers.
    b.  the notochord.
    c.  lobes of the liver.
\*   d.  lungs.
    e.  vocal cords.

M **22.** The ostracoderms were
    a  an ancient group of spiny, thin echinoderms.
    b.  a group of primitive protochordates.
\*   c.  primitive fishes without jaws.
    d.  one of the first terrestrial vertebrates.
    e.  reptiles with a bony skin.

M **23.** Ostracoderms lost out in evolutionary competition to animals
    a  with more protective body coverings.
    b.  who were filter feeders.
    c.  with lungs.
\*   d.  that had begun to develop jaws.
    e.  with an exoskeleton.

M **24.** Placoderms were the first fishes to display
\*   a  jaws.
    b.  gill openings.
    c.  cartilaginous skeletons.
    d.  a and b only
    e.  a, b, and c

M **25.** Which of the following classes is represented only by fossil forms?
    a  Agnatha
    b.  Amphibia
    c.  Aves
\*   d.  Placodermi
    e.  Chondrichthyes

M **26.** The chief advance of the placoderms was the development of
    a  paired fins for efficient movement.
\*   b.  paired jaws that enabled them to bite and feed.
    c.  bony plates for protection.
    d.  an efficient set of lungs.
    e.  a strengthened notochord.

M **27.** The most primitive, but still existing, vertebrates are members of the class
\*   a  Agnatha.
    b.  Amphibia.
    c.  Chondrichthyes.
    d.  Aves.
    e.  Osteichthyes.

M  28.  Which of the following was the first class to evolve?
   a   Aves
   b.  Reptilia
   c.  Osteichthyes
*  d.  Agnatha

## EXISTING, JAWLESS FISHES

M  29.  The feeding habits of lampreys are best described as
   a   suspension feeding.
   b.  predatory.
*  c.  parasitic.
   d.  scavenging.
   e.  all of the above

M  30.  Which of the following was the first class to evolve?
   a   Aves
   b.  Reptilia
   c.  Osteichthyes
*  d.  Agnatha

D  31.  The term *agnathan* could be used to describe
   a   ostracoderms.
   b.  placoderms.
   c.  hagfish.
*  d.  a and c only
   e.  b and c only

## EXISTING, JAWED FISHES

E  32.  Sharks differ from most other fish in that they lack
   a   lungs.
   b.  scales.
*  c.  bone.
   d.  paired appendages.

E  33.  Sharks, rays, and skates belong to what group?
   a   birds
   b.  amphibians
*  c.  cartilaginous fish
   d.  bony fish
   e.  reptiles

M  34.  The feeding behavior of true fishes is dependent on highly developed
   a   parapodia.
   b.  notochords.
*  c.  sense organs.
   d.  gill slits.
   e.  motile organs.

E  35.  In true fishes the gills primarily serve which function?
*  a   gas exchange
   b.  feeding
   c.  water elimination
   d.  both feeding and gas exchange
   e.  all of the above

E  36.  The vertebrate lung first appeared in which organism?
*  a   fishes
   b.  amphibians
   c.  reptiles
   d.  birds
   e.  mammals

E  37.  Sharks, rays, and skates belong to the class
   a   Aves.
   b.  Amphibia.
*  c.  Chondrichthyes.
   d.  Osteichthyes.
   e.  Reptilia.

D  38.  All but which of the following have cartilaginous skeletons?
   a   sharks
   b.  lampreys
*  c.  perch
   d.  rays

M  39.  Which of the following is associated with lobe-finned fish?
   a   cartilage
   b.  replaceable teeth
   c.  dermal rays
*  d.  lungs
   e.  none of the above

M  40.  The feeding behavior of true fishes selected for highly developed
   a   parapodia.
   b.  notochords.
*  c.  sense organs.
   d.  gill slits.
   e.  motile organs.

M  41.  In true fishes, the gills primarily serve which function?
*  a   gas exchange
   b.  feeding
   c.  water elimination
   d.  both feeding and gas exchange
   e.  all of the above

M  42.  Which of the following statements is false?
   a   Shark's teeth are modified scales that are continuously shed and replaced.
   b.  Many fish use a swim bladder to provide buoyancy control.
*  c.  The bony fishes were the ancestors of the cartilaginous fishes.
   d.  The ray-finned fishes are the most numerous and diverse of the fish groups.
   e.  The lobe-finned fish gave rise to the ray-finned fish.

**AMPHIBIANS**

E   43. Exchange of respiratory gases through the skin is a characteristic of many
    a   fish.
    * b   amphibians.
    c   reptiles.
    d   mammals.

D   44. Amphibians most likely evolved from
    * a   fish with lobed fins.
    b   ray-finned fish.
    c   reptiles.
    d   agnathans.
    e   placoderms.

E   45. Amphibians are completely dependent on an aquatic environment for
    a   respiration.
    b   feeding.
    * c   reproduction.
    d   a and c only
    e   a, b, and c

M   46. Amphibians are distinguished from earlier vertebrates by
    a   the development of eggs capable of hatching on land.
    b   metamorphosis.
    * c   the development of limbs capable of moving on land.
    d   the presence of scales to prevent desiccation.
    e   absence of gills in any stage of development.

M   47. A water environment provides more of all but which one of the following than does air?
    a   support
    b   buoyancy
    c   constancy of temperature
    * d   oxygen
    e   resistance to movement

M   48. Members of the _____ are noted for the ability of larval forms to reproduce sexually.
    a   Aves
    b   Osteichthyes
    * c   Amphibia
    d   Reptilia
    e   Mammalia

M   49. In which group are retention of larval characteristic and sexual maturity seen in the same body?
    a   toads
    * b   salamanders
    c   frogs
    d   caecilians

**REPTILES**

M   50. Which of the following is most responsible for freeing vertebrates from dependence on watery habitats?
    a   lungs
    b   paired appendages
    * c   the shelled, amniote eggs
    d   the four-chambered heart
    e   scales

E   51. The first group to exhibit an amniotic egg belonged to the
    a   Aves.
    b   Amphibia.
    * c   Reptilia.
    d   Osteichthyes.
    e   Mammalia.

D   52. Reptiles resemble _____ in not being able to _____.
    a   fish; leave the water
    b   birds; breathe using lungs
    c   ostracoderms; utilize their jaws
    * d   amphibians; maintain a constant body temperature

M   53. The reptiles differ from the amphibians in that they
    a   have a more developed cerebral cortex.
    b   have scales that prevented desiccation.
    c   have internal fertilization.
    d   use a shelled amniotic egg.
    * e   all of the above

M   54. Which of the following statements is false?
    * a   Lizards are a very small component of the present-day reptiles.
    b   Lizards gave rise to the snakes.
    c   Lizards are primarily insect eaters.
    d   Lizards can break off their tails to serve as a distraction to predators.
    e   Lizards are most numerous in deserts and tropical forests.

**BIRDS**

D   55. An organism that possesses feathers must also possess
    a   malpighian tubules.
    b   a three-chambered heart.
    * c   a dorsal nerve cord.
    d   a pseudocoelom.
    e   replaceable teeth

E   56. Birds differ from earlier vertebrates by
    a   their lack of scales.
    b   the land egg.
    * c   the ability to maintain a constant body temperature.
    d   the ability to fertilize eggs internally.
    e   their possession of a dorsal nerve cord.

D  57. Birds and mammals share which of the following characteristics?
   a  ectothermy (body temperature regulated by environment)
   b. body hair
 * c. four-chambered heart
   d. lung design
   e. amniotic egg

M  58. Adaptations for flight in birds include all but which of the following?
 * a  sound production
   b. lightweight bones
   c. feathers
   d. efficient respiration
   e. four-chambered heart

## MAMMALS

E  59. Which feature do mammals share in common with all vertebrates?
   a  hair
 * b. a column of individual backbones
   c. milk
   d. internal development

E  60. Mammals are the only vertebrates that possess
   a  teeth.
   b. a backbone.
   c. brain
 * d. mammary glands
   e. sensory organs

M  61. A mammal with well-developed premolars and molars would likely be eating mostly
   a  meat.
 * b. plant matter.
   c. insects.
   d. decayed materials.
   e. none of these

M  62. Egg-laying mammals
   a  cannot feed their young with milk.
 * b. have no teeth.
   c. are hairless.
   d. are confined to South America.
   e. bear their young into pouches.

D  63. Which of the following statements concerning the placenta is incorrect?
   a  It nourishes the young in the uterus.
   b. Nutrients pass to the fetus.
 * c. It is entirely a maternal structure.
   d. It promotes faster growth than does the pouch of marsupials.
   e. It cleans the fetal blood of impurities.

E  64. All of these are types of mammalian teeth except
   a  canines.
   b. molars.
   c. premolars.
 * d. cusps.
   e. incisors.

## EVOLUTIONARY TRENDS AMONG THE PRIMATES

E  65. Which is NOT an anthropoid?
   a  orangutan
 * b. lemur
   c. spider monkey
   d. gibbon
   e. chimpanzee

M  66. Humans are least closely related to the
   a  chimpanzee.
   b. orangutan.
   c. gorilla.
 * d. tarsier.
   e. gibbon.

M  67. Which group includes all the others?
   a  tarsioids
   b. hominoids
   c. prosimians
   d. anthropoids
 * e. primates

M  68. Humans belong to all but which one of the following?
   a  hominids
   b. hominoids
 * c. prosimians
   d. anthropoids
   e. primates

E  69. Which of the following can be included in the group called "hominids"?
   a  monkeys
 * b. humans
   c. apes
   d. b and c only
   e. a, b, and c

E  70. Bipedalism is most highly developed in
   a  hominoids.
   b. apes.
 * c. humans.
   d. monkeys.
   e. prosimians.

M  71. In the course of the evolution of existing primate groups, there has been a general decrease in
 * a  number of offspring produced by a female.
   b. body size.
   c. life span.
   d. duration of infant dependency.

E  72. All but which factor were important evolutionary adaptations in primates?
   a  enhanced daytime vision
   b. upright walking
   c. an opposable thumb
 * d. the development of a restricted or specialized diet
   e. brain expansion and elaboration

M 73. Which feature is NOT characteristic of the evolutionary trends in primates?
    a longer life span
    b. longer gestation period
    c. longer infant dependency
    d. longer periods between pregnancies
 * e. larger litters

M 74. Which characteristic is NOT considered to have been a key character in early primate evolution?
    a eyes adapted for discerning color and shape in a three-dimensional field
    b. body and limbs adapted for tree climbing
 * c. greater jaw and dental specialization
    d. eyes adapted for discerning movement in a three-dimensional field
    e. opposable thumb and forefinger

E 75. The evolutionary trend of bipedalism refers to the
    a ability of only humans to ride a bicycle.
 * b. human ability to habitually walk on two feet.
    c. use of two hands to swing through the trees as monkeys do.
    d. development of a prehensile hand.
    e. use of feet as well as hands for grasping.

E 76. Well-developed molars would be most valuable to
    a cats.
    b. meat-eaters.
 * c. cows.
    d. dogs.
    e. birds.

M 77. Behavioral trends in primate evolution include
    a longer life spans.
    b. longer learning period and dependence on parents.
    c. lower reproductive rate.
    d. longer periods between pregnancies.
 * e. all of the above

M 78. Which feature is NOT characteristic of the evolutionary trends in primates?
    a longer life span
    b. longer gestation period
    c. longer infant dependency
    d. longer periods between pregnancies
 * e. larger litters

E 79. The ability to grasp objects by wrapping the hand around them is termed
    a opposable.
    b. grabbing.
 * c. prehensile.
    d. grappling.
    e. hooking.

E 80. The ability to hold a paintbrush as an artist does is to the thumb and fingers being
    a prehensile.
    b. in line with each other.
    c. bendable.
    d. muscular.
 * e. opposable.

M 81. The most recent level of evolution in primates is considered to be in
    a brain expansion.
 * b. behavior and culture.
    c. dentition.
    d. hand grip.
    e. daytime vision.

M 82. The location of the eyes on the front of the head in later primates was especially important in
    a seeing color.
    b. detecting light intensity.
    c. predatory behavior.
 * d. seeing in three dimensions.
    e. mating.

## FROM PRIMATES TO HOMINIDS

M 83. The primates first arose about how many million years ago?
    a 75
 * b. 60
    c. 50
    d. 40
    e. 30

M 84. The most primitive living primate is the
    a Old World monkey.
    b. lemur.
    c. New World monkey.
 * d. tree shrew.
    e. tarsier.

M 85. Primitive primates generally live
 * a in tropical and subtropical forest canopies.
    b. in temperate savanna and grassland habitats.
    c. near rivers, lakes, and streams in the East African Rift Valley.
    d. in caves with abundant supplies of insects.
    e. all of the above

M 86. The diet of the direct ancestors of primates did NOT include
 * a grass.
    b. insects.
    c. fruits.
    d. seeds.

M 87. The first known primates were characterized as
 * a arboreal and nocturnal.
    b. ground-dwelling and nocturnal.
    c. arboreal and diurnal.
    d. ground-dwelling and diurnal.

M 88. In comparison to the Oligocene, the climate at the start of the Miocene
a remained the same.
b. became wetter and warmer.
* c. became drier and cooler.
d. became wetter and cooler.
e. became drier and warmer.

M 89. The anthropoids of the Oligocene lived in
a hot, dry deserts.
b. grassy, savannas.
* c. forests.
d. the watery swamps.
e. cool, and pleasant mountains.

M 90. Hominids evolved when the climate was becoming
a wetter and hotter.
b. wetter and cooler.
c. drier and hotter.
* d. drier and cooler.

D 91. How long ago did the hominid evolutionary line diverge from that leading to the great apes?
a about 3 million years ago
* b. somewhere between 6 million and 4 million years ago
c. during the Eocene epoch
d. less than 2 million years ago
e. about 1.5 million years ago

E 92. Hominids are characterized as being
a insectivores.
b. herbivores.
c. carnivores.
* d. omnivores.
e. none of the above

E 93. The early hominid fossils are found in
* a Africa.
b. Asia.
c. Australia.
d. the South Pacific.
e. Europe.

M 94. Which is a hominid?
a chimpanzee
* b. *Australopithecus*
c. baboon
d. a and b
e. a, b, and c

M 95. Fossils of the earliest known hominids are how many million years old?
a more than 20
b. about 10
* c. between 4 and 2
d. less than 0.5

M 96. The conclusion that early hominids were bipedal is based on examination of
a the angles made by the bones that articulate with the pelvis.
b. fossil footprints.
c. imprints of motor cortex in fossilized craniums.
* d. a and b
e. a, b, and c

M 97. The primate fossil named Lucy was a(n)
a dryopith.
* b. australopith.
c. cercopith.
d. prosimian.
e. hominid.

## EMERGENCE OF HUMANS

M 98. It is thought that the earliest tools were employed by hominids to
a assist in locomotion.
b. provide protection.
* c. facilitate the processing of food.
d. ward off predators.

E 99. The oldest "manufactured" tools have been found in
a North America.
b. Eurasia.
* c. Africa.
d. Australia.

M 100. The first toolmakers were
a *Australopithecus africanus.*
b. *Australopithecus robustus.*
c. *Australopithecus boisei.*
* d. *Homo habilis* (early *Homo*).
e. *Homo erectus.*

M 101. The first to make use of controlled fires were
a *Australopithecus africanus.*
b. *Australopithecus robustus.*
c. *Australopithecus boisei.*
d. *Homo habilis* (early *Homo*).
* e. *Homo erectus.*

D 102. Although the phylogenetic lineages for hominids are not definitive, which of the following statements is NOT a possibility?
* a *Homo* preceded *Australopithecus.*
b. *Homo sapiens* is the most recent.
c. *Australopithecus* is probably more ancient than *Homo.*
d. *Homo erectus* preceded *Homo sapiens.*
e. *Homo* and *Australopithecus* may have evolved at the same time.

M 103. The geographical distribution of hominids changed dramatically during the Pleistocene due to the migrations of
a Australopithecus robustus.
b. Australopithecus boisei.
* c. Homo erectus.
d. Homo sapiens.

M 104. Fossil evidence suggests the earliest members of the genus Homo were
a social.
b. omnivorous.
c. tool makers.
d. a and b
* e. a, b, and c

M 105. Which statement about Neanderthals is false?
a The oldest Neanderthal fossils are 500,000 years old.
b. Neanderthal settlements show little evidence of tools.
c. Neanderthal brains were larger than those of modern humans.
* d. a and b are false
e. a, b, and c are all false

M 106. Neandertals were members of
a Australopithecus robustus.
b. Australopithecus boisei.
c. Homo habilis (early Homo).
d. Homo erectus.
* e. Homo sapiens.

D 107. "Long, chinless face, thick-walled skull, and heavy-browed" would partially describe
a Australopithecus robustus.
b. Australopithecus boisei.
c. Homo habilis (early Homo).
* d. Homo erectus.
e. Homo sapiens.

D 108. "Smaller teeth and jaws, presence of a chin, thin facial bones, larger brain, and rounder, higher skull" would be a partial description
a Australopithecus robustus.
b. Australopithecus boisei.
c. Homo habilis (early Homo).
d. Homo erectus.
* e. Homo sapiens.

M 109. The species Homo sapiens is thought to be how many years old?
a 10,000–25,000
b. 30,000–60,000
c. 60,000–95,000
d. 85,000–120,000
* e. 200,000–300,000

M 110. About 40,000 years ago, what kind of evolution replaced biological evolution in the shaping of modern humans?
* a cultural
b. behavioral
c. chemical
d. psychological
e. morphological

M 111. A hominid of Europe and Asia that became extinct about 35,000 years ago was
a a dryopith.
b. Australopithecus.
c. Homo erectus.
* d. Neanderthals.

## Matching Questions

D 112. Matching I. Choose the one most appropriate letter for each blank.

1. ___ birds
2. ___ bony fishes
3. ___ caecilians
4. ___ humans
5. ___ lampreys
6. ___ lancelets
7. ___ opossum
8. ___ ostracoderms
9. ___ placoderms
10. ___ platypus
11. ___ salamanders
12. ___ sharks
13. ___ snakes
14. ___ tunicates

A. cartilaginous skeleton; jaws
B. jawless fishes; now extinct
C. placental mammal
D. legless amphibian
E. invertebrate chordate; no metamorphosis
F. endotherm with feathers
G. limbless reptile
H. most primitive fishes with jaws
I. modern-day parasitic agnathan
J. marsupial
K. adult is called "sea squirt"
L. egg-laying mammal
M. swim bladder for buoyancy
N. may be sexually mature but not adult

Answers:

| | | | | | |
|---|---|---|---|---|---|
| 1. | F | 2. | M | 3. | D |
| 4. | C | 5. | I | 6. | E |
| 7. | J | 8. | B | 9. | H |
| 10. | L | 11. | N | 12. | A |
| 13. | G | 14. | K | | |

D    113.    Matching II. Choose the one most appropriate answer for each.

1. ___    *Australopithecus*
2. ___    *Homo erectus*
3. ___    *Homo sapiens*
4. ___    Neandertals

A.    lived from approximately 100,000 to 30,000 years ago; skilled toolmakers and artisans

B.    lived about 1.5 million years ago until 300,000 years ago; cranial capacity approximately 1,000 cubic centimeters; bipedal

C.    lived about 30 million years ago near Fayum

D.    humans since 300,000 years ago

E.    Lucy; between 3.8 to 1 million years ago

*Answers:*    1. E    2. B    3. D
4. A

## Classification Questions

Answer questions 114- 118 in reference to the five classes listed below:

a    Agnatha
b.    Chondrichthyes
c.    Osteichthyes
d.    Amphibia
e.    Reptilia

E    114.    Members of this class are fully terrestrial except for reproduction.

M    115.    Ostracoderms could qualify for membership in this class.

M    116.    Members of this class have cartilaginous skeletons but also possess jaws.

M    117.    Some species of this class live in water but are not dependent upon an aquatic environment.

D    118.    Members of one unusual class may have been ancestors of amphibians.

*Answers*    114. d    115 . a    116. b
117. e    118. c

Answer questions 119-122 in reference to the four hominids listed below:

a    *Homo habilis*
b.    *Homo erectus*
c.    *Homo sapiens*
d.    *Australopithecus afarensis*

M    119.    The Neandertals belong to this species.

M    120.    Our own species evolved from this species.

M    121.    This species was the first known to use fire.

D    122.    This species was the first definitely known to use tools.

*Answers*    119. c    120. b    121. b
122. a

## Selecting the Exception

D    123.    Four of the five answers listed below are members of a common group. Select the exception.
a    lancelet
b.    jawed fish
c.    jawless fish
d.    sea squirt
*    e.    squid

M    124    Four of the five answers below are members of the same group. Select the exception.
*    a.    lampreys
b.    sharks
c.    rays
d.    skates
e.    chimaeras

D    125.    Four of the five answers below are correct pairings of group name and common name. Select the exception.
a    Chondrichthyes – sharks
*    b.    Urochordata – lancelets
c.    Amphibia – toads
d.    Reptilia – lizards
e.    Agnatha – hagfish

M    126.    Four of the five answers below are classes of living chordates. Select the exception.
a    Agnatha
b.    Osteichthyes
c.    Reptilia
*    d.    Placodermi
e.    Chondrichthyes

M    127.    Four of the five answers below are related by a common group. Select the exception.
a    frogs
b.    toads
*    c.    tuataras
d.    salamanders
e.    caecilians

M 128. Four of the five answers below are principal characteristics of all chordates. Select the exception.
   a. tail
 * b. bony vertebra
   c. notochord
   d. nerve cord
   e. pharyngeal gill slits

M 129. Four of the five answers below are breathing mechanisms in chordates. Select the exception.
   a. skin
   b. gills
 * c. tracheas
   d. lungs
   e. lining of pharynx and mouth

M 130. Four of the five answers below characterize a group of chordates. Select the exception.
   a. feathers
 * b. ectothermic
   c. four-chambered heart
   d. hollow skeleton
   e. no teeth

M 131. Three of the four answers listed below are prosimians. Select the exception.
   a. tree shrews
 * b. monkey
   c. lemurs
   d. lorises

E 132. Four of the five answers listed below are anthropoids. Select the exception.
 * a. tarsier
   b. Old World monkey
   c. human
   d. ape
   e. gorilla

M 133. Three of the four answers listed below are trends in hominid evolution. Select the exception.
   a. strong social bonding
   b. enhanced vision
 * c. upright vertebral column
   d. omnivorous feeding behavior

D 134. Four of the five answers listed below are related by a similar evolutionary characteristic in *Homo*. Select the exception.
   a. small thin face
   b. high skull
   c. large cranial capacity
   d. larger body size
 * e. specialized teeth

# CHAPTER 22
# PLANT TISSUES

## Multiple-Choice Questions

### OVERVIEW OF THE PLANT BODY

E **1.** Approximately how many species of plants are known?
   a. 100,000
   b. 180,000
   * c. 265,000
   d. 360,000
   e. 480,000

M **2.** Perpetually young tissues where cells retain the ability to divide are
   a. vascular.
   * b. meristematic.
   c. protective.
   d. photosynthetic.
   e. all of the above

E **3.** Which of the following is most extensive in the plant body?
   * a. ground tissue
   b. dermal tissue
   c. epidermal tissue
   d. vascualr tissue
   e. transport tissue

M **4.** Increases in stem length occur at
   a. vascular cambium.
   b. cork cambium.
   c. secondary tissues.
   * d. apical meristem.
   e. lateral meristem.

### TYPES OF PLANT TISSUES

M **5.** Plant tissue noted for photosynthesis, storage, and secretion is
   a. vascular cambium.
   * b. parenchyma.
   c. collenchyma.
   d. sclerenchyma.
   e. none of the above

M **6.** Parenchyma cells are specialized for and involved in all of the following activities EXCEPT
   a. photosynthesis.
   b. structure of fruits.
   * c. conduction of food.
   d. secretion.
   e. food storage.

M **7.** The chewy, stringy cells in celery are which cells?
   a. xylem
   * b. collenchyma
   c. phloem
   d. sclerenchyma
   e. parenchyma

E **8.** The substance that strengthens and waterproofs cell walls is
   a. cutin.
   * b. lignin.
   c. pectin.
   d. suberin.
   e. chitin.

M **9.** The gritty stone cells of pears, the hard cells of seed coats, and plant fibers are examples of
   a. xylem.
   b. collenchyma.
   c. phloem.
   * d. sclerenchyma.
   e. parenchyma.

E **10.** Cells that are the main water-conducting cells of a plant are
   a. sclereids.
   * b. xylem tubes.
   c. sieve tubes.
   d. parenchyma.
   e. all of the above

M **11.** The cells that function with the sieve tubes are the
   a. vessels.
   * b. companion cells.
   c. adjunct cells.
   d. sclereids.
   e. periderm.

E **12.** The cell walls of epidermal cells are filled with which of the following to reduce water loss?
   * a. cutin
   b. pectin
   c. lignin
   d. suberin
   e. chitin

E **13.** Gaseous exchange occurs in plants through these structures in the epidermis.
   a. cotyledons
   b. companion cells
   * c. stomata
   d. tracheids
   e. sclereids

E 14. A cotyledon is which of the following?
   a. embryonic root
   b. seed cover
   c. flower part
   * d. seed leaf
   e. fruit

M 15. Which statement is NOT generally true of monocot stems?
   a. They do not undergo secondary growth.
   b. They are not tapered along their length.
   c. Their vascular bundles are scattered throughout the ground tissue.
   * d. Monocot stems have a single central vascular cylinder.
   e. all of the above

## SHOOT PRIMARY STRUCTURE

M 16. Leaf primordia arise
   a. as part of the periderm.
   b. as part of secondary growth.
   * c. at the nodes.
   d. as a result of differentiation of cambium cells.
   e. from the lateral, not the apical, meristem.

E 17. Buds are produced
   a. in the angles where leaves attach to stems.
   b. at the very ends of stems.
   c. at the nodes.
   d. by the apical meristem.
   * e. all of the above

M 18. The stalk that supports the individual dicot leaf is the
   a. vascular bundle.
   * b. petiole.
   c. node.
   d. bundle sheath.
   e. stomata.

E 19. Deciduous plants
   a. are nonvascular.
   b. are evergreen.
   c. shed their leaves as winter approaches.
   d. may retain their dead brown leaves over the winter and shed them only when new leaves emerge.
   * e. both c and d

## A CLOSER LOOK AT LEAVES

E 20. The main photosynthetic area of a leaf is composed of
   * a. mesophyll.
   b. cortex.
   c. xylem.
   d. epidermis.
   e. none of the above

M 21. Photosynthesis takes place in the
   a. stomata.
   b. vascular bundles.
   c. cuticle.
   d. lower and upper epidermis.
   * e. mesophyll tissue.

## ROOT PRIMARY STRUCTURE

E 22. Roots are involved in all the following activities EXCEPT
   a. support.
   b. food storage.
   * c. food production.
   d. anchorage.
   e. absorption and conduction.

M 23. Adventitious roots can be described using any of the following except
   a. arise from stems.
   b. fibrous.
   * c. single.
   d. similar in size.
   e. grasses.

M 24. The carrot
   a. has a taproot system.
   b. uses food stored in the root to produce flowers, fruits, and seeds.
   c. takes two years to complete its life cycle.
   d. does not develop adventitious roots and has very limited lateral roots.
   * e. all of the above

E 25. Mitosis takes place in which region of the root?
   a. zone of maturation
   b. root cap
   c. zone of elongation
   * d. apical meristem region
   e. region of differentiation

M 26. Which gives rise to lateral roots?
   a. endodermis
   b. cortex
   c. epidermis
   * d. pericycle
   e. pith

## WOODY PLANTS

M 27. If all of the phloem were stripped from around a tree in a process known as girdling,
   a. the plant would stop growing.
   b. the vascular cambium would be destroyed so that the plant could no longer grow.
   c. the shoot system would get no moisture or minerals.
   * d. the roots would starve and eventually the plant would die.
   e. there would be no problems unless the tree became infected by insects and fungi.

M 28. Which is part of the lateral meristem?
* a. cork cambium
b. procambium
c. protoderm
d. ground meristem
e. all of the above

M 29. Annual growth rings are formed in woody stems principally through the activities of the
a. pericycle.
b. pith.
* c. vascular cambium.
d. mesophyll.
e. endodermis.

M 30. Secondary xylem is formed in association with the
a. pith.
* b. inner face of vascular cambium.
c. outer face of vascular cambium.
d. inner face of cork cambium.
e. outer face of cork cambium.

M 31. Which provides horizontal transport of material in stems and roots?
* a. ray cells
b. vessels
c. the pericycle
d. the cortex
e. the secondary phloem

M 32. Which environment would be most likely to produce trees without annual rings?
* a. tropical rain forest
b. northern evergreen forest
c. areas with alternating wet and dry seasons
d. temperate-deciduous forests
e. none of the above, because annual rings are characteristic of all trees

M 33. Which tissue will not be crushed or sloughed off by the growing of the stem?
* a. vascular cambium
b. epidermis
c. cortex
d. pith
e. endodermis

M 34. Lateral meristems
a. are groups of dividing cells.
b. are responsible for increases in the width of a stem or root.
c. are called cambium.
d. produce secondary growth only.
* e. all of the above

## Matching Questions

D 35. Choose the one most appropriate answer for each.

1 _____ companion cells
2 _____ cork cambium
3 _____ fusiform initials
4 _____ meristems
5 _____ mesophyll
6 _____ pericycle
7 _____ primordium
8 _____ sclereids
9 _____ sieve tube members
10 _____ vascular bundles
11 _____ xylem vessels
12 _____ collenchyma
13 _____ bark
14 _____ endodermis
15 _____ epidermis
16 _____ parenchyma
17 _____ periderm
18 _____ phloem
19 _____ pith
20 _____ sclerenchyma
21 _____ stoma
22 _____ vascular cambium
23 _____ xylem

A. collection of strands of all types of conducting tissue

B. cells that help sieve tube members

C. a part of the vascular column just inside endodermis; gives rise to lateral roots

D. ground tissue that is "stringy" in consistency

E. living cells that conduct food from photosynthetic source to storage sink

F. tissue providing support; example is hemp fibers

G. gives rise to periderm

H. tissue transporting water and minerals upward

I. unspecialized plant tissue that will form specific organs later

J. outer layer of cells over primary plant body

K. replaces the epidermis in plants that undergo secondary growth

L. openings for air and water vapor movement into/out of leaf

M. produce vascular tissue arranged parallel to stem axis

N. individual dead cells that conduct water

O. tissue transporting food from source to sink

P. the thickest and principal photosynthetic region of the leaf

Q. single layer of cells that controls water movement into xylem

R. regions of high mitotic activity

S. tissue specializing in photosynthesis, storage, secretion

T. cells with thick walls; abundant in shells of nuts and "stones" of fruit

U. ground tissue located centrally within a ring of vascular bundles

V. all living and nonliving tissues between vascular cambium and stem surface

W. develops into secondary xylem and phloem

*Answers:*

| | 1. | B. | 2. | G | 3. | M |
|---|---|---|---|---|---|---|
| 4. | R | 5. | P | 6. | C | 7. | I |
| 8. | T | 9. | E | 10. | A | 11. | N |
| 12. | D | 13. | V | 14. | Q | 15. | J |
| 16. | S | 17. | K | 18. | O | 19. | U |
| 20. | F | 21. | L | 22. | W | 23. | H |

## Classification Questions

Answer questions 36–40 in reference to the five plant tissues listed below:

 a. parenchyma
 b. collenchyma
 c. sclerenchyma
 d. xylem
 e. phloem

M 36. This is a ground tissue of plants which forms hardened cells often found in nut shells.

E 37. This vascular tissue that conducts and distributes food to plant cells.

E 38. This vascular tissue that conducts water and dissolved salts throughout a plant.

D 39. This vascular tissue of a plant composed of dead cells with recesses, pits, open ends.

M 40. This plant tissue involved in photosynthesis and storage.

*Answers:*

| 36. | c | 37. | e | 38. | d |
|---|---|---|---|---|---|
| 39. | d | 40. | a | | |

Answer questions 41-46 in reference to the plant tissues listed below:

 a. vascular cambium
 b. cork cambium
 c. pericycle
 d. ground tissue
 e. dermal tissue

D 41. This tissue gives rise to periderm.

D 42. This tissue gives rise to the protective covering that forms the bark of a tree.

M 43. This tissue makes up the bulk of the plant body.

M 44. This tissue gives rise to secondary phloem and xylem.

M 45. This tissue gives rise to lateral roots.

D 46. This tissue gives rise to the xylem and phloem of an older tree.

*Answers:*

| 41. | b | 42. | b | 43. | d |
|---|---|---|---|---|---|
| 44. | a | 45. | c | 46. | a |

## Selecting the Exception

M 47. Four of the five answers listed below are related by a common region of the plant body. Select the exception.
 a. leaf
 * b. root cap
 c. node
 d. axillary bud
 e. stem

M 48. Four of the five answers listed below are characteristic of monocots. Select the exception.
 a. flower parts in threes or multiples of three
 b. pollen grains have one pore
 c. one cotyledon in seed
 * d. vascular tissue arranged in a ring
 e. veins in leaf are parallel

D 49. Four of the five answers listed below are characteristic of dicots. Select the exception.
 a. secondary growth
 b. net venation
 c. flower parts in fours or fives
 d. two seed leaves
 * e. pollen grains with one pore or furrow

M 50. Four of the five answers listed below are types of ground tissue. Select the exception.
 a. ground tissue
 * b. xylem
 c. sclerenchyma
 d. parenchyma
 e. collenchyma

D 51. Four of the five answers listed below are functions of parenchyma tissue. Select the exception.
* a. support
b. wound healing
c. food storage
d. conduct photosynthesis
e. regeneration of lost parts

D 52. Four of the five answers listed below are characteristic of sclerenchyma cells. Select the exception.
a. sclereid
b. found in seed coats
* c. retain the ability to divide after differentiation
d. gritty texture of pear cells
e. used in manufacture of paper, textiles, and rope

D 53. Four of the five answers listed below are characteristics of xylem. Select the exception.
a. dead at maturity
b. cell walls impregnated with waterproofing substances
* c. conducts dissolved food
d. help support plant body
e. have pits in the walls of the cells

D 54. Four of the five answers listed below are characteristics of phloem. Select the exception.
* a. consists only of cell walls
b. characterized by channels across plant cell walls
c. sieve plates found between some cells
d. include accessory companion cells
e. transports sugar

D 55. Four of the five answers listed below are tissues capable of cell division. Select the exception.
a. cork cambium
b. apical meristem
c. procambium
* d. periderm
e. vascular cambium

M 56. Four of the five answers listed below are limited to the node region. Select the exception.
a. leaf axil
b. node
* c. vascular bundle
d. lateral bud
e. leaf primordia

M 57. Four of the five answers listed below are parts of tissue found in a cross section of root. Select the exception.
a. cortex
* b. pith
c. pericycle
d. endodermis
e. epidermis

M 58. Four of the five answers listed below are related to vascular tissue. Select the exception.
a. conducts water and minerals
b. vascular bundle
c. translocation
d. vein
* e. pith

M 59. Four of the five answers listed below possess chloroplasts. Select the exception.
a. mesophyll cell
* b. epidermal cell
c. sclereid cell
d. palisade cell
e. spongy cell

M 60. Four of the five answers listed below are functions of roots. Select the exception.
a. support
* b. synthesis of food
c. absorption of water and minerals
d. conduction of water and solutes
e. anchorage

M 61. Four of the five answers listed below are related by a similar nature. Select the exception.
a. adventitious
b. tap
c. fibrous
d. lateral
* e. insectivorous

D 62. Four of the five answers listed below are features of the pericycle. Select the exception.
a. outermost tissue in the vascular column
b. origins of branch roots
c. found in the root, but not in stem
* d. site for food storage
e. located inside the endodermis

D 63. Four of the five answers listed below are parts of a leaf. Select the exception.
a. stoma
b. cuticle
c. mesophyll
* d. node
e. petiole

# CHAPTER 23
# PLANT NUTRITION AND TRANSPORT

## Multiple-Choice Questions

### FLIES FOR DINNER

E 1. The concentration of carbon dioxide in the atmosphere approximates how many parts per million?
- a. 3.5
- b. 35
- * c. 350
- d. 3,500
- e. 35,000

E 2. Plants in general require a total of how many essential elements for their growth and survival?
- a. 6
- b. 12
- * c. 16
- d. 22
- e. 28

E 3. Which of the following elements required by plants do NOT come directly from the soil?
- * a. carbon
- b. nitrogen
- c. magnesium
- d. potassium
- e. iron

M 4. Which element is found as a component of amino acids, proteins, nucleic acids, and coenzymes?
- * a. nitrogen
- b. potassium
- c. sulfur
- d. phosphorus
- e. magnesium

M 5. Which element activates enzymes used in protein, starch, or sugar synthesis and helps maintain water–solute balance?
- a. nitrogen
- * b. potassium
- c. sulfur
- d. phosphorus
- e. magnesium

D 6. Which element is a component of two vitamins and most proteins?
- a. nitrogen
- b. potassium
- * c. sulfur
- d. phosphorus
- e. magnesium

D 7. Which element is a component of chlorophyll and activates enzymes used in photosynthesis, respiration, and protein synthesis?
- a. nitrogen
- b. potassium
- c. sulfur
- d. phosphorus
- * e. magnesium

M 8. Chlorosis and leaf droop are caused by a deficiency of
- a. nitrogen.
- b. potassium.
- c. sulfur.
- d. phosphorus.
- * e. magnesium.

E 9. Which is a micronutrient?
- a. sulfur
- b. calcium
- c. phosphorus
- * d. manganese
- e. magnesium

E 10. Chlorotic leaves turn
- * a. yellow.
- b. black.
- c. orange.
- d. red.
- e. transparent.

D 11. A plant will become chlorotic due to a lack of any of the following EXCEPT
- a. nitrogen.
- * b. phosphorus.
- c. magnesium.
- d. manganese.
- e. iron.

E 12. Most of the macronutrients and micronutrients function as
- a. food for plants.
- b. structural components for cells.
- c. elements needed for the development of mycorrhizae.
- * d. enzyme activators.
- e. all of the above

### UPTAKE OF WATER AND NUTRIENTS AT THE ROOTS

E 13. Nodules found on the roots of leguminous plants are involved in supplying which element for the plant?
- a. aluminum
- b. boron
- c. magnesium
- * d. nitrogen
- e. chlorine

E	14.	Mycorrhizae are
	a	roots.
	b.	bacteria.
*	c.	fungus-roots.
	d.	isolated plants.
	e.	small animals found in agricultural soils.

M	15.	Mycorrhizae
	a	increase plant growth.
	b.	are symbionts.
	c.	allow a plant to absorb more water.
	d.	increase the surface area for absorption of water and minerals.
*	e.	all of the above

M	16.	Which statement is false?
	a	Annual grasses have fibrous root systems.
	b.	Most dicots have a large taproot system.
	c.	Mycorrhizae are mutually beneficial to the plants they infect.
*	d.	Roots explore the soil and actively search for water.
	e.	In mycorrhizal infection the fungus absorbs sugar and nitrogen compounds from the host plant.

M	17.	The Casparian strip is associated with the
	a	epidermis.
	b.	vascular tissue.
	c.	cortex.
	d.	root hairs.
*	e.	endodermis.

M	18.	The water and minerals absorbed by the roots usually first enter the
	a	pericycle.
	b.	vascular tissue.
	c.	cortex.
*	d.	root hairs.
	e.	endodermis.

E	19.	The relationships of organisms in root nodules and mycorrhizae can be described as
	a	unfortunate.
	b.	cohesion
*	c.	symbiotic
	d.	parasitic
	e.	exploitive

M	20.	Mineral uptake in plants occurs by way of
	a	leaves.
*	b.	roots.
	c.	stems.
	d.	phloem.
	e.	flowers.

## CONSERVATION OF WATER IN STEMS AND LEAVES

M	21.	Most of the water moving into a leaf is lost through
	a	osmotic gradients.
*	b.	evaporation.
	c.	pressure flow forces.
	d.	translocation.
	e.	all of the above

E	22.	Of all the water moving into a leaf, about what percent is used in photosynthesis, membrane functions, and other activities?
	a	1
*	b.	2
	c.	10
	d.	70
	e.	90

M	23.	Which of the following causes transpiration?
	a	hydrogen bonding
*	b.	the drying power of air
	c.	cohesion
	d.	turgor pressure
	e.	all of the above

E	24.	The waxy covering of the leaf is the
*	a	cuticle.
	b.	epidermis.
	c.	Casparian strip.
	d.	stomata.
	e.	none of the above

E	25.	The openings in leaves that function to exchange gases are called
	a	cuticles.
*	b.	stomata.
	c.	guard cells.
	d.	pits.
	e.	pores.

E	26.	The cells that surround stomata are
	a	endodermal cells.
*	b.	guard cells.
	c.	mesophyll cells.
	d.	vascular bundle cells.
	e.	vessel cells.

E	27.	Carbon dioxide enters most plants
	a	at night.
	b.	when transpiration occurs.
	c.	when the guard cells are turgid.
	d.	when potassium ions leave the guard cells.
*	e.	both b and c

E	28.	The cuticle
	a	conserves water.
	b.	reduces absorption of carbon dioxide by the plant.
	c.	reduces transpiration.
	d.	helps prevent wilting.
*	e.	all of the above

M 29. Guard cells
    a  surround the stoma.
    b.  control the opening to the interior of the leaf.
    c.  become turgid when it becomes light if environmental conditions are not too hot or dry.
    d.  absorb water from surrounding epidermal cells.
*    e.  all of the above are true

M 30. Usually, during the daytime
    a  carbon dioxide accumulates in leaf cells.
    b.  turgor pressure in the guard cell decreases.
*    c.  water and potassium move into the guard cell.
    d.  the guard cells close.
    e.  water is conserved.

M 31. Water uptake depends on
    a  abscisic acid.
    b.  cohesion.
*    c.  the concentration gradient.
    d.  active transport.
    e.  potassium pump.

## A THEORY OF WATER TRANSPORT

M 32. Most of the water that enters the plant
    a  leaves the plant through the root system.
*    b.  is lost through transpiration.
    c.  remains in the plant to form the high concentration of water in plant tissue.
    d.  remains in the plant to function in translocation.
    e.  is used up in cellular metabolism.

M 33. Which theory of water transport states that hydrogen bonding allows water molecules to maintain a continuous fluid column as water is pulled from roots to leaves?
    a  pressure flow
    b.  evaporation
*    c.  cohesion
    d.  abscission
    e.  fusion

E 34. Water inside all of the xylem cells is being pulled upward by
    a  turgor pressure.
*    b.  negative pressures (tensions).
    c.  osmotic gradients.
    d.  pressure flow forces.
    e.  all of the above

M 35. Water moves through a plant because of
    a  transpirational pull.
    b.  the cohesion of water molecules.
    c.  the strength of hydrogen bonds holding water molecules together.
    d.  the replacement of lost water molecules.
*    e.  all of the above

M 36. Water tension in a transpiring plant
    a  is exerted on a continuous column of water throughout the plant.
    b.  is the result of the polar nature of water molecules.
    c.  results in the loss of over 90 percent of the water the plant absorbs.
    d.  will exert a pull on water molecules lower down in the plant's vascular system.
*    e.  all of the above

## DISTRIBUTION OF ORGANIC COMPOUNDS THROUGH THE PLANT

M 37. The most common form of sugar transported to the roots is
    a  glucose.
    b.  fructose.
*    c.  sucrose.
    d.  ribose.
    e.  starch.

E 38. Carbohydrates are stored in plants in the form of
    a  cellulose.
    b.  sucrose.
*    c.  starch.
    d.  fats.
    e.  glucose.

E 39. Movement of soluble organic material through plants is known as
*    a  translocation.
    b.  active transport.
    c.  passive transport.
    d.  transpiration.
    e.  none of the above

E 40. Sugars are carried throughout the plant in which tissue?
    a  cortex
    b.  parenchyma
    c.  xylem
*    d.  phloem
    e.  cambium

E 41. Insects used to study the process of translocation in plants are the
*    a  aphids.
    b.  fruit flies.
    c.  cockroaches.
    d.  termites.
    e.  grasshoppers.

D 42. The fluid in the phloem
    a  is under negative pressure.
    b.  moves by active transport.
*    c.  is under pressure equivalent to the air in a tire or greater.
    d.  is responsible for the transpiration pull of material from roots.
    e.  is chiefly water with dissolved minerals.

M 43. A car parked under a tree that gets spattered by sticky droplets has been covered by
   a. water and minerals that have been exuded from the tips of leaves.
  * b. droplets of honeydew that have been forced out of aphids.
   c. feces from herbivorous insects.
   d. material released from mistletoe in the upper limbs.
   e. drops of water produced by transpiration.

E 44. The movement of materials already in the phloem is described as
   a. source-to-sink.
   b. pressure flow.
   c. cohesion.
   d. active transport.
  * e. both a and b

M 45. The source region in the pressure flow explanation of phloem transport is most often the
   a. root.
   b. flower.
   c. stem.
  * d. leaf.
   e. soil.

M 46. The sink region in the pressure flow explanation of phloem transport could be
   a. growing leaves.
   b. seeds.
   c. fruits.
   d. roots.
  * e. all of the above

M 47. Large pressure gradients arise in sieve tube systems by means of
   a. vernalization.
   b. abscission.
  * c. osmosis.
   d. transpiration.
   e. all of the above

## Matching Questions

D 48. Choose the one most appropriate letter for each.
1 _____ companion cells
2 _____ legumes
3 _____ mycorrhiza
4 _____ nodules
5 _____ sieve tube members
6 _____ stylet
7 _____ tracheids and vessels
8 _____ translocation
9 _____ transpiration

A. mouthpart of an aphid

B. pipelines of the xylem

C. a mutually beneficial association between a fungus and a young root

D. structures on roots that house nitrogen-fixing bacteria

E. pipelines of the phloem

F. evaporation from stems and leaves

G. actively transport sucrose into sieve tube members

H. dicot plants that tend to establish symbiotic relationships with nitrogen-fixing bacteria

I. transport of organic molecules from source region to sink

*Answers:*
| 1. G | 2. H | 3. C |
| 4. D | 5. E | 6. A |
| 7. B | 8. I | 9. F |

## Classification Questions

Answer questions 49–53 in reference to the five plant macronutrients listed below:
   a. nitrogen
   b. potassium
   c. calcium
   d. magnesium
   e. phosphorus

M 49. This nutrient helps to maintain turgor pressure.

E 50. This nutrient is an extremely important part of ATP.

M 51. This nutrient is an important part of the backbone structure of DNA.

D 52. This nutrient helps to cement cell walls together.

M 53. This nutrient is essential to formation of chlorophyll and acts as a cofactor for many enzymes.

*Answers:*
| 49. b | 50. e | 51. e |
| 52. c | 53. d | |

Answer questions 54-58 in reference to the five plant micronutrients listed below:

    a. iron
    b. boron
    c. manganese
    d. zinc
    e. copper

D    **54.** This nutrient is used in synthesis of auxins.

M    **55.** This nutrient plays an important role in flowering and germination.

M    **56.** This nutrient is a cofactor in enzymes involved in carbohydrate metabolism.

E    **57.** This nutrient is an essential component of proteins involved in electron transport.

D    **58.** This nutrient plays an important role in the movement of plant hormones.

*Answers*:
| 54. d | 55. b | 56. e |
|-------|-------|-------|
| 57. a | 58. b | |

## Selecting the Exception

M    **59.** Four of the five answers listed below are macronutrients. Select the exception.
   *   a. manganese
      b. potassium
      c. calcium
      d. magnesium
      e. phosphorus

M    **60.** Four of the five answers listed below are micronutrients. Select the exception.
      a. molybdenum
      b. copper
   *   c. nitrogen
      d. iron
      e. chlorine

M    **61.** Four of the five answers listed below are related by a common chemical nature. Select the exception.
      a. protein
   *   b. calcium carbonate
      c. carbohydrate
      d. lipid
      e. nucleic acid

D    **62.** Four of the five answers listed below are elements whose deficiency symptoms include chlorosis. Select the exception.
   *   a. phosphorus
      b. iron
      c. chlorine
      d. copper
      e. magnesium

M    **63.** Four of the five answers listed below are related by their participation in water movement through plants. Select the exception.
      a. hydrogen bonds
      b. transpiration
      c. cohesion
      d. tension in xylem
   *   e. photosynthesis

D    **64.** Four of the five answers listed below are associated with transpiration. Select the exception.
      a. potassium ions pumped into guard cells
      b. water pressure builds up in guard cells
      c. photosynthesis occurs in guard cells
      d. carbon dioxide enters leaf
   *   e. presence of cuticle

M    **65.** Four of the five answers listed below are actions that cause stomata to open. Select the exception.
   *   a. sunlight decreases
      b. potassium ions build up guard cells
      c. water moves from epidermal cells to guard cells
      d. turgor pressure increases in guard cells
      e. guard cells carry on photosynthesis

M    **66.** Four of the five answers listed below are sinks for solute deposition. Select the exception.
      a. fruits
      b. roots
   *   c. flower blossoms
      d. seeds
      e. rapidly growing tissue

# CHAPTER 24

# PLANT REPRODUCTION AND DEVELOPMENT

## Multiple-Choice Questions

### A COEVOLUTIONARY TALE

M    **1.** The first seed-bearing plants were produced in the Devonian, about how many million years ago?
- a. 50
- b. 150
- c. 250
- * d. 390
- e. 450

M    **2.** Ovules and pollen sacs first arose on the surface of scales that were
- a. stems.
- b. leaves.
- c. flowers.
- d. found in cones.
- * e. both b and d, but not a or c

M    **3.** The evolution of flowers and insects is an example of
- a. parallel evolution.
- b. regressive evolution.
- * c. coevolution.
- d. convergent evolution.
- e. divergent evolution.

E    **4.** Insects are attracted to flowers by
- a. nectaries.
- b. specific colors.
- c. specific color patterns.
- d. floral odors.
- * e. all of the above

E    **5.** Bees use what wavelength to see patterns in flowers that humans cannot see?
- a. infrared light
- b. visible light
- * c. ultraviolet light
- d. gamma radiation
- e. X-rays

E    **6.** Which color are most insects unable to see?
- a. yellow
- b. blue
- * c. red
- d. green
- e. orange

M    **7.** Foul-smelling flowers may be pollinated by
- a. birds.
- * b. beetles and flies.
- c. bees and bumblebees.
- d. wasps.
- e. bugs and butterflies.

M    **8.** Bees will NOT visit flowers of what color?
- * a. red
- b. blue
- c. yellow
- d. purple
- e. white

### REPRODUCTIVE STRUCTURES OF FLOWERING PLANTS

E    **9.** Which statement is false?
- a. Flowers are reproductive shoots.
- * b. Trees are gametophytes.
- c. Sporophyte plants reproduce asexually.
- d. Cells produced by mitosis are clones.
- e. Gametophytes are haploid.

M    **10.** The least specialized part of the flower is a
- a. carpel.
- b. stamen.
- c. petal.
- * d. sepal.
- e. pistil.

E    **11.** Which of the following develops into seed?
- a. flower
- b. ovary
- c. carpel
- * d. ovule
- e. pistil

E    **12.** The male part of a flower is the
- a. carpel.
- * b. stamen.
- c. petal.
- d. sepal.
- e. pistil.

E    **13.** The male part of a flower includes the
- a. carpel.
- b. stigma.
- c. filament.
- d. anther.
- * e. both c and d, but not a or b

E    **14.** The various flower parts are attached to the
- a. style.
- * b. receptacle.
- c. stigma.
- d. filament.
- e. sepal.

E    **15.** Stamens contain
- a. petals.
- b. sepals.
- c. stigmas.
- d. ovules.
- * e. anthers.

E　　16.　A stamen is
　　　　　　a　composed of a stigma, a style, and an ovary.
　　　　　　b.　the mature male gametophyte.
　　*　　c.　the site where microspores are produced.
　　　　　　d.　part of the vegetative phase of an
　　　　　　　　angiosperm.
　　　　　　e.　none of the above

E　　17.　The corolla is made up of
　　　　　　a　sepals.
　　*　　b.　petals.
　　　　　　c.　pistils.
　　　　　　d.　pollen grains.
　　　　　　e.　anthers.

M　　18.　Which forms the outermost whorl of flower
　　　　　parts?
　　*　　a　sepals
　　　　　　b.　petals
　　　　　　c.　anthers
　　　　　　d.　pistils
　　　　　　e.　stamens

## A NEW GENERATION BEGINS

E　　19.　The process during which the diploid set of
　　　　　chromosomes become haploid is
　　　　　　a　metastasis.
　　　　　　b.　fertilization.
　　　　　　c.　cleavage.
　　*　　d.　meiosis.
　　　　　　e.　none of the above

E　　20.　Which of the following are produced within the
　　　　　anthers?
　　　　　　a　ovules
　　　　　　b.　stamens
　　*　　c.　microspores
　　　　　　d.　female gametophytes
　　　　　　e.　none of the above

M　　21.　The protective layers covering the ovule are the
　　　　　　a　nucellus.
　　　　　　b.　endosperm.
　　*　　c.　integuments.
　　　　　　d.　micropyle.
　　　　　　e.　embryo sac.

M　　22.　Megaspores
　　　　　　a　are haploid.
　　　　　　b.　are found in the embryo sac.
　　　　　　c.　will develop into the gametophyte.
　　　　　　d.　are female rather than male.
　　*　　e.　all of the above

D　　23.　The megaspore eventually divides into how
　　　　　many cells to form the embryo sac prior to
　　　　　fertilization?
　　　　　　a　3
　　　　　　b.　4
　　*　　c.　7
　　　　　　d.　8
　　　　　　e.　16

E　　24.　The female gametophyte is the
　　　　　　a　nucellus.
　　　　　　b.　ovule.
　　*　　c.　embryo sac.
　　　　　　d.　endosperm.
　　　　　　e.　ovary.

E　　25.　The egg is
　　　　　　a　diploid.
　　　　　　b.　tetraploid.
　　　　　　c.　polyploid.
　　　　　　d.　triploid.
　　*　　e.　haploid.

E　　26.　The primary function of the endosperm is
　　　　　　a　protection.
　　　　　　b.　reproduction.
　　　　　　c.　growth.
　　*　　d.　nutrition.
　　　　　　e.　water absorption.

E　　27.　Pollination occurs on the
　　　　　　a　micropyle.
　　*　　b.　stigma.
　　　　　　c.　style.
　　　　　　d.　anther.
　　　　　　e.　embryo sac.

D　　28.　In flowering plants one sperm nucleus fuses with
　　　　　that of an egg and a zygote forms that develops
　　　　　into an embryo. Another sperm nucleus
　　　　　　a　fuses with a primary endosperm cell to
　　　　　　　　produce three cells, each with one nucleus.
　　　　　　b.　fuses with a primary endosperm cell to
　　　　　　　　produce one cell with one triploid nucleus.
　　*　　c.　fuses with the diploid endosperm mother
　　　　　　　　cell, forming a primary endosperm cell with
　　　　　　　　a single triploid nucleus.
　　　　　　d.　fuses with one of the smaller megaspores to
　　　　　　　　produce what will eventually become the
　　　　　　　　seed coat.
　　　　　　e.　none of the above

E　　29.　The pollen tube grows to or through which of the
　　　　　following?
　　　　　　a　stigma
　　　　　　b.　style
　　　　　　c.　ovary
　　　　　　d.　micropyle
　　*　　e.　all of the above

E　　30.　The endosperm is
　　　　　　a　diploid.
　　　　　　b.　tetraploid.
　　　　　　c.　polyploid.
　　*　　d.　triploid.
　　　　　　e.　haploid.

E　　31.　The zygote is
　　*　　a　diploid.
　　　　　　b.　tetraploid.
　　　　　　c.　polyploid.
　　　　　　d.　triploid.
　　　　　　e.　haploid.

## FROM ZYGOTE TO SEED

M  32. Wind-pollinated plants
    a  include grasses.
    b.  include deciduous trees.
    c.  are usually found in dry, windy areas.
    d.  do not have large, showy flowers and may not even have petals.
  * e.  all of the above

E  33. The seed is produced by the development of the
    a  embryo.
  * b.  ovule.
    c.  ovary.
    d.  zygote.
    e.  pollen.

M  34. The seed coat forms from the
    a  zygote.
    b.  cotyledon.
    c.  nucellus.
  * d.  integuments.
    e.  micropyle.

M  35. What kind of fruit is formed from carpels of several associated flowers?
    a  aggregate
    b.  simple
  * c.  multiple
    d.  fleshy
    e.  dry

E  36. Fruit is produced from the development of the
    a  zygote.
    b.  ovule.
    c.  flowers.
    d.  cotyledon.
  * e.  ovary.

E  37. A seed leaf is which of the following?
    a  embryo
    b.  coleoptile
    c.  endosperm
  * d.  cotyledon
    e.  suspensor

M  38. Each of the following is a simple fruit EXCEPT
    a  pea.
    b.  maple.
  * c.  strawberry.
    d.  wheat.
    e.  sunflower.

M  39. The seeds of fleshy fruits are most likely to be spread by
  * a  animals.
    b.  water.
    c.  wind.
    d.  explosion.
    e.  insects.

## ASEXUAL REPRODUCTION OF FLOWERING PLANTS

E  40. Strawberries reproduce by
  * a  runners.
    b.  corms.
    c.  bulbs.
    d.  tubers.
    e.  rhizomes.

M  41. Which is NOT primarily related to asexual reproduction?
    a  rhizomes
  * b.  pollination
    c.  runner formation
    d.  cloning and tissue culture
    e.  all of the above

E  42. Grasses reproduce by
    a  runners.
    b.  corms.
    c.  bulbs.
    d.  tubers.
  * e.  rhizomes.

## PATTERNS OF GROWTH AND DEVELOPMENT

M  43. The most critical factor affecting seed germination is
    a  increasing day length.
    b.  oxygen availability.
  * c.  water absorption.
    d.  warmth.
    e.  none is most critical; all are equal.

E  44. The signaling chemicals produced by one group of cells that affect distant target cells are called
    a  secretions.
  * b.  hormones.
    c.  steroids.
    d.  polymers.
    e.  enzymes.

E  45. The resumption of growth after a period of arrested embryonic development is
    a  senescence.
  * b.  germination.
    c.  imbibition.
    d.  parthenogenesis.
    e.  thigmotropism.

## PLANT HORMONES

M  46. Synthetic auxins are used as
    a  pesticides.
  * b.  herbicides.
    c.  fungicides.
    d.  insecticides.
    e.  all of the above

M 47. 2,4-D, a potent dicot weed killer, is a synthetic
  * a auxin.
    b. gibberellin.
    c. cytokinin.
    d. phytochrome.
    e. none of the above

M 48. The most common synthetic "hormone" is
    a 3,7-C.
  * b. 2,4-D.
    c. 1,5-K.
    d. 3,6-T.
    e. 1,4-X.

M 49. The plant hormone that is gaseous is
    a. auxin.
    b. gibberellin.
    c. cytokinin.
    d. florigen.
  * e. ethylene.

M 50. The plant hormone that promotes cell division is
    a. auxin.
    b. gibberellin.
  * c. cytokinin.
    d. florigen.
    e. ethylene.

M 51. The plant hormone that promotes fruit ripening is
    a. auxin.
    b. gibberellin.
    c. cytokinin.
    d. florigen.
  * e. ethylene.

D 52. A plant hormone whose existence is conjectured but that has NOT been isolated or identified is
    a. auxin.
    b. gibberellin.
    c. cytokinin.
  * d. florigen.
    e. ethylene.

M 53. The plant hormone that promotes dormancy in plants and seeds is
  * a. abscisic acid.
    b. auxin.
    c. gibberellin acid.
    d. ethylene.
    e. none of the above

M 54. The plant hormone thought to be involved with tropism is
    a. abscisic acid.
  * b. auxin.
    c. gibberellin acid.
    d. ethylene.
    e. none of the above

M 55. The function of a coleoptile is
    a. food production.
    b. food storage.
  * c. protection.
    d. translocation.
    e. absorption of water and minerals.

M 56. Studies on the growth of coleoptiles involve
    a. florigen.
    b. ethylene.
  * c. auxin.
    d. abscisic acid.
    e. gibberellin.

## ADJUSTMENTS IN THE RATE AND DIRECTION OF GROWTH

M 57. What is the principal substance that causes phototropism in stems or leaves?
  * a. auxin
    b. gibberellin acid
    c. abscisic acid
    d. ethylene
    e. all of the above

M 58. The primary root of a seedling grows down
    a. to avoid light.
    b. in response to gravity.
    c. because the cells on the top of the root grow faster than those on the bottom of the root.
    d. in response to different concentrations of auxin.
  * e. all except a

M 59. Which substance is involved in thigmotropism?
  * a. auxin
    b. gibberellin acid
    c. abscisic acid
    d. florigen
    e. none of the above

## BIOLOGICAL CLOCKS AND THEIR EFFECTS

M 60. Which of the following is NOT promoted by the active form of phytochrome?
    a. seed germination
  * b. root growth
    c. leaf expansion
    d. stem branching
    e. flower formation

D 61. Compared with young trees growing out in the open, young trees growing in a darker forest understory tend to have longer, thinner trunks with less branching; this developmental pattern is principally caused by
    a. phototropism.
    b. thigmotropism.
  * c. activated phytochrome being converted to inactive phytochrome.
    d. inactive phytochrome being converted to active phytochrome.
    e. none of the above

M 62. The pigment responsible for photoperiodism is
a chlorophyll.
b. xanthophyll.
c. anthocyanin.
* d. phytochrome.
e. photoerythrin.

E 63. Rhythms that are repeated every 24 hours are collectively and specifically known as
a sleep movements.
b. tropisms.
c. biorhythms.
* d. circadian rhythms.
e. the biological clock.

M 64. The active form of phytochrome is known as
a Pp.
b. Pr.
* c. Pfr.
d. Pl.
e. Pst.

M 65. Active phytochrome controls
a flowering and seed set.
b. seed germination.
c. stem branching and elongation.
d. expansion of leaves.
* e. all of the above

M 66. The value of a plant's sleep movements is possibly that they
a block moonlight from the lower leaves.
b. reduce the amount of heat lost from the plant at night.
c. allow heat transfer between leaves.
d. speed the process of translocation between plant parts.
* e. a and b, but not c and d

M 67. Phytochrome is converted from the inactive to the active form by being exposed to light of what color?
a far red
* b. red
c. yellow
d. white
e. blue

E 68. In the dark, plants cannot
a grow.
b. respire.
c. move.
* d. form chlorophyll.
e. form carotenoid pigment.

M 69. Day-neutral plants are
a short-day plants.
* b. able to bloom when they are old enough.
c. night-blooming plants.
d. triggered to bloom by cold weather.
e. none of the above

M 70. Which statement is true?
* a Long-day plants will never bloom in the tropics.
b. Short-day plants bloom around noon.
c. Short-day plants bloom in midsummer.
d. Cocklebur is an example of a long-day plant.
e. The flowering of day-neutral plants is controlled by the duration of darkness, not the duration of light.

M 71. Short-day plants
a flower in late summer.
b. will not bloom until they have been exposed to a dark period longer than a critical length.
c. flower in the fall.
d. will not bloom if their dark period is interrupted by two to five minutes of light.
* e. all of the above

M 72. "Day-neutral plants
a only grow at night.
b. require equal periods of light and darkness.
* c. flower when mature.
d. require shady areas to grow.

## LIFE CYCLES END, AND TURN AGAIN.

E 73. All the processes that lead to the death of a plant or any of its organs are called
a dormancy.
b. vernalization.
c. abscission.
* d. senescence.
e. none of the above

E 74. The aging of a plant is known as
* a senescence.
b. vernalization.
c. abscission.
d. dormancy.
e. chlorosis.

M 75. Senescence may be counteracted by
a auxins.
b. abscisic acid.
* c. cytokinin.
d. gibberellin acid.
e. florigen.

# Matching Questions

D    **76.**   Matching I. Choose the one most appropriate answer for each.

1 _____ aggregate fruit

2 _____ anther

3 _____ carpel

4 _____ embryo sac

5 _____ endosperm mother cell

6 _____ megaspores

7 _____ micropyle

8 _____ microspores

9 _____ multiple fruit

10 _____ ovary

11 _____ ovule

12 _____ petal

13 _____ pollen grain

14 _____ sepal

15 _____ stigma

A.   meiospores of anthers

B.   site where pollen tube usually penetrates the ovule

C.   after fertilization ripens into fruit tissue

D.   a 2$n$ cell that will help form nutrients for the developing plant embryo

E.   cluster of matured ovaries attached to a common receptacle

F.   modified leaves with pigments and fragrance-producing cells

G.   immature male gametophyte

H.   female reproductive organ

I.   landing platform for pollen

J.   pollen-bearing structure

K.   meiospores of ovule

L.   outermost whorl of leaf parts on a receptacle; generally green, but sometimes pigmented

M.   female gametophyte

N.   matured ovaries of several flowers fused together into a single mass (for example, pineapple, fig)

O.   after fertilization will form a seed

*Answers:*

| 1. E | 2. J | 3. H |
|------|------|------|
| 4. M | 5. D | 6. K |
| 7. B | 8. A | 9. N |
| 10. C | 11. O | 12. F |
| 13. G | 14. L | 15. I |

D    **77.**   Matching II. Choose the one most appropriate answer for each.

1 _____ abscisic acid

2 _____ annual

3 _____ biennial

4 _____ coleoptile

5 _____ ethylene

6 _____ florigen

7 _____ gibberellin acid

8 _____ phytochrome

9 _____ short-day plant

10 _____ target cell

11 _____ long-day plant

A.   has receptor sites for a particular hormonal message

B.   a hollow, cylindrical organ that protects young leaves growing within it

C.   blue-green pigment that absorbs light energy

D.   stimulates stomata closure and might trigger seed and bud dormancy

E.   stimulates fruit ripening

F.   reproduce in spring

G.   produces only roots, stems, and leaves the first growing season and produces flowers the second year

H.   flowers in autumn

I.   possible hormone that controls flowering

J.   lives for only one growing season

K.   promotes stem elongation in dwarf plants

*Answers:*

| 1. D | 2. J | 3. G |
|------|------|------|
| 4. B | 5. E | 6. I |
| 7. K | 8. C | 9. H |
| 10. A | 11. F | |

## Classification Questions

Answer questions 78–82 in reference to the five flower parts listed below:

    a   anther
    b.  stigma
    c.  ovule
    d.  ovary
    e.  stamen

E    **78.** During fertilization of a flowering plant, the male gamete first adheres to this structure.

M    **79.** A pollen tube ultimately grows into this structure.

M    **80.** Fertilization of a flowering plant occurs inside this structure.

E    **81.** This structure produces pollen.

M    **82.** Male gametogenesis occurs in this structure.

*Answers:*

| 78. | b | 79. | c | 80. | c |
|-----|---|-----|---|-----|---|
| 81. | a | 82. | a | | |

Answer questions 83–87 in reference to the five flower parts listed below:

    a   megaspore
    b.  microspore mother cell
    c.  ovule
    d.  ovary
    e.  seed

M    **83.** This structure gives rise to the female gametophyte.

E    **84.** This structure is female and haploid.

M    **85.** This structure gives rise to haploid pollen grains.

D    **86.** The egg is ultimately derived from this structure.

M    **87.** During early development the plant embryo is most intimately associated with this structure.

*Answers:*

| 83. | a | 84. | a | 85. | b |
|-----|---|-----|---|-----|---|
| 86. | a | 87. | c | | |

Answer questions 88–92 in reference to the five plant hormones listed below:

    a   auxins
    b.  gibberellins
    c.  cytokinins
    d.  abscisic acid
    e.  ethylene

M    **88.** These hormones are most closely associated with cell division.

M    **89.** These hormones are involved in stem elongation and closely related chemically to certain weed killers like 2,4-D.

D    **90.** This hormone controls rate of transpiration.

E    **91.** This hormone is a gas that promotes ripening.

M    **92.** This hormone promotes bud and seed dormancy.

*Answers:*

| 88. | c | 89. | a | 90. | d |
|-----|---|-----|---|-----|---|
| 91. | e | 92. | d | | |

## Selecting the Exception

E    **93.** Four of the five answers listed below are related by gender. Select the exception.
    a   carpel
    b.  ovary
*   c.  stamen
    d.  style
    e.  stigma

M    **94.** Four of the five answers listed below are types of flower whorls. Select the exception.
*   a   receptacle
    b.  stamen
    c.  carpel
    d.  petal
    e.  sepal

E    **95.** Four of the five answers listed below are haploid. Select the exception.
    a   gametophyte
*   b.  zygote
    c.  sperm
    d.  microspore
    e.  gamete

E    **96.** Four of the five answers listed below are nonreproductive parts of a flower. Select the exception.
    a   receptacle
*   b.  anther
    c.  corolla
    d.  petal
    e.  sepal

M    **97.** Four of the five answers listed below are related by a common gender. Select the exception.
    a   micropyle
    b.  integument
    c.  embryo sac
*   d.  microspore
    e.  egg

E  **98.** Four of the five answers listed below are the results of fertilization. Select the exception.
   a  fruit
   b.  seed
   c.  embryo
 * d.  pollen
   e.  endosperm

E  **99.** Four of the five answers listed below are useful to flowers as means to attract vectors. Select the exception.
   a  nectar
   b.  flower color
   c.  color patterns
   d.  pollen
 * e.  wind

M  **100.** Four of the five answers listed below are parts of a seed. Select the exception.
 * a  ovary
   b.  cotyledon
   c.  meristem
   d.  coleoptile
   e.  endosperm

M  **101.** Four of the five answers listed below are defined as simple fruits. Select the exception.
 * a  pineapple
   b.  maple
   c.  pea
   d.  lemon
   e.  banana

E  **102.** Four of the five answers listed below are adaptations to aid in dispersal of fruit. Select the exception.
   a  hooks
   b.  spines
 * c.  smooth surface
   d.  hairs
   e.  sticky substances

D  **103.** Three of the four answers listed below are effects caused by auxin. Select the exception.
   a  used as herbicide
 * b.  promotes cell division
   c.  promotes cell elongation
   d.  functions in tropism

D  **104.** Three of the four answers listed below are effects caused by gibberellin. Select the exception.
   a  breaks dormancy in seeds in buds
   b.  causes stem elongation
 * c.  triggers flower production
   d.  overcomes genetic dwarfing

M  **105.** Four of the five answers listed below are characteristics of ethylene. Select the exception.
   a  triggers dropping of leaves and fruits
   b.  promotes fruit ripening
 * c.  triggers cell division
   d.  a gas
   e.  effects observed by ancient Chinese

M  **106.** Four of the five answers listed below are stimulators that evoke plant tropisms. Select the exception.
   a  gravity
   b.  touch
   c.  mechanical stress
   d.  light
 * e.  electrical current

M  **107.** Four of the five answers listed below are flower responses that follow 24-hour cycles. Select the exception.
   a  sleep movements
   b.  flowers open in the morning
   c.  circadian rhythm
 * d.  photoperiodism
   e.  flowers close at night

M  **108.** Four of the five answers listed below are plant activities affected by phytochrome. Select the exception.
 * a  tropism
   b.  stem elongation
   c.  seed germination
   d.  leaf expansion
   e.  formation of flowers, fruits, and seeds

# CHAPTER 25
# TISSUES, ORGAN SYSTEMS, AND HOMEOSTASIS

## Multiple-Choice Questions

### EPITHELIAL TISSUE

E    1.  Chemical and structural bridges link groups or
         layers of like cells, uniting them in structure and
         function as a cohesive
         a   organ.
         b.  organ system.
      *  c   tissue.
         d.  cuticle.

E    2.  The tissue that lines internal surfaces of the body
         is
      *  a   epithelial.
         b.  loose connective.
         c   supportive connective.
         d.  fibrous.
         e.  adipose.

M    3.  Epithelial cells are specialized for all the
         following functions EXCEPT
         a   secretion.
         b.  protection.
         c   filtration.
      *  d.  contraction.
         e.  absorption.

D    4.  Adhering and gap junctions are found at the
         a   endoplasmic reticulum.
         b.  nuclear membrane.
      *  c   plasma membrane.
         d.  Golgi apparatus.
         e.  ribosomes.

M    5.  Which junction influences the passage of ions
         and small molecules between cells?
      *  a   gap
         b.  adhering
         c   loose
         d.  tight
         e.  plasma

E    6.  The secretion of tears, milk, sweat, and oil are
         functions of what tissue?
      *  a   epithelial
         b.  loose connective
         c   lymphoid
         d.  nervous
         e.  adipose

M    7.  Which epithelial cell is modified for diffusion?
         a   cuboidal
      *  b.  simple squamous
         c   simple columnar
         d.  stratified squamous
         e.  stratified columnar

M    8.  The type of epithelial cell found in the lining of
         the stomach, intestinal tract, and part of the
         respiratory tract is
         a   simple cuboidal.
         b.  simple squamous.
      *  c   simple columnar.
         d.  stratified.
         e.  stratified columnar.

E    9.  Exocrine glands secrete
         a   enzymes.
         b.  sweat.
         c   milk.
         d.  saliva.
      *  e.  all of the above

### CONNECTIVE TISSUE

M    10. Which of the following is NOT included in
         connective tissues?
         a   bone
      *  b.  skeletal muscle
         c   cartilage
         d.  collagen
         e.  blood

E    11. What type of tissue is blood?
         a   epithelial
         b.  muscular
      *  c   connective
         d.  adipose
         e.  noncellular fluid

M    12. An extracellular ground substance is
         characteristic of
         a   muscle tissue.
         b.  epithelial tissue.
      *  c   connective tissue.
         d.  nervous tissue.
         e.  embryonic tissue.

M    13. Connective tissues include all the following
         EXCEPT
         a   cartilage.
         b.  blood.
         c   bone.
         d.  fat.
      *  e.  outer layer of skin.

E    14. Dense fibrous tissues that connect muscle to
         bone are called
         a   muscles.
         b.  cartilage.
         c   ligaments.
      *  d.  tendons.
         e.  all of the above

M 15. Collagen fibers are characteristic of which tissue?
   a muscle
   b. epithelial
* c. connective
   d. nervous
   e. embryonic

M 16. Tendons connect
   a bones to bones.
   b. bones to ligaments.
* c. muscles to bones.
   d. bones to cartilage.
   e. all of the above

M 17. Bones are linked together at skeletal joints by
   a. tendons.
   b. intercellular junctions.
* c. ligaments.
   d. cartilage.
   e. collagen.

E 18. Cartilage is found
   a. in the nose.
   b. at the ends of bones.
   c. in the external ear.
   d. between vertebrae.
* e. all of the above

E 19. Adipose tissue cells are filled with
   a. minerals.
* b. fat.
   c. cartilage.
   d. fibers.
   e. muscles.

## MUSCLE TISSUE

M 20. If its cells are striated and fused at the ends so that the cells contract as a unit, the tissue is
   a. smooth muscle.
   b. dense fibrous connective.
   c. supportive connective.
* d. cardiac muscle.
   e. none of the above

E 21. Muscle that is NOT striped and is involuntary is
   a. cardiac.
   b. skeletal.
   c. striated.
* d. smooth.
   e. both a and d, but not b or c

E 22. Cardiac muscle cells are
   a. involuntary.
   b. voluntary.
   c. striated.
   d. slow contracting.
* e. both a and c

E 23. Smooth muscles are
   a striated and voluntary.
   b. isolated, spindle-shaped cells.
   c. found in the walls of hollow structures such as blood vessels and the stomach.
   d. involuntary and nonstriated.
* e. all except a

## NERVOUS TISSUE

E 24. Rapid communication throughout the body is accomplished by
* a. neurons.
   b. blood.
   c. hormones.
   d. muscles.
   e. connective tissue.

## ORGAN SYSTEMS

E 25. Chemical and structural bridges link groups or layers of like cells, uniting them in structure and function as a cohesive
   a. organ.
   b. organ system.
* c. tissue.
   d. cuticle.

E 26. Which of the following represents the correct hierarchy of organization in the human body?
   a cells —> tissues —> organ systems —> organs
* b. cells —> tissues —> organs —> organ systems
   c. tissues —> cells —> organs —> organsystems
   d. tissues —> organs —> cells —> organsystems

D 27. A cell in the pancreas is unaffected by which of the following features of muscle or bone tissue?
   a. Contraction of muscle cells aids in circulation of blood and lymph.
   b. Bone tissue serves as a reservoir for certain minerals such as calcium and potassium.
   c. Muscle contraction during a reflex action helps to avoid a falling piano.
   d. Bone tissue through hemopoesis results in blood cell production.
* e. None of the above, because all directly or indirectly affect any given cell in the pancreas.

M 28. Of the following organs, which is NOT in the abdominal cavity?
   a. stomach
   b. liver
* c. heart
   d. intestine
   e. pancreas

E    29. What we usually call the "back" of the human
         body is really the
         a    anterior.
     *   b.   posterior.
         c.   inferior.
         d.   superior.

E    30. Muscle cells are produced by
         a    the ectoderm.
         b.   the endoderm.
     *   c.   the mesoderm.
         d.   the ectoderm and endoderm.
         e.   all of the germ layers.

E    31. The lining of the intestinal tract is produced by
         a    the ectoderm.
     *   b.   the endoderm.
         c.   the mesoderm.
         d.   the endoderm and mesoderm.
         e.   all of the germ layers.

E    32. The nervous system is produced by
     *   a    the ectoderm.
         b.   the endoderm.
         c.   the mesoderm.
         d.   the endoderm and ectoderm.
         e.   all of the germ layers.

E    33. The external covering of the body is produced by
     *   a    the ectoderm.
         b.   the endoderm.
         c.   the mesoderm.
         d.   the ectoderm and mesoderm.
         e.   all of the germ layers.

M    34. Somatic cells can form all but which of the
         following?
     *   a    gametes
         b.   epithelia
         c.   muscles
         d.   digestive organs
         e.   Somatic cells form all of the above.

E    35. The endocrine system functions in
         a    conduction.
         b.   contraction.
     *   c.   hormonal control of body functioning.
         d.   protection against disease.
         e.   cell production.

E    36. Maintaining the volume and composition of body
         fluids is the direct responsibility of
         which system?
         a    integumentary
         b.   immune
         c.   digestive
     *   d.   urinary
         e.   circulatory

M    37. Which system is involved with body movement?
         a    endocrine system
         b.   nervous system
     *   c.   muscular system
         d.   respiratory system
         e.   skeletal system

E    38. Integration of body functions is controlled by the
         a    respiratory system.
         b.   nervous system.
         c.   endocrine system.
         d.   defense system.
     *   e.   both b and c, but not a and d

M    39. Which system produces blood cells?
         a    endocrine
     *   b.   skeletal
         c.   muscular
         d.   defense
         e.   integumentary

## HOMEOSTASIS AND SYSTEMS CONTROL

M    40. Extracellular fluid would NOT include
         a    plasma.
         b.   blood.
         c.   interstitial fluid.
     *   d.   cytoplasm.
         e.   any of the above

D    41. When nutrients are supplied to a cell, the last
         fluid through which they must pass before
         encountering the plasma membrane is the
         a    plasma.
     *   b.   interstitial fluid.
         c.   blood.
         d.   intracellular fluid.
         e.   cerebrospinal fluid.

E    42. Which of the following is most directly
         associated with a stimulus?
         a    integrators
     *   b.   receptors
         c.   effectors
         d.   central nervous system
         e.   all of the above

M    43. Which are examples of integrators?
     *   a    brain, spinal cord
         b.   muscles, glands
         c.   sensory cells in eye, tongue, and ear
         d.   bones
         e.   none of the above

E    44. The control of the temperature of the body is an
         example of which of the following?
         a    homeostatic mechanism
         b.   positive feedback system
         c.   endocrine function
         d.   negative feedback system
     *   e.   both a and d, but not b or c

M    **45.** Which is the correct sequence involved in the regulation of organ systems?

     a   stimulus, receptor, integrator, response, effector

     b.   stimulus, response, integrator, receptor, effector

  *    c.   stimulus, receptor, integrator, effector, response

     d.   stimulus, integrator, receptor, effector, response

     e.   stimulus, effector, integrator, receptor, response

M    **46.** An effector is a

     a   muscle.

     b.   nerve.

     c.   gland.

     d.   receptor.

  *    e.   both a and c

M    **47.** Which involves a positive feedback stimulation?

     a   temperature control

  *    b.   sexual stimulation

     c.   glucose concentration

     d.   absorption of toxins

     e.   muscle concentration

## Matching Questions

D    **48.** Choose the one most appropriate answer for each.

    1 _____   adipose tissue

    2 _____   blood

    3 _____   dense connective tissue

    4 _____   glandular epithelium

    5 _____   loose connective tissue

    6 _____   interstitial fluid

    7 _____   neuron

    8 _____   epidermis

    A.   tendons are made of this

    B.   contains collagen and elastin; acts as a packing material that supports internal organs

    C.   receives, conducts, and initiates signals in response to environmental changes

    D.   stores fatty reserves

    E.   offers resistance to mechanical injury and loss of internal fluids; also a barrier against microorganisms

    F.   secretes extracellular products such as sweat, mucus, tears, and shells

    G.   fluid ground substance plus free cells; involved in transport, pH, and temperature stability

    H.   extracellular fluid that bathes cells and tissues

*Answers:*

| 1. D | 2. G | 3. A |
|------|------|------|
| 4. F | 5. B | 6. H |
| 7. C | 8. E | |

## Classification Questions

Answer questions 49– 53 in reference to the five types of connective tissue listed below:

    a   loose tissue

    b.   dense tissue

    c.   adipose tissue

    d.   cartilage

    e.   blood

E    **49.** Tendons are composed of this.

E    **50.** The elasticity of skin is due to the presence of this kind of tissue.

M    **51.** This tissue plays an important role in stabilizing body temperature.

E    **52.** This tissue provides nourishment to each of the other connective tissues.

M    **53.** This tissue plays a particularly important role in the thermoregulation of marine mammals.

*Answers*

| 49. b | 50. a | 51. e |
|-------|-------|-------|
| 52. e | 53. c | |

Answer questions 54–58 in reference to the five organ systems listed below:

    a   circulatory

    b.   lymphatic

    c.   digestive

    d.   endocrine

    e.   respiratory

E    **54.** The first line of defense against infectious bacteria found in food lies in this system.

E    **55.** The immune response is part of this system.

M    **56.** Airborne allergens are first encountered by this system.

E    **57.** Antibodies are distributed throughout the body by this system.

E    **58.** The recovery of excess interstitial fluid is the responsibility of this system.

*Answers*

| 54. c | 55. b | 56. e |
|-------|-------|-------|
| 57. a | 58. b | |

## Selecting the Exception

M   **59.** Three of the four answers listed below are germ
layers. Select the exception.
   a   ectoderm
   b.   mesoderm
* c   blastoderm
   d.   endoderm

M   **60.** Four of the five answers listed below are secreted
by an exocrine gland. Select the exception.
   a   wax
   b.   saliva
* c   hormone
   d   milk
   e.   mucus

D   **61.** Four of the five answers listed below are related
by a common tissue type. Select
the exception.
   a   adipose
   b.   bone
   c   cartilage
   d   blood
* e   epithelium

M   **62.** Four of the five answers listed below are
functions of the skeleton. Select the exception.
* a   controls body temperature
   b.   produces blood cells
   c   protection
   d   storage sites for calcium and phosphorus
   e.   muscle attachment

# CHAPTER 26
# PROTECTION, SUPPORT, AND MOVEMENT

## Multiple-Choice Questions

### INTEGUMENTARY SYSTEM

E    **1.** The word *integument* is derived from the word for
- a protection.
- b. support.
- \* c. covering.
- d. contraction.
- e. resistance.

E    **2.** The body covering of arthropods is
- a a secreted cuticle.
- b. made of hardened cells.
- c. also its skeleton.
- \* d. a and c only
- e. a, b, and c

E    **3.** Melanin protects the skin from
- a desiccation.
- b. abrasion.
- \* c. ultraviolet radiation.
- d. stretching.
- e. invasion by bacteria.

E    **4.** The integumentary system is responsible for all but which of the following?
- a protection against bacterial attack
- b. protection against abrasion
- c. synthesis of certain vitamins
- \* d. blood cell formation
- e. control of temperature and prevention of desiccation

E    **5.** The largest organ of the vertebrate body is which of the following?
- a lungs
- b. liver
- c. stomach
- \* d. skin
- e. small intestines

E    **6.** Vitamin D is required for _____ metabolism.
- a sulfur
- b. phosphorus
- \* c. calcium
- d. potassium
- e. zinc

M    **7.** Which of the following is NOT found in the epidermis?
- a stratified epithelium
- \* b. blood vessels
- c. tight cell junctions
- d. keratin
- e. melanin

E    **8.** Which of the following statements is false concerning the outermost layer of the epidermis?
- a It is the first to feel any abrasion.
- b. Keratin provides waterproofing.
- c. Millions of cells are worn off daily.
- \* d. Its cells are undergoing rapid cell division.
- e. It is called the stratum corneum.

M    **9.** Which of the following components of the dermis is incorrectly matched with its function?
- a blood vessels – nutrient supply
- \* b. sweat glands – hormone secretion
- c. oil glands – lubrication of hair and skin
- d. hairs – insulation
- e. receptors – pain

### SKELETAL SYSTEMS

M    **10.** Organisms with external skeletons are exemplified by
- a octopuses and earthworms.
- b. mollusks.
- c. sea anemones.
- \* d. insects and crabs.
- e. vertebrates.

E    **11.** Which organisms have a hydrostatic skeleton with a soft body wall?
- \* a sea anemones
- b. spiders
- c. sponges
- d. crabs
- e. vertebrates

E    **12.** Which organisms have a somewhat rigid internal skeleton and many muscles?
- a octopuses
- b. earthworms
- c. sea anemones
- d. insects
- \* e. vertebrates

M    **13.** The human axial skeleton includes all of the following EXCEPT
- a skull.
- b. ribs.
- \* c. pectoral girdle.
- d. sternum.
- e. vertebral column.

E    **14.** Which of the following is NOT part of the appendicular skeleton?
- a clavicle
- b. scapula
- c. fibula
- \* d. ribs
- e. patella

E     15.    The bone in the upper arm is the
        a    radius.
        b.   ulna.
        c.   tibia.
  *     d.   humerus.
        e.   femur.

E     16.    Bones in fingers or toes are called
        a    hyoid.
        b.   patella.
        c.   scapula.
        d.   clavicle.
  *     e.   phalanges.

E     17.    The kneecap is the
        a    hyoid.
  *     b.   patella.
        c.   scapula.
        d.   clavicle.
        e.   phalanx.

E     18.    The collarbone is the
        a    hyoid.
        b.   patella.
        c.   scapula.
  *     d.   clavicle.
        e.   phalanx.

E     19.    The shoulder blade is the
        a    hyoid.
        b.   patella.
  *     c.   scapula.
        d.   clavicle.
        e.   phalanx.

## A CLOSER LOOK AT BONES AND THE JOINTS BETWEEN THEM

E     20.    The mineral stored in greatest quantity in bones is
        a    phosphorus.
        b.   iron.
        c.   magnesium.
  *     d.   calcium.
        e.   sulfur.

E     21.    In spongy bone tissue the spaces are filled with
        a    air.
        b.   blood.
        c.   cartilage.
  *     d.   marrow.
        e.   lymph.

M    22.    Haversian canals are characteristic of which tissue?
        a    adipose
  *     b.   bone
        c.   cartilage
        d.   epithelial
        e.   muscular

D     23.    All but which of the following are associated with bone formation?
        a    osteoblasts
        b.   cartilage
  *     c.   osteoporosis
        d.   marrow cavity formation
        e.   calcium

E     24.    Bones such as the humerus and femur are examples of which kind of bones?
  *     a    long
        b.   short
        c.   flat
        d.   irregular
        e.   all of the above

M    25.    The nonmoving joints between skull bones are examples of what kind of joints?
        a    synovial
  *     b.   fibrous
        c.   cartilaginous
        d.   hinge
        e.   none of the above

M    26.    What kind of joints are freely movable and the bones are separated by a fluid-filled cavity?
  *     a    synovial
        b.   fibrous
        c.   cartilaginous
        d.   hinge
        e.   none of the above

M    27.    The vertebral discs with small amounts of movement are examples of what kind of joints?
        a    synovial
        b.   fibrous
  *     c.   cartilaginous
        d.   hinge
        e.   none of the above

M    28.    Growth of long bones
        a    follows the cartilage model.
        b.   occurs in the middle at first, then at both ends.
        c.   is characterized by bone tissue replacing calcified cartilage.
        d.   is characterized by the persistence of cartilage at both ends of the shaft.
  *     e.   all of the above

M    29.    Which statement is false?
        a    Calcium is the most important mineral involved with bone tissue turnover.
        b.   Osteocytes and osteoclasts are involved with the reabsorption and repair of bones.
        c.   Bone mass decreases with age.
  *     d.   Males have greater problems with loss of bone tissue than females do.
        e.   Marrow fills the cavities in the spaces of the spongy bone and in the center of the shaft of the bone almost as quickly as the spaces are formed.

## SKELETAL–MUSCULAR SYSTEMS

E **30.** Each muscle fiber is also called a
&ast;    a muscle.
    b. muscle cell.
    c. myofibril.
    d. sarcomere.
    e. all of the above

M **31.** The ability to extend a leg originates from
    a contraction of ligaments and tendons.
&ast;    b. contraction of a muscle.
    c. lengthening of a muscle.
    d. combination of push and pull by antagonistic muscle pairs.

D **32.** Reciprocal innervation of reflexes between antagonistic muscle pairs
&ast;    a is the usual basis of coordinated contractions.
    b. is the means by which rods prevent cones from being stimulated.
    c. refers to the lens adjustments that bring about precise focusing onto the retina.
    d. explains the mechanism for the operation of the calcium pump.
    e. all of the above

E **33.** Smooth muscle is
&ast;    a involuntary and nonstriated.
    b. responsible for movement of the skeleton.
    c. involved in contraction of the heart.
    d. connected to bones by tendons.
    e. both a and c

M **34.** The gastrocnemius muscle is located
    a in the forelimb.
    b. on the back.
    c. in the hip area.
&ast;    d. in the lower leg.
    e. in the neck.

E **35.** The pectoralis major muscle is located
&ast;    a in the chest.
    b. on the back.
    c. near the hips.
    d. in the upper leg.
    e. in the lower leg.

## MUSCLE STRUCTURE AND FUNCTION

M **36.** Which of the following includes all the others?
    a actin
    b. myofibril
    c. myosin
    d. myofilament
&ast;    e. muscle cell

M **37.** During muscle contractions
    a the myofibrils shorten.
    b. the actin and myosin filaments slide over each other.
    c. the actin filaments move toward the middle of the sacromere during contraction and away on relaxation.
    d. the muscle thickens.
&ast;    e. all of the above

D **38.** During contraction
    a cross-bridges of muscle filaments are broken and reformed.
    b. ATP is used to form cross-bridges.
    c. muscle cells use glycogen as their energy source.
    d. if there is a poor supply of oxygen, glycogen depletion by glycolysis will lead to fatigue.
&ast;    e. all of the above

D **39.** In their action, muscles would be most like
&ast;    a ropes.
    b. levers.
    c. push rods.
    d. screws.
    e. hammers.

## CONTROL OF MUSCLE CONTRACTION

M **40.** The element specifically associated with muscle contraction is
    a phosphorus.
    b. potassium.
&ast;    c. calcium.
    d. sodium.
    e. chlorine.

E **41.** Functionally, the plasma membrane of a muscle cell is most like that of a
    a bone cell.
&ast;    b. nerve cell.
    c. cartilage cell.
    d. pancreatic islet cell.
    e. epidermal cell.

D **42.** Which of the following statements does NOT describe normal activity in a motor system?
    a All motor systems require the presence of some medium or structural element against which force can be applied.
    b. In a skeletal muscle system, coordinated contraction depends on reciprocal innervation of motor neurons to antagonistic muscle pairs.
    c. In vertebrates, only skeletal muscle acts to move the body through the environment.
&ast;    d. In a resting muscle, energy is stored in the form of tropomyosin.
    e. all of the above

## PROPERTIES OF WHOLE MUSCLES

M    **43.** A motor neuron and all the muscles under its control is called what kind of unit?
   - a  end
   - b.  movement
   - c.  muscle
   - *  d.  motor
   - e.  coordination

M    **44.** An active, nonfatiguing muscle would be expected to have
   - a  aerobic respiration.
   - b.  numerous mitochondria.
   - c.  moderate rates of contraction.
   - d.  a and c only
   - *  e.  a, b, and c

M    **45.** The mechanical force that resists gravity in the lifting of an object is
   - a  muscle fatigue.
   - b.  a motor unit.
   - *  c.  muscle tension.
   - d.  a muscle twitch.
   - e.  tetanus.

## ATP FORMATION AND LEVELS OF EXERCISE

E    **46.** The most immediate, but necessarily limited, source of energy for reformation of ATP in muscle cells is
   - a  aerobic respiration.
   - b.  mitochondrial pathways.
   - c.  electron transport phosphorylation.
   - *  d.  creatine phosphate.
   - e.  anaerobic fermentation.

E    **47.** Muscle fatigue is a result of
   - *  a  accumulation of lactic acid.
   - b.  exhaustion of available ATP.
   - c.  reduction in lactic acid and oxygen debt.
   - d.  failure of calcium channels to open after prolonged use.

## Classification Questions

Answer questions 48- 52 in reference to the five bones listed below:
   - a  clavicle
   - b.  lumbar vertebra
   - c.  tibia
   - d.  metatarsal
   - e.  metacarpal

E    **48.** This bone is not part of the appendicular skeleton.

M    **49.** This bone is part of the wishbone of birds.

M    **50.** If one had a slipped disk, that disk might be next to this bone.

D    **51.** This bone is a toe bone in birds.

M    **52.** This bone connects to the femur.

*Answers*    48.  b    49.  a    50.  b
              51.  d    52.  c

Answer questions 53- 57 in reference to the five muscles listed below:
   - a  pectoralis major
   - b.  deltoid
   - c.  rectus femoris
   - d.  triceps
   - e.  gastrocnemius

D    **53.** This muscle is a principal muscle of the upper leg.

M    **54.** This muscle is located on the upper shoulder.

M    **55.** This muscle is antagonistic to the action of the biceps.

D    **56.** The Achilles' tendon attaches this muscle to the heel bones.

D    **57.** This muscle is the principal flight muscle of birds.

*Answers*    53.  c    54.  b    55.  d
              56.  e    57.  a

## Selecting the Exception

M    **58.** Four of the five answers listed below possess the same type of skeleton. Select the exception.
   - a  butterfly
   - b.  fly
   - *  c.  earthworm
   - d.  crab
   - e.  grasshopper

M 59. Four of the five answers listed below are parts of the same anatomical area. Select the exception.
   a   humerus
 * b.  fibula
   c.  radius
   d.  clavicle
   e.  scapula

M 60. Four of the five answers listed below are parts of the same skeletal division. Select the exception.
   a   cranium
   b.  ribs
   c.  sternum
   d.  vertebrae
 * e.  phalanges

M 61. Four of the five answers listed below are regions of the vertebral column. Select the exception.
   a   cervical
 * b.  appendicular
   c.  lumbar
   d.  thoracic
   e.  sacral

E 62. Four of the five answers listed below are types of bones. Select the exception.
 * a   immovable
   b.  long
   c.  short
   d.  flat
   e.  irregular

E 63. Four of the five answers listed below are muscles. Select the exception.
   a   pectoralis
 * b.  patella
   c.  gastrocnemius
   d.  deltoid
   e.  sartorius

D 64. Four of the five answers listed below are molecules that participate in muscle contraction. Select the exception.
 * a   sarcolemma
   b.  ATP
   c.  calcium
   d.  actin
   e.  myosin

# CHAPTER 27
# CIRCULATION

## Multiple-Choice Questions

### CIRCULATORY SYSTEMS—AN OVERVIEW

M   1. Which of the following is usually NOT present in an open circulation system?
*   a   veins
  b.   the heart
  c.   arteries
  d.   blood
  e.   arterioles

E   2. Which of the following has a closed circulatory system?
  a   clam
*   b.   earthworm
  c.   spider
  d.   snail
  e.   insect

M   3. Which of the following statements is false?
  a   The systemic circuit carries oxygenated blood.
*   b.   Humans have an open circulatory system.
  c.   The function of the heart is to generate pressure to make the blood flow through the circulatory system.
  d.   The rate of blood flow varies throughout the circulatory system.
  e.   The interstitial fluid is returned to the circulatory system through the lymphatic system.

D   4. Which of the following systems is the only one to have direct interactions with the other three?
  a   digestive
  b.   urinary
*   c   circulatory
  d.   respiratory

E   5. Which of the following possesses a three chambered heart?
  a   human
*   b.   frog
  c.   mammal
  d.   bird
  e.   fish

D   6. Which of the following is true of the pulmonary circuit?
  a   Blood is pumped to the digestive system.
  b.   Oxygen-poor blood is received by the left atrium of the heart.
*   c   The right ventricle pumps oxygen-poor blood.
  d.   It bypasses the lungs.
  e.   It exists only in fishes.

E   7. Which of the following is NOT a function of the lymph system?
  a   fighting infection
*   b.   transporting dissolved gases
  c.   reclaiming fluids
  d.   harboring white blood cells
  e.   All are functions of the lymph system.

### CHARACTERISTICS OF BLOOD

E   8. Which of the following makes up the greatest percentage of human plasma?
  a   albumin
  b.   red blood cells
  c.   white blood cells
*   d   water
  e.   dissolved ions, sugars, hormones, etc.

M   9. Which cell is NOT the same type as the others?
*   a   erythrocytes
  b.   neutrophils
  c.   lymphocytes
  d.   eosinophils
  e.   monocytes

M   10. Which cell is NOT involved with the defense response?
*   a   erythrocytes
  b.   neutrophils
  c.   lymphocytes
  d.   eosinophils
  e.   monocytes

M   11. Which cell is the most abundant in the human body?
  a   lymphocytes
  b.   basophils
*   c   erythrocytes
  d.   neutrophils
  e.   platelets

M   12. Which cell produces the fibrin used in blood clots?
  a   lymphocytes
  b.   basophils
  c.   erythrocytes
  d.   neutrophils
*   e   platelets

E   13. In humans, which cell does NOT have a nucleus when mature?
*   a   erythrocytes
  b.   lymphocytes
  c.   neutrophils
  d.   eosinophils
  e.   monocytes

E **14.** Most of the oxygen in the blood is transported by
    a. plasma.
    b. serum.
    c. platelets.
    * d. hemoglobin.
    e. leukocytes.

E **15.** Red blood cells originate in the
    a. liver.
    b. spleen.
    c. kidneys.
    * d. bone marrow.
    e. thymus gland.

M **16.** How long does the average red blood cell live?
    a. 4 days
    b. 4 weeks
    * c. 4 months
    d. 1 year
    e. 4 years

E **17.** About how many quarts of blood does a normal, 150-pound, human male have?
    a. 2–3
    b. 3–4
    * c. 4–5
    d. 5–6
    e. 6–7

E **18.** What percent of the total blood volume does plasma normally amount to?
    a. 15 to 25
    b. 33 to 40
    * c. 50 to 60
    d. 66 to 75
    e. about 80

E **19.** Hemoglobin contains which element?
    a. chlorine
    b. sodium
    * c. iron
    d. copper
    e. magnesium

M **20.** Megakaryocytes fragment to produce
    a. red blood cells.
    b. lymphocytes.
    * c. platelets.
    d. eosinophils.
    e. neutrophils.

E **21.** Blood rich in oxygen is what color?
    a. yellow
    b. pink
    * c. bright red
    d. blue
    e. purple

## BLOOD TYPING AND BLOOD TRANSFUSIONS

M **22.** Type A blood will NOT agglutinate when mixed with
    a. type B blood.
    b. type A blood.
    c. type AB blood.
    d. type O blood.
    * e. both A and AB, but will clump with types B and O.

E **23.** Which blood type is the universal donor?
    a. A+
    b. B
    c. AB+
    d. AB
    * e. O

E **24.** Which blood type is the universal recipient?
    a. A
    b. B+
    c. AB+
    * d. AB
    e. O+

D **25.** In the Rh disease
    a. the mother must be positive and her first and second children positive.
    * b. the mother must be negative and her first and second children positive.
    c. the mother must be negative and her first and second children negative.
    d. the mother must be positive and her first and second children negative.
    e. the mother and the father must both be negative and the child positive.

D **26.** If you are blood type A,
    * a. you carry antibodies for type B blood.
    b. you carry markers for type B blood.
    c. you can donate blood to a person with type O blood.
    d. you can receive blood from a person with type AB blood.
    e. none of the above

## HUMAN CARDIOVASCULAR SYSTEM

M **27.** The pulmonary circulation
    a. involves the hepatic portal vein.
    b. moves oxygen-rich blood to the kidneys.
    c. includes the coronary arteries.
    * d. leads to, through, and from the lungs.
    e. all of the above

M **28.** In the human systemic circuit, blood will pass through all but which of the following?
    a. liver
    b. limbs
    * c. lungs
    d. digestive organs
    e. brain

E   29.   In its travel through the human body, blood
          usually continues on from capillaries to enter
          a   arterioles.
    *     b.   venules.
          c.   arteries.
          d.   veins.
          e.   other capillaries.

D   30.   Which of the following statements is true?
          a   Arteries carry only oxygenated blood.
    *     b.   The systemic circuit leaves the heart from
               the left ventricle.
          c.   Blood passes through only one capillary bed
               on its trip through the systemic circuit.
          d.   Platelets survive a longer time than
               erythrocytes.
          e.   The heart is able to pick up the oxygen it
               needs as the blood flows through it.

M   31.   Blood in arteries
    *     a   always travels away from the heart.
          b.   travels away from the heart only if it is
               oxygen-rich.
          c.   always travels toward the heart.
          d.   travels from the lungs.
          e.   is always oxygen-rich.

E   32.   The receiving zone of a vertebrate heart is
          a   a plaque.
          b.   the aorta.
    *     c.   an atrium.
          d.   a capillary bed.
          e.   all of the above

M   33.   The aorta leaves the
          a   left atrium.
          b.   right atrium.
    *     c.   left ventricle.
          d.   right ventricle.

M   34.   The pulmonary artery carries blood away from
          the
          a   aorta.
          b.   right atrium.
    *     c.   right ventricle.
          d.   left atrium.
          e.   left ventricle.

E   35.   Blood from the body is first received by the heart
          in the
          a   coronary vein.
          b.   left atrium.
          c.   right ventricle.
    *     d.   right atrium.
          e.   left ventricle.

## THE HEART IS A LONELY PUMPER

M   36.   The heart
    *     a   will contract as a result of stimuli from the
               sinoatrial node.
          b.   contracts only as a result of nerve
               stimulation from the central nervous system.
          c.   is activated primarily through the autonomic
               nervous system.
          d.   pulse is primarily under the control of the
               atrioventricular node.
          e.   is completely independent of all nervous
               control.

M   37.   Heart excitation originates in the
          a   atrioventricular node.
          b.   intercalated disk.
    *     c.   sinoatrial node.
          d.   pericardium.
          e.   all of the above

M   38.   What occurs during systole?
          a   Oxygen-rich blood is pumped to the lungs.
    *     b.   The heart muscle tissues contract.
          c.   The atrioventricular valves suddenly open.
          d.   Oxygen-poor blood from all body regions
               except the lungs flows into the right atrium.
          e.   all of the above

M   39.   The pacemaker is which of the following nodes?
    *     a   sinoatrial
          b.   semilunar
          c.   atrioventricular
          d.   inferior vena cava
          e.   superior vena cava

D   40.   If a physician hears two "lub" sounds instead of
          one, then which of these is true?
          a   The semilunar valves are not closing
               simultaneously.
          b.   The atrial blood is flowing backward and
               causing the extra sound.
    *     c.   The atrioventricular valves are not closing
               at the same time.
          d.   The AV and semilunar valves are not
               closing at the same time.
          e.   No such double sound has ever been heard.

M   41.   The coronary vessels
    *     a   supply and drain the heart muscle.
          b.   bypass the heart ventricles.
          c.   send blood directly to the lungs.
          d.   are not really necessary because the heart
               can get its blood supply from the "inside."
          e.   lead directly from the atria to the ventricles.

M 42. Which of the following statements is false?
   a A heart will stop beating when the nerves to the heart are severed.
   b. Some cardiac muscle cells are self-excitatory.
   c. The pacemaker of the heart is the sinoatrial node.
   d. Cardiac muscles join end to end to allow rapid communication.
   e. Cardiac muscles contract essentially in unison.

## BLOOD PRESSURE IN THE CARDIOVASCULAR SYSTEM

M 43. Blood pressure is highest in the
   a aorta.
   b. pulmonary artery.
   c. capillary bed.
   d. subclavian vein.
   e. lower vena cava.

E 44. The greatest volume of blood is found in the
   a aorta and arteries.
   b. capillaries.
   * c. veins.
   d. lungs.
   e. heart.

E 45. Which of the following has the highest blood pressure?
   a right ventricle
   b. right atrium
   * c. left ventricle
   d. left atrium
   e. pulmonary circulation

M 46. Which of the following is NOT found in an arteriole?
   a elastic layer
   b. basement membrane
   c. smooth muscle
   * d. valve
   e. endothelium

M 47. The diastolic pressure for a normal young adult would be
   a 60 mmHg.
   * b. 80 mmHg.
   c. 100 mmHg.
   d. 120 mmHg.
   e. 140 mmHg.

E 48. By controlling their musculature, which can vary the resistance to blood flow?
   a arteries
   b. veins
   c. capillaries
   * d. arterioles
   e. all of the above

M 49. Because of their great elasticity, which of the following can function as blood volume reservoirs during times of low metabolic output?
   * a veins and venules
   b. arteries
   c. arterioles
   d. capillaries
   e. all of the above

E 50. Which controls the distribution of blood?
   a arteries
   * b. arterioles
   c. capillaries
   d. venules
   e. veins

E 51. Which are pressure reservoirs with low resistance to flow?
   * a arteries
   b. arterioles
   c. capillaries
   d. venules
   e. veins

E 52. Which are highly distensible reservoirs for blood volume?
   a arteries
   b. arterioles
   c. capillaries
   d. venules
   * e. veins

M 53. The greatest drop in blood pressure occurs in the
   a arteries.
   * b. arterioles.
   c. capillaries.
   d. venules.
   e. veins.

M 54. The most common vascular disease is
   a phlebitis.
   * b. hypertension.
   c. leukemia.
   d. sickle cell anemia.
   e. a stroke.

E 55. A stroke is a rupture of a blood vessel in the
   a leg.
   * b. brain.
   c. heart.
   d. lung.
   e. internal organs.

M 56. In atherosclerosis
   a abnormal multiplication of smooth muscle cells in blood vessels occurs.
   b. the arterial walls fill with connective tissue.
   c. the lipids in the bloodstream become embedded in the walls of the endothelial lining.
   d. a fibrous net covers the entire abnormal area.
   * e. all of the above

M    57.   The mineral associated with atherosclerosis is
            a    iron.
            b.   magnesium.
            c.   cobalt.
         *  d.   calcium.
            e.   iodine.

M    58.   Cholesterol is believed to be carried by
            a    albumin.
            b.   high-density lipoproteins.
            c.   low-density lipoproteins.
            d.   triglycerides.
         *  e.   both b and c

## HEMOSTASIS

D    59.   Hemostasis in vertebrates includes all of the
           following EXCEPT
            a    blood clot formation.
            b.   vessel constriction.
         *  c    release of iron to aid in the clumping of
                 platelets.
            d.   vessel spasms.
            e    platelets releasing substances that cause
                 them to attract each other.

M    60.   Which of the following is NOT involved in the
           formation of a blood clot?
         *  a    plasma cells
            b.   fibrinogen
            c    thrombin
            d    fibrin
            e    All of the above are involved.

## LYMPHATIC SYSTEM

M    61.   Which of the following is transported in greater
           quantities in the lymphatic system than in the
           blood?
            a    red blood cells
            b.   wastes
         *  c    fats
            d    amino acids
            e    white blood cells

M    62.   Which statement is NOT true of the lymph
           vascular system? The lymph vascular system
            a    transports lipids absorbed from the small
                 intestine to the bloodstream.
            b.   recovers and transports interstitial fluid back
                 to the bloodstream.
         *  c    absorbs glucose from the small intestine and
                 transports it to the brain.
            d    serves the body's system of defenses against
                 bacteria and other infectious agents.
            e    performs all of the above functions.

M    63..  The lymphoid organs include all but the
            a    spleen.
         *  b.   stomach.
            c    thymus.
            d    tonsils and adenoids.
            e    appendix.

E    64.   The system that reclaims fluids and proteins that
           have escaped from blood capillaries is the
            a    cardiovascular.
            b.   pulmonary.
         *  c    lymphatic.
            d    sinoatrial.
            e.   venous.

E    65.   Areas where lymphocytes congregate as they
           cleanse the blood of foreign materials are called
            a    stem cells.
            b.   SA nodes.
            c    capillary beds.
         *  d.   lymph nodes.
            e.   antibodies.

## Classification Questions

Answer questions 66- 70 in reference to the five
components of mammalian blood listed below:
            a    red blood cells
            b.   basophils
            c    platelets
            d    serum albumin protein
            e    sodium and potassium chloride

E    66.   This blood component plays a central role in
           clotting blood following a wound.

E    67.   This blood component contains hemoglobin.

D    68.   This blood component plays a role in the
           inflammatory response and shows anticlotting
           activity.

E    69.   This blood component plays a role in
           maintaining the ionic balance of the body.

E    70.   Oxygen is transported throughout the body by
           this blood component.

*Answers* :     66.  c        67.  a        68.  b
                69.  e        70.  a

Answer questions 71–75 in reference to the four structures of the heart listed below:

    a   right atrium
    b.  left atrium
    c.  left ventricle
    d.  right ventricle

M    **71.**    Blood from the superior and inferior vena cavas enters the heart via this structure.

M    **72.**    Blood passes to the lungs from this structure.

M    **73.**    Deoxygenated blood exits the heart from this structure.

M    **74.**    Oxygenated blood enters the heart via this structure.

M    **75.**    Blood is pumped to the majority of the body by this structure.

*Answers*:    71.  a     72.  d     73.  d
               74.  b     75.  c

## Selecting the Exception

M    **76.**    Four of the five answers listed below designate organisms with open circulations. Select the exception.
    a   insects
    b.  snails
    c.  spiders
    d.  clams
  *  e.  frogs

M    **77.**    Four of the five answers listed below are related by a common property. Select the exception.
    a   neutrophil
  *  b.  erythrocyte
    c.  lymphocytes
    d.  monocyte
    e.  basophil

M    **78.**    Four of the five answers listed below are blood proteins. Select the exception.
  *  a   epinephrine
    b.  globulin
    c.  hemoglobin
    d.  fibrinogen
    e.  albumin

M    **79.**    Four of the five answers listed below are characteristics of most veins. Select the exception.
    a   blood volume reservoir
    b.  contain valves
    c.  low resistance-transport tubes
  *  d.  transport oxygen
    e.  low blood pressure

M    **80.**    Three of the four answers listed below are related by a common function. Select the exception.
  *  a   gamma globulin
    b.  prothrombin
    c.  fibrin
    d.  fibrinogen

D    **81.**    Four of the five answers listed below are related by a common feature. Select the exception.
    a   A
    b.  B
    c.  AB
  *  d.  Rh+
    e.  O

D    **82.**    Four of the five answers listed below are related by a common function. Select the exception.
  *  a   heart
    b.  spleen
    c.  thymus
    d.  tonsils
    e.  lymph node

# CHAPTER 28
# IMMUNITY

## Multiple-Choice Questions

### RUSSIAN ROULETTE, IMMUNOLOGICAL STYLE

E  **1.** The first disease for which a successful vaccination was developed was
  - a  the plague.
  - * b.  smallpox.
  - c.  rabies.
  - d.  chicken pox.
  - e.  diphtheria.

E  **2.** The person who developed and demonstrated the first successful vaccine was
  - a  Pasteur.
  - b.  Koch.
  - c.  Lister.
  - * d.  Jenner.
  - e.  Erhlich.

E  **3.** The word *vaccination* comes from the Latin word for
  - a  germ.
  - * b.  cow.
  - c.  chicken.
  - d.  rabbit.
  - e.  rat.

### THREE LINES OF DEFENSE

M  **4.** The barrier to invasion by microbes involves
  - a  urine.
  - b.  the symbiotic microorganisms already in the body.
  - c.  ciliated mucous membranes.
  - d.  lysozyme and other enzymes.
  - * e.  all of the above

E  **5.** All but which of the following are good barriers to invasion by microbes?
  - a  mucous membranes
  - b.  eye secretions
  - * c.  broken skin
  - d.  urine
  - e.  gut bacteria

M  **6.** Lysozyme
  - a  is secreted by endocrine glands in the skin.
  - * b.  destroys the cell wall of invading bacteria.
  - c.  is produced in the lymph nodes and actively disables bacteria.
  - d.  has proved to be a very effective defense against viruses.
  - e.  is active within the circulatory system.

### COMPLEMENT PROTEINS

M  **7.** Which system involves plasma proteins activated when they contact a bacterial cell?
  - a  infection
  - * b.  complement
  - c.  bodyguard
  - d.  enhancer
  - e.  defender

D  **8.** Which of the following would NOT be the result of the action of the complement system?
  - a  lysis of a pathogen's membrane
  - * b.  trapping of pathogens in tangled protein threads
  - c.  marking of pathogens for destruction by macrophages
  - d.  attraction of phagocytes to scene of pathogen invasion

M  **9.** The complement system
  - a  includes a group of about 20 plasma proteins.
  - b.  induces a cascade of proteins that counteract invasion by coating the invading cells.
  - c.  attracts phagocytic leukocytes to attack invading cells.
  - d.  causes the lysis of the plasma membranes of invading cells.
  - * e.  all of the above

### INFLAMMATION

M  **10.** Phagocytes are derived from stem cells in the
  - a  spleen.
  - b.  thymus.
  - * c.  bone marrow.
  - d.  blood.
  - e.  liver.

M  **11.** All but which of the following types of cells can be called "phagocytes"?
  - a  monocytes
  - * b.  erythrocytes
  - c.  neutrophils
  - d.  eosinophils
  - e.  macrophages

M  **12.** Histamine causes
  - a  blood vessels to contract.
  - b.  capillaries to lose their permeability.
  - * c.  an outward flow of fluids from the capillaries.
  - d.  a destruction of mast cells.
  - e.  an opening of the area of infection, through which the body's defense system can enter.

M 13. Which event does NOT occur in the inflammatory response?
    a Tissue swells because of outflow from capillary beds.
    * b. Blocking antibodies inactivate the resident mast cells.
    c. White blood cells are attracted to the area by chemotaxis.
    d. Complement proteins help identify invading material.
    e. The foreign invaders are engulfed and destroyed by phagocytosis.

M 14. Inflammation
    * a leads to the release of histamine, which causes capillaries to become "leaky."
    b. is accentuated by the administration of antihistamine drugs.
    c. does not occur during allergic reactions.
    d. is initiated by the buildup of dead cells and bacteria.
    e. is not affected by the action of the complement system.

D 15. An antihistamine drug would have as its SPECIFIC action which of the following?
    * a constriction of the capillaries
    b. decreased redness
    c. reduced warmth
    d. promotion of clotting
    e. attraction of phagocytes

D 16. Interleukins
    a are secreted by macrophages.
    b. trigger any B cell that has become sensitive to the specific antigen (the one inducing interleukin production) to divide.
    c. are the chemical triggers that cause tissue to release antihistamine.
    d. are effective only on pathogens that have invaded body cells.
    * e. both a and b, but not c or d

## THE IMMUNE SYSTEM

M 17. Terms that describe the immune response include all of the following EXCEPT
    a specific.
    b. rapid.
    c. memory.
    * d. general.
    e. effective.

E 18. Which cells are divided into two groups: T cells and B cells?
    a macrophages
    * b. lymphocytes
    c. complement cells
    d. platelets
    e. all of the above

M 19. Which cells produce and secrete antibodies that set up bacterial invaders for subsequent destruction by macrophages?
    a phagocytes
    b. macrophages
    * c. B cells
    d. T cells
    e. all of the above

M 20. Which of the following are NOT generally targets of T cells?
    a transplants of foreign tissue
    b. cancer
    c. infections caused by viruses
    * d. infections caused by bacteria
    e. all of the above

M 21. Which cells produce antibodies?
    a helper T
    b. suppressor T
    c. cytotoxic T
    d. natural killer
    * e. B

M 22. Which cells cause rapid division of the lymphocytes?
    * a helper T
    b. suppressor T
    c. cytotoxic T
    d. memory
    e. B

M 23. Which cells are held in reserve to be used for a rapid response to subsequent intruders of the same type?
    a helper T
    b. suppressor T
    c. cytotoxic T
    * d. memory
    e. B

M 24. Body cells have self-markers located
    a in their nuclei.
    b. in the endoplasmic reticulum.
    c. in the mitochondria.
    * d. on the plasma membrane.
    e. inside the Golgi bodies.

M 25. The markers for each cell in a body are referred to by the letters
    * a MHC.
    b. HTC.
    c. ADS.
    d. RSW.
    e. AKA.

M 26. Which cells are the longest lasting in the body?
    a helper T
    b. natural killer cells
    c. cytotoxic T
    * d. memory
    e. B

M 27. Which of the following would be ignored in most instances by lymphocytes?
   a. cells coated with complement proteins
   b. cells with antigens on their surface
   * c. "self" cells with MHC markers
   d. cells with both antigen and self-MHC markers
   e. cells with damaged or mutant self-MHC markers

## LYMPHOCYTE BATTLEGROUNDS

M 28. Phagocytes perform their services in
   a. the blood.
   b. tissue spaces.
   c. the lymph system.
   d. a and b only
   * e. a, b, and c

M 29. Which of the following is NOT a lymphoid organ?
   a. tonsils
   b. nodules
   * c. thyroid
   d. spleen
   e. thymus

M 30. Which of the following is mostly likely to happen in a lymph node?
   a. oxygenation of the interstitial fluid
   b. production of B and T lymphocytes
   * c. phagocytosis of organisms foreign to the body
   d. attachment of MHC markers to self cells
   e. red blood cells are destroyed and their contents recycled

## CELL-MEDIATED RESPONSES

M 31. Which cells are similar to cytotoxic cells in their mode of action?
   a. helper T
   * b. natural killer
   c. cytotoxic T
   d. memory
   e. B

M 32. Which cells directly destroy body cells infected by viral or fungal parasites?
   a. helper T
   b. suppressor T
   * c. cytotoxic T
   d. memory
   e. B

M 33. Mutant and cancerous cells are destroyed by which cells?
   a. helper T
   b. suppressor T
   * c. cytotoxic T
   d. memory
   e. B

M 34. Cell-mediated response
   * a. involves cytotoxic T cells.
   b. involves the action of antibodies to destroy invaders.
   c. acts only on extracellular clues.
   d. results in the production of clones of plasma cells.
   e. all of the above

M 35. Most organ transplants fail because
   a. of poor vascular connection between host and donor tissue.
   b. the migrating leukocytes attack the tissue adjacent to the transplant.
   * c. cytotoxic T cells enter the transplant through the connecting blood vessels and kill the individual transplant tissue.
   d. introduced tissues produce antibodies that cause a massive reaction.
   e. all of the above

M 36. Effector cells
   a. are fully differentiated lymphocytes.
   b. manufacture and secrete antibodies.
   c. can develop from either T or B cells.
   d. secrete antibodies or interleukins depending on their origin.
   * e. all of the above

## ANTIBODY-MEDIATED RESPONSES

E 37. Antibodies are shaped like the letter
   a. C.
   b. E.
   c. H.
   d. K.
   * e. Y.

E 38. Antibodies are
   * a. proteins.
   b. steroids.
   c. polysaccharides.
   d. lipoproteins.
   e. all of the above

E 39. Antibodies belong to a group of compounds known as
   a. self-recognizing compounds.
   * b. immunoglobulins.
   c. histosaccharides.
   d. antisteroids.
   e. virulent bases.

M 40. Which immunoglobulin is able to pass the placenta to protect the fetus from pathogens?
   * a. IgG
   b. IgA
   c. IgD
   d. IgM
   e. IgE

M 41. Which immunoglobulin is the first to be secreted and initiates the complement cascade?
   a IgG
   * b. IgA
   c IgD
   d. IgM
   e IgE

D 42. Which statement is NOT true?
   a When an invading bacterium is destroyed by a macrophage, its antigens are preserved.
   * b. Antibodies attack and destroy invading antigens.
   c Helper T cells recognize the major histocompatibility complex and antigens on the surface of macrophages.
   d. Self cells have major histocompatibility complex markers or antigens.
   e Helper T cells secrete lymphokines, which help the cells of the immune system communicate with each other.

M 43. Effector (plasma) cells
   a die within a week of production.
   b. manufacture and secrete antibodies.
   c do not divide and form clones.
   d. develop from B cells.
   * e all of the above

## IMMUNE SPECIFICITY AND MEMORY

E 44. The antibody molecule consists of how many polypeptide chains, including light and heavy chains?
   a 2
   b. 3
   * c 4
   d. 5
   e 6

M 45. Clones of B or T cells are
   a being produced continually.
   b. interchangeable.
   * c produced only when their surface proteins recognize specific protein.
   d. known as memory cells.
   e produced and mature in the bone marrow.

M 46. The antigen binds to the _____ region of an antibody.
   a constant
   b. curved
   * c variable
   d. Z
   e Q

D 47. The infinite variety of antibodies that can be generated by B cells is due to
   a the infinite variety of genes in these cells.
   * b. the shuffling of genes to produce an infinite variety of proteins.
   c the recombination of genes due to crossing over.
   d. a and c only
   e a, b, and c

M 48. The primary immune response
   a is shorter in duration than a secondary response.
   b. is quicker than a secondary response.
   c depends on random construction of appropriate antibodies.
   d. is the result of a reproduction of an appropriate lymphocyte resulting in a sensitive clone.
   * e both c and d

D 49. After a primary immune response
   a a clone of sensitive lymphocytes is ready for any subsequent invasion of the same antigen.
   b. some of the clone cells will remain alive for decades.
   c clone cells may be modified to attack new invaders.
   d. clone cells are continually reproduced to confer immunity against subsequent invasion.
   * e both a and b

## IMMUNITY ENHANCED, MISDIRECTED, OR COMPROMISED

E 50. A vaccine contains
   a killed pathogen.
   b. weakened pathogen.
   c noninfective fragments of a pathogen.
   d. full-strength pathogen.
   * e all except d may be used

M 51. Passive immunity can be obtained by
   a having the disease.
   b. receiving a vaccination against the disease.
   c receiving antibodies by injection.
   d. receiving antibodies from mother at birth.
   * e either c or d

D 52. The purpose of a vaccine is to
   a produce a mild case of the disease.
   b. stimulate the immune response.
   c cause memory cells to be formed.
   d. b and c only
   * e a, b, and c

M 53. Whenever the body is reexposed to a sensitizing agent, the IgE antibodies cause
   * a the production of prostaglandins and histamine.
   b. the release of antihistamines.
   c. the suppression of the inflammatory response.
   d. the production of clonal cells.
   e. all of the above

M 54. A person sensitive to bee stings might die minutes after a sting due to
   a a collapse of the immune system.
   b. a clogging of the capillaries.
   * c a release of excessive fluids from the capillary beds.
   d. respiratory distress caused by excessive mucus.
   e. the extremely sharp rise in blood pressure.

E 55. Rheumatoid arthritis is
   a sexually transmitted.
   * b. an autoimmune disease.
   c. one of the diseases associated with AIDS.
   d. caused by a bacterial infection.
   e. preventable by vaccination.

M 56 When the body's defenses turn against its own cells, the disorder is called
   * a an autoimmune response.
   b. anaphylactic shock.
   c. acquired immune deficiency syndrome.
   d. passive immunity.
   e. an inflammatory response.

E 57. The reason AIDS is so serious is that
   a the excessive immune reaction leads to death.
   b. it is so highly contagious.
   * c it is fatal.
   d. it is caused by a retrovirus.
   e. many natural reservoirs may spread the disease at any time.

E 58. Kaposi's sarcoma is characteristic of people who have
   * a AIDS.
   b. allergic reactions.
   c. a hypersensitive immune system.
   d. ancestors who come from Cyprus.
   e. herpes.

E 59. Of the following, AIDS is usually transferred by
   a casual contact.
   b. food.
   c. water.
   * d. sexual intercourse.
   e. insect bites.

M 60. The human immunodeficiency virus (HIV-1) primarily destroys which cells?
   a B
   b. M
   c. Tl
   * d. CD4
   e. suppressor T

## Matching Questions

D 61. Matching. Include the most appropriate letter in each blank at the left.

1. ___ antigens
2. ___ B lymphocytes
3. ___ perforin
4. ___ clone
5. ___ complement proteins
6. ___ cytotoxic T lymphocytes
7. ___ interleukins
8. ___ macrophages
9. ___ memory cells
10. ___ plasma cells
11. ___ retroviruses
12. ___ stem cells
13. ___ natural killer cells
14. ___ vaccine

A. cells that do not divide, die in less than a week, and secrete large quantities of antibodies

B. cells that directly destroy body cells already infected by viral or fungal parasites, as well as mutant and cancerous cells

C. lymphocytes that are held in reserve, circulate in the bloodstream, and enable a rapid response to subsequent encounters with the same type of invader

D. able to lyse cells by forming pore complexes

E. cells that are produced in the bone marrow and are never changed by the thymus; these cells produce antibodies

F. able to destroy cells but not dependent on recognition of antigen-MHC complexes

G. a class of proteins that help cells of the immune system communicate with each other

H. "big eaters" that alert other lymphocytes to the invasion of specific antigens

I immature cells that may or may not be committed to develop into one of several mature cell types

J. a group of cells that are all produced asexually from one original parent cell

K. surface patterns of nonself molecules or particles

L. proteins released by cytotoxic T cells to destroy target cell membranes

M. preparation injected into the body to elicit a primary immune response

N. one of this group has been identified as the causative agent of AIDS

## Classification Questions

Answer questions 62–66 in reference to the five types of white cells listed below:

    a  macrophages
    b.  helper T cells
    c.  B cells
    d.  cytotoxic T cells
    e.  natural killer cells

D    **62.**  These cells kill tumor cells but are not B or T lymphocytes.

M    **63.**  These cells scavenge dead cells and attack bacteria directly.

D    **64.**  These cells destroy cells infected by viruses.

D    **65.**  These cells recognize cell surface antigens and initiate the proliferation of lymphocytes.

M    **66.**  Antibody production occurs in these cells.

Answers:      62.  e        63.  a        64.  d
              65.  b        66.  c

Answer questions 67–71 in reference to the five items listed below:

    a  antigens
    b.  antibodies
    c.  helper T cells
    d.  cytotoxic T cells
    e.  memory B cells

E    **67.**  These bind, as in a lock-and-key mechanism, to foreign proteins?

M    **68.**  These produce immunoglobulins in response to the reinvasion by a virus?

D    **69.**  These directly attack the foreign cells of an incompatible skin graft?

M    **70.**  An $Rh^+$ molecule in the body of an $Rh^-$ woman is an example of these.

D    **71.**  Bacteria and viruses in the blood are attacked by proteins produced by these.

Answers:      67.  b        68.  e        69.  d
              70.  a        71.  e

## Selecting the Exception

M    **72.**  Four of the five answers listed below are barriers to invasion. Select the exception.
    a  intact skin
    b.  mucous membrane
    c.  gastric juices
*    d.  blood plasma
    e.  lysozyme

D    **73.**  Four of the five answers listed below are characteristic reactions of the complement system to invaders. Select the exception.
    a  causes an amplifying cascade of reactions to invaders
*    b.  triggers the secretion of histamines
    c.  causes invading cells to lyse
    d.  enhances the recognition of invaders by phagocytes
    e.  creates gradients that attract phagocytes

D    **74.**  Four of the five answers listed below are events of the inflammatory response. Select the exception.
    a  increases capillary permeability
    b.  release of histamine
    c.  blood vessels dilate
*    d.  temperature of the affected areas drops
    e.  phagocytes migrate toward the affected area

E    **75.**  Four of the five answers listed below are targets of the immune system. Select the exception.
    a  virus
*    b.  normal cells
    c.  cancer cells
    d.  bacteria
    e.  debris and dead cells

# CHAPTER 29
# RESPIRATION

## Multiple-Choice Questions

### THE NATURE OF RESPIRATION

E      1.  The most abundant gas in the earth's atmosphere is
           a   oxygen.
           b.  water vapor.
           c.  argon.
        *  d.  nitrogen.
           e.  carbon dioxide.

E      2.  The oxygen content of air is approximately
        *  a   21 percent.
           b.  78 percent.
           c.  0.04 percent.
           d.  0.96 percent.
           e.  100 percent.

E      3.  The concentration of nitrogen in the earth's atmosphere is approximately
        *  a   78 percent.
           b.  66 percent.
           c.  50 percent.
           d.  33 percent.
           e.  20 percent.

E      4.  The concentration of carbon dioxide in the earth's atmosphere is
           a   0.004 percent.
        *  b.  0.04 percent.
           c.  0.4 percent.
           d.  4.0 percent.
           e.  40 percent.

M      5.  Exchange across a membrane requires
           a   moisture.
           b.  transport proteins.
           c.  pressure gradients.
        *  d.  a and c only
           e.  a, b, and c

M      6.  The movement of both oxygen and carbon dioxide in the body is accomplished by
           a   exocytosis and endocytosis.
           b.  bulk flow.
           c.  osmosis.
        *  d.  diffusion.
           e.  facilitated diffusion.

D      7.  As an animal grows larger, the surface area increases by the mathematical _____ of its dimensions.
           a   cube
        *  b.  square
           c.  square root
           d.  doubling
           e.  quotient

M      8.  Ventilation is defined as
           a   bailing water over the gills.
           b.  movement of water past cells by using flagella.
           c.  moving air in and out of lungs.
           d.  tracheal exchanges.
        *  e.  all of the above

### INVERTEBRATE RESPIRATION

E      9.  For the surface of an animal to function in the integumentary exchange of gases it must
           a   be thin and soft.
           b.  have a high number of blood vessels.
           c.  have mucus or moist covering.
        *  d.  all of the above

E     10.  External gills are characteristic of
           a   larval insects.
           b.  larval amphibians.
           c.  most fish.
           d.  all of the above
        *  e.  only a and b

M     11.  Adult insects exchange respiratory gases primarily by means of
           a   spiracles.
        *  b.  tracheae.
           c.  lungs.
           d.  gills.
           e.  body surface.

### VERTEBRATE RESPIRATION

M     12.  Blood and water flowing in opposite directions, in conjunction with respiratory systems, is a mechanism that explains how
        *  a   oxygen uptake by blood capillaries in fish gills occurs.
           b.  ventilation occurs.
           c.  sounds originating in the vocal cords of the larynx are formed.
           d.  intrapleural pressure is established.
           e.  all of the above

E     13.  The group of animals with the most efficient respiratory system is the
           a   amphibians.
        *  b.  birds.
           c.  mammals.
           d.  reptiles.
           e.  fish.

M  14. Birds
   a. breathe through air sacs.
   b. exchange gas with their lungs as they breathe in or out.
   c. have exceptionally large and flexible lungs.
   d. have four air sacs for each lung that behave like bellows.
 * e. both b and d

## HUMAN RESPIRATORY SYSTEM

M  15. What is the proper sequence in the flow of air in mammals?
   a. nasal cavities, larynx, pharynx, bronchi, trachea
   b. nasal cavities, pharynx, bronchi, larynx, trachea
 * c. nasal cavities, pharynx, larynx, trachea, bronchi
   d. nasal cavities, larynx, pharynx, trachea, bronchi
   e. nasal cavities, bronchi, larynx, trachea, pharynx

M  16. The last mammalian structure that air moves through before the alveoli is the
   a. larynx.
   b. glottis.
 * c. bronchioles.
   d. trachea.
   e. pharynx.

D  17. During inhalation,
   a. the pressure in the thoracic cavity is greater than the pressure within the lungs.
 * b. the pressure in the thoracic cavity is less than the pressure within the lungs.
   c. the diaphragm moves upward and becomes more curved.
   d. the chest cavity volume decreases.
   e. all of the above

D  18. When humans breathe using only the mouth, which of the following is most diminished?
 * a. filtering
   b. warming
   c. moisturizing
   d. texturizing

M  19. Food and drink are prevented from entering the respiratory passageways during swallowing by means of the
   a. glottis.
   b. pharynx.
 * c. epiglottis.
   d. larynx.
   e. trachea.

M  20. When you swallow, the epiglottis covers the opening to the
   a. pharynx.
   b. esophagus.
 * c. larynx.
   d. bronchus.
   e. alveoli.

E  21. The human vocal cords are located in the
   a. glottis.
   b. pharynx.
   c. trachea.
 * d. larynx.
   e. bronchus.

M  22. In pleurisy,
   a. some of the alveoli fill with fluid.
 * b. the pleural membrane becomes inflamed and swollen and causes painful breathing.
   c. the diaphragm develops muscular cramps.
   d. the vagus nerve is irritated.
   e. the intercostal muscles become inflamed and cause pain during deep breathing.

E  23. Actual exchange of gases in the lungs occurs in the
   a. bronchi.
 * b. alveoli.
   c. bronchioles.
   d. tracheas.
   e. glottis.

M  24. Which of the following is NOT found in lung tissue?
   a. blood capillaries
   b. alveolar sacs
   c. interstitial fluid
   d. connective tissue
 * e. muscle

## GAS EXCHANGE AND TRANSPORT

M  25. Oxygen moves from alveoli to the bloodstream
 * a. because the concentration of oxygen is greater in alveoli than in the blood.
   b. mainly due to the activity of carbonic anhydrase in the red blood cells.
   c. by using the assistance of carbaminohemoglobin.
   d. through active transport.
   e. all of the above

M  26. Hemoglobin
   a. tends to give up oxygen in regions where partial pressure of oxygen exceeds that in the lungs.
   b. tends to hold onto oxygen when the pH of the blood drops.
   c. tends to release oxygen where the temperature is lower.
 * d. releases oxygen more readily in highly active tissues.
   e. all of the above

M  27. Which statement is NOT true?
   a   Carbon dioxide is more soluble in fluid than in oxygen.
   b.  Carbon dioxide diffuses more rapidly across the respiratory surface than does oxygen.
   c.  The major muscle involved in breathing is the diaphragm.
*  d.  Oxygen is carried primarily by blood plasma.
   e.  Carbon dioxide is carried by the blood plasma.

M  28. Oxyhemoglobin gives up $O_2$ when
*  a   carbon dioxide concentrations are high.
   b.  body temperature is lowered.
   c.  pH values are high.
   d.  $CO_2$ concentrations are low.
   e.  all of the above

M  29. Most of the carbon dioxide produced by the body is transported to the lungs in
   a   a gaseous form.
   b.  blood plasma.
   c.  potassium carbonate ions.
*  d.  bicarbonate ions.
   e.  carbonic acid.

M  30. The enzyme responsible for converting free carbon dioxide in the blood into forms in which it can be transported in the blood is
*  a   carbonic anhydrase.
   b.  carboxypeptidase.
   c.  carbonase.
   d.  decarboxylase.
   e.  dehydrogenase.

M  31. Which statement is true?
   a   Breathing rate and depth are completely under voluntary control.
   b.  A person can commit suicide by holding one's breath.
   c.  The contraction of the diaphragm and muscle of the rib cage are under the control of areas of the brain.
   d.  There are chemoreceptors in the brain that monitor carbon dioxide content in the blood and control breathing.
*  e.  both c and d

E  32. Carbon monoxide
   a   has a very low affinity or attraction to hemoglobin.
   b.  is unlikely to be transported by the circulatory system.
   c.  is not the cause of death of people who breathe excessive amounts of automobile exhausts.
*  d.  can arise from cigarette smoke.
   e.  both c and d

E  33. The cessation of smoking
   a   can reduce the risk of stillbirth.
   b.  reduces the chances of cancer.
   c.  reduces the chances of coronary disease.
   d.  improves lung functioning.
*  e.  all of the above

E  34. Smoking has been shown to cause
   a   bronchitis.
   b.  emphysema.
   c.  lung cancer.
   d.  coronary disease.
*  e.  all of the above

E  35. Decompression sickness is caused by
   a   a rapid rise of carbon dioxide in the blood.
   b.  lack of oxygen in the tissues.
*  c.  bubbles of nitrogen in the blood.
   d.  glucose deficiency.
   e.  descending too rapidly into deep water.

## Matching Questions

D  36. Choose the one most appropriate answer for each.

   1 _____  alveoli
   2 _____  bronchi
   3 _____  diaphragm
   4 _____  epiglottis
   5 _____  intercostal rib muscles
   6 _____  larynx
   7 _____  pharynx
   8 _____  trachea

   A.  flexible windpipe reinforced with cartridges
   B.  contains two true vocal cords
   C.  move the ribs
   D.  throat cavity behind the mouth
   E.  connect trachea to lungs
   F.  flaplike structure that points upward and allows air to enter trachea; closed during swallowing
   G.  contraction moves it downward
   H.  microscopically small pockets lined with moist epithelium

   Answers:
   1. H     2. E     3. G
   4. F     5. C     6. B
   7. D     8. A

## Classification Questions

Answer questions 37–41 in reference to the five components of respiratory systems listed below:

  a pharynx
  b. larynx
  c. trachea
  d. bronchiole
  e. alveolus

E  **37.** The voice box is located here.

M  **38.** This is the last component of the human lung that air flows into.

M  **39.** Gas exchange between the air in the lungs and their blood supply occurs here.

E  **40.** Air moves from the nasal cavity into this component.

M  **41.** Spent air moves from the bronchial tubes back to this component.

*Answers:*  37. b  38. e  39. e
      40. a  41. c

## Selecting the Exception

E  **42.** Four of the five answers listed below are parts of the same body system. Select the exception.
    a trachea
 * b. esophagus
    c. alveoli
    d. bronchiole
    e. glottis

M  **43.** Four of the five answers listed below are components of the human respiratory system. Select the exception.
    a thoracic cavity
    b. trachea
    c. diaphragm
 * d. spiracle
    e. larynx

D  **44.** Four of the five answers listed below are related by the same function. Select the exception.
    a blood plasma
    b. carbaminohemoglobin
 * c. oxyhemoglobin
    d. carbonic acid
    e. bicarbonate ions

# CHAPTER 30

# DIGESTION AND HUMAN NUTRITION

## Multiple-Choice Questions

### THE NATURE OF DIGESTIVE SYSTEMS

E  **1.** Ruminants need special enzymes to digest
   a. starch.
   b. proteins.
   * c. cellulose.
   d. lignin.
   e. catin.

M  **2.** Which of the following possess an incomplete digestive system?
   a. annelids
   * b. flatworms
   c. mollusks
   d. arthropods
   e. echinoderms

M  **3.** The process that moves nutrients into the blood or lymph is
   * a. absorption.
   b. assimilation.
   c. digestion.
   d. ingestion.
   e. all of the above

E  **4.** The process that releases digestive enzymes is
   a. mobility.
   * b. secretion.
   c. digestion.
   d. absorption.
   e. elimination.

E  **5.** The muscular digestive organ in which food is ground into small bits is the
   a. lumen.
   * b. gizzard.
   c. crop.
   d. stomach.
   e. cloaca.

E  **6.** Earthworms and birds have a crop that is modified for
   a. digestion of cellulose.
   * b. food storage.
   c. mechanical breakdown of food.
   d. digestion of fats.
   e. storage and elimination of undigested food.

### OVERVIEW OF THE HUMAN DIGESTIVE SYSTEM

E  **7.** Which of the following organs of the digestive system is different from the other four because it does NOT produce any secretions that aid in the digestive process?
   a. stomach
   b. liver
   * c. colon
   d. pancreas
   e. salivary gland

E  **8.** Which of the following stores feces immediately prior to elimination?
   a. small intestine
   b. liver
   c. appendix
   d. gall bladder
   * e. rectum

D  **9.** Which of the following is NOT an active participant in the digestive process?
   a. small intestine
   * b. esophagus
   c. pancreas
   d. mouth
   e. liver

### INTO THE MOUTH, DOWN THE TUBE

E  **10.** Chewing
   a. breaks food down into smaller pieces.
   b. physically and mechanically breaks up the food.
   c. increases the surface area of food exposed to digestive enzymes.
   d. actually mixes some enzymes with the food.
   * e. all of the above

E  **11.** A bolus is formed in the
   * a. mouth.
   b. esophagus.
   c. stomach.
   d. small intestine.
   e. large intestine.

E  **12.** The digestion of which class of foods begins in the mouth?
   * a. carbohydrates
   b. proteins
   c. lipids
   d. amino acids
   e. nucleic acids

M    13. During the process of swallowing, the
        a   esophagus is temporarily closed by the glottis.
*     b.   epiglottis closes the trachea leading to the lungs.
        c.   pharynx restricts food entry to the esophagus.
        d.   epiglottis seals the esophagus.
        e.   none of the above

## DIGESTION IN THE STOMACH AND SMALL INTESTINE

M    14. Which process propels the food down the esophagus into the stomach?
        a   glycolysis
        b.   plasmolysis
        c.   emulsion
*     d.   peristalsis
        e.   all of the above

M    15. Sphincters
        a   are circular muscles.
        b.   prevent backflow.
        c.   are smooth muscles.
        d.   are found at the beginning and end of the stomach.
*     e.   all of the above

E    16. The digestion of proteins begins in the
*     a   stomach.
        b.   pancreas.
        c.   small intestine.
        d.   large intestine.
        e.   esophagus.

E    17. Chyme is formed in the
        a   mouth.
        b.   esophagus.
*     c.   stomach.
        d.   small intestine.
        e.   large intestine.

E    18. The acid released in the stomach is
        a   carbonic acid.
*     b.   hydrochloric acid.
        c.   nitric acid.
        d.   sulfuric acid.
        e.   phosphoric acid.

D    19. Which of the following is NOT an active form of an enzyme?
        a   trypsin
        b.   amylase
        c.   pepsin
*     d.   pepsinogen
        e.   chymotrypsin

M    20. Which of the following factors does NOT stimulate the stomach to pass on its contents to the small intestine?
*     a   depression and fear
        b.   stimulation of mechanoreceptors in the stomach wall following a large meal
        c.   reduced fat or acid content of chyme in the duodenum
        d.   elation and relaxation
        e.   all of the above

E    21. The digestion of fats mostly occurs in the
        a   stomach.
        b.   pancreas.
*     c.   small intestine.
        d.   lymph vascular system.
        e.   liver.

M    22. Which of the following does NOT digest proteins?
        a   trypsin
        b.   chymotrypsin
        c.   aminopeptidase
        d.   pepsin
*     e.   lipase

E    23. Ducts from the pancreas and liver enter the
        a   stomach.
        b.   colon.
*     c.   small intestine.
        d.   gall bladder.
        e.   rectum.

M    24. Which of the following is NOT found in bile?
        a   salts
        b.   cholesterol
        c.   pigments
*     d.   digestive enzymes
        e.   lecithin

M    25. Bile
        a   has no effect on digestion.
*     b.   helps in the digestion of fats.
        c.   helps in the digestion of carbohydrates.
        d.   helps in the digestion of proteins.
        e.   both c and d

E    26. Fats are digested by which of the following?
        a   aminopeptidase
        b.   disaccharidases
        c.   amylase
*     d.   lipase
        e.   trypsin

M    27. High stomach acidity
        a   creates ideal conditions for carbohydrate digestion.
        b.   promotes emulsification of fats.
*     c.   favors protein digestion.
        d.   blocks the release of histamine, thereby favoring production of peptic ulcers.
        e.   converts lipases into their active forms.

M  28. Stomach motility
    a  decreases following a heavy meal.
*   b. controls the amount of material leaving the
       pyloric sphincter.
    c  is unaffected by emotional state or external
       environmental factors.
    d. may be retarded when stretch receptors on
       the stomach wall are activated.
    e. is increased by hormones released in
       response to high stomach acidity.

M  29. Which of the following is NOT a secretion of the
       stomach?
    a  pepsinogen
    b. mucus
    c. gastrin
    d. hydrochloric acid
*   e. lipase

E  30. The first part of the small intestine is the
*   a  duodenum.
    b. ileum.
    c. colon.
    d. cecum.
    e. jejunum.

M  31. Ducts from the pancreas and liver enter the
    a  stomach.
    b. colon.
*   c. duodenum.
    d. jejunum.
    e. ileum.

D  32. Which of the following is NOT a hormone?
    a  gastrin
    b. secretin
*   c. mucin
    d. cholecystokinin
    e. All of the above are hormones.

D  33. Which of the following chemicals is the first
       hormone secreted by the intestinal tract in
       response to the presence of food?
    a  salivary amylase
    b. cholecystokinin
    c. glucose insulinotropic peptide (GIP)
*   d. gastrin
    e. secretin

M  34. Which of the following acts enzymatically rather
       than hormonally?
    a  cholecystokinin
*   b. pepsin
    c. secretin
    d. gastrin
    e. all of the above

M  35. Which of the following stimulates the
       gallbladder to contract?
    a  salivary amylase
*   b. cholecystokinin
    c. glucose insulinotropic peptide (GIP)
    d. gastrin
    e. secretin

**ABSORPTION IN THE SMALL INTESTINE**

E  36. Of the following the greatest amount of nutrient
       absorption takes place in the
    a  stomach.
*   b. small intestine.
    c. colon.
    d. pancreas.
    e. esophagus.

M  37. Which of the following are absorbed by the
       lymphatic system?
    a  monosaccharides
    b. amino acids
    c. monoglycerides
    d. fatty acids
*   e. both c and d

M  38. Movement of glucose through the membranes of
       the small intestine is primarily by
    a  osmosis.
    b. bulk flow.
*   c. active transport.
    d. diffusion.
    e. all of the above

D  39. Which of the following are tiny projections of
       the mucosal wall?
    a  microvilli
    b. mucins
*   c. villi
    d. submucosa
    e. jejunum

M  40. Which of the following layers lies next to the
       lumen of the intestinal tract?
    a  longitudinal muscles
    b. circular muscle layer
    c. submucosa
*   d. mucosa
    e. serosa

M  41. Peristalsis
    a  is an adverse reaction to improper food.
*   b. occurs in the digestive tract from the
       esophagus to the large intestine.
    c. occurs only in humans.
    d. is a defensive mechanism that reduces the
       bacterial invasion of the digestive tract.
    e. is an inflammation of the intestinal mucosa.

D  42. The function of segmentation is to
    a  move the food through the digestive tract.
    b. churn the food and mix the contents with
       the digestive tract.
    c. bring the contents to the wall of the tract,
       where they could be absorbed.
    d. produce a wavelike push of the gut contents
       through the system.
*   e. both b and c, but not a or d

E    **43.** The digestion of fats mostly occurs in the
     a.   stomach.
     b.   pancreas.
\*   c.   small intestine.
     d.   lymph vascular system.
     e.   liver.

## DISPOSITION OF ABSORBED ORGANIC COMPOUNDS

E    **44.** The organ that stores and detoxifies different organic compounds is the
     a.   pancreas.
     b.   small intestine.
\*   c.   liver.
     d.   spleen.
     e.   gall bladder.

M    **45.** The liver is associated with all of the following functions EXCEPT
     a.   formation of urea.
     b.   formation of bile.
     c.   detoxification of poisons.
\*   d.   secretion of bicarbonate ions.
     e.   carbohydrate metabolism.

M    **46.** The liver is associated with all of the following functions EXCEPT
     a.   inactivation of drugs.
     b.   assembly and storage of fats.
     c.   assembly and disassembly of certain proteins.
     d.   degradation of worn-out blood cells.
\*   e.   formation of glucagon.

M    **47.** During, or shortly after a meal, most cells use which of the following as a source of energy?
     a.   fat
     b.   amino acids
\*   c.   glucose
     d.   glycogen
     e.   any of the above, depending on the concentration of the particular organic compound

## THE LARGE INTESTINE

M    **48.** Bulk in the diet
     a.   increases the length of time material is in the colon.
     b.   increases the chance of cancer.
\*   c.   prevents diarrhea and irritable colon syndrome.
     d.   may increase the incidence of appendicitis in the people who eat too much bulk.
     e.   is characteristic of people in urban areas.

E    **49.** The primary function of the large intestine is
     a.   storage of feces.
     b.   retention of water.
     c.   manufacture of vitamin K.
     d.   digestion of fats.
\*   e.   absorption of water.

D    **50.** What the structure located at the junction of the small and large intestines?
\*   a.   cecum
     b.   rectum
     c.   anus
     d.   villus
     e.   pharynx

## HUMAN NUTRITIONAL REQUIREMENTS

M    **51.** The ideal diet consists of all of the following EXCEPT
     a.   bulk.
\*   b.   few complex carbohydrates.
     c.   little salt and sugar.
     d.   little red meat.
     e.   fish, poultry, and legumes.

M    **52.** Which of the following should be present in the human diet in the highest percentage?
     a.   protein
\*   b.   carbohydrate
     c.   lipid
     d.   vitamins
     e.   minerals

M    **53.** Lipids can serve in all but which of the following capacities?
\*   a.   enzymes
     b.   energy
     c.   membrane structure
     d.   insulation
     e.   It can serve in all of the above capacities.

E    **54.** Of the 20 amino acids, how many are considered to be essential in that the human body cannot synthesize them?
     a.   2
     b.   5
\*   c.   8
     d.   10
     e.   12

## VITAMINS AND MINERALS

M    **55.** Which of the following vitamins is fat-soluble and can be stored in the body?
\*   a.   A
     b.   $B_1$ (thiamine)
     c.   C (ascorbic acid)
     d.   $B_2$ (riboflavin)
     e.   niacin

E    **56.** Which vitamin functions in forming a blood clot?
     a.   A
     b.   E
\*   c.   K
     d.   B
     e.   all of the above

M 57. A deficiency of which vitamin produces rickets in children and osteomalcia in adults?
    a. A
    b. B
    c. C
   * d. D
    e. E

M 58. A deficiency of vitamin C may give rise to
    a. beriberi.
   * b. scurvy.
    c. pellagra.
    d. hypothyroidism.
    e. all of the above

M 59. Which of the following statements is NOT true concerning mineral metabolism?
    a. Sodium and potassium are needed for maintaining osmotic balances.
   * b. Zinc is important in building strong bones and teeth.
    c. Sodium and potassium are needed for muscle and nerve functioning.
    d. Iron is needed for building cytochromes and heme groups.
    e. all the statements are true

E 60. Lack of which element can lead to thyroid problems?
    a. iron
   * b. iodine
    c. calcium
    d. zinc
    e. magnesium

M 61. The element needed for blood clotting, nerve transmission, and bone and tooth formation is
    a. iron.
    b. iodine.
   * c. calcium.
    d. zinc.
    e. magnesium.

E 62. The constituent of hemoglobin whose absence leads to anemia is
   * a. iron.
    b. iodine.
    c. calcium.
    d. zinc.
    e. magnesium.

## Matching Questions

D 63. Choose the one most appropriate answer for each.

1 _____ amylase
2 _____ bile
3 _____ disaccharidase
4 _____ gastrin
5 _____ lipase
6 _____ monosaccharides
7 _____ pepsin
8 _____ amino- and carboxypeptidase
9 _____ sphincter
10 _____ trypsin

A. made in the small intestine and pancreas; acts on protein fragments
B. glucose, fructose, and galactose
C. made in the pancreas; acts on fats
D. made by the pancreas and salivary glands; acts on starch
E. made by the small intestine; acts on double sugars
F. made by the pancreas; acts on proteins and polypeptides
G. contains cholesterol; helps emulsify fats
H. made in the stomach; acts on proteins
I. stimulates hydrochloric acid secretion
J. separates the stomach from the small intestine

Answers:
| 1. D | 2. G | 3. E |
|------|------|------|
| 4. I | 5. C | 6. B |
| 7. H | 8. A | 9. J |
| 10. F | | |

## Classification Questions

Answer questions 64–68 in reference to the five components of the gastrointestinal tract listed below:

    a.  stomach
    b.  gall bladder
    c.  small intestine
    d.  appendix
    e.  large intestine

D    **64.**  Many organisms, such as birds, have ceca (digestive pouches) in which bacteria break down difficult-to-digest plant materials. These ceca are homologous to this in humans.

M    **65.**  This organ absorbs about 95 percent of the water that enters the human body, either as fluids or as part of food being eaten.

M    **66.**  Enzymatic digestion of proteins occurs primarily in this organ.

E    **67.**  Bile salts, bile pigments, cholesterol, and lecithin are stored by this structure.

E    **68.**  The digestion of cellulose occurs in this part of the digestive system of the cow?

*Answers*:    64.  d    65.  c    66.  c
               67.  b    68.  a

Answer questions 69–73 in reference to the four glands or structures of the mammalian gastrointestinal tract listed below:

    a.  salivary glands
    b.  stomach lining
    c.  intestinal lining
    d.  pancreas

M    **69.**  This is where the enzyme pepsin is produced.

D    **70.**  This is where the enzyme carboxypeptidase is produced.

D    **71.**  This is where the fat-digesting enzyme, lipase, is formed.

D    **72.**  This is where the peptide-digesting enzyme, aminopeptidase, is produced.

M    **73.**  This is where the protein-digesting enzyme, trypsin, is produced.

*Answers*:    69.  b    70.  d    71.  d
               72.  c    73.  d

Answer questions 74–78 in reference to the five vitamins listed below:

    a.  Vitamin $B_1$
    b.  Vitamin $B_2$
    c.  Niacin
    d.  Vitamin $B_6$
    e.  Vitamin $B_{12}$

D    **74.**  This vitamin is a coenzyme involved in amino acid metabolism and obtained from meat, potatoes, even spinach.

D    **75.**  This vitamin is a component of the coenzyme thiamine pyrophosphate.

M    **76.**  This vitamin is a constituent of the coenzymes $NAD^+$ and $NADP^+$.

M    **77.**  This vitamin is more commonly known as riboflavin.

D    **78.**  This vitamin acts as a coenzyme in nucleic acid metabolism.

*Answers*:    74.  d    75.  a    76.  c
               77.  b    78.  e

## Selecting the Exception

E    **79.**  Four of the five answers listed below are structures through which ingested foodstuffs travel. Select the exception.
      a.  crop
  *  b.  liver
      c.  gizzard
      d.  rectum
      e.  small intestine

E    **80.**  Four of the five answers listed below possess a complete digestive system. Select the exception.
      a.  human
      b.  bird
      c.  earthworm
  *  d.  planaria
      e.  fish

M    **81.**  Four of the five answers listed below are functions of the digestive organs. Select the exception.
  *  a.  excretion
      b.  absorption
      c.  motility
      d.  secretion
      e.  digestion

M    **82.**  Four of the five answers listed below release secretions that assist digestion. Select the exception.
      a.  salivary gland
  *  b.  esophagus
      c.  pancreas
      d.  gall bladder
      e.  liver

D       **83.** Four of the five answers listed below are
        hormones associated with digestion. Select the
        exception.
    *    a    bile
         b.   gastrin
         c.   secretin
         d.   cholecystokinin
         e.   glucose insulinotropic peptide

D       **84.** Four of the five answers listed below are end -
        products of digestion ready for intestinal
        absorption. Select the exception.
         a    monoglyceride
         b.   nucleotides
    *    c.   disaccharides
         d.   amino acids
         e.   free fatty acids

M       **85.** Four of the five answers listed below digest the
        same class of foods. Select the exception.
         a    aminopeptidase
         b.   pepsin
    *    c.   amylase
         d.   trypsin
         e.   chymotrypsin

M       **86.** Four of the five answers listed below perform
        their task in the same workplace. Select
        the exception.
    *    a    pepsin
         b.   lipase
         c.   carboxypeptidase
         d.   nuclease
         e.   disaccharidase

M       **87.** Four of the five answers listed below are all of
        the same class of vitamins. Select
        the exception.
         a    Vitamin A
         b.   Vitamin K
    *    c.   Vitamin C
         d.   Vitamin D
         e.   Vitamin E

D       **88.** Four of the five answers listed below are
        functions performed by the same organ. Select
        the exception.
    *    a    regulates pH of body fluids
         b.   removes toxic substances from the blood
         c.   stores and interconverts carbohydrates, fats,
              and proteins
         d.   inactivates hormones
         e.   forms urea from nitrogenous waste

# CHAPTER 31
# THE INTERNAL ENVIRONMENT

## Multiple-Choice Questions

E    **1.**  Animals began invading land how many million years ago?
- a  800
- b.  600
- \*  c.  375
- d.  250
- e.  150

M    **2.**  How much of the total water gain does the kangaroo rat get from metabolic water?
- a  5 percent
- b.  12 percent
- c.  33 percent
- d.  65 percent
- \*  e.  90 percent

D    **3.**  Extracellular fluid is defined as
- a  blood only.
- b.  interstitial fluid only.
- \*  c.  both blood and interstitial fluid.
- d.  urine.
- e.  sweat.

## URINARY SYSTEM OF MAMMALS

M    **4.**  All but which of the following are significant routes for water loss from the body?
- a  excretion in urine
- \*  b.  sneezing
- c.  sweating
- d.  elimination in feces
- e.  evaporation from respiratory surfaces

E    **5.**  The process that normally exerts the greatest control over the water balance of an individual is
- a  sweating.
- b.  elimination in feces.
- \*  c.  urinary excretion.
- d.  evaporation through the skin.
- e.  respiratory loss.

D    **6.**  Which of the following does NOT dispose of a type of waste directly to the environment?
- a  digestive system
- b.  respiratory system
- c.  integumentary system
- \*  d.  circulatory system
- e.  urinary system

D    **7.**  Humans gain the least amounts of water by what route?
- \*  a  metabolism
- b.  ingestion of liquids
- c.  ingestion of solids
- d.  All of the above contribute equal amounts of water.

D    **8.**  Toxic substances, such as ammonia and urea which are routinely found in the blood, are metabolites of
- a  carbohydrates.
- \*  b.  proteins.
- c.  lipids.
- d.  minerals.
- e.  vitamins.

E    **9.**  The subunit of a kidney that purifies blood and restores solute and water balance is called a
- a  glomerulus.
- b.  loop of Henle.
- \*  c.  nephron.
- d.  ureter.
- e.  all of the above

M    **10.**  In the kidney, the ducts from the nephrons empty immediately into the
- a  renal cortex.
- b.  renal medulla.
- \*  c.  renal pelvis.
- d.  ureter.
- e.  urethra.

E    **11.**  The last portion of the excretory system through which urine passes before it is eliminated from the body is the
- a  glomerulus.
- b.  ureter.
- \*  c.  urethra.
- d.  bladder.
- e.  rectum.

E    **12.**  The functional unit of the kidney is the
- a  Bowman's capsule.
- \*  b.  nephron.
- c.  glomerulus.
- d.  urinary bladder.
- e.  urethra.

M    **13.**  Which of the following processes is under voluntary control?
- a  filtration
- b.  reabsorption
- \*  c.  urination
- d.  secretion
- e.  excretion

M 14. Filtration occurs in which section of mammalian nephrons?
* a glomerulus
  b. loops of Henle
  c. proximal tubules
  d. distal tubules
  e. peritubular capillaries

E 15. The tube leading from each kidney to the bladder is the
  a glomerulus.
* b. ureter.
  c. urethra.
  d. bladder.
  e. rectum.

E 16. Filtrate that is removed from the blood is collected by the
  a loop of Henle.
  b. glomerulus.
  c. distal tubule.
  d. proximal tubule.
* e. Bowman's capsule.

D 17. After the blood leaves the glomerular capillaries, it next goes to the
  a renal vein.
  b. renal artery.
* c. peritubular capillaries.
  d. vena cava.
  e. heart.

## URINE FORMATION

M 18. Which of the following are most permeable to water and small molecules?
* a glomerular capillaries.
  b. peritubular capillaries.
  c. proximal tubules.
  d. ureters.
  e. collecting ducts

D 19. The process of filtration in the glomerulus is driven by
  a active transport.
* b. hydrostatic pressure.
  c. osmosis.
  d. dialysis.
  e. sodium-potassium pumps.

M 20. The process during which potassium and hydrogen ions, penicillin, and some toxic substances are put into the urine by active transport is called
* a secretion.
  b. reabsorption.
  c. filtration.
  d. osmosis.
  e. excretion.

E 21. Which of the following substances is NOT filtered from the bloodstream?
  a water
* b. plasma proteins
  c. urea
  d. glucose
  e. sodium

M 22. What is the name given to the fluid removed from the blood but not yet processed by the nephron tubules?
  a urine
  b. water
  c. uretrial fluid
* d. filtrate
  e. renal plasma

E 23. A kidney machine removes solutes from the blood by means of
  a osmosis.
  b. diffusion.
* c. dialysis.
  d. active transport.
  e. bulk flow.

M 24. The antidiuretic hormone
  a promotes processes that lead to an increase in the volume of urine.
* b. promotes processes that lead to a decrease in the volume of urine.
  c. acts on the proximal tubules of nephrons in the kidney.
  d. is produced by the adrenal cortex.
  e. all of the above

M 25. Reabsorption is the movement of water and solutes from the _____ to the _____.
  a interstitial fluid; tubules
  b. glomerular capillaries; Bowman's capsule
  c. Bowman's capsule; nephron tubules
* d. nephron tubules; capillaries
  e. glomerular capillaries; peritubular capillaries

E 26. In reabsorption,
  a plasma proteins are returned to the blood.
  b. excess hydrogen ions are removed from the blood.
  c. excess water is passed on to the urine.
* d. nutrients and salts are selectively returned to the blood.
  e. drugs and foreign substances are passed into the urine.

E 27. About what percent of the fluid removed from the blood is eventually returned to the blood?
  a 59
  b. 90
* c. 98
  d. 0.9
  e. 9

D    **28.** Most of the water and sodium is reabsorbed in the
     a   glomerulus.
*    b.   proximal tubule.
     c.   distal tubule.
     d.   loop of Henle.
     e.   collecting duct.

D    **29.** The reabsorption of solutes is the result of active transport of
     a   potassium.
*    b.   sodium.
     c.   carbonate.
     d.   chloride.
     e.   all of the above

M    **30.** The hormone that influences sodium reabsorption in the kidney is
     a   antidiuretic hormone.
     b.   cortisone.
*    c.   aldosterone.
     d.   corticotropic hormone.
     e.   adrenalin.

E    **31.** The hormone that controls the concentration of urine is
     a   insulin.
     b.   glucagon.
*    c.   the antidiuretic hormone.
     d.   thyroxine.
     e.   epinephrine.

D    **32.** A rise in sodium levels and extracellular volume leads to a rise in blood pressure. As a result
     a   renin levels rise, but aldosterone levels fall.
     b.   renin levels fall, but aldosterone levels rise.
     c.   renin and aldosterone levels rise.
*    d.   renin and aldosterone levels drop.

M    **33.** The hormonal control over excretion occurs in the
     a   Bowman's capsule.
     b.   proximal tubule.
*    c.   distal tubule.
     d.   loop of Henle.
     e.   urinary bladder.

D    **34.** Ethanol (drinking alcohol) is an inhibitor of ADH. Therefore, a person consuming a couple of mixed drinks should excrete
     a   less water because ADH promotes reabsorption.
     b.   the alcohol because ADH cannot degrade it.
     c.   ketone bodies formed from the alcohol.
*    d.   more water because ADH normally promotes reabsorption.
     e.   more water plus the alcohol due to the ADH inhibition.

E    **35.** Which of the following does NOT belong with the others?
     a   ADH
     b.   aldosterone
     c.   renin
*    d.   insulin

E    **36.** In humans, the thirst center is located in the
     a   adrenal cortex.
*    b.   hypothalamus.
     c.   anterior pituitary.
     d.   glomerulus.
     e.   stomach.

## THE BODY'S ACID–BASE BALANCE

D    **37.** The urinary system helps to maintain the extracellular fluid pH by
     a   synthesizing buffers.
     b.   retaining carbon dioxide in the filtrate.
*    c.   excreting hydrogen ions as water.
     d.   combining hydrogen ions with urea.

D    **38.** Which of the following does NOT influence the pH of the blood and extracellular fluids?
     a   respiration
     b.   blood proteins
     c.   bicarbonate ions
*    d.   filtration by glomerulus
     e.   phosphate and ammonia ions

## ON FISH, FROGS, AND KANGAROO RATS

M    **39.** Excess salts of saltwater fish are excreted
     a   by relatively large kidneys.
     b.   through the skin.
     c.   through the eyes.
     d.   through special salt glands located in the tail.
*    e.   through the gills.

## MAINTAINING BODY TEMPERATURE

E    **40.** The usual upper temperature limit before proteins are denatured is
     a   35°C.
*    b.   40°C.
     c.   45°C.
     d.   50°C.
     e.   55°C.

M    **41.** The rate of a chemical reaction is cut in half for a drop of every
     a   5°C.
*    b.   10°C.
     c.   15°C.
     d.   20°C.
     e.   25°C.

E   42. Heat loss by direct exchange of energy between molecules is called
    * a conduction.
      b. radiation.
      c. convection.
      d. metabolism.
      e. evaporation.

M   43. Which of the following processes is able to move heat in one direction only—away from the body?
      a convection
    * b. evaporation
      c. conduction
      d. radiation
      e. collection

E   44. The transfer of heat by air or water is called
      a radiation.
      b. conduction.
    * c. convection.
      d. denaturing.
      e. evaporation.

E   45. Endothermic animals
      a use up more energy than ectotherms.
      b. have more stamina than ectotherms.
      c. have a higher metabolic rate than ectotherms.
      d. have layers of fat to reduce heat loss.
    * e. all of the above

M   46. Which of the following statements is false?
      a Endotherms have a higher metabolic rate than ectotherms.
      b. Endotherms can regulate their temperature through behavior.
      c. Ectotherms regulate their temperatures through behavior.
      d. Heterotherms may function as either an ectotherm or an endotherm.
    * e. Ectotherms do better in cold climates.

M   47. Ectothermic animals
      a are more likely to use metabolism for heat.
      b. shun the sun during the daylight hours.
      c. are more adapted to cold.
    * d. are more likely to use behavioral temperature regulation.
      e. all of the above

M   48. Which of the following is NOT a response to low temperature that increases the chance for survival?
    * a hypothermia
      b. shivering
      c. production of brown fat
      d. pilomotor response
      e. increased metabolism

M   49. The primary thermostat of the body is located in the
      a heart.
    * b. hypothalamus.
      c. medulla oblongata.
      d. cerebellum.
      e. thyroid gland.

M   50. Which of the following is NOT part of the initial response to cold temperature?
    * a opening of peripheral blood vessels
      b. shivering
      c. increased respiration
      d. shunting of the blood to the core regions of the body
      e. increased metabolism

E   51. Responses to heat stress include
      a reduction in muscle contraction.
      b. increased sweating.
      c. dilation of peripheral blood vessels.
      d. loss of salts and liquids.
    * e. all of the above

## Matching Questions

D    **52.** Matching. Choose the one most appropriate answer for each.

1. ___ nephron
2. ___ aldosterone
3. ___ secretion
4. ___ ADH
5. ___ conduction
6. ___ convection
7. ___ pilomotor response
8. ___ ectothermic
9. ___ evaporation
10. ___ glomerular filtration
11. ___ hemodialysis
12. ___ hypothermia
13. ___ heterothermic
14. ___ radiation
15. ___ tubular reabsorption

A. do not maintain the same body temperature at all times; are capable of internal heat production

B. heat energy is released to the air when water escapes from the body surfaces

C. bulk flow of protein-free plasma from capillaries into Bowman's capsule

D. animals with more or less constant body temperature

E. infrared wavelengths released from body surface when environmental temperature is lower

F. movement of ions from peritubular capillaries into nephron tubules

G. loss of too much body heat

H. heat next to the body's surface undergoes mass transport by air or water currents

I. active and passive transport of solutes from peritubular capillaries into the nephron

J. a long, slender tubular unit in the vertebrate kidney that forms urine

K. body temperatures rise and fall with environmental changes

L. secreted by adrenal glands; influences sodium reabsorption

M. passive transport of water; active and passive transport of solutes out of the nephron into peritubular capillaries

N. heat energy is transferred from high to low temperature regions due to collisions between adjacent molecules

O. released from the posterior lobe of the pituitary in response to hypothalamic signals

P. toxic substances are extracted from blood circulating in cellophane tubes suspended in a warm-water bath

Q. erection of hairs and feathers by smooth muscles in the skin

*Answers:*

| 1. | J | 2. | L | 3. | F |
|----|---|----|---|----|---|
| 4. | O | 5. | N | 6. | H |
| 7. | Q | 8. | K | 9. | B |
| 10. | C | 11. | P | 12. | G |
| 13. | A | 14. | E | 15. | M |

## Classification Questions

Answer questions 53-57 in reference to the four regions of a nephron listed below:

a. Bowman's capsule
b. proximal tubule
c. descending portion of loop of Henle
d. distal tubule

M    **53.** Sodium ions are actively transported out of the nephron from this region.

E    **54.** Filtration of the blood occurs in association with this structure.

D    **55.** Antibiotics are secreted from this structure.

M    **56.** Permeability to water is regulated by antidiuretic hormone in this structure.

E    **57.** The glomerular capillaries are intimately associated with this structure.

*Answers*

| 53. | b | 54. | a | 55. | d |
|-----|---|-----|---|-----|---|
| 56. | d | 57. | a | | |

## Selecting the Exception

D    **58.** Four of the five answers listed below are potentially toxic waste products of metabolism. Select the exception.

   a. urea
 * b. water
   c. uric acid
   d. carbon dioxide
   e. ammonia

M    **59.** Four of the five answers listed below are parts of the same organ. Select the exception.

   a. distal tubule
   b. loop of Henle
 * c. ureter
   d. proximal tubule
   e. Bowman's capsule

M     **60.** Four of the five answers listed below are functions of the nephron. Select the exception.
- a   filtration
- \*    b.   dilution
- c.   excretion
- d.   reabsorption
- e.   secretion

D     **61.** Four of the five answers listed below are the result of ADH (antidiuretic hormone) secretion. Select the exception.
- a   water is reabsorbed in the distal tubule
- b.   fluid volume of blood increases
- \*    c.   rise in solute concentration in blood
- d.   distal tubule and collecting duct become more permeable to water
- e.   solutes concentration decreases

E     **62.** Four of the five answers listed below are methods by which the body exchanges heat into the environment. Select the exception.
- \*    a   muscle contraction
- b.   radiation
- c.   evaporation
- d.   convection
- e.   conduction

E     **63.** Four of the five answers listed below are ectotherms. Select the exception.
- a   snail
- b.   snake
- c.   spider
- d.   frog
- \*    e.   bird

E     **64.** Four of the five answers listed below are habits of desert animals. Select the exception.
- a   spend time in shade
- b.   spend daytime hours in underground burrows
- c.   are active mainly at night
- d.   have low metabolism during day
- \*    e.   spend nighttime sleeping

M     **65.** Four of the five answers listed below are responses of the body to heat. Select the exception.
- a   increased sweating
- \*    b.   increased retention of blood on the core region
- c.   decreased rate of muscle activity
- d.   increased water loss
- e.   dilation of peripheral blood vessels

# CHAPTER 32
# NEURAL CONTROL AND THE SENSES

## Multiple-Choice Questions

### WHY CRACK THE SYSTEM?

E    **1.** The basic unit of the nervous system is
  *    a    the neuron.
       b.   neuroglia.
       c.   the brain.
       d.   a nerve.
       e.   a nerve impulse.

M    **2.** Which of the following is NOT true concerning sensory neurons?
       a    They have receptor regions for detection of stimuli.
  *    b.   They lie in the pathway between the interneurons and motor neurons.
       c.   They relay information to the spinal cord.
       d.   They are part of a reflex arc.
       e.   They are one of three types of neurons.

E    **3.** Which of the following sequences is correct?
       a    receptors——>sensory neurons——>motor neurons——>interneurons
       b.   sensory neurons ——>receptors——> motor neurons
       c.   motor neurons——>integrators——> sensory neurons
       d.   receptors——>motor neurons——> interneurons——>sensory neurons
  *    e.   sensory neurons——>interneurons——> motor neurons

### INVERTEBRATE BEGINNINGS

D    **4.** In terms of evolution, which of the following is considered to be the oldest?
       a    cephalization
       b.   information storage
       c.   eyes
  *    d.   reflexes
       e.   reasoning

M    **5.** A jellyfish has
       a    radial symmetry.
       b.   a "nerve net."
       c.   tentacles.
       d.   a single opening to the digestive tract.
  *    e.   all of the above

D    **6.** Which of the following is incorrect concerning a nerve net?
       a    found in animals with radial symmetry
       b.   used in reflex actions
  *    c.   shows evolution of cephalization
       d.   operates cells with contractile properties
       e.   utilizes sensory cells

M    **7.** A planula is
       a    a polyp with tentacles.
       b.   a portion of the nerve net of a cnidarian.
       c.   radially symmetrical.
  *    d.   a free-swimming larva.
       e.   a sessile polyp stage in the life cycle of a cnidarian.

M    **8.** Cephalization refers to a
       a    type of symmetry.
       b.   type of segmentation characteristic of lower forms of life.
       c.   group of protective cells found in the tentacles of a polyp.
       d.   transitional state in the life cycle of a jellyfish.
  *    e.   none of the above

M    **9.** Which of the following is the more advanced nervous system?
       a    a diffuse system with scattered nerves
       b.   a bilaterally symmetrical system
       c.   a radially symmetrical system
  *    d.   paired nerves, paired sensory structures, and paired brain centers
       e.   a nerve net

E    **10.** Clusters of cell bodies of neurons outside the central nervous system are known as
       a    nerve cords.
  *    b.   ganglia.
       c.   a plexus.
       d.   notochords.
       e.   nerves.

M    **11.** The beginnings of cephalization may have occurred in a
       a    earthworm.
  *    b.   planula.
       c.   jellyfish.
       d.   vertebrate.
       e.   grasshopper.

### NEURONS—THE COMMUNICATION SPECIALISTS

E    **12.** The single long process that extends from a typical motor nerve cell is the
  *    a    axon.
       b.   neuron.
       c.   synapse.
       d.   dendrite.
       e.   both a and d, but not b or c

E    13. The input zone of a neuron is the
        a.  axon.
        b.  axonal terminals.
        c.  cell body.
        d.  dendrite.
     *  e.  both c and d, but not a or b

D    14. Within a single neuron, the direction an impulse follows is
        a.  dendrite —> axon —> cell body.
        b.  axon —> dendrite —> cell body.
     *  c.  dendrite —> cell body —> axon.
        d.  cell body —> dendrite —> axon.
        e.  cell body —> axon —> dendrite.

M    15. Functionally speaking, a nerve impulse is
        a.  a flow of electrons along the outside of the plasma membrane of a neuron.
        b.  the movement of cytoplasmic elements through the core of the neuron.
     *  c.  a series of changes in membrane potentials.
        d.  a lengthening and shortening of the membrane extensions of an individual neuron.

M    16. When a neuron is at rest
        a.  there is a voltage difference across the membrane of about 70 millivolts.
        b.  the interior is negatively charged.
        c.  it is not responding to a stimulus.
        d.  the fluid outside the membrane has more sodium and less potassium than the cytoplasm.
     *  e.  all of the above

M    17. At rest, a nerve cell has a high concentration of _____ inside and a high concentration of _____ outside.
        a.  acetylcholine; chlorine
        b.  sodium; potassium
     *  c.  potassium; sodium
        d.  calcium; phosphorous
        e.  phosphorus; calcium

D    18. Active transport
        a.  helps establish the resting potential of a neuron.
        b.  counters the process of diffusion.
        c.  allows transport of atoms across the plasma membrane of the neuron against the concentration gradient.
        d.  both a and b, but not c
     *  e.  a, b, and c

E    19. The resting potential of a neuron is approximately
        a.  70 microvolts.
     *  b.  70 millivolts.
        c.  70 volts.
        d.  70 electrovolts.
        e.  70 megavolts.

M    20. The membrane-bound enzyme system that restores and maintains the resting membrane potential is which of the following pumps?
        a.  sodium-phosphorus
     *  b.  sodium-potassium
        c.  sodium-chlorine
        d.  phosphorus-calcium
        e.  phosphorus-chlorine

## ACTION POTENTIALS

D    21. The term that best describes what happens to a neuron as an impulse passes along it is
        a.  polarization-depolarization.
     *  b.  depolarization-repolarization.
        c.  ionization-depolarization.
        d.  hypopolarization.
        e.  transpolarization.

D    22. Which of the following is the first response a neuron makes to a stimulus?
     *  a.  Sodium ions enter the cell.
        b.  Sodium ions leave the cell.
        c.  Potassium ions enter the cell.
        d.  Potassium ions leave the cell.
        e.  a and c above

D    23. An action potential is brought about by
        a.  a sudden membrane impermeability.
        b.  the movement of negatively charged proteins through the neuronal membrane.
        c.  the movement of lipoproteins to the outer membrane.
     *  d.  a local change in membrane permeability caused by a greater-than-threshold stimulus.
        e.  all of the above

M    24. Disturbances in sensory neurons will result in an action potential if the
        a.  stimulus is graded.
        b.  stimulus remains local.
     *  c.  graded stimulus reaches a trigger zone.
        d.  localized stimuli do not spread too far.
        e.  stimuli become downgraded to localized ones.

D    25. Which of the following terms most accurately describes the cellular activity associated with the actual passage of a nerve impulse?
        a.  electrical discharge
        b.  action of sodium-potassium pump
     *  c.  wave of depolarization
        d.  repolarization
        e.  active transport of ions

D     **26.** The reason that an action potential is so brief is that

*    a. a wave of repolarization immediately follows an action potential.
     b. the opening of potassium gates allows the voltage difference across the neural membrane to be restored.
     c. the protein channels for sodium movement remain open.
     d. the sodium-potassium pump restores the electrical gradients.
     e. the membrane limits electrical activity.

D     **27.** The occurrence of an action potential can best be compared to a

*    a. switch to turn a lamp on and off.
     b. volume control on a stereo.
     c. door to the classroom.
     d. room light dimmer switch.

E     **28.** Before another action potential "spike" can occur

*    a. there must be a very brief restoration of the resting conditions in the membrane.
     b. the membrane voltage must drop to zero.
     c. the sodium-potassium pump must cease temporarily.
     d. all of the membrane gates must be closed at the same time.

D     **29.** During the short recovery period before another action potential

     a. the threshold value is increased.
     b. the threshold value is reduced.
*    c. the sodium gates are shut and the potassium gates are opened.
     d. both sodium and potassium gates are shut.
     e. the nerve is said to be at the resting potential.

D     **30.** During the passage of a nerve impulse

     a. sodium ions pass through gated channels.
     b. positive feedback causes more sodium ions to enter the cell.
     c. the interior of the cell becomes positive.
     d. changing voltage increases the number of open gates.
*    e. all of the above

D     **31.** The phrase "all or nothing," as used in conjunction with discussion about an action potential, means that

     a. a resting membrane potential has been received by the cell.
*    b. nothing can stop the action potential once the threshold is reached.
     c. the membrane either achieves total equilibrium or remains as far from equilibrium as possible.
     d. propagation along the neuron proceeds from node to node.
     e. none of the above

**CHEMICAL SYNAPSES**

M     **32.** Transmitter substances

     a. are expelled from the presynaptic cells.
     b. tend to destroy acetylcholine.
     c. enter the presynaptic cell to continue the passage of the impulse.
     d. interact with membrane receptors of the postsynaptic cells.
*    e. both a and d

E     **33.** Which is a junction between two neurons?

     a. Schwann cell
*    b. chemical synapse
     c. node
     d. sodium gate
     e. all of the above

M     **34.** Which bridges the gap between a neuron sending a message and the neuron receiving it?

     a. threshold value
     b. action potential
*    c. transmitter substance
     d. neurohormone
     e. all of the above

M     **35.** Transmitter substances

     a. include acetylcholine.
     b. change the permeability of postsynaptic cells.
     c. may be excitatory or stimulatory.
     d. may participate in synaptic integration.
*    e. all of the above

D     **36.** Which of the following neurotransmitters is mismatched?

     a. acetylcholine—muscle contraction
     b. endorphin—pain perception
     c. norepinephrine—emotions, dreaming, awakening
*    d. serotonin—sexual function
     e. dopamine and GABA—act on the brain

D     **37.** At an inhibitory synapse,

     a. no transmitter substances are released by the sending cell.
*    b. a transmitter substance produces changes in the receiving cell that drive the membrane potential away from threshold.
     c. no transmitter substance can bind to the receiving cell.
     d. a transmitter substance produces changes in the receiving cell that drive the membrane potential closer to threshold.
     e. both a and c

D  38. An excitatory postsynaptic potential
   a.  is only one of several types of graded
       potential.
   b.  has a hyperpolarizing effect.
   c.  will drive the membrane away from its
       potential.
 * d.  is summed with an inhibitory postsynaptic
       potential at the input zone of a neuron in a
       process known as synaptic integration.
   e.  none of the above

D  39. At an inhibitory synapse
   a.  no transmitter substances are released by the
       sending cell.
 * b.  a transmitter substance produces changes in
       the receiving cell that drive the membrane
       potential away from threshold.
   c.  no transmitter substance can bind to the
       receiving cell.
   d.  a transmitter substance produces changes in
       the receiving cell that drive the membrane
       potential closer to threshold.
   e.  a and c above

M  40. Synaptic integration means that
   a.  all positive or excitatory stimuli are added
       together.
   b.  the positive and negative ions neutralize
       each other.
 * c.  excitatory and inhibitory signals are
       combined in a neuron.
   d.  adjacent neurons interact so that excitatory
       and inhibitory stimuli cancel each other.
   e.  all of the above

D  41. The presynaptic neuron and postsynaptic neuron
       do not directly contact each other because
   a.  one would inhibit the actions of the other.
   b.  they never grow to sufficient length.
   c.  the synaptic vesicles keep them apart.
 * d.  this would cause continuous impulse
       transmission.
   e.  acetylcholine prevents this action.

## PATHS OF INFORMATION FLOW

M  42. By definition, a "nerve" is
 * a.  a bundle of axons.
   b.  a single extension of a neuron.
   c.  the same as a neuron within the central
       nervous system.
   d.  a dendrite.
   e.  a fiber more than 10 inches in length.

M  43. The myelin sheath
   a.  is formed by the Schwann cell.
   b.  speeds up the transmission of impulses.
   c.  does not surround all nerves.
   d.  extends from node to node.
 * e.  all of the above

M  44. The spaces that separate adjacent Schwann cells
       are called
   a.  neuroglia.
   b.  myelin sheaths.
 * c.  nodes.
   d.  dendrites.
   e.  synapses.

D  45. A deterioration in the myelin sheaths of motor
       axons to the lower leg would be expected to
   a.  remove the restraints to ion movement and
       speed up impulse transmission.
   b.  cause immobility of the leg due to cessation
       of impulses to leg muscles.
 * c.  slow the rate of transmission and cause lack
       of motor control.
   d.  have little effect because the sheaths are for
       insulation only.

M  46. What is the name of the condition in which there
       is a deterioration of the myelin sheaths of the
       neurons in the spinal cord?
   a.  muscular dystrophy
   b.  cancer
   c.  diabetes
   d.  multiple sclerosis
   e.  Alzheimer disease

E  47. The simplest nerve pathway
   a.  is located in the midbrain.
 * b.  is the reflex arc.
   c.  is found in the lower part of the brain.
   d.  is found in the autonomic nervous system.
   e.  is in the flow of information from a sense
       receptor to the brain.

M  48. One example of a simple reflex arc involves the
 * a.  contraction of a muscle when it is stretched.
   b.  conscious message to move part of the
       body.
   c.  receptor, the brain, and the effector.
   d.  muscle action in a salute when a
       noncommissioned combatant sees an
       officer.
   e.  contraction of an antagonistic muscle when
       its opposite muscle relaxes.

M  49. The stretch reflex is
   a.  an adaptation that enables humans to stand
       upright.
   b.  activated by stretch-sensitive receptors
       inside the muscle spindles.
   c.  a simple, stereotyped, and repeatable motor
       action.
   d.  elicited by a sensory stimulus.
 * e.  all of the above

M 50. In the knee-jerk reflex arc, the synapse between a sensory neuron and a motor neuron occurs where?
   a  in the brain
   b.  between the receptor and the spinal cord
   c.  within the muscle of the leg
  * d.  within the spinal cord
   e.  in the nerve leading to the spinal cord

M 51. Which statement is false?
   a  Reflexes are the simplest of all nervous reactions.
   b.  The nervous system required sense organs before organisms could perceive their environment.
  * c.  Motor neurons lead toward the brain or central nervous system.
   d.  Reflex actions are stereotyped and repeatable.
   e.  All of the above statements are true.

M 52. *Clostridium tetani*
   a  causes lockjaw.
   b.  produces a nerve toxin.
   c.  is an anaerobic bacterium.
   d.  interferes with the inhibitory synapses on motor neurons.
  * e.  all of the above

M 53. In lockjaw
  * a  a muscle cannot relax.
   b.  nerve impulses in involuntary muscles are blocked.
   c.  nerve impulses cannot be propagated along a neuron.
   d.  acetylcholine is destroyed.
   e.  the impulse cannot pass across a synapse.

## FUNCTIONAL DIVISIONS OF VERTEBRATE NERVOUS SYSTEMS

E 54. The midbrain includes the
   a  thalamus.
   b.  pineal gland.
  * c.  tectum.
   d.  medulla oblongata.
   e.  olfactory lobes.

E 55. The hindbrain includes the
   a  thalamus.
   b.  pineal gland.
   c.  cerebellum.
   d.  medulla oblongata.
  * e.  both c and d

E 56. The pituitary gland is controlled by the
   a  pineal gland.
   b.  medulla.
  * c.  hypothalamus.
   d.  thalamus.
   e.  cerebrum.

E 57. The center of consciousness and intelligence is the
   a  medulla.
   b.  thalamus.
   c.  pons.
   d.  cerebellum.
  * e.  cerebrum.

E 58. Which part of the mammalian brain is disproportionately larger than the corresponding part of a fish brain?
   a  medulla
   b.  thalamus
   c.  pons
   d.  cerebellum
  * e.  cerebrum

E 59. Which structure forms the roof of the midbrain where visual and auditory signals are integrated?
   a  ventricles
   b.  meninges
  * c.  tectum
   d.  olfactory and optic bulbs
   e.  pineal gland

E 60. The part of the brain that connects one brain center with another is the
   a  cerebrum.
  * b.  pons.
   c.  cerebellum.
   d.  fissure of Rolando.
   e.  hypothalamus.

E 61. The part of the brain that deals with the basic drives such as hunger, sex, and thirst is the
   a  cerebrum.
   b.  pons.
   c.  cerebellum.
   d.  thalamus.
  * e.  hypothalamus.

E 62. The major relay center of the brain is the
   a  cerebrum.
   b.  olfactory area.
   c.  cerebellum.
  * d.  thalamus.
   e.  hypothalamus.

E 63. The center for balance and coordination is the
   a  cerebrum.
   b.  pons.
  * c.  cerebellum.
   d.  thalamus.
   e.  hypothalamus.

E 64. The part of the brain that controls the basic responses necessary to maintain life processes (breathing, heartbeat) is the
  * a  medulla.
   b.  corpus callosum.
   c.  fissure of Rolando.
   d.  cerebellum.
   e.  cerebral cortex.

M 65. The two MAJOR divisions of the vertebral nervous system are the
    a. autonomic and peripheral systems.
    b. sympathetic and parasympathetic systems.
    c. cranial and spinal nerves.
*    d. central and peripheral nervous systems.
    e. brain and spinal cord.

D 66. Which of the following terms is NOT directly associated with the nervous system?
*    a. spinal column
    b. spinal cord
    c. neural tube
    d. nerve cord
    e. All of the above are associated with the nervous system.

M 67. Which of the following would NOT be a part of the central nervous system?
    a. brain
    b. cerebellum
    c. medulla
*    d. spinal nerves
    e. neuroglia cells

## THE MAJOR EXPRESSWAYS

M 68. The two principal divisions of the peripheral nervous system are the
*    a. somatic and autonomic systems.
    b. sympathetic and parasympathetic systems.
    c. peripheral and central systems.
    d. afferent and autonomic systems.
    e. cranial and skeletal nerves.

M 69. Which of the following statements concerning the peripheral nervous system is false?
    a. Spinal nerves lead to and from the spinal cord.
    b. There are 31 pairs of spinal nerves.
*    c. Cranial nerves lead from the brain directly to the spinal cord.
    d. Some nerves carry only sensory information.
    e. Some nerves are both sensory and motor.

E 70. All nerves that conduct impulses away from the central nervous system are
*    a. motor only,
    b. sensory only.
    c. motor or sensory depending body location.
    d. spinal nerves.
    e. cranial nerves.

M 71. The autonomic subdivision of the vertebrate nervous system would innervate all but which of the following?
    a. intestinal muscles
*    b. skeletal muscles
    c. heart
    d. pancreas
    e. liver

E 72. The autonomic subdivision consists specifically of
    a. central and peripheral nerves.
*    b. parasympathetic and sympathetic.
    c. somatic and involuntary.
    d. brain and spinal cord.
    e. spinal and cranial nerves.

M 73. Which nerves generally dominate internal events when environmental conditions permit normal body functioning?
    a. ganglia
    b. pacemaker
    c. sympathetic
*    d. parasympathetic
    e. all of the above

D 74. Which statement is true?
    a. Both the parasympathetic and sympathetic nervous systems send nerves to all organs.
    b. The sympathetic nervous system that supplies an organ will also provide parasympathetic nerves to it.
    c. Both the sympathetic and parasympathetic have either excitatory or inhibitory effects.
*    d. The sympathetic branch of the autonomic system usually speeds up the activities of the body.
    e. The parasympathetic system usually speeds up the activities of the body.

E 75. Signals from the parasympathetic nervous system cause which of the following?
    a. rise in blood pressure
    b. increase in pulse rate
*    c. increase in digestive system movements
    d. rise in blood sugar level
    e. rise in metabolic rate

M 76. The parasympathetic nervous system includes the
    a. cranial and thoracic nerves.
    b. thoracic and lumbar nerves.
    c. lumbar and sacral nerves.
    d. cervical and lumbar nerves.
*    e. cranial and sacral nerves.

M 77. The sympathetic nervous system includes the
    a. cranial and thoracic nerves.
*    b. thoracic and lumbar nerves.
    c. lumbar and sacral nerves.
    d. cervical and lumbar nerves.
    e. cranial and sacral nerves.

D 78. The word that best describes the interaction of sympathetic and parasympathetic systems is
*    a. antagonistic.
    b. cooperation.
    c. overriding.
    d. subversive.
    e. ineffective.

M   79. The part of the central nervous system that is composed of parts that are antagonistic to each other is the
    * a  autonomic nervous system composed of the sympathetic and parasympathetic subsystems.
      b  central nervous system composed of the brain and spinal cord.
      c  peripheral nervous system composed of the cranial and spinal nervous system.
      d  none of the above; the muscular system is the only system with antagonistic subsets.

D   80. During the "fight-flight" response, which of the following would be in use?
      a  sympathetic nervous system
      b  parasympathetic nervous system
      c  epinephrine
    * d  a and c
      e  b and c

M   81. Activation of the sympathetic nervous system
    * a  causes the pupils of the eye to dilate.
      b  increases the flow of watery saliva.
      c  stimulates peristaltic contractions of the intestinal system.
      d  slows heartbeat and lowers blood pressure.
      e  allows the body to relax rather than prepare for fight or flight.

D   82. All but which of the following are true of the spinal cord?
      a  houses connections between sensory and motor neurons
      b  serves as a reflex center
    * c  its gray matter serves as passageway for nerve tracts to brain
      d  is covered with meninges
      e  is enclosed by vertebrae

E   83. Areas of the spinal cord appear glistening white because of
      a  naked dendrites.
      b  cell bodies.
      c  neuroglia cells.
      d  lack of meninges.
    * e  myelin sheaths.

E   84. Interneurons are found in the
      a  dorsal root.
    * b  spinal cord.
      c  sensory neurons.
      d  motor neurons.
      e  autonomic nervous system.

M   85. The ascending and descending axons
      a  are found in the gray matter of the spinal cord.
      b  are found in the white matter of the spinal cord.
      c  are covered with myelin sheaths.
      d  are both sensory and motor.
    * e  all except a are correct

E   86. The brain and spinal cord are covered by the protective
      a  ventricles.
    * b  meninges.
      c  tectum.
      d  olfactory and optic bulbs.
      e  pineal gland.

**THE HUMAN BRAIN**

E   87. The gray matter of the brain is associated with the
    * a  cerebral cortex.
      b  pons.
      c  optic chiasm.
      d  corpus callosum.
      e  thalamus.

D   88. Destruction of the motor areas in the left cerebral cortex results in the loss of
      a  sensation on the right side of the body.
      b  sensation on the left side of the body.
      c  voluntary movement on the left side of the body.
    * d  voluntary movement on the right side of the body.

E   89. The part of the brain that shows the greatest proportional increase in size from the lower vertebrates to humans is the increase in the
      a  cerebellum.
    * b  cerebrum.
      c  medulla oblongata.
      d  hypothalamus.

D   90. What is the name given to the network of interneurons that extends from the medulla to the cerebrum and is responsible for message integration?
      a  tectum
    * b  reticular formation
      c  hypothalamus
      d  cerebral cortex.
      e  meninges.

E   91. The occipital lobe of the brain is responsible for
      a  coordination of hands and fingers.
      b  speech.
      c  memory.
      d  sense of taste and smell.
    * e  vision.

E   92. The cerebral hemispheres communicate with each other by means of the
      a  cerebral cortex.
      b  corpora cardiaca.
      c  corporothalamus.
    * d  corpus callosum.
      e  corpus allata.

D    93. If the motor cortex on the right side of the brain is destroyed by a stroke, what would be impaired?
- a   movement on both sides of the body
- b. reception of sensory information from the left side of the body
- c. movement by the right side of the body
- * d. movement by the left side of the body
- e. all of the above

M    94. To produce a split-brain individual, an operation would need to cut the
- * a   corpus callosum.
- b. reticular formation.
- c. hypothalamus.
- d. fissure of Rolando.
- e. pons.

M    95. The left hemisphere of the brain is responsible for
- a   music.
- b. artistic ability.
- c. spatial relationships.
- * d. language skills.
- e. abstract abilities.

M    96. The right hemisphere of the cerebrum is specialized for
- a   verbal ability.
- b. mathematics.
- * c. music interpretation.
- d. control over the right side of the body.

D    97. The primary hearing interpretation portion of the brain is located
- * a   at the rear of the brain.
- b. midway from front to back.
- * c. in the "temple" area.
- d. behind the forehead.
- e. in the cerebellum.

E    98. The sleep center of the brain is the
- a   pons.
- b. thalamus.
- c. hypothalamus.
- * d. reticular activating system.
- e. medulla.

M    99. High levels of which chemical in the sleep centers of the brain induce drowsiness and sleep?
- a   norepinephrine
- * b. serotonin
- c. adrenalin
- d. enkephalin
- e. cyclic AMP

## MEMORY

D    100. Studies of memory indicate that
- a   short-term memory is the product of chemical changes in neurons.
- b. long-term memory is limited to a few years' duration.
- c. long-term memories are lost more frequently in amnesia.
- * d. long-term memory depends on structural or chemical changes in the brain.
- e. short-term memory is limited to several hundred bits of information.

## FOCUS ON HEALTH: DRUGS, THE BRAIN, AND BEHAVIOR

E    101. Active chemicals found in chocolate, tea, coffee, and soft drinks are examples of which of the following?
- a   depressant
- * b. stimulant
- c. narcotic analgesic
- d. hallucinogen or psychedelic
- e. antipsychotic

E    102. Pain relievers such as endorphins and enkephalins are
- a   depressants.
- b. stimulants.
- * c. analgesics.
- d. hallucinogens or psychedelics.
- e. antipsychotics.

E    103. Substances that lower the activity of the brain and inhibit transmission at a synapse are
- * a   depressants.
- b. stimulants.
- c. narcotic analgesics.
- d. hallucinogens or psychedelics.
- e. antipsychotics.

E    104. Substances that could be called hypnotics and that induce sleep are
- * a   depressants.
- b. stimulants.
- c. narcotic analgesics.
- d. hallucinogens or psychedelics.
- e. antipsychotics.

M    105. A chemical substance that behaves as a natural analgesic is
- a   an amphetamine.
- b. LSD.
- c. epinephrine.
- * d. endorphin.
- e. none of the above

M 106. A group of chemicals that at low doses reduce fatigue and heighten awareness but at high doses elicit anxiety and irritability while mimicking the effect of norepinephrine are
   a  depressants.
   b.  stimulants.
   c.  narcotic analgesics.
*  d.  hallucinogens or psychedelics.
   e.  antipsychotics.

E 107. Substances that alter sensory perception, cause disorientation, and inhibit the ability to perform complex tasks are
   a  depressants.
   b.  stimulants.
   c.  narcotic analgesics.
*  d.  hallucinogens or psychedelics.
   e.  antipsychotics.

E 108. Barbiturates are
*  a.  depressants.
   b.  stimulants.
   c.  narcotic analgesics.
   d.  hallucinogens or psychedelics.
   e.  antipsychotics.

E 109. Substances that sedate the body and relieve pain are
   a.  depressants.
   b.  stimulants.
*  c.  narcotic analgesics.
   d.  hallucinogens or psychedelics.
   e.  antipsychotics.

## SENSORY SYSTEMS

M 110. A sensory system includes
   a  a sensory receptor.
   b.  nerve pathways from the receptor to the brain.
   c.  brain regions where the sensory information is processed.
   d.  a and b only
*  e.  a, b, and c

D 111. The difference in "sensation" and "perception" when referring to a stimulus lies in
   a  the type of receptor stimulated.
*  b.  understanding the significance of the stimulus.
   c.  the number of receptors that depolarize.
   d.  feeling exactly what is happening at the site.
   e.  responding to the stimulus.

M 112. In order for snakes such as pythons to capture prey at night, they are equipped with
   a  extra-sensitive hearing.
   b.  extraordinary sight.
*  c.  pits that are sensitive to heat.
   d.  a strong sense of smell located in the tongue.
   e.  special organs that detect vibrations so that they can detect nearby movement.

M 113. Differences in intensity of a stimulus
   a  do not affect the impulse transmitted.
   b.  are indicated by the number of nerves activated.
   c.  control the part of the brain that receives the stimulus.
   d.  are encoded in the frequency of action potentials on a single axon.
*  e.  both b and d, but not a or c

E 114. Which sense uses mechanical energy?
   a  sense of touch
   b.  acceleration
   c.  sense of pain
   d.  sense of balance
*  e.  all of the above

E 115. Infrared receptors are classified as
   a  chemoreceptors.
   b.  mechanoreceptors.
   c.  photoreceptors.
*  d.  thermoreceptors.
   e.  none of the above

M 116. Which statement is true?
   a  All action potentials for the same nerve are alike.
   b.  Receptors respond by graded potential.
   c.  Different nerves convey different information by going to different areas of the brain.
   d.  Differences in intensities may be due to the number of receptors and nerves involved in response.
*  e.  all of the above

E 117. Receptors in the human nose are
*  a  chemoreceptors.
   b.  mechanoreceptors.
   c.  photoreceptors.
   d.  nocireceptors.
   e.  none of the above

E 118. Eyes are
   a  chemoreceptors.
   b.  mechanoreceptors.
*  c.  photoreceptors.
   d.  nocireceptors.
   e.  none of the above

## SOMATIC SENSATIONS

E 119. The Pacinian corpuscle is used in detecting
   a  sound.
*  b.  pressure.
   c.  chemicals.
   d.  sight.
   e.  chemical differences.

E    120.  Mechanoreceptors are located in
          a   internal organs.
          b.  skin.
          c.  joints.
          d.  tendons.
      *   e.  all of the above

E    121.  A stretch receptor is classified as a
          a   chemoreceptor.
      *   b.  mechanoreceptor.
          c.  photoreceptor.
          d.  thermoreceptor.
          e.  all of the above

E    122.  The pain produced in an internal organ may be
          perceived as occurring somewhere else. This is
          called
          a   mixed nerve messages.
      *   b.  referred pain.
          c.  phantom pain.
          d.  psychosomatic pain.
          e.  hypochondria.

M    123.  The somatic senses include all but which one of
          the following sensations?
      *   a   balance
          b.  pain near the body surface
          c.  temperature
          d.  touch
          e.  pressure

## HEARING AND BALANCE

E    124.  The organ of Corti is a
          a   chemoreceptor.
      *   b.  mechanoreceptor.
          c.  photoreceptor.
          d.  nocireceptor.
          e.  all of the above

E    125.  Hair cells are important in the sense of
          a   equilibrium.
          b.  hearing.
          c.  taste.
          d.  smell.
      *   e.  both a and b

E    126.  The sense of equilibrium can detect
          a   motion.
          b.  acceleration.
          c.  gravity.
          d.  position.
      *   e.  all of the above

E    127.  The semicircular canals are
          a   empty.
          b.  filled with gas.
      *   c.  filled with a liquid.
          d.  filled with bones or stones.
          e.  filled with sand grains.

E    128.  The principal place in the human ear where
          sound waves are amplified by means of the
          vibrations of tiny bones is the
          a   pinna.
          b.  ear canal.
      *   c.  middle ear.
          d.  organ of Corti.
          e.  all of the above

M    129.  The place where vibrations are translated into
          patterns of nerve impulses is the
          a   pinna.
          b.  ear canal.
          c.  middle ear.
      *   d.  organ of Corti.
          e.  none of the above

E    130.  The organ of Corti is located in the
          a   thoracic cavity.
      *   b.  inner ear.
          c.  abdominal cavity.
          d.  brain stem.
          e.  semicircular canals.

D    131.  In hearing, the last place that pressure or sound
          waves pass through is the
          a   bones of the middle ear.
          b.  tympanic membrane.
          c.  oval window.
      *   d.  round window.
          e.  tectorial membrane.

E    132.  How many coiled and fluid-filled ducts are found
          in each cochlea?
          a   1
          b.  2
      *   c.  3
          d.  4
          e.  5 or more

## VISION

M    133.  Which of the following has receptors for
          ultraviolet light?
          a   bears
      *   b.  bees
          c.  birds
          d.  reptiles
          e.  amphibians

E    134.  The layer of the eye where photoreceptors are
          located is the
          a   lens.
          b.  cornea.
          c.  pupil.
          d.  iris.
      *   e.  retina.

E    135.  The repeating units of a compound eye are called
          a   ocelli.
          b.  lenses.
          c.  rhabdomeres.
      *   d.  ommatidia.
          e.  pupils.

E   136. The adjustable ring of contractile and connective tissues that controls the amount of light entering the eye is the
a   lens.
b.   cornea.
c.   pupil.
*   d.   iris.
e.   retina.

E   137. The white protective fibrous tissue of the eye, often called the white of the eye, is the
a   lens.
*   b.   sclera.
c.   pupil.
d.   iris.
e.   retina.

E   138. The dark middle layer of the eye that prevents the scattering of light is the
a   fovea.
b.   retina.
c.   sclera.
*   d.   choroid.
e.   cornea.

E   139. The outer transparent protective cover of the eyeball is the
a   fovea.
b.   retina.
c.   sclera.
d.   choroid.
*   e.   cornea.

E   140. The part of the eye that may be colored (for example, brown, blue, green, or gray) is the
a   retina.
b.   sclera.
c.   choroid.
d.   cornea.
*   e.   iris.

## CASE STUDY—FROM SIGNALING TO VISUAL PERCEPTION

E   141. Rods and cones are located in the
a   lens.
b.   cornea.
c.   pupil.
d.   iris.
*   e.   retina.

E   142. The highest concentration of cones is in the
*   a   fovea.
b.   blind spot.
c.   sclera.
d.   ommatidium.
e.   choroid.

M   143. In the human eye, what provides the greatest visual acuity (the precise discrimination between adjacent points in space)?
a   photoreceptors in the sclera
*   b.   photoreceptors in the fovea
c.   protein filaments in the lens
d.   photoreceptors in the optic nerve
e.   none of the above

E   144. Cones are
a   sensitive to red light.
b.   sensitive to green light.
c.   sensitive to blue light.
d.   relatively insensitive to dim light.
*   e.   all of the above

M   145. Where are bipolar, amacrine, and ganglion cells located?
a   sclera
b.   thalamus
c.   organ of Corti
*   d.   retina
e.   all of the above

## Matching Questions

D **146.** Matching I. Choose the BEST response.

1 _____ effector

2 _____ ganglion

3 _____ integrator

4 _____ stretch receptor

5 _____ myelin sheath

6 _____ neuroglia

7 _____ receptor

8 _____ rest period

9 _____ response

10 _____ sodium-potassium pump

11 _____ stimulus

12 _____ transmitter substance

A. cells that nurture and support neurons

B. a neuron cannot propagate an action potential during this time

C. acetylcholine

D. interneuron in brain or spinal cord

E. establishes basis of resting membrane potential

F. sheathed muscle cells that contain receptors

G. input

H. modified dendrite of a neuron

I. output

J. muscle or gland

K. produced by a specific kind of Schwann cell

L. cluster of cell bodies from different neurons

*Answers:*

| 1. | J | 2. | L | 3. | D |
|----|---|----|---|----|---|
| 4. | F | 5. | K | 6. | A |
| 7. | H | 8. | B | 9. | I |
| 10. | E | 11. | G | 12. | C |

D **147.** Matching. II Choose the one most appropriate answer for each.

1. _____ autonomic nervous system

2. _____ frontal lobe

3. _____ cerebellum

4. _____ corpus callosum

5. _____ ganglion

6. _____ hypothalamus

7. _____ limbic system

8. _____ medulla oblongata

9. _____ midbrain

10. _____ nerve net

11. _____ peripheral nervous system

12. _____ reticular formation

13. _____ meninges

14. _____ transmitter substances

15. _____ white matter

A. integrates body position, motions, balance

B. in cnidarians; based on reflex pathways devoted to swimming and feeding

C. messages from here arouse the brain and maintain wakefulness

D. the cortical region that coordinates muscles required for speech

E. all parts of nerve cells outside the brain and spinal cord

F. acetylcholine is an example

G. reflex control center for breathing, heart rate, and blood pressure

H. axons of the central nervous system that are sheathed with fatty myelin

I. at top of the brainstem bordering the cerebral hemispheres; influences learning and emotional behavior

J. motor neurons that are divided into sympathetic and parasympathetic divisions

K. membrane coverings over brain spinal cord

L. contains the optic lobes; receives and integrates sensory information that is largely sent on to the forebrain for further neural processing

M. connects right and left cerebral hemispheres

N. group of nerve cell bodies encased in connective tissue; forms integrative centers

O. contains centers concerned with body temperature regulation and with salt and water balance

*Answers:*

| 1. | J | 2. | D | 3. | A |
|----|---|----|---|----|---|
| 4. | M | 5. | N | 6. | O |
| 7. | I | 8. | G | 9. | L |
| 10. | B | 11. | E | 12. | C |
| 13. | K | 14. | F | 15. | H |

D      **148.**   Matching III. Choose the one most appropriate answer for each.

     1 _____ amplitude

     2 _____ cochlea

     3 _____ eardrum

     4 _____ iris

     5 _____ oval window

     6 _____ rhodopsin

     7 _____ pitch

     8 _____ retina

     9 _____ round window

   10 _____ semicircular canals

     A.   dissipates excess vibrational energy to the middle ear

     B.   contains the organ of Corti

     C.   separates the outer and middle ears

     D.   membrane-covered gateway to inner ear

     E.   consists of tissue containing rods and cones

     F.   peak height and valley depth of sound waves are its basis

     G.   maintain balance and position; detect acceleration

     H.   depends on how many wave changes per second occur

     I.   visual pigment

     J.   regulates size of pupil and amount of incoming light

*Answers:*

| | | |
|---|---|---|
| 1. F | 2. B | 3. C |
| 4. J | 5. D | 6. I |
| 7. H | 8. E | 9. A |
| 10. G | | |

## Classification Questions

Answer questions 149- 153 in reference to the four cell types listed below:

     a   sensory neurons
     b.   interneurons
     c.   motor neurons
     d.   Schwann cells

M     **149.**   These are nerve cells transmit signals to muscle cells.

M     **150.**   These are a type of neuroglial cells.

E     **151.**   Myelin is formed by these.

E     **152.**   An animal brain is composed mostly of this cell type.

E     **153.**   This cell type picks up environmental signals.

*Answers:*

| | | |
|---|---|---|
| 149. c | 150. d | 151. d |
| 152. b | 153. a | |

Answer questions 154- 158 in reference to the autonomic nervous system associated with the five regions of the human vertebral column listed below:

     a   cervical
     b.   thoracic
     c.   lumbar
     d.   sacral
     e.   coccygeal

D     **154.**   Sympathetic nerves from this region innervate the bladder, uterus, and genitals.

D     **155.**   Sympathetic nerves from this region innervate the kidney.

D     **156.**   Parasympathetic nerves from this region innervate the rectum.

D     **157.**   Sympathetic nerves from this region innervate the heart.

D     **158.**   Sympathetic nerves from this region pass through the celiac ganglion.

*Answers:*

| | | |
|---|---|---|
| 154. c | 155. b | 156. d |
| 157. b | 158. b | |

Answer questions 159–163 in reference to the five regions of the vertebrate brain listed below:

     a   cerebrum
     b.   hypothalamus
     c.   pons
     d.   cerebellum
     e.   medulla oblongata

D     **159.**   This region of the brain contains the reflex centers involved in respiration.

D     **160.**   This region of the brain controls neural-endocrine activities such as temperature control.

D     **161.**   This region of the brain controls carbohydrate metabolism.

M     **162.**   This part of the brain controls the complex coordination of motor activity and limb movement.

D     **163.**   This region of the brain contains parasympathetic nerves that innervate the heart and lungs.

*Answers:*

| | | |
|---|---|---|
| 159. e | 160. b | 161. b |
| 162. d | 163. e | |

Answer questions 164–168 in reference to the five kinds of energy listed below:

    a   chemical
    b.  mechanical
    c.  thermal
    d.  light
    e.  wavelike form of mechanical energy

E    **164.**   Receptors on the tongue detect variation in this kind of energy.

M    **165.**   Olfactory receptors detect this kind of energy.

D    **166.**   Ears monitor this kind of energy.

E    **167.**   Ultraviolet radiation detected by insects is in this category.

E    **168.**   The pain you feel from fire is a result of detecting this kind of energy.

*Answers:*    164.  a      165.  a      166.  e
               167.  d      168.  b

Answer questions 169–173 in reference to the five eye structures listed below:

    a   cornea
    b.  lens
    c.  retina
    d.  ommatidium
    e.  vitreous body

D    **169.**   This structure is found in the compound eyes of insects but not in the eyes of octopi.

M    **170.**   This structure is composed of photoreceptor cells.

E    **171.**   This structure primarily acts to focus light waves.

M    **172.**   This structure is composed of rod- and cone-shaped cells in mammals and birds.

M    **173.**   This structure acts to maintain the shape of the eye and to transmit light to other structures.

*Answers:*    169.  d      170.  c      171.  b
               172.  c      173.  e

## Selecting the Exception

M    **174.**   Four of the five answers listed below are actively involved in nerve impulse transmission. Select the exception.
   *   a   neuroglia
        b.  neuron
        c.  ganglia
        d.  nerves
        e.  tracts

M    **175.**   Four of the five answers listed below are true of a neuron at resting potential. Select the exception.
   *   a   interior of neuron is positive
        b.  interior of neuron has negative charge
        c.  more sodium ions outside neuron
        d.  more potassium ions inside neuron
        e.  membrane of neuron is polarized

M    **176.**   Four of the five answers listed below are used in descriptions of neuron membranes. Select the exception.
        a   gate
        b.  pump
        c.  wave of depolarization
        d.  channel
   *   e.  synaptic cleft

M    **177.**   Four of the five answers listed below are used in descriptions of the nerve sheath. Select the exception.
        a   Schwann cell
   *   b.  threshold
        c.  myelin sheath
        d.  node–to–node conduction
        e.  layered

M    **178.**   Four of the five answers listed below are participants in a common function. Select the exception.
        a   sensory neuron
   *   b.  medulla oblongata
        c.  interneuron
        d.  effector
        e.  receptor

D    **179.**   Four of the five answers listed below are characteristic of bilaterally symmetrical forms. Select the exception.
   *   a   sessile, nonmoving
        b.  segmentation
        c.  cephalization
        d.  paired nerves, muscles, sensory structures
        e.  right and left halves of the body

M    **180.**   Four of the five answers listed below are parts of the central nervous system. Select the exception.
        a   spinal cord
        b.  medulla oblongata
   *   c.  ganglia
        d.  cerebellum
        e.  cerebrum

M    **181.**   Four of the five answers listed below are parts of the same nerve grouping. Select the exception.
   *   a   cranial nerve
        b.  thoracic nerve
        c.  lumbar nerve
        d.  cervical nerve
        e.  sacral nerve

E 182. Four of the five answers listed below are innervated by the autonomic nervous system. Select the exception.
* a skeletal muscles
b. smooth muscles
c. heart
d. endocrine glands
e. exocrine glands

D 183. Four of the five answers listed below are actions mediated by the sympathetic nervous system. Select the exception.
a pulse increase
* b. blood glucose levels drop
c. metabolism increases
d. digestion slows down
e. dilates pupils of the eye

D 184. Four of the five answers listed below are located within the spinal cord. Select the exception.
* a dorsal root ganglion
b. interneurons between sensory input motor outputs
c. major ascending and descending nerve tracts
d. interneurons connecting with other neurons
e. direct reflex connections between sensory and motor neurons

M 185. Four of the five answers listed below are parts of the forebrain. Select the exception.
a limbic system
b. thalamus
c. olfactory lobes
* d. cerebellum
e. cerebrum

E 186. Four of the five answers listed below are lobes of the brain. Select the exception.
a parietal
* b. squamosal
c. frontal
d. occipital
e. temporal

D 187. Four of the five answers listed below are classified as white matter. Select the exception.
a myelin sheath
b. descending tracts
c. corpus callosum
* d. cerebrum
e. ascending tract

M 188. Four of the five answers listed below are stimulants. Select the exception.
* a heroin
b. caffeine
c. nicotine
d. cocaine
e. amphetamine

M 189. Four of the five answers listed below are depressants. Select the exception.
a alcohol
b. barbiturates
c. Valium
* d. marijuana
e. Quaalude

D 190. Four of the five answers listed below are analgesics. Select the exception.
a endorphin
b. opium
c. heroin
d. enkephalin
* e. lithium

M 191. Four of the five answers listed below are related by a similar sense receptor. Select the exception.
a touch or pressure
* b. olfaction
c. balance (equilibrium)
d. hearing
e. pain

M 192. Four of the five answers listed below are somatic senses. Select the exception.
* a light
b. pressure
c. touch
d. temperature
e. pain

M 193. Four of the five answers listed below are parts of the inner ear. Select the exception.
* a eardrum
b. oval window
c. scala tympani
d. basilar membrane
e. cochlea

M 194. Three of the four answers listed below are functionally connected to each other. Select the exception.
a hammer
* b. pinna
c. stirrup
d. anvil

M 195. Four of the five answers listed below are parts of the same sense organ. Select the exception.
a choroid
b. retina
c. vitreous humor
* d. ampulla
e. sclera

M 196. Four of the five answers listed below are parts of the same sense organ. Select the exception.
* a cochlea
b. cornea
c. sclera
d. choroid
e. fovea

D    197.  Three of the four answers listed below are colors
           for which the cone cells have pigments. Select
           the exception.
           a   red
     *     b.  yellow
           c   blue
           d.  green

# CHAPTER 33

# INTEGRATION AND CONTROL: ENDOCRINE SYSTEMS

## Multiple-Choice Questions

### THE ENDOCRINE SYSTEM

E    **1.** The first hormone to be discovered was
   a  insulin.
   b.  gastrin.
   * c  secretin.
   d.  thyroxine.
   e.  estrogen.

E    **2.** The word *hormone* comes from the Greek word meaning
   a  target.
   b.  response.
   c  secretion.
   * d.  set in motion.
   e.  internal gland.

M    **3.** Target cells
   a  are found only in specific endocrine glands.
   b.  are equipped with specific receptor molecules.
   c  are muscle cells.
   d.  may occur in any part of the body.
   * e.  both b and d, but not a or c

E    **4.** Which glands secrete pheromones?
   * a  exocrine
   b.  ductless
   c  sebaceous
   d.  endocrine
   e.  digestive

D    **5.** Pheromones are used primarily for
   a  signaling target cells in the vicinity of the secreting cells.
   b.  use as transmitter substances in certain synapses.
   * c  arousing interest in a potential mate.
   d.  causing a response in a part of the body some distance from the site of secretion.
   e.  all of the above, depending on the species

M    **6.** When Bayliss and Starling conducted experiments to determine what caused secretion of pancreatic juice, they
   a  cut the blood supply to the upper digestive tract.
   b.  added acid to the small intestine and got secretions of pancreatic juices.
   c  cut the nerve supply to the upper digestive tract.
   d.  got a response from the pancreas using extracts of cells lining the intestinal tract.
   * e.  All except a are true.

E    **7.** Hormones are distributed throughout the body by the
   a  exocrine system.
   b.  lymphatic system.
   c  nervous system.
   * d.  blood system.
   e.  integumentary system.

M    **8.** The primary purpose of the endocrine system is to
   a  provide a mechanism for rapid response to changes in the body.
   * b.  maintain a relatively constant internal environment.
   c  ensure proper growth and development.
   d.  allow for a mechanism to control gene action.
   e.  all of the above

### SIGNALING MECHANISMS

M    **9.** Which is the predominant second messenger involved in regulating glucose metabolism?
   a  insulin
   b.  glucagon
   c  adenyl cyclase
   * d.  cyclic AMP
   e.  all of the above

M    **10.** Second messengers are molecules of
   a  steroid compounds.
   * b.  cyclic AMP.
   c  ADP.
   d.  prostaglandin.
   e.  intermedin.

M    **11.** In the testicular feminization syndrome
   a  no testosterone is produced.
   b.  chemicals circulating in the blood deactivate the male hormone.
   * c  the cellular receptor for testosterone in the target cells is defective.
   d.  the male with this defect is normal in all respects except that he is sterile.
   e.  all of the above

M    **12.** Water-soluble hormones
   a  have to be transported by specific carriers in the blood.
   b.  have no trouble entering the target cells.
   c  find and react with the surface receptor molecules.
   d.  sometimes elicit the production of a second messenger.
   * e.  all except b

M    **13.** Steroid hormones do not require a membrane receptor because they
   - a   are small enough to pass directly through the membrane.
   - *   b.   are lipid-soluble in the bilayer.
   - c.   pass through special channels.
   - d.   are water-soluble.
   - e.   dissolve in the cholesterol of the membranes.

M    **14.** The release of cyclic AMP as a second messenger is a response to
   - a   peptide hormones.
   - b.   steroid hormones.
   - c.   glycoprotein hormones.
   - *   d.   both a and c, but not b
   - e.   a, b, and c

## THE HYPOTHALAMUS AND PITUITARY GLAND

E    **15.** Which gland is often called the master gland?
   - a   pineal
   - *   b.   pituitary
   - c.   thyroid
   - d.   adrenal
   - e.   pancreas

E    **16.** The pituitary gland is controlled by the
   - a   pons.
   - b.   corpus callosum.
   - c.   medulla.
   - d.   thalamus.
   - *   e.   hypothalamus.

M    **17.** Which is an example of an organ that is nervous in origin, structure, and function but secretes substances into the bloodstream?
   - a   anterior pituitary
   - *   b.   posterior pituitary
   - c.   pancreas
   - d.   adrenal cortex
   - e.   testis

D    **18.** The hypothalamus and pituitary link the activities of the endocrine system and nervous system by
   - *   a   neurohormones being secreted in response to the summation of neural messages that enter the hypothalamus.
   - b.   shifts in hormonal concentrations being detected by the anterior pituitary.
   - c.   pheromones being secreted as a response to photoperiodic stimuli.
   - d.   the nervous tissue of the anterior lobe of the pituitary sending stimuli to the glandular tissue of the posterior pituitary to produce hormones that will be secreted by the hypothalamus.
   - e.   all of the above

M    **19.** Which statement is true?
   - a   The anterior pituitary gland is essentially nervous tissue.
   - b.   The anterior pituitary gland secretes only two hormones.
   - c.   The posterior pituitary gland is the master gland.
   - *   d.   The posterior pituitary gland only stores hormones produced by the hypothalamus.
   - e.   all of the above

E    **20.** If you were cast up on a desert island with no fresh water to drink, the level of which of the following would rise in your bloodstream in an effort to conserve water?
   - a   erythropoietin
   - b.   oxytocin
   - c.   insulin
   - *   d.   antidiuretic hormone
   - e.   glucose

M    **21.** The antidiuretic hormone
   - a   controls water balance.
   - b.   controls the concentration of urea in the urine.
   - c.   influences blood pressure.
   - d.   changes the permeability of the urine-conducting tubules so that the interstitial fluid increases.
   - *   e.   all of the above

E    **22.** Oxytocin affects the
   - *   a   uterine wall.
   - b.   voluntary muscles throughout the body.
   - c.   nervous tissue.
   - d.   target cells in the brain.
   - e.   target cells in the digestive tract.

E    **23.** The anterior pituitary secretions produce their effects in the
   - a   gonads.
   - b.   thyroid glands.
   - c.   adrenal glands.
   - d.   mammary glands.
   - *   e.   all of the above

M    **24.** The pituitary hormone associated most directly with metabolic rate and with growth and development is
   - a   ACTH.
   - *   b.   TSH.
   - c.   FSH.
   - d.   LH.
   - e.   ADH.

M    **25.** The most general of the pituitary hormones, in that it may affect almost any cell in the body, is
   - a   the adrenocorticotropic hormone.
   - b.   the thyroid-stimulating hormone.
   - c.   gonadotropin.
   - *   d.   somatotropin.
   - e.   prolactin.

M 26. Prolactin
* a stimulates the mammary glands to produce milk.
b. causes the development of breasts and other secondary sexual characteristics in the male.
c. acts in concert with FSH to produce milk.
d. has secondary effects on reducing the size of the uterus after birth.

E 27. The growth hormone is
a prolactin.
b. adrenalin.
c. thyroxine.
d. ACTH.
* e. somatotropin.

M 28. The melanocyte-stimulating hormone
a affects kidney functions.
b. causes melanoma if there is excess secretion.
c. is found only in humans.
* d. controls pigmentation in the external protective tissue.
e. maintains normal reproductive or estrus cycle.

M 29. ACTH
a is secreted by the posterior pituitary.
b. has target cells in the autonomic nervous system.
* c. has target cells in the adrenal cortex.
d. has target cells in the adrenal medulla.
e. initiates the autoimmune response.

M 30. The luteinizing hormone
* a stimulates ovulation.
b. has no function in males.
c. is produced by the corpus luteum.
d. stimulates milk production.
e. promotes sperm formation.

M 31. The control over milk production, water balance, and labor in childbirth is mediated by the _____ gland.
a pineal
b. anterior pituitary
* c. posterior pituitary
d. parathyroid
e. thyroid

E 32. The immediate stimulus for the release of milk from the female breast is the
a culmination of the maternal instinct.
b. excessive accumulation of milk.
* c. mechanical stimulation of the breast by sucking.
d. time of day.
e. interaction of hormones.

D 33. Antidiuretic hormone and oxytocin are products of
a endocrine glands.
* b. neurosecretory cells.
c. blood capillaries.
d. the anterior pituitary.
e. kidney and uterine wall cells, respectively.

D 34. The secretion of each of the hormones from the anterior pituitary requires
a stimulation from the posterior pituitary.
b. that they first be secreted from the neurons of the hypothalamus.
c. two capillary beds.
d. the action of minute amounts of releasing hormones.
* e. both c and d

## EXAMPLES OF ABNORMAL PITUITARY OUTPUT

E 35. Dwarfism may be due to insufficient production of
a mineralocorticoid.
b. glucocorticoid.
c. calcitonin.
* d. somatotropin.
e. the parathyroid hormone.

E 36. Acromegaly is the result of excessive secretion of which of the following by adults?
a mineralocorticoid
b. glucocorticoid
c. thyroxine
d. testosterone
* e. somatotropin

## SOURCES AND EFFECTS OF OTHER HORMONES

M 37. Which hormone prepares and maintains the uterine lining for pregnancy?
a estrogen
b. progesterone
c. follicle-stimulating hormone
d. luteinizing hormone
* e. both a and b

E 38. Which hormone is produced by the liver?
a calcitonin
b. norepinephrine
* c. somatomedin
d. erythropoietin
e. angiotensin

M 39. Calcitonin acts in opposition to
* a the parathyroid hormone.
b. thyroxine.
c. glucagon.
d. the adrenal medulla.
e. all of the above

E  40. Angiotensin is produced in the
      a   bloodstream.
      b.  adrenal cortex.
      c.  adrenal medulla.
  *   d.  kidneys.
      e.  heart.

D  41. You have just moved from Norfolk, Virginia (sea
       level), to Taos, New Mexico (high in the
       mountains), and you find yourself out of breath
       climbing a small hill. Three months later,
       climbing the same hill, you have no difficulty. In
       the interim you have not altered your level of
       activity or diet. Which hormone has been at
       work?
      a   angiotensin
  *   b.  erythropoietin
      c.  aldosterone
      d.  estrogen
      e.  none of the above

M  42. Which gland promotes body immune response as
       its primary function?
      a   pineal
  *   b.  thymus
      c.  thyroid
      d.  gonads
      e.  adrenal

M  43. A group of hormones that are believed to affect
       the membrane surface receptors of lymphocytes
       are
  *   a   thymosins.
      b.  prostaglandins.
      c.  erythropoietin.
      d.  secretin.
      e.  none of the above

M  44. Which gland is involved in the maturation of
       lymphocytes?
      a   thyroid
      b.  adrenal
      c.  kidney
  *   d.  thymus
      e.  parathyroid

## FEEDBACK CONTROL OF HORMONE SECRETIONS

E  45. Which gland secretes sex hormones?
  *   a   testis
      b.  adrenal medulla
      c.  thyroid
      d.  kidney
      e.  pancreas

M  46. Glucocorticoids
      a   are secreted by the adrenal cortex.
      b.  influence carbohydrate, fat, and protein
          metabolism.
      c.  function during infection and injury as part
          of the defense response.
      d.  are exemplified by cortisol.
  *   e.  all of the above

D  47. A friend tells you that her husband has been
       feeling guilty and stressed for the past month.
       During the same time interval he has felt fatigued
       most of the time and many foods now seem to
       upset his stomach. Doctors have already checked
       for ulcers, cancer, blood pressure changes, and
       other blood irregularities, but these apparently
       are normal. You are an endocrinologist, so you
       suggest that he be tested for the most likely
       endocrine malfunction, which would be
      a   androgen/estrogen levels in the
          bloodstream.
  *   b.  glucocorticoid levels in the bloodstream.
      c.  calcitonin level in the bloodstream.
      d.  melatonin level in the bloodstream.
      e.  none of the above

E  48. The adrenal medulla produces
      a   mineralocorticoids.
  *   b.  epinephrine.
      c.  cortisol.
      d.  testosterone.
      e.  glucocorticoids.

E  49. A goiter is an enlarged form of which gland?
      a   adrenal
      b.  pancreas
  *   c.  thyroid
      d.  parathyroid
      e.  thymus

E  50. The gonads are another name for the
      a   parathyroid and thyroid.
  *   b.  ovary and testis.
      c.  adrenal cortex and medulla.
      d.  anterior and posterior pituitary.
      e.  none of the above

M  51. The hormone whose levels remain high when the
       body is suffering from inflammation and stress is
  *   a   cortisol.
      b.  somatotropin.
      c.  thymosin.
      d.  prolactin.
      e.  parathyroid hormone.

D  52. The only endocrine gland whose secretory
       function is under direct control by sympathetic
       nerves is the
      a   pancreas.
      b.  thyroid.
  *   c.  adrenal medulla.
      d.  thymus.
      e.  testis.

D  53. A goiter is caused by a deficiency in
      a   thyroxine.
      b.  triiodothyronine.
      c.  calcium.
  *   d.  iodine.
      e.  both a and b

## RESPONSES TO LOCAL CHEMICAL CHANGES

E  **54.** Glucagon is produced by the
   a  adrenal cortex.
   b.  adrenal medulla.
   c.  thyroid.
   d.  kidneys.
   *  e.  pancreas.

M  **55.** The hormone that is antagonistic in action to glucagon is
   a  norepinephrine.
   *  b.  insulin.
   c.  thyroxine.
   d.  epinephrine.
   e.  mineralocorticoids.

M  **56.** Which of the following does NOT affect blood sugar levels?
   a  glucagon
   b.  epinephrine
   *  c.  parathyroid hormones
   d.  glucocorticoids
   e.  insulin

M  **57.** If you eliminated all sources of calcium (dairy products, some vegetables) from your diet, the level of which of the following would rise in an attempt to supply calcium stored in your body to the tissues that need it?
   a  aldosterone
   b.  calcitonin
   c.  mineralocorticoids
   *  d.  parathyroid hormone
   e.  all of the above

E  **58.** The normal individual has how many parathyroid glands?
   a  2
   b.  3
   *  c.  4
   d.  5
   e.  6

M  **59.** Which gland is both an exocrine and endocrine gland?
   *  a  pancreas
   b.  adrenal
   c.  ovary
   d.  thyroid
   e.  pituitary

E  **60.** Excess glucose is converted into glycogen in the
   a  pancreas.
   *  b.  liver.
   c.  thymus.
   d.  thyroid.
   e.  none of the above

M  **61.** Specialized islet cells that secrete hormones are found scattered throughout the
   a  adrenal cortex.
   b.  liver.
   c.  thymus.
   d.  adrenal medulla.
   *  e.  pancreas.

D  **62.** If you skip a meal, which of the following conditions would prevail?
   a  Insulin levels would rise.
   b.  Glucagon levels would rise.
   c.  Glycogen would be converted to glucose.
   d.  a and c
   *  e.  b and c

D  **63.** Which of the following is true of "type 1 diabetes"?
   a  Insulin levels are near normal.
   b.  Target cells do not respond to insulin.
   c.  It is the more common form of diabetes.
   *  d.  It is thought to be an autoimmune disease.
   e.  It usually occurs in middle-aged people.

M  **64.** Prostaglandins
   a  affect blood flow by acting on smooth muscles in the blood cells.
   b.  cause menstrual cramps.
   c.  may produce strong allergic reactions.
   d.  are produced by the corpus luteum if pregnancy does not follow ovulation.
   *  e.  all of the above

## HORMONAL RESPONSES TO ENVIRONMENTAL CLUES

E  **65.** Which gland is the remnant of the third eye?
   *  a  pineal
   b.  pituitary
   c.  thyroid
   d.  parathyroid
   e.  thymus

E  **66.** The gland that functions in controlling the reproductive cycle is the
   a  thyroid.
   *  b.  pineal.
   c.  thymus.
   d.  pancreas.
   e.  kidney.

M  **67.** Which gland is associated with biological clocks or biorhythms?
   *  a  pineal
   b.  parathyroid
   c.  hypothalamus
   d.  pituitary
   e.  thymus

D    **68.** Based on evolutionary evidence in higher animals, the search for hormones in insects should focus on
     a   the digestive system.
     b.   exocrine glands.
*     c.   the nervous system.
     d.   muscles.
     e.   the exoskeleton.

E    **69.** The molting hormone of insects is
     a   corticotropin.
     b.   MSH.
     c.   oxytocin.
*     d.   ecdysone.
     e.   adrenalin.

## Matching Questions

D    **70.** Choose the one most appropriate answer for each.

1 _____     adrenal cortex
2 _____     adrenal medulla
3 _____     anterior lobe of pituitary
4 _____     exocrine glands
5 _____     endocrine cells in gastrointestinal tract
6 _____     gonad
7 _____     hypothalamus
8 _____     intermediate lobe of pituitary
9 _____     kidneys
10 _____     pancreatic islets
11 _____     parathyroid gland
12 _____     pineal gland
13 _____     posterior lobe of pituitary
14 _____     thymus gland
15 _____     thyroid gland

A.     secretes one hormone that increases the metabolic rate and another that inhibits calcium release from bone storage sites

B.     secrete insulin and glucagon

C.     secretes hormones that prepare accessory reproductive structures for reproduction

D.     involved in lymphocyte maturation

E.     secretes tropic hormones, growth hormone, and prolactin

F.     secretes mineralocorticoids and glucocorticoids

G.     in many vertebrates, help to determine the amount and distribution of dark pigments in the skin

H.     secrete enzymes that help to form angiotensin and erythropoietin

I.     participates in reproductive physiology and senses photoperiods

J.     secretes (releases into bloodstream) oxytocin and antidiuretic hormone

K.     secretes a hormone that promotes calcium release from bone storage sites

L.     produces oxytocin and antidiuretic hormone

M.     secretes secretin and gastrin

N.     secretes epinephrine and norepinephrine

O.     secrete pheromones, milk, tears, sweat, and mucus

*Answers:*

| 1. F. | 2 N | 3. E |
|-------|-----|------|
| 4. O | 5. M | 6. C |
| 7. L | 8. G | 9. H |
| 10. B | 11. K | 12. I |
| 13. J | 14. D | 15. A |

## Classification Questions

Answer questions 71-75 in reference to the five endocrine glands listed below:

     a   pituitary
     b.   adrenal
     c.   pancreas
     d.   thyroid
     e.   thymus

M    **71.** This gland is the target for corticotropin (ACTH).

E    **72.** In this gland oxytocin is produced.

M    **73.** In this gland antidiuretic hormone is produced.

M    **74.** This gland produces a hormone that controls metabolism MOST directly.

E    **75.** Insulin is produced in this gland.

*Answers:*

| 71. b | 72. a | 73. a |
|-------|-------|-------|
| 74. d | 75. c | |

Answer questions 76-80 in reference to the five pituitary hormones listed below:

    a. estrogen
    b. luteinizing hormone
    c. somatotropin
    d. oxytocin
    e. antidiuretic hormone

M    **76.** This hormone controls water retention and loss.

M    **77.** The mammary glands are the target for this hormone.

D    **78.** This hormone induces protein synthesis and cell division in young animals.

D    **79.** The kidneys are the target for this hormone.

M    **80.** Uterine contractions are induced by this hormone.

*Answers:*    76. e    77. d    78. c
              79. e    80. d

Answer questions 81-85 in reference to the five endocrine glands listed below:

    a. adrenal cortex
    b. ovary
    c. pineal
    d. thyroid
    e. thymus

D    **81.** This gland controls circadian rhythms.

M    **82.** This gland plays a central role in the immune response.

D    **83.** This gland secretes a hormone that prepares and maintains the uterus for pregnancy.

M    **84.** Progesterone is produced by this gland.

M    **85.** Calcium concentration in the blood is controlled by this glands.

*Answers:*    81. c    82. e    83. b
              84. b    85. d

## Selecting the Exception

E    **86.** Four of the five answers listed below are endocrine glands. Select the exception.
    a. thymus gland
   * b. salivary gland
    c. parathyroid gland
    d. thyroid gland
    e. pituitary gland

D    **87.** Four of the five answers listed below are produced by the same lobe of the pituitary. Select the exception.
   * a. antidiuretic hormone
    b. prolactin
    c. corticotropin
    d. somatotropin
    e. luteinizing hormone

M    **88.** Four of the five answers listed below are related by a common source. Select the exception.
    a. glucocorticoids
    b. sex hormones
    c. cortisol
   * d. adrenalin
    e. mineralocorticoid

M    **89.** Four of the five answers listed below affect blood glucose level. Select the exception.
   * a. calcitonin
    b. glucagon
    c. glucocorticoid
    d. insulin
    e. epinephrine

D    **90.** Four of the five answers listed below directly affect another endocrine gland. Select the exception.
   * a. cortisol
    b. corticotropin
    c. luteinizing hormone
    d. follicle-stimulating hormone
    e. angiotensin

D    **91.** Four of the five answers listed below are true of hyperthyroidism. Select the exception.
    a. excessive weight loss
   * b. excessive water loss through urination
    c. intolerance of heat
    d. increased heart rate and blood pressure
    e. excessive sweating

M    **92.** Four of the five answers listed below are related by a similar source. Select the exception.
   * a. prolactin
    b. progesterone
    c. androgen
    d. estrogen
    e. testosterone

D    **93.** Four of the five answers listed below are related by a similar gland. Select the exception.
    a. goiter
    b. deficiency of iodine in the diet
    c. hypothyroidism
   * d. rickets
    e. excessive stimulation of the thyroid gland

D    **94.** Four of the five answers listed below are related by the same action. Select the exception.
    a. activates vitamin D
    b. induces resorption of calcium by the kidney
    c. removes calcium and phosphate from bones
   * d. regulates blood volume
    e. involved in the biofeedback control of extracellular calcium

# CHAPTER 34
# REPRODUCTION AND DEVELOPMENT

## Multiple-Choice Questions

### THE BEGINNING: REPRODUCTIVE MODES

M **1.** Which of the following is NOT true of asexual reproduction?
- a It is more suitable for reproduction in animals in stable environments.
- b. It results in offspring that are identical to each other.
- * c. It promotes genetic variation in each successive generation.
- d. Budding is one type of asexual reproduction.
- e. The offspring are genetically identical to the parents.

M **2.** Which of the following statements is NOT an advantage of asexual reproduction?
- a Asexual reproduction is more efficient than sexual reproduction.
- b. An individual organism can reproduce asexually by itself.
- * c. Asexual reproduction promotes variation.
- d. Asexual reproduction produces fewer offspring than sexual reproduction.

D **3.** Which of the following is NOT one of the factors contributing to the high cost of sexual reproduction?
- a specialized reproductive structures such as the male penis
- b. production of excessive numbers of gametes
- c. development of elaborate courtship rituals
- * d. production of the cytoplasm for millions of reproductive buds
- e. nourishment of offspring

D **4.** Which of the following animals would fit this description: "Eggs fertilized outside the body, minimum of yolk, rapid development?"
- a bird
- * b. sea urchin
- c. bony fish
- d. reptile
- e. human

### STAGES OF DEVELOPMENT—AN OVERVIEW

M **5.** At the end of gastrulation, which of the following are produced?
- a hollow balls of cells
- * b. embryos with germ layers
- c. solid balls of cells
- d. maternal messages
- e. all of the above

E **6.** Which stage in development occurs first?
- a cleavage
- b. morula
- c. gastrula
- * d. zygote
- e. blastula

E **7.** The germ layers are formed in which of the following stages?
- a cleavage
- b. morula
- * c. gastrula
- d. zygote
- e. blastula

E **8.** The heart, muscles, bones, and blood develop primarily from
- a ectoderm.
- * b. mesoderm.
- c. endoderm.
- d. the placenta.
- e. the gray crescent.

E **9.** The process of cleavage most commonly produces a
- a zygote.
- * b. blastula.
- c. gastrula.
- d. puff.
- e. third germ layer.

M **10.** Which embryonic tissue is incorrectly associated with its derivative?
- * a skin from mesoderm
- b. nervous system from ectoderm
- c. liver from endoderm
- d. circulatory system from mesoderm

E **11.** Muscles differentiate from which tissue?
- a ectoderm
- b. endoderm
- * c. mesoderm
- d. all of the above

E **12.** Shortly after fertilization, successive cell divisions convert the zygote into a multicellular embryo during a process known as
- a meiosis.
- b. parthenogenesis.
- c. embryonic induction.
- * d. cleavage.
- e. invagination.

M   13.   The mesoderm is responsible for the formation of all of the following adult tissues EXCEPT
         a   reproductive system.
         b.  circulatory system.
    *    c   nervous system.
         d.  muscle system.
         e.  excretory system.

E   14.   In the following list of developmental events, which occurs last?
    *    a   tissue specialization
         b.  gamete formation
         c   gastrulation
         d.  cleavage
         e.  organ formation

D   15.   In the human, which of the following events would occur over the longest period of time?
         a   sperm production
         b.  cleavage
         c   fertilization
         d.  gastrulation
    *    e   growth and tissue specialization

## A VISUAL TOUR OF FROG AND CHICK DEVELOPMENT

E   16.   Which of the following statements is NOT true?
         a   It is an advantage for eggs to complete their development as quickly as possible to avoid predation.
         b.  The amount of yolk in an egg varies from one species to another.
    *    c   Bird egg shells are present before fertilization occurs.
         d.  Human eggs have almost no yolk.
         e.  Yolk is composed of fats and proteins and is high in nutritive value.

## EARLY MARCHING ORDERS

D   17.   Before gastrulation the future phenotype of cell lineages is largely established by which of the following acquired during cleavage?
         a   the genotype
    *    b.  the portion of egg cytoplasm
         c   surface recognition factors on the plasma membrane
         d.  the number and type of organelles
         e.  all of the above

M   18.   Which of the following affects the developmental pathways that different embryonic cells eventually will follow?
         a   sperm nucleus
         b.  egg nucleus
         c   sperm cytoplasm
    *    d.  egg cytoplasm
         e.  both b and c

D   19.   Which of the following statements is false?
         a   Most of the genes of the nucleus are inactive during cleavage.
         b.  The particular sector of the egg cytoplasm helps control the differences among cells.
         c   The amount of yolk present in the egg influences cleavage patterns.
    *    d.  The cells of the animal pole are larger than the cells of the vegetal pole.
         e.  There is so much yolk in the eggs of reptiles and birds that cleavage is restricted to a very small region of the animal pole.

M   20.   The gray crescent is
         a   formed where the sperm penetrates the egg.
    *    b.  formed opposite from where the sperm enters the egg.
         c   the portion of the egg where the yolk is found.
         d.  located next to the dorsal lip of the blastopore.
         e.  the point where the first cleavage occurs.

D   21.   The stimulus for the formation of the gray crescent is
         a   provided by the RNA transcripts in the egg.
    *    b.  the entry of the sperm.
         c   the responsibility of oocyte components.
         d.  determined by the polarity of the egg.
         e.  determined in part by all of the above except b.

D   22.   Which of the following statements is false?
         a   The cells in the animal pole are smaller than those in the vegetal pole.
    *    b.  The gray crescent is formed where the sperm enters the egg.
         c   The archenteron is formed by the process of invagination.
         d.  In most mammals, the blastula has a group of cells that will eventually develop into the placenta.
         e.  In mutant *Drosophila* embryos, if the polar granules do not migrate properly, the adult produced will be sterile.

E   23.   Which of the following is a single-layered, hollow ball of cells?
         a   cleavage
         b.  morula
         c   gastrula
         d.  zygote
    *    e   blastula

D   24.   In the process of blastula formation,
         a   the size of individual cells decreases.
         b.  the number of cells increases.
         c   the total amount of cytoplasm remains about the same.
         d.  only a and b are possible
    *    e   a, b, and c are all possible

## HOW SPECIALIZED TISSUES AND ORGANS FORM

M  25. During which of the following stages do cells of identical genetic makeup become structurally and functionally different from one another according to the genetically controlled developmental program of the species?
  a  cleavage
* b. cell differentiation
  c. morphogenesis
  d. metamorphosis
  e. ovulation

M  26. In the process of cell differentiation,
  a  some daughter cells usually receive varying assortments of genes.
* b. cells with identical assortments of genes come to have different individual genes expressed.
  c. cells become specialized as a result of meiosis.
  d. daughter cells acquire different characteristics as a result of mutations that have occurred.
  e. all of the above

D  27. Which of the following statements is false?
  a  Cell migration during embryonic development is an example of chemotaxis.
  b. Schwann cells follow adhesive cells as they migrate along the axons of neurons.
* c. Cells continue migrating throughout the entire embryonic process.
  d. Morphogenesis depends upon local growth.
  e. Controlled cell death leads to morphogenesis.

M  28. Cells migrate during morphogenesis in response to
  a  chemical gradients.
  b. recognition proteins.
  c. adhesive cues.
  d. a and c only
* e. a, b, and c

D  29. Complex maneuvers such as the folding involved in formation of the neural tube are accomplished primarily by
  a  adhesive cues.
  b. chemical gradients.
* c. microtubules and microfilaments.
  d. controlled cell death.
  e. chemotaxis.

M  30. Patterns that involve controlled cell death include
  a  formation and hollowing out of tubes.
  b. opening of the eyes and mouth.
  c. formation of fingers and toes.
  d. destruction of certain specific cells.
* e. all of the above

M  31. The differentiation of a body part in response to signals from an adjacent body part is
  a  contact inhibition.
  b. ooplasmic localization.
* c. embryonic induction.
  d. pattern formation.
  e. all of the above

M  32. The mechanism of embryonic induction involves
* a  chemicals.
  b. electrical signals.
  c. touch.
  d. a and c only
  e. b and c only

M  33. The process in which the fate of a group of cells is controlled by substances produced by other embryonic cells is known as
* a  embryonic induction.
  b. cytoplasmic localization.
  c. cellular differentiation.
  d. morphogenesis.
  e. formation of the gray crescent.

M  34. Homeobox genes
  a  cause lethal mutations.
* b. control blocks of genes necessary for pattern formation.
  c. are found only in fruit flies where they are responsible for odd placement of appendages.
  d. are also known as "fate maps."
  e. operate only in individuals with two genes of the same kind.

M  35. Signaling molecules responsible for embryonic induction are called
  a  crystallins.
* b. morphogens.
  c. mutagens.
  d. inducagens.
  e. homeoboxes.

## REPRODUCTIVE SYSTEM OF HUMAN MALES

M  36. The male and female sex organs begin to differentiate during which week of gestation?
  a  fourth week
* b. seventh week
  c. twelfth week
  d. twentieth week
  e. twenty-eighth week

E  37. In the human male several hundred million sperm are produced by spermatogenesis occurring in
  a  interstitial cells.
  b. the prostate.
* c. seminiferous tubules.
  d. the vas deferens.
  e. epididymis.

E   38.   Sperm are produced in the
    *    a   testes.
         b.  vas deferens.
         c.  epididymis.
         d.  prostate gland.
         e.  penis.

M   39.   Seminal fluid is produced by the
         a   prostate gland.
         b.  seminal vesicle.
         c.  bulbourethral gland.
         d.  urinary bladder.
    *    e.  all except d

D   40.   The seminal vesicles ("sperm vessels") are misnamed. Sperm are actually stored in the
         a   vas deferens.
    *    b.  epididymis.
         c.  prostate.
         d.  scrotum.
         e.  urethra.

D   41.   Which of the following is the site where sperm are stored?
         a   ureter
         b.  urethra
         c.  vas deferens
         d.  vas efferens
    *    e.  epididymis

D   42.   If the vas deferens tubes are cut and tied (vasectomy), the semen will not contain
         a   fructose.
         b.  buffers.
         c.  mucus.
    *    d.  sperm.
         e.  any of the above

M   43.   Which of the following is the last structure that a sperm travels through as it leaves the body?
         a   ureter
    *    b.  urethra
         c.  vas deferens
         d.  vas efferens
         e.  epididymis

**MALE REPRODUCTIVE FUNCTION**

M   44.   Which of the following cells are diploid?
         a   spermatids
         b.  primary spermatocytes
         c.  secondary spermatocytes
         d.  spermatogonia
    *    e.  both b and d

M   45.   Which cells are produced during meiosis I?
         a   spermatids
         b.  primary spermatocytes
    *    c.  secondary spermatocytes
         d.  spermatids
         e.  sperm

M   46.   Sperm become fully motile in the
         a   vas deferens.
         b.  epididymis.
         c.  seminiferous tubules.
    *    d.  vagina.
         e.  seminal fluid.

M   47.   Testosterone
         a   stimulates sperm production.
         b.  promotes the normal development and maintenance of sexual behavior.
         c.  is responsible for secondary sexual characteristics.
         d.  is responsible for the development of the male genitalia.
    *    e.  all of the above

D   48.   The secretions of the interstitial cells (Leydig cells) eventually pass into the
         a   semen.
         b.  vagina.
    *    c.  blood.
         d.  a and b only
         e.  a, b, and c

M   49.   All but which of the following hormones are in some way responsible for the production of sperm?
         a   luteinizing hormone
         b.  follicle-stimulating hormone
         c.  gonadotropic releasing hormone
         d.  testosterone
    *    e.  human chorionic gonadotropin

D   50.   All but which of the following are the products of meiosis?
         a   male gametes
         b.  spermatids
         c.  sperm
         d.  secondary spermatocytes
    *    e.  spermatogonia

D   51.   Which of the following is NOT involved in a feedback loop in the male reproductive system?
         a   anterior pituitary
         b.  hypothalamus
    *    c.  adrenal gland
         d.  Sertoli cells
         e.  interstitial cells

D   52.   The release of testosterone requires
         a   luteinizing hormone.
         b.  GnRH.
         c.  Sertoli cells.
    *    d.  a and b only
         e.  a, b, and c

## REPRODUCTIVE SYSTEM OF HUMAN FEMALES

E 53. The female reproductive system includes all the following EXCEPT
  a  clitoris.
  b.  vagina.
  c.  oviduct.
  d.  ovary.
  * e.  mammary gland.

E 54. The primary reproductive organ in the human female is the
  a  uterus.
  * b.  ovary.
  c.  vagina.
  d.  clitoris.
  e.  vulva.

M 55. Which mammal does NOT exhibit seasonal sexual activities?
  a  whale
  b.  cats
  * c.  primates
  d.  horses
  e.  dogs

E 56. The passageway that channels ova from the ovary into the uterus is known as
  a  a vagina.
  b.  a uterus.
  * c.  an oviduct.
  d.  an endometrium.
  e.  all of the above

M 57. The surface of which of the following is covered with fingerlike projections that produce a sweeping action?
  a  ovary
  b.  uterus
  c.  vagina
  * d.  oviduct
  e.  follicle

E 58. The cervix is part of the
  a  vulva.
  b.  ovary.
  * c.  uterus.
  d.  oviduct.
  e.  vagina.

E 59. In most mammals a predictably recurring time when the female becomes sexually receptive to the male is called
  * a  estrus.
  b.  endometrium.
  c.  menstruation.
  d.  coitus.
  e.  parturition.

M 60. Which of the following statements is false?
  a  A female has more oocytes before she is born than at any time during her life.
  b.  Meiosis II will not occur in an oocyte unless it is fertilized.
  * c.  Fertilization occurs in the vagina.
  d.  Implantation occurs in the uterus.
  e.  The vagina serves as the birth canal.

M 61. Which of the following hormones is exclusively female?
  a  follicle-stimulating hormone
  b.  luteinizing hormone
  * c.  progesterone
  d.  a and c only
  e.  a, b, and c

D 62. Which of the following is NOT essential to the reproductive process?
  a  ovary
  b.  oviduct
  * c.  clitoris
  d.  vagina
  e.  uterus

## FEMALE REPRODUCTIVE FUNCTION

M 63. Which of the following statements is NOT true of the human female?
  a  She produces all the eggs that she ever will before she is born.
  b.  The process of meiosis may take thirty to fifty years to complete.
  c.  The primary oocytes lay dormant until puberty.
  * d.  She will produce more gametes than her male counterpart.
  e.  It is possible that more than one egg will be released at ovulation.

E 64. Menstrual flow results in the discharge of
  a  the follicle.
  b.  the corpus luteum.
  * c.  the endometrial lining.
  d.  surface cells from the vagina.
  e.  blood from the blood vessels on the outer surface of the uterus.

E 65. Ovulation is triggered primarily by
  * a  a surge of LH that occurs halfway through the menstrual cycle.
  b.  the falling levels of estrogen and progesterone.
  c.  the rising levels of progesterone.
  d.  both a and c

M 66. Ovulation involves the
  a  production of the first polar body.
  * b.  release of a secondary oocyte.
  c.  beginning of the follicular phase of the menstrual cycle.
  d.  suspension of the meiotic process.
  e.  deterioration of the corpus luteum.

D 67. Which of the following serves to end the menstrual cycle?
    a a surge in luteinizing hormone
    b. the secretion of human chorionic gonadotropin
*   c the secretion of prostaglandins by the corpus luteum that lead to its self-destruction
    d. a rise in the level of progesterone
    e. a drop in the level of gonadotropic hormones in the blood

D 68. Using your knowledge of the feedback loops of human female hormones, which of the following would you predict is the result of high levels of estrogen and progesterone in the blood?
    a lack of growth of the corpus luteum
*   b. absence of monthly ovulation
    c increased secretion of FSH
    d increased levels of LH
    e all of the above

M 69. Destruction of the corpus luteum, if pregnancy does NOT occur, results from the action of
    a chorionic gonadotropism.
    b. the luteinizing hormone.
    c progesterone.
*   d prostaglandins.
    e estrogen.

## VISUAL SUMMARY OF THE MENSTRUAL CYCLE

M 70. FSH and LH are secreted by the
    a hypothalamus.
    b. ovaries.
*   c anterior pituitary.
    d testes.
    e uterus.

M 71. Ovulation is triggered by
*   a high levels of LH.
    b. low levels of LH.
    c high levels of chorionic gonadotropin.
    d high levels of estrogen.
    e high levels of progesterone.

E 72. Menstrual flow begins in response to
    a rising levels of FSH and LH.
    b. falling levels of estrogen.
    c falling levels of progesterone.
*   d both b and c

## PREGNANCY HAPPENS

M 73. Orgasm is necessary for
*   a ejaculation of semen.
    b. pregnancy.
    c erection.
    d sexual arousal.
    e all of the above

E 74. Fertilization in mammals occurs in the
    a ovary.
    b. uterus.
    c vagina.
*   d oviduct.
    e follicle.

E 75. The average number of sperm that are deposited in the vagina during an ejaculation is between
    a 150,000 and 350,000.
    b. 1.5 and 3.5 million.
    c 15 and 35 million.
*   d 150 and 350 million.
    e 1.5 and 3.5 billion.

## FORMATION OF THE EARLY EMBRYO

E 76. The embryo is recognizable as human and is called a fetus by which week of pregnancy?
*   a eighth
    b. twelfth
    c sixteenth
    d twentieth
    e twenty-fourth

M 77. During a human pregnancy, implantation occurs at which stage?
    a zygote
    b. early cleavage
*   c blastocyst
    d gastrula
    e morula

E 78. Implantation occurs in the
    a ovary.
*   b. uterus.
    c vagina.
    d oviduct.
    e follicle.

M 79. The first several cleavages after fertilization occur in the
    a uterus.
    b. ovary.
    c vagina.
*   d oviduct.
    e any of the above except vagina

M 80. Which of the following statements is false?
    a Ovulation occurs when the follicle ruptures and releases an egg.
    b. Cleavage occurs when the zygote divides.
    c Fertilization occurs in the upper regions of the oviduct.
    d The blastocyst implants in the endometrial lining of the uterus.
*   e Implantation occurs about 36 hours after fertilization.

M 81. In the eggs of birds and reptiles, the waste products are stored in the
* a allantois.
b placenta.
c chorion.
d amnion.
e yolk sac.

M 82. In humans, the fluid immediately surrounding the embryo is contained in the
a allantois.
b placenta.
c chorion.
* d amnion.
e yolk sac.

M 83. The outermost membrane that forms the majority of the placenta is the
a amnion.
b allantois.
* c chorion.
d yolk sac.
e umbilical cord.

M 84. The presence of which hormone in a mother's urine indicates that she is pregnant?
a luteinizing hormone
b follicle-stimulating hormone
* c chorionic gonadotropin
d progesterone
e estrogen

M 85. Which of the following hormones is produced only when a woman is pregnant?
a testosterone
b gonadotropic-releasing hormone
* c human chorionic gonadotropin
d estrogen
e progesterone

M 86. Implantation of a blastocyst on the uterine wall can be detected by the presence of
* a human chorionic gonadotropin.
b progesterone.
c estrogen.
d testosterone.
e second polar body.

## EMERGENCE OF THE VERTEBRATE BODY PLAN

E 87. During human development, which of the following gives rise to the embryo?
a trophoblast
b amnion
* c embryonic disk
d chorion
e placenta

M 88. Which of the following systems is the first of those listed to begin development in the human embryo?
* a nervous system
b excretory system
c reproductive system
d skeletal system
e endocrine system

## ON THE IMPORTANCE OF THE PLACENTA

M 89. The membrane that forms the majority of the placenta is the
a amnion.
b allantois.
* c chorion.
d yolk sac.
e umbilical cord.

M 90. Which of the following would be expected to diffuse in greater amounts from the fetal blood to the mother's blood?
a oxygen
* b urea
c hormones
d antibodies
e nutrients

## EMERGENCE OF DISTINCTLY HUMAN FEATURES

D 91. Which of the following does NOT occur in the first trimester?
a formation of a heart
b disappearance of the tail
c formation of internal organs
* d detection of movement of the fetus
e segmentation and development of somites

E 92. In humans, the embryonic development of a four-chambered heart and the nerve cord is present by which week?
a third
* b fourth
c fifth
d sixth
e seventh

## FROM BIRTH ONWARD

M 93. The female hormones that participate in milk production for the newborn are
* a prolactin and oxytocin.
b prolactin and estrogen.
c prolactin and progesterone.
d oxytocin and estrogen.
e oxytocin and progesterone.

M 94. Milk production in women is stimulated by
a estrogen.
* b prolactin.
c oxytocin.
d prostaglandin.
e progesterone.

D  95.  Which of the following is NOT currently a possible explanation of the process of aging?
   a  limited number of mitosis cycles
   b.  autoimmune attack
 * c  increased mutation rate
   d.  gene deterioration
   e.  limited division potential

**CONTROL OF HUMAN FERTILITY**

E  96.  Which of the following is the most effective in helping prevent venereal disease?
 * a  condoms
   b.  the Pill
   c  douching
   d.  the IUD
   e.  rhythm

E  97.  Of the following, which is the least successful method of birth control?
   a  early withdrawal
   b.  a condom alone
   c  a spermicidal jelly or foam alone
 * d.  douching
   e.  the Pill

M  98.  A contraceptive pill contains
   a  estrogen.
   b.  progesterone.
   c  the follicle-stimulating hormone.
   d.  the luteinizing hormone.
 * e.  both a and b

D  99.  Which of the following is the most effective contraceptive approach of those listed?
   a  withdrawal
 * b.  diaphragm
   c  cheap condoms
   d.  douche
   e.  rhythm method

E  100.  The type of contraception that functions by preventing implantation (even after successful fertilization) is
   a  tubal ligation.
   b.  spermicidal jelly.
   c  birth control pills.
 * d.  RU-486.
   e.  diaphragm.

E  101.  The type of contraception that works because ovulation is prevented is
   a  rhythm.
   b.  tubal ligation.
 * c  birth control pills.
   d.  diaphragm.
   e.  condom.

M  102.  Which of the following is NOT an effective temporary method of contraception?
   a  birth-control pills
 * b.  vasectomy
   c  condoms
   d.  IUD plus spermicide
   e.  spermicidal jelly or foam

## Matching Questions

D  103.  Matching I. Choose the one most appropriate answer for each.

1  _____  abortion
2  _____  abstention
3  _____  coitus
4  _____  douching
5  _____  ejaculation
6  _____  implantation
7  _____  lactation
8  _____  menopause
9  _____  menstruation
10  _____  miscarriage
11  _____  orgasm
12  _____  ovulation
13  _____  tubal ligation
14  _____  vasectomy

A.  the production and secretion of milk
B.  sloughing off of endometrium stops permanently
C.  birth control exercised after development begins
D.  an abortion that occurs spontaneously
E.  the burrowing of the blastocyst into the uterus
F.  the release of an egg from the ovary
G.  the release of seminal fluid from the male reproductive tract
H.  a 100 percent effective method of preventing conception
I  a highly unreliable form of birth control
J.  the periodic elimination of the uterine lining
K.  characterized by involuntary muscle contractions, release of tension, and warmth
L.  sexual intercourse
M.  sperm and egg cannot meet because section of oviduct is missing
N.  cutting and tying of vas deferens

*Answers*:
| 1. C | 2. H | 3. L |
| 4. I | 5. G | 6. E |
| 7. A | 8. B | 9. J |
| 10. D | 11. K | 12. F |
| 13. M | 14. N | |

D    **104.**    Matching II. Choose the one most appropriate answer for each.

1  _____  acrosome
2  _____  allantois
3  _____  blastocyst
4  _____  cervix
5  _____  clitoris
6  _____  endometrium
7  _____  epididymis
8  _____  FSH
9  _____  Leydig cells of testis
10 _____  LH
11 _____  placenta
12 _____  seminal vesicles
13 _____  vas deferens

A.  in females, acts on ruptured follicle to produce corpus luteum

B.  structures that secrete mucus and nutrients absorbable by sperm; open into the ejaculatory duct

C.  forms as an outgrowth of the embryonic gut; becomes part of umbilical cord and placenta

D.  two of these connect seminiferous tubules with vasa deferentia

E.  opening between uterus and vagina

F.  organ that supplies the embryo/fetus with nutrients and removes waste products

G.  connect epididymides with ejaculatory duct

H.  cap over the head of a sperm; contains lytic enzymes that help penetrate egg membrane

I.  inner cell mass plus trophoblast; attaches to uterine wall

J.  testosterone produced here

K.  part of vulva; develops from same embryonic tissues as does the penis in males

L.  the uterine lining

M.  acts on gonad to help mature gametes; released from anterior lobe of pituitary

*Answers:*

| 1. | H | 2. | C | 3. | I |
|----|---|----|---|----|---|
| 4. | E | 5. | K | 6. | L |
| 7. | D | 8. | M | 9. | J |
| 10. | A | 11. | F | 12. | B |
| 13. | G |  |  |  |  |

## Classification Questions

Answer questions 105–109 in reference to the five stages of development listed below:

a  zygote
b.  blastula
c.  morula
d.  gastrula
e.  embryo

M    **105.**    This stage appears as a multicellular, hollow bal.

E    **106.**    This is the fertilized egg.

M    **107.**    This stage might be described as a "solid ball".

D    **108.**    The gut cavity of an animal forms during this stag.

D    **109.**    The major germ layers are formed during this stage.

*Answers:*

| 105. | b | 106. | a | 107. | c |
|------|---|------|---|------|---|
| 108. | d | 109. | d |  |  |

Answer questions 110–114 in reference to the five stages of sperm development listed below:

a  spermatogonia
b.  secondary spermatocyte
c.  primary spermatocyte
d.  spermatid
e.  sperm

D    **110.**    At this stage of development the male sex cell has been reduced to the haploid condition for the first time.

M    **111.**    These cells continue to undergo mitosis throughout the reproductive life of the male.

D    **112.**    This represents the product of the first meiotic division.

D    **113.**    This is a mitotic product, but then undergoes meiosis.

M    **114.**    At this stage of development the male sex cell is fully motile.

*Answers:*

| 110. | b | 111. | a | 112. | b |
|------|---|------|---|------|---|
| 113. | c | 114. | e |  |  |

Answer questions 115-119 in reference to the five stages and structures involved in the development of the human egg:

    a  oogonium
    b.  primary oocyte
    c.  secondary oocyte
    d.  polar body
    e.  secondary follicle

M    **115.**  This structure becomes the mature egg only after fertilization is begun.

D    **116.**  This structure contains the first sex cell stage to be in the haploid state.

M    **117.**  This structure contains a full haploid set of chromosomes, but will never be fertilized.

M    **118.**  This structure divides by mitosis during the fetal stages of development until all of the approximately 2 million potential eggs have been formed.

D    **119.**  This stage lies dormant between birth and puberty.

*Answers:*    115.  c    116.  c    117.  d
                  118.  a    119.  b

## Selecting the Exception

M    **120.**  Four of the five answers listed below are events occurring after fertilization. Select the exception.
        a  cleavage
   *  b.  gametogenesis
        c.  blastula
        d.  gastrulation
        e.  organogenesis

M    **121.**  Four of the five answers listed below are produced by the same germ layer. Select the exception.
   *  a  nervous system
        b.  muscle system
        c.  circulatory system
        d.  reproductive system
        e.  excretory system

M    **122.**  Three of the four answers listed below produce portions of the seminal fluid. Select the exception.
   *  a  epididymis
        b.  prostate
        c.  seminal vesicle
        d.  bulbourethral gland

M    **123.**  Three of the four answers listed below are related by the number of chromosomes present. Select the exception.
        a  sperm
   *  b.  spermatogonia
        c.  secondary spermatocyte
        d.  spermatids

E    **124.**  Three of the four answers listed below are all parts of a sperm. Select the exception.
        a  flagella
        b.  midpiece
        c.  acrosome
   *  d.  polar body

D    **125.**  Four of the five answers listed below are related by a common quantity. Select the exception.
   *  a  urethra
        b.  testis
        c.  ejaculatory duct
        d.  vas deferens
        e.  epididymis

D    **126.**  Four of the five answers listed below are true of testosterone. Select the exception.
        a  promotes secondary sex characteristics
        b.  controls sexual behavior
        c.  necessary for growth and function of male reproductive tract
        d.  stimulates spermatogenesis
   *  e.  produced by spermatogonia cells

M    **127.**  Four of the five answers listed below are related by a common location. Select the exception.
        a  follicle
        b.  corpus luteum
   *  c.  cervix
        d.  oogonium
        e.  primary oocyte

D    **128.**  Four of the five answers listed below are related by a matching feature. Select the exception.
   *  a  blastocyst
        b.  amnion
        c.  allantois
        d.  yolk sac
        e.  chorion

M    **129.**  Four of the five answers listed below are related by a similar effectiveness. Select the exception.
        a  pill
        b.  tubal ligation
        c.  vasectomy
   *  d.  douching
        e.  IUD

# CHAPTER 35
# POPULATION ECOLOGY

## Multiple-Choice Questions

### CHARACTERISTICS OF POPULATIONS

E    **1.** Which of the following includes all the others?
     a.   ecosystem
\*    b.   biosphere
     c.   community
     d.   individual
     e.   population

E    **2.** A group of individuals of the same species occupying a given area defines a
     a.   community
     b.   ecosystem
\*    c.   population
     d.   biosphere
     e.   habitat

M    **3.** A population
     a.   is the unit of evolution.
     b.   consists of interbreeding members of the same species.
     c.   shares the same gene pool.
     d.   grows at an exponential rate when the birth rate exceeds the death rate at a constant differential, no matter how slight the difference.
\*    e.   all of the above

E    **4.** The total number of individuals of the same species that occupy a given area at a given time is the
     a.   population distribution.
     b.   population growth.
     c.   population birth rate.
\*    d.   population size.
     e.   carrying capacity.

M    **5.** The average number of individuals of the same species per unit of surface area at a given time is the
\*    a.   population density.
     b.   population growth.
     c.   population birth rate.
     d.   population size.
     e.   carrying capacity.

M    **6.** What distribution pattern is the most common in the natural world?
     a.   random
     b.   uniform
\*    c.   clumped
     d.   stratified or layered
     e.   bimodal

M    **7.** To a person studying utilization of classroom space on campus, the most useful data concerning students in a classroom would be expressed by the number of
     a.   total individuals.
\*    b.   individuals per square yard.
     c.   individuals per room.
     d.   rooms per building.
     e.   students of each age.

D    **8.** Which of the following would provide a chicken rancher using a noncaged arrangement for his flock the data necessary to ensure maximum survival of his hens?
\*    a.   distribution
     b.   number of individuals
     c.   individuals per square foot
     d.   size of room
     e.   age structure

M    **9.** The distribution of the human population in the United States is
\*    a.   clumped.
     b.   random.
     c.   uniform.
     d.   constant.

M    **10.** Uniform distribution of human habitats would likely be the result of _____ , whereas habitats of other animals would be due to _____ .
     a.   competition; social interaction
\*    b.   law; competition
     c.   social interaction; chemical avoidance
     d.   limited mobility; contact inhibition

### POPULATION SIZE AND EXPONENTIAL GROWTH

M    **11.** The maximum rate of increase of a population is its
\*    a.   biotic potential.
     b.   carrying capacity.
     c.   exponential growth.
     d.   distribution.
     e.   reproductive base.

D    **12.** The biotic potential
     a.   varies from one species to another.
     b.   is controlled by the timing of the first reproduction.
     c.   is controlled by the frequency of reproduction.
     d.   is controlled by the number of offspring produced.
\*    e.   all of the above

E    **13.** Population size depends upon
- a   deaths.
- b.   births.
- c.   migration.
- d.   immigration.
- \*   e.   all of the above

M    **14.** Populations of most species
- \*   a   are relatively constant over time.
- b.   gradually decrease over time.
- c.   gradually increase over time.
- d.   vary rapidly, depending upon environmental conditions.

M    **15.** Zero population growth is achieved when
- a   a population reaches the carrying capacity of the environment.
- \*   b.   the population size has been stabilized for a long time.
- c.   births exceed deaths.
- d.   deaths exceed births.
- e.   migration is prevented.

M    **16.** A situation in which the birth rate equals the death rate is called
- a   an intrinsic limiting factor.
- b.   exponential growth.
- c.   saturation.
- \*   d.   zero population growth.
- e.   geometric growth.

D    **17.** The rate of increase for a population ($r$) refers to what kind of relationship between birth rate and death rate?
- a   their sum
- b.   their product
- c.   the doubling time between them
- \*   d.   the difference between them
- e.   reduction in each of them

E    **18.** Which characteristic of a population is a convenient way to express the rate of change within a population?
- a   size
- \*   b.   growth
- c.   density
- d.   carrying capacity
- e.   age

E    **19.** A population that is growing exponentially in the absence of limiting factors can be illustrated by which curve?
- a   S-shaped
- \*   b.   J-shaped
- c.   one that terminates in a plateau phase
- d.   bimodal
- e.   binomial

M    **20.** Which concept is a way to express the growth rate of a given population?
- \*   a   doubling time
- b.   population density
- c.   population size
- d.   carrying capacity
- e.   all of the above

D    **21.** In a population growing exponentially,
- a   the number of individuals added to the population next year is greater than the number added this year.
- b.   the population growth rate increases year after year.
- c.   net reproduction per individual increases year after year.
- \*   d.   a and b
- e.   a, b, and c

## LIMITS ON THE GROWTH OF POPULATIONS

M    **22.** Populations
- a   are limited by only one factor at a time.
- b.   increase arithmetically.
- c.   increase indefinitely.
- \*   d.   are limited by the carrying capacity.
- e.   are represented by a minimum of two different sizes.

D    **23.** Limiting factors
- a   produce more pronounced effects as a population grows.
- b.   prevent a population from producing a J-shaped curve.
- c.   can be either density-dependent or density-independent.
- d.   act together in concert to form the environmental resistance to population growth.
- \*   e.   all of the above

D    **24.** A J-shaped growth curve is converted to an S-shaped one
- a   when the parents are past reproductive age.
- b.   if the data are plotted in reverse.
- \*   c.   when the carrying capacity is reached.
- d.   if reproduction stops.
- e.   only for fast-growing populations such as bacteria.

D    **25.** The carrying capacity of an environment is determined by
- a   the net rate of reproduction of the female members.
- b.   an S-shaped curve.
- c.   the predation rate on the females.
- d.   diseases suffered by both sexes.
- \*   e.   the sustainable supply of resources it provides.

M 26. Interaction between resource availability and a population's tolerance to prevailing environmental conditions defines
* a the carrying capacity of the environment.
b. exponential growth.
c. the doubling time of a population.
d. density-independent factors.
e. all of the above

D 27. In natural communities, feedback mechanisms called _____ operate when the size of a population changes.
a density-dependent factors
b. density-independent factors
c. biotic factors
d. physical factors
* e. both a and c, but not b or d

D 28. In natural communities some feedback mechanisms operate whenever populations change in size; they are
* a density-dependent factors.
b. density-independent factors.
c. always within the individuals of the community.
d. always outside the individuals of the community.
e. none of the above

M 29. A change in a population that is NOT related strictly to the size of the population is best described as
a density-dependent.
* b. density-independent.
c. within.
d. an S-shaped curve.
e. a J-shaped curve.

M 30. In itself, a flood that washes away an entire population of rabbits is
a a density-dependent factor.
b. a limiting factor dependent on the individuals.
c. a consequence of exponential growth.
* d. density-independent.
e. all of the above

M 31. Which density-dependent factor controls the size of a population?
a wind velocity
b. light intensity
* c. nutrient supply
d. rainfall
e. wave action in an intertidal zone

E 32. Which is NOT a density dependent, growth-limiting factor?
a predation
* b. drought
c. parasitism
d. competition

E 33. Density-independent controls over population growth include
a parasites.
* b. temperature.
c. disease.
d. competition.
e. all of the above

M 34. As population density increases, the chance of _____ also increases.
a parasitism
b. pathogens
c. predation
d. competition
* e. all of the above

**LIFE HISTORY PATTERNS**

M 35. A cohort is
* a a group of newborn individuals of the same species.
b. any member of the same species.
c. any member of the same species and sex within a population.
d. a sexual mate.
e. a litter mate or sibling within a large population.

E 36. Life tables provide data concerning
a expected life span.
b. reproductive age.
c. death rate.
d. birth rate.
* e. all of the above

M 37. A type III survivorship curve is characteristic of
a monkeys.
b. horses.
c. eagles.
* d. sea urchins.

M 38. Organisms that demonstrate a type I survivorship curve are characterized by
a high $r$, small offspring.
b. low $r$, small offspring.
* c. low $r$, large offspring.
d. high $r$, large offspring.

M 39. A type III survivorship curve (mortality high at birth and decreasing with age) is characteristic of all but which species?
a flies
* b. humans
c. frogs
d. reptiles
e. fish

D   **40.** Type II survivorship curves
   a   are characteristic of humans and elephants.
   * b.   typify a population in which all ages have an equal chance of surviving.
   c.   indicate a high mortality rate in the very young.
   d.   show that very few young are produced, that each is given parental support, and that most individuals live a relatively long life and die of old age.
   e.   are typical of annual plants.

## HUMAN POPULATION GROWTH

E   **41.** The leading cause of human deaths is
   a   heart disease.
   b.   cancer.
   * c.   malnutrition and starvation.
   d.   war.
   e.   accidents.

D   **42.** All of the following are the reasons for the rapid population explosion of humans EXCEPT
   a   increases in carrying capacity.
   b.   expansion into new habitats.
   c.   removal of limiting factors.
   d.   reproduction occurring earlier in the life cycle.
   * e.   longer generation times.

M   **43.** The tremendous increase in the number of human beings over the course of the past 100 years is attributable to
   a   immunization and vaccination programs.
   b.   colonization of previously underutilized habitat.
   c.   more equal distribution of scattered resources.
   d.   a and b
   * e.   a, b, and c

M   **44.** Which of the following is NOT a factor that has led to the dramatic increase in the human population?
   a   increase of carrying capacity
   b.   removal of several limiting factors
   c.   human invasion of new habitats and climatic zones
   * d.   an increase in the levels of pollution in the world
   e.   the development of public health and the germ theory of disease

M   **45.** The earliest human populations were found in
   a   tropical rain forests.
   b.   deserts.
   c.   the taiga.
   * d.   the savanna.
   e.   temperate deciduous forests.

M   **46.** Which of the following groups of plants formed the basis for the development of agriculture and the spread of civilization?
   * a   grasses
   b.   legumes
   c.   potato-tomato family
   d.   sunflower family
   e.   none of the above

E   **47.** The greatest reduction of human population in recorded history was the result of
   a   a global ice age.
   b.   two world wars.
   * c.   bubonic plague.
   d.   family planning.
   e.   ozone depletion.

## CONTROL THROUGH FAMILY PLANNING

M   **48.** If the reproductive rate drops to the maintenance level (zero population growth), how many year(s) would it take for world population to stop growing?
   a   1
   b.   20
   c.   50
   * d.   60
   e.   150

M   **49.** The most reasonable method of limiting human population growth is
   a   increasing carrying capacity.
   * b.   decreasing birth rate.
   c.   decreasing competition.
   d.   increasing death rate.
   e.   exploiting outer space.

E   **50.** Which of the following countries has established the most extensive family-planning program in the world?
   a   the United States
   b.   Brazil
   * c.   China
   d.   Japan
   e.   Pakistan

E   **51.** When the human population growth of the world is calculated, the doubling time is
   a   about the same as it was 20 years ago.
   * b.   decreasing at an accelerated pace.
   c.   increasing slowly.
   d.   in a gradual decline.
   e.   about 1.8%.

## POPULATION GROWTH AND ECONOMIC DEVELOPMENT

M   **52.** As the twenty-first century draws near, the continent with the highest potential for human population growth rate was _____ and that with the lowest was _____.
- a   North America, Asia
- b.  Asia, North America
- \*  c.   Africa, Europe
- d.  Africa, Asia

D   **53.** In which demographic model is population growth the fastest?
- a   preindustrial
- \*  b.  transitional
- c.   industrial
- d.  postindustrial

E   **54.** Which of the following countries has a population that is farthest from zero population growth?
- a   Sweden
- \*  b.  Mexico
- c.   United Kingdom
- d.  Germany
- e.  Hungary

### SOCIAL IMPACT OF NO GROWTH

M   **55.** The age structure diagram for rapidly growing populations
- a   is in the form of a pyramid.
- b.  is characterized by a large percentage of the population in the postreproductive years.
- c.  has a very broad base showing a large number of young.
- d.  has about equal distribution between all age groups.
- \*  e.  both a and c

D   **56.** If reproduction occurs early in the life cycle, what occurs?
- \*  a   Population growth rate increases.
- b.  Population size declines.
- c.   Population size is not affected.
- d.  Generation time increases.
- e.  Growth rate remains unchanged.

## Matching Questions

D   **57.** Choose the one most appropriate answer for each.
- 1 _____ age structure
- 2 _____ population growth rate
- 3 _____ J-shaped curve
- 4 _____ limiting factor

- A.  describes a population that is experiencing unrestrained growth
- B.  the birth rate minus the death rate plus any inward or minus any outward migration
- C.  how individuals are distributed at each age level for a population
- D.  the amount of glucose in a culture flask containing bacteria

*Answers:*   1.  C     2.  B     3.  A
              4.  D

## Classification Questions

Answer questions 58-62 in reference to the four levels of organization listed below:
- a   population
- b.  community
- c.   ecosystem
- d.  biosphere

E   **58.** This is composed of living organisms (biotic) and the abiotic environment.

E   **59.** This constitutes all of the individuals of a single species living in a region.

M   **60.** This is a group of different species living together in a single habitat.

M   **61.** This is the basic functional unit of ecology.

E   **62.** This contains all of the others.

*Answers:*   58.  c     59.  a     60.  b
             61.  c     62.  d

Answer questions 63–67 in reference to the five terms listed below that are used by ecologists:

    a  carrying capacity
    b.  net reproductive rate
    c.  age structure
    d.  survivorship
    e.  growth rate

D    **63.**  The average number of offspring born to each female over her reproductive lifetime is known as this.

M    **64.**  The number of individuals in each of several age categories is known as this.

M    **65.**  The maximum number of individuals that a given habitat can support is known as this.

D    **66.**  A change in the available food supply in a habitat will affect all of the above except this.

E    **67.**  This term is equal to the birth rate minus the death rate of a species.

*Answers:*    63.  b    64.  c    65.  a
                  66.  c    67.  e

## Selecting the Exception

E    **68.**  Four of the five answers listed below are components of the abiotic environment. Select the exception.
        a  soil
        b.  rainfall
   *   c.  competitors
        d.  temperature
        e.  sunlight

E    **69.**  Four of the five answers listed below are factors that affect population size. Select the exception.
        a  births
   *   b.  distribution
        c.  emigration
        d.  immigration
        e.  deaths

D    **70.**  Four of the five answers listed below follow a type II survivorship curve. Select the exception.
        a  songbirds
   *   b.  large mammals with extended parental care
        c.  small mammals
        d.  lizards
        e.  seed prior to germination

D    **71.**  Four of the five answers listed below follow a type III survivorship curve. Select the exception.
        a  most insects
        b.  most reptiles
        c.  many fish
   *   d.  humans
        e.  most marine invertebrates

M    **72.**  Four of the five answers listed below are density-independent factors. Select the exception.
   *   a  nutrient supply
        b.  temperature drop
        c.  drought
        d.  volcanic eruption
        e.  hard freeze

# CHAPTER 36
# COMMUNITY INTERACTIONS

## Multiple-Choice Questions

### FACTORS THAT SHAPE COMMUNITY STRUCTURE

E    **1.** Which is an example of a habitat?
   - a   predator
   - * b.   intestinal tract
   - c.   parasite
   - d.   producer
   - e.   decomposer

M    **2.** All of the populations of different species that occupy and are adapted to a given area are referred to by which term?
   - a   biosphere
   - * b.   community
   - c.   ecosystem
   - d.   niche
   - e.   habitat

M    **3.** What term denotes the range of all factors that influence whether a species can obtain resources essential for survival and reproduction?
   - a   habitat
   - * b.   niche
   - c.   carrying capacity
   - d.   ecosystem
   - e.   community

M    **4.** Which of the following would be more likely to affect an animal's habitat than its niche?
   - * a   rainfall
   - b.   prey abundance
   - c.   predators
   - d.   defense mechanisms

M    **5.** When Shakespeare wrote about the world as a stage and each of us being players, he was unknowingly referring to the biological concept of
   - a   succession.
   - * b.   the niche.
   - c.   different habitats.
   - d.   feeding levels.
   - e.   interspecific competition.

E    **6.** A relationship in which two species are dependent on each other for survival is
   - a   neutral interaction.
   - b.   commensalism.
   - c.   competitive exclusion.
   - * d.   mutualism.
   - e.   parasitism.

E    **7.** A one-way relationship in which one species benefits at the expense of another is called
   - a   commensalism.
   - b.   symbiosis.
   - * c.   parasitism.
   - d.   mutualism.
   - e.   all of the above

D    **8.** Which of the following is NOT characteristic of parasites?
   - a   They are specialists and usually are able to affect only one variety of hosts.
   - * b.   They inflict serious injury and kill their hosts.
   - c.   Some reside inside their hosts, whereas others live outside their hosts.
   - d.   Their host may be a plant as well as an animal.

M    **9.** The weakest symbiotic attachment, in which one species simply lives better in the presence of another species that is relatively unaffected, is called
   - * a   commensalism.
   - b.   competitive exclusion.
   - c.   mutualism.
   - d.   predation.
   - e.   parasitism.

M    **10.** Fruit flies probably have what type of relationship with humans?
   - a   parasitic
   - b.   mutualistic
   - c.   predatory
   - * d.   commensal
   - e.   neutral interaction

E    **11.** In the food chain, grass —> rabbit —> eagle, the reaction between the grass and eagle is
   - a   predation.
   - b.   commensalism.
   - c.   competition.
   - * d.   neutral.
   - e.   mutualism.

E    **12.** The interaction in which one species benefits and the second species is neither harmed nor benefited is
   - a   mutualism.
   - b.   parasitism.
   - * c.   commensalism.
   - d.   competition.
   - e.   predation.

M   13. The interaction between two species in which both species are harmed is known as
     a   mutualism.
     b   parasitism.
     c   commensalism.
*    d   competition.
     e   predation.

E   14. The interaction between two species in which one species benefits and the other species is harmed is
     a   mutualism.
     b   commensalism.
     c   competition.
*    d   predation.
     e   none of the above

## MUTUALISM

M   15. The relationship between an insect and the plants it pollinates is best described as
*    a   mutualism.
     b   competitive exclusion.
     c   parasitism.
     d   commensalism.
     e   all of the above

E   16. The relationship between the yucca plant and the yucca moth that pollinates it is best described as
     a   camouflage.
     b   commensalism.
     c   competitive exclusion.
*    d   mutualism.
     e   all of the above

M   17. In mixed assemblages, baboons sometimes see predators that impala do not hear, and impala sometimes hear predators that baboons do not see. In both cases, the flight of one species alerts the other to danger. This interaction is an example of
     a   a neutral relationship.
     b   commensalism.
*    c   mutualism.
     d   competition.

E   18. An interaction between two species in which both species benefit is known as
*    a   mutualism.
     b   parasitism.
     c   commensalism.
     d   competition.
     e   predation.

## COMPETITIVE INTERACTIONS

M   19. Niche overlap initially leads to
     a   mutualism.
     b   commensalism.
*    c   competition.
     d   predation.
     e   parasitism.

M   20. Competitive exclusion is the result of
     a   mutualism.
     b   commensalism.
*    c   competition.
     d   predation.
     e   parasitism.

D   21. A male wolf who is courting a female bares his teeth when a second male approaches the same female. The second male retreats. This series of events provides an example of
     a   a neutral interaction.
     b   exploitation competition.
*    c   intraspecific competition.
     d   competitive exclusion.

D   22. The construction of a fence around your yard would establish a relationship with the neighbor's dog that would be described as
     a   succession.
*    b   interspecific competition.
     c   commensalism.
     d   mutualism.
     e   niche.

D   23. In most cases of interspecific interference competition, the inferior competitor displaced from an area of niche overlap is
     a   smaller.
     b   slower.
     c   more specialized in its niche requirements.
*    d   less specialized in its niche requirements.

M   24. In Gause's experiments with *Paramecium* growing in test tubes, he demonstrated that
     a   organisms with similar niches will evolve enough to survive in different niches.
     b   organisms with slightly different feeding habits will change to become exclusive competitors.
*    c   organisms with similar feeding habits may compete to the point of extinction.
     d   both b and c
     e   both a and c

M   25. Gause's exclusion principle refers to
     a   isolation.
*    b   competition.
     c   habitat preference.
     d   physiological adaptation.

M   26. The concept of competitive exclusion is based on the idea that
     a   one species will hold some sort of advantage over the other one.
     b   no two species can completely occupy the same niche.
*    c   both of the above
     d   neither of the above

M  **27.** The "final result" of community interaction when viewed by an ecologist observer is
   a  competition.
   b  social parasitism.
   c  predation.
   d  mimicry.
   * e  resource partitioning.

M  **28.** Which one of the following is the final consequence of the others?
   * a  resource partitioning
   b  competition
   c  predation
   d  parasitism

## PREDATION AND PARASITISM

E  **29.** A goat eating by pulling a plant out of the ground is an example of
   a  parasitism.
   * b  predation.
   c  competition.
   d  commensalism.
   e  mutualism.

M  **30.** Conditions of stable coexistence between predator and prey include
   a  high predator reproductive rate relative to that of the prey.
   b  a carrying capacity for prey that is not high.
   c  large predator size relative to that of the prey.
   * d  a and b
   e  a, b, and c

M  **31.** Humans hunt the black rhinoceros, which is rapidly approaching extinction as a result of this predation. What accounts for the absence of stable coexistence between the two species?
   a  Predator and prey have not coevolved.
   b  Human predation is not necessarily density-dependent.
   c  The prey reproductive rate is greater than that of the predator.
   * d  a and b
   e  a, b, and c

M  **32.** In general, a predator is _____ than its _____.
   a  smaller; host
   b  larger; host
   c  smaller; prey
   * d  larger; prey

D  **33.** In contrast to a predator, a parasite usually
   * a  does not kill the animal on which or in which it lives.
   b  kills its host.
   c  is a short-term visitor.
   d  is larger than its host.
   e  both a and d

D  **34.** Ladybugs are effective natural control agents against pest insects, but as gardeners soon find out, they do not reduce pest populations to zero because
   a  they can't fly to find pests on nearby plants.
   b  of their very selective feeding habits.
   * c  to do so would jeopardize their own existence.
   d  they don't live long enough.
   e  their reproductive capacity is nonexistent.

D  **35.** Without intervention by humans, cockroaches will overrun a kitchen until
   a  the carrying capacity is reached.
   b  predators attack.
   c  parasites invade the roaches' bodies.
   d  density-independent factors such as cold intervene.
   * e  all of the above

M  **36.** Which of the following statements about predation is true?
   a  It can result in an increase in species diversity within a community.
   b  It can cause extinction of a prey species within a community.
   c  It can prevent extinction of a prey species within a community.
   d  both a and b
   * e  a, b, and c

M  **37.** Which of the following statements about parasites is true?
   a  Parasites usually do not kill their hosts.
   b  The parasite species that infects a particular host species becomes less virulent over evolutionary time.
   c  Warm-blooded animals are commonly infected by parasites.
   d  both a and b
   * e  a, b, and c

M  **38.** Which is an adaptation against predation?
   a  thorns
   b  camouflage
   c  mimicry
   d  a and b
   * e  a, b, and c

E  **39.** Chemicals in both plants and animals serve as which of the following to predators?
   a  warnings
   b  repellents
   c  poisons
   d  bad tastes
   * e  all of the above

M  **40.** Which is an example of warning coloration?
   a  the dark brown mane of a lion
   b  the bright green and blue feathers of a peacock
   * c  the black and yellow bands of a wasp
   d  the black and white stripes of a zebra

## FORCES CONTRIBUTING TO COMMUNITY STABILITY

D  **41.** During the process of community succession,
   a. the total mass of living things remains constant.
   * b. there are increasing possibilities for resource partitioning.
   c. the pioneer community gives way quickly to the climax community, followed by a succession of more diverse arrays of organisms.
   d. nutrients cycle more rapidly with time.
   e. all of the above

E  **42.** Populations are held in check by
   a. resource partitioning.
   b. predation.
   c. social parasitism.
   d. competition.
   * e. all of the above

M  **43.** Most dominant plant species in a climax community
   a. become quickly reestablished in a cleared area because they are adapted specifically to that geographic region.
   * b. cannot grow or develop fully except as part of a certain integrated community structure.
   c. grow faster in areas exposed to sunlight by clear-cutting.
   d. both a and c
   e. all of the above

M  **44.** Which statement is false?
   a. Succession is highly predictable.
   b. Pioneer species have wide ranges of tolerances.
   c. Pioneer plant species are usually small annuals with an abundance of easily dispersed seeds.
   * d. The succession that occurs after a large fire is primary succession.
   e. Climax species are those that are best adapted to the specific climate where the succession occurs.

M  **45.** Secondary succession is likely to occur
   a. in a deciduous forest.
   b. on an eroded, bare hillside.
   c. in an abandoned field.
   d. a and b
   * e. a, b, and c

M  **46.** Pioneer plant species are usually characterized by
   a. small size.
   b. efficient dispersal mechanisms.
   c. long life cycles.
   * d. a and b
   e. a, b, and c

M  **47.** Which of the following represent an early stage in primary succession?
   a. pine trees
   * b. moss and lichens on bare rock
   c. weedy annual plants in an open field
   d. climax species in succession

D  **48.** Which of the following statements concerning climax communities is true?
   a. A climax community is always a result of primary succession.
   * b. When compared to early successional communities, climax communities usually possess more species.
   c. The species of the climax community require long periods of environmental stability to ensure continued survival in the community.
   d. both a and b
   e. a, b, and c

M  **49.** The plants and animals now present on acreage from which the trees were removed ten years earlier represent
   a. primary succession.
   b. a climax forest.
   c. pioneer species.
   * d. secondary succession.
   e. species introductions.

D  **50.** Farmland that is under regular and continued tillage will not
   a. undergo succession.
   * b. produce a climax community.
   c. experience competition.
   d. suffer from the effects of disturbance.
   e. develop species diversity.

M  **51.** The climax community
   a. is formed by species with the greatest range of environmental tolerance.
   b. is the most common community found in an area.
   c. changes over time.
   * d. is well adapted to the climate and persists until the climate changes.

M  **52.** In 1882, the tropical volcanic island Krakatoa exploded and was reduced to an abiotic island covered by a thick layer of volcanic ash. By 1933, populations of all of the following organisms were present. Which population was probably established after all the others?
   a. ferns
   b. bacteria
   c. insects
   * d. rodents

C

## OMMUNITY INSTABILITY

M 53. Which exotic organism was NOT intentionally introduced to this country?
* a Japanese beetle
b. English house sparrow
c. carp
d. water hyacinth
e. starling

M 54. Many introduced species have had deleterious effects on communities and ecosystems because
* a coevolved parasites and competitors are absent.
b. the introduced species are long-lived.
c. predators prefer the introduced species, and the local prey therefore proliferate to dangerously high levels.
d. the communities from which they came lose an important predator, competitor, or parasite.

E 55. A keystone species is
a a single dominant species.
b. in control of the prey species.
c. exemplified by the sea star.
d. a and c only
* e. a, b, and c

## PATTERNS OF BIODIVERSITY

M 56. Of the following four islands at the same latitude, the one that possesses the fewest number of species is
a 1,000 square kilometers and 300 km from the mainland.
b. 3,000 square kilometers and 100 km from the mainland.
* c. 100 square kilometers and 3,000 km from the mainland.
d. 300 square kilometers and 1,000 km from the mainland.

M 57. Stable coexistence between predator and prey is least likely to occur on an island that is
* a small and distant from the mainland.
b. small and close to the mainland.
c. large and close to the mainland.
d. large and distant from the mainland.

M 58. In the United States, the number of breeding bird species increases from
* a Minnesota to Texas.
b. mainland Florida to the Florida Keys.
c. low mountain altitudes to high mountain altitudes.
d. both a and b
e. a, b, and c

D 59. There are more insect species per square kilometer in a Brazilian rain forest than there are in a redwood forest of the Pacific Northwest of the United States. According to contemporary ecological hypotheses, an explanation for this finding is
a the tropics have been climatically stable for a longer period of time than have temperate areas.
b. niches in the tropics are smaller than those in temperate areas.
c. on average, insects are smaller in the tropics than they are in temperate areas.
* d. a and b
e. a, b, and c

M 60. An equilibrium population of 5 individuals on an island is more likely to go extinct than an equilibrium population of 50 individuals because
a intraspecific competition is more intense in smaller groups.
* b. density-independent factors are more likely to eliminate smaller rather than larger groups.
c. there is more ecological space for predators if there are fewer numbers of prey.
d. predation pressure increases as prey populations decrease.

## Matching Questions

D 61. Choose the one most appropriate answer for each.

1 _____ camouflage
2 _____ commensalism
3 _____ competitive exclusion
4 _____ habitat
5 _____ mimicry
6 _____ mutualism
7 _____ parasitism
8 _____ primary succession
9 _____ climax community
10 _____ secondary succession
11 _____ succession

A. blending in and being hidden by the background

B. where an organism is generally located in an environment

C. organism benefits at another organism's expense

D. a self-sustaining array of interacting organisms that is best suited for a particular environment

E. lichens on newly hardened, newly cooled lava

F. robins and human populations

G. the yucca moth and the yucca

H. one species is forced from an area of niche overlap

I. a tasty viceroy butterfly resembles a bad-tasting monarch butterfly

J. the process that converts a pioneer community to a climax community

K. natural reforestation of burned over forest

*Answers:*

| 1. A | 2. F | 3. H |
|------|------|------|
| 4. B | 5. I | 6. G |
| 7. C | 8. E | 9. D |
| 10. K | 11. J | |

## Classification Questions

Answer questions 62–66 in reference to the five kinds of species interactions listed below:

a competition
b. predation
c. mutualism
d. commensalism
e. parasitism

E 62. In this interaction, one species benefits while the other is neither harmed nor benefited.

M 63. In this interaction between two species, both species are harmed in some way.

M 64. In this interaction, both species benefit.

E 65. In this interaction, one individual or species usually is killed while the other benefits by eating the first.

E 66. In this interaction one species is harmed, but usually not killed, to the benefit of the other that lives on or in the first.

*Answers:*  62. d    63. a    64. c
66. b    66. e

Answer questions 67–71 in reference to the five kinds of species interactions listed below:

a competition
b. predation
c. mutualism
d. commensalism
e. parasitism

E 67. The relationship between a dog and a wood tick is this kind of relationship.

M 68. The interaction between termites and the cellulose-digesting protozoans in the termite gut is this kind of relationship.

M 69. This is the likely interaction between two closely related species of woodpeckers that live in a temperate forest.

M 70. If a wasp lays its eggs inside the larva of a fly, the type of interaction is this.

M 71. When a tropical bird places its nest in association with a wasp nest on the same tree, the type of interaction is this.

*Answers:*  67. e    68. c    69. a
70. e    71. d

## Selecting the Exception

M  72. Four of the five answers listed below are
relationships in which at least one of the
interactants benefits. Select the exception.
*   a   competition
    b.  parasitism
    c.  mutualism
    d.  commensalism
    e.  predation

D  73. Four of the five answers listed below are
examples of mutualism. Select the exception.
    a   plants and pollinators
    b.  plants and seed dispersal by seed-eating
        animals
    c.  mycorrhiza
*   d.  antibiotic
    e.  lichen

E  74. Four of the five answers listed below are
examples of prey defense. Select the exception.
    a   display behavior
    b.  chemicals
    c.  camouflage
*   d.  albinism
    e.  mimicry

E  75. Four of the five answers listed below are defense
chemicals. Select the exception.
*   a   perfume
    b.  warning odors
    c.  poisons
    d.  alarm substances
    e.  repellents

M  76. Four of the five answers listed below are exotic
or introduced species. Select the exception.
    a   Argentine fire ant
*   b.  cockroach
    c.  starling
    d.  water hyacinth
    e.  chestnut blight

M  77. Four of the five answers listed below are events
that lead to secondary succession. Select
the exception.
    a   opening the canopy in a tropical rain forest
    b.  abandoning a cotton field
*   c.  retreat of a glacier in Alaska
    d.  following a fire
    e.  growth of weeds in an unmowed lawn

# CHAPTER 37
# ECOSYSTEMS

## Multiple-Choice Questions

### THE NATURE OF ECOSYSTEMS

M    **1.** Which statement about ecosystems is false?
     a   The rate of energy flow depends on the ratio of producers to consumers.
     b.   The requirements of an ecosystem change with age.
     c.   The larger the ecosystem, the more flexible it is.
     *   d.   The smaller the ecosystem, the more stable it is.
     e.   The more efficient the producers are, the more energy must be put in and the more energy is available for the next trophic level.

M    **2.** A network of interactions that involve the cycling of materials and the flow of energy between a community and its physical environment is which of the following?
     a   population
     b.   community
     *   c.   ecosystem
     d.   biosphere
     e.   species

M    **3.** A community differs from an ecosystem in that the former does NOT include
     a   unicellular organisms.
     b.   decomposers.
     *   c.   abiotic (nonliving) factors.
     d.   a and b
     e.   a, b, and c

E    **4.** In a natural community, the primary consumers are
     *   a   herbivores.
     b.   carnivores.
     c.   scavengers.
     d.   decomposers.
     e.   all of the above

E    **5.** Which is usually a primary carnivore?
     a   chicken
     b.   cow
     c.   rabbit
     *   d.   wolf
     e.   squirrel

M    **6.** Which is a primary consumer?
     *   a   cow
     b.   dog
     c.   hawk
     d.   fox
     e.   snake

M    **7.** All living organisms are dependent upon plants because
     a   plants produce oxygen as a by-product of photosynthesis.
     *   b.   as producers, they form the base of food chains.
     c.   they function to prevent erosion and reduce desertification.
     d.   as they remove carbon dioxide from the atmosphere, they reduce the problems generated by the greenhouse effect.

D    **8.** Which of the following combinations of organisms could be expected to survive in isolation from other forms of life available?
     *   a   producers and decomposers
     b.   producers and carnivores
     c.   carnivores and decomposers
     d.   herbivores, carnivores, and decomposers

M    **9.** Wastes would accumulate and most nutrients would stop cycling if the _____ in the ecosystem died.
     a   protozoans and protistans
     *   b.   bacteria and fungi
     c.   flatworms, roundworms, and earthworms
     d.   insects

D    **10.** Which of the following is NOT dependent on the others as a food supply?
     a   carnivores
     b.   herbivores
     *   c.   producers
     d.   detritivores
     e.   decomposers

E    **11.** Which of the following is the correct word meaning "to feed"?
     a   tropic
     *   b.   trophic
     c.   topic
     d.   trophic
     e.   tropical

M    **12.** The primary consumer is also
     a   the second link in a food chain.
     b.   a herbivore.
     c.   an animal.
     d.   only b and c
     *   e.   a, b, and c

D    **13.** A secondary consumer could eat
     a   only herbivores.
     b.   only primary producers.
     c.   primary carnivores.
     *   d.   anything "below" it in the food web.

D    14. Food chains rarely have more than three levels of consumers because
     a   the animals are too large to search for prey.
     b.   the growing season of plants is not long enough.
     c.   pyramids do not go that high.
*    d.   the amount of energy still available is too small.

E    15. Herbivores represent the
*    a   primary consumers.
     b.   secondary consumers.
     c.   tertiary consumers.
     d.   primary producers.
     e.   secondary producers.

M    16. Chemosynthetic organisms are
     a   primary consumers.
     b.   secondary consumers.
     c.   tertiary consumers.
*    d.   primary producers.
     e.   secondary producers.

E    17. The ultimate source of all energy in a terrestrial ecosystem is
     a   the organic matter in all the organisms of the ecosystem.
     b.   water.
*    c.   sunlight.
     d.   carbon dioxide.

M    18. Primary carnivores are
     a   tertiary consumers in the third trophic level.
*    b.   secondary consumers in the third trophic level.
     c.   secondary consumers in the second trophic level.
     d.   tertiary consumers in the fourth trophic level.

E    19. In the Antarctic, blue whales feed mainly on
     a   petrels.
*    b.   krill.
     c.   seals.
     d.   fish and small squid.
     e.   penguins.

M    20. Which cannot be placed in a single trophic level?
     a   oak tree
     b.   zebra
*    c.   mushroom
     d.   rabbit

## ENERGY FLOW THROUGH ECOSYSTEMS

D    21. Net primary productivity is the
     a   rate of photosynthesis.
     b.   rate of energy flow.
     c.   amount of energy stored in the ecosystem.
     d.   amount of energy utilized.
*    e.   amount of energy stored in the plant tissue in excess of that used by autotrophs in respiration.

E    22. Most of the energy within an ecosystem is lost
     a   when organisms disperse.
     b.   when organisms die.
*    c.   as a result of metabolism.
     d.   by organisms at the top of the food web.

E    23. Of the energy that enters one trophic level, approximately what percent (average) becomes available for the next trophic level?
     a   100
*    b.   10
     c.   1
     d.   0.1
     e.   0.01

M    24. The difference between gross primary productivity and net primary productivity is
     a   the amount of sunlight reflected by plants.
     b.   the rate of photosynthesis of autotrophs.
*    c.   the rate of respiration of autotrophs.
     d.   the rate of herbivorous consumption of autotrophs.

M    25. Detritivores are
     a   bacteria.
     b.   plants.
     c.   fungi.
*    d.   animals.
     e.   a and c

M    26. About what percent of the solar energy reaching the earth's surface is stored as organic material?
*    a   1–2
     b.   5–6
     c.   10–12
     d.   15–18
     e.   25

M    27. The simple food chain, grass —> zebra —> lion, provides a good example of a pyramid of
     a   energy.
     b.   height.
     c.   biomass.
     d.   a and b
*    e.   a and c

M    28. Detritus specifically includes
     a   organic wastes.
     b.   toxic materials.
     c.   dead and partially decayed material.
     d.   living bacteria and fungi.
*    e.   both a and c

D    29. The amount of energy that flows through a detrital food web is _____ that which flows through a grazing web.
     a   the same as
*    b.   greater than
     c.   less than
     d.   the sum of
     e.   the difference of

M 30. Decomposers perform their recycling efforts on organisms
   a  at the end of a food chain.
   b.  on the top of a pyramid.
   c.  that are producers.
   d.  that are consumers.
*   e.  all of the above

E 31. Decomposers
   a  are able to enter a food chain at any trophic level.
   b.  are the most numerous organisms in an ecosystem.
   c.  include bacteria and fungi.
*   d.  all of the above

E 32. At the bottom or base of a pyramid of energy are the
*   a  primary producers.
   b.  secondary producers.
   c.  primary consumers.
   d.  secondary consumers.
   e.  tertiary consumers.

E 33. At the top of a pyramid of biomass are the
   a  primary producers.
   b.  secondary producers.
   c.  primary consumers.
   d.  secondary consumers.
*   e.  tertiary consumers.

M 34. The biomass of a community is the weight of the
   a  material decomposed in a year.
   b.  producers.
*   c.  living organisms.
   d.  consumers.
   e.  decomposers.

M 35. Of the following, which must always have a base larger than the other components?
   a  pyramid of numbers
*   b.  pyramid of energy
   c.  pyramid of biomass
   d.  a and b
   e.  a, b, and c

D 36. Energy pyramids are characteristic of ecosystems because
   a  not all of what is eaten is absorbed by a consumer.
   b.  not all of what is killed is eaten by a predator.
   c.  not all of what is produced in one trophic level is consumed by organisms in the next highest trophic level.
   d.  both a and b
*   e.  a, b, and c

E 37. Energy flow in an ecosystem is
   a  cyclical.
*   b.  one-way.
   c.  two-way.
   d.  reversible under different conditions.

## BIOGEOCHEMICAL CYCLES—AN OVERVIEW

E 38. Materials in sedimentary cycles
   a  pass through both a solid and a gaseous phase.
*   b.  are never present as gases in the ecosystem.
   c.  are present as liquids in the earth but as gases in the atmosphere.
   d.  both a and c
   e.  a, b, and c

E 39. Which of the following does NOT cycle through an ecosystem?
   a  water
   b.  carbon
*   c.  energy
   d.  phosphorus
   e.  nitrogen

M 40. The chemical elements that are available to producers are usually in what form?
*   a  ions
   b.  gases
   c.  solids
   d.  compounds
   e.  hydrocarbons

D 41. Which of the following statements is false?
   a  Ecologists use models to represent relationships between biogeochemical cycles and most ecosystems.
*   b.  The physical environment has virtually no reservoir for most elements.
   c.  Inputs from the physical environment and recycling made possible by decomposers and detritivores maintain the nutrient reserves in an ecosystem.
   d.  In most major ecosystems, the amount of nutrients that is cycled within the ecosystem is greater than the amount entering or leaving the ecosystem in a given year.
   e.  Once elements are in the biological compartments of the biogeochemical cycles, they are unlikely to leave until the organism dies.

## HYDROLOGIC CYCLE

M 42. The Hubbard Brook watershed studies revealed the importance of tree roots in preventing loss of calcium from an ecosystem. Calculation of calcium loss is performed by sampling
   a  the roots of the trees.
   b.  the soil of the watershed.
*   c.  the stream exiting the watershed.
   d.  a and b
   e.  a, b, and c

M  43. Most of the water vapor in the earth's atmosphere comes from evaporation from
   a  lakes.
   b.  rivers.
   c.  land.
   * d.  oceans.
   e.  plants.

## CARBON CYCLE

M  44. Which gas is increasing in the atmosphere and threatening the world with the greenhouse effect?
   * a.  carbon dioxide
   b.  carbon monoxide
   c.  ozone
   d.  fluorocarbons
   e.  oxygen

E  45. Carbon is stored in what form?
   a  biomass
   b.  fossil fuels
   c.  limestone rocks
   d.  shells of animals
   * e.  all of the above

M  46. A significant fraction of the earth's carbon is found in all but which of the following?
   a  carbonate
   b.  carbon dioxide
   c.  cellulose
   * d.  carbon monoxide

D  47. Carbon enters the biomass of animal bodies in the form of
   a  carbon dioxide.
   b.  carbon monoxide.
   * c.  carbohydrates.
   d.  fossil fuels.
   e.  calcium carbonate.

M  48. In which of the following locations does carbon remain for the shortest time?
   a  peat bogs
   * b.  tropical forests
   c.  marshes
   d.  sea shells
   e.  fossil fuels

M  49. Carbon is introduced into the atmosphere by all of the following means EXCEPT
   a  respiration.
   b.  volcanic eruptions.
   c.  burning of fossil fuels.
   * d.  wind erosion.

## NITROGEN CYCLE

M  50. Which is NOT part of the nitrogen cycle?
   a  denitrification
   * b.  deammonification
   c.  nitrogen fixation
   d.  ammonification
   e.  assimilation and biosynthesis

D  51. Nitrification
   * a  converts ammonia into nitrates.
   b.  reduces nitrates to nitrites.
   c.  converts nitrogenous compounds into free nitrogen.
   d.  is a synonym for nitrogen fixation.

M  52. Some nitrogenous waste products or organic remains of organisms are decomposed by soil bacteria and fungi. The bacteria and fungi use the amino acids for their own growth and, in turn, release the excess as $NH_3$ or ammonium ion. This process is
   a  nitrification.
   * b.  ammonification.
   c.  denitrification.
   d.  nitrogen fixation.
   e.  hydrogenation.

E  53. The greatest concentration of nitrogen on the planet Earth is found in
   a  living organisms, including bacteria.
   * b.  the atmosphere.
   c.  soil minerals.
   d.  fossil fuels.
   e.  oceans.

E  54. Nitrogen is released into the atmosphere by
   a  nitrogen fixation.
   * b.  denitrification.
   c.  nitrification.
   d.  ammonification.
   e.  decomposition.

E  55. Which plants are planted to increase the amount of nitrogen in the soil?
   a  watermelon and cantaloupe vines
   * b.  legumes
   c.  mints
   d.  grasses
   e.  heaths

M  56. Plant cells assimilate nitrogen in the form of
   a  ammonia and $N_2$.
   b.  $N_2$ and nitrite.
   * c.  nitrate and ammonia.
   d.  urea and nitrate.

M  57. Nitrifying bacteria convert
   * a  ammonia ———> nitrite ———> nitrate
   b.  nitrate ———> nitrite ———> nitrogen gas
   c.  nitrate ———> ammonia
   d.  urea ———> ammonia

E  58. If agricultural soil has been depleted of nitrates, a good crop to plant and subsequently plow under is
   a   wheat.
   b   corn.
*  c   clover.
   d   sugar beets.

## PHOSPHORUS CYCLE

D  59. Animals obtain minerals such as phosphorus
   a   primarily dissolved in drinking water.
   b   by inhalation.
   c   in meats.
   d   by eating plants.
*  e   both c and d

## PREDICTING THE IMPACT OF CHANGE IN ECOSYSTEMS

E  60. In biological magnification
*  a   poisons accumulate in the high ends of food chains and webs.
   b   there is a tendency for an environment to change when organisms first invade.
   c   more highly evolved forms are able to build large populations under favorable conditions.
   d   parasites spread rapidly through congested populations.
   e   sediments fill in aquatic environments so that succession will occur if organisms disturb the aquatic habitat.

M  61. Biological magnification refers to the
   a   increase in size of animals as they progress through a food chain.
   b   increase in size of organisms as they progress through ecological succession.
   c   increase in the efficiency of energy utilization as organisms progress through a food chain.
*  d   accumulation of toxic pollutants as animals pass through a food chain.

M  62. The release of DDT into the environment to control some insect pests will result in the highest detectable concentrations
   a   at the bottom of the food chain.
   b   in the targeted insect pest.
   c   in the middle of the food chain.
*  d   at the end of the food chain.

M  63. Long-lasting pesticides such as DDT
   a   are target-specific.
   b   are the most effective control over pests.
*  c   build up in concentration as they pass through a food chain.
   d   break down after the organism that receives the pesticide dies.

M  64. Which substance is magnified during transfers in ecosystems?
*  a   fat-soluble pesticides
   b   carbohydrates
   c   inorganic phosphates
   d   a and b
   e   a, b, and c

## Matching Questions

D  65. Choose the one most appropriate answer for each.
   1 _____ biological magnification
   2 _____ detritus
   3 _____ legumes
   4 _____ net primary production
   5 _____ primary productivity
   6 _____ webs
   7 _____ gross primary production

   A.   rate at which energy becomes stored in organic compounds through photosynthesis
   B.   total amount of solar energy stored in organic compounds during photosynthesis
   C.   interconnected food chains
   D.   the potential chemical energy remaining (after aerobic respiration by autotrophs) that can still be passed on to other trophic levels
   E.   DDT spraying program in Borneo
   F.   a kind of plant that often harbors symbiotic nitrogen fixers in its roots
   G.   particles of organic waste products, dead or partly decomposed tissues

Answers:   1. E      2. G      3. F
           4. D      5. A      6. C
           7. B

## Classification Questions

Answer questions 66–70 in reference to the five trophic categories of an ecosystem listed below:

     a.  producer
     b.  herbivore
     c.  primary carnivore
     d.  secondary carnivore
     e.  decomposer

M    **66.**  This is a primary consumer.

M    **67.**  A Venus flytrap plant obtains its nitrogen when it functions as this.

M    **68.**  Most mushrooms function as this.

D    **69.**  A bear feeding on a salmon is functioning as this.

E    **70.**  A bear feeding on blueberries is functioning as this.

*Answers:*    66.  b     67.  c     68.  e
               69.  d     70.  b

Answer questions 71–75 in reference to the four steps of the nitrogen cycles listed below:

     a.  nitrogen fixation
     b.  nitrification
     c.  denitrification
     d.  ammonification

M    **71.**  The action of bacteria on urea occurs during this process.

M    **72.**  The action of bacteria on ammonia, ultimately converting it to nitrate, occurs during this process.

E    **73.**  The action of bacteria on nitrates, converting them to gaseous nitrogen, occurs during this process.

E    **74.**  This is the process whereby gaseous nitrogen is first converted to ammonia and then to other nitrogenous compounds.

M    **75.**  The process whereby nitrite is converted to nitrate is an important part of this process.

*Answers:*    71.  d     72.  b     73.  c
               74.  a     75.  b

## Selecting the Exception

E    **76.**  Three of the four answers listed below are related by a common theme. Select the exception.
      a.  numbers
  *  b.  nutrients
      c.  biomass
      d.  energy

M    **77.**  Four of the five answers listed below are heterotrophic. Select the exception.
      a.  consumers
      b.  carnivores
      c.  herbivores
      d.  parasites
  *  e.  producers

M    **78.**  Four of the five answers listed below are related by a common action. Select the exception.
      a.  volcanic eruption
  *  b.  photosynthesis
      c.  respiration
      d.  fire
      e.  decomposition

D    **79.**  Four of the five answers listed below are related by a common action that retains nitrogen in the biomass. Select the exception.
      a.  decomposition
      b.  ammonification
      c.  nitrification
      d.  nitrogen fixation
  *  e.  denitrification

# CHAPTER 38
# THE BIOSPHERE

## Multiple-Choice Questions

### AIR CIRCULATION PATTERNS AND REGIONAL CLIMATES

E    **1.** The amount of ultraviolet radiation hitting the earth's surface is greatly reduced by which gas in the atmosphere?
*    a.   ozone
     b.   oxygen
     c.   water vapor
     d.   carbon dioxide
     e.   nitrogen

E    **2.** An important gas in the absorption of ultraviolet radiation is
     a   $N_2$.
*    b.   $O_3$.
     c   $CO_2$.
     d.   $SO_2$.

M    **3.** The amount of solar energy that any spot on the surface of the earth receives is controlled by the
     a   photoperiod or duration of light.
     b.   angle at which the sun strikes the earth.
     c.   amount of atmosphere above the spot.
     d.   particulate matter and pollution in the atmosphere.
*    e.   all of the above

M    **4.** At how many degrees north and south of the equator does air rise as a result of differential heating and cooling?
     a   10
     b.   30
     c.   40
*    d.   60
     e.   75

M    **5.** The tradewinds in the zone from 0 to 30 degrees north latitude are generally from the
     a   north.
     b.   northwest.
*    c.   northeast.
     d.   southeast.
     e.   southwest.

M    **6.** Major air masses rise from the earth's surface at
     a   the equator and 30 degree latitudes.
     b.   30 degree and 60 degree latitudes.
*    c.   the equator and 60 degree latitudes.
     d.   30 degree latitudes and the poles.

M    **7.** Which factor has the least effect on the amount of incoming light that strikes an area?
     a   latitude
*    b.   temperature
     c.   the degree that a slope is exposed to the incoming light
     d.   the amount of recurring cloud cover
     e.   all of the above

### THE OCEAN, LAND FORMS, AND REGIONAL CLIMATES

E    **8.** What portion of the earth's surface is covered by oceans?
     a   less than 10%
     b.   more than 80%
     c.   about 50%
     d.   approximately 70%
     e.   barely 20%

M    **9.** Water in the oceans tends to move in great currents from
     a   north pole to south pole
     b.   equator to poles
*    c.   poles to equator
     d.   south pole to north pole
     e.   poles to equator and back again

M    **10.** A mountain rain shadow is the
     a   arid area on the windward slope.
     b.   wet area on the windward slope.
*    c.   arid area on the leeward slope.
     d.   wet area on the leeward slope.

M    **11.** Mountains produce
     a   rain shadows on the windward sides.
     b.   precipitation on the leeward sides.
*    c.   deserts on the leeward sides.
     d.   extensive grasslands on the windward sides.
     e.   all of the above

M    **12.** A wind system that influences large climatic regions and reverses direction seasonally, producing dry and wet seasons, is referred to as
     a   a geothermal ecosystem.
     b.   an upwelling.
     c.   a taiga.
*    d.   a monsoon.
     e.   a hurricane.

M    **13.** The formation of mountains affects the climate and vegetation of the surrounding areas to the greatest extent by influencing
     a   temperature.
*    b.   moisture relationships.
     c.   light regimens.
     d.   wind.

M 14. The windward side of a mountain range
   a. supports arid types of vegetation typical of a desert.
 * b. is subjected to high precipitation levels.
   c. is located in a rain shadow.
   d. is protected from the effects of the wind.
   e. has essentially identical climates and vegetation as the leeward side.

M 15. Temperature variations during the course of a year tend to increase with
 * a. increasing distance from the equator and increasing distance from the oceans.
   b. increasing distance from the equator and decreasing distance from the oceans.
   c. decreasing distance from the equator and decreasing distance from the oceans.
   d. decreasing distance from the equator and increasing distance from the oceans.

## THE WORLD'S BIOMES

M 16. In general, which list places the terms in order of increasing size?
   a. ecosystem, biogeographical realm, biome, biosphere
   b. ecosystem, biome, biosphere, biogeographical realm
   c. biome, ecosystem, biogeographical realm, biosphere
 * d. ecosystem, biome, biogeographical realm, biosphere

E 17. Productivity of a biome increases as
   a. water availability increases and elevation increases.
   b. water availability decreases and elevation increases.
 * c. water availability increases and elevation decreases.
   d. water availability decreases and elevation decreases.

M 18. Which is NOT a biogeographical realm?
   a. Palearctic
   b. Ethiopian
 * c. Pantropical
   d. Neotropical
   e. Nearctic

D 19. The first two scientists to divide the world into biogeographical realms were
   a. Lamarck and Cuvier.
   b. Linnaeus and Ray.
   c. Darwin and Huxley.
   d. Elowitz and Whipple.
 * e. Sclater and Wallace.

E 20. The first widely accepted attempt at an analysis of biogeographical distribution of life used six
   a. biomes.
 * b. realms.
   c. ecosystems.
   d. biotas.
   e. life zones.

M 21. Biogeographical realms
   a. are composed of different biomes.
   b. were first proposed by W. Sclater and then Alfred Wallace, the codiscoverer of evolution.
   c. are primarily based upon geography rather than climate.
   d. would be entirely different if continental drift had not occurred.
 * e. all of the above

M 22. Distribution of biomes tends to be influenced by all but which one of the following?
   a. topography
   b. soil
   c. latitude
 * d. longitude
   e. climate

M 23. Which of the following factors is most important in determining the type of biomes found in a particular region?
   a. soil type
   b. light intensity
 * c. temperature
   d. type of animals in the region

M 24. A particular biome is characterized by
   a. climate.
   b. vegetation.
   c. animals.
   d. b and c only
 * e. a, b, and c

D 25. Similarity of one biome to another may be due to
   a. altitude.
   b. latitude.
   c. longitude.
 * d. a and b only
   e. a, b, and c

## SOILS OF MAJOR BIOMES

E 26. The soil described as a mixture of sand, silt, clay, and humus is
   a. humus.
   b. sand.
   c. soil.
 * d. loam.
   e. silt.

E   **27.** The most productive soil is
   a. humus.
   b. sand.
   c. soil.
 * d. loam.
   e. silt.

M   **28.** Which of the following would be the least suitable for conversion to agriculture?
   a. grassland
 * b. tropical forests
   c. deciduous forest
   d. prairie
   e. silted in lake

## DESERTS

M   **29.** At which latitudes are deserts usually found?
   a. 0–15
   b. 15–25
 * c. 25–40
   d. 40–60
   e. 60–90

M   **30.** The only one of the following characteristics that all deserts have in common is
 * a. low rainfall amounts.
   b. heat.
   c. sand.
   d. lack of vegetation.
   e. cacti.

D   **31.** The biome most in danger of desertification is
   a. desert.
 * b. grassland.
   c. deciduous forest.
   d. tropical rain forest.
   e. taiga.

E   **32.** Most desert biomes are in close proximity to what other biome?
   a. tundra
 * b. grasslands
   c. deciduous forests
   d. evergreen forests

M   **33.** The biome with the greatest range of daily temperature extremes is the
   a. tundra.
   b. taiga.
   c. tropical rain forest.
 * d. desert.
   e. grassland.

M   **34.** The biome that is currently increasing in size most rapidly is
   a. tundra.
   b. taiga.
   c. tropical rain forest.
 * d. desert.
   e. grassland.

## DRY SHRUBLANDS, DRY WOODLANDS, AND GRASSLANDS

M   **35.** In shrublands,
 * a. cool winters are followed by prolonged drought.
   b. primary production is abundant throughout the year.
   c. there are constant cool temperatures throughout the year.
   d. winters are mild and summers are wet.
   e. precipitation occurs evenly year round.

D   **36.** Fire in the dry shrublands does not kill the small bushy plants most probably because
   a. the plants have a tough protective bark.
   b. the leaves are very heavy and wet.
 * c. there is not much to "feed" the fire and thus it moves rapidly through the area.
   d. humans live close by and have fire-fighting equipment.

E   **37.** The biome with the greatest amount of topsoil and the richest, most fertile soil is
   a. tundra.
   b. taiga.
   c. tropical rain forest.
   d. desert.
 * e. grassland.

M   **38.** The Dust Bowl of the 1930s was the result of destruction of
   a. desert
   b. chaparral.
   c. tallgrass prairie.
 * d. shortgrass prairie.
   e. temperate deciduous forest.

M   **39.** Which of the following biomes would support and be characterized by the greatest number and diversity of herbivores?
   a. tundra
   b. taiga
 * c. grassland
   d. chaparral
   e. desert

D   **40.** Grassland biomes around the earth vary in several ways, but the chief factor causing the variation is
 * a. rainfall amounts.
   b. vegetation.
   c. soil type.
   d. the animals present.
   e. prevailing winds.

M   **41.** A biome with grasses as primary producers and scattered trees adapted to prolonged dry spells is known as a
   a. warm desert.
 * b. savanna.
   c. tundra.
   d. taiga.
   e. chaparral.

M 42. The biome most closely associated with fire (and later, mudslides) is the
    a. desert.
    b. tropical rain forest.
\*   c. chaparral (dry shrublands).
    d. temperate deciduous forest.
    e. taiga.

## TROPICAL RAINFORESTS AND OTHER BROADLEAF FORESTS

E 43. In tropical rain forests,
\*   a. competition for available sunlight is intense.
    b. diversity is limited because the tall forest canopy shuts out most of the incoming light.
    c. conditions are extremely favorable for growing luxuriant food crops.
    d. there is little competition for resources.
    e. habitat partitioning is minimal.

E 44. The biome with the greatest diversity of life forms is
    a. tundra.
    b. taiga.
\*   c. tropical rain forest.
    d. desert.
    e. grassland.

E 45. In which biome is plant and animal life greatly "layered"?
    a. tundra
    b. taiga
\*   c. tropical rain forest
    d. desert
    e. grassland

M 46. The removal of trees from tropical rain forest for the purpose of large-scale food crop agriculture is not recommended because
    a. the soil is poor in organic nutrients.
    b. erosion rates accelerate when trees are removed.
    c. the soil has few decomposers.
\*   d. both a and b
    e. a, b, and c

E 47. Which biome is characterized by plants whose leaves drop off in the wintertime?
    a. coniferous forest
    b. tundra
\*   c. temperate deciduous forest
    d. tropical rain forest
    e. all of the above

M 48. Concerning biomes where maple and beech trees are the dominant vegetation, which statement is true?
    a. Winters are mild.
    b. Rainfall is low.
    c. Rate of evaporation is low.
\*   d. Soil nutrient concentration is high.

D 49. Which is NOT true of a mature temperate deciduous forest?
    a. Larger predators and herbivores use the forest more for shelter than for food; they tend to feed in clearings.
    b. Extensive tree roots prevent a great deal of soil erosion.
\*   c. The principal producers are the bushes and low lying grasses.
    d. The mature trees are the primary energy foundation for the entire community and play a key role in recycling nutrients.
    e. all of the above are not true

## TUNDRA

E 50. Which biome is a treeless plain that occurs around the Arctic Circle?
    a. chaparral
    b. taiga
    c. desert
    d. grassland
\*   e. tundra

M 51. Permafrost and low rainfall are characteristic of which biome?
    a. boreal forest
    b. montane coniferous forest
\*   c. tundra
    d. evergreen coniferous forest

M 52. Low temperature, short growing seasons, limited rainfall, dwarf trees, and herbaceous plants characterize the
\*   a. tundra.
    b. taiga.
    c. temperate deciduous forest.
    d. grassland.
    e. tropical montane forests.

E 53. The word *permafrost* is associated with which biome?
\*   a. tundra
    b. taiga
    c. temperate deciduous forest
    d. grassland
    e. montane forest

M 54. The biome at the top of a very tall mountain at the equator would be
\*   a. alpine tundra.
    b. taiga (boreal forest).
    c. tropical rain forest.
    d. temperate deciduous forest.
    e. chaparral (shrublands).

## CONIFEROUS FORESTS

E 55. The largest biome in North America is the
\*   a. taiga (evergreen coniferous).
    b. tundra.
    c. temperate grassland.
    d. temperate deciduous forest.
    e. chaparral (shrublands).

E 56. The taiga could best be described as what type of forest?
  a  deciduous
  b  thorn
* c  evergreen coniferous
  d  broad-leafed
  e  shrub

D 57. Evergreen trees are found in the
  a  tropics.
  b  temperate zones.
  c  taiga.
  d  b and c only
* e  a, b, and c

## FRESHWATER PROVINCES

M 58. The greatest diversity of organisms in lake ecosystems is found in what zone?
  a  profundal
  b  limnetic
  c  thermocline
* d  littoral

E 59. Freshwater lakes will turn over in the
  a  fall.
  b  winter.
  c  spring.
  d  summer.
* e  both a and c

M 60. In a lake, the open sunlit water with its suspended phytoplankton is referred to as which zone?
  a  epipelagic
* b  limnetic
  c  littoral
  d  profundal
  e  benthic

M 61. The profundal zone is characterized by
  a  plankton.
  b  algae.
  c  plants and animals.
* d  decomposers.
  e  all of the above

M 62. Thorough mixing of oxygen and nutrients within a lake occurs in
  a  winter and summer.
  b  winter and spring.
  c  spring and summer.
* d  spring and autumn.
  e  summer and autumn.

E 63. The upper and lower levels of a lake are separated by the
  a  limnetic zone.
* b  thermocline.
  c  littoral zone.
  d  lentic zone.
  e  eutrophic zone.

E 64. A lake in which minerals are scarce is
  a  profundal.
* b  oligotrophic.
  c  eutrophic.
  d  benthic.
  e  pelagic.

M 65. Oligotrophic lakes are characterized by all but which of the following?
  a  deep water
  b  steep banks
  c  abundant oxygen
  d  low nutrients
* e  high production of fish

M 66. Eutrophication refers to which change in a lake?
  a  decrease in depth
* b  increase in dissolved nitrogen and phosphorus
  c  increase in species diversity
  d  decrease in nutrient concentrations

E 67. Riffles, pools, and runs are words used to describe
  a  estuaries.
  b  sandy shores.
  c  coral reefs.
* d  streams.
  e  lake ecosystems.

E 68. The region where fresh water and salt water mix is the
  a  neteric zone.
* b  estuary.
  c  lotic zone.
  d  littoral region.
  e  pelagic zone.

## THE OCEAN PROVINCES

M 69. Because thermal stratification is _____ prevalent in tropical oceans, they exhibit _____ productivity when compared to oceans in temperate regions.
  a  more; higher
* b  more; lower
  c  less; higher
  d  less; lower

M 70. Which zone of the ocean is found above the continental shelf?
  a  abyssal
  b  benthic
  c  pelagic
* d  neritic
  e  oceanic

M 71. Differences in which factor determine the distribution of producer organisms in marine ecosystems?
    a. the intensity of incoming solar radiation
    b. the salinity of surface waters
    c. the availability of nutrients
*   d. all of the above

M 72. The organisms that occupy the first trophic level near hydrothermal vents are
    a. detritivores.
*   b. chemosynthetic bacteria.
    c. decomposers.
    d. photosynthetic bacteria.

D 73. The Galápagos Rift is a geothermal ecosystem 2,500 meters beneath the ocean's surface that has which of the following as its primary producers?
    a. blue-green algae
    b. protistans
    c. nitrogen-fixing organisms
*   d. chemosynthetic organisms
    e. vascular plants

M 74. Which of the following factors would be likely to be limiting in the open ocean?
*   a. nutrients
    b. temperature
    c. oxygen
    d. light
    e. wind

M 75. The ocean zone that exhibits the greatest degree of species diversity is
    a. estuary.
    b. rocky intertidal.
*   c. neritic.
    d. continental shelf.

## CORAL REEFS AND BANKS

E 76. The words "fringing," "barrier," and "atoll" describe
    a. streams.
    b. lakes.
*   c. reefs.
    d. upwellings.
    e. coastal ecosystems.

M 77. Coral reefs include
    a. skeletons of corals.
    b. living corals.
    c. algae.
    d. invertebrate animals.
    e. all of these

## LIFE ALONG COASTS

M 78. Estuaries often exhibit a great degree of species diversity because
    a. saltwater and freshwater species are present.
    b. many species of the open ocean spend a portion of their life cycles in estuarine waters.
    c. there is a continued upwelling of nutrients.
*   d. a and b
    e. a, b, and c

M 79. Water draining from the land mixes with seawater carried in on tides in which of the following?
    a. abyssal zone
    b. rift zone
    c. upwelling
*   d. estuary
    e. pelagic zone

M 80. Which are nursery grounds for shrimp and many marine forms?
    a. photic zones
    b. benthic zones
*   c. estuaries
    d. pelagic zones
    e. limnetic areas

D 81. Upwelling
*   a. increases productivity by bringing nutrient-rich cool water to the surface of the ocean.
    b. occurs in freshwater lakes when the thermocline is destroyed by changing temperatures.
    c. refers to the accumulation of pollution in certain estuaries.
    d. occurs when warm ocean currents approach the edge of continents.
    e. generates the major climatic changes in the Pacific Ocean known as El Niño.

## Matching Questions

D   **82.**   Choose the one most appropriate answer for each.

1   _____   benthic province
2   _____   biome
3   _____   cold deserts
4   _____   hydrothermal vents
5   _____   estuary
6   _____   savanna
7   _____   shortgrass prairie
8   _____   taiga
9   _____   tallgrass prairie
10  _____   deciduous forest
11  _____   littoral zone
12  _____   tropical rain forest
13  _____   tundra
14  _____   upwellings
15  _____   warm deserts

A.   northern coniferous forest

B.   strong vertical currents

C.   Steinbeck and Michener lamented their disruption

D.   mosaics of tall, coarse grasses, shrubs, and low trees, even humid forests; rainfall varies

E.   shallow area near lakeshores

F.   buffalo, Indians, and future fields of corn and wheat

G.   includes sediments and rocks of ocean bottom

H.   sagebrush communities of the western United States; frost and arid conditions

I.   stratified communities with vines, orchids, and monkeys

J.   where hot water spews from fissures

K.   large daily temperature fluctuations; prickly pear cacti, ocotillo

L.   dwarf willows, mosses, lichens, caribou, and lemmings

M.   *Spartina*, eelgrass, and diatoms

N.   a large region characterized by its large array of dominant primary producers

O.   Southern Appalachian mountains; moderate rain, cold snowy winters; deer kept in check by hunters

*Answers:*   

| | | | | | |
|---|---|---|---|---|---|
| 1. | G | 2. | N | 3. | H |
| 4. | J | 5. | M | 6. | D |
| 7. | C | 8. | A | 9. | F |
| 10. | O | 11. | E | 12. | I |
| 13. | L | 14. | B | 15. | K |

## Classification Questions

Answer questions 83–87 in reference to the five biomes listed below:

   a.   tundra
   b.   grassland
   c.   desert
   d.   taiga (boreal forest)
   e.   savanna

M   **83.**   A tropical plant community composed primarily of shrubby trees widely spaced and surrounded by grasses is this biome.

M   **84.**   A community composed of herbaceous plants, no trees, a very short growing season, and relatively few animal species is likely to be this biome.

E   **85.**   This biome is characterized by variable daily temperatures and plants that are highly resistant to desiccation.

M   **86.**   This biome has the richest soils.

E   **87.**   Conifers are most likely to be found in this biome.

*Answers:*   

| | | | | | |
|---|---|---|---|---|---|
| 83. | e | 84. | a | 85. | c |
| 86. | b | 87. | d | | |

Answer questions 88–92 in reference to the five biomes listed below:

   a.   tundra
   b.   chaparral
   c.   desert
   d.   taiga (coniferous forest)
   e.   deciduous forest

M   **88.**   In this biome you could find a black spruce.

E   **89.**   In this biome you are most likely to find sagebrush.

M   **90.**   In this biome you would expect to find caribou.

E   **91.**   This biome would be most likely to have a black oak.

M   **92.**   This biome is most likely to have a population of moose.

*Answers:*   

| | | | | | |
|---|---|---|---|---|---|
| 88. | d | 89. | b | 90. | a |
| 91. | e | 92. | d | | |

## Selecting the Exception

D   **93.**   Four of the five answers below are related by inclusion in the same type of biome. Select the exception.

   a.   shortgrass prairie
   b.   monsoon grassland
   c.   savanna
\*   d.   chaparral
   e.   tallgrass prairie

E    94.   Four of the five answers listed below are
           characteristics of the tropical rain forest. Select
           the exception.
           a    slash and burn
           b.   great diversity
           c.   highly stratified
           d.   lack of nutrients
      *    e.   large herds of herbivores

E    95.   Four of the five answers listed below are related
           by a common biome. Select the exception.
           a    no trees
           b.   permafrost
           c.   short growing seasons
      *    d.   found in the rain shadows
           e.   may be found above Arctic Circle or at top
                of mountains

D    96.   Four of the five answers listed below are related
           by a similar habitat. Select the exception.
           a    neritic zone
      *    b.   littoral zone
           c.   benthic province
           d.   pelagic province
           e.   abyssal zone

# CHAPTER 39
# HUMAN IMPACT ON THE BIOSPHERE

## Multiple-Choice Questions

### AIR POLLUTION—PRIME EXAMPLES

M   1. Carbon dioxide is a pollutant because it
    a   is absorbed by the ocean and converted into insoluble carbonates.
    b.   is liberated when fossil fuel is burned.
    c.   is a waste product of respiration.
   * d.   cannot be recycled at a rate equal to its present production.

M   2. In the United States, how many metric tons of pollutants are discharged into the atmosphere each day?
    a   1,000
    b.   100,000
   * c.   700,000
    d   5 million
    e.   15 to 30 million

E   3. Air pollution
    a   reduces visibility.
    b.   corrodes buildings.
    c.   causes various human diseases.
    d.   damages plants.
   * e.   all of the above

E   4. Air pollution may cause
    a   lung cancer.
    b.   emphysema.
    c.   bronchitis.
    d.   burning eyes.
   * e.   all of the above

M   5. Which acid is a severe air pollutant?
    a   carbonic acid
   * b.   nitric acid
    c.   hydrofluoric acid
    d.   hydrochloric acid
    e.   boric acid

M   6. Acid rain occurs when
    a   carbon dioxide combines with water in the atmosphere.
    b.   phosphorus-rich water in lakes evaporates to form phosphoric acid.
   * c.   sulfur released in burning fossil fuels combines with water in the atmosphere.
    d.   excess hydrogen is released into the atmosphere where ozone is formed.

M   7. Acid rain
    a   increases the mobility of toxic heavy metals.
    b.   is the major reason for the production of sterile lakes around the world.
    c.   is rainwater with a pH above 7.
    d.   is primarily the result of industrial pollution.
   * e.   All but choice c are correct.

M   8. The two chemical elements associated with acid deposition are
    a   nitrogen and oxygen.
    b.   sulfur and oxygen.
   * c.   nitrogen and sulfur.
    d.   carbon and oxygen.
    e.   nitrogen and carbon.

E   9. Acid rain
    a   attacks nylons.
    b.   attacks marble statues.
    c.   causes toxic metals to become motile in the ecosystem.
    d.   can be reduced in the local area by tall smokestacks.
   * e.   all of the above

M   10. Each of the following substances contributes to acid rain EXCEPT
   * a.   ozone.
    b.   waste products from the burning of coal.
    c.   nitrogen fertilizers.
    d.   waste products from the burning of gasoline.

M   11. Acid rain is NOT a serious problem in some areas because of the presence of which substance in the soil?
    a   granite
   * b.   carbonate
    c.   clay
    d.   sand

M   12. The unequal distribution of acid rain over the United States is closely correlated with
    a   per capita energy use.
    b.   fertilizer use.
   * c.   burning fossil fuels.
    d.   average summer temperatures.

M   13. The region of the United States most affected by acid rain is the
    a   Northwest.
    b.   Southwest.
   * c.   Northeast.
    d.   Southeast.

E   14. Transportation-produced smog causes air to turn
    a   gray.
    b.   black.
   * c.   brown.
    d.   red.
    e.   blue.

M  15.  A thermal inversion refers to
    a  an abnormal occurrence not predicted by meteorologists.
    b.  an Indian summer.
    c.  an unusually quick change in weather patterns.
    d.  the process of cool air drainage at night.
  *  e.  a layer of cool air trapped underneath a warm air blanket.

E  16.  When fossil-fuel burning gives off particulates and sulfur oxides, we have
    a  photochemical smog.
  *  b.  industrial smog.
    c.  a thermal inversion.
    d.  both a and c
    e.  all of the above

E  17.  Industrial smog causes air to turn
  *  a  gray.
    b.  black.
    c.  brown.
    d.  red.
    e.  blue.

M  18.  Which city has brown fog?
    a  London
  *  b.  Los Angeles
    c.  Chicago
    d.  New York
    e.  Pittsburgh

M  19.  When fossil-fuel burning gives off particulates and sulfur oxides, what results?
    a  photochemical smog
  *  b.  industrial smog
    c.  a thermal inversion
    d.  both a and c, but not b
    e.  all of the above

M  20.  Which factor is NOT characteristic of a city primarily plagued by industrial smog?
    a  high concentration of sulfur oxides
    b.  dependence on fossil fuel for manufacturing
    c.  cold, wet winters
  *  d.  high concentration of nitrogen oxides

M  21.  Which factor is NOT characteristic of a city primarily plagued by photochemical smog?
  *  a  high concentration of sulfur oxides
    b.  high concentration of nitrogen oxides
    c.  significant amounts of PANs
    d.  large numbers of internal combustion engines

M  22.  In brown air fog, which substance combines with nitrogen dioxide in the sunlight to form photochemical smog?
    a  carbon monoxide
    b.  water vapor
  *  c.  hydrocarbons
    d.  sulfuric acid
    e.  all of the above

D  23.  What results when nitrogen dioxide and hydrocarbons react in the presence of sunlight?
  *  a  photochemical smog
    b.  industrial smog
    c.  a thermal inversion
    d.  both a and c
    e.  all of the above

## OZONE HOLES—GLOBAL LEGACIES OF AIR POLLUTION

M  24.  Chlorofluorocarbons (CFCs) are pollutants because
  *  a  biogeochemical mechanisms for their removal have not yet appeared in the biosphere.
    b.  they combine with water to form hydrochloric and hydrofluoric acids.
    c.  they are found in smog.
    d.  they are photochemical oxidants.

M  25.  The atmosphere above which region is known to have a hole in the ozone layer?
  *  a  Antarctica
    b.  Eastern North America
    c.  Northern Europe
    d.  the western Pacific

M  26.  Each factor appears to be correlated with a decrease in atmospheric ozone EXCEPT
    a  suppression of the immune system.
    b.  decreased rates of photosynthesis.
    c.  increased incidence of skin cancers.
  *  d.  decreased levels of atmospheric carbon dioxide.

M  27.  Uses of chlorofluorocarbons include each of the following EXCEPT
  *  a  gasoline additives.
    b.  aerosol propellants.
    c.  refrigeration coolants.
    d.  plastic packaging.

## WHERE TO PUT SOLID WASTES, WHERE TO PRODUCE FOOD

E  28.  About how many beverage containers sold in the United States each year are nonreturnable cans and bottles, many of which are discarded in public places?
    a  25 million
    b.  25 billion
    c.  50 million
  *  d.  50 billion
    e.  100 million

E  29.  What percentage of urban wastes are paper products?
    a  10
    b.  20
  *  c.  50
    d.  75
    e.  more than 90

E    30. Using recycled paper could reduce the air
         pollution that results from paper manufacturing
         by
         a   50 percent
    *    b.  95 percent
         c.  5 percent
         d.  zero percent.
         e.  75 percent

E    31. Landfills should contain
         a   all garbage.
         b.  nonbiodegradable wastes.
    *    c.  nonrecycled solid wastes.
         d.  glass and metallic debris.
         e.  organic litter.

E    32. How many trees are required just to print all the
         Sunday newspapers in the United States?
         a   1 million
         b.  100,000
    *    c.  500,000
         d.  2 billion
         e.  none because all the paper is recycled

M    33. Approximately 50 percent of the billions of tons
         of solid wastes produced in the United States is
         a   glass.
    *    b.  paper.
         c.  aluminum.
         d.  plastic.

M    34. Of the earth's land, what is the maximum
         percentage now being used for agriculture?
         a   10
    *    b.  21
         c.  50
         d.  75

M    35. The new high-yield crops require which of the
         following that cannot be supplied by subsistence
         agriculture?
         a   irrigation
         b.  pesticides
         c.  fertilizers
         d.  fossil fuel energy
    *    e.  all of the above

D    36. Subsistence agriculture does not utilize
         a   human labor.
         b.  sunlight.
         c.  available soil.
    *    d.  synthetic fertilizers.
         e.  water.

M    37. For a given crop yield, modern agricultural
         practices require how many times more energy
         and mineral resources than is required by
         subsistence agricultural practices?
         a   .01
         b.  .25
         c.  4
         d.  25
    *    e.  100

## DEFORESTATION-CONCERTED ASSAULT ON FINITE RESOURCES

M    38. Tropical plants or their products have provided
         humans with all of the following EXCEPT
         a   medicines.
    *    b.  grain.
         c.  spices.
         d.  fuel.

M    39. Deforestation results in
         a   increased air temperatures.
         b.  decreased soil fertility.
         c.  altered rainfall patterns.
         d.  a and b
    *    e.  a, b, and c

D    40. The soils in the tropical rain forest are nutrient-
         poor because
         a   they are located near the equator.
         b.  the trees remove most of the good things.
    *    c.  decomposition of organic matter is very
             rapid.
         d.  leaching occurs even before tree cutting.
         e.  of shifting cultivation.

M    41. At current rates of clearing and degradation, the
         disappearance of the tropical rain forest biome
         may be complete by the year
    *    a   2035.
         b.  2100.
         c.  2150.
         d.  2200.

## TRADING GRASSLANDS FOR DESERTS

M    42. The primary cause of desertification in the world
         today is
         a   increased salinity resulting from irrigation
             practices.
    *    b.  overgrazing of marginal lands.
         c.  clearing and degradation of tropical forests.
         d.  herbicide and fertilizer runoff.

## A GLOBAL WATER CRISIS

E    43. For every million liters of water in the world,
         only about _____ liters are in a form that
         can be used for human consumption or
         agriculture.
    *    a   6
         b.  60
         c.  600
         d.  6,000

D    44. Of all the water on the earth's surface, most of it
         is NOT fit for human consumption because it
         contains
         a   microbial pollutants.
    *    b.  salt.
         c.  heavy metals.
         d.  pesticides.
         e.  CFCs.

D 45. Of the following, which would probably be the safest source of drinking water?
    a municipal water supply
    b. clear mountain stream
    * c. deep well
    d. shallow well
    e. rainwater

E 46. Primary treatment of sewage involves
    * a. filtration and sedimentation, which physically treats water.
    b. the biological degradation of the organic material.
    c. the most expensive sewage treatment process.
    d. the chemical treatment of the water to neutralize its effects.
    e. chlorination or ultrasonic vibration, removal of nitrogen from ammonia, and precipitation of phosphate compounds.

M 47. After secondary sewage treatment, the water may contain all of the following EXCEPT
    a. viruses.
    b. oxygen-demanding wastes.
    c. nitrates and phosphates.
    * d. large suspended solids.
    e. pesticides and industrial chemicals.

M 48. Which process is NOT generally considered a component of tertiary wastewater treatment?
    * a. microbial action
    b. precipitation of suspended solids
    c. reverse osmosis
    d. absorption of dissolved organic compounds

M 49. Primary treatment of wastewater does NOT involve using which of the following?
    a. sedimentation tanks
    * b. aeration with pure oxygen
    c. mechanical screens
    d. chemicals such as aluminum sulfate

M 50. Which is NOT a result or effect of irrigation?
    a. increased food production
    b. waterlogging of soil
    c. raised water tables
    * d. alteration of soil type

## A QUESTION OF ENERGY INPUTS

E 51. The most harmful element in coal that causes serious pollution problems is
    a. nitrogen.
    b. silver.
    c. carbon.
    * d. sulfur.
    e. chlorine.

E 52. Fossil fuels
    a. are renewable natural resources.
    * b. will be commercially depleted within the next 100 years.
    c. can be utilized without any environmental degradation.
    d. are essentially pure carbon deposits.

E 53. Carbon dioxide in the atmosphere
    a. is destroying the ozone layer.
    * b. has dramatically increased in the last few decades.
    c. is one of the prime reasons for acid rain.
    d. is a waste gas produced by respiration and has no biological use.

M 54. Which of the following is the most reliable source of energy for the next few hundred or thousands of years?
    a. oil
    b. coal
    * c. sun
    d. natural gas
    e. nuclear

M 55. If one kind of plutonium isotope is not removed, the wastes from a nuclear power reactor must be kept out of the environment for how many years before they are safe?
    a. 25
    b. 250
    * c. 250,000
    d. 1 million

M 56. Which statement about nuclear power plants is true?
    * a. Their net energy production is relatively low.
    b. Their waste products lead to the production of acid rain.
    c. Their waste products are not radioactive.
    d. a and b
    e. a, b, and c

M 57. Problems associated with the extraction or use of coal as a large-scale source of energy include all of the following EXCEPT
    a. production of sulfur oxides.
    b. stripmining in fragile semiarid environments.
    * c. limited reserves.
    d. amplification of the general warming trend of the earth.

## ALTERNATIVE ENERGY SOURCES

M 58. To produce power from fusion,
    a. breeder reactors must convert uranium to plutonium.
    b. hydrogen and oxygen are combined to yield water.
    * c. hydrogen atoms are joined to form helium.
    d. a and b
    e. a and c

M 59. Which of the following accurately describes the concept of solar-hydrogen energy?
   a   Hydrogen gas is trapped by solar cells.
   b.  Solar energy is used to fuse hydrogen atoms into helium atoms.
   c.  Electricity is produced by the splitting of hydrogen atoms using sunlight power.
 * d.  Sunlight produces electricity which is used to produce hydrogen fuel.
   e.  Solar power is tapped for use in hydrogen-breeder reactors.

## Matching Questions

D 60. Matching. Choose the one most appropriate answer for each.

   1. ___   solar-hydrogen energy
   2. ___   dry acid depositions
   3. ___   fossil fuels
   4. ___   salination
   5. ___   fusion power
   6. ___   chlorofluorocarbons
   7. ___   meltdown
   8. ___   shifting cultivation
   9. ___   primary treatment
   10. ___  PANS
   11. ___  reverse osmosis
   12. ___  thermal inversion
   13. ___  secondary treatment

   A.  a process that is part of tertiary wastewater treatment
   B.  could happen in a conventional nuclear fission reactor
   C.  coal, oil, gas
   D.  photochemical smog component, like tear gas
   E.  dense air trapped beneath a layer of warm air
   F.  its reactions resemble those occurring in the sun
   G.  depends on microbial action
   H.  slash and burn
   I.  forms sludge from coarse, suspended solids
   J.  uses photovoltaic cells to generate burnable gas
   K.  can cause depletion of ozone
   L.  tiny particles that attack marble and cause crop damage
   M.  salt deposition that results from irrigating arid-zone soils

Answers:
   1. J        2. L        3. C
   4. M        5. F        6. K
   7. B        8. H        9. I
   10. D       11. A       12. E
   13. G

## Selecting the Exception

E 61. Four of the five answers listed below are particulate wastes. Select the exception.
   a   smoke
   b.  soot
   c.  asbestos
   d.  dust
 * e.  ozone

E 62. Four of the five answers listed below are nonrenewable resources. Select the exception.
 * a   biomass
   b.  coal
   c.  natural gas
   d.  oil
   e.  nuclear

M 63. Four of the five answers listed below are effects of acid rain. Select the exception.
   a   attacks marble, metals, mortar, nylons
 * b.  causes air inversion and pollution events
   c.  makes toxic heavy metals more mobile
   d.  has different effects in different watersheds
   e.  produces sterile lakes

M 64. Four of the five answers listed below could increase the earth's carrying capacity. Select the exception.
 * a   desertification
   b.  recycling
   c.  green revolution
   d.  irrigation
   e.  conservation

# CHAPTER 40
# ANIMAL BEHAVIOR

## Multiple-Choice Questions

### THE HERITABLE BASIS OF BEHAVIOR

M    1.    Which statement is false?
a    Behavior is controlled by the environmental stimuli an organism receives.
b.    Behavior is partially genetic so that it undergoes natural selection and evolution.
*    c.    Behavior refers only to responses to external stimuli.
d.    Behavior sometimes is nonadaptive.
e.    Behavior patterns can be learned.

M    2.    The pineal gland responds to
a    light intensity.
*    b.    light duration or photoperiod.
c.    flashes of light.
d.    red light.
e.    different colors of light.

M    3.    Melatonin specifically controls or interacts to control
a    the growth of the gonads of birds.
b.    migration.
c.    sexual behavior patterns.
d.    singing and territorial behavior.
*    e.    all of the above

M    4.    Which hormone activates the song system when a bird sings?
a    melatonin
*    b.    testosterone
c.    thyroxin.
d.    calcitonin
e.    epinephrine

M    5.    Each statement concerning behavior is true EXCEPT
a    the knee-jerk reflex is a behavior.
*    b.    a behavior such as a complex courtship ritual is encoded by a single gene.
c.    behaviors are products of natural selection.
d.    behaviors are adaptive.

M    6.    Behavior is the result of
a    neural networks.
b.    hormonal interactions.
c.    genetic predisposition.
d.    environmental cues.
*    e.    all of the above

M    7.    Bird song
a    has to be heard before a bird can sing it.
b.    is learned during early life.
c.    is specific for each bird species.
d.    has a genetic component.
*    e.    all of the above

M    8.    The cells surrounding milk-producing cells in the female mammary gland contract shortly after the female hears the cry of an infant. This is an example of
a    a response that is not a behavior.
*    b.    instinctive behavior.
c.    imprinting behavior.
d.    learned behavior.

M    9.    Instinctive behavior is
a    stereotyped.
b.    unlearned.
c.    induced each and every time the stimulus is presented.
d.    triggered by limited sets of clues.
*    e.    all of the above

E    10.    To get a young baby to smile, simply present a
a    parent's smiling face.
b.    parent's nonsmiling face.
c.    person's face or a mask.
d.    picture of a face.
*    e.    representation of a face, so long as it has two recognizable eyes.

### LEARNED BEHAVIOR

D    11.    Learned behavior is recognizable by the _____ the animal makes in its responses.
a    fixed patterns
*    b.    changes
c.    stereotyping
d.    repetitions
e.    false starts

E    12.    Konrad Lorenz is noted for his studies on
a    prenatal marking.
b.    mating behavior.
*    c.    imprinting.
d.    habituation.
e.    insight learning.

E    13.    Newly hatched baby geese follow any large moving objects to which they are exposed shortly after hatching. This is an example of
a    homing behavior.
*    b.    imprinting.
c.    piloting.
d.    migration.
e.    none of the above

M    **14.** Recent studies in humans have shown there is a close relationship between poor nutrition and poor learning ability. These studies suggest that
     a   there is only a minor genetic component to learned behavior.
*    b.   behavior is modified by the environment.
     c.   learning is adaptive.
     d.   learning is instinctive.

E    **15.** Learning by use of landmarks is
*    a   spatial
     b.   insight
     c.   operant
     d.   habituation
     e.   imprinting

M    **16.** In classical conditioning,
*    a   two different stimuli elicit the same response.
     b.   two different stimuli elicit two different responses.
     c.   one stimulus elicits one response.
     d.   one stimulus elicits two different responses.

M    **17.** A child grabs a dog's ear, and the dog responds by biting the child. Both behaviors are repeated once again the next day, and again a day later. The child never grabs a dog's ear again. This sequence of events is an example of
     a   insight learning.
     b.   latent learning.
*    c.   operant conditioning.
     d.   imprinting.

E    **18.** The ability of a rat to solve a maze to obtain a reward is increased if it has the chance to explore the maze before the test begins. This is an example of
     a   insight learning.
*    b.   latent learning.
     c.   associative learning.
     d.   conditioning.
     e.   extinction.

D    **19.** Horticulturists use periodic discharges of loud sounds to scare birds away from their fruit trees. After several days birds can be seen ignoring the sounds due to
*    a   habituation.
     b.   imprinting.
     c.   conditioning.
     d.   insight learning.
     e.   instinct.

D    **20.** Humans, and other primates to some extent, differ from other animals in their ability to learn by
     a   conditioning.
     b.   imprinting.
     c.   habituation.
*    d.   insight.
     e.   latent learning.

## THE ADAPTIVE VALUE OF BEHAVIOR

M    **21.** The example used to demonstrate that Darwinian natural selection explains some behavioral traits better than group selection does is
     a   the dilution effect in wildebeest and zebra populations.
     b.   siblicide among egrets.
     c.   courtship behavior in albatrosses.
*    d.   the dispersal of Norwegian lemmings when population densities became extremely high.
     e.   all of the above

D    **22.** During aggressive encounters between members of the same species,
     a   the strong members are always victorious.
     b.   the invader into a territory is able to replace the current resident of the territory unless he has already mated.
*    c.   opponents usually settle the dispute without bloodshed.
     d.   a fight to the death occurs, with the one higher in the pecking order being successful more often.

## COMMUNICATION SIGNALS

E    **23.** In the termite colony described in the text, the soldier termites defend the colony by
     a   stinging the invaders.
     b.   removing the legs of the invaders.
     c.   blinding the invaders.
*    d.   covering the invaders with a sticky substance.
     e.   decapitating the invaders after an exhausting combat.

E    **24.** Pheromones are
*    a   used in nonverbal communication.
     b.   found only in the invertebrates.
     c.   signals to members of other species.
     d.   types of internal hormones that control maturation.

E    **25.** Pheromones are advantageous because
     a   they work in the dark.
     b.   they are often unique to individual species.
     c.   only small amounts are needed.
     d.   they do not trigger a response in other species.
*    e.   all of the above

M    **26.** Communication by means of visual signals has a minimum requirement of
     a   daylight.
     b.   short distance.
*    c.   a clear line of sight.
     d.   keen eyesight.
     e.   sharp hearing.

E 27. The communication signal requiring the most minimal distance between the sender and receiver animals is
    a  visual.
    b.  chemical.
    c.  acoustical.
*     d.  tactile.

E 28. Social behavior among insects depends on
    a  genetic similarity.
    b.  bonding early in youth.
*     c.  communication.
    d.  diversity.
    e.  polymorphism.

E 29. The initial alarm signal given by workers to indicate that the termite nest has been broken is
    a  odor.
    b.  taste.
    c.  sound.
*     d.  a set of vibrations.
    e.  contact between antennae.

E 30. Which scientist won the Nobel Prize for his research on the behavior of bees and the discovery of the way bees communicated the location of a food source?
*     a  Karl von Frisch
    b.  Nicholas Tinbergen
    c.  Konrad Lorenz
    d.  Skinner
    e.  Pavlov

E 31. Bees learn the direction to a distant source of food by
    a  following the foraging scout.
    b.  following a trail pheromone.
*     c.  observing the tail-wagging dance.
    d.  observing the round dance.
    e.  both c and d, but not a or b

M 32. Bees use which information for locating food and the hive?
    a  local topographic features
    b.  wind direction
    c.  magnetism
*     d.  the angle of the sun
    e.  distance between plants

## MATING, PARENTING, AND REPRODUCTIVE SUCCESS

M 33. In many bird and mammal species, males compete for females, but females do NOT compete for males because
    a  males are larger than females.
    b.  females are larger than males.
*     c.  females produce fewer gametes than males do.
    d.  females compete for territory.

D 34. Which of the following statements is false?
    a  Territorial pairs of ravens feed silently.
    b.  Single nonterritorial ravens proclaim the discovery of a food source.
    c.  Sexual selection through competition for mates leads to evolutionary change.
*     d.  Reproductive success is based upon the same criteria for both sexes.
    e.  Males that do not have territorial or sexual status sometimes employ strategies that allow them to mate.

D 35. During aggressive encounters between members of the same species,
    a  the strong members are always victorious.
    b.  the invader into a territory is able to replace the current resident of the territory unless he has already mated.
*     c.  opponents usually settle the dispute without bloodshed.
    d.  a fight to the death occurs, with the one higher in the pecking order being successful more often.

## COSTS AND BENEFITS OF BELONGING TO SOCIAL GROUPS

M 36. When researchers attempt to answer the question of why various animals exist in such a diversity of social units from solitary to complex societies, they use
    a  genetic analysis.
    b.  habitat data.
*     c.  cost-benefit analysis.
    d.  environmental studies.
    e.  time-density data.

D 37. All but which of the following are disadvantages to sociality?
*     a  predator avoidance
    b.  cannibalism
    c.  food depletion
    d.  contagious diseases
    e.  parasite infestation

D 38. The presence of the strongest competitors in the center of a group of animals may qualify the group for status as a(n)
    a  altruistic society.
*     b.  selfish herd.
    c.  kin group.
    d.  dominance hierarchy.

## SOCIAL LIFE AND SELF-SACRIFICING BEHAVIOR

M 39. Which statement concerning subordinate behavior as exemplified by interactions among members of wolf packs is true?
    a It is gradually being removed by natural selection.
    * b. It is adaptive.
    c. It is self-sacrificing.
    d. It is inexplicable in terms of reproductive success.

E 40. A submissive animal that exposes its throat or genitals to a dominant member of the same group is said to be engaging in what type of behavior?
    * a appeasement
    b. avoidance
    c. ritualized
    d. dispersive
    e. all of the above

M 41. The example used to demonstrate that competitive interactions lead to the formation of dominance hierarchies involved
    a albatrosses.
    b. a honeybee colony.
    * c. baboon troops.
    d. greylag geese.
    e. all of the above

E 42. Altruistic behavior is
    a selfish.
    b. sexually directed behavior.
    * c. self-sacrificing behavior.
    d. aggressive behavior.
    e. nonreactive, such as freezing at the sign of danger.

M 43. In highly integrated insect societies
    a natural selection favors individual behaviors that lead to greater diversity among members of the society.
    b. there is scarcely any division of labor.
    * c. cooperative behavior predominates.
    d. patterns of behavior are flexible, and learned behavior predominates.

E 44. A female insect can often be distinguished from the male by her
    a wing patterns.
    b. mating calls.
    * c. larger size.
    d. bigger antennae.
    e. longer feet.

D 45. Altruism in animals other than humans is
    * a probably a perception by human observers.
    b. gene-based.
    c. a conscious effort to preserve the species.
    d. just lucky behavior.

## AN EVOLUTIONARY VIEW OF HUMAN SOCIAL BEHAVIOR

D 46. Only in judging human behaviors does the concept of "_____" supplant "adaptation."
    a self-sacrifice.
    b. altruism
    c. judgment
    * d. morality

## Matching Questions

D 47. Choose the one most appropriate answer for each. Some letters may not be used.

1 _____ altruism
2 _____ insight
3 _____ instinctive behavior
4 _____ imprinting
5 _____ learning
6 _____ Lorenz
7 _____ lek

A. communal display ground
B. imprintings in baby geese
C. capacity of an animal to complete complex, stereotyped responses to first-time encounters to key stimuli
D. problem solving without trial and error
E. an adaptive change in behavior
F. occurs during a sensitive period in which a following response or social attachment becomes fixed on a particular moving object
G. self-sacrificing behavior

*Answers:*
| 1. G | 2. D | 3. C |
| 4. F | 5. E | 6. B |
| 7. A | | |

# Classification Questions

Answer questions 48-52 in reference to the five kinds of behavior listed below:

    a  imprinting
    b.  sexual selection
    c.  anti-predator behavior
    d.  female-defense behavior
    e.  altruism

M    **48.**  The extreme variation observed among the males of various species of ducks is thought to be due to this kind of behavior.

E    **49.**  Organisms increasing their apparent size when startled by another is an example this behavior.

E    **50.**  If the young of newly hatched birds (for example, chickens or ducks) are continually shown a large moving object during the first few days of their lives, and they will follow that object then this kind of behavior is seen.

M    **51.**  The adult male who jumps overboard to save a drowning niece is exhibiting this behavior.

M    **52.**  Two male bison butting one another during the breeding season are probably exhibiting this behavior.

*Answers*:    48.  b    49.  c    50.  a
                51.  e    52.  d

Answer questions 53-57 in reference to the four processes listed below associated with learning:

    a  conditioning
    b.  latent learning
    c.  insight learning
    d.  habituation

M    **53.**  This process is a synthesis of previous experiences to provide novel solutions to a problem.

M    **54.**  The process whereby an individual's performance on some task or activity improves following a period of inactivity or involvement in some other activity is known as:

M    **55.**  Trial-and-error learning is a subcategory of this.

M    **56.**  The ability of an animal to connect a novel experience with one that is familiar is known as this.

E    **57.**  A person ignoring a repetitive noise is an example of this.

*Answers:*    53.  c    54.  b    55.  a
                56.  a    57.  d

Answer questions 58-62 in reference to the four kinds of reception listed below that are used by social animals:

    a  tactile
    b.  auditory
    c.  visual
    d.  chemical

M    **58.**  This sensory modality is used by honey bees during the waggle dance.

E    **59.**  The sex pheromone emitted by a female gypsy moth relies on this sense in the male.

E    **60.**  The elaborate posturing displays of male birds of paradise utilize this sense in the female.

D    **61.**  The primary signal sent out by receptive female primates is likely to be this.

D    **62.**  The alarm signal one snail sends to another is most likely to be this.

*Answers*:    58.  a    59.  d    60.  c
                61.  d    62.  d

Answer questions 63-67 in reference to the four kinds of social behavior listed below:

    a  altruism
    b.  cooperation
    c.  self-sacrifice
    d.  kin selection

D    **63.**  The offspring of one brood of Florida scrubjays helping their parents in taking care of their siblings in the next brood, is an example of this behavior.

M    **64.**  A bluejay giving an alarm call at the intrusion of a crow into a woodlot, is an example of this behavior.

E    **65.**  Two or more female lions attacking a wildebeest together, is an example of this behavior.

M    **66.**  A female woodcock fluttering off her nest exhibiting a cripple-wing display to distract a predator is an example of this behavior.

M    **67.**  An example of this is when a woman raises her brother's children.

*Answers*:    63.  d    64.  a    65.  b
                66.  c    67.  d

## Selecting the Exception

E    **68.** Four of the five answers listed below are behaviors that are inborn. Select the exception.
- \*   a   modified by the environment
- b.   stereotyped
- c.   performed the first time stimulus is presented
- d.   innate
- e.   automatic

M    **69.** Four of the five answers listed below are castes of termites. Select the exception.
- \*   a   drone
- b.   king
- c.   queen
- d.   soldier
- e.   worker

M    **70.** Four of the five answers listed below are activities of the same type of bee. Select the exception.
- \*   a   lay eggs
- b.   feed larvae
- c.   guard hive
- d.   clean and maintain nest
- e.   forage for food

M    **71.** Four of the five answers listed below are pheromone signals. Select the exception.
- a   sex
- b.   alarm or attack
- c.   territory
- \*   d   threat
- e.   trail

# Interactive Electronic
# Study Guide Questions

# Interactive Electronic Study Guide Questions Contents

| | | |
|---|---|---|
| 1 | Methods and Concepts in Biology | 1 |
| 2 | Chemical Foundations for Cells | 7 |
| 3 | Cell Structure and Function | 14 |
| 4 | Ground Rules of Metabolism | 20 |
| 5 | Energy-Acquiring Pathways | 23 |
| 6 | Energy-Releasing Pathways | 28 |
| 7 | Cell Division and Mitosis | 33 |
| 8 | Meiosis | 36 |
| 9 | Observable Patterns of Inheritance | 40 |
| 10 | Chromosomes and Human Genetics | 46 |
| 11 | DNA Structure and Function | 53 |
| 12 | From DNA to Proteins | 58 |
| 13 | Recombinant DNA and Genetic Engineering | 64 |
| 14 | Microevolution | 71 |
| 15 | Speciation | 78 |
| 16 | The Macroevolutionary Puzzle | 83 |
| 17 | The Origin and Evolution of Life | 87 |
| 18 | Bacteria, Viruses, and Protistans | 92 |
| 19 | Plants and Fungi | 100 |
| 20 | Animals: The Invertebrates | 106 |
| 21 | Animals: The Vertebrates | 111 |
| 22 | Plant Tissues | 115 |
| 23 | Plant Nutrition and Transport | 119 |

**24** Plant Reproduction and Development 123

**25** Tissues, Organ Systems, and Homeostasis 130

**26** Protection, Support, and Movement 136

**27** Circulation 142

**28** Immunity 150

**29** Respiration 158

**30** Digestion and Human Nutrition 165

**31** The Internal Environment 172

**32** Neural Control and the Senses 178

**33** Integration and Control: Endocrine Systems 186

**34** Reproduction and Development 192

**35** Population Ecology 199

**36** Community Interactions 203

**37** Ecosystems 209

**38** The Biosphere 215

**39** Human Impact on the Biosphere 221

**40** Animal Behavior 223

# CHAPTER 1

# METHODS AND CONCEPTS IN BIOLOGY

1.	The instructions for each trait passed on from one generation to another is found in
	a.	blood.
	b.	semen.
	c.	deoxyribonucleic acid.
	d.	proteins.

	a.	no; an old wives' tale, blood has no impact on heredity
	b.	no; this is only the fluid which contains sperm
*	c.	yes; the chemical name for a gene
	d.	no; proteins are complex organic chemicals that have a large number of functions but heredity is not one of them

2.	Diversity found in living organisms is a result of
	a.	natural selection.
	b.	biogenesis.
	c.	biosynthesis.
	d.	life.

*	a.	yes; the environment influences which forms will survive
	b.	no; living organisms produce living organisms, but is not a sufficient explanation by itself for the differences we see
	c.	no; different biosynthetic pathways result in different end-products, but this does not explain all the differences we see
	d.	no; does not explain the source of diversity

3.	Life is
	a.	a way of capturing and using energy and materials.
	b.	a commitment to programs of growth and development and a capacity for reproduction.
	c.	adaptive both in the short term and through subsequent generations.
	d.	all of the above

	a.	no; a partial answer; a more complete answer is available
	b.	no; a partial answer; a more complete answer is available
	c.	no; a partial answer; a more complete answer is available
*	d.	yes; all of the above are correct

4.	Which of the following is alive?
	a.	a single cell swimming around on a microscope slide
	b.	an accident victim with no brain activity that's maintained on life support instruments
	c.	a blastocyst that has recently been implanted on the uterus of a teenager
	d.	the answer depends upon the definition of life

	a.	no; a more appropriate answer is available; but the single cell exhibits many features characteristic of life
	b.	no; a more appropriate answer is available; at one time, death was said to occur when the heart stopped beating
	c.	no; a more appropriate answer is available; this distractor is at the heart of the pro life/pro-choice controversy
*	d.	yes; your history and experiences might cause you to consider this question differently than others

5.	Life is
	a.	a way of sensing and responding to changes in the environment.
	b.	the capacity to reproduce, grow, and develop.
	c.	a way of capturing and using energy and raw materials.
	d.	all of the above

	a.	no; a partial answer; a more complete answer is available
	b.	no; a partial answer; a more complete answer is available
	c.	no; a partial answer; a more complete answer is available
*	d.	yes; all of the above answers are correct

6.	Any consideration of life must include
	a.	the evolutionary process that produced it.
	b.	the series of chemical and physical activities known as metabolism.
	c.	the control over biological activities imposed by molecules of deoxyribonucleic acid.
	d.	all of the above

a. no; a partial answer; a more complete answer is available
b. no; a partial answer; a more complete answer is available
c. no; a partial answer; a more complete answer is available
* d. yes; all of the above are correct

7. Which of the following statements is false?
a. All living organisms are unique in some of their traits.
b. The diversity of life includes some traits that are no longer functional and led to the extinction of those that possessed those traits.
c. the theory of evolution does not help explain the meaning of life's diversity.
d. Many millions of species of organisms are now extinct.

a. no; this statement is true
b. no; this statement is true
* c. yes; this statement is false; the theory of evolution provides explanations for the origin and persistence or extinction of different forms of life
d. no; this statement is true

8. A cell
a. is the basic living unit.
b. is able to survive and live on its own.
c. requires DNA, energy, and nutrients (raw materials).
d. all of the above

a. no; a partial answer; a more complete answer is available
b. no; a partial answer; a more complete answer is available
c. no; a partial answer; a more complete answer is available
* d. yes; all of the above are correct

9. The basic unit of life is a(n)
a. population.
b. organ.
c. cell.
d. ecosystem.

a. no; a group of living and interbreeding members of the same species
b. no; a group of living tissues united to perform common functions
* c. yes; the fundamental unit of life whether considering unicellular or multicellular organisms
d. no; consists of both living and non-living components

10. Which of the following is the simplest unit that can survive and live on its own?
a. cell
b. organelle
c. tissue
d. organ

* a. yes; individual cells can be cultured and are able to live and reproduce on their own
b. no; organelles are only able to function for a short time and quickly die when isolated from cells
c. no; tissues are able to survive, but cells are simpler units
d. no; organs are able to survive but cells are simpler units

11. A biological system such as the circulatory, excretory, endocrine or nervous system is most appropriately described as being composed of
a. cells.
b. organs.
c. tissues.
d. organelles.

a. no; although these systems are composed of cells there is a more appropriate unit
* b. yes; organ systems are made up of two or more organs that interact to perform a function
c. no; although these systems are composed of tissues there is a more appropriate unit
d. no; organelles are microscopic units that perform specific functions for individual cells

12. Which of the following is the most inclusive?
a. community
b. population
c. ecosystem
d. biosphere

a. no; it is part of an ecosystem
b. no; part of a community
c. no; part of the biosphere
* d. yes; includes all of the ecosystems

13. A community is composed of
a. individual organisms.
b. different species.
c. various populations.
d. all of the above

a. no; composed of groups of interacting individuals (populations), a better choice is available
b. no; different species are found in communities, a better choice is available
c. no; all the populations of an area form a community, a better choice is available
* d. yes; all of the above are correct

14. Which of the following levels of organization include the chemical and physical environment as well as the living components?
a. individual organisms
b. ecosystems
c. communities
d. populations

a. no; only the single organism
* b. yes; includes both the physical features and the organisms
c. no; only living populations
d. no; only interacting individuals of same species

15. A group of organisms of the same kind that live and reproduce together is called a
    a. community.
    b. species.
    c. population.
    d. ecosystem.

    a. no; a community is composed of many different kinds of organisms
    b. no; a species is a taxonomic concept and members of the same species may live in many widely separated habitats
    * c. yes; by definition, a population is a group of individuals of the same species that live together and interbreed
    d. no; an ecosystem is a more complex unit that consists of many different species and also includes facets of the physical environment

16. Metabolism refers to all but which of the following?
    a. the capacity of a cell to extract and convert energy from its surroundings
    b. transfer energy
    c. the use energy to carry on life process
    d. the ability to grow

    a. no; one of the aspects of metabolism
    b. no; metabolism involves transfer of energy
    c. no; metabolism uses energy to carry on life processes
    * d. yes; growth results from metabolism, but in a separate process

17. Which of the following is a "metabolic worker" that enables cells to put together or breakdown compounds?
    a. ATP
    b. DNA
    c. enzymes
    d. all of the above

    a. no; the energy currency of the cell that may be involved inmetabolism
    b. no; the molecules that carry the blueprints or instructions for life
    * c. yes; enzymes are organic catalysts that allow chemical compounds to be metabolized
    d. no; a common distractor; but only one of the above answers is correct

18. Metabolism refers to
    a. chemical reactions only.
    b. energy transfers within cells.
    c. utilization of energy.
    d. physical controls over cellular activities.

    a. no; this choice leaves out the physical aspects of metabolism
    * b. yes; the most appropriate of all the choices because it is the most inclusive, and metabolism does involve transfer of energy
    c. no; this choice omits energy production or catabolic processes
    d. no; this choice omits the chemical aspects of metabolism

19. Organisms that capture energy and make it available to all other forms of life are known as
    a. consumers.
    b. decomposers.
    c. producers.
    d. all of the above

    a. no; they ultimately get their energy from plants
    b. no; they get their energy from the protoplasm of other organisms
    * c. yes; they capture solar energy by photosynthesis and convert it into energy-rich compounds used by other forms of life
    d. no; a common distractor; only one of the above is correct

20. The entry points for the flow of energy throughout the biosphere are
    a. microorganisms.
    b. consumers.
    c. producers.
    d decomposers.

    a. no; although some microorganisms may serve as the foundation for some ecosystems (i.e. phytoplankton provide energy for many aquatic ecosystems)
    b. no; these organisms utilize food that is already captured
    * c. yes; through photosynthesis producers are able to capture and store energy that may be used throughout the biosphere
    d. no; decomposers represent a way for nutrients to be recycled in the ecosystem

21. Which of the following statements is false?
    a. Energy is the ability to do work.
    b. The kind of energy found in living things is different from the energy used in inanimate things.
    c. Energy binds atoms together.
    d. Energy must be expended to maintain a constant internal environment for living organisms.

    a. no; this statement is true
    * b. yes; this statement is false; the physical laws are constant throughout the universe, although there may be some physical laws that are applicable to living organisms
    c. no; this statement is true
    d. no; this statement is true; the maintenance of a steady-state internal environment is called homeostasis

22. Which of the following statements is false?
    a. Energy exhibits a continuous cycle throughout the ecosystem
    b. All energy captured from the sun flows through the environment.
    c. Materials such as nutrients cycle recycle throughout the biosphere
    d. Elephant dung contains both energy and nutrients that may become available to other organisms in the ecosystem.

\*  a. yes; this statement is false; energy exhibits a one-way flow through the biosphere and does not cycle

b. no; this statement is true; the energy that is captured by living organisms will eventually escape into the environment as low grade energy

c. no; this statement is true materials or nutrients such as chemical elements cycle through the various compartments in the biosphere, sometimes being found in the living organisms, other times in the atmosphere, hydrosphere or lithosphere

d. no; this statement is false; elephant dung contains undigested food that could be used as energy or nutrients by organisms such as dung beetles.

23. The term used to describe the interconnection of all living organisms to each other is a
a. web.
b. network.
c. chain, such as a food chain.
d. ladder.

\*  a. yes; the web is an appropriate symbol
b. no; not used, but could be an appropriate choice
c. no; food chains are too limited and simplistic
d. no; although this symbolism is partially used in some ecological considerations of energy found in nature

24. The great pattern of organization in nature is maintained by
a. flow of energy from the sun.
b. the annual climatic changes.
c. the action of animals in the control of nature.
d. the activity of microorganisms.

\*  a. yes; essentially all energy comes from the sun
b. no; may affect natural phenomena, but not responsible for its organization
c. no; may contribute, but other factors are at work
d. no; important controlling factor in some facets of nature

25. The compound most intimately associated with energy transfer in living organisms is
a. oxygen.
b. ATP.
c. glucose.
d. fat.

a. no; anaerobic respiration involves the liberation of energy without free oxygen
\*  b. yes; adenosine triphosphate has high energy phosphate bonds which can be transferred from one compound to another
c. no; glucose may function as a source of energy, but is not a transfer agent
d. no; fats represent an effective way to store, but not to transfer energy

26. Homeostasis is the
a. maintenance of a constant internal environment.
b. application of a positive feedback system in living organisms.
c. use of the buffer system of the body.
d. recovery from stress.

\*  a. yes; by definition homeostasis involves the maintenance of a dynamic equilibrium
b. no; negative feedback systems are usually involved
c. no; only an example of one facet of a homeostatic system
d. no; homeostasis may be involved in recovery, but this concept is more appropriately termed resiliency

27. Homeostasis
a. is part of the internal control over body function.
b. is exhibited by inanimate objects as well as living things.
c. may only be exhibited by living organisms.
d. is the general name given to the responses an organism makes to changes in the external environment.

\*  a. yes; it is a system that maintains a constant internal environment (allows minor changes within prescribed limits)
b. no; inanimate objects only reflect changes in the external environments
c. no; it is possible with the help of instrumentation and machines to maintain a constant environment
d. no; organisms use the nervous system to sense and respond to the external environment; homeostasis refers to control over the internal environment

28. Which stage in the metamorphosis of a moth involves extensive remodeling and reorganization of moth tissue
a. egg
b. adult
c. larva
d. pupa

a. no; a stage of inactivity
b. no; the organism is mature
c. no; a period of active growth and development
\*  d. yes; may involve change in appearance, habitat, life style, etc.

29. In which stage of metamorphosis does reproduction occur?
a. egg
b. pupa
c. adult
d. larvae

a. no; reproduction has already occurred
b. no; a period of reorganization and remodeling
\*  c. yes; only adults may reproduce
d. no; too immature, the sex organs have not yet developed

30. An agent used to kill an insect pest
    a. may target any stage in the life cycle.
    b. might prevent a larvae from completing metamorphosis.
    c. could function by preventing reproduction by the adults.
    d. all of the above

    a. no; a partial answer; a more complete answer is available
    b. no; a partial answer; a more complete answer is available
    c. no; a partial answer; a more complete answer is available
    * d. yes; all of the above answers are correct

31. Light-colored moths
    a. are protected during the day by resting on light-colored backgrounds.
    b. are males, while dark-colored moths are female
    c. have an advantage in some environments and a disadvantage in others
    d. both (a) and (c), but not (b)

    a. no; a partial answer; a more complete answer is available
    b. no; a moth's color is not controlled by sex
    c. no; a partial answer; a more complete answer is available
    * d. yes; both (a) and (c) are true, but (b) is not

32. Most mutations are
    a. harmful.
    b. beneficial.
    c. neutral.
    d. none of the above

    * a. yes; any change in a functional gene that has withstood natural selection over evolutionary time is most likely to be non-adaptive and therefore harmful
    b. no; there may be a number of mutations that do not have any harmful effect but they would be hard to identify
    c. no; if most mutations were beneficial then organism's phenotypes (physical characteristics) would be highly volatile and organisms would be subjected to continual change
    d. no; choice (a) is correct

33. Which of the following is the least inclusive of those taxonomic categories listed?
    a. class
    b. family
    c. phylum
    d. order

    a. no; all related orders belong to the same class
    * b. yes; all related genera (not listed) are placed in the same family
    c. no; all related classes belong to the same phylum
    d. no; all related families belong to the same order

34. The plural for genus is
    a. genus.
    b. geni.
    c. genuses.
    d. genera.

    a. no; not the plural form
    b. no; not the plural form
    c. no; not the plural form
    * d. yes; the plural of genus is genera

35. Members of closely related families are placed in the same
    a. class.
    b. order.
    c. genus.
    d. phylum.

    a. no; too inclusive
    * b. yes; related families are placed in the same order
    c. no; related genera are placed in the same family
    d. no; too inclusive

36. The simplest forms of life belong to the Kingdom _____.
    a. Plantae
    b. Fungi
    c. Protista
    d. Monera

    a. no; eukaryotic, multicellular
    b. no; eukaryotic, multicellular
    c. no; eukaryotic, unicellular
    * d. yes; prokaryotic, lack a nucleus and membrane-bound organelles

37. Which of the following is a more accurate characterization of evolution?
    a. It is the result of natural selection.
    b. It is the result of mutation.
    c. It is the result of changes in the environment.
    d. It results in changes in gene frequency in subsequent generations.

    a. no; a partial answer; a more complete answer is available
    b. no; a partial answer; a more complete answer is available
    c. no; a partial answer; a more complete answer is available
    * d. yes; the other three distractors contain elements necessary for evolution and are partially correct; but regardless of the cause, evolution results in changes in gene frequencies in subsequent populations

38. Charles Darwin cited breeding experiment with _____ to show how selection could occur in a population.
    a. pigeons
    b. cats
    c. fruit flies
    d. dogs

  \*
a. yes; a common pet used in competitive shows, similar to cat and dog shows
b. no; available, but not used by Darwin
c. no; used by Thomas H. Morgan and others in the twentieth century in genetic research
d. no; a commonly used example but not used by Darwin

39. Which of the following points apply to the process of evolution?
a. More organisms are produced than can possibly survive.
b. Differential reproduction is a form of natural selection.
c. Over time the characteristics of a species may change.
d. all of the above

a. no; a partial answer; a large number of organisms may lead to a decline in necessary support systems.
b. no; a partial answer; the environment (through natural selection) determines which members of a population will have the greatest and least genetic impact on the next generation.
c. no; a partial answer; this statement could be used as a short definition for evolution.
  \*
d. yes; all statements are true.

40. A tentative explanation to account for an observation is a _____.
a. theory
b. hypothesis
c. principle
d. law

a. no; a generalization used to explain a series of observations
  \*
b. yes; a statement, often in form of a question that can be tested
c. no; a generalization used to explain a series of observations
d. no; a generalization used to explain a series of observations

41. A scientific theory
a. is a testable explanation about the cause(s) of a broad range of related phenomena.
b. is a question formulated to explain natural phenomena.
c. can be verified with certainty by scientific experimentation.
d. is not as broad as a scientific law or principle.

  \*
a. yes; by definition
b. no; this distractor describes a hypothesis
c. no; it may be falsified but not proven in all possible cases
d. no; there are few principles or laws that are as far-reaching as the theory of evolution, and physicists often apply the term law to physical phenomena, such as the laws of motion, Boyle's law, Charles's law, or Ohm's law

42. Biology is based upon
a. observations.
b. hypotheses and predictions.
c. tests and experiments.
d. all of the above

a. no; a partial answer; a more complete answer is available
b. no; a partial answer; a more complete answer is available
c. no; a partial answer; a more complete answer is available
  \*
d. yes; all of the above answers are correct

# CHAPTER 2

# CHEMICAL FOUNDATIONS FOR CELLS

1.  The process of photosynthesis is more than
    _____ years old.
    a.  100,000,000
    b.  300,000,000
    c.  1 billion
    d.  3 billion

    a.  no; much older
    b.  no; much older
    c.  no; much older
    * d.  yes; at least 3 billion years

2.  We began using synthetic pesticides in
    a.  the early 1800s.
    b.  1905.
    c.  1925.
    d.  1945.

    a.  no; too early
    b.  no; too early
    c.  no; too early
    * d.  yes; in 1945

3.  Most insecticides act upon the pest's _____
    system.
    a.  digestive
    b.  nervous
    c.  circulatory
    d.  respiratory

    a.  no; another system is more often attacked
        by pesticides
    * b.  yes; the pesticides kill by affecting the
        nervous system
    c.  no; another system is more often attacked
        by pesticides
    d.  no; another system is more often attacked
        by pesticides

4.  Ions are
    a.  charged atoms or molecules that have
        gained or lost electrons.
    b.  radioactive isotopes that give off alpha,
        beta, or gamma radiation.
    c.  electrically neutral fragments of a molecule
        that has been split apart.
    d.  both (a) and (c) are correct, but (b) is
        incorrect

    * a.  yes; the loss of an electron makes them
        positive or cations, and the gain of an
        electron makes them negative or anions
    b.  no; isotopes give off radiation and may or
        may not be ionized
    c.  no; ions are charged particles
    d.  no; (b) and (c) are incorrect, while (a) is
        correct

5.  There are ___ naturally occurring elements
    found on earth.
    a.  forty-seven
    b.  sixty-three
    c.  ninety-two
    d.  114

    a.  no; too few
    b.  no; too few
    * c.  yes; there are 92 naturally occurring
        elements
    d.  no; too many

6.  Which of the following is a trace element needed
    only in a very small quantity?
    a.  hydrogen
    b.  oxygen
    c.  copper
    d.  nitrogen

    a.  no; one of the four major elements
    b.  no; one of the four major elements
    * c.  yes; used in extremely small amounts as in
        enzymes but is essential for total normal
        growth
    d.  no; one of the four major elements

7.  A compound is
    a.  a physical mixture of two or more elements.
    b.  a chemical combination of elements whose
        proportions do not vary.
    c.  any substance that will dissolve in water.
    d.  the smallest unit of matter.

    a.  no; called a mixture, such as the physical
        combination of salt and sugar
    * b.  yes; the combination is the result of a
        chemical reaction and the proportion of the
        ingredients do not vary
    c.  no; individual elements as well as
        molecules may dissolve in water, and some
        will not dissolve in water
    d.  no; the smallest unit of matter is an atom

8. The half-life of a radioactive substance
   a. is the length of time it takes for one-half of a radioactive sample to undergo decay.
   b. cannot be modified by heat, pressure, chemical reactions, or other known pressures.
   c. enables us to date artifacts and fossils with a high degree of precision.
   d. all of the above

   a. no; a partial answer; a more complete answer is available
   b. no; a partial answer; a more complete answer is available
   c. no; a partial answer; a more complete answer is available
   * d. yes; all of the answers are complete

9. Which of the following is *not* a use of a radioactive isotope as a tracer?
   a. uncovering the details of photosynthesis using radioactive carbon.
   b. using uranium isotope to date the age of the earth
   c. injecting radioactive iodine to analyze thyroid function
   d. the use of radioisotope to investigate the characteristic metabolism of cancer cells

   a. no; an example of use of an isotope to track or study normal activities using a radioactive isotope to locate and follow their reactions
   * b. yes; the use of radioactive dating only tells how old a particular feature is but is not a use of a radioactive tracer
   c. no; an example of use of an isotope to track or study normal activities using a radioactive isotope to locate and follow their reaction
   d. no; an example of use of an isotope to track or study normal activities using a radioactive isotope to locate and follow their reactions

10. Which of the following statements is false?
    a. A mole of glucose weighs more than a mole of water.
    b. The simplest atom is hydrogen.
    c. Electrons found near the center of the atom have the highest energy levels.
    d. Hydrogen is the only atom to have a naturally occurring atom with an orbital with two electrons.

    a. no; this statement is true
    b. no; this statement is true
    * c. yes; this statement is false, the closer an electron is to the center of an atom, the lower is its energy
    d. no; this statement is true

11. How many electrons does sodium have in its outermost shell if it has eleven protons?
    a. one
    b. two
    c. four
    d. six

    * a. yes; two in the first orbital, eight in the second and one in the third
    b. no; does not conform to the number of electrons/orbitals
    c. no; does not conform to the number of electrons/orbitals
    d. no; does not conform to the number of electrons/orbitals

12. Chlorine with an atomic number of 17 would be expected to have ___ electrons in its outer shell.
    a. one
    b. three
    c. five
    d. seven

    a. no; not enough
    b. no; not enough
    c. no; not enough
    * d. yes; two in the first shell, eight in the second, and seven in the third

13. Which of the following statements is true?
    a. There are two ionic bonds in water.
    b. There are two polar covalent bonds in water.
    c. There is one covalent and one ionic bond in water.
    d. Electrons are less attracted to oxygen than hydrogen.

    a. no; the water molecule has only covalent polar bonds
    * b. yes; the hydrogen bonds produce a slight polar bond
    c. no; both bonds are polar
    d. no; electrons are more attracted to hydrogen than water

14. Which of the following statements is false?
    a. Polar molecules are attracted to water and are hydrophilic.
    b. Water tends to repel oil and nonpolar substances.
    c. Water tends to stabilize temperature of substances that contain it.
    d. Only during evaporation do hydrogen bonds in water break apart.

    a. no; this statement is true
    b. no; this statement is true
    c. no; this statement is true
    * d. yes; this statement is false; when water is in a liquid form, hydrogen bonds will break and form continuously

15. Which of these terms is *not* appropriate to describe water?
    a. solvent
    b. covalent
    c. cohesive
    d. nonpolar

    a. no; water is sometimes called a universal solvent
    b. no; water has covalent bonds, not ionic bonds
    c. no; water tends to cohere to other water molecules, resulting in surface tension
    * d. yes; water is polar, not nonpolar

16. A pH of 3 is ___ times more acidic than a pH of 5.
    a. 2
    b. 10
    c. 20
    d. 100

    a. no; not great enough difference
    b. no; not great enough difference
    c. no; not great enough difference
* d. yes; pH is a logarithmic scale to the base ten so that a difference of two is actually a difference of $10^2$ or 100

17. All forms of matter are made up of one or more naturally occurring fundamental substances called
    a. atoms.
    b. molecules.
    c. compounds.
    d. none of the above

    a. no; the smallest unit of matter unique to an element
    b. no; a unit consisting of two or more atoms of the same element
    c. no; a unit consisting of two or more atoms of different elements
* d. yes; none of the above is correct; the answer is element, the fundamental substance

18. The negatively charged subatomic particle is the
    a. nucleus.
    b. neutron.
    c. electron.
    d. proton.

    a. no; contains neutron and proton
    b. no; uncharged subatomic particle
* c. yes; negatively charged subatomic particle
    d. no; positively charged subatomic particle

19. Isotopes of an element differ from other isotopes of the same element by the
    a. number of protons.
    b. number of neutrons.
    c. functions of the isotope in a biological organism.
    d. chemical properties of the isotope.

    a. no; atoms with the same number of protons are the same and fit in the same place (iso/ tope = equal/place) in a periodic table
* b. yes; isotopes have different atomic weights due to a difference in the number of neutrons
    c. no; isotopes behave the same biologically
    d. no; isotopes have same number of protons so they behave the same chemically, but not physically

20. If a person were injected with some radioactive iodine, it would appear in a radioisotope scan of the ___ gland.
    a. pancreas
    b. adrenal
    c. thyroid
    d. parotid

    a. no; not a site for iodine metabolism
    b. no; neither the adrenal medulla nor cortex concentrates iodine
* c. yes; iodine is an element used in the manufacture of thyroid hormones
    d. no; the parotid gland is one of the salivary glands and does not use or concentrate iodine

21. In an excited molecule,
    a. the atoms making up the molecule become disassociated.
    b. an electron moves to an orbital closer to the nucleus of one of the atoms in the molecule.
    c. an electron is ejected from an inner to an outer electron shell.
    d. the nucleus captures a new neutron.

    a. no; this occurs in ionization
    b. no; this would reduce the energy in the molecule
* c. yes; it returns to ground (unexcited) state when the electron returns to its normal site closer to the nucleus
    d. no; neutron capture may induce radioactivity but is not the same as excitation

22. In ionic bonding, the electrons of two or more atoms are
    a. shared.
    b. exchanged.
    c. lost or gained.
    d. attracted to positive charges of other atoms.

    a. no; typical of covalent bonding
    b. no; does not affect the characteristics of the atoms
* c. yes; the two atoms become ionized
    d. no; this happens in the formation of polar bonds

23. Which of the following compounds could be used as an example of an ionic bond?
    a. hydrochloric acid
    b. glucose
    c. molecular nitrogen
    d. proteins

* a. yes; the molecule will dissociate to form ions
    b. no; the carbon, hydrogen, and oxygen share electrons
    c. no; the nitrogen atoms share electrons
    d. no; the atoms are bound together by sharing electrons

24. Hydrophobic molecules tend to be
    a. inorganic minerals.
    b. nonpolar.
    c. ionic.
    d. water-soluble.

    a. no; tend to form ionic compounds that would be water-soluble
* b. yes; do not mix with water
    c. no; readily dissociate in water, therefore hydrophilic
    d. no; water-soluble substances dissolve in water easily

25. Normal rainfall has a pH of _____.
    a. 3.8
    b. 5.6
    c. 7.0
    d. 8.1

    a. no; but "acid precipitation" may be even
       more acidic
*   b. yes; the pH of rain is slightly acid
    c. no; a pH of 7 is neutral; dissolved materials
       make rain acidic
    d. no; slightly basic, too much so for normal
       rainfall

26. Which of the following atoms or molecules
    found in the body do not contain carbon as a
    basic element?
    a. proteins
    b. fats or lipids
    c. nucleic acids
    d. minerals

    a. no; proteins are composed of amino acids
       that contain carbon
    b. no; fats and lipids have a central carbon
       backbone
    c. no; nucleic acids contain carbon atoms
*   d. yes; minerals are inorganic compounds that
       generally do not have carbon atoms

27. Which of the following includes the others?
    a. atoms
    b. electrons
    c. protons
    d. neutrons

*   a. yes; atoms are composed of electrons,
       protons, and neutrons
    b. no; one of the three subatomic particles
    c. no; one of the three subatomic particles
    d. no; one of the three subatomic particles

28. Any substance that cannot be broken down into
    a different substance is a(n)
    a. atom.
    b. molecule.
    c. compound.
    d. element.

    a. no; the smallest unit of matter that is unique
       to a particular element
    b. no; molecules are composed of two or more
       atoms
    c. no; composed of two or more elements
*   d. yes; the stem is the definition of an element

29. The simplest atom is an atom of
    a. oxygen.
    b. hydrogen.
    c. helium.
    d. carbon.

    a. no; the largest of the four elements listed
*   b. yes; consists of one proton and one electron
    c. no; consists of an atom with two protons,
       two neutrons, and two electrons
    d. no; consists of an atom with six protons,
       six neutrons, and six electrons

30. Which of the following elements is found to be
    the most common in the earth's crust?
    a. iron
    b. oxygen
    c. silicon
    d. nitrogen

    a. no; but the most common in the earth's core
*   b. yes; highest concentration in the earth's
       crust is the form of silicon dioxide and
       oxygenated compounds such as nitrates,
       sulfates, and phosphates
    c. no; only one atom of silicon to two atoms of
       oxygen in sand
    d. no; although it is the most common element
       in the atmosphere

31. Which of the following does not belong?
    a. liquid
    b. gas
    c. element
    d. solid

    a. no; a physical state of matter
    b. no; a physical state of matter
*   c. yes; not one of the physical states of matter
    d. no; a physical state of matter

32. A molecule of pure water
    a. consists of atoms of different elements.
    b. is a physical mixture of hydrogen and
       oxygen.
    c. is an example of matter with the same
       number of atoms of different elements.
    d. is a neutral ion composed of two parts
       oxygen, one part hydrogen.

*   a. yes; it is a molecule composed of two atoms
       of hydrogen, one part oxygen
    b. no; mixtures can be made in any
       proportion, but water is a chemical
       combination of hydrogen and oxygen in a
       two to one ratio
    c. no; water is an example of matter, but the
       number of atoms of hydrogen and oxygen
       are not equal
    d. no; ions are electrically charged fragments
       of molecules, and the proportion of atoms is
       wrong

33. The negatively charged part of an atom is the
    a. nucleus.
    b. neutron.
    c. proton.
    d. electron.

    a. no; contains both neutrons and protons,
       neither of which is negatively charged
    b. no; neutrons have no charge
    c. no; protons are positively charged
*   d. yes; electrons are negatively charged
       subatomic particles

34. The only atom that has a nucleus with no
    neutrons is
    a. argon.
    b. carbon.
    c. oxygen.
    d. hydrogen.

a. no; an inert gas with many neutrons in its nucleus
b. no; an element commonly with six neutrons
c. no; an element commonly with eight neutrons
* d. yes; the common form of hydrogen has only one proton and no neutrons in its nucleus

35. Which of the following statements about an atom is true?
a. The atomic number refers to the number of protons and neutrons it has.
b. The mass number refers to the number of protons and electrons it has.
c. The atomic number is the same as its atomic weight.
d. The atomic number is equal to the number of protons it has.

a. no; the number of protons and neutrons refers to its atomic weight
b. no; electrons are not used in calculating mass number
c. no; these are different numbers except for hydrogen which has an atomic number and an atomic weight of 1
* d. yes; the atomic number is determined by the number of protons an atom has

36. Which of the following statements is false?
a. The atomic number controls the chemical characteristics of an element.
b. The weight of an electron does not contribute significantly to the atomic mass number.
c. The electron is found outside the nucleus of an atom.
d. An element can lose, gain, or share protons.

a. no; the statement is true; the number of protons determines the chemical nature of any element
b. no; the statement is true; the atomic mass number includes only the contribution of the particles in the nucleus
c. no; the statement is true; the electron is in continual motion in orbit around the nucleus
* d. yes; this statement is false; only the electrons can be lost, gained, or shared.

37. The number of ___ determines the number of electrons in an atom.
a. bonds
b. protons
c. neutrons
d. orbitals

a. no; bonds are characteristic of compounds
* b. yes; the number of protons and electrons are the same so that an atom is electrically neutral
c. no; the number of neutrons does not affect the number of protons
d. no; the number of orbitals determines the maximum number of electrons an atom may hold

38. Which of the following statements is true?
a. All isotopes have the same number of protons.
b. All isotopes have the same number of neutrons.
c. Al isotopes are radioactive.
d. All isotopes give off subatomic particles or gamma radiation.

* a. yes; the number of protons determines the chemical nature of the element and its position in the periodic table
b. no; the number of neutrons can vary between isotopes of the same element
c. no; there are stable isotopes that are not radioactive
d. no; only radioactive isotopes give off subatomic particles (alpha, beta, neutron, or gamma radiation)

39. Orbitals
a. are pathways for the movement of protons.
b. have room for one or two electrons.
c. are mechanisms for the release of radiation.
d. are synonymous for electron shells.

a. no; the protons remain inside the nucleus of an atom
* b. yes; by definition
c. no; has no impact on release of radiation because that is controlled in the nucleus
d. no; electron shells contain varying number of orbitals

40. The maximum number of orbitals in most shells around a nucleus is
a. one.
b. two.
c. three.
d. four.

a. no; more orbitals in a shell
b. no; more orbitals in a shell
c. no; more orbitals in a shell
* d. yes; four orbitals with a maximum of eight electrons

41. The innermost shell around an atomic nucleus has a maximum of ___ orbitals.
a. one.
b. two.
c. three.
d. four.

a. no; more orbitals
* b. yes; the innermost shell has two orbitals
c. no; less orbitals
d. no; less orbitals

42. All isotopes of a particular element
a. behave the same chemically and biologically but not the same physically.
b. are radioactive.
c. have the same number of electrons as neutrons.
d. can be detected using a Geiger counter or scintillation detector.

* a. yes; the physical difference allows a way to distinguish between isotopes while the biological and chemical similarity allows them to be used as tracers
b. no; many isotopes are stable, but difference in the number of neutrons allows their detection by a mass spectrometer
c. no; there is no relationship between the number of neutrons and electrons even though the number of protons and electrons are the same
d. no; these instruments only detect radioactive isotopes by the ionization their radioactive decay produces

43. Position emission tomography (PET) involves
a. a series of X-ray photographs at different levels of an organ.
b. the use of a cobalt isotope in radiation therapy of some tumors.
c. a scanner that maps the deposition of isotopes in the body.
d. internal scanning of the digestive tract.

a. no; this is known as a CAT scan
b. no; this is one of the approaches used in radiation therapy
* c. yes; PET follows tracers that have been administered by the radiation they give off
d. no; it can be used anywhere a tracer is found in the body

44. Which of the following atomic numbers indicates the element with the most electrons in its outer shell?
a. 5
b. 7
c. 10
d. 15

a. no; the outer shell has three electrons
b. no; the outer shell has five electrons
* c. yes; the outer shell has eight electrons
d. no; the outer shell has five electrons

45. The atoms in molecules of $O_2$ or $N_2$ are held together by
a. ionic bonds.
b. polar covalent bonds.
c. nonpolar covalent bonds.
d. hydrogen bonds.

a. no; the atoms do not ionize but share electrons
b. no; neither part of these diatomic molecules is more electronegative than the other
* c. yes; these atoms share electrons
d. no; these atoms are not bound together by hydrogen bonds

46. The two parallel strands of DNA are held together by _____ bonds.
a. ionic
b. hydrogen
c. nonpolar
d. covalent

a. no; electrons are not lost or gained in this bond
* b. yes; a negative atom of the DNA strand is weakly attracted to a hydrogen atom of the other DNA strand
c. no; nonpolar bonds are not involved
d. no; a better choice is available

47. A pH of 3 is _____ times as acidic as a pH of 7.
a. 4
b. 20
c. 100
d. 10,000

a. no; higher
b. no; higher
c. no; higher
* d. yes; pH is a logarithmic scale so that a difference of 4 is equivalent to a difference of 10,000

48. Which of the following has the lowest pH?
a. lemon juice
b. bananas
c. black coffee
d. saliva

* a. yes; lemon juice is actually citric acid and has a pH of 3
b. no; has a pH of 4.6, and there is one choice lower
c. no; has a pH of 5, and there are two choices lower
d. no; has a pH range of 6.2–7.4, and all other choices have lower pH values

49. The range for the pH of human blood and most tissues is
a. 5.35–5.45.
b. 6.35–6.45.
c. 7.35–7.45.
d. 8.35–8.45.

a. no; too acidic
b. no; too acidic
* c. yes; the normal range
d. no; too alkalinic

50. Electric power plants produce acid precipitation because of the _____ they release.
a. sulfur dioxide
b. carbon monoxide
c. nitrous oxide
d. carbon dioxide

* a. yes; sulfur dioxide combines with water to form sulfuric acid
b. no; not a source of acid precipitation
c. no; nitrous oxide will combine with water to form nitric acid, but a power plant is not the most common source
d. no; not an acid producer

51.  When acids react with a base, a(n) ___ is formed.
   a.  organic acid
   b.  salt
   c.  solute
   d.  buffer

   a.  no; this reaction will not produce another acid
*  b.  yes; salt and water are produced in this reaction
   c.  no; not a specific answer, but the substance produced could become a solute in the water produced by the reaction
   d.  no; buffers are chemicals that control pH

52.  The N—H bond in an amino acid is an example of a(n)
   a.  ionic bond.
   b.  hydrogen bond.
   c.  polar covalent bond
*  d.  nonpolar covalent bond.

   a.  no; neither nitrogen nor hydrogen loses or gains an electron
   b.  no; if the hydrogen bond was electrically attracted to some other atom, it would be a hydrogen bond
*  c.  yes; there is a differential pull on the shared electrons between nitrogen and hydrogen
   d.  no; the atoms of nitrogen and hydrogen exert a different amount of attraction for the shared electrons

# CHAPTER 3

# CELL STRUCTURE AND FUNCTION

1. All cells are characterized by all but which of the following?
   a. nucleus
   b. plasma membrane
   c. cytoplasm
   d. ribosomes

   * a. correct; prokaryotes have DNA molecules, but no definite nucleus
   b. incorrect; all cells have plasma membrane to control internal composition
   c. incorrect; all cells have cytoplasm (even prokaryotes)
   d. incorrect; all cells have ribosomes (even prokaryotes)

2. Which of the following is *not* one of the premises of the cell theory?
   a. All living organisms are made of cells.
   b. Only plants and animals are composed of cells.
   c. Cells come from preexisting cells.
   d. Cells are the basic structural and functional units of life.

   a. incorrect; this part of the cell theory
   * b. correct; fungi are multicellular and monera and some protista are unicellular
   c. incorrect; this is part of the cell theory
   d. incorrect; this is part of the cell theory

3. In 1665, Robert Hooke saw a _____ in a microscope and named it a cell.
   a. red blood cell
   b. bacterium
   c. cork cell
   d. liver cell

   a. no
   b. no
   * c. yes
   d. no

4. Which of the following gives the greatest magnification?
   a. scanning electron microscope
   b. transmitting electron microscope
   c. compound light microscope
   d. interference contrast microscope

   a. no; very useful to study surface characteristics
   * b. yes; gives the greatest magnification
   c. no; maximum magnification is around 2,000x
   d. no; maximum magnification is around 2,000x

5. The most widely accepted current concept that best explains the functioning of a plasma membrane is a
   a. protein–lipid sandwich.
   b. lipid bilayer.
   c. fluid mosaic model.
   d. porous phospholipid lining.

   a. no, the membrane is made of both, but not accurately described as a sandwich
   b. no, not a complete explanation
   * c. yes, most recent explanation
   d. no, not a complete concept

6. Cellular gates or channels are
   a. openings through membrane proteins.
   b. spaces between cells.
   c. gaps in the nuclear envelope.
   d. none of the above

   * a. yes; their characteristics are influenced by the protein
   b. no; gap junctions may be involved
   c. no; pores may exist, but not usually referred to as gates or channels
   d. no; one of the above is correct

7. Which of the following organelles is involved in lipid synthesis?
   a. Golgi bodies
   b. lysosomes
   c. endoplasmic reticulum
   d. mitochondria

   a. no; involved in cellular secretion
   b. no; involved in cellular digestion
   c. yes; involved in both lipid and protein synthesis
   * d. no; involved in cellular respiration

8. Which of the following is one of the types of vesicles produced by the Golgi body?
   a. lysosomes
   b. ribosomes
   c. nucleolus
   d. chromatin

   * a. yes; contains digestive enzymes that destroy wastes and foreign particles
   b. no; associated with endoplasmic reticulum
   c. no; RNA-containing organelle in the nucleus
   d. no; nuclear material containing DNA

9. Which of the following is NOT associated with the internal transport system of a cell?
   a. vacuoles
   b. mitochondria
   c. microsomes
   d. endoplasmic reticulum

   a. incorrect; formed during endocytosis
   * b. correct; organelle associated with cellular respiration
   c. incorrect; formed as buds from endoplasmic reticulum and contain enzymes
   d. incorrect; the cytomembrane system through which many substances travel

10. Which organelle of a cell is shaped like a stack of pancakes?
    a. Golgi body
    b. mitochondrion
    c. chromatin
    d. nuclear envelope

    * a. yes; often molecules are packaged in secretory vesicles that break off from the Golgi body
    b. no; has an internal membrane but shaped more like a hot dog roll or a sphere
    c. no; a dispersed threadlike material filling the nucleus
    d. no; a double membrane surrounding the nucleus

11. The stacks of disks containing chlorophyll in a chloroplast are the
    a. grana.
    b. microfilaments.
    c. plastids.
    d. stroma.

    * a. yes; contains pigments and enzymes associated with photosynthesis
    b. no; part of the cytoskeleton
    c. no; name given to pigmented organelles in plants such as chloroplasts
    d. no; fluid surrounding the grana

12. Which organelle is characterized by possessing pores?
    a. nuclear envelope
    b. mitochondria
    c. chloroplasts
    d. nucleolus

    * a. yes; found in the double-walled membrane that allows material to enter and leave the nucleus
    b. no; pores are not found in this organelle
    c. no; pores are not found in this organelle
    d. no; pores are not found in this organelle

13. If the forty-six genetic molecules in a human cell were stretched out end-to-end, they would extend about
    a. 1 inch.
    b. 5 inches.
    c. 15 inches.
    d. 40 inches.

    a. no; too short
    b. no; too short
    c. no; too short
    * d. yes; about one meter

14. Phagocytic cells
    a. eat cells and cellular debris.
    b. are used in asexual reproduction.
    c. do not contain a nucleus.
    d. are cells equipped with locomotive organs such as cilia and flagella.

    * a. yes; such as leucocytes
    b. no; not used in reproduction
    c. no; they contain a nucleus
    d. no; although many move by pseudopods

15. Amyloplasts
    a. have no pigments.
    b. are abundant in potato tubers and many seeds.
    c. often store starch grains.
    d. all of the above

    a. no; a partial answer; a more complete answer is available
    b. no; a partial answer; a more complete answer is available
    c. no; a partial answer; a more complete answer is available
    * d. yes; all of other answers are correct

16. Large storage structures often found in plant cells are
    a. Golgi bodies.
    b. central vacuoles.
    c. mitochondria.
    d. plastids.

    a. no; an organ that produces many kinds of products often for secretion
    * b. yes; the central vacuole stores many things
    c. no; the site for ATP production during aerobic respiration
    d. no; bodies that usually contain pigments

17. The microtubule organizing centers are associated with the
    a. mitochondrion.
    b. central vacuole.
    c. ribosome.
    d. centriole.

a. no; another organelle
b. no; another organelle
c. no; another organelle
* d. yes; the centriole is involved in organizing the microtubules during mitosis.

18. _____ are found in flagella and cilia.
   a. Microtubules
   b. Intermediate filaments
   c. Microfilaments
   d. Spindle fibers

* a. yes; there is a definite pattern of microtubules found inside the filaments
   b. no; part of the cytoskeleton in some specialized animal cells
   c. no; found in muscle fibers
   d. no; involved in moving chromosomes during mitosis

19. Which of the following does *not* have cell walls?
   a. plant cells
   b. fungal cells
   c. bacteria
   d. animal cells

   a. no; have cell walls that give them shape
   b. no; have cell walls that give them shape
   c. no; cell walls give shape to bacteria
* d. yes; do not have cell walls

20. Which of the following statements is false?
   a. Different cells in the body have the same environments.
   b. Different cells have different structures and functions.
   c. Cells are able to control what enters and leaves through their membranes.
   d. Cells control their own internal activities.

* a. yes; this statement is false because cells live in different environments (for example, liver, muscle, and bone marrow all present different environments)
   b. no; this statement is true
   c. no; this statement is true
   d. no; this statement is true

21. The cells of higher organisms differ from a bacterial cell by
   a. the presence of DNA.
   b. their size, complexity, and many isolated organelles.
   c. the presence of a plasma membrane.
   d. the presence of a semifluid substance called cytoplasm.

   a. no; both possess DNA, but in the eukaryotes the DNA is enclosed by a membrane that forms a nucleus
* b. yes; eukaryotic cells are much more complex and larger and have many types of organelles
   c. no; both have plasma membranes to control what goes into and out of the cells
   d. no; both bacteria and eukaryotic cells have cytoplasm

22. Which of the following statements is false?
   a. Some cells are large enough to be seen by the unaided eye.
   b. Cells with infoldings and outfoldings of their plasma membranes are able to move substances more rapidly in and out of cells.
   c. All cells are round, hexagonal, or shaped like cubes.
   d. Eukaryotic cells have a central nucleus that controls activities throughout the cell.

   a. no; the statement is true, and cells in some fruits or some eggs are large enough to be seen by the naked eye
   b. no; the statement is true; those cells with large surface-to-volume ratios efficiently transfer materials in and out of cells
* c. yes; this statement is false; because nerve cells and muscle cells are often long and fiberlike
   d. no; the statement is true; eukaryotic cells have a central nucleus that controls the activities of the cell

23. The first type of cells ever seen were ___ cells observed through a compound microscope by Robert Hooke.
   a. red blood
   b. fish sperm
   c. cork
   d. human skin

   a. no; make another choice
   b. no; make another choice
* c. yes; cells from the bark of the cork oak tree
   d. no; make another choice

24. The first cells were seen in the ___ century.
   a. seventeenth
   b. eighteenth
   c. nineteenth
   d. twentieth

* a. yes; the first cells were seen more than 300 years ago
   b. no; earlier than the eighteenth century
   c. no; earlier than the nineteenth century
   d. no; earlier than the twentieth century

25. The ultimate limit of a light microscope's ability to show small objects is
   a. the amount of light that can be made available.
   b. the maximum magnification is about 100 times the object's actual size.
   c. the ability to resolve between two closely placed objects.
   d. the ability of the object viewed to transmit light.

   a. no; light brightness is not usually a limiting factor
   b. no; maximum magnification approximately 2,000 times
* c. yes; the margins of two close objects begin to blur together (objects appear larger but not clearer)
   d. no; opaque substances can be magnified

26. Which of the following organelles are filled with digestive enzymes?
    a. Golgi bodies
    b. lysosomes
    c. ribosomes
    d. mitochondria

    a. no; primarily involved in formation and processing polypeptides
    * b. yes; breaks down large molecules and cellular debris
    c. no; involved in the production of polypeptides
    d. no; the site where ATP is produced

27. Which of the following organelles would be most likely found in secretory cells?
    a. mitochondria
    b. lysosome
    c. nucleoli
    d. Golgi bodies

    a. no; involved in production of ATP and would be common in brain neurons and skeletal muscles
    b. no; used in digestion and would be found in leukocytes
    c. no; nuclear organelle rich in RNA
    * d. yes; Golgi bodies are involved in secretion and would be common in exocrine and endocrine glands

28. DNA is stored in the
    a. nucleus.
    b. nucleolus.
    c. endoplasmic reticulum.
    d. vesicles.

    * a. yes; found on chromosomes in the nucleus
    b. no; the site for RNA, not DNA
    c. no; the site for synthesis of polypeptides and lipids
    d. no; temporary storage sites in the cytoplasm

29. Ribosomes are formed in the
    a. chromosomes.
    b. endoplasmic reticulum.
    c. Golgi bodies.
    d. nucleolus.

    a. no; chromosomes are the sites for genes
    b. no; ribosomes are found lining the rough endoplasmic reticulum where polypeptides are synthesized
    c. no; Golgi bodies modify and secrete polypeptides
    * d. yes; the nucleolus constructs polypeptides and subunits of ribosomes

30. Which of the following is *not* part of the cytomembrane system?
    a. Golgi apparatus
    b. chromatin material
    c. endoplasmic reticulum
    d. certain vesicles

    a. no; part of the cytomembrane system
    * b. yes; the threadlike material that condenses to form a chromosome found in the nucleus
    c. no; part of the cytomembrane system
    d. no; part of the cytomembrane system

31. Lipid synthesis occurs in the
    a. smooth endoplasmic reticulum.
    b. mitochondrion.
    c. lysosome.
    d. rough endoplasmic reticulum.

    * a. yes; the major site for lipid synthesis
    b. no; produces ATP
    c. no; digests cellular waste products
    d. no; site for polypeptide synthesis

32. Peroxisomes have enzymes that digest all but which one of the following?
    a. ethyl alcohol
    b. amino acids
    c. fatty acids
    d. polysaccharides

    a. no; this chemical is digested in peroxisomes
    b. no; this chemical is digested in peroxisomes
    c. no; this chemical is digested in peroxisomes
    * d. yes; polysaccharides are not acted upon by peroxisomes

34. Which of the following organelles has its own DNA and ribosomes?
    a. mitochondria
    b. Golgi bodies
    c. lysosomes
    d. all of the above

    * a. yes; have both DNA and ribosomes
    b. no; does not have its own DNA
    c. no; contains enzymes, but not DNA
    d. no: a common distractor; only one of the above is correct

35. Cristae form the internal membranes of the
    a. centriole.
    b. mitochondrion.
    c. Golgi body.
    d. endoplasmic reticulum.

    a. no; has microtubules
    * b. yes; separates the mitochondrion into two parts
    c. no; there is no internal membrane
    d. no; a double membrane that extends throughout the cell

36. The term *9 + 2 array* refers to
    a. microtubules.
    b. intermediate filaments.
    c. spindles.
    d. microfilaments.

    * a. yes; characteristic of cilia, flagella, and centrioles
    b. no; composed of proteins found in many types of cells
    c. no; temporary tubulin units used to move chromosomes around during cell division
    d. no; not arranged in 9 + 2 array as in the actin and myosin filaments of myofibrils

37. Cilia are found
    a. on cells lining the respiratory tract.
    b. on cells lining the upper reaches of the female reproductive tract.
    c. on cells surrounding the blood capillaries.
    d. both (a) and (b), but not (c)

    a. no; a partial answer
    b. no; a partial answer
    c. no; not found in capillaries
    * d. yes; both (a) and (b) are correct

# CHAPTER 4

# GROUND RULES OF METABOLISM

1.    Enzymes are
      a. proteins.
      b. carbohydrates.
      c. nucleotides.
      d. steroids.

*     a. yes; the vast majority are proteins
      b. no; another compound
      c. no; although there have been a *few* DNA
         molecules discovered that function as
         enzymes
      d. no; another compound

2.    The sum total of all the chemical and physical
      activities of a cell is called
      a. synthesis.
      b. homeostasis.
      c. metabolism.
      d. cellular growth.

      a. no; not all living processes synthesize
         complex molecules and store energy, for some
         break down their own substances and
         release energy
      b. no; the maintenance of a constant internal
         environment is not the total of all
         cellular activities
*     c. yes; by definition metabolism includes both
         constructive and destructive physical and
         chemical processes
      d. no; cellular growth is just one result of
         cellular activities

3.    Superoxide dismutase and catalase
      a. are enzymes that break down toxic
         substances to form hydrogen peroxide,
         oxygen, and water and oxygen respectively.
      b. are enzymes that tend to accumulate during
         old age.
      c. form free radicals and toxins.
      d. are common examples in biochemical
         laboratories but are not found in most
         animals.

*     a. yes; they are antiaging enzymes
      b. no; their formation declines with age
      c. no; they break these substances down
      d. no; these are common enzymes found in
         humans

4.    Which of the following statements is false?
      a. After energy is used, it is lost.
      b. The amount of energy in the universe now is
         the same as the first day of the universe.
      c. Energy can neither be created nor destroyed,
         but it can be converted from one form
         to another.
      d. Energy may be stored in the bonds between
         the elements that make up chemical
         compounds.

*     a. yes; this statement is false; energy is not lost,
         but it may be dissipated into low-quality
         energy that is no longer useful
      b. no; this statement is true
      c. no; this statement is true
      d. no; this statement is true

5.    Which of the following statements is false?
      a. There is an one-way flow of energy into the
         world and out of it.
      b. Energy released in energy conversions is
         usually dissipated as heat.
      c. Life is a pocket of resistance to energy flow
         and does not follow the second law of
         thermodynamics.
      d. The world of life maintains a high degree of
         organization, only because it is being
         resupplied with energy.

      a. no; this statement is true
      b. no; this statement is true
*     c. yes; this statement is false; life does follow
         the second law of thermodynamics, for
         energy has to be captured and transferred
         for organisms to survive
      d. no; this statement is true.

6.    Which of the following is part of the first law
      of thermodynamics?
      a. Some energy is lost when it is transferred.
      b. The amount of energy in the universe is
         decreasing.
      c. The amount of energy in the universe is
         constant.
      d. The amount of energy in the universe is
         increasing.

a. no; true but appropriate to the second law of thermodynamics

b. no; energy may disperse and be less useful (entropy increases), but the amount is the same

* c. yes; the law is often referred to as the law of conservation of matter and energy

d. no; there is no source for additional energy input for the universe

7. The amount of high-quality energy in the universe
   a. is constantly increasing.
   b. is called entropy.
   c. is constant.
   d. continually declines.

   a. no; the direction is to reduce high-quality energy
   b. no; entropy refers to the decrease in high-quality energy
   c. no; high-quality energy is in high demand
   * d. yes; high-quality energy is continually used and converted to low-quality energy

8. Which of the following is an example of low-quality energy?
   a. atomic reactor
   b. starch in a potato
   c. heat in the atmosphere
   d. a barrel of crude oil

   a. no; represents high-quality energy, which can be used to do work
   b. no; high-quality chemical energy that can be used as energy to contract muscles
   * c. yes; not concentrated and not a useful form of energy in a dispersed state
   d. no; a source of high-quality energy that can be used to power an internal combustion engine

9. Which of the following statements is false?
   a. The amount of entropy is increasing.
   b. The ultimate end of material things in the universe will be a state of maximum entropy.
   c. Billions of years from now the universe will consist of isolated hot spots, with the remainder at a common low temperature.
   d. Living organisms do not represent a temporary exception to entropy.

   a. incorrect; this statement is true; energy is being dispersed continually
   b. incorrect; this statement is true; energy will be completely dispersed (maximum entropy)
   c. correct; this statement is false; all energy will be evenly dispersed
   * d. incorrect; this statement is true; they are able to concentrate energy, but it has to be continually supplied from elsewhere (the sun)

10. Cellular gates or channels are
    a. openings through membrane proteins.
    b. spaces between cells.
    c. gaps in the nuclear envelope.
    d. none of the above

* a. yes
   b. no; gap junctions may be involved
   c. no; pores may exist but are not usually referred to as gates or channels
   d. no; one of the above is correct

11. Transport proteins located in the plasma membrane serve as ___ for water-soluble molecules.
    a. open or gated channels
    b. carriers
    c. pumps
    d. all of the above

    a. no; a partial answer; a more complete answer is available
    b. no; a partial answer; a more complete answer is available
    c. no; a partial answer; a more complete answer is available
    * d. yes; all of the answers are correct

12. Which of the following statements about a carrier protein is false?
    a. A carrier protein must receive an energy boost before it will actively jump its cargo across the membrane.
    b. A carrier protein differs from a channel protein in that it is always open.
    c. A carrier protein undergoes a change in shape before its gates are opened.
    d. A carrier protein allows water-soluble molecules to enter and leave a cell.

    a. no; this statement is true
    * b. yes; this statement is false; they open and close depending upon conditions surrounding them.
    c. no; this statement is true
    d. no; this statement is true

13. Osmosis is based upon
    a. tonicity.
    b. concentration.
    c. differential pressure.
    d. all of the above

    a. no; a partial answer; a more complete answer is available
    b. no; a partial answer; a more complete answer is available
    c. no; a partial answer; a more complete answer is available
    * d. yes; all of the answers are correct

14. Plants will wilt
    a. after a prolonged drought.
    b. when fertilized heavily.
    c. when internal cells lose turgor pressure.
    d. all of the above

    a. no; a partial answer; a more complete answer is available
    b. no; a partial answer; a more complete answer is available
    c. no; a partial answer; a more complete answer is available
    * d. yes; all of the answers are correct

15. There is no net movement of water when a cell is placed in a(n)
    a. hypertonic solution.
    b. hypotonic solution.
    c. isotonic solution.
    d. both (a) and (c) are correct

    a. no; under these conditions, water would leave the cell
    b. no; under these conditions, water would enter the cell
    * c. yes; the same amount of water would enter and leave the cell
    d. no; only one answer is correct

16. A red blood cell placed in a hypotonic solution will
    a. shrink.
    b. exhibit no change.
    c. swell or explode.
    d. form a sickle shape.

    a. no; this happens in a hypertonic solution
    b. no; there is no change in an isotonic solution
    * c. yes; as osmosis occurs, water moves from high concentration outside the cell to lower concentration inside
    d. no; happens to some red blood cells under oxygen tension

17. Phenylketones in the genetic disorder phenylketonuria (PKU) lead to
    a. weight accumulation.
    b. accumulation of phenylalanine.
    c. mental retardation.
    d. none of the above.

    a. no; not an obvious effect of phenylketones
    b. no; phenylalanine is a precursor to phenylketones
    * c. yes; the phenotypic expression of PKU includes mental retardation
    d. no; one of the above is correct

18. Reactions in which the energy found in the product is greater than that in the reactants are known as ____ reactions.
    a. reversible
    b. endergonic
    c. exergonic
    d. dynamic equilibrium

    a. no; energy may or may not be greater
    * b. yes; there is a net gain in energy
    c. no; there is a net loss in energy
    d. no; a result of a reaction, not the name of a type of reaction

19. Which of the following is an endergonic reaction?
    a. photosynthesis
    b. digestion
    c. protein synthesis
    d. phosphorylation

    a. no; stores solar energy as chemical energy
    * b. yes; breaks down complex compounds to release energy
    c. no; production of larger, more complex molecule stores energy
    d. no; the addition of high-energy phosphate increases the energy available in a compound

20. In reversible biological reactions,
    a. the direction is dependent upon the concentration of the reactants and the products.
    b. the direction is dependent upon the metabolic condition of the organism.
    c. the rates for forward and reverse reactions are the same in a dynamic equilibrium.
    d. all of the above

    a. no; a partial answer; a more complete answer is available
    b. no; a partial answer; a more complete answer is available
    c. no; a partial answer; a more complete answer is available
    * d. yes; all of the above are correct

21. Which of the following is an energy carrier?
    a. enzymes
    b. adenosine triphosphate
    c. reactant
    d. cofactors

    a. no; organic catalysts that enable a reaction to occur
    * b. yes; the energy currency of a cell
    c. no; a possible source for the energy in high-energy bonds
    d. no; necessary component in enzyme systems

22. Metabolic pathways may be
    a. linear.
    b. cyclic.
    c. branched.
    d. all of the above

    a. no; a partial answer; a more complete answer is available
    b. no; a partial answer; a more complete answer is available
    c. no; a partial answer; a more complete answer is available
    * d. yes; all of the above are correct

23. Enzymes
    a. are the only way some biological reactions could occur.
    b. are nonspecific and can mediate a great many different reactions.
    c. are altered or used up by the reactions they control.
    d. act by lowering the activation energy required for a reaction to occur.

a. no; enzymes only affect the speed of a reaction that would happen anyway
b. no; enzymes are highly specific and limited in the type of reactions they can control
c. no; enzymes can be used over and over again
* d. yes; activation energy can be supplied by the enzyme or by other sources, such as heat

24. The activation site of an enzyme
   a. can be altered by excessive change in pH.
   b. may be distorted so that it will not bind with a substrate.
   c. can be destroyed by high temperatures such as occur in high fevers.
   d. all of the above

   a. no; a partial answer; a more complete answer is available
   b. no; a partial answer; a more complete answer is available
   c. no; a partial answer; a more complete answer is available
   * d. yes; all of the above are correct

25. The characteristic dark color of the tail, ears, face, and paws of a Siamese cat is due to
   a. an enzyme inhibitor that blocks the expression of the light color in these regions.
   b. the higher temperature tending to reduce the activity of the enzyme controlling the production of melanin pigment, therefore, the central body has a lighter color.
   c. the lower temperatures found in these regions denaturing the enzyme necessary for the production of color.
   d. all of the above

   a. no; an enzyme inhibitor is not involved
   * b. yes; the reduction in melanin pigment occurs in the center of the body because the higher temperature in the center of the body reduces the activity of the enzyme controlling melanin pigment production
   c. no; the lower temperature favors melanin pigment production
   d. no; one of the above is correct

26. The sugar associated with ATP is
   a. glucose.
   b. ribose.
   c. deoxyribose.
   d. fructose.

   a. no
   * b. yes; a component of adenosine
   c. no
   d. no

27. Which statement about an energy transport system is true?
   a. Bioluminescence is a manifestation of electron transport.
   b. ATP is a precursor of ADP.
   c. Oxidized acceptors have more energy than do reduced forms.
   d. A reduced cytochrome molecule may accept electrons from another molecule in the electron transport series.

* a. yes; energy is given off in the form of light
b. no; ADP becomes ATP by adding a high-energy phosphate
c. no; reduced acceptors release energy when they are oxidized or give up electrons
d. no; oxidized acceptors become reduced when they accept an electron

# CHAPTER 5

# ENERGY-ACQUIRING PATHWAYS

1.  The Sahel Desert, site of drought and starvation is found in
    a.  Asia.
    b.  Australia.
    c.  Africa.
    d.  South America.

    a.  no; another continent
    b.  no; another continent
    *   c.  yes; the drought has lead to massive starvation in Biafra, Ethiopia, and Somalia
    d.  no; another continent

2.  The source of our food is
    a.  a farm.
    b.  a refrigerator.
    c.  a grocery store.
    d.  the sun.

    a.  no; we grow food on a farm
    b.  no; we store food in a refrigerator
    c.  no; we sell food in a grocery store
    *   d.  yes; the energy needed to produce food comes from the sun

3.  Organisms capable of extracting carbon and energy directly from the environment are called (select the best answer)
    a.  plants.
    b.  heterotrophs.
    c.  autotrophs.
    d.  photosynthesizers.

    a.  no; generally acceptable, but many plants are parasitic or saphrophytic
    b.  no; heterotrophs obtain their energy and carbon from other organisms
    *   c.  yes; autotrophs include all organisms (plants, protists, and monerans) that synthesize their own food
    d.  no; this choice leaves out those organisms that gain energy through chemosynthesis

4.  The carbon source of autotrophs is
    a.  organic compounds in dead bodies.
    b.  carbonates in the soil.
    c.  carbon dioxide.
    d.  methane.

    a.  no; decomposers use this carbon source
    b.  no; not the primary source for carbon
    *   c.  yes; absorbed by the plant and used in photosynthesis
    d.  no; plants do not use methane

5.  The plant's main carbohydrates include all but which one of the following?
    a.  glucose
    b.  sucrose
    c.  starch
    d.  cellulose

    *   a.  yes; a transitory carbohydrate
    b.  no; the common form in which carbohydrates are transported
    c.  no; starch is the way plants store carbohydrates
    d.  no; the major component in plant cell walls

6.  Photoautotrophs include all but which one of the following?
    a.  green plants
    b.  certain protistans
    c.  certain chemoautotrophs
    d.  certain bacteria

    a.  no; members of these groups produce food through photosynthesis
    b.  no; members of these groups produce food through photosynthesis
    *   c.  yes; chemosynthetic forms use other energy sources than light
    d.  no; some bacteria can carry on photosynthesis

7.  Photosynthesis occurs in cytoplasmic organelles called
    a.  Golgi bodies.
    b.  chloroplasts.
    c.  chromoplasts.
    d.  mitochondria.

    a.  no; specialized for secretion
    *   b.  yes; organelles with chlorophyll
    c.  no; colored plastids lend colors to flowers and fruits
    d.  no; cellular organelles associated with respiration

8. In plants, photosynthesis takes place in the
   a. stroma.
   b. cytoplasm.
   c. grana.
   d. both (a) and (c)

   a. yes; a partial answer; only the light dependent reactions of photosynthesis occurs here
   b. no; photosynthesis occurs only in association with chloroplasts
   c. yes; a partial answer; only the light-independent reactions of photosynthesis occurs here
   * d. yes; both (a) and (c) are correct; photosynthesis includes both light-dependent and light-independent reactions

9. Which of the following is *not* part of the light-dependent reaction of photosynthesis?
   a. carbon dioxide is fixed
   b. oxygen is released
   c. light energy is absorbed in the light-independent reactions
   d. water is split in two

   * a. yes; takes place in the light-independent reactions
   b. no; part of the light-dependent reaction that occurs when water is split
   c. no; light energy is absorbed by chlorophyll in the light-dependent reaction
   d. no; photolysis of water occurs during the light-dependent reactions

10. Which of the following statements is false?
    a. The light-independent reactions take place in the thylakoid membrane.
    b. The light-dependent reactions take place in the thylakoid membrane.
    c. The interior of a chloroplast is the stroma.
    d. The light-independent reactions takes place in the stroma.

    a. no; this statement is true
    * b. yes; this statement is false, for the light-dependent reactions take place in the thylakoid membrane system
    c. no; this statement is true
    d. no; this statement is true

11. The hydrogen (electron) acceptor in the light dependent reaction is
    a. FAD.
    b. oxygen.
    c. NADP.
    d. glucose.

    a. no; an acceptor in aerobic respiration
    b. no; an acceptor in aerobic respiration
    * c. yes; the hydrogen (electron) acceptor
    d. no; part of the light-independent reactions

12. The carotenoids absorb ____ light.
    a. yellow
    b. orange
    c. red
    d. blue-violet

    a. no; reflect this color so that it appears to be this color
    b. no; reflect this color so that it appears to be this color
    c. no; reflect this color so that it appears to be this color
    * d. yes; absorb light in the blue-violet wavelengths

13. Which color of light is reflected by chlorophyll?
    a. red
    b. blue
    c. orange
    d. green

    a. no; absorbed radiant energy converted to chemical energy
    b. no; absorbed radiant energy converted to chemical energy
    c. no; absorbed radiant energy converted to chemical energy
    * d. yes; this is why leaves appear green —we see the reflected green light

14. Which of the following is *not* one of the pigments commonly found in the leaves of plants that turn yellow or golden in the autumn?
    a. anthocyanin
    b. carotene
    c. chlorophyll
    d. xanthophyll

    * a. correct; pigment responsible for red or purple colors, not found in the yellow or golden leaves
    b. incorrect; the orange pigment found in these leaves
    c. incorrect; this green pigment masks the presence of the other pigments while the leaf is green in the summer
    d. incorrect; this is the yellow pigment that becomes visible in the fall

15. Which plant pigment changes color when the pH changes?
    a. chlorophyll
    b. anthocyanin
    c. phycobilin
    d. carotenoids

    a. no; does not change color
    * b. yes; turns red under acidic conditions and blue when alkalinic
    c. no; does not change color
    d. no; does not change color

16. Engleman was able to get different colors of light for his photosynthesis experiment by using
    a. different colored light bulbs.
    b. stained glass the color he wanted.
    c. a prism.
    d. different color cellophane wrappings.

a. no; although these would produce different colors, he had a simpler method
b. no; although these would produce different colors, he had a simpler method
* c. yes; the prism broke the white light into a full spectrum of color
d. no; although these would produce different colors, he had a simpler method

17. Which of the following was *not* part of Englemann's classic experiment to elucidate the nature of photosynthesis?
a. a prism
b. carbon dioxide labeled with carbon 14
c. elodea, a water plant
d. aerobic bacteria

a. incorrect; a prism was used to separate light into different colors (wavelengths) in the experiment
* b. correct; radioactive carbon not available in 1882; part of later research on the nature of photosynthesis
c. incorrect; this water plant liberated oxygen bubbles during photosynthesis in the experiment
d. incorrect; the aerobic bacteria clustered around areas of active photosynthesis (dependent on the wavelength of the light hitting the cells) in the experiment

18. The bubbles that arise on bright sunny days on the surface of the leaves of plants immersed in water are bubbles of
a. carbon dioxide.
b. water vapor.
c. hydrogen sulfide.
d. oxygen.

a. no; carbon dioxide would be released in respiration
b. no; this would quickly dissolve in the water
c. no; a gas produced during putrefaction-anaerobic respiration
* d. yes; oxygen liberated during photolysis

19. The oxygen liberated in photosynthesis comes from
a. atmospheric oxygen.
b. carbon dioxide.
c. water.
d. glucose.

a. no; not used in photosynthesis
b. no; carbon dioxide is fixed by ribulose bisphosphate
* c. yes; during photolysis of water
d. no; the other product of photosynthesis (in addition to oxygen)

20. The portion of the electromagnetic spectrum absorbed by chlorophyll is
a. x-ray.
b. ultraviolet.
c. visible light.
d. infrared.

a. no; enough energy to produce ionization and destroy cells
b. no; enough energy to excite some molecules, but not involved in photosynthesis
* c. yes; this electromagnetic energy is converted in chemical energy
d. no; heat energy that does not contribute directly to photosynthesis

21. The carbon dioxide in the light-independent reactions becomes fixed to
a. phosphoglycerate (PGA).
b. phosphoglyceraldehyde (PGAL).
c. ribulose bisphosphate (RuBP).
d. oxaloacetate.

a. no; formed by this reaction
b. no; a compound formed after carbon dioxide fixation occurs
* c. yes; combines with carbon dioxide to form an unstable intermediate compound that eventually forms PGA
d. no; C4 photosynthesis

22. In photorespiration, oxygen becomes attached to
a. PGA.
b. PGAL.
c. RuBP.
d. oxaloacetate.

a. no; formed by photorespiration
b. no; found in both photorespiration and the Calvin-Benson cycle
* c. yes; to form one PGA and one phosphoglycolate
d. no; part of the C4 cycle

23. The products of the light-independent reaction in photosynthesis
a. are complex carbohydrates.
b. are not used in the light-independent reaction.
c. include glucose molecules and the by-product oxygen.
d. are phosphoglyceraldehyde molecules that may be converted into glucose and ribulose biphosphate.

a. no; these are formed as polymers of glucose or other monomers
b. no; the energy from the light-dependent reaction is used to convert PGA to PGAL
c. no; glucose might be produced from PGAL after the dark reaction is completed, while oxygen is released in the light-dependent phase
* d. yes; PGAL is appropriately considered the end product of the light-independent reaction

24. The light-independent reaction of photosynthesis
    a. fixes carbon dioxide.
    b. involves the liberation of oxygen.
    c. cannot occur in light.
    d. all of the above

  * a. yes; ribulose biphosphate reacts with carbon dioxide
    b. no; oxygen is released during the light phase
    c. no; it is called the dark reaction to distinguish it from the light reaction, which requires the energy from light; it may occur in either light or darkness
    d. no; only one of the above is correct

25. The light reaction of photosynthesis
    a. involves photolysis of water.
    b. occurs in mitochondria.
    c. consist of the fixation of carbon dioxide.
    d. produces phosphoglyceric acid as its first stable compound.

  * a. yes; the energy from light splits water by noncyclic photophosphorylation
    b. no; occurs in the inner membranes of the chloroplast
    c. no; carbon dioxide fixation with ribulose biphosphate occurs in the dark reaction
    d. no; PGA in the first stable compound of the dark reaction

26. Through photolysis and electron transport a(n) ___ is created across the thylakoid membrane.
    a. electric gradient
    b. concentration gradient
    c. hydrogen ion gradient
    d. all of the above

    a. no; a partial answer; a more complete answer is available
    b. no; a partial answer; a more complete answer is available
    c. no; a partial answer; a more complete answer is available
  * d. yes; all of the answers are correct

27. Which of the following is associated with cyclic photophosphorylation?
    a. photosystem I
    b. photosystem II
    c. light of 680 nanometers
    d. both (b) and (c)

  * a. yes; the system that captures and passes on the energy used in cyclic photophosphorylation
    b. no; the system involved in noncyclic photophosphorylation
    c. no; 680 nanometers used in noncyclic photophosphorylation; 700 nanometers used in cyclic photophosphorylation
    d. no; only (a) is correct for cyclic photophosphorylation

28. The oldest means of ATP production is thought to be
    a. glycolysis.
    b. noncyclic photophosphorylation.
    c. cyclic photophosphorylation.
    d. aerobic respiration.

    a. no; characteristic of anaerobic organisms. both uses and produces ATP
    b. no; a more complex process associated with photosynthesis and though to arise later
  * c. yes; the simple way for primitive organisms to tap the continual influx of energy from the sun
    d. no; dependent on the availability of free oxygen, which is dependent upon the prior existence of noncyclic photophosphorylation

29. ATP is formed in the chemiosmotic process by (choose best answer)
    a. enzymes in the stroma surrounding the chlorophyll.
    b. photosystem I.
    c. enzymes in a protein channel in the thylakoid membrane.
    d. enzymes in thylakoid compartment where the hydrogen ions accumulate.

    a. no; enzymes are associated with protein channels between the thylakoid compartment and the stroma
    b. yes; but not as good an answer as one of the more detailed choices
  * c. yes; ATP formation occurs as the protons flow through the channel in response to an electrical and concentration gradient
    d. no; hydrogen ions accumulate in the compartment, but ATP syntheases are associated with the protein channel

30. In noncyclic photophosphorylation, which of the following compounds are produced?
    a. oxygen
    b. ATP
    c. NADPH
    d. all of the above

    a. yes; a partial answer; during photolysis
    b. yes; a partial answer; during chemiosmosis
    c. yes; a partial answer; as an electron acceptor
  * d. yes; all of the above are correct

31. Which of the following people discovered the pathway of carbon in photosynthesis?
    a. Calvin
    b. Hill
    c. Benson
    d. both (a) and (c)

a. yes; partial answer
b. no
c. yes; partial answer
* d. yes; both (a) and (c)

32. A bloom of algae in the ocean most often occurs in the
    a. spring.
    b. summer.
    c. fall.
    d. winter.

* a. yes; when the winter currents bearing nutrients reach the surface
  b. no; a different season
  c. no; a different season
  d. no; a different season

33. Stomata are
    a. openings in the surface of leaves for gas exchange.
    b. the liquid centers of chloroplasts.
    c. specialized pores found only in $C_4$ plants.
    d. none of the above

* a. yes; the site for entry of carbon dioxide into a leaf
  b. no; the center of a chloroplast is the stroma
  c. no; the pores in $C_4$ plants are also called stomata
  d. no; one of the above answers is correct

34. Which of the following statements is false?
    a. Bundle sheath cells are characteristic of $C_4$ plants.
    b. $C_4$ plants are likely to lose more water than $C_3$ plants and must therefore be found in moist environments.
    c. $C_4$ plants fix carbon dioxide twice.
    d. Mesophyll cells convert carbon dioxide into oxaloacetate.

  a. no; this statement is true
* b. yes; this statement is false; $C_4$ plants fix carbon more efficiently than $C_3$ plants because they have smaller/fewer stomata and therefore lose less water
  c. no; this statement is true
  d. no; this statement is true

35. Which of the following would have the best chances to survive on a desert?
    a. $C_3$ plants
    b. $C_4$ plants
    c. CAM plants
    d. all of the above have equal chances; survival in the desert is not dependent on the type of photosynthesis

a. no; the least likely to survive
b. no; although $C_4$ plants do well in the hot summer
* c. yes; adapted to keeping their stomata closed during the day
d. no; one has a much better chance for survival

36. Which of the following compounds is found exclusively in $C_4$ plants?
    a. phosphoglyceraldehyde
    b. phosphoglycerate
    c. oxaloacetate
    d. ribulose biphosphate

a. no; found in $C_3$ and $C_4$ plants
b. no; found in $C_3$ and $C_4$ plants
* c. yes; characteristic intermediate in $C_4$ plants
d. no; found in $C_3$ and $C_4$ plants

# CHAPTER 6

# ENERGY-RELEASING PATHWAYS

1.     Which of the following is a coenzyme?
       a. NAD
       b. iron
       c. cobalt
       d. copper

*      a. yes; a large organic compound that
          functions with an enzyme
       b. no; these minerals are known as
          cofactors and activate an enzyme
       c. no; these minerals are known as
          cofactors and activate an enzyme
       d. no; these minerals are known as
          cofactors and activate an enzyme

2.     FAD (flavin adenine dinucleotide) and
       NAD (nicotinamide adenine dinucleotide)
       are well known examples of
       a. substrates.
       b. reactants.
       c. coenzymes.
       d. products.

       a. no; although FAD and NAD could be
          substrates, they have a much better
          known role
       b. no; although FAD and NAD could be
          reactants, they have a much better
          known role
*      c. yes; FAD and NAD are coenzymes and
          cofactors involved in the transfer of an
          electron
       d. no; although FAD and NAD could be
          end products, they have a much better
          known role

3.     Which of the following compounds has
       more energy than the others?
       a. ATP
       b. pyruvate
       c. glucose
       d. oxaloacetate

       a. no; thirty-six ATP molecules released
          when glucose is oxidized
       b. no; an intermediate compound in the
          breakdown of glucose
*      c. yes; the most energy is found in glucose
       d. no; an intermediate compound in the
          breakdown of glucose, found at the
          beginning of the Krebs cycle

4.     Which of the following molecules has the
       most carbon atoms?
       a. phosphoglyceraldehyde
       b. glucose
       c. oxaloacetate
       d. pyruvate

       a. no; contains three carbon atoms
*      b. yes; contains six carbon atoms
       c. no; contains four carbon atoms
       d. no; contains three carbon atoms

5.     When a molecule accepts an electron, it is
       said to be
       a. oxidized.
       b. phosphorylated.
       c. reduced.
       d. hydrolyzed.

       a. no; a molecule is oxidized when oxygen
          is added to it or the molecule loses an
          electron
       b. no; a molecule is phosphorylated when
          a high-energy phosphate bond is added
          to it
*      c. yes; molecules are reduced when they
          pick up an electron
       d. no; a molecule is hydrolyzed when the
          molecule is split by the chemical
          addition of water

6.     The number of molecules of ATP produced
       by the complete aerobic breakdown of a
       molecule of glucose is
       a. 2.
       b. 32.
       c. 36.
       d. 52.

       a. no; the number produced by glycolysis
          or by the Krebs cycle
       b. no; too few, the number produced in
          electron transport phosphorylation
*      c. yes; 36 is the usual amount, but could be
          more
       d. no; too many

7. The aerobic breakdown of glucose known as respiration involves
   a. the Krebs Cycle.
   b. glycolysis.
   c. electron transport phosphorylation.
   d. all of the above

   a. yes; a partial answer; intermediate reactions
   b. yes; a partial answer; the initial stage
   c. yes; a partial answer; the final process in aerobic respiration
   * d. yes; all three reaction series are involved

8. The last molecule formed in glycolysis is
   a. phosphoglyceraldehyde.
   b. fructose bisphosphate.
   c. pyruvate.
   d. citric acid.

   a. no; an intermediate formed by the splitting of fructose bisphosphate
   b. no; an intermediate formed during the phosphorylation of glucose
   * c. yes; the end product of glycolysis
   d. no; the first compound in the Krebs cycle

9. Glycolysis takes place in the
   a. ribosomes.
   b. cytoplasm.
   c. mitochondria.
   d. all of the above

   a. no; site for protein synthesis
   * b. yes; the enzymes and intermediate products are found in the cytoplasm
   c. no; the site for aerobic respiration
   d. no; one of the above is correct

10. Which of the following reactions takes place in the cristae of mitochondria?
    a. glycolysis
    b. Krebs cycle
    c. oxidative phosphorylation
    d. both (b) and (c), but not (a)

    a. no; glycolysis occurs in the cytoplasm
    b. no; a partial answer; the Krebs cycle occurs in the cristae
    c. no; a partial answer; the oxidative phosphorylation occurs in the cristae
    * d. yes; both (b) and (c) are correct, but (a) is not

11. Ribose is part of the _____ molecule.
    a. glucose
    b. ATP
    c. phosphoglycerate
    d. glycogen

    a. no; glucose is a hexose (six-carbon sugar) while ribose is a pentose (five-carbon sugar)
    * b. yes; ATP is made up of adenine, ribose, and phosphate groups
    c. no; only has three carbons and is part of the glycolysis of glucose
    d. no; a complex carbohydrate composed of many glucose molecules

12. Fermentation is part of
    a. glycolysis.
    b. electron transport phosphorylation.
    c. Krebs cycle.
    d. none of the above

    * a. yes; fermentation is an anaerobic continuation of pyruvate metabolism
    b. no; requires oxygen
    c. no; requires oxygen
    d. no; one of the above is correct

13. Which of the following is not produced by fermentation?
    a. ethyl alcohol
    b. whipping cream
    c. sour cream
    d. yeast breads and cakes

    a. no; ethyl alcohol is produced by the fermentation of some sugar sources
    * b. yes; whipping cream is high in butter fat and comes from cows
    c. no; sour cream is produced by fermentation of lactose to produce lactic acid
    d. no; fermentation produces carbon dioxide, which allows breads and cakes to rise

14. Fermentation will occur in humans when there is an insufficient supply of
    a. pyruvates.
    b. oxygen.
    c. glucose.
    d. carbon dioxide.

    a. no; more pyruvate would be manufactured from dietary foods or stored supplies
    * b. yes; if there is insufficient oxygen, there is no final hydrogen acceptor so that all acceptors become reduced; the pyruvate is unable to form acetyl COA and is therefore broken down by anaerobic respiration
    c. no; additional glucose can be produced from the diet or body supplies
    d. no; carbon dioxide is a waste product and is given off as a gas

15. Which of the following statements is false?
    a. Six molecules of carbon dioxide are produced for each molecule of glucose entering aerobic respiration.
    b. Glycolysis forms NADH, a reusable coenzyme.
    c. The glucose molecule is broken down to form three molecules of acetyl CoA.
    d. Some ATP is used to initiate the glycolysis reactions.

    a. incorrect; statement is true; six-carbon compound combines with six molecules of oxygen to form six molecules of carbon dioxide.
    b. incorrect; statement is true and NADH functions as a proton/electron carrier.
* c. correct; statement is false, only two acetyl CoAs are formed from the two pyruvates produced at the end of the glycolysis of a single glucose molecule.
    d. incorrect; statement is true; the deficit of 2 ATP involved in the phosphorylation of glucose to fructose bisphosphate is compensated by the production of 4 ATP in glycolysis to give a net yield of 2 ATP.

16. The compound that enters a mitochondrion to undergo aerobic respiration is
    a. phosphoglyceraldehyde.
    b. acetyl CoA.
    c. oxaloacetate.
    d. pyruvate.

    a. no; part of glycolysis found in the cytoplasm
    b. no; transitional compound formed in the mitochondria
    c. no; compound already found in mitochondria
* d. yes; pyruvate enters the mitochondria

17. Oxaloacetate is
    a. regenerated by passage through the Krebs cycle.
    b. the first compound in electron transport phosphorylation.
    c. the compound produced immediately in the first step in the degradation of citric acid.
    d. a compound limited to anaerobic organisms.

* a. yes; at the end of the Krebs cycle, oxaloacetate may combine with Acetyl CoA to form citric acid to start the Krebs cycle again
    b. no; not an electron acceptor
    c. no; at the end of the Krebs cycle
    d. no; found in the Krebs cycle, which is part of aerobic respiration

18. The first compound formed in the Krebs cycle is
    a. acetyl COA.
    b. oxaloacetic acid or oxaloacetate.
    c. citric acid or citrate.
    d. malic acid or malate.

    a. no; acetyl is the two-carbon molecule formed from pyruvic acid and the COA is its carrier
    b. no; oxaloacetate is considered to be the compound that combines with the acetyl group to begin the Krebs cycle
* c. yes; the four-carbon oxaloacetate combines with two-carbon acetyl group to form the six-carbon citric acid
    d. no; a four-carbon intermediate in the Krebs cycle

19. The second stage of aerobic respiration
    a. loads many coenzymes with hydrogen ions and electrons.
    b. produces ATP by substrate-level phosphorylation.
    c. produces the same number of ATP as does the first stage of aerobic respiration.
    d. all of the above

    a. yes; a partial answer; the hydrogen is produced in the breakdown of compounds in the Krebs cycle
    b. yes; a partial answer; involves GDP and GTP
    c. yes; a partial answer; a total of two, one for each turn of the cycle
* d. yes; all of the above statements are true

20. The final hydrogen acceptor in the electron transport system is
    a. NAD.
    b. FAD.
    c. a cytochrome.
    d. free oxygen.

    a. no; the common acceptor that picks up hydrogen from compounds in the Krebs cycle
    b. no; a primary acceptor from succinate in the Krebs cycle
    c. no; cytochromes are intermediates in the electron transport system
* d. yes; the final acceptor, oxygen combines with hydrogen to form water

21. The electron acceptors in the electron transport system are found
    a. in the cytoplasm.
    b. on the external membrane of the mitochondria.
    c. on the internal membrane of the mitochondria.
    d. in the matrix of the mitochondria.

    a. no; electron transport is associated with the mitochondria
    b. no; located elsewhere
* c. yes; embedded in the internal membrane of the mitochondria
    d. no; located elsewhere

22. The production of ATP in a mitochondrion
   a. is referred to as chemiosmotic theory.
   b. occurs when free hydrogen ions outside the mitochondrion leak inside through protein channels.
   c. is dependent on ATP synthease, an enzyme found dissolved in the inner compartment of the mitochondrion.
   d. both (a) and (c)

   * a. yes; the chemiosmotic theory is the current explanation for ATP production in the mitochondrion
   b. no; the free hydrogen ions are found inside the mitochondrial membrane
   c. no; ATP synthease is found in the protein channel between the inner and outer compartment of the mitochondrion
   d. no; only (a) is correct, both (b) and (c) are incorrect

23. The main storage form for glucose in animals is
   a. fat.
   b. glycogen.
   c. complex carbohydrates.
   d. none of the above

   a. no; a different compound than fat is used to store glucose
   * b. yes; the body contains about a 24–hour supply
   c. yes; but the *specific* carbohydrate is glycogen
   d. no; one of the answers is correct

24. If a person were to go on a hunger strike, the energy source of last resort would be
   a. glucose.
   b. fat.
   c. protein and tissue.
   d. glycogen.

   a. no; there is only about a twenty-four hour supply of glucose readily available
   b. no; one of the last resorts, but the glycogen supply of the liver would be used first
   * c. yes; proteins and actual tissue are the last resort
   d. no; when the glucose level drops, glycogen is the first thing broken down to supply glucose

25. In alcoholic fermentation, the final hydrogen acceptor is
   a. oxygen.
   b. acetaldehyde.
   c. lactic acid or lactate.
   d. pyruvate.

   a. no; characteristic of aerobic respiration
   * b. yes; the hydrogen reacts with acetaldehyde to form ethyl alcohol
   c. no; the hydrogen acceptor in lactate fermentation
   d. no; not a hydrogen acceptor

26. In alcoholic fermentation, the end-products are ethyl alcohol and
   a. hydrogen.
   b. water.
   c. acetyl CoA.
   d. carbon dioxide.

   a. no; hydrogen is not released
   b. no; no oxygen available to form water
   c. no; formed from pyruvate in aerobic respiration
   * d. yes; as bubbles in beer or sparkling wine (champagne)

27. Adipose tissue is
   a. a tissue which is found evenly dispersed throughout the body.
   b. the tissue where fat is stored.
   c. a type of glandular tissue.
   d. a tissue limited to humans.

   a. no; the amount of fat varies in different parts of the body
   * b. yes; a connective tissue where fat is stored
   c. no; simply a place to store excess energy in the form of fat
   d. no; many animals have fat

28. In the complete aerobic breakdown of proteins to carbon dioxide and water the chemical fragments enter the aerobic pathway for metabolism of complex carbohydrates
   a. in glycolysis.
   b. in the Krebs cycle.
   c. in electron transport phosphorylation.
   d. as simple carbohydrates.

   a. no; restricted to simple compounds
   * b. yes; enters as an intermediate in the Krebs cycle
   c. no; only hydrogen enters the electron transport system
   d. no; as amino acids converted into elements of the Krebs cycle

29. Which of the following is *not* one of the three phases of aerobic respiration?
   a. glycolysis
   b. photolysis
   c. hydrogen transfer series
   d. citric acid cycles

   a. incorrect; the first step in aerobic respiration
   * b. correct; this is not part of aerobic respiration, but the light-dependent phase of photosynthesis
   c. incorrect; the part of respiration that liberates the majority of ATP
   d. incorrect; the part of respiration that produces hydrogen and carbon dioxide

30. Which of the following is *not* a synonym for the other terms and does not describe the cycle characteristic of aerobic respiration?
    a. citric acid
    b. tricarboxylic
    c. Krebs
    d. photophosphorylation

    a. incorrect; one of the synonyms
    b. incorrect; one of the synonyms
    c. incorrect; one of the synonyms
    * d. correct; one of the aspects of photosynthesis

31. Which of the following reactions in respiration involves oxygen?
    a. phosphorylation
    b. Krebs cycle
    c. hydrogen transfer series
    d. glycolysis

    a. no; adds high-energy phosphate to glucose
    b. no; starts with citric acid and ends with oxaloacetic acid
    * c. yes; oxygen is the final hydrogen acceptor and forms water at the end of the hydrogen transfer series
    d. no; ends with pyruvic acid

32. Which of the following cells is unable to derive as much energy from glucose molecules as the others?
    a. liver cells
    b. muscle cells
    c. kidney cells
    d. heart cells

    a. no; they have an $NAD^+$ shuttle in their mitochondria and produce thirty-eight ATP molecules
    * b. yes; they lack the $NAD^+$ shuttle in their mitochondria and produce thirty-six ATP molecules
    c. no; kidney cells have the $NAD^+$ shuttle in their mitochondria and produce thirty-eight ATP molecules
    d. no; they have $NAD^+$ shuttle in their mitochondria and produce thirty-eight ATP molecules

33. The efficiency of aerobic respiration is about _____ percent.
    a. 20
    b. 40
    c. 60
    d. 80

    a. no; too little
    * b. yes; thirty-six ATP molecules x 7.5 kilocalories = 686 kilocalories in glucose
    c. no; too much
    d. no; too much

34. Robins gets drunk from eating the fermenting fruits of
    a. cherry trees.
    b. persimmon trees.
    c. pyracantha bushes.
    d. plum trees.

    a. no; another fruit
    b. no; another fruit
    * c. yes; wild yeast ferments the sugars present
    d. no; another fruit

35. Which of the following utilizes alcoholic fermentation for energy?
    a. elephants
    b. yeast
    c. bacteria that sours milk
    d. human muscle cells

    a. no; too large an organism to depend upon anaerobic respiration
    * b. yes; both wild yeast and cultivated ones used in the production of beer and wine
    c. no; uses lactate fermentation, which causes milk to sour
    d. no; uses lactate fermentation under anaerobic condition

36. Which of the following is *not* a product of anaerobic respiration in yeast?
    a. water
    b. pyruvate
    c. carbon dioxide
    d. ethanol

    * a. correct; water is not formed because oxygen is not used
    b. incorrect; pyruvate is produced by glycolysis
    c. incorrect; carbon dioxide is given off as bubbles and causes bread to rise
    d. incorrect; yeast uses alcohol, not lactic fermentation

# CHAPTER 7

# CELL DIVISION AND MITOSIS

1.  Which of the following cells is produced by a type of division different from the other cells listed?
    a.  nerve cells
    b.  egg cells
    c.  muscle cells
    d.  pancreatic cells

    a.  no; not produced by meiosis
    * b.  yes; produced by meiosis, others by meiosis
    c.  no; not produced by meiosis
    d.  no; not produced by meiosis

2.  Mitosis and meiosis do not occur in
    a.  insects.
    b.  bacteria.
    c.  fungi.
    d.  red and brown algae.

    a.  incorrect; insects undergo mitosis and meiosis as do all eukaryotes
    * b.  correct; prokaryotes do not undergo mitosis or meiosis
    c.  incorrect; fungi and all eukaryotes undergo mitosis and meiosis
    d.  incorrect; both types of algae are eukaryotes and undergo mitosis and meiosis

3.  _____ attaches to chromosomes at the centromere.
    a.  A sister chromatid
    b.  A spindle apparatus
    c.  A microfilament
    d.  The nuclear membrane

    a.  no; two chromatids may be connected at the centromere
    * b.  yes; the site where the spindle fibers attach
    c.  no; microtubules, not microfilaments, are involved with chromosomes in cell division
    d.  no; no relationship; the chromosomes may appear anywhere inside the nucleus

4.  The division of the mother cell's cytoplasm is called
    a.  mitosis.
    b.  meiosis.
    c.  karyokinesis.
    d.  cytokinesis.

    a.  no; commonly called cell division but actually only refers to the division of the nucleus
    b.  no; a specialized nuclear division that reduces the number of chromosome in each daughter cell by one-half
    c.  no; karyokinesis refers to the division of the nucleus only
    * d.  yes; cytokinesis refers to the division of the cytoplasm

5.  In most sexually reproducing organisms, the cells of the adult organisms are
    a.  triploid.
    b.  haploid.
    c.  diploid.
    d.  tetraploid.

    a.  no; three sets of chromosomes, organism usually sterile
    b.  no; one set of chromosome, characteristic of gametes or haploid life cycle
    * c.  yes; two sets of chromosomes per cell—one paternal, one maternal
    d.  no; four sets of chromosomes; a few domesticated varieties of plants are tetraploid, most are diploid

6.  A cell spends the majority of time of the cell cycle in
    a.  interphase.
    b.  metaphase.
    c.  telophase.
    d.  prophase.

    * a.  yes; the majority of the time in the cell cycle is spent in interphase, only a small portion is spent in mitosis
    b.  no; only a small part of the cell cycle is spent in mitosis
    c.  no; only a small part of the cell cycle is spent in mitosis
    d.  no; only a small part of the cell cycle is spent in mitosis

7. A set of chromosomes (a genome) is indicated by the letter
   a. a.
   b. f.
   c. g.
   d. n.

   a. no; another letter is used
   b. no; another letter is used
   c. no; another letter is used
 * d. yes; as in 1n, 2n, etc.

8. The two parts of a duplicated chromosome are called _____ chromatids.
   a. mother and daughter
   b. sister
   c. maternal and paternal
   d. brother

   a. no; used to describe mother cell and daughter cell produced by meiosis
 * b. yes
   c. no; applies to the pair of homologous chromosomes
   d. no

9. Which of the following phases of the cell cycle occurs after the genetic material has been replicated and prepares the cells for division?
   a. M
   b. $G_1$
   c. $G_2$
   d. S

   a. no; the actual division process
   b. no; period of growth before DNA duplication
 * c. yes; occurs immediately after DNA duplication
   d. no; the actual replication stage

10. Which of the following events does not occur in prophase?
    a. The spindle apparatus form.
    b. The centromeres divide.
    c. The centrioles separate and move to poles of the cell.
    d. The chromosomes become visible as separate entities.

    a. incorrect; the spindle fibers appear in prophase
 *  b. correct; the division of the centromeres marks the beginning of anaphase
    c. incorrect; this is the first step of mitosis and occurs in prophase
    d. incorrect; the chromosomes first appear during prophase

11. The chromosomes are first aligned along the spindle equator during
    a. telophase.
    b. anaphase.
    c. prophase.
    d. metaphase.

    a. no; the chromosomes have already separated into two groups, one at each pole
    b. no; the chromosomes have begun to separate although they may still be at the spindle equator
    c. no; the chromosomes and spindle fibers first appear; there has not been enough time to arrange the chromosomes in the center
 *  d. yes; the chromosomes move to the center of the cell before the centromeres divide

12. Which of the following processes occur during telophase?
    a. The chromosomes decondense to become chromatin threadlike forms.
    b. The nuclear envelope disappears.
    c. The spindle fibers move the chromosomes to the center of the spindle.
    d. The two chromatids divide and separate,

 *  a. yes; in preparation for their functioning in interphase
    b. no; this event occurs during prophase
    c. no; this event occurs during metaphase
    d. no; the chromosome is made up of two chromatids until the centromere divides during anaphase

13. Which of the phases of mitosis is the least complex?
    a. anaphase
    b. prophase
    c. telophase
    d. metaphase

    a. no; during this phase the centromeres divide and the chromosomes separate and move toward the poles
    b. no; probably the most complex involving construction of the spindle, condensation of the chromosomes, and disappearance of the nucleolus and nuclear membrane
    c. no; the reverse of the events of prophase
 *  d. yes; all that has to happen is to move the chromosomes to the center of the spindle

14. The hereditary material becomes separated from the cytoplasm during
    a. metaphase.
    b. prophase.
    c. telophase.
    d. anaphase.

a. no; the chromosomes are in the center of the cell surrounded by the cytoplasm and the spindle

b. no; at the beginning, the hereditary material is isolated by the nuclear membrane, but it quickly disappears

\* c. yes; toward the end of telophase, the nuclear membrane reforms, thus isolating the genetic material

d. no; the chromosomes are pulled through the cytoplasm by the spindle fibers but remain in contact with the cytoplasm

15. A cell spindle furrow is characteristic of cytokinesis in
    a. animals.
    b. bacteria.
    c. plants.
    d. fungi.

\* a. yes; no cell wall is involved with cytokinesis

b. no; no mitosis but fission

c. no; a cell plate forms

d. no; sometime cytokinesis does not occur, but when it does, a cell wall is involved

16. DNA
    a. is found on chromosomes.
    b. is responsible for the production of proteins.
    c. of the proper kind is necessary for any cell to function.
    d. all of the above are true

a. no; a partial answer; a more complete answer is available

b. no; a partial answer; a more complete answer is available

c. no; a partial answer; a more complete answer is available

\* d. yes; all of the above are correct

17. Cells produced by mitosis are called _____ cells.
    a. germinal
    b. reproductive
    c. somatic
    d. haploid

a. no; germinal cells are produced by meiosis

b. no; reproductive cells are produced by meiosis

\* c. yes; the new cells will use both old organelles and new ones they produce

d. no; DNA is involved in producing additional organelles

18. A centromere
    a. is the site where microtubules attach to a chromosome.
    b. is the place where two sister chromatids are connected.
    c. appears at different locations on different chromosomes.
    d. all of the above are correct

a. no; a partial answer, a more complete answer is available

b. no; a partial answer, a more complete answer is available

c. no; a partial answer, a more complete answer is available

\* d. yes; all of the above are correct

19. The DNA is replicating during the ___ stage of the cell cycle.
    a. M
    b. G1
    c. G2
    d. S

a. no; this is the stage of mitosis

b. no; the period of growth before replication

c. no; the period of preparation for cell division that occurs after the replication of the genetic material

\* d. yes; the period when the chromosomes and genetic material is replicated

20. Henrietta Lacks
    a. died of cancer, but her cells were the basis for human cell culture.
    b. developed a technique to allow tissue culture of human cells.
    c. discovered that humans had forty-six chromosomes.
    d. is the first known human triploid individual.

\* a. yes; her cancer cells are widely used in cancer research

b. no; not a researcher, but a woman from Baltimore who developed cancer

c. no; did not count human chromosomes or do karyotypes

d. no; there are no known triploid humans

# CHAPTER 8

# MEIOSIS

1.  In Slipper limpets
    a.  the sex of a larva depends upon whether it hatches at night or during the day.
    b.  the females reproduce asexually and there are no males.
    c.  a larva develops into a female if it matures alone and into a male if it is near others.
    d.  the sex of the adult depends upon the salinity of the water where it lives.

    a.  no; the timing of hatching does not influence sex
    b.  no; this animal reproduces sexually
    *   c.  yes; the females develop all alone, and then if others are nearby, subsequent maturations produce a pile of males on top of a single female
    d.  no; salinity does not affect sex

2.  Asexual reproduction
    a.  is the common form of reproduction in higher organisms.
    b.  requires only one parent.
    c.  produces wide variety of offspring.
    d.  both (b) and (c)

    a.  no; natural selection favored sexual reproduction in higher organisms
    *   b.  yes; and the offspring resembles the parent
    c.  no; offspring are alike
    d.  no; only (b) is correct

3.  When compared to asexual reproduction sexual reproduction.
    a.  is more efficient.
    b.  produces more variety in the offspring.
    c.  requires only one parent.
    d.  produces more offspring.

    a.  no; asexual reproduction is more simple in that it does not require that gametes meet and a single cell can reproduce
    *   b.  yes; clearly the correct answer; variety is the chief advantage of sexual reproduction and the reason why it is favored by natural selection
    c.  no; although a very few hermaphroditic sexually reproducing forms might be able to reproduce alone
    d.  no; the number of offspring is not controlled by the type of reproduction; some sexually reproducing parasites and spore-producing fungi may exceed 1 million offspring

4.  In animals, meiosis occurs to produce
    a.  somatic cells.
    b.  gametes.
    c.  cells of the sex organs.
    d.  diploid cells.

    a.  no; body cells are produced by mitosis
    *   b.  yes; gametes are formed by meiosis in gametogenesis
    c.  no; a possible answer since germ cells are in the sex organs but most cells are produced by mitosis; another choice is a much better answer
    d.  no; majority of animals are diploid so that meiosis would produce haploid cells

5.  The sex chromosomes in humans are referred by
    a.  A and B.
    b.  M and F.
    c.  X and O.
    d.  X and Y.

    a.  no
    b.  no
    c.  no
    *   d.  yes; female by X and male by Y

6.  In meiosis, DNA replication occurs
    a.  during interphase.
    b.  between meiosis I and meiosis II.
    c.  during prophase I.
    d.  after meiosis II.

\*     a.    yes; as is the case in mitosis
      b.    no; usually meiosis II follows meiosis I so rapidly there is not enough time for replication
      c.    no; this is the time for synapsis
      d.    no; this would restore the diploid condition and negate the reduction in chromosomes that occurred in meiosis

7.    Synapsis occurs
      a.    during interphase.
      b.    between meiosis I and meiosis II.
      c.    during prophase I.
      d.    during prophase II.

      a.    no; replication takes placed in interphase before chromosomes condense and move around
      b.    no; synapsis has already occurred
\*     c.    yes; at the beginning of meiosis
      d.    no; synapsis has already occurred

8.    Sister chromatids of each chromosome are separated from each other during
      a.    interphase.
      b.    prophase I.
      c.    anaphase I.
      d.    anaphase II.

      a.    no; the phase when the chromosomes are replicated
      b.    no; the phase when pairing occurs
      c.    no; the homologues separate during anaphase I
\*     d.    yes; the sister chromatids separate during anaphase II

9.    During crossing over, ___ undergo breakage and exchange segments.
      a.    sister chromatids
      b.    nonsister chromatids of a homologous pair
      c.    nonhomologous chromatids
      d.    X and Y chromosomes

      a.    no; there would be no change because they are replicates
\*     b.    yes; this allows new combinations of paternal and maternal alleles
      c.    no; different genes on different chromosomes do not pair
      d.    no; although these chromosomes pair, they pair only at one end and do not exchange

10.    ____ results in recombination of genes.
      a.    Crossing over
      b.    Pairing
      c.    Duplication
      d.    none of the above

\*     a.    yes; breakage and exchange take place
      b.    no; pairing only produces conditions that allow recombination
      c.    no; just duplicates the existing genes, does nothing to reshuffle them
      d.    no; one of the above is correct

11.    The centromeres divide during
      a.    prophase I.
      b.    anaphase I.
      c.    prophase II.
      d.    anaphase II.

      a.    no; synapsis occurs
      b.    no; homologues separate but chromatids remain attached by centromeres
      c.    no; centromeres do not divide during prophase
\*     d.    yes; centromeres divide and chromatids become chromosomes and move toward the poles

12.    If a diploid organism has a genome consisting of 4 chromosomes, it can produce _____ different combinations of maternal and paternal chromosomes disregarding crossing over.
      a.    4
      b.    8
      c.    16
      d.    32

      a.    no; not enough
      b.    no; not enough
\*     c.    yes; 2 to the 4th power is 16
      d.    no; too many

13.    A single pair of chromosomes consisting one maternal and one paternal chromosome and possessing genes for the same traits are called
      a.    autosomes.
      b.    homologous chromosomes.
      c.    chromatids.
      d.    somatic chromatids.

      a.    no; name given to nonsex chromosomes
\*     b.    yes; same except for different alleles and they come from different parents
      c.    no; name given to replicated chromosomes
      d.    no; somatic refers to body tissues

14.    The ultimate reason that two chromosomes are called homologous is that they
      a.    possess genes for the same traits.
      b.    possess the same traits.
      c.    are the same length and have their centromeres in the same place.
      d.    pair or synapse during meiosis.

a. no; essentially correct but does not address X and Y chromosomes that are said to be homologous (better answer given)
b. no; not necessarily true, as one homologous chromosome could have a dominant allele while the other carries a recessive one
c. no; true of all homologous chromosomes except the X and Y chromosomes (better answer given)
* d. yes; homologous chromosomes by definition pair during synapsis. The other statements may be partially true, but they do not apply to the sex chromosome, which are homologous but quite different in appearance and the genes they carry

15. The paired homologous chromosomes are found at the spindle equator during
a. metaphase I.
b. telophase I.
c. prophase II.
d. anaphase II.

* a. yes; the homologues separate during anaphase I
b. no; the homologues have already separated
c. no; the homologues have already separated
d. no; the homologues have already separated

16. When oocytes undergo meiosis, they produce a total of _____ polar body (bodies)
a. one
b. two
c. three
d. four

a. no; only one polar body is produced after meiosis I
b. no; would be the correct answer if only the primary and secondary oocytes produce polar bodies, but the first polar body also divides
* c. yes
d. no; one of the four cells produced is the egg; not all can be polar bodies

17. Which of the following statements about meiosis is *not* true?
a. Meiosis produces clones.
b. Meiosis reduces the number of chromosomes.
c. Meiosis promotes variation.
d. Meiosis produces gametes.

* a. correct; this statement is not true; meiosis produces differences not similarity
b. incorrect; statement is true
c. incorrect; statement is true
d. incorrect; statement is true

18. The reason that sexually reproducing organisms produce offspring different from themselves is
a. crossing over.
b. random arrangement of chromosomes from the spindle equator.
c. fertilization is a chance mix of genetically different gametes.
d. all of the above

a. no; a partial answer; a more complete answer is available
b. no; a partial answer; a more complete answer is available
c. no; a partial answer; a more complete answer is available
* d. yes; all statements are true

19. Which of the following statements is false?
a. Crossing over occurs during cell division.
b. The fusion of two haploid cells produces a diploid cell.
c. Meiosis of a diploid cell produces haploid cells.
d. The fusion of two haploid cells occurs in sexual reproduction and is known as fertilization.

* a. yes; crossing over occurs only during meiosis
b. no; this statement is true
c. no; this statement is true
d. no; this statement is true

20. Asexual reproduction is accomplished by
a. gametogenesis.
b. mitosis.
c. fusion of sex cells.
d. all of the above

a. no; refers to the production of gametes used in sexual reproduction
* b. yes; in many plants and animals and other eukaryotic organisms
c. no; fusion of sex cells occurs during sexual reproduction
d. no; only one of the above answers is correct

21. It can be said with certainty that if you are normal, you inherited
a. twenty-two autosomes and a Y chromosome from your father.
b. twenty-two autosomes and a X chromosome from your mother.
c. forty-four chromosomes from both parents.
d. none of the above can be stated with certainty

a. no; this statement cannot be said by a female
* b. yes; both males and females inherit an X chromosomes and twenty-two autosomes from their mother
c. no; you also had to inherit sex chromosomes from both parents
d. no; it is certain that everyone inherits an X chromosome from their mother and twenty-two maternal autosomes

22. Meiosis is similar to mitosis in that
    a. synapsis is a characteristic event.
    b. spindle fibers control movement of chromosomes.
    c. the daughter cells are identical.
    d. haploid cells are produced.

    a. no; synapsis occurs only during meiosis
\*  b. yes; spindle fibers are responsible for chromosome movement
    c. no; the daughter cells are identical in mitosis but differ in meiosis
    d. no; if diploid cells undergo meiosis, haploid cells result, and haploid cells are produced in mitosis only if haploid cells undergo mitosis

23. Genetic recombination
    a. is the result of crossing over.
    b. is the major advantage of sexual reproduction.
    c. provides a mechanism for adaptation and evolution in changing environments.
    d. all of the above

    a. no; a partial answer; a more complete answer is available
    b. no; a partial answer; a more complete answer is available
    c. no; a partial answer; a more complete answer is available
\*  d. yes; all of the above are correct

24. Disjunction occurs during
    a. interphase.
    b. mitotic anaphase.
    c. anaphase I.
    d. anaphase II.

    a. no; chromosomes are replicated during interphase
    b. no; synapsis and crossing over do not occur during mitosis
\*  c. yes; disjunction or separation of homologous chromosomes occurs during anaphase I
    d. no; disjunction has already occurred

25. The diploid number is restored by
    a. mitosis.
    b. fertilization.
    c. meiosis.
    d. nondisjunction.

    a. no; the chromosome number is maintained
\*  b. yes; the two sets of chromosomes fuse to restore the diploid number
    c. no; the chromosome number is cut in half by meiosis
    d. no; nondisjunction occurs when chromosomes do not separate and the result is often a genome with an extra chromosome

# CHAPTER 9

# OBSERVABLE PATTERNS OF INHERITANCE

1.  The allele for detached earlobes in humans
    a.  involves an allele that calls for cell death during embryonic development.
    b.  is a recessive allele.
    c.  may be passed on to children by parents that have either attached or detached ears.
    d.  requires that both inherited alleles be alleles for detached ears.

    *
    a.  yes; the cells between the earlobe and the skull die so that the earlobe becomes free
    b.  no; detached earlobes are controlled by a dominant allele and attached earlobes are controlled by a recessive allele
    c.  no; parents with attached earlobes must have both recessive alleles and therefore do not have an allele for detached earlobes
    d.  no; only one allele for detached earlobes has to be present because it is a dominant allele

2.  The discoverer of the laws of genetics was
    a.  Alfred Wallace.
    b.  Jean-Baptiste LeMarck.
    c.  Gregor Mendel.
    d.  Charles Darwin.

    a.  no; coauthor of evolution theory, did not know of genetics
    b.  no; proposed the inheritance of acquired characteristics
    *   c.  yes; proposed the laws of genetics
    d.  no; coauthor of evolution theory, did not know of genetics

3.  Gregor Mendel lived in
    a.  Germany.
    b.  Czechoslovakia.
    c.  Albania.
    d.  Poland.

    a.  no; another country
    *   b.  yes; he was born in Czechoslovakia
    c.  no; another country
    d.  no; another country

4.  Gregor Mendel discovered
    a.  sex-linked inheritance.
    b.  chromosomes.
    c.  the law of independent assortment.
    d.  mutations.

    a.  no; discovered later using fruit flies
    b.  no; discovered later using fruit flies
    *   c.  yes; Mendel discovered that genes for different characteristics were inherited independently of each other
    d.  no; discovered later by DeVries, one of the rediscoverers of Mendel's laws

5.  Which of the following was discovered by Mendel?
    a.  linkage
    b.  relationship of genetic behavior to laws of probability
    c.  the location of genes on chromosomes
    d.  role of chromosomes in sex determination

    a.  no; no evidence to show that he understood this phenomenon
    *   b.  yes; his detailed statistical evidence to support this observation
    c.  no; the role of chromosomes not discovered until much later
    d.  no; the relationship of chromosomes to genetics was not known in Mendel's time

6.  Which of the following is *not* one of the principles of heredity proposed by the father of genetics?
    a.  law of dominance
    b.  law of incomplete dominance
    c.  law of independent assortment
    d.  law of segregation

    a.  no; Mendel proposed the law of dominance
    *   b.  yes; Mendel did not propose a law for incomplete dominance
    c.  no; Mendel proposed the law of independent assortment
    d.  no; Mendel proposed the law of segregation

7.  In his research, Gregor Mendel used
    a.  snap dragons.
    b.  fruit flies.
    c.  chickens.
    d.  none of the above

a.  no; not widely used plant for genetic crosses
b.  no; used later by T. H. Morgan
c.  no; although the pattern of inheritance for a number of traits is well-known
*  d.  yes, Mendel restricted his genetic work to garden peas

8.  At Mendel's time, the conventional wisdom stated
    a.  the sperm controlled the development of an individual.
    b.  the egg controlled the development of an individual.
    c.  blood was the factor that controlled genetics.
    d.  characteristics of the parents blended together in the offspring.

    a.  no; an earlier theory of preformation that stated the sperm had miniature adults preformed in them
    b.  no; an earlier theory of preformation held that the egg had miniature adults preformed in them
    c.  no; "bad blood" and "blue blood" were often used, but this was not the dominant theory (they are still referred to today)
*  d.  yes; people believed in blending inheritance

9.  Which of the following statements is *not* one of Mendel's tenets?
    a.  There are discrete units of inheritance called factors.
    b.  Organisms inherit two factors, one from each parent.
    c.  Different factors assort independently into gametes.
    d.  Characteristics of the parents blend together in their offspring.

    a.  no; this was one of Mendel's tenets
    b.  no; this was one of Mendel's tenets
    c.  no; this was one of Mendel's tenets
*  d.  yes; this was not one of Mendel's tenets; this was the conventional wisdom of Mendel's time

10.  An individual homozygous at a particular locus
    a.  has the same alleles located at the homologous locus.
    b.  has the same genotype as its parents.
    c.  can be identified by examining its phenotype.
    d.  will contribute different alleles to its offspring.

*  a.  yes; they have the same alleles
    b.  no; not necessarily—two heterozygotes could produce a homozygote
    c.  no; this would be possible for a recessive, but not a dominant individual
    d.  no; all gametes will receive the same alleles

11.  If Mendel crossed two purple pea plants chosen at random (purple is dominant to white)
    a.  the offspring would be hybrids.
    b.  the offspring could have some white flowers among the offspring.
    c.  they would breed true.
    d.  both (b) and (c)

    a.  no; hybrids are the offspring of two pure-breeding organisms with different phenotypes
    b.  yes; a partial answer; if the two purples were heterozygous
    c.  yes; a partial answer; the only way that could happen would be if the two purple plants were homozygous
*  d.  yes; both (b) and (c) are possible

12.  The cytological basis for segregation may be seen during _____ of meiosis.
    a.  prophase I
    b.  anaphase I
    c.  prophase II
    d.  anaphase II

    a.  no; too early; homologous chromosomes have not separated
*  b.  yes; the homologous chromosomes separate during anaphase I
    c.  no; too late; the chromosomes have already separated
    d.  no; too late; the chromosomes have already separated

13.  Rose comb is dominant to single comb in chickens. If the $F_1$ (of the cross of pure-breeding rose and pure-breeding single chickens) were crossed, the next generation would have
    a.  all rose-combed chickens.
    b.  one-fourth rose, three-fourths single.
    c.  one-half rose, one-half single.
    d.  one-fourth single, three-fourths rose.

    a.  no; the $F_2$ would contain some homozygous recessives
    b.  no; there should be more rose and less single
    c.  no; the ratio obtained from a testcross
*  d.  yes; the typical 3:1 ratio with the large number attributed to the dominant trait

14.  In garden peas, Mendel found that green pods are dominant to yellow pods and yellow seeds are dominant to green seeds. Which of the phenotypes would be more common in the second generation of a cross of a plant with yellow seeds and pods with a plant with green seeds and pods?
    a.  yellow seeds, yellow pods
    b.  yellow seeds, green pods
    c.  green seeds, green pods
    d.  green seeds, yellow pods

a. no; 3/16 of the offspring
* b. yes; 9/16 of the offspring
c. no; 3/16 of the offspring
d. no; 1/16 of the offspring

15. In garden peas, round and yellow seeds are controlled by dominant alleles while wrinkled and green are controlled by recessive alleles. If you found a plant with round and yellow seeds and wanted to determine its genotype, you would cross this plant with a plant that is pure breeding for
a. round and yellow seeds.
b. round and green seeds.
c. wrinkled and green seeds.
d. wrinkled and yellow seeds.

a. no; unable to determine the genotype of either trait
b. no; unable to determine the genotype of the round seeds
* c. yes; a cross called a testcross; if a recessive trait appears, the unknown is heterozygous for it; otherwise it would be homozygous for the dominant trait
d. no; unable to determine the genotypes of the yellow seeds

16. If a cross produces a 1:1 phenotypic ratio, the genotype of the parents were
a. both homozygous.
b. both heterozygous.
c. one homozygous dominant, the other heterozygous.
d. one homozygous recessive, the other heterozygous.

a. no; if both parents were homozygous dominant all offspring would have dominant phenotypes, and if both parents were homozygous recessive all offspring would have recessive phenotypes
b. no; the ratio would be 3 dominant to 1 recessive
c. no; two possible genotypes, but the phenotypes would all be dominant
* d. yes; one-half would be heterozygous expressing the dominant trait. whereas the others would be homozygous recessive

17. Which of the following can be determined with monohybrid crosses?
a. the law of dominance.
b. the law of independent assortment.
c. the law of segregation.
d. both (a) and (c)

a. yes; a partial answer
b. no; need a pair of genes to test
c. yes; a partial answer
* d. yes; both (a) and (c) are correct

18. If an organism had a genotype of AaBbCc, how many different gametes could it form according to the law of independent assortment?
a. four
b. eight
c. twelve
d. sixteen

a. no; more different gametes are possible
* b. yes; ABC, ABc, AbC, Abc, aBC, aBc, abC, abc ($2^3$=8)-two different choices for three different genes
c. no; fewer gametes are possible
d. no; fewer gametes are possible

19. Which of the following $F_2$ phenotypic ratio would support the law of independent assortment?
a. 3:1
b. 9:3:3:1
c. 1:2:1
d. 7:1:1:7

a. no; law of dominance
* b. yes; derived from the Punnett square
c. no; a genotypic ratio or a monohybrid ratio showing incomplete dominance
d. no; results produced by linkage, not independent assortment

20. A 1:2:1 phenotypic ratio in which the two individuals represent a blend of the other two phenotypes is best explained by
a. codominance.
b. incomplete dominance.
c. multiple alleles.
d. dominance.

a. no; the ratio could be obtained, but the phenotype would not be a blend
* b. yes; not enough product to give full phenotype expressed by the extreme
c. yes; but other ratios can be obtained and blending not necessarily a result
d. no; in dominance the phenotypic ratio would be 3:1

21. Which of the following statements is false?
a. Two or more genes may influence a single trait.
b. Some genes may influence more than one trait.
c. Genes are independent of each other and do not interact.
d. Genes are located on a specific spot on a chromosome.

a. no; this statement is true
b. no; this statement is true
* c. yes; this statement is false; genes do interact with each other to modify their expression
d. no; this statement is true

22. Which of the following statements is false?
   a. The sorting of all genes in the formation of gametes is independent of what happens to all other genes during gamete formation.
   b. If two alleles are different, one may have a more pronounced effect on the trait than the other.
   c. All cells in the body (with the exception of the gametes) have two alleles for each gene controlling a trait.
   d. Genes are units of information about traits that can be inherited.

 * a. yes; this statement is false; alleles on the same chromosome tend to be inherited together, or are said to be linked, and do not exhibit independent assortment
   b. no; this statement is true; such as in dominant and recessive alleles
   c. no; this statement is true; one inherited from each parent
   d. no; this statement is true

23. If a person with blood type AB were crossed to a person with blood type O, the offspring would be
   a. AB or O.
   b. AB only.
   c. A or B, but not AB or O.
   d. none of the above

   a. no; no way for an individual to inherit both traits from one parent
   b. no; offspring has to inherit an O, therefore cannot be type AB
 * c. yes; would inherit an A or B from one parent and an O from the other
   d. no; a common distractor; one of the above is correct

24. Pleiotropy refers to
   a. the extent to which a gene is expressed in an individual.
   b. a gene that has multiple effects.
   c. a condition in which one gene masks the expression of another gene.
   d. a gene that has a lethal effect.

   a. no; refers to expressivity
 * b. yes; such as sickle-cell anemia
   c. no; refers to epistasis
   d. no; lethal genes

25. A Punnett square
   a. gives the genotypes of the possible offspring produced by a genetic cross.
   b. indicates the gametes that can be produced by the parents involved in a cross.
   c. enables a person to determine the probability that particular genotypes would be found in the offspring and in what proportion.
   d. all of the above

   a. no; a partial answer; a more complete answer is available
   b. no; a partial answer; a more complete answer is available
   c. no; a partial answer; a more complete answer is available
 * d. yes; all of the above are correct

26. Cystic fibrosis is controlled by a recessive allele. If two normal parents have a child with cystic fibrosis, the chance that their next child will have cystic fibrosis is
   a. zero.
   b. 1/4.
   c. 3/4.
   d. unable to predict.

   a. no; there is a chance for the child to inherit the defective gene from the parents regardless of what happened in previous crosses
 * b. the probability remains the same regardless of previous crosses
   c. no; the chances for a normal child would be 3 in 4
   d. no; it is possible to predict 1 chance in 4 because of the laws of probability

27. Which of the following statements is false?
   a. A testcross is used when the genotypes of the parents are unknown.
   b. A testcross is used when the phenotypes of the parents are unknown.
   c. A testcross is used when the genotypes of the offspring are unknown.
   d. none of the above

 * a. yes; a testcross can be used to determine the genotype of the parents
   b. no; the phenotypes can be determined by visual inspection
   c. no; unable to determine genotype without more information
   d. no; only one of the above is correct

28. Chin fissure is controlled by a dominant allele and a smooth chin by a recessive allele. Dimples are controlled by a dominant allele and no dimples by a recessive allele. If the parents were heterozygous for each trait, the chance to produce a child with a chin fissure and no dimples would be
   a. 12/16.
   b. 9/16.
   c. 3/16.
   d. 1/16.

   a. no; too great a chance
   b. no; too great a chance
 * c. yes; 3/4 chance for each child to have a chin fissure "times" 1/4 chance to have no dimples equals 3/16
   d. no; too small a chance

29. Chin fissure is controlled by a dominant allele and a smooth chin by a recessive allele. Dimples are controlled by a dominant allele and no dimples by a recessive allele. If the parents were heterozygous for each trait, the chance to produce a child with a chin fissure and dimples would be
   a. 12/16.
   b. 9/16.
   c. 3/16.
   d. 1/16

   a. no; too great a chance
 * b. yes; 3/4 chance for each child to have a chin fissure "times" 3/4 chance to have a dimple equals 9/16
   c. no; too small a chance
   d. no; too small a chance

30. Chin fissure is controlled by a dominant allele and a smooth chin fissure by a recessive allele. Dimples are controlled by a dominant allele and no dimples by a recessive allele. If the father was *Ccdd* and the mother *CcDd*, what are the chances that a child will have a chin fissure and dimples?
   a. 9/16
   b. 6/16
   c. 3/16
   d. 2/16

   a. no; too great a chance
 * b. yes; 3/4 chance for chin fissure "times" 2/4 chance for dimples equals 6/16
   c. no; too small a chance
   d. no; too small a chance

31. If two heterozygous parents, *CcDd*, were crossed, there are ___ different combinations of genotypes in the offspring.
   a. sixteen
   b. nine
   c. six
   d. four

   a. no; too many
 * b. yes; *CCDD, CCDd, CcDD, CcDd, ccDD, ccDd, CCdd, Ccdd, and ccdd*
   c. no; not enough
   d. no; not enough

32. If two heterozygous parents *CcDd* were crossed, there are ___ different pure breeding offspring produced.
   a. sixteen
   b. nine
   c. six
   d. four

   a. no; too many
   b. no; too many
   c. no; too many
 * d. yes; *CCDD, CCdd, ccDD, ccdd*

33. Which of the following would produce phenotypic results different from those predicted by Mendel?
   a. genes with codominant alleles
   b. linked genes
   c. multiple genes
   d. all of the above

   a. no; a partial answer; a more complete answer is available
   b. no; a partial answer; a more complete answer is available
   c. no; a partial answer; a more complete answer is available
 * d. yes; all of the above

34. The ABO blood types have ___ different genotypes.
   a. three
   b. four
   c. six
   d. sixteen

   a. no; not enough
   b. no; not enough
 * c. yes; $I^AI^A$, $I^AI^B$, $I^Ai$, $I^BI^B$, $I^Bi$, ii
   d. no; too many

35. The ABO blood types have ___ different phenotypes.
   a. two
   b. four
   c. six
   d. sixteen

   a. no; not enough
 * b. yes; A, B, AB, O
   c. no; too many
   d. no; too many

36. If a woman has blood type AB and has a child with blood type AB, to which blood type could the father *not* belong?
   a. A
   b. B
   c. AB
   d. O

   a. no; in each case it would be possible for the child to inherit an A or a B from the mother and an A or a B from the father
   b. no; in each case it would be possible for the child to inherit an A or a B from the mother and an A or a B from the father
   c. no; in each case it would be possible for the child to inherit an A or a B from the mother and an A or a B from the father
 * d. yes; the father has to pass on either an A or a B depending upon what the child received from the mother; if the father were blood type O, the child could not get an A or a B from the father

37. If a child was blood type O, his father could *not* belong to blood type
    a. A.
    b. B.
    c. AB.
    d. O.

    a. no; this blood type could produce a child with blood type O
    b. no; this blood type could produce a child with blood type O
    * c. yes; the child would have to inherit blood type A or B from his father
    d. no; this blood type could produce a child with blood type O

38. If a child belonged to blood type O, the child could *not* have had which one of the following parents?
    a. a type A mother and a type B father
    b. a type AB mother and a type O father
    c. a type O mother and a type B father
    d. a type A mother and a type O father

    a. no; the child could inherit type O blood from each parent
    * b. yes; the child would have to inherit $I^A$ or $I^B$ from his mother and belong to blood type A or blood type B
    c. no; the child would inherit O from the mother and could inherit O from the father
    d. no; the child could inherit O from the mother and would inherit O from the father

39. Blood types are controlled by
    a. multiple alleles.
    b. multiple genes.
    c. pleiotropic genes.
    d. none of the above

    * a. yes; there are three alternate forms of the allele to govern blood types
    b. no; a type of genetics in which many different genes interact to produce the phenotype
    c. no; pleiotropic genes affect more than one characteristic
    d. no; one of the above is correct

40. Codominance is exhibited in
    a. body height.
    b. sickle-cell anemia.
    c. polydactyl.
    d. phenylketonuria.

    a. no; controlled by multiple genes
    * b. yes; an example of codominance
    c. no; a trait controlled by a dominant allele
    d. no; a trait controlled by a recessive allele

41. In sickle-cell anemia, red blood cells will form a sickled shape when
    a. exposed to excess oxygen.
    b. the blood pH drops too low.
    c. when there is insufficient oxygen.
    d. both (a) and (b), but not (c)

    a. no; excess oxygen will not affect blood cell shape
    b. no; pH will not affect blood cell shape
    * c. yes; when a red blood cell of a person with sickle-cell anemia is exposed to a deficiency in oxygen, it will form a sickled shape
    d. no; both (a) and (b) are false, while (c) is correct

42. Which of the following statements is false?
    a. The gene for sickle-cell anemia produces an abnormal hemoglobin molecule possibly leading to many symptoms and damage to the body.
    b. Only people with sickle-cell anemia show symptoms; those that are heterozygous are clear from the disease.
    c. A carrier for sickle-cell anemia is able to produce both normal and abnormal hemoglobin.
    d. Children homozygous for sickle-cell anemia often die early in life.

    a. no; this statement is true
    * b. yes; this statement is false; those that have sickle-cell trait may also show symptoms
    c. no; this statement is true
    d. no; this statement is true

43. Sickle-cell anemia may result in
    a. damage to heart and lungs.
    b. local failure in blood supply.
    c. damage to brain and kidneys.
    d. all of the above

    a. no; a partial answer; a more complete answer is available
    b. no; a partial answer; a more complete answer is available
    c. no; a partial answer; a more complete answer is available
    * d. yes; all the above are correct

44. Polygenic traits are
    a. controlled by many different genes.
    b. control quantitative traits that express continuous variation in traits.
    c. produce a bell-shaped curve when the characteristics of individuals in a population are plotted on a graph.
    d. all of the above

    a. no; a partial answer; a more complete answer is available
    b. no; a partial answer; a more complete answer is available
    c. no; a partial answer; a more complete answer is available
    * d. yes; all of the above are true

# CHAPTER 10

# CHROMOSOMES AND HUMAN GENETICS

1. In 1882 Walter Fleming discovered
   a. penicillin.
   b. sex linkage.
   c. chromosomes.
   d. the first human genetic disorder.

   a. no; Alexander Fleming made this discovery almost fifty years later
   b. no; coworkers of T. H. Morgan made this discovery
   * c. yes
   d. no; many genetic traits were known to be passed on from parents even though the mechanism was still unknown

2. In the 1880s, efforts to uncover the mysteries of heredity were triggered by
   a. the discovery of Mendel's research paper.
   b. Weismann's proposal that meiosis occurred and that each sex contributed one-half of the hereditary information to the offspring.
   c. the frequency of hemophilia in the royal families descending from Queen Victoria.
   d. the development of many research prizes such as the Nobel prize, the Award of the Royal Society of London, the French Pasteur prize, and the Elowitz prize.

   a. no; did not occur until 1900
   * b. yes; Weismann's theory and the newly discovered chromosomes provided a physical mechanism to explain some of the biological mysteries of heredity
   c. no; not a major research stimulus
   d. no; some of these are fictitious

3. The characteristics of autosomes and sex chromosomes can best be studied during ____, when they are in their most condensed state.
   a. interphase
   b. telophase
   c. anaphase
   d. metaphase

   a. no; chromosome are dispersed
   b. no; chromosomes begin to decondense and are gathered together at the pole
   c. no; the division of centromere makes it hard to separate twice as many chromosomes as they move toward the poles
   * d. yes; they are easier to see and distinguish

4. A karyotype is
   a. a visual presentation of the chromosomes from the largest to the smallest.
   b. a visual representation of how genes combine to form the genotypes of the next generation.
   c. a visual presentation of how a human trait is inherited in a family.
   d. none of the above

   * a. yes; used in diagnosis of chromosomal diseases
   b. no; a Punnett square used to show genetic combinations
   c. no; a pedigree chart used to study human genetic patterns
   d. no; a common distractor; one of the above is correct

5. Which of the following statements is false?
   a. Humans have forty-six chromosomes with forty-four autosomes.
   b. Both males and females have the same number and kinds of chromosomes.
   c. The gene sequence on a chromosome does not necessarily remain the same.
   d. Alterations in chromosome numbers can result in genetic disorders.

   a. no; this statement is true
   * b. yes; this statement is false; males have an X and a Y while females have two Xs
   c. no; the statement is true; crossing over may rearrange the gene sequence
   d. no; the statement is true; an extra chromosome may lead to Down syndrome

6. A chromosome can be distinguished from other chromosomes based on its
   a. length.
   b. centromere position.
   c. banding patterns.
   d. all of the above

a. no; a partial answer; not definitive by itself
b. no; a partial answer; not definitive by itself
c. no; a partial answer; an important discriminating feature
* d. yes, all of the above are correct

7. Which of the following statements is false?
a. Genes are arranged in linear order on chromosomes.
b. Meiosis and sexual reproduction lead to changes in chromosome numbers.
c. Diploid cells have pairs of homologous chromosomes.
d. The number of autosomes varies for each sex.

a. no; this statement is true
b. no; this statement is true
c. no; this statement is true
* d. yes; this statement is false; both sexes have twenty-two pairs of autosomes

8. The chemical used in developing a karyotype is
a. colchicine.
b. chloramphenicol.
c. hexosaminilase.
d. testosterone.

* a. yes; interferes with microtubules so that chromosome movement is arrested
b. no; not used during karyotyping
c. no; not used during karyotyping
d. no; not used during karyotyping

9. Which of the following statements is false?
a. Most of the genes located on the X chromosome are involved in controlling sexual characteristics.
b. In the absence of the gene product of Sry (the gene carried on the Y chromosome), ovaries will develop.
c. The Y chromosome is smaller and carries fewer genes than the X chromosome.
d. Genes located on the X or the Y chromosome are called sex-linked genes.

* a. yes; this statements is false; most genes on the sex chromosome deal with nonsexual traits
b. no; this statement is true
c. no; this statement is true
d. no; this statement is true

10. Crossing over occurs between
a. nonhomologous chromosomes.
b. sister chromatids.
c. nonsister chromatids.
d. daughter chromatids.

a. no; this would be called translocation and would be a chromosome aberration
b. no; there would be no effect if sister chromatids exchanged parts
* c. yes; results in swapping maternal and paternal chromatid segments
d. no; there would be no effect if they exchanged segments

11. Linkage
a. increases variability.
b. refers to the tendency of genes found on the same chromosome to be inherited together.
c. is an exception to the law of segregation.
d. is unaffected by crossing over.

a. no; tends to reduce it because certain traits would be inherited together
* b. yes
c. no; rather an exception to the law of independent assortment
d. no; crossing over breaks up linkage relationships

12. Which of the following is *not* one of the traits that would be desirable in an organism used for genetic experimentation?
a. high fertility with large number of offspring
b. long life cycle
c. inexpensive and easy to raise
d. many easily recognizable phenotypic variations

a. no; large number of offspring is desirable
* b. yes; it would be a disadvantage—need short generation time
c. no; this would be a definite advantage to reduce the cost of research
d. no; an important feature needed by organisms used for genetic research

13. The carriers of a sex-linked recessive trait are ____ that do not express the recessive trait they carry.
a. homozygous individuals of either sex
b. heterozygous individuals of either sex
c. heterozygous males
d. heterozygous females

a. no; homozygous individuals would express the recessive alleles they possess
b. no; males cannot be heterozygous for a sex-linked trait
c. no; males cannot be heterozygous for a sex-linked trait
* d. yes; heterozygous females can carry a recessive sex-linked allele that is masked by the dominant allele found on the other X chromosome

14. If a male carries a X-linked recessive trait and his mate is homozygous normal,
    a. all sons will be affected.
    b. all daughters will be carriers.
    c. all daughters will be affected.
    d. the recessive gene will be expressed in all of the offspring.

    a. no; the sons will inherit the normal gene from their mother
    * b. yes; the daughters inherit the normal gene from their mother and the recessive gene from their father
    c. no; the mother will pass on a normal dominant gene so that all females will unaffected
    d. no; the recessive gene will not be expressed in any offspring

15. Red eye is dominant to white eye in *Drosophila*. It is an X-linked gene, (located on the X chromosome). A mutation to white eye in a population of pure-breeding red-eyed fruit flies would be phenotypically expressed first in
    a. a male.
    b. a female.
    c. either sex—it would be impossible to predict.
    d. whichever sex the mutation occurred—the fly's eye color would turn white.

    * a. yes; since it only has one X chromosome, whenever a male inherits the X chromosome with the white-eye gene it will be expressed
    b. no; the presence of a wild-type allele on the other sex chromosome would mask the expression of white eye
    c. no; it can be predicted on the basis that the male only has one sex chromosome
    d. no; white eye is a recessive trait and would not affect the red eye color

16. Red eye is a sex-linked dominant gene; white eye is its recessive allele. If a red-eyed male were crossed to a white-eyed female the F$_1$ generation would consist of
    a. all female flies red-eyed and all males white-eyed.
    b. all female flies white-eyed and all males red-eyed.
    c. all female flies red-eyed and 1/2 males red other 1/2 white-eyed.
    d. 1/2 females red-eyed, 1/2 white-eyed and 1/2 males red-eyed, 1/2 white-eyed.

    * a. yes
    b. no; there would be no red-eyed males or white-eyed females
    c. no; there would be no red-eyed males or white-eyed females
    d. no; there would be no red-eyed males or white-eyed females

17. Red eye is a sex-linked dominant gene; white eye is its recessive allele. If a red-eyed male were crossed to a white-eyed female the F$_2$ generation would consist of
    a. all female flies red-eyed and all males white-eyed.
    b. all female flies white-eyed and all males red-eyed.
    c. all female flies red-eyed and 1/2 males red other 1/2 white-eyed.
    d. 1/2 females red-eyed, 1/2 white-eyed and 1/2 males red-eyed, 1/2 white-eyed.

    a. no; the phenotype of the F$_1$ generation
    b. no; the phenotype of both sexes would be mixed in the F$_2$
    c. no; the phenotype of both sexes would be mixed in the F$_2$
    * d. yes; the phenotype of both sexes would be mixed in the F$_2$

18. Human males inherit their sex-linked traits
    a. from their mother.
    b. from their father.
    c. from both parents.
    d. it depends upon the laws of chance

    * a. yes; they inherit their X-linked traits from the alleles on her X chromosome
    b. no; the X chromosome comes from their mother; the alleles on the Y chromosome are called holandric and are only found in males
    c. no; determined by the X chromosome they inherit from their mother
    d. no; it depends on the inheritance of the X chromosome from the mother

19. The genes responsible for the secondary sex characteristics are carried on the
    a. X chromosome.
    b. Y chromosome.
    c. the autosomes.
    d. all of the chromosomes.

    a. no; a partial answer; the X chromosome carries some secondary sex characteristics and all sex-linked alleles (a better answer available)
    b. no; a partial answer; the Y chromosome carries male fertility genes and genes associated with the secondary sex characteristics of the male (a better answer available)
    c. no; a partial answer; many of the secondary sexual traits are carried on autosomes (a better answer available)
    * d. yes; all of the chromosomes have genes that influence the expression of secondary sex characteristics

21. Which of the following statements about linkage is false?
    a. The closer two genes are located on a chromosome, the more likely they are to be inherited together.
    b. The further apart two genes are on a chromosome, the less likely they will be involved in recombination.
    c. The number of linkage groups is equal to the number of chromosomes found in a gamete.
    d. Two genes located far apart appear to assort independently.

    a. no; the statement is true because the closer two genes are, the less likely crossing over will occur between them
    * b. yes; this statement is false; if the two genes are located fifty units or more apart, they behave as if they were on separate chromosomes
    c. no; this statement is true; all the genes on one chromosome are linked together and represent the maternal or paternal contribution for that chromosome
    d. no; the statement is true; the genes appear not to be linked

22. In a pedigree chart, the clear circles indicate
    a. an affected male.
    b. an unaffected male.
    c. an affected female.
    d. an unaffected female.

    a. no; affected males are indicated darkened squares
    b. no; unaffected males are indicated by clear squares
    c. no; affected females are indicated by darkened circles
    * d. yes; unaffected females are indicated by clear circles

23. Which of the following statements is false?
    a. Pedigree charts use lines between males and females to indicate a marriage or mating.
    b. Pedigree charts use a diamond shape to indicate an offspring whose sex is unknown.
    c. Pedigree charts can only be used to determine answers to questions about human heredity.
    d. Pedigree charts use roman numerals to stand for each generation and arabic numbers for each child in sequence.

    a. no; this statement is true
    b. no; this statement is true
    * c. yes; this statement is false; pedigree analysis provides information about inheritance patterns that can be used for any organism
    d. no; this statement is true

24. The European monarch associated most with hemophilia was
    a. Queen Victoria.
    b. Queen Elizabeth.
    c. King Louis XIV.
    d. King Henry VIII.

    * a. yes; a carrier that transmitted the gene to subsequent generations
    b. no; a different monarch
    c. no; a different monarch
    d. no; a different monarch

25. Which of the following statements is false?
    a. If two normal parents have a child that expresses a recessive genetic defect, there is a 25 percent chance that the next child will have the same defect.
    b. A carrier expresses the dominant trait and may never know that he/she carries the recessive trait.
    c. A carrier is homozygous for the trait in question.
    d. A carrier may pass on either a dominant or a recessive allele to his/her child.

    a. no; this statement is true
    b. no; this statement is true
    * c. yes; this statement is false; a carrier is heterozygous
    d. no; this statement is true

26. Phenylketonuria
    a. is a disease controlled by a dominant gene.
    b. will not be present in the children of two normal parents.
    c. is a sex-linked disorder.
    d. may be partially controlled by diets low in phenylalanine.

    a. no; PKU is caused by the homozygous condition of two recessive genes
    b. no; two carriers may each pass on a defective recessive gene to produce a homozygous recessive child that expresses PKU
    c. no; occurs with equal frequency in both sexes
    * d. yes; diets low in phenylalanine prevent the buildup of phenylpyruvic acid that produces the problems in PKU

27. Which of the following genetic diseases is controlled by a recessive allele?
    a. Huntington's disease
    b. progeria
    c. Tay-Sachs disease
    d. familial hypercholesterolemia

    a. no; controlled by a dominant allele
    b. no; controlled by a dominant allele
    * c. yes; controlled by a recessive allele
    d. no; controlled by a dominant allele

28. Genetic screening utilizes
    a. amniocentesis.
    b. chorionic villi sampling.
    c. embryo testing.
    d. all of the above

a. no; a partial answer; a more complete choice is available
b. no; a partial answer; a more complete choice is available
c. no; a partial answer; a more complete choice is available
* d. yes; all of the above are correct

29. It would be possible to eliminate Huntington's disease in one generation by
a. testing the entire population for the presence of genetic markers on chromosome 4.
b. preventing those people who have the disease from having children.
c. not allowing the children of parents who develop Huntington's disease to have children.
d. using genetic therapy to replace the defective gene.

a. no; this approach could be used, but it would prove to be too costly
b. no; too many people who will develop the disease will already have children before they develop symptoms
* c. yes; the only way a person develops the disease is to inherit it from a parent and if those that have the chance to inherit the gene (children of affected parents) never have children of their own, the gene would be eliminated in one generation
d. no; the possibility of genetic therapy is still in the future

30. Eight percent of human males develop red/green color blindness, a sex-linked recessive trait. The chance of a female having this trait is
a. zero—there is no chance.
b. 8 in 100, the same chance as a male.
c. 16 in 100 because she has two X chromosomes; she should have twice the chance to develop the disease.
d. 64 in 10,000.

a. no; there is a chance for a female to inherit the disease.
b. no; males are XY and females XX; for a female to express the trait she would have to be homozygous recessive, a chance of 8 percent "times" 8 percent
c. no; with two X chromosomes she could have a dominant normal allele and mask the inheritance of a recessive allele
* d. yes; the chances that an X chromosome would carry the recessive allele is 8/100; the chances that both would be recessive is 8/100 "times" 8/100 which equals 64/10,000

31. If a female expresses the red/green color blindness, we know that
a. both father and mother are normal.
b. the father is color-blind; the mother may be a carrier or color-blind.
c. the father is normal; the mother may be a carrier or color-blind.
d. nothing can be said about the parents.

a. no; the female must inherit the allele for color blindness from both parents
* b. yes; this is the only way that a daughter could inherit the allele from both parents
c. no; the father must be color-blind for his daughter to inherit the allele for color blindness from him
d. no; it is possible to identify the genotype of the father and know that the mother has the allele to pass on to her daughter

32. Which of the following is (are) true of Huntington's disorder, an example of an autosomal dominant inheritance?
a. An individual with this trait will pass it on to all of his/her offspring.
b. Defective genes are able to persist in high frequencies in a population because people with the gene are able to survive to reproduction.
c. An individual with the disorder will often have completed reproduction before any symptoms of the disease appear.
d. both (b) and (c), but not (a)

a. no; this statement is false; only a 50-50 chance of passing on the trait
b. no; this statement is true, but only a partial answer; organisms with this defect reproduce normally,
c. no; this statement is true but only a partial answer; the onset of the disease is usually after age forty
* d. yes; both (b) and (c) are true statements

33. The transfer of a fragment of one chromosome to a nonhomologous chromosome is called
a. translocation.
b. inversion.
c. deletion.
d. duplication.

* a. yes; part of one chromosome becomes attached to nonhomologous chromosome
b. no; the sequence of genes on the same chromosomes is reversed
c. no; some genes are simply lost from a chromosome
d. no; involves duplicating a segment on the same chromosome so that there are two such sequences on the chromosome

34. The failure of chromosomes to separate during meiosis I or II is a
a. deletion.
b. duplication.
c. nondisjunction.
d. mutation.

a. no; involves the loss of a segment of a chromosome
b. no; involves a duplication of a segment of a chromosomes
* c. yes; the homologous chromosomes fail to separate and are inherited together
d. no; an inheritable change in a gene

35. Down Syndrome
    a. is known as trisomy 21.
    b. individuals live longer than normal unaffected individuals.
    c. may be treated by gene therapy.
    d. is not a genetic but an embryonic effect.

    * a. yes; a Down syndrome individual has three chromosomes 21
    b. no; usually a Down syndrome child has a shorter life span
    c. no; the condition results from an extra chromosome
    d. no; although some manifestations of the syndrome may have an embryonic basis, the majority are the result of an extra chromosome

36. Which of the following chromosomal modifications has evolutionary consequences?
    a. duplication
    b. translocation
    c. deletion
    d. inversion

    * a. yes; allow the development of mutations in the duplicated segment that could survive because of the availability of a normal allele
    b. no; might result in trisomy that could reduce survival and adaptability
    c. no; the loss of genes is often fatal and may lose the buffering affect of a normal gene if the one left on the remaining chromosome is a lethal gene
    d. no; may reduce fertility because of problems involved in synapsis

37. Turner's syndrome is
    a. produced by mutation.
    b. produced by nondisjunction of an autosome.
    c. produced by nondisjunction of a X chromosome.
    d. trisomy X.

    a. no; mutations generally produce one effect rather than a large group of effects characteristic of a syndrome
    b. no; does not involve an autosome
    * c. yes; producing an XO individual, a female with only one sex chromosome
    d. no; this condition is possible, but is not called Turner syndrome

38. A person with Turner's syndrome has a sex chromosome makeup of
    a. XXY.
    b. XYY.
    c. XXX.
    d. XO.

    a. no; Klinefelter's syndrome
    b. no; a male with two Y chromosomes
    c. no; a metafemale
    * d. yes; an abnormal female with only one X chromosome known as Turner's syndrome

39. *Cri du chat* is a genetic disease brought about by
    a. nondisjunction.
    b. chromosome deletion.
    c. chromosomal translocation.
    d. chromosomal inversion.

    a. no; not caused by failure of chromosomes to separate
    * b. yes; loss of a portion of chromosome 5
    c. no; there is no exchange of chromosome parts
    d. no; not caused by an inversion in the order of genes on a chromosome

40. Duplications of nucleotide sequences
    a. are inconsequential.
    b. lead to genetic disorders such as the fragile X syndrome.
    c. result in amplification of the proteins produced by the gene.
    d. do not have genetic effects; it is the deletion of nucleotides that produces disease by the inability to produce a product.

    a. no; may produce disease
    * b. yes; fragile X disease is the result of duplication of nucleotides
    c. no; although this may happen if the total gene is repeated, but duplication usually involves only a fragment of a gene
    d. no; there are definite effects attributed to duplications of nucleotides

41. The problem associated with chromosome aberrations is
    a. the inability to replicate the aberrant part.
    b. the inability for proper pairing of genes during synapsis.
    c. the changes in the location of the genes produce major changes in gene expression.
    d. the tendency for the chromosomes to break again in the same place.

    a. no; there is no problem with replication of nucleotides
    * b. yes; the physical changes make it hard for each gene to pair up gene for gene during synapsis
    c. no; although there is a position effect for some genes, it is not considered to be a major problem
    d. no; if the chromosomes broke again in the same place, it is likely that they would be restored to their original configuration or that they would be reconstituted so that the same aberration was reestablished

42. If there were two chromosomes with segments labeled ABCDEFG and LMNOP, the appearance of chromosomes ABCNOP and LMDEFG would be an example of a(n)
    a. deletion.
    b. duplication.
    c. translocation.
    d. inversion.

a. no; there is no loss of any segment
b. no; there is no duplication of any segment
* c yes; segments DEFG and NOP have exchanged places
d. no; there is no change in segment sequencing

a. no; is genetically male but phenotypically female
* b. yes; there are no receptors for testosterone, so that the individual appears to be female but has a XY sex chromosome makeup
c. no; appears female but does not have female sex organs
d. no; only one of the choices is correct

43. If there were two chromosomes with segments labeled ABCDEFG and LMNOP, the appearance of chromosomes ABEDCFG and LMNOP would indicate that a(n) ____ had occurred.
a. deletion
b. duplication
c. translocation
d. inversion

a. no; there are no segments missing
b. no; there are no segments duplicating
c. no; there are no segments that have been exchanged between chromosomes
* d. yes; the sequence in the first chromosome has been inverted or turned around

44. Aneuploidy
a. occurs when an individual has one extra chromosome.
b. occurs when an individual has one less chromosome.
c. results in a large number of the miscarriages that occur.
d. all of the above are correct

a. no; a partial answer; a more complete choice is available
b. no; a partial answer; a more complete choice is available
c. no; a partial answer; a more complete choice is available
* d. yes; all of the above are correct

45. Down syndrome is an example of
a. polyploidism.
b. trisomy.
c. monosomy.
d. abnormality in embryonic development.

a. no; there are only two sets of chromosomes with one extra chromosome
* b. yes; Down syndrome is often called trisomy 21—resulting from an extra twenty-first chromosome
c. no; there is an extra chromosome, not the loss of a chromosome
d. no; although Down syndrome may have some developmental abnormalities, the chief cause is the presence of an extra chromosome

46. In testicular feminizing syndrome the affected person
a. appears male but is genetically female.
b. inherits a sex-linked gene that results in defective receptors for testosterone.
c. is a sterile hermaphrodite.
d. all of the above are true

# CHAPTER 11

# DNA STRUCTURE AND FUNCTION

1.  When Fred Griffith discovered bacterial transformation, he was
    a.  attempting to develop a vaccine against a bacteria that produced pneumonia in humans.
    b.  conducting experiments on bacteriophages.
    c.  attempting to understand how antibiotics prevented the growth of bacteria.
    d.  using in vitro (glassware) methods to elucidate the chemical nature of the gene.

    *   a.  yes; discovery of transformation was an unexpected bonus
        b.  no; was not involved in viral research
        c.  no; even though penicillin was discovered at approximately the same time
        d.  no; this was the experiment conducted by Avery and his coworkers and followed Griffith's experiment

2.  Which of the following would *not* kill a mouse under test conditions?
    a.  injection of rough bacteria
    b.  injection of smooth bacteria
    c.  injection of rough bacteria and heat-killed smooth bacteria
    d.  both (a) and (c), but not (b)

    *   a.  yes; rough bacteria are nonvirulent
        b.  no; smooth bacteria are pathogenic
        c.  no; this combination would kill a mouse because of genetic transformation
        d.  no; injection of rough bacteria and heat-killed smooth bacteria would kill the mouse

3.  The conversion of rough bacteria to smooth bacteria is known as
    a.  transcription.
    b.  translocation.
    c.  translation.
    d.  transformation.

    a.  no; this is the production of RNA from instructions in DNA
    b.  no; this is the exchange of genetic material between nonhomologous chromosomes
    c.  no; this is the manufacture of a protein from instructions in RNA
    *   d.  yes; this is a permanent change from a rough to a smooth form because of the incorporation of the gene for S bacteria

4.  The first person(s) to isolate from the nucleus a previously unknown substance that came to be known as DNA was (were)
    a.  Miescher.
    b.  Avery.
    c.  Watson and Crick.
    d.  Hershey and Chase.

    *   a.  yes; isolated and identified nucleic acids
        b.  no; in vitro analysis of genetic transformation
        c.  no; proposed the double helix theory of DNA structure
        d.  no; studied bacteriophages

5.  In the Hershey and Chase experiment with bacteriophages, the most important clue to the chemical nature of the gene was the
    a.  entrance of radioactive sulfur into the bacteria.
    b.  entrance of radioactive phosphorus into the bacteria.
    c.  accumulation of phosphorus on the surface of the bacteria.
    d.  accumulation of sulfur on the surface of the bacteria.

    a.  no; sulfur does not enter the bacteria; it remains outside with the protein coat
    *   b.  yes; phosphorus is an element found in DNA, and its entrance indicated that nucleic acid was the active portion
    c.  no; phosphorus does not accumulate outside the bacteria but enters with nucleic acids to participate in bacterial metabolic activities
    d.  no; the fact that it accumulates outside the bacteria indicates that protein does not participate in cellular activities

6. The sequence of activity in bacteriophage multiplication ends with
   a. the attachment of a virus to the surface of a bacterium.
   b. the rupture of the bacterial wall and release of viruses.
   c. the injection of DNA into a bacterium.
   d. the virus controlling the metabolic machinery of a bacterium to produce more viruses.

   a. no; the first step
 * b. yes; the fourth (last) step
   c. no; the second step
   d. no; the third step

7. Which of the following is *not* a component of a nucleotide?
   a. amino acid
   b. phosphate group
   c. pentose sugar
   d. nitrogenous base

 * a. correct; not part of a nucleotide, but part of proteins
   b. incorrect; found in all nucleic acids
   c. incorrect; either ribose or deoxyribose is present, depending on whether considering RNA or DNA nucleotides
   d. incorrect; five possibilities—adenine, cytosine, guanine, thymine, uracil—are found in nucleotides

8. The presence of which of the following nitrogenous bases would indicate that the nucleic acid being analyzed was a molecule of DNA and not RNA?
   a. adenine
   b. uracil
   c. cytosine
   d. thymine

   a. no; found in both DNA and RNA
   b. no; found only in RNA
   c. no; found in both DNA and RNA
 * d. yes; found only in DNA

9. Which of the following was *not* involved in the identification of the structure of DNA?
   a. James Watson
   b. Rosalind Franklin
   c. Francis Crick
   d. Oswald Avery

   a. incorrect; proposed the double helix
   b. incorrect; worked on X-ray diffraction
   c. incorrect; proposed the double helix
 * d. correct; reported the probable chemical nature of the gene

10. The amount of uracil in a molecule of RNA is balanced by an equal amount of
    a. adenine.
    b. guanine.
    c. cytosine.
    d. thymine.

 * a. yes; uracil pairs with adenine
   b. no; cytosine pairs with guanine
   c. no; guanine pairs with cytosine
   d. no; thymine appears only in DNA and does not pair with uracil

11. Which of the following techniques was used in the early 1950s to determine the structure of DNA?
    a. use of radioactive isotopes in autoradiography (using radiation from isotopes to take pictures)
    b. electron microscopy
    c. X-ray diffraction
    d. all of the above

    a. no; not important in determining structure of DNA
    b. no; not powerful enough to be useful
 *  c. yes; indicated DNA is a long, thin molecule of uniform diameter
    d. no; only one of the above is correct

12. Which factor is most critical to the role of DNA in protein synthesis?
    a. the number of chains involved in the molecule
    b. the number of nucleotides in the molecule
    c. the sequence of the nucleotides in the molecule
    d. the pattern of nitrogenous base pairing

    a. no; only two chains are found in the double helix
    b. no; the number is essentially immaterial as long as it is possible to produce a functional protein
 *  c. yes; the sequence controls the coding for the amino acid sequences found in the protein
    d. no; the pattern of pairing of nucleotides is standard and does not change

13. The chemical responsible for genetic information in a cell is
    a. protein.
    b. DNA.
    c. RNA.
    d. polysaccharides.

    a. no; although it is the most complex of the chemicals and was long thought to be the gene, it turned out not to be the gene
 *  b. yes; DNA contains the essential instructions to control the activities of a cell
    c. no; RNA is an intermediate in the action of genes
    d. no; polysaccharides do not carry genetic information

14. Which of the following persons did *not* receive a Nobel prize for establishing that DNA was the genetic material and explaining how it operated?
    a. Crick
    b. Pauling
    c. Wilkins
    d. Watson

a. no; one of the three people honored with the Nobel prize for the discovery that DNA was the genetic material
* b. yes; won his Nobel prize for the discovery that sickle-cell anemia was caused by a single genetic material
c. no; one of the three people honored with the Nobel prize for the discovery that DNA was the genetic material
d. no; one of the three people honored with the Nobel prize for the discovery that DNA was the genetic material

15. The contribution of Wilkins and Franklin to the understanding of the DNA structure was
a. the understanding of how amino acids formed proteins.
b. information about how nucleoproteins were organized.
c. the physical shape of the DNA molecule from X-ray diffraction evidence.
d. that RNA was used to record the information contained in DNA.

a. no; basic information discovered many years earlier
b. no; came much later
* c. yes; X-ray diffraction indicated that DNA was a spiral molecule of uniform diameter
d. no; this was information developed by Watson and Crick

16. Which of the following statements is false?
a. Genes are specific regions of DNA that encode for information of how to build proteins.
b. The information contained in DNA is encoded in linear sequence of nucleotides.
c. The code words of DNA are sequences of DNA bases read three at a time.
d. DNA consists of a single isolated strand of nucleotides.

a. no; this statement is true
b. no; this statement is true
c. no; this statement is true
* d. yes; composed of two attached strands that are twisted to form a helix or spiral

17. The five-carbon sugar found in DNA is
a. arabinose.
b. deoxyribose.
c. ribose.
d. xylose.

a. no; another five-carbon sugar
* b. yes; the reason that DNA is called DNA is that it has deoxyribose
c. no; ribose is found in RNA
d. no; another five-carbon sugar

18. The two strands of DNA are held together by
a. hydrogen bonds.
b. covalent bonds.
c. polar bonds.
d. ionic bonds.
* a. yes; the two strands are held together by hydrogen bonds
b. no; hold the nucleotides together
c. no; a more specific answer is available
d. no; there are no ionic bonds involved

19. Guanine pairs with
a. adenine.
b. thymine.
c. cytosine.
d. uracil.

a. no; another nucleotide
b. no; another nucleotide
* c. yes; guanine pairs with cytosine with hydrogen bonds
d. no; another nucleotide

20. Which of the following nitrogenous bases is found exclusively in DNA?
a. adenine
b. thymine
c. cytosine
d. uracil

a. no; found in both DNA and RNA
* b. yes; found in DNA, not RNA
c. no; found in both DNA and RNA
d. no; found in RNA only

21. Which of the following nitrogenous bases is found exclusively in RNA?
a. adenine
b. thymine
c. guanine
d. uracil

a. no; found in both DNA and RNA
b. no; found only in DNA
c. no; found in both DNA and RNA
* d. yes; found only in RNA

22. Replication of DNA is described as
a. semiconservative.
b. regenerative.
c. complementary.
d. alternative.

* a. yes; part of the new DNA molecule is new and part from the old DNA
b. no; not an accurate adjective
c. no; not an accurate adjective
d. no; not an accurate adjective

23. Thymine dimmers
a. can be induced by exposure to ultraviolet light.
b. are usually repaired in the DNA repair process.
c. result from the covalent bonding of adjacent thymine nucleotides.
d. all of the above

a. no; a partial answer; a more complete answer is available
b. no; a partial answer; a more complete answer is available
c. no; a partial answer; a more complete answer is available
* d. yes; all of the above are correct

24. The process of replication is controlled by the enzyme
a. ligase.
b. reverse transcriptase.
c. DNA polymerase.
d. restriction endonuclease.

a. no; ties genes together
b. no; converts RNA into DNA
* c. yes; replicates DNA
d. no; the enzyme called a genetic scissor that cuts DNA at specific points

25. The enzyme that proofreads and repairs errors in DNA is
a. ligase.
b. reverse transcriptase.
c. DNA polymerase.
d. restriction endonuclease.

a. no; ties genes together
b. no; converts RNA into DNA
* c. yes; reads the DNA molecule and keeps it unchanged and free of errors
d. no; the enzyme called a genetic scissor that cuts DNA at specific points

26. For replication to occur
a. a stockpile of free nucleotides is available to be used in the assembling.
b. a separation of the two strands of DNA must occur.
c. the replication process produces a double-stranded molecule, one strand of which is new and the other old.
d. all of the above

a. yes; there must be a supply of new nucleotides available for the new strand of DNA (partial answer)
b. yes; must be separated so that pairing of new nucleotides can be processed (partial answer)
c. yes; this makes for uniformity in DNA throughout time (partial answer)
* d. yes; all of the above statements are true

27. DNA polymerases
a. are enzymes that are involved in replication.
b. are available for proofreading assembled genes.
c. govern the assembly of nucleotides on the parent strand.
d. all of the above

a. yes; an enzyme is needed to be able to assemble the new DNA molecules fast enough to be effective (partial answer)
b. yes; on the average 1 mistake out of 100,000,000 nucleotide pairs represents an error in the base pair (partial answer)
c. yes; the enzyme controls complementary pairing and therefore the sequence of complementary nucleotides as specified by the existing DNA strand (partial answer)
* d. yes; all of the above are true

28. The proteins most characteristically associated with DNA in the nucleosomes are
a. globulins.
b. enzymes.
c. cytochromes.
d. histones.

a. no; globulins are proteins associated with blood proteins (immunoglobulins, hemoglobins, and so on)
b. no; the DNA has the blueprint of nucleotide sequence for the enzymes, but otherwise enzymes have little connection with DNA
c. no; these proteins are associated with the electron transport system
* d. yes; the histones are closely associated with nucleic acids, often serving as a spool to wind up segments of DNA (nucleosomes)

29. The folding of DNA in a chromosome results in the production of
a. spindles.
b. segments.
c. coils or loops.
d. all of the above

a. no, spindles are microtubule complexes involved in chromosome movement
b. no; an invalid distractor
* c. yes; the packing unit may allow the clustering of common genes
d. no; a common distractor; only one of the above is correct

30. The fusion of nucleotide fragments during DNA replication
a. is called proofreading.
b. is controlled by the enzyme ligase.
c. is haphazard and unorganized.
d. does not occur; rather, the new DNA strand is assembled one nucleotide at a time.

a. no; proofreading involves checking and correcting base pairs
* b. yes; ligase is the enzyme that connects nucleotide fragments
c. no; is highly organized and structured
d. no; does occur with fusion of Okazaki fragments on one DNA strand, whereas continuous assembly on one nucleotide at a time characterizes the DNA replication on the other side of the replication fork

31. The manufacture of RNA from DNA is called
    a. polymerization.
    b. translation.
    c. transcription.
    d. replication.

    a. no; a general term for the production of large molecules from small repeating units
    b. no; the manufacture of proteins from RNA codes
* c. yes; the production of RNA from DNA

    d. no; the duplication of DNA

34. During transcription, DNA's cytosine pairs with RNA's
    a. adenine.
    b. cytosine.
    c. uracil.
    d. guanine.

    a. no; thymine would pair with adenine
    b. no; does not pair with itself
    c. no; adenine would pair with uracil
* d. yes; cytosine pairs with guanine

# CHAPTER 12

# FROM DNA TO PROTEINS

1.  The DNA strand that is used as the instruction to generate a RNA strand is known as a(n)
    a.  exon.
    b.  codon.
    c.  template.
    d.  replicate.

    a.  no; the expressed portion of a gene
    b.  no; a sequence of three nucleotides that specify an amino acid
    *   c.  yes; provides information to form the complementary strand
    d.  no; a replicate is a copy, not a complementary strand

2.  The manufacture of RNA from DNA is called
    a.  polymerization.
    b.  translation.
    c.  transcription.
    d.  replication.

    a.  no; a general term for the production of large molecules from small repeating units
    b.  no; the manufacture of proteins from RNA codes
    *   c.  yes; writing the genetic instructions in a "working form"
    d.  no; the duplication of DNA

3.  Transcription starts at
    a.  the initiator.
    b.  the promoter.
    c.  the end of the previous gene.
    d.  any site where the RNA polymerase enzyme can bind.

    a.  no; not the proper term
    *   b.  yes; the site of the base sequence that signals the start of a gene is known as the promoter
    c.  no; often there are gaps between genes filled with proteins or meaningless nucleotides
    d.  no; the transcription process begins only at the beginning of a gene

4.  During transcription, DNA's cytosine pairs with RNA's ___
    a.  adenine.
    b.  cytosine.
    c.  uracil.
    d.  guanine.

    a.  no; thymine would pair with adenine
    b.  no; does not pair with itself
    c.  no; adenine would pair with uracil
    *   d.  yes; cytosine pairs with guanine

5.  The enzyme used during transcription is
    a.  reverse transcriptase.
    b.  DNA polymerase.
    c.  RNA polymerase.
    d.  ligase.

    a.  no; used to convert RNA into DNA
    b.  no; used during replication
    *   c.  yes; the enzyme involved in transcription
    d.  no; used to tie DNA fragments together

6.  A promoter is
    a.  the site where RNA polymerase binds.
    b.  an active part of a RNA molecule.
    c.  an enzyme that turns on a gene to transcribe a RNA molecule.
    d.  all of the above

    *   a.  yes; the place where transcription begins
    b.  no; part of the DNA molecule, not the RNA molecule
    c.  no; not an enzyme, but part of a DNA molecule
    d.  no; only one of the above is correct

7.  The type of RNA that provides the site for a protein synthesis is
    a.  messenger RNA.
    b.  ribosomal RNA.
    c.  promoter RNA.
    d.  transfer RNA.

    a.  no; the RNA that carries the message from the DNA code
    *   b.  yes; in the ribosome
    c.  no; not a type of RNA
    d.  no; the RNA that brings the amino acid to the site of protein synthesis

8. RNA differs from DNA
   a. in the specific sugar found in the nucleotides.
   b. in that it is composed of two instead of just one strand.
   c. by the presence of thymine rather than uracil.
   d. all of the above

 * a. yes; RNA contains ribose, DNA has deoxyribose
   b. no; RNA has one strand, DNA has two strands
   c. no; RNA has uracil, DNA has thymine
   d. no; only one of the above is correct

9. Mature RNA refers to
   a. RNA that has left the nucleus.
   b. RNA in which introns have been removed and the exons spliced together and a cap and tail added.
   c. RNA in which exons have been removed and the introns spliced together and a cap and tail added.
   d. both (a) and (b), but not (c)

   a. no; a partial answer; a more complete answer is available; the mature messenger RNA does not leave the nucleus until the introns have been removed
   b. no; a partial answer; a more complete answer is available
   c. no; exons are the expressed portion of the genetic message and would not be eliminated
 * d. yes; both (a) and (b) are correct, and (c) is incorrect

10. A mature messenger RNA
    a. contains a sequence of triplet codons that specify amino acids.
    b. has eliminated noncoding introns.
    c. leaves the nucleus and carries out its function in the cytoplasm.
    d. all of the above

    a. yes; a partial answer
    b. yes; a partial answer
    c. yes; a partial answer
 *  d. yes; all of the above

11. Which of the following is *not* part of a mature RNA molecule?
    a. tail
    b. exon
    c. cap
    d. intron

    a. no; a nucleotide with functional groups added to the RNA molecule
    b. no; the expressed portion of RNA
    c. no; a string of adenine nucleotides added to the RNA molecule
 *  d. yes; introns are parts of the DNA code that are not used and are not translated as amino acids in the protein synthesized by RNA

12. There are six codons that specify three of the amino acids. Which of the following is *not* one of the amino acids specified by six codons?
    a. leucine
    b. arginine
    c. serine
    d. tryptophan

    a. no; there are six codons that may specify this amino acid
    b. no; there are six codons that may specify this amino acid
    c. no; there are six codons that may specify this amino acid
 *  d. yes; there is only one codon specifying tryptophan

13. Which of the three nucleotides is the least sensitive, that is, if it were to be changed, it would be least likely to change the amino acid specified?
    a. first nucleotide in the codon
    b. second nucleotide in the codon
    c. third nucleotide in the codon
    d. all are equally sensitive; in other words, the change in any nucleotide is just as likely to change the amino acid specified as any other nucleotide

    a. no; not the least sensitive
    b. no; not the least sensitive, but the most likely to change the amino acid specified
 *  c. yes; the majority of the redundancy in the nuclear code is in the third nucleotide of the codon; produces the wobble effect
    d. no; one nucleotide is less sensitive

14. Which of the following statements is true?
    a. Changing the first nucleotide in a codon is most likely to result in a change in the amino acid specified.
    b. Changing the second nucleotide in a codon is most likely to result in a change in the amino acid specified.
    c. Changing the third nucleotide in a codon is most likely to result in a change in the amino acid specified.
    d. All changes have the same chance of producing another amino acid.

    a. no; this statement is false; a change in the first codon produces five or six different amino acids
    b. no; this statement is false; a change in the second codon produces four to seven different amino acids
 *  c. yes; this statement is true; a change in the third codon produces twelve to fifteen different amino acids
    d. no; this statement is false; the number of amino acids varies

15. The greatest effect on gene translation would be caused by the
    a. insertion of three nucleotides into a gene sequence.
    b. addition or deletion of one nucleotide in a codon.
    c. substitution of one nucleotide in a codon.
    d. substitution of two nucleotides in a codon.

    a. no; the addition of one codon leads to a protein with one additional amino acid
  * b. yes; results in a mutation that changes the way the whole DNA molecule is read after the insertion or deletion (called a frameshift mutation)
    c. no; may change one of the amino acids
    d. no; may change one of the amino acids

16. Anticodons are part of
    a. DNA templates.
    b. messenger RNA.
    c. transfer RNA.
    d. ribosomal RNA.

    a. no; only codons
    b. no; only codons
  * c. yes; anticodons are present to match the codons in messenger RNA
    d. no; no anticodons in ribosomal RNA

17. Anticodons are associated with
    a. nonsense messages.
    b. transcription.
    c. replication.
    d. translation.

    a. no; nonsense messages are the complementary half of template DNA or introns found in template DNA or in immature RNA before they are removed
    b. no; template DNA converted to messenger RNA
    c. no; DNA codons are replicated exactly with no anticodons involved
  * d. yes; anticodons on transfer RNA match the messenger RNA codons, so that the sequence of amino acids in protein synthesis is correct

18. Which of the following is *not* an anticodon?
    a. AUG
    b. CCG
    c. TAG
    d. UUC

    a. no; this could be an anticodon
    b. no; this could be an anticodon
  * c. yes; TAG is not an anticodon because it has thymine, not uracil
    d. no; this could be an anticodon

19. If two DNA codons read TAGTCA, the two anticodons would read
    a. AUCAGU.
    b. UAGUCA.
    c. UUCUGU.
    d. TUCTGU.

    a. no; the messenger RNA codons
  * b. yes; the appropriate anticodons
    c. no; improper changing of nucleotides
    d. no; anticodons cannot possess thymine as a nitrogenous base

20. Which of the following is false?
    a. There are sixty-four different codons.
    b. All codons specify a specific amino acid.
    c. Some codons are used for initiation or termination of a gene.
    d. There are more codons than amino acids so that the code is redundant.

    a. incorrect; this statement is true
  * b. correct; this statement is false; some are initiators or terminators
    c. incorrect; this statement is true
    d. incorrect; this statement is true

21. Barbara McClintock's "jumping" genes, or transposable elements, functioned by
    a. enabling genes to skip a generation.
    b. inactivating genes that are found next to them when they are inserted into a new location.
    c. producing changes in phenotypes.
    d. both (b) and (c), but not (a)

    a. no; does not happen (may happen to recessive genes in some mating condition)
    b. yes; a partial answer
    c. yes; a partial answer
  * d. yes; both (b) an (c), but not (a)

22. Mutations are
    a. rare.
    b. random.
    c. inherited.
    d. all of the above

    a. no; a partial answer; a more complete answer is available
    b. no; a partial answer; a more complete answer is available
    c. no; a partial answer; a more complete answer is available
  * d. yes; all of the above are correct

23. Mutations may be produced by
    a. ultraviolet radiation.
    b. mutagenic chemicals.
    c. viruses.
    d. all of the above

    a. yes; a partial answer; a more complete answer is available
    b. yes; a partial answer; a more complete answer is available
    c. yes; a partial answer; a more complete answer is available
  * d. yes; all of the above are correct

24. Which of the following is *not* a stage in translation?
    a. initiation
    b. substitution
    c. elongation
    d. termination

    a. no; the start of protein synthesis
  * b. yes; not part of translation
    c. no; the bulk of protein synthesis involving the sequencing of amino acids
    d. no; the cessation of protein synthesis

25. A polysome is
    a. a group of ribosomes that are arranged in sequence to make multiple copies of proteins.
    b. a group of proteins manufactured by ribosomes.
    c. the part of the nucleolus that manufactures ribosomes.
    d. a group of nucleosomes located on a looped domain.

  * a. yes; an assembly line designed to produce large amounts of proteins
    b. no; does not refer to the protein manufactured by RNA
    c. no; not found in the nucleolus
    d. no; not associated with chromosomes

26. Mutagens
    a. cause mutations.
    b. often are carcinogens.
    c. include ultraviolet radiation, viruses, some chemicals, and free radicals.
    d. all of the above

    a. no; a partial answer; a more complete answer is available
    b. no; a partial answer; a more complete answer is available
    c. no; a partial answer; a more complete answer is available
  * d. yes; all of the above are correct

27. Which of the following would be the most damaging?
    a. a point mutation
    b. a substitution of one nucleotide for another
    c. a frameshift mutation
    d. none of the above; all have the same level of effect

    a. no; produces minimal damage and in some cases, the changed nucleotide might not change the amino acid specified
    b. no; produces minimal damage and in some cases, the changed nucleotide might not change the amino acid specified
  * c. yes; would change all of the amino acids downstream of the mutation
    d. no; one of the above has a greater effect

28. Which of the following statements is false?
    a. Mutagens may alter the rate of mutations.
    b. A mutation must occur in the gametes for it to be inherited.
    c. A mutation occurs spontaneously.
    d. Although the rate of a mutation may change with changes in the environment, all genes have the same chance of undergoing mutations.

    a. no; this statement is true
    b. no; this statement is true
    c. no; this statement is true
  * d. no; some genes are more unstable than others, and mutation rates vary from one gene to another

29. Cells in a single organism differ from one another based on
    a. the repressors and operators that are active in each cell.
    b. the kinds of genes that they possess.
    c. the rates but not the types of transcription that occur in the cells.
    d. none of the above

  * a. yes; this is one of the factors that serve
    to make cells different
    b. no; cells possess the same kinds of genes
    c. no; *both* the rates and the types of transcriptions control the type of cells
    d. no; one of the above is correct

30. An operator is found
    a. on a different chromosome than the one that contains the gene loci it controls.
    b. between a promoter and the gene it activates.
    c. in the ribosome responsible for the protein being synthesized by the gene.
    d. covering the repressor protein that turns off the gene.

    a. no; this would produce wide variation in response and not give satisfactory control
  * b. yes; here the operator can control initiation
    c. no; no particular ribosomes are involved in producing specific proteins
    d. no; perhaps this could be a way to prevent repression but not a way to stimulate induction

31. An operon consists of an
    a. operator gene and repressor protein.
    b. operator gene and promoter.
    c. operator gene, a promoter, and a gene or functioning set of genes.
    d. any set of genetic material or protein associated with an operator gene.

a. no; the repressor is antagonistic to the operator gene
b. no; are only two of the three parts of an operon
* c. yes; the three interact to form an operon
d. no; too general and incomplete a choice

32. In the "lac operon" of *E. coli,*
a. lactose functions as a repressor.
b. galactose and glucose react to form lactose.
c. the three genes associated in the operon are enzymes that digest lactose and its products.
d. RNA polymerase is blocked by the presence of lactose.

a. no; repressors are proteins; lactose is a disaccharide
b. no; this reaction may happen, but the "lac operon" controls the reverse of this reaction
* c. yes; this statement is correct
d. no; lactose bends (distorts) the repressor to allow RNA polymerase to initiate transcription

33. In the "lac operon," when the repressor is altered the
a. concentration of lactose is low.
b. genes for three digestive enzymes cannot be transcribed.
c. repressor cannot bind to the promoter or operator.
d. all of the above

a. no; the repressor is altered when lactose concentrations are high
b. no; they are actively transcribed while the repressor is altered and cannot work
* c. yes; therefore the process of transcription can proceed
d. no; only one of the above is correct

34. Differentiation
a. arises through selective gene expression in different cells.
b. results from differences in genes in different tissue of an organism.
c. occurs only during embryonic development.
d. both (a) and (c)

* a. yes; the induction of specific genes in different cells could cause these cells to become different
b. no; the genes are the same in all tissues of the same organism
c. no; induction may occur at various times throughout an organism's life cycle
d. no; only one of the above choices is correct

35. Anhidrotic ectodermal dysplasia
a. occurs only in heterozygous females.
b. is the result of inactivation of one of the female's sex chromosomes.
c. results in patches of skin that are unable to perspire.
d. all of the above are correct

a. yes; a partial answer
b. yes; a partial answer
c. yes; a partial answer
* d. yes; all of the above are correct

36. Which of the following statements is true?
a. Metastasis is the conversion of a benign tumor into a malignant one.
b. Oncogenes are responsible for the repression and remission of cancers.
c. Cancer is a fatal disease only in humans.
d. Cancer may be caused by chemicals called carcinogens.

a. no; this statement is false; metastasis refers to the migration of cancer cells
b. no; this statement is false; oncogenes are responsible for the production of cancer
c. no; this statement is false; many animals, including laboratory mice, may be killed by cancer
* d. yes; this statements is true; carcinogens are chemicals in the environment that may induce cancer

37. Cancer kills one in ___ in the United States.
a. four
b. five
c. seven
d. nine

a. no; too many
* b. yes; one in five
c. no; too few
d. no; too few

38. An oncogene is
a. a cancer-causing gene.
b. a tumor-suppressing gene.
c. a gene responsible for self-signals on cell membranes.
d. a gene that only functions during embryonic development.

* a. yes; a gene that causes cancer
b. no; produces tumors rather than suppressing them
c. no; such genes are not called oncogenes
d. no; an oncogene may be a gene that normally operates during embryonic development but somehow gets turned on after birth to induce cancer

39. Which of the following statements is false?
a. Proto-oncogenes are cancer genes.
b. Proto-oncogenes are normal genes that regulate cell growth and development.
c. Proto-oncogenes code for regulatory proteins that involve cell adhesions.
d. Proto-oncogenes code for proteins that signal other cells to divide.

*   a.   yes; this is false; proto-oncogenes are precursors of oncogenes that function as cancer genes
    b.   no; this statement is true
    c.   no; this statement is true
    d.   no; this statement is true

40.   *Escherichia coli*
    a.   lives in the intestinal tract of mammals.
    b.   uses lactose in milk as an energy source.
    c.   only produces the enzymes necessary to digest lactose when lactose is present in the digestive system.
    d.   all of the above

    a.   no; a partial answer; a more complete answer is available
    b.   no; a partial answer; a more complete answer is available
    c.   no; a partial answer; a more complete answer is available
*   d.   yes; all of the answers are correct

41.   Which of the following statements is false?
    a.   Anytime lactose is present in the intestinal tract, the enzymes used to break it down are secreted.
    b.   The genes used to digest glucose are transcribed continuously by *Escherichia coli*.
    c.   At high concentrations, lactose induces transcription by binding to and distorting the repressor by expressing the promoter.
    d.   The lactose operon is under negative control.

*   a.   yes; this statement is false; the enzyme will be produced when glucose is absent
    b.   no; this statement is true
    c.   no; this statement is true
    d.   no; this statement is true

42.   The chemical that turns on the activator protein called CAP is
    a.   cAMP.
    b.   lactose.
    c.   glucose.
    d.   RNA polymerase.

*   a.   yes; leads to positive control over the lactose operon
    b.   no; will trigger the lactose operon if there is little or no glucose available
    c.   no; the presence of glucose inhibits the lactose operon
    d.   no; used to transcribe RNA to produce lactose

43.   The addition of polypeptide groups in the cytomembrane system is part of the cellular control that occurs during
    a.   replication.
    b.   transcription.
    c.   translation.
    d.   post-translation.

    a.   no; this would be gene amplification
    b.   no; many mRNA molecules could be produced
    c.   no; many proteins could be produced by the ribosomes
*   d.   yes; the completion of a finish protein is part of a post-translational process

44.   A Barr body is
    a.   the inactive X chromosome found on the nuclear membrane.
    b.   a cluster of proteins produced by polysomes.
    c.   an accumulation of nonsoluble waste products.
    d.   the structure that produces caps for mature RNA.

*   a.   yes; discovered by Murray Barr; it is characteristic of cells with more than one X chromosome
    b.   no; such proteins usually move through the cytomembrane system and are exported one at a time from the cell
    c.   no; there is no definite body that accumulates nonsoluble wastes inside
    d.   no; there is no specific structure that performs this function

45.   Which of the following statements is false?
    a.   Calico cats are female.
    b.   Calico cats exhibit mosaicism.
    c.   The color of a patch of a calico cat's fur is dependent upon which chromosome is inactivated.
    d.   The color pattern of calico cats is controlled by incompletely dominant genes.

    a.   no; this statement is usually true, although through non-disjunction some XXY males may be calico
    b.   no; this statement is true
    c.   no; this statement is true
*   d.   yes; this statement is false; color is dependent on an X-linked gene.

# CHAPTER 13

# RECOMBINANT DNA
# AND GENETIC ENGINEERING

1.  In recombinant DNA experiments, which of the following events occurs last?
    a.  Genes are inserted into an organism.
    b.  Genes are isolated.
    c.  Genes produces functional proteins.
    d.  Genes are modified.

    a.  no; occurs third
    b.  no; occurs first
    *c.  yes; occurs last
    d.  no; occurs second

2.  The enzyme responsible for fusing fragments of DNA together is
    a.  DNA polymerase.
    b.  reverse transcriptase.
    c.  ligase.
    d.  restriction endonuclease.

    a.  no; used in DNA replication
    b.  no; used in production of DNA from RNA
    *c.  yes; enzyme that seals two DNA fragments together
    d.  no; enzyme that cuts DNA into fragments

3.  Plasmids
    a.  are small circular DNA molecules.
    b.  enable bacterial conjugation to occur.
    c.  may become incorporated in the main chromosome.
    d.  all of the above

    a.  yes; a partial answer
    b.  yes; a partial answer
    c.  yes; a partial answer
    *d.  yes; all of the above are correct

4.  Circular molecules of DNA in bacteria are called
    a.  plasmids.
    b.  vectors.
    c.  chromosomes.
    d.  pili.

    *a.  yes; a circular molecule containing many genes
    b.  no; name given to any organism used to transfer DNA molecules
    c.  no; name for the large continual DNA molecules that contain the majority of the bacteria's DNA
    d.  no; a filament that allows a bacterium to adhere to a substrate

5.  All the DNA found in a haploid set of chromosomes is a
    a.  plasmid.
    b.  DNA library.
    c.  genome.
    d.  none of the above

    a.  no; a small circular DNA molecule
    b.  no; a collection of DNA fragments
    *c.  yes; a complete set of chromosomes
    d.  no; one of the above is correct

6.  Which of the following enzymes cuts a chromosome into fragments with sticky ends?
    a.  restriction nuclease
    b.  DNA ligase
    c.  reverse transcriptase
    d.  DNA polymerase

    *a.  yes; cuts DNA at particular sites
    b.  no; seals two fragments together
    c.  no; enzymes that produce DNA from RNA
    d.  no; enzyme involved in replication of DNA

7.  Which of the following enzyme is used to manufacture DNA from RNA?
    a.  restriction nuclease
    b.  DNA ligase
    c.  reverse transcriptase
    d.  DNA polymerase

    a.  no; cuts DNA at particular sites
    b.  no; seals two fragments together
    *c.  yes; produces DNA from RNA
    d.  no; involved in replication of DNA

8. cDNA refers to
   a. chromosomal DNA.
   b. copied DNA from mRNA.
   c. cytoplasmic DNA.
   d. none of the above

   a. no; no such term, simply described as DNA
 * b. yes; any DNA molecule copied from mRNA
   c. no; usually referred to by the organelle it is associated with (e.g., mitochondrial DNA)
   d. no; one of the above is correct

9. Amplification refers to the
   a. introduction of DNA into a plasmid.
   b. multiple replications of a gene.
   c. manufacture of many protein products.
   d. the production of many molecules of any type.

   a. no; called insertion or splicing
 * b. yes; the most common method employs polymerase chain reaction
   c. no; production of product dependent on demand
   d. no; control over transcription is one mechanism of control

10. Which of the following statements is true?
    a. No two humans that have the same "genetic fingerprint".
    b. Pattern variations in "genetic fingerprints" can be detected with a radioactive probe.
    c. Biopsies providing a tissue sample of an individual, is needed to run a genetic fingerprint.
    d. Semen or blood samples are insufficient to make a "genetic fingerprint."

    a. no; this statement is false; identical twins have the same genetic fingerprint
 *  b. yes; this statement is true; the standard method used
    c. no; this statement is false; other kinds of samples can be used
    d. no; this statement is false; either could be used for a genetic fingerprinting

11. Recombinant DNA technology grew out of research on
    a. bacteria.
    b. laboratory rats.
    c. corn.
    d. viruses.

 *  a. yes; work with plasmids led to recombinant DNA technology
    b. no; with another organism
    c. no; with another organism
    d. no; with another organism

12. An agent that carries a gene from one organism to a site in another organism is called a(n)
    a. plasmid.
    b. phage.
    c. vector.
    d. accessory.

    a. no; a circular molecule of DNA found in bacteria
    b. no; a shorter version of bacteriophage, a virus that enters and destroys bacteria
 *  c. yes; the appropriate name regardless of the organism that is involved in the transfer
    d. no; a distractor that does not refer to recombinant DNA technology

13. Restriction fragment length polymorphisms
    a. are used in genetic fingerprinting.
    b. are used in reassembling exons into a functional gene.
    c. are a method used to compare closely related species.
    d. refer to similarities in the primary structure of proteins.

 *  a. yes; the common technique to compare a person's genes to a tissue, blood, or semen sample
    b. no; restriction enzymes and ligases are used to assemble a functional mRNA
    c. no; called melting of DNA in which single-stranded DNA is tested to see if it is complementary to test strands of DNA from other organisms
    d. no; primary structure of proteins refers to the sequence of amino acids

14. Restriction enzymes
    a. are used in recombinant DNA technology.
    b. are naturally occurring enzymes that bacteria may use to defend itself against invading viruses.
    c. could be described as molecular scissors that cut molecules of DNA.
    d. all of the above

    a. no; a partial answer; a more complete answer is available
    b. no; a partial answer; a more complete answer is available
    c. no; a partial answer; a more complete answer is available
 *  d. yes; all of above are correct

15. Which of the following statements is false?
    a. Restriction endonucleases cut only one type of DNA molecule.
    b. Restriction endonucleases cut DNA at a specific sequence of bases.
    c. Restriction endonucleases leave short single-stranded ends of DNA where other appropriate fragments can be attached.
    d. It takes two actions or cuts in a DNA molecule to produce fragments unless the enzyme acts close to the end of a DNA molecule.

* a. yes; this statement is false; the enzyme acts on a specific sequence wherever it occurs in the genome
  b. no; this statement is true
  c. no; this statement is true
  d. no; this statement is true

16. A collection of DNA fragments produced by restriction enzymes and inserted in plasmids or some other cloning tool is known as a
  a. library.
  b. vector.
  c. clone.
  d. both (a) and (b), but not (c)

* a. yes; the collection of DNA fragments is a library
  b. no; the organism used to transfer DNA
  c. no; a group of cells with identical genotypes
  d. no; only one answer is correct

17. The reproduction of massive amounts of the same DNA molecule is known as
  a. cloning.
  b. amplification.
  c. replication.
  d. regeneration.

  a. no; growth of colonies of cells with identical genotypes
* b. yes; with appropriate enzymes, a molecule of DNA can be reproduced over and over again
  c. no; replication refers to a single exact duplication of a DNA molecule
  d. no; refers to the replacement of lost parts to restore a structure to a facsimile of the original

18. Which of the following statements is false?
  a. The same restriction enzyme used to cut the DNA in a bacterial chromosome is also used to cut the plasmid.
  b. The DNA fragment is inserted into a bacterial plasmid by using a ligase enzyme.
  c. If DNA technology is trying to clone a human gene, yeast may be used.
  d. none of the above, all of the above are true

  a. no; this statement is true
  b. no; this statement is true
  c. no; this statement is true
* d. yes; none of the above are false

19. Which of the following statements is false?
  a. DNA primers are single strands of DNA.
  b. DNA polymerase is used for amplification.
  c. DNA polymerase is derived from bacteria that thrive in hot springs.
  d. DNA polymerase is used in genetic fingerprinting.

* a. yes; this statement is false; DNA primers are double strands of DNA
  b. no; this statement is true
  c. no; this statement is true
  d. no; this statement is true

20. The polymerase chain reaction
  a. builds a DNA library.
  b. amplifies a gene.
  c. generates protein products.
  d. results in hybrid DNA sequence.

  a. no; uses restriction enzymes to generate DNA fragments
* b. yes; polymerase is an enzyme that replicates DNA
  c. no; polymerase does not involve transcription
  d. no; does not produce new sequences

21. When DNA is mixed with bacteria, the bacteria that pick up the DNA are said to be
  a. transcribed.
  b. transformed.
  c. transferred.
  d. translated.

  a. no; refers to converting the DNA code to a RNA molecule
* b. yes; the bacteria are transformed into new forms with new genes
  c. no; does not refer to action by DNA or RNA
  d. no; refers to the production of protein by RNA

22. Which of the following statements is false?
  a. DNA probes are radioactive.
  b. DNA probes are used to identify transformed colonies of cells.
  c. DNA probes exhibit nucleic acid hybridization.
  d. DNA probes are part of a genetic library.

  a. no; this statement is true
  b. no; this statement is true
  c. no; this statement is true
* d. yes; this statement is false; a genetic library consists of many different DNA fragments

23. The way to identify transformed bacteria is to
  a. use antibiotics that match resistant genes located in the plasmid with the transferred gene.
  b. use radioactive probes.
  c. use only the bacteria that produce the product desired.
  d. both (a) and (b), but not (c)

a. no; a partial answer; the plasmid contains a gene that makes the bacteria resistant to an antibiotic so that those that survive the exposure to the antibiotic contain the resistance gene and the desired gene
b. no; DNA probes base pair with part of the gene being studied
c. no; a partial answer; there is no easy way in a large colony of bacteria to identify those bacteria that possess the ability to produce a product
* d. yes; both (a) and (b) are correct, but (c) is not

24. By using radioactive probes in association with restriction fragment length polymorphism, it is possible to
a. distinguish between identical twins.
b. detect certain mutant or defective alleles.
c. clone certain human genes.
d. all of the above

a. no; identical twins are genetically identical and cannot be separated
* b. yes; a technique that is useful in diagnosing certain genetic defects
c. no; a different technique is involved
d. no; a common distractor, only one is correct

25. Which of the following is the last step in locating a specific gene in a bacteria?
a. replica plating is used to produce colonies of bacteria
b. DNA probes are added
c. solutions are added to rupture cells, fix released DNA, and make double-stranded DNA unwind
d. isolate bacteria with antibiotic-resistant genes in their plasmids

a. no; replica plating is the second step after the antibiotic-resistant forms are isolated
* b. yes; the radioactive probes designate which DNA fragments are the ones you are interested in
c. no; the DNA has to be released from the cell before probes are added
d. no; the isolation of antibiotic-resistant forms is the first step

26. Many researchers feel that there is no danger in recombinant DNA research because
a. the genes involved are relatively harmless.
b. the organisms used have been altered to prevent their survival outside the laboratory environment.
c. the researchers generally use techniques that prevent dangerous forms from escaping.
d. all of the above

a. no; a partial answer; special safeguards would be established if they would be likely to become harmful
b. no; a partial answer; mutations restrict the organism to survival only under tightly prescribed conditions
c. no; a partial answer otherwise the pathogens scientists work with would escape
* d. yes; all of the above are correct

27. Lindow's ice-minus bacteria
a. infects a plant and prevent ice crystals from forming within leaf tissues.
b. add electrolytes to cells to raise the freezing point of cell solutions.
c. competes with bacteria that naturally occur on the surface of a leaf or stem.
d. have had a dangerous gene removed from its genome.

a. no; remains on the surface of the plant
b. no; not the method of reaction
c. no; may actually occur, but this is not the important characteristic
* d. yes; that is why it is called *ice-minus* — they lack the genetic information to form the proteins involved in ice formation

28. Gene therapy refers to
a. removing a defective gene.
b. inserting potentially desirable genes.
c. substituting a normal gene for a defective one.
d. developing new genes through a gene machine.

a. no; usually a functional gene would have to be available to provide a needed protein or enzyme
b. no; called eugenic engineering and generally not considered ethical
* c. yes; a desirable way to eliminate a genetic defect
d. no; not yet possible and not the thrust of genetic research

29. The production of cDNA from mRNA is known as
a. transcription.
b. reverse transcription.
c. translation.
d. amplification.

a. no; the production of mRNA from DNA
* b. yes; the enzyme reverse transcriptase produces cDNA from mRNA
c. no; involves manufacturing proteins from mRNA
d. no; involves DNA producing more DNA

30. Plasmids in bacteria are the sites for many human genes that produce a large amount of useful human
a. proteins.
b. antibodies.
c. medicines.
d. food.

* a. yes; the function of a gene is to produce a protein, and human genes produce human proteins
b. no; not a major role of transformed bacteria, but the potential is there if the gene that produces the antibody needed can be found
c. no; not a common function, although some proteins such as interferon are used for medicine
d. no; not currently a function of transformed bacteria

31. Some plants that are unable to grow from seeds may be cloned by
a. incorporating their genes in a bacterium.
b. substituting the nucleus of a desired plant into a rapidly growing healthy plant.
c. taking somatic cells from the parent plant and growing them in tissue culture.
d. transplanting the embryo from the plant to another seed that germinates easily.

a. no; would not help
b. no; not an effective technique
* c. yes; tissue culture is a common technique used in cloning some plants
d. no; embryo transplanting is not a technique used in propagation

32. Although some say that man should not alter lives of any organism,
a. nature alters DNA all the time.
b. if benefits are derived from the process and no ill effects are produced, most people would say that man should alter the lives of other organisms.
c. much profit can be generated for biotechnology companies.
d. all of the above

a. no; a partial answer; a more complete answer is available
b. no; a partial answer; a more complete answer is available
c. no; a partial answer; a more complete answer is available
* d. yes; all of the above answers are correct

33. Which of the following objections to using genetic engineering in nature is currently obviated by federal regulations?
a. The creation of more desirable humans by inserting genes that would make them more desirable.
b. Transgenic bacteria could mutate and become super pathogens that would endanger man.
c. Crop plants with resistance to insects could cause insects to evolve and set in motion an evolutionary seesaw.
d. Transgenic fish could displace natural species, disrupting the ecological balance.

a. no; there are no specific regulations to safeguard against this potential problem, but the use of bioengineered products would be monitored to keep this from happening
* b. yes; federal guidelines require that transgenic bacteria have built-in safeguards to keep them from escaping and breeding in nature
c. no; there are no specific regulations to safeguard against this potential problem, but the use of bioengineered products would be monitored to keep this from happening
d. no; there are no specific regulations to safeguard against this potential problem, but the use of bioengineered products would be monitored to keep this from happening

34. Which of the following statements is true?
a. No two humans have the same genetic fingerprinting.
b. Pattern variations in the genetic fingerprint can be detected with a radioactive probe.
c. A biopsy providing a tissue sample of an individual is needed to run a genetic fingerprint.
d. Semen or blood samples are insufficient to make a genetic fingerprint.

a. no; identical twins have the same genetic fingerprint
* b. yes; this statement is true; it describes the standard method used
c. no; it is possible to use either blood or semen samples
d. no; either sample could be used for genetic fingerprinting

35. The test that showed that the growth hormone gene was effectively transferred into a mouse egg was
a. the use of appropriate genetic probes.
b. the isolation of the inserted gene from the adult nucleus.
c. the fact that the mouse grew much larger than normal mice.
d. the change in the nucleotide sequences in the mouse chromosome.

a. no; a simpler test was available
b. no; a simpler test was available
* c. yes; the reason that the mouse grew much larger than normal was that not only was the gene transferred but also the gene functioned by producing the growth hormone that resulted in dramatic increase in size
d. no; a simpler test was available

36. The human growth hormone has been transferred to
a. mice.
b. chicken.
c. cattle.
d. Guinea pigs.

* a. yes; transferred to mice
 b. no; another animal
 c. no; another animal
 d. no; another animal

37. The human genes that code for the production of tissue plasminogen activator have been transferred to a
 a. pig.
 b. goat.
 c. bacterium.
 d. dog.

 a. no; another organism
* b. yes; it has been transferred to a goat
 c. no; another organism
 d. no; another organism

38. Somatotropin is a human hormone that controls
 a. growth.
 b. blood pressure.
 c. pancreatic secretion.
 d. calcium metabolism.

* a. yes; somatotropin is the human growth hormone
 b. no; has another function
 c. no; has another function
 d. no; has another function

39. The interest in "barnyard biotechnology" or the use of farm animals rather than bacteria in bioengineering is because
 a. of the excessive regulation on the growth of biogenetically engineered bacteria.
 b. the farm animals may produce large quantities of the wanted material faster and cheaper than bacteria.
 c. of pressure by the U.S. Department of Agriculture to use farm animals.
 d. there are fewer problems raising farm animals than bacteria.

 a. no; another reason
* b. yes; farm animals produce more product quicker and cheaper
 c. no; another reason
 d. no; another reason

40. Objections to the human genome project include
 a. the limited gene pool used to obtain the sequence of nucleotides may not represent the diversity in the human race.
 b. some scientists and biotechnology firms may reap a tremendous commercial gain from public money used to develop the project.
 c. other things such as cancer or AIDS research could make more effective use of the funds invested in the human genome project.
 d. all of the above

 a. no; a partial answer; a more complete answer is available
 b. no; a partial answer; a more complete answer is available
 c. no; a partial answer; a more complete answer is available
* d. yes; all of the above answers are correct

42. RFLP research uses ____ to detect pattern variation.
 a. chromatography
 b. electrophoresis
 c. X-ray diffraction
 d. radioisotopes

 a. no; a method used to separate material based upon differential solubility
* b. yes; a method based upon separation of molecular fragments by size and charge
 c. no; a technique used in determining shape of molecules
 d. no; a technique used in tracing physiological activities

43. RFLPs can be used to
 a. produce genetic fingerprints and place criminals at the site of a crime.
 b. locate mutant alleles responsible for genetic disorders.
 c. identify the proper parents in case of identification problems with babies.
 d. all of the above

 a. no; a partial answer; a more complete answer is available
 b. no; a partial answer; a more complete answer is available
 c. no; a partial answer; a more complete answer is available
* d. yes; all of the above answers are correct

44. Genetic fingerprints rely on the activity of
 a. ligases.
 b. restriction enzymes.
 c. DNA polymerases.
 d. reverse transcriptase.

 a. no; used to tie two cut ends of DNA together
* b. yes; produces a group of DNA fragments of different lengths based upon where the enzyme cuts the DNA
 c. no; used to replicate DNA
 d. no; used to manufacture DNA from RNA

45. The use of DNA fingerprinting in court cases
 a. is limited because its scientific complexity may be too much for untrained jurors.
 b. is more often used to prove that a person is innocent than guilty.
 c. would be invalid if the suspect had an identical twin brother.
 d. all of the above are correct

a. no; a partial answer; a more complete answer is available
b. no; a partial answer; a more complete answer is available
c. no; a partial answer; a more complete answer is available
* d. yes; all other answer are correct

46. Gene therapy involves
a. modification of the diet to prevent the expression of a defective allele such as PKU (phenylketonuria).
b. pedigree analysis and risk analysis to reduce the chance of a couple producing a defective child.
c. the insertion of appropriate normal gene into the gamete so that the offspring produce would be normal.
d. the substitution of a normal gene to replace a defective gene.

a. no; a typical type of therapy used to counteract some defective genes
b. no; this describes standard process in genetic counseling
c. no; this might be an advanced form of gene therapy to be developed in the future, but gene therapy is being developed now
* d. yes; normal genes are introduced into defective individuals by various vectors and once the normal gene is in place, it produces the normal gene and hopefully replaces the defective gene

47. Gene therapy refers to
a. removing a defective gene.
b. inserting potentially desirable genes.
c. substituting a normal gene for a defective one.
d. developing a new gene through the use of a gene machine.

a. no; usually there would need to be a functional gene available to provide a needed protein or enzyme
b. no; called eugenic engineering and generally not considered ethical
* c. yes; a desirable way to eliminate a genetic defect
d. no; not the thrust of gene therapy

# CHAPTER 14

# MICROEVOLUTION

1.  Evolution refers to changes in
    a.  the characteristics of an individual.
    b.  responses to environmental differences.
    c.  heritable lines of descent.
    d.  species composition of an area.

    a.  no; these changes, which include growth, development, and disease are part of the life cycle
    b.  no; organisms may respond to environmental changes without undergoing evolution; examples are migration, and growth of thicker hair in response to cold temperature
  * c.  yes; the changes are passed on to subsequent generations
    d.  no; this could be ecological succession or fortuitous changes

2.  Aristotle
    a.  viewed nature as a continuum of organization from lifeless matter through complex forms of plant and animal life.
    b.  used an explanation of life that depended upon the intervention of supernatural beings.
    c.  simply collected information in great detail but failed to synthesize ideas.
    d.  proposed a rigid authoritarian concept known as the Chain of Being that extended from lower forms to humans and onto spiritual beings.

  * a.  yes; although he realized that each kind was distinct from the rest, he saw the similarity in living forms
    b.  no; the conventional wisdom of his day evoked the presence and participation of supernatural beings
    c.  no; he made separate explanations on the order of nature
    d.  no; the Chain of Being was the product of many centuries of application of Aristotle's thoughts into a rigid, authoritarian scheme

3.  The theory of catastrophism was proposed by
    a.  deBuffon.
    b.  Cuvier.
    c.  Lamarck.
    d.  Lyell.

    a.  no; thought that organisms originated in different places and perhaps became modified over time
  * b.  yes; said there was only one time of creation, but that catastrophes wiped out many forms of life that were replaced by survivors
    c.  no; proposed the theory of the inheritance of acquired characteristics
    d.  no; proposed the theory of uniformity

4.  The person who developed the same explanation for natural selection as Darwin was
    a.  Henslow.
    b.  Lyell.
    c.  Wallace.
    d.  Malthus.

    a.  no; a botanist that got Darwin his job on the *Beagle*
    b.  no; a geologist who proposed the theory of uniformity
  * c.  yes; a biogeographer who developed the same ideas and is considered a cofounder with Darwin for the theory of evolution
    d.  no; an economist and clergyman who considered the problems of populations exceeding their resource base

5. By the mid-eighteenth century, fossils were used as evidence to support all but which of the following?
   a. All organisms were created in one place at the same time.
   b. Imperfections meant that species were not unalterably perfect and perhaps became modified over time.
   c. Simple forms were restricted to lower layers while those in upper strata were complex.
   d. Different layers held different kinds of fossils.

   * a. yes; not supported by the widespread occurrence of fossils; if they were created at the same time and place, the barriers would have stopped their spread
   b. no; supported by fossil evidence showing changes
   c. no; supported by the stratification of fossils
   d. no; supported by the fossil variation through the sediments

6. The mission of the ship HMS *Beagle* was to
   a. collect biological specimens from all over the world.
   b. supply British naval forts.
   c. map the coastline of South America.
   d. study geological processes such as volcanism (volcanic activities).

   a. no; although Darwin did make some collections
   b. no; not that type of ship
   * c. yes; a scientific expedition to complete mapping that had already started
   d. no; although some observations were made, this was not a major objective of the trip

7. Observations of which of these animals supplied Darwin with the most convincing evidence for his theory of natural selection?
   a. rabbits
   b. armadillos
   c. fishes
   d. finches

   a. no; although he noted similarities of rabbits and hares
   b. no; although he did observe these unusual creatures
   c. no; not a major animal studied by Darwin
   * d. yes; from the Galapagos Islands

8. Darwin's finches had distinctive ____, unlike those of other finches.
   a. color patterns
   b. feet
   c. feathers
   d. beaks

   a. no; these finches were relatively nondescript
   b. no; they had rather common generic-type feet
   c. no; nothing distinctive about feathers
   * d. yes; variation in beaks allow finches to feed upon different seeds, thereby reducing competition

9. The person who suggested that a population tends to outgrow its resource base was
   a. Malthus.
   b. Lyell.
   c. LaMarck.
   d. Henslow.

   * a. yes; economist and clergyman who indicated population grows faster than food supply
   b. no; a geologist who proposed the long time required for geological processes
   c. no; suggested the theory of use and disuse or the inheritance of acquired characteristics
   d. no; a botanist who got Darwin his job as naturalist aboard the *Beagle*

10. In his writing Lyell presented arguments for the slow, gradual occurrences of all but one of the following?
    a. erosion
    b. mountain formation
    c. formation of fossils
    d. volcanic activity

    a. incorrect; a slow process
    b. incorrect; a slow process
    * c. correct; did not express an opinion on this idea
    d. incorrect; a slow process

11. Natural selection is due to
    a. differential reproductive rates.
    b. differential survival resulting in change in a population.
    c. competition.
    d. all of the above

    a. yes; a partial answer; a more complete answer is available
    b. yes; a partial answer; a more complete answer is available
    c. yes; a partial answer; a more complete answer is available
    * d. yes; all of the above

12. *Archaeopteryx*
    a. is an example of a "missing link."
    b. was an animal with teeth and a long, bony tail.
    c. is a fossil reptile with feathers.
    d. all of the above

    a. yes; a partial answer; a more complete answer is available
    b. yes; a partial answer; a more complete answer is available
    c. yes; a partial answer; a more complete answer is available
    * d. yes; all of the above

13. Darwin was
    a. strongly encouraged to publish his work by his friends because of Wallace's similar conclusions.
    b. the first person to propose a theory of evolution.
    c. one of several people to suggest the concept of natural selection.
    d. quick to publish his ideas in both scientific papers and in a book.

    * a. yes; Darwin's colleagues encouraged him to publish
    b. no; several people had suggested evolution, but Darwin's contribution was to provide a mechanism for it to happen
    c. no; Darwin and Wallace shared this idea
    d. no; Darwin's voyage started in 1831 and his paper was published in 1858

14. Which of the following is *not* an observation that Darwin made?
    a. Human populations grow faster than their food supply.
    b. Organisms produce more offspring than can possibly survive.
    c. Related organisms need the same limited resources.
    d. Some organisms are better equipped to extract resources from their surroundings than others.

    * a. yes; Darwin did *not* work with human populations—this was a conclusion of Thomas Malthus
    b. no; this concept, known as biotic potential is characteristic of all thriving populations
    c. no; refers to the fact that there is competition between organisms and refers to the "struggle for existence"
    d. no; refers to the concept of adaptations and is known as the "survival of the fittest"

15. Which of the following features of *Archaeopteryx* is avian, not reptilian?
    a. long, bony tail
    b. possession of feathers
    c. a mouth with teeth
    d. bipedal locomotion

    a. no; birds' tails are composed of feathers, not bones
    * b. yes; possession of feathers is restricted only to birds
    c. no; reptiles had teeth, but birds did not
    d. no; both reptiles and birds used their hind legs for movements

16. Which of the following sources of variation does *not* result from shuffling existing genes?
    a. gene mutation
    b. crossing over
    c. genetic recombination
    d. independent assortment of chromosomes

    * a. yes; creates new genes, not new combinations
    b. no; breaks linkage relationships and increases genetic variation
    c. no; combines the potential variation of both parents (if one was 8 million, the combination would be 65 trillion)
    d. no; there are $2^{23}$ (8,000,000+) ways to arrange the chromosomes of humans by independent assortment alone

17. The variation found in a population arises from
    a. sexual recombination of traits.
    b. independent assortment of genes during the formation of gametes.
    c. crossing over during gamete formation.
    d. all of the above

    a. no; a partial answer; a more complete answer is available
    b. no; a partial answer; a more complete answer is available
    c. no; a partial answer; a more complete answer is available
    * d. yes; all of the above answers are correct

18. A gene pool is composed of different
    a. traits.
    b. alleles.
    c. phenotypes.
    d. species.

    a. no; refers to differences in physical appearance
    * b. yes; refers to the genes that control the appearance of members of a population
    c. no; refers to differences in physical appearance
    d. no; a species is a group of individuals that share the same gene pool

19. Which of the following does *not* result in variation in alleles from one generation to the next?
    a. changes in chromosome numbers and structure
    b. crossing over during meiosis
    c. asexual reproduction
    d. independent assortment of alleles during gametogenesis

    a. no; results in change through polyploidy, aneuploidy, or chromosomal aberrations
    b. no; results in change in offspring because of changes in linkage
    * c. yes; in asexual reproduction, the offspring are all alike
    d. no; independent assortment leads to new combinations of genes in offspring

20. Changes in allelic frequency occur because of differential survival, and reproduction is caused by
    a. mutation.
    b. natural selection.
    c. genetic drift.
    d. gene flow.

* a. no; an inheritable change in a gene
* b. yes; nature determines the contribution to the next generation by selecting those that survive and the amount they reproduce (number of offspring)
c. no; refers to change in genetic frequency in small populations just by chance
d. no; refers to change in gene frequency because of migration

21. Which of the following statements is true?
    a. Natural selection operates on genotypes.
    b. Offspring inherit phenotypes.
    c. Differences in genotypes result in differences in phenotypes.
    d. Variation in phenotypes is entirely attributable to genes.

    a. no; phenotypes, not genotypes, are selected
    b. no; organisms inherit genotypes
* c. yes; different genotypes produce different phenotypes
    d. no; the environment or other factors may modify the phenotypic expression of a genotype

22. Uniformitarianism refers to
    a. constant rate of geological processes.
    b. constant rate of new species being produced.
    c. period of stasis or little change followed by periods of rapid speciation.
    d. uniform rate of movement of the continents.

* a. yes; the process of erosion and weathering and other such events occur at a relatively constant rate
    b. no; rates of evolution are not uniform but vary according to conditions
    c. no; refers to punctuated equilibrium
    d. no; movement of continents is variable

23. Which of the following is mismatched?
    a. stratified–layered
    b. fossil–dig
    c. evolution–change
    d. Glyptodonts–sloths

    a. no; matched correctly; strata are layers of rock or sediments
    b. no; matched correctly; fossil is derived from the Latin word for dig
    c. no; matched correctly; evolution is characterized by change
* d. yes; these are mismatched; Glyptodonts were extinct fossil forms that resembled armadillos

24. Which of the following are mismatched?
    a. Cuvier–catastrophism
    b. Lamarck–gradualist or slow evolution
    c. Aristotle–Chain of Being
    d. Wallace–natural selection

    a. no; matched correctly; Cuvier proposed there was only one creation, but many catastrophes
* b. yes; Lamarck proposed the Inheritance of Acquired Characteristics while gradualism was accepted as the way evolution occurred
    c. no; matched correctly
    d. no; matched correctly; a codiscoverer with Darwin of the theory of natural selections

25. The Galapagos Islands
    a. lie on the equator.
    b. are 600 miles west of South America and isolated from other land masses.
    c. had a volcanic origin.
    d. all of the above

    a. yes; a partial answer; a more complete answer is available
    b. yes; a partial answer; a more complete answer is available
    c. yes; a partial answer; a more complete answer is available
* d. yes; all of the above

26. Most mutations are
    a. harmful.
    b. lethal.
    c. neutral.
    d. beneficial.

* a. yes; a change in the instructions in a gene will usually result in the formation of a protein with one or more different amino acids, which would result in a different enzyme; since enzymes are specific, this new enzyme might not work
    b. no; many changes may produce minor changes and the organisms possessing it does not necessarily die from a defective protein; example: sickle-cell hemoglobin
    c. no; there are many types of hemoglobin, some of which are simple molecular variations that do not affect its functioning
    d. no; some mutations may produce conditions that are favorable to a changed environment, such as the one suggested by the text in which an enzyme that functioned at a higher temperature is favored if the temperature rises

27. The reason that most mutations are harmful is that
   a. if a mutation were beneficial when the mutation first occurred, it would have been selected for and become part of the gene pool of the population.
   b. a mutation would produce an aberrant product that would not supply the protein produced before the mutation arose and the organism would not be able to survive.
   c. a mutation produces a change that would not be functional unless the environment changed in a direction that would favor the new mutation.
   d. all of the above are correct

   a. no; a partial answer; a more complete answer is available
   b. no; a partial answer; a more complete answer is available
   c. no; a partial answer; a more complete answer is available
   * d. yes; all of the answers above are correct

28. If the frequency of expression of a recessive gene in a population was 16 percent, the frequency of the heterozygote carriers would be
   a. 36 percent.
   b. 60 percent.
   c. 40 percent.
   d. 48 percent.

   a. no; the frequency of the homozygous dominant individuals in the population
   b. no; the frequency of the dominant allele in the population
   c. no; the frequency of the recessive allele in the population
   * d. yes; 2$\underline{pq}$: 2 "times" (60%) (40%) = 48%

29. To determine the frequency of the different genotypes for a particular allele in a population following the Hardy-Weinberg equilibrium, the first thing that you would need to do would be to determine the value of
   a. $p^2$ or the homozygous dominant individuals.
   b. $q^2$ or the homozygous recessive individuals.
   c. 2$\underline{pq}$ or the heterozygous individuals.
   d. $\underline{p}$ or the frequency of the dominant allele.

   a. no; unable to distinguish which is homozygous and which is heterozygous by looking at dominant individuals
   * b. yes; all homozygous individuals, and only homozygous individuals will express the recessive trait, and from this value all other values in the Hardy-Weinberg equations can be calculated
   c. no; unable to distinguish between homozygous dominant and heterozygous forms expressing dominant trait
   d. no; no way to determine this information without doing step (b) first

30. Which of the following would *not* drive a population away from a genetic equilibrium?
   a. random mating in a large population
   b. genetic drift
   c. gene flow
   d. natural selection

   * a. correct; a large population that mates randomly eliminates the influence of chance in changing gene frequencies
   b. incorrect; in a small population, genetic drift can result in change simply by chance
   c. incorrect; migration or the introduction or loss of alleles from a population could result in change
   d. incorrect; differences in reproductive rates or survival with reference to one or more alleles could result in change in the genetic composition of a population

31. If a population that is in genetic balance has a frequency of 49 percent for the expression of the recessive allele, then the frequency of the dominant allele would be
   a. 30 percent.
   b. 50 percent.
   c. 70 percent.
   d. none of the above

   * a. yes; if $q^2$ = 49%; $\underline{q}$ = 70%; $\underline{p}$ then equals 30%
   b. no; for this value to be correct $q^2$ would have to be 25%
   c. no; for this value to be correct $q^2$ would have to be 9%
   d. no; a common distractor, but one of the above is correct

32. Which of the following will prevent genetic drift from happening?
   a. genetic isolation
   b. random mating
   c. large population
   d. the founder effect or the bottleneck effect

a. no; genetic isolation would tend to support genetic drift by keeping the population small
b. no; random mating is a requirement for genetic drift
* c. yes; a large population would tend to prevent the frequency of an allele from changing drastically or being eliminated from a population
d. no; both are examples of genetic drift

33. Which of the following inferences can be drawn from the following observations: organisms produce more offspring than can survive, quantities of resources remain relatively constant, environmental resources limit population growth?
   a. competition
   b. survival of the fittest
   c. biotic potential
   d. extinction is the ultimate fate of a species

* a. yes; there is competition among a growing population for limited resources
b. no; this happens because the fittest have the best chance in competition
c. no; this addresses only the first observation
d. no; a conclusion that may be based on a great number of observations, including those given but dependent on other observations

34. Which type of selection would tend to reduce the variability present in a natural population and favor the persistence of existing phenotypes?
   a. artificial selection
   b. disruptive selection
   c. directional selection
   d. stabilizing selection

a. no; used in controlling features of a domesticated form
b. no; would tend to separate the population into two different groups
c. no; would result in a change in the phenotype of the population in favor of one type over all others
* d. yes; stabilizing selection eliminates extremes and tends to promote uniformity

35. In sickle-cell anemia
   a. both homozygous forms have less chance of survival in tropical and subtropical Africa than heterozygotes.
   b. the different forms represent balanced polymorphism.
   c. one-third of the population in central Africa may be heterozygous for the trait.
   d. all of the above

a. no; a partial answer; a more complete answer is available
b. no; a partial answer; a more complete answer is available
c. no; a partial answer; a more complete answer is available
* d. yes; all of the above are correct

36. Which of the following inferences is *not* supported by the observation that organisms exhibit highly variable traits that are inherited from earlier generations?
   a. Over generations populations change and evolve.
   b. There is differential reproduction.
   c. Organisms tend to exceed their natural limit of numbers.
   d. Some heritable traits are more adaptive than others.

a. incorrect; this inference is supported by the observation
b. incorrect; this inference is supported by the observation
* c. correct; there is nothing in the observation to support this inference
d. incorrect; this inference is supported by the observation

37. Which of the following is responsible for the changing frequencies of the alleles controlling the color of the peppered moths in England?
   a. artificial selection
   b. stabilizing selection
   c. disruptive selection
   d. directional selection

a. no; humans did not direct the selection of peppered moths as they might with domesticated animals
b. no; there was an increase in the frequency of one form over the other
c. no; did not result in bimodal distribution
* d. yes; the color pattern of the dark form was favored because of environmental changes following the onset of the industrial revolution

38. Which type of selection is operating when any particular trait gives an organism competitive advantage over others in selecting a mate and producing offspring?
   a. disruptive selection
   b. directional selection
   c. sexual selection
   d. stabilizing selection

a. no; results in two different forms such as found in sexual dimorphism
b. no; results in organisms at one extreme having advantage over the others
* c. yes; the female mate selects males on the basis of sexual features
d. no; refers to the type of selection that eliminates the extremes and reduces variability

39. Which of the following would *not* lead to
an accidental or random change in the gene
frequency in a population?
a. the founder effect
b. a bottleneck effect
c. nonrandom mating
d. a small isolated population

a. no; these would lead to genetic drift
b. no; these would lead to genetic drift
* c. yes; nonrandom mating could lead to a
directional change in gene frequency
d. no; a small population could lead to
genetic drift

40. Pest resurgences are the result of
a. the development of pesticide resistance
by natural populations.
b. the introduction of exotic forms.
c. domesticated forms interbreeding with
wild populations.
d. all of the above

* a. yes; many pests become resistant to
pesticides by selection of survivors
from indiscriminate use of pesticides
b. no; these organisms may become pests
once they are introduced, but it is
improper to refer to resurgence
c. no; although this breeding may occur,
it would simply broaden the gene pool
of the domesticated forms
d. no; a common distractor; but one of the
above is correct

41. Researchers at the National Zoo retrieve
DNA from unfertilized eggs of dead females
as a way to increase the genetic diversity
in ___ that have undergone the bottleneck
effect.
a. buffaloes
b. California condors
c. Florida panthers
d. cheetahs

a. no; although the population declined
severely, it has recovered dramatically
and does not require extraordinary
efforts
b. no; a population that has undergone
the bottleneck effect, but egg pulling
has restored some genetic diversity
* c. yes; the unfertilized eggs from roadkill
and genetic engineering will be used to
increase genetic diversity
d. no; cheetahs have undergone the
bottleneck effect, but there is no ready
source of eggs

# CHAPTER 15

# SPECIATION

1. The process of evolution occurs in
   a. individuals.
   b. populations.
   c. species.
   d. families.

   a. no; individuals may change over time (such as aging), but this is not evolution because gene frequencies do not change
 * b. yes; a group of interbreeding organisms evolve
   c. no; segments of species, the populations evolve and may lead to new species
   d. no; this chapter deals with microevolution, which is evolution at the population level or lower; the evolution of higher taxa is known as macroevolution

2. Evolution basically involves changes in
   a. genes.
   b. individuals.
   c. populations.
   d. species.

   a. no; mutations allow evolution to occur but must include selection
   b. no; individuals may change throughout life and only the changes in the germ plasm have a chance to be passed on to offspring
 * c. yes; changes in isolated populations may eventually be great enough to prevent members from interbreeding, resulting in speciation (the production of a new species)
   d. no; different species are already different and do not interbreed; so change may produce variation, but not new species

3. _____ leads to speciation.
   a. Evolution
   b. Isolation
   c. Divergence
   d. all of the above

   a. no; a partial answer; a more complete answer is available; if it results in changes in populations sufficient to prevent interbreeding
   b. no; a partial answer; a more complete answer is available; if sufficient changes occur during isolation to prevent interbreeding
   c. no; a partial answer; a more complete answer is available; refers to the accumulation of differences in populations
 * d. yes; all of the above are correct

4. Polyploidy
   a. can result in the immediate formation of species.
   b. leads to geographical isolation of population.
   c. only occurs in animals.
   d. is the end result of natural selection.

 * a. yes; prevents interbreeding or results in formation of sterile hybrids, thereby separating the two populations as different species
   b. no; polyploid has no specific relationship to geographic distribution
   c. no; less likely to occur in animals but does occur in plants and may persist through asexual reproduction
   d. no; polyploids may or may not be better adapted than diploids, but it is not correct to say that natural selection leads to polyploidy

5. Which of the following statements is false?
   a. Populations of a species have a shared genetic history and are evolving independently of other species.
   b. Speciation requires irreversible genetic divergence of one population from others, accompanied by isolating mechanisms that maintain genetic divergence.
   c. A species consists of interbreeding populations, regardless of origin or location.
   d. The timing, rate, and direction of speciation is essentially the same for all species located in the same environment.

a.  no; this statement is true
b.  no; this statement is true
c.  no; this statement is true
*  d.  yes; this statement is false; evolution of different species is independent of each other, and they may react differently to variations in the same environmental factor

6.  No matter how extensive the phenotypic variation is in the population of one species, individuals remain members of the same species as long as their ___ remain(s) the same.
a.  ability to interbreed
b.  morphological characteristics
c.  behavioral features
d.  physiology

*  a.  yes; interbreeding is the ultimate criteria to determine if two organisms belong to the same species.
b.  no; morphological characteristics may vary widely within a species
c.  no; behavioral features may vary widely within a species
d.  no; the physiology of individuals may vary widely within a species

7.  Zebroids are interspecific hybrids between zebras and
a.  horses.
b.  antelopes.
c.  donkeys.
d.  asses.

*  a.  yes; zebras and horses are able to cross in captivity
b.  no; genetically quite different from zebras
c.  no; members of the same family, but do not normally interbreed
d.  no; members of the same family, but do not normally interbreed

8.  Which of the following would be classified as a postzygotic type of isolating mechanism?
a.  temporal isolation
b.  gametic mortality
c.  hybrid sterility
d.  behavioral isolation

a.  no; the gametes never unite because they mature at different times
b.  no; mortality before the formation of a zygote would be classified as prezygotic isolation
*  c.  yes; if the hybrid is unable to breed, the species remains separate even though a zygote was formed
d.  no; behavioral isolation results in the failure of two animals to attempt to mate

9.  The cicadas are insects that exhibit a classical example of ___ isolation.
a.  behavioral
b.  temporal
c.  mechanical
d.  genetic

a.  no; another type of isolation
*  b.  yes; they reproduce every thirteen or seventeen years
c.  no; another type of isolation
d.  no; another type of isolation

10.  Most interspecific hybrids
a.  are weak and have reduced chances of survival.
b.  express the best features of the individuals that produced them.
c.  are stronger than their progenitors.
d.  are highly fertile and reproduce more vigorously that the organisms that produced them.

*  a.  yes; most are not as well adapted to their environment as their parents
b.  no; it is unusual that the best features are expressed, more often the undesirable traits will appear
c.  no; the mule is an exception, but most are weaker
d.  no; do not reproduce as well as their parents

11.  The development of daughter species occurs on the common border between two populations in
a.  allopatric speciation.
b.  sympatric speciation.
c.  parapatric speciation.
d.  all of the above

a.  no; the two populations are geographically isolated
b.  no; the daughter species could arise wherever the distribution of the two species overlap
*  c.  yes; in parapatric speciation species share a common border
d.  no; a common distractor; but one of the above is correct

12.  Geographic isolation occurs in
a.  allopatric speciation.
b.  sympatric speciation.
c.  parapatric speciation.
d.  all of the above

*  a.  yes; the two populations are geographically isolated
b.  no; there is a place where the two species come in contact
c.  no; there is a place where the two species come in contact
d.  no; one of the above answers is correct

13.  Physical barriers are likely to come into play in ___ isolation.
a.  behavioral
b.  ecological
c.  temporal
d.  geographical

a.  no; the barrier is the failure to recognize courtship patterns
b.  no; the barrier is based upon habitat preference and response to environmental variables
c.  no; the isolation is based upon difference in the timing of sexual maturity
* d.  yes; the barrier may be physical, such as an ocean, mountain range, desert, or a road

14. Factors leading to evolution include all but which one of the following?
a.  mutation
b.  natural selection
c.  genetic equilibrium
d.  reproductive isolation

a.  incorrect; it is the driving force of evolution that provides change
b.  incorrect; this is the guiding force of evolution that determines which of the various adapted individuals survive
* c.  correct; when a population reaches genetic equilibrium, it is stable and does not undergo evolution
d.  incorrect; speciation may occur if isolated populations become so different that they are not longer able to interbreed

15. The monotremes or egg-laying mammals are limited to Australia, Tasmania, and New Guinea because
a.  they were once wide-ranging forms but have been killed off in other habitats.
b.  the ecological adaptations of these animals are only met in these places.
c.  they evolved there and the isolation of this area did not allow them spread to other areas.
d.  God created them for a particular habitat.

a.  no; they were never widespread forms
b.  no; artificial environments can support them and they may be able to survive in other parts of the world where they have yet to be been introduced
* c.  yes; the most likely explanation available
d.  no; no evidence to support this supposition, because the environment is continually changing

16. Which of the following would most likely cause sympatric forms to speciate?
a.  ecological partitioning of the environment
b.  development of morphological differences
c.  development of polyploidy
d.  development of physical barriers

a.  no; this could be a way to develop speciation, but one of the other choices is more compelling
b.  no; unlikely to produce speciation unless the morphological change resulted in mechanical isolation
* c.  yes; polyploidy would give rise to an immediate genetic barrier
d.  no; it would take a considerable amount of time for two physically isolated populations to develop sufficient genetic differences to produce speciation

17. Which of the following statements is false?
a.  Animals are more likely to exhibit polyploidy than plants.
b.  Plants are able to carry extra genes with no apparent harm.
c.  Most hybrids between plant species are sterile.
d.  Even polyploid plants may not be able to reproduce sexually, but asexual reproduction may allow new chromosome combinations to survive.

* a.  yes; this statement is false; polyploidy in animals usually upsets normal developmental processes resulting in death in these forms
b.  no; this statement is true
c.  no; this statement is true
d.  no; this statement is true

18. A hybrid zone is characteristic of
a.  allopatric speciation.
b.  sympatric speciation.
c.  parapatric speciation.
d.  all of the above

a.  no; there is no physical contact and the populations remain physically separate
b.  no; if hybrids occur, they could occur anywhere throughout the range of the species
* c.  yes; the hybrid zone occurs where the parapatric forms share a common border
d.  no; a common distractor; only one of the above is correct

19. In ____, a species accumulates changes in allelic frequencies until it is recognized by authorities to be a different species.
a.  cladogenesis
b.  anagenesis
c.  punctuated equilibrium
d.  temporal isolation

a. no; divergence or branching results in the formation of new species
* b. yes; a species forms by the gradual accumulation of features as it develops along an evolutionary road
c. no; characterized by a dramatic change in the rate of evolution, such as the immediate isolation and rapid change in one path of evolution
d. no; temporal isolation refers to the failure of organisms to reproduce because of the fact that their gametes mature at different times

20. Punctuated equilibrium is *not* supported by the concept of
a. the bottleneck effect.
b. rapid transitions due to strong direction selection.
c. the founder effect.
d. the slow accumulation of small minor changes leading to eventual divergence.

a. no; this would favor the idea of punctuated equilibrium
b. no; this would favor the idea of punctuated equilibrium
c. no; this would favor the idea of punctuated equilibrium
* d. yes; this distractor describes the conditions favoring the concept of gradualism

21. Punctuated equilibrium
a. may be the result of major climatic changes.
b. states that there are long periods of little or no change interrupted by bursts of rapid evolution.
c. explains why the fossil record contains very few transitional forms and fails to show a continuum of gradual changes.
d. all of the above

a. no; a partial answer; a more complete answer is available
b. no; a partial answer; a more complete answer is available
c. no; a partial answer; a more complete answer is available
* d. yes; all the above answers are correct

22. Adaptive radiation
a. is a burst of microevolutionary activity, resulting in development of new species in many different habitats.
b. is simply the process of gene flow between two populations that have been isolated for long periods of time.
c. is solely a macroevolutionary process.
d. occurs when an exotic is able to invade a new habitat where it did not previously live.

* a. yes; the concept involves the spread of an ancestral form into new environments and the development of new adaptations that allow it to exploit the new adaptive zone
b. no; refers to gene flow that may introduce new genes into a population
c. no; not necessarily limited to major evolutionary events, it may occur at the level of speciation
d. no; often exotics are able to become established simply because there is not enough competition, and the exotic may not undergo any change in its gene pool or response to the physical environment

23. Adaptive radiation in a phylogenetic tree is indicated by a
a. single-angled branch.
b. horizontal branch of a vertical lineage.
c. continuation of a vertical lineage.
d. great many branches along a vertical lineage all close to the same point.

a. no; illustrative of a gradual divergence
b. no; indicative of a rapid change producing a new species
c. no; indicative that no change has taken place
* d. yes; indicates that many changes known as adaptive radiation have occurred

24. The development of wings by insects represents
a. a physical access to an adaptive zone.
b. an evolutionary access to an adaptive zone.
c. an ecological access to an adaptive zone.
d. all of the above

a. no; a partial answer; a more complete answer is available
b. no; a partial answer; a more complete answer is available
c. no; a partial answer; a more complete answer is available
* d. yes; all of the above answers are correct

25. Mammals invaded the adaptive zone that was once occupied by
a. reptiles.
b. amphibians.
c. birds.
d. all of the above

* a. yes; mammals assumed the place held by the dinosaurs
b. no; few mammals live in both water and land
c. no; mammals have not really invaded the aerial environment to any great extent
d. no; one of the above answers is correct

26. A key innovation may lead to ____ access to an adaptive zone.
    a. physical
    b. ecological
    c. evolutionary
    d. chronological

    a. no; the organism simply must reach in a given area
    b. no; this occurs when one organism is able to outcompete another, but it does not necessarily require a key innovation
    * c. yes; permits the exploitation of an adaptive zone in an innovative way
    d. no; timing is not a factor in key innovations

27. A species is
    a. a group of organisms sharing the same gene pool.
    b. a group of organisms that can interbreed with each other.
    c. able to produce fertile offspring after two of its members breed.
    d. all of the above

    a. no; a partial answer; a more complete answer is available
    b. no; a partial answer; a more complete answer is available
    c. no; a partial answer; a more complete answer is available
    * d. yes; all of the above answers are correct

28. Reproductive isolating mechanisms occur when organisms
    a. are separated geographically.
    b. perform different courtship rituals so that their reproductive behavior does not elicit an appropriate response.
    c. produce their gametes at different times.
    d. all of the above

    a. no; a partial answer; a more complete answer is available
    b. no; a partial answer; a more complete answer is available
    c. no; a partial answer; a more complete answer is available
    * d. yes; all of the above answers are correct

# CHAPTER 16

# THE MACROEVOLUTIONARY PUZZLE

1. Fossils
   a. may be used as a geological mapping tool.
   b. are evidences of life that lived in the distant past.
   c. are found in distinct layers or strata.
   d. all of the above are correct

   a. no; a partial answer; a more complete answer is available
   b. no; a partial answer; a more complete answer is available
   c. no; a partial answer; a more complete answer is available
   * d. yes; all the above answers are correct

2. Which of the following is an example of macroevolution?
   a. the development of a new species
   b. the invasion of land by the labyrinthodont amphibia
   c. the buildup of genetic differences in an isolated population to the extent that they could not interbreed
   d. genetic drift

   a. no; speciation is a microevolutionary event
   * b. yes; led to the evolution of terrestrial forms, a major step in evolution
   c. no; an example of a microevolutionary advance
   d. no; genetic drift leads to change in gene frequencies in small populations just by chance and is a microevolutionary change

3. Which of the following would represent an area where fossils would be unlikely to form and be preserved?
   a. shallow seas with continuous deposits of sediments
   b. tar pits
   c. swamps and floodplains
   d. rivers, hillsides, sites of rapid erosion

   a. no; fossils are often well preserved under these conditions
   b. no; animals are trapped, as in quicksand, and are preserved by the tar
   c. no; these sites favor preservation, particularly if decomposition does not occur
   * d. yes; areas of disturbance are unlikely to provide a stable situation where material can fossilize or be preserved

4. The word *fossil* comes from the Latin word for
   a. layered.
   b. old.
   c. preserved.
   d. dig.

   a. no; strata refers to the layers of sediment where fossils are found
   b. no; does not refer to age
   c. no; does not refer to preserved
   * d. yes; from the Latin word meaning to dig

5. Fossils are found in
   a. metamorphic rock.
   b. igneous rock.
   c. sedimentary rock.
   d. all of the above

   a. no; the heat and pressure to form these rocks destroy fossils as occurs when limestone metamorphoses to become marble
   b. no; originates from the heated core of the earth
   * c. yes; dead organisms are covered, and as long as they are not destroyed, they may be preserved
   d. no; only one of the above is correct

6. Which is the probable explanation for the difference in the adult skulls of humans and chimpanzees?
   a. The difference reflects different adaptation to the different habitats where they live.
   b. A regulatory gene that controlled the growth rate for bones mutated in the early ancestor and then a second regulator gene mutated to block the rapid growth in humans.
   c. A mutation in a gene expressed during embryonic development is responsible for such profound differences.
   d. A series of mutations led to gradual changes now manifested in the two different skulls.

   a. no; there are no major habitat differences to account for this much difference
   * b. yes; changes in genes that affect the growth rate can produce major differences
   c. no; the two skulls are alike at birth, and the differences occur later
   d. no; a possible explanation, but the limited fossil record does not support this

7. Vertebrates are all placed in the same phylum because
   a. they all possessed gills as embryos or subadults.
   b. they have similar structural features that demonstrate their kinship.
   c. they exhibit many homologous structures.
   d. all of the above

   a. no; a partial answer; a more complete answer is available
   b. no; a partial answer; a more complete answer is available
   c. no; a partial answer; a more complete answer is available
   * d. yes; all the above are correct

8. Which of the following structures are analogous?
   a. wing of a bird and wing of a butterfly
   b. wing of a bat and arm of a man
   c. wing of a bird and leg of a horse
   d. leg of a horse and the arm of a man

   * a. yes; these structures are analogous
   b. no; these structures are homologous
   c. no; these structures are homologous
   d. no; these structures are homologous

9. Organisms sharing analogous structures
   a. have a common ancestor.
   b. evolved from the same prototype form.
   c. exhibit structures that perform the same function, even if the two forms are not closely related embryologically.
   d. none of the above

   a. no; statement would be true if homologous structures were considered
   b. no; statement would be true if homologous structures were considered
   * c. yes; by definition analogous structures share the same function—for example, the wing of a bird and the wing of an insect
   d. no; a common distractor; only one of the above is correct

10. Homologous structures
    a. are found in animals that share a common ancestor.
    b. share a common function.
    c. are no longer functional and are appropriately called vestigial structures.
    d. are limited to vertebrate animals.

    * a. yes; the process of divergence reveals the similarity in structure that originated the common ancestor
    b. no; the similarity in function characteristic of analogous structures
    c. no; homologous structures may or may not be vestigial
    d. no; homologous structures may be found in vertebrates

11. Which of the following animals have wings that are not homologous to the others?
    a. pterosaurs
    b. bats
    c. insects
    d. birds

    a. no; the wings are homologous with two of the others
    b. no; the wings are homologous with two of the others
    * c. yes; the insect wings do not have bones and are not homologous with the others
    d. no; the wings are homologous with two of the others

12. Sharks, penguins, and porpoises exhibit _____ evolution.
    a. divergent
    b. convergent
    c. parallel
    d. regressive

    a. no; these organisms become more similar
    * b. yes; these unrelated forms developed similar adaptations
    c. no; these forms were not related and underwent changes appropriate to another type of evolution
    d. no; in regressive evolution, there is the loss of an advanced feature

13. A cladogram
   a. is a diagram that provides direct information about ancestors and descendants.
   b. portrays relative relationships among organisms based on the sharing of homologous structures.
   c. is based solely on morphological traits and makes wide use of available fossil material.
   d. all of the above

   a. no; demonstrates relationships but not direct lineages
 * b. yes; indicates which organisms are close relatives
   c. no; behavioral and other traits may be used in a cladogram
   d. no; only one of the above answers are correct

14. Cytochrome c is a protein
   a. used in controlling cell division.
   b. that functions in the electron transport chain.
   c. that enables muscles to contract.
   d. used in neurotransmission.

   a. no; it has another function
 * b. yes; is a hydrogen acceptor in the hydrogen transfer system in aerobic organisms
   c. no; it has another function
   d. no; it has another function

15. Which of the following organisms does *not* possess cytochrome c?
   a. a raccoon
   b. an oak tree
   c. an anaerobic bacteria
   d. a mosquito

   a. no; as aerobic organisms they use cytochrome c in the electron transport chain
   b. no; as aerobic organisms they use cytochrome c in the electron transport chain
 * c. yes; anaerobic bacteria do not have an electron transport chain, and therefore do not possess cytochrome c
   d. no; as aerobic organisms they use cytochrome c in the electron transport chain

16. Which of the following statements is false?
   a. DNA-DNA hybridization is used to compare the similarity of two DNA molecules.
   b. The more similarity in the primary structure of two similar proteins from different individuals, the more closely related they are.
   c. Analogous structures demonstrate evolutionary relationships.
   d. Homologous structures are the same body parts that are modified in different ways in different lines of descent from a common ancestor.

   a. no; this statement is true
   b. no; this statement is true
 * c. yes; this statement is false; analogous structures resemble each other because they share a common function, not a common ancestor
   d. no; this statement is true

17. The way to tell how similar two hybridized DNA molecules are is to
   a. compare the primary sequences of the proteins they code for.
   b. expose the hybridized DNA to different amounts of heat; the more closely similar the molecules are, the more heat it takes to separate them.
   c. expose the hybridized DNA to an acid; the more acid that has to be added to separate them, the more closely related the DNA molecules are.
   d. all of the above

   a. no; although this technique could be productive, it is not used to compare DNA molecules
 * b. yes; the heat breaks the bonds
   c. no; this technique would not work
   d. no; a common distractor, but only one of the above is correct

18. The endangered giant panda has been shown to be related to the ___ by DNA-DNA hybridization experiments.
   a. bear
   b. raccoon
   c. dog
   d. hyena

 * a. yes; bears and giant pandas are closely related
   b. no; DNA-DNA hybridization does not indicate that this animal is closely related to the giant panda
   c. no; DNA-DNA hybridization does not indicate that this animal is closely related to the giant panda
   d. no; DNA-DNA hybridization does not indicate that this animal is closely related to the giant panda

19. The most inclusive taxa used in the current classification system is
   a. genus.
   b. order.
   c. kingdom.
   d. phyla.

   a. no; a more inclusive group is available
   b. no; a more inclusive group is available
 * c. yes; the most inclusive group is the kingdom
   d. no; a more inclusive group is available

20. Phylum or division is composed of related
   a. classes.
   b. families.
   c. orders.
   d. genera.

\*　　a.　yes; classes are the subdivisions of phylum
　　　b.　no; orders are the subdivisions of class
　　　c.　no; genera are the subdivisions of family
　　　d.　no; species are the subdivisions of genus

21.　Which of the following includes related orders?
　　　a.　class
　　　b.　phylum
　　　c.　family
　　　d.　genus

\*　　a.　yes; related orders are in the same class
　　　b.　no; phyla are composed of related classes
　　　c.　no; family are composed of related genera
　　　d.　no; genera are composed of related species

22.　Which of the following is false?
　　　a.　Morphological convergence leads to analogous structures.
　　　b.　A neutral mutation has no measurable effect on the survival and reproduction of the organism that bears it.
　　　c.　The ancestors of the modern horse had five toes, not one.
　　　d.　A molecular clock is based on the number of substantive rather than neutral mutations that occur over time.

　　　a.　incorrect; this statement is true; structures show adaptations to their environment
　　　b.　incorrect; this statement is true; a simple definition of a neutral mutation
　　　c.　incorrect; this statement is true
\*　　d.　correct; this statement is false; neutral mutations are used rather than substantive mutations, which might modify survival rates and the number of mutations produced (i.e. major mutations might be attended by a number of minor ones and throw off the accuracy of a molecular clock of evolution)

# CHAPTER 17

# THE ORIGIN AND EVOLUTION OF LIFE

1. The first organisms were
   a. primitive eukaryotes.
   b. aerobic forms.
   c. heterotrophs.
   d. photosynthetic.

   a. no; they were prokaryotes; the eukaryotes originated during the Proterozoic 1.2 billion years ago
   b. no; they were anaerobic forms most likely using fermentation pathways because there was no oxygen available
   * c. yes; absorbed their food from their environment
   d. no; photosynthesis developed later, between 3.2 and 3.5 billion years ago

2. The accumulation of oxygen in the atmosphere was the result of
   a. the action of stromatolites.
   b. the evolution of cyclic pathways of photosynthesis.
   c. the development of the synthesis phase of photosynthesis.
   d. the evolution of the noncyclic pathway of photosynthesis.

   a. no; did not release free oxygen
   b. no; did not release free oxygen
   c. no; this reaction fixes carbon dioxide but does not release free oxygen
   * d. yes; the process began changing the atmosphere 3.5 billion years ago

3. The first life appeared on earth approximately ___ billion years ago.
   a. between 1/2 and 1
   b. between 1 1/2 and 2
   c. between 2 1/2 and 3
   d. between 3 1/2 and 4

   a. no; not old enough
   b. no; not old enough
   c. no; not old enough
   * d. yes; the first living forms originated between 3 1/2 and 4 billion years ago

4. Which of the following gases was not one of the gases found in the early atmosphere of the earth?
   a. hydrogen
   b. oxygen
   c. carbon monoxide
   d. carbon dioxide

   a. no; hydrogen was present
   * b. yes; there was little or no oxygen in the early atmosphere
   c. no; there was carbon monoxide
   d. no; there was carbon dioxide

5. Which of the following statements is false?
   a. A combination of methane, water, ammonia, and hydrogen reacted in experiments to form amino acids.
   b. Experiments showed that formaldehyde could form glucose, ribose, deoxyribose, and other sugars.
   c. Experiments demonstrated that nucleotides could be formed from formaldehyde and methane.
   d. Adenine triphosphate could be formed from hydrogen cyanide.

   a. no; this statement is true
   b. no; this statement is true
   c. no; this statement is true
   * d. yes; no experiments have been done demonstrating this result; one substance that is lacking is phosphorus that is needed to form the nucleotide found in ATP

6. Proteins were first formed by amino acids in the primitive earth under the influence of
   a. enzymes.
   b. clay.
   c. iron ions.
   d. heavy metals.

   a. no; there were no enzymes at this time
   * b. yes; the clays formed a lattice that allowed amino acids to become organized and joined together
   c. no; this did not influence protein formation
   d. no; this did not influence protein formation

7. Which of the following statements is false?
   a. Water and lipid mixture will spontaneously form lipid sacs that contain water.
   b. Heated amino acids formed protein chains and when they cooled, they formed microspores.
   c. RNA may have functioned as an enzyme.
   d. DNA was one of the very first organic compounds and was essential for the early stages of chemical evolution.

   a. no; this statement is true
   b. no; this statement is true
   c. no; this statement is true
   * d. yes; this statement is false; the origin and place for DNA is still unknown

8. Which of the following ingredients was deemed necessary for the origin of life on earth?
   a. free oxygen
   b. water in a liquid form
   c. the absence of sunlight for parts of a day
   d. all of the above

   a. no; free oxygen actually would be antagonistic to the formation of some organic compounds
   * b. yes; liquid water was necessary to form salt solutions and a medium where life could flourish
   c. no; no need for either light or darkness in the beginning because photosynthesis had not evolved
   d. no; a common distractor, but one of the above is correct

9. The first templates (structural patterns) for protein synthesis were most likely
   a. complex polysaccharides.
   b. nucleic acids.
   c. clay.
   d. inorganic crystals.

   a. no; no evidence to support this
   b. no; these came later
   * c. yes; long chains of proteins could be formed with inherent stability to keep them from breaking apart
   d. no; structural pattern would not permit this

10. Which of the following is the least likely mechanism leading to the establishment of membranes around cells?
    a. Fragments of cellulose (the most common organic compound in the world) joined together to form the first membrane.
    b. Lipid molecules self-assembled into small water-filled sacs.
    c. Membranes arose spontaneously and involved both amino acids and lipids.
    d. Chains of amino acids self-assembled into small stable spheres that later added lipids at their surface.

* a. yes; cellulose was not available at this time
    b. no; one plausible explanation of the origin of membranes
    c. no; one plausible explanation of the origin of membranes
    d. no; one plausible explanation of the origin of membranes

11. Stanley Miller's early experiments and others like them demonstrate that
    a. a protein chain will form from amino acids as they dry on clay substrates.
    b. RNA can function as an enzyme.
    c. many simple organic compounds can be formed from mixtures of gases thought to be found in the early atmosphere of the earth if appropriate conditions are available.
    d. DNA is formed and replicated easily under primitive conditions, such as those that existed when life first evolved.

    a. no; this was demonstrated by experiments by Sidney Fox
    b. no; not demonstrated by these experiments on early chemical evolution
    * c. yes; molecules such as amino acids, simple sugars, and nitrogenous bases may be formed
    d. no; has not been demonstrated

12. Which of the following were *not* one of the four gases used in Stanley Miller's simulation of the synthesis of organic compounds on the early earth?
    a. methane
    b. ammonia
    c. water vapor
    d. carbon dioxide

    a. no; methane was used
    b. no; ammonia was used
    c. no; water vapor are used
    * d. yes; carbon dioxide was not one of the four gases used

13. Porphyrin rings are found in
    a the cytochrome system of the electron transport system.
    b. the central portion of the chlorophyll molecule.
    c. ATP molecules.
    d. both (a) and (b), but not (c)

    a. no; a partial answer; a more complete answer is available
    b. no; a partial answer; a more complete answer is available
    c. no; not found in ATP
    * d. yes; (a) and (b) are correct, and (c) is incorrect

14. The appearance of oxygen in the Proterozoic atmosphere was dependent upon
    a. action of methanogens.
    b. the synthesis of organic compounds.
    c. the evolution of photosynthetic bacteria.
    d. the appearance of heterotrophic organism.

    a. no; would produce methane
    b. no; would not generate free oxygen
    * c. yes; would produce oxygen as a byproduct
    d. no; would consume free oxygen

15. The first eukaryotes were the
    a. archaebacteria.
    b. protista.
    c. fungi.
    d. plants.

    a. no; these are primitive prokaryotes
    * b. yes; single-celled organisms
    c. no; multicellular forms
    d. no; multicellular forms

16. The most widely accepted explanation for the origin of organelles is
    a. the gradual isolation of functions to different parts of the cytoplasm.
    b. infoldings of the plasma membranes.
    c. incorporation of microorganisms that functioned as symbionts.
    d. genes evolved that specified for the production of internal membranes.

    a. no; there is no way to segregate functions into separate parts of the cytoplasm without the existence of membranes
    b. no; although this does represent an alternative to the endosymbiont hypothesis
    * c. yes; the endosymbiont hypothesis proposed by Margulis
    d. no; no evidence to support this suggestion

17. The endosymbiont hypothesis is supported by the fact that
    a. mitochondria replicate their own DNA.
    b. the code for mitochondrial DNA is slightly different from nuclear DNA.
    c. mitochondria are the size of bacteria and the inner mitochondrial membrane is similar to a bacterial plasma membrane.
    d. all of the above

    a. no; a partial answer; a more complete answer is available
    b. no; a partial answer; a more complete answer is available
    c. no; a partial answer; a more complete answer is available
    * d. yes; all of the above answers are correct

18. Evolutionary access to an adaptive zone may occur
    a. through an extinction which provides a vacancy in that zone.
    b. if the invading organism is able to out compete the resident species.
    c. with the development of a key innovation.
    d. all of the above

    a. yes; (a better answer is available)
    b. yes; (a better answer is available)
    c. yes; (a better answer is available)
    * d. yes; all of the above could result in invasion of an adaptive zone

19. The most recent period of the six periods of the Paleozoic era was the
    a. Cambrian.
    b. Permian.
    c. Carboniferous.
    d. Devonian.

    a. no; the oldest of the six periods
    * b. yes; the most recent of the six periods
    c. no; the fifth oldest of six periods
    d. no; the fourth oldest of the six periods

20. The fossil fuels were formed during the
    a. Cretaceous.
    b. Cambrian.
    c. Cenozoic.
    d. Carboniferous.

    a. no; part of Mesozoic
    b. no; too early, first of the Paleozoic
    c. no; too late, the most recent geological era
    * d. yes; the term means carbon bearing

21. Which of the following periods was *not* characterized by giant reptiles?
    a. Permian
    b. Triassic
    c. Cretaceous
    d. Jurassic

    * a. correct; the large dinosaurs had not yet developed
    b. incorrect; the reptiles were dominant forms
    c. incorrect; the reptiles were dominant forms
    d. incorrect; the reptiles were dominant forms

22. The flowering plants arose and underwent major radiation during the ____ period.
    a. Permian
    b. Triassic
    c. Cretaceous
    d. Quarternary

    a. no; too early
    b. no; too early
    * c. yes; during a brief ten million year span
    d. no; too later

23. Which of the following epochs was *not* part of the tertiary period?
   a. Pleistocene
   b. Eocene
   c. Miocene
   d. Pliocene

   * a. correct; part of the quarternary period
   b. incorrect; part of the tertiary period
   c. incorrect; part of the tertiary period
   d. incorrect; part of the tertiary period

24. The earliest and longest period of the Paleozoic was the
   a. Ordovician.
   b. Silurian.
   c. Cambrian.
   d. Carboniferous.

   a. no; there was an earlier period
   b. no; there was an earlier period
   * c. yes; both the first and longest period of the Paleozoic
   d. no; there was an earlier period

25. The lobe-finned fish invaded land during the
   a. Permian.
   b. Cambrian.
   c. Carboniferous.
   d. Devonian.

   a. no; earlier
   b. no; later
   c. no; earlier
   * d. yes; the age of fishes

26. Which group of plants was not present during the Permian?
   a. cycads
   b. ginkgos
   c. conifers
   d. flowering plants

   a. no; these plants were part of the flora of the Permian
   b. no; these plants were part of the flora of the Permian
   c. no; these plants were part of the flora of the Permian
   * d. yes; arose during the Mesozoic

27. The giant asteroid hit ___ 65 million years ago.
   a. Yucatan peninsula
   b. Hudson Bay in Canada
   c. the continent Atlantis causing it to sink
   d. Pacific Ocean

   * a. yes; in Mexico
   b. no; not in Canada
   c. no; there is no evidence to support this theory
   d. no; although there could be other asteroids that hit there

28. The mineral that is typical of deposits of 65 million years ago that is found in asteroids but is not a common mineral on earth is
   a. platinum.
   b. iridium.
   c. plutonium.
   d. radium.

   a. no; a common mineral found in the earth's crust
   * b. yes; not a common mineral on earth but found on meteors and asteroids
   c. no; a common mineral found in the earth's crust
   d. no; a common mineral found in the earth's crust

29. Dinosaurs are thought to have become extinct by
   a. climatic changes.
   b. the rise of the mammals.
   c. the impact of one or several meteors.
   d. the result of a worldwide epidemic of parasites.

   a. no; although the climate may have become much colder after one or a group of meteors hit the earth because the dust would block the heat from the sun
   b. no; the adaptive radiation of mammals occurred after the massive extinction of dinosaurs
   * c. yes; the impact produced massive clouds that cooled off the temperature of the earth, which killed the dinosaurs
   d. no; no evidence to support this viewpoint

30. The large land mass that started breaking up during the Mesozoic era and is still moving apart today was
   a. Gondwana.
   b. Pangea.
   c. Eurasia.
   d. Nazca plate.

   a. no; an early land mass that formed part of Pangea
   * b. yes; the large common land mass
   c. no; a tectonic plate that includes much of Europe and Asia
   d. no; a tectonic plate located west of South America in the Pacific Ocean

31. At the beginning of geological eras there were
   a. massive extinctions.
   b. catastrophic climatic and geological events.
   c. periods of recovery, adaptive radiation, and filling of vacant niches and adaptive zones.
   d. periods of stasis with minimal biotic change.

a. no; marked the closing of a previous era rather than marking the beginning of a new one
b. no; marked the closing of a previous era rather than marking the beginning of a new one
* c. yes; many vacant niches existed following the massive extinctions and organisms adapted to new environmental conditions
d. no; period of intense evolutionary activity

# CHAPTER 18

# BACTERIA, VIRUSES, AND PROTISTANS

1. There are _____ nanometers in a meter.
   a. 10,000
   b. 1,000,000
   c. 1,000,000,000
   d. 100,000,000,000

   a. no; too few
   b. no; too few
   * c. yes; there are 1 billion nanometers in a meter
   d. no; too many

2. Bacteria may be described as
   a. pathogens.
   b. photosynthesizers.
   c. decomposers.
   d. all of the above

   a. no; a partial answer; a more complete answer is available
   b. no; a partial answer; a more complete answer is available
   c. no; a partial answer; a more complete answer is available
   * d. yes; all of the above answers are correct

3. Which of the following is *not* a hydrogen source for the photoautotrophic bacteria using a cyclic pathway?
   a. water
   b. hydrogen gas
   c. hydrogen sulfide
   d. inorganic compounds in the environment

   * a. yes; water is the source of hydrogen in the noncyclic pathway, not the cyclic pathway
   b. no; hydrogen may be taken from hydrogen gas
   c. no; hydrogen may come from hydrogen sulfides
   d. no; hydrogen may be derived from other organic compounds

4. The photoheterotrophs do *not* obtain their carbon from
   a. fatty acids.
   b. carbohydrates.
   c. carbon dioxide.
   d. other organic compounds produced by the photosynthetic bacteria.

   a. no; carbon may come from fatty acids
   b. no; carbon may come from carbohydrates
   * c. yes; atmospheric carbon dioxide is not the source for carbon for photoheterotrophs
   d. no; carbon may be obtained from organic compounds

5. Which of the following statements is false?
   a. Bacterial cells have a single circular chromosome plus some plasmids.
   b. The cell wall of a bacteria is composed of chitin.
   c. Most bacteria reproduce by binary fission.
   d. Collectively, bacteria show a great diversity in their modes of metabolism.

   a. no; this statement is true
   * b. yes; this statement is false; the cell wall is composed of peptidoglycan
   c. no; this statement is true
   d. no; this statement is true

6. Which of the following names refers to a chain of cells?
   a. staphylococcus
   b. streptococcus
   c. spirilla
   d. bacillia

   a. no; refers to a sheetlike cluster of cells
   * b. yes; refers to a chain of cocci
   c. no; refers to a bacteria with a spiral pattern
   d. no; name refers to a rodlike bacteria

7. Gram-positive bacteria are
   a. larger than average-sized bacteria.
   b. bacteria that retain a purple dye even after being washed with alcohol.
   c. pink in color after being exposed to Gram's stain and an alcohol wash.
   d. ones that have a nucleus that stains dark after begin exposed to Gram's stain and an alcohol wash.

   a. no; the gram does not refer to weight of the bacteria
   * b. yes; the bacteria that retain the purple dye from Gram stain are said to be Gram-positive
   c. no; these bacteria are Gram-negative
   d. no; bacteria do not have a nucleus

8. Bacterial conjugation
   a. involves the transfer of plasmid DNA from one cell to another.
   b. involves mutation in response to exposure to ultraviolet radiation.
   c. is another name for binary fission.
   d. involves the removal of the wall of a bacteria.

   * a. yes; another form of sexual reproduction
   b. no; does not involve radiation or mutation
   c. no; is the same as binary fission
   d. no; does not affect the bacterial wall

9. Which of the following is *not* classified as a *Eubacteria*?
   a. Archaebacteria
   b. Gram-positive bacteria
   c. Cyanobacteria
   d. nitrifying, sulfur-oxidizing, and iron-oxidizing bacteria

   * a. yes; more primitive than eubacteria
   b. no; a chemoheterotrophic eubacteria
   c. no; a photoautotrophic eubacteria
   d. no; a chemoautotrophic eubacteria

10. Which of the following bacteria are well represented in the fossil record?
    a. methanogens
    b. the green and purple sulfur bacteria
    c. stromatolites
    d. Actinomyces

    a. no; not well represented by fossils
    b. no; not well represented by fossils
    * c. yes; the bacteria and sediments were often fossilized
    d. no; not well represented by fossils

11. Which statement is false?
    a. Bacteria lack an organized nucleus.
    b. Bacteria have a plasma membrane, but lack membranes to surround the organelles.
    c. Bacteria lack ribosomes.
    d. Bacteria are prokaryotic, rather than eukaryotic.

    a. True. They have one long chromosome but it is not surrounded by nuclear membrane.
    b. True. They lack membrane-bound organelles.
    * c. False. They possess ribosomes and use them to produce proteins.
    d. True. They are primitive forms of life.

12. The majority of bacteria are
    a. photosynthetic autotrophs.
    b. chemosynthetic autotrophs.
    c. pathogens.
    d. heterotrophs.

   a. no; a small number function this way
   b. no; an even smaller number function as chemosynthesizers
   c. no; disease producing bacteria are a minority
   * d. yes; vast majority are decomposers and derive their food heterotrophically

13. Extra circular pieces of chromosome found in bacteria are called
    a. pili.
    b. peptidoglycans.
    c. flagella.
    d. plasmids.

    a. no; a conjugation tube
    b. no; the ingredient in the walls of bacteria
    c. no; organelles used for movement
    * d. yes

14. Which of the following is *not* closely related to the other three?
    a. extreme halophiles
    b. methanogens
    c. Gram-positive bacteria
    d. thermoacidophiles

    a. no; a representative of the Archaebacteria
    b. no; a representative of the Archaebacteria
    * c. yes; one of the types of eubacteria
    d. no; a representative of the Archaebacteria

15. The halophiles are
    a. the "heat-lovers" found in hot springs.
    b. "salt-lovers" found near hot vents on the seafloor.
    c. characteristic of swamps and sewage treatment plants.
    d. involved in the nitrogen cycle.

    a. no; the "heat-lovers" are called thermophiles
    * b. yes; halophiles are found in habitats with high salinity
    c. no; this describes the methanogens
    d. no; the halophiles do not have anything to do with the nitrogen cycle

16. Antibiotics are produced by
    a. some pathogenic bacteria.
    b. Actinomyces.
    c. *E. coli.*
    d. spirochetes.

    a. no; some pathogens produce toxins
    * b. yes; mostly soil organisms including *Actinomycetes* and *Streptomyces*
    c. no; a common bacteria found in the intestinal tracts of humans and farm animals
    d. no; some parasitic free-living organisms that do not produce antibiotics

17. Which of the following statements is false?
    a. Penicillin interferes with the cell walls of bacteria.
    b. Antibiotics are useful in treating viral disorders.
    c. Prescription leads to the development of resistance in pathogens.
    d. Streptomycins block protein synthesis by pathogens.

    a. no; this statement is true
  * b. yes; this statements is false; antibiotics are ineffective against viruses
    c. no; this statement is true
    d. no; this statement is true

18. Lyme disease is spread by
    a. fleas.
    b. spiders.
    c. ticks.
    d. mosquitoes.

    a. no; does not spread Lyme disease
    b. no; does not spread Lyme disease
  * c. yes; tick bites spread this disease, caused by a spirochete
    d. no; do not spread Lyme disease

19. An endospore is
    a. a type of asexual reproduction.
    b. a method to escape extremes in the environment.
    c. a sexual gamete.
    d. a vegetative cell.

    a. no; although the spore will germinate to form a new vegetative cell
  * b. yes; endospores enable the bacteria to resist heat, boiling, drying, and radiation
    c. no; is not involved with sexual reproduction
    d. no; not a normal vegetative cell, but a specialized resistant one

20. The methanogens are responsible for all but which one of the following?
    a. chemosynthetic production of food
    b. the production of swamp gas
    c. production of gas in sewage treatment facilities
    d. production of gases by cattle and similar organisms

  * a. yes; not a chemosynthetic bacteria
    b. no; decomposition leads to production of methane
    c. no; methane is produced in sewage plants
    d. no; cattle are a major source of methane

21. Bacteriorhodopsin is a bacterial _____.
    a. vitamin
    b. light-trapping pigment
    c. food storage product
    d. metabolic waste product

    a. no; not dietary food necessity
  * b. yes
    c. no; food stored in various compounds
    d. no; these are numerous waste products produced by bacteria including strong toxins but this is not one of them

22. Heterocysts are cells in the cyanobacteria that
    a. fix nitrogen.
    b. anchor the plant.
    c. develop into spores.
    d. develop into gametes.

  * a. yes
    b. no; such cells are called holdfasts
    c. no; such cells are called sporangia
    d. no; such cells are called gametangia

23. The monerans and protists are alike in that they are essentially
    a. unicellular.
    b. producers.
    c. eukaryotic.
    d. motile.

  * a. yes; protists and majority of bacteria are unicellular
    b. no; many parasitic and heterotrophic forms, not all are producers
    c. no; monerans are prokaryotic
    d. no; motility varies among these organisms and is not an important or diagnostic feature

24. A virus
    a. takes over the control of a host cell and forces it to make more virus particles.
    b. is a naked molecule of nucleic acid.
    c. is a living obligate parasite of certain animals.
    d. is a chemical poison that disrupts the normal metabolic processes of a cell.

  * a. yes; typical of the lytic cycle of viral infection
    b. no; viruses have a protective protein coat or sometimes may be encased in a lipid envelope
    c. no; viruses are not alive and may infect a wide range of hosts including bacteria, fungi, and plants
    d. no; this distractor could be true of a number of chemical toxins

25. A virus can replicate
    a. while attached to a receptor on the surface of a cell.
    b. only after its DNA/RNA has entered the host cell and started to control the biosynthetic machinery of the cell.
    c. under a wide range of environmental conditions, thus making viruses extremely dangerous pathogens.
    d. only in warm blooded animals and a few insect vectors.

a. no; unable to replicate unless it enters a living cell
* b. yes
c. no; only under very specific conditions inside a cell
d. no; may infect and reproduce in a wide variety of host cells

26. Which of the following activities occurs first during the invasion of a cell by a virus?
    a. the DNA or RNA is injected into the cell
    b. the virus locks onto a specific receptor molecule on the surface of a host cell
    c. the virus gains control over the cells' metabolic machinery
    d. viral nucleic acids are replicated and viral proteins produced

    a. no; second
* b. yes; first
    c. no; third
    d. no; fourth

27. Viroids are infective units composed of
    a. DNA fragments.
    b. RNA fragments.
    c. viral proteins.
    d. proteins and nucleic acids.

    a. no; fragment of a gene, not a virus
* b. yes; cause plant diseases and certain types of cancer
    c. no; not infective by themselves
    d. no; a virus contain nucleic acid and proteins not a viroid which is a naked strand of RNA

28. Which of the following statements is false?
    a. A virus is alive.
    b. Viruses have protein coats and a nucleic acid core.
    c. A virus cannot reproduce itself.
    d. (a) and (c) are false; but (b) is true

* a. yes; this statement is false
    b. no; this statement is true
    c. no; this statement is true
    d. no; only (a) is false; (b) and (c) are true

29. Which of the following is a RNA virus?
    a. hepatitis virus
    b. papovavirus such as those causing warts
    c. AIDS virus
    d. smallpox and cowpox

    a. no; a DNA virus
    b. no; a DNA virus
* c. yes; the AIDS virus is a retrovirus or one with an RNA core
    d. no; a DNA virus

30. Which of the following is *not* an RNA or retrovirus?
    a. chicken pox virus
    b. influenza virus
    c. viruses that cause rabies and the common cold
    d. herpes virus

    a. no; this is an example of an RNA virus
    b. no; this is an example of an RNA virus
    c. no; this is an example of an RNA virus
* d. yes; the herpes virus is a DNA virus

31. Infectious protein particles are known as
    a. viruses.
    b. viroids.
    c. prions.
    d. both (b) and (c), but not (a)

    a. no; viruses have nucleic acids
    b. no; viroids are strands or circles of RNA and have no protein coat
* c. yes; infectious proteins
    d. no; only (c) is correct

32. Which of the following steps occurs last?
    a. Virus enters the host cell.
    b. Infected cells release viruses.
    c. Viral nucleic acid directs host cells to produce viruses.
    d. Viral nucleic acids and proteins are assembled into a new virus.

    a. no; the first step
* b. yes; the last step
    c. no; the second step
    d. no; the third step

33. Flagellated, photosynthetic protistans that are capable of living heterotrophically are members of the
    a. Chrysophytes.
    b. Euglenids.
    c. Paramecia.
    d. Sporozoans.

    a. no; autotrophic only
* b. yes; able to produce food or exist heterotrophically
    c. no; ciliated protistans unable to photosynthesize
    d. no; incapable of independent movement or autotrophic nutrition

34. The walls of the diatoms and some other Chrysophyta contain
    a. peptidoglycan.
    b. silica.
    c. calcium carbonate.
    d. cellulose.

    a. no; found in bacterial cell walls
* b. yes; forms the shells
    c. no; found in shells of other marine animals
    d. no; found in plants and dinoflagellates

35. The red tides kill fish by
    a. suffocation through the production of excess oxygen.
    b. clogging the fish gills with a large number of organisms.
    c. a nerve poison (neurotoxin).
    d. a chemical that paralyzes the large swimming muscles of the fish.

a. no; not an apparent problem
b. no; not an apparent problem
* c. yes; correct
d. no; not an apparent problem

36. The chytrids are most similar to
a. algae.
b. fungi.
c. bacteria.
d. Protozoa.

a. no; do not produce food
* b. yes; heterotrophic organisms that are saprobes or parasites
c. no; structurally, they are quite different
d. no; lack the diversity and internal organelles

37. Which of the following diseases is due to a water mold?
a. late blight of potatoes
b. late blight of corn
c. Dutch elm disease
d. Chestnut blight

* a. yes; a chytrid is responsible
b. no; caused by a fungus
c. no; caused by a fungus
d. no; caused by a fungus

38. "Spores germinate to produce living amoebas that stream together and form a mobile slug." The previous description fits a
a. water mold.
b. slime mold.
c. fungus.
d. all of the above

a. no; forms a mycelium only
* b. yes; a weird and different form of life
c. no; forms a mycelium only
d. no; a common distractor, but only one of the above is true

39. Single-celled predators and parasites are examples of
a. protozoa.
b. chrysophytes.
c. cyanophytes.
d. diatoms.

* a. yes; unicellular heterotrophic organisms
b. no; a type of algae
c. no; the blue-green algae
d. no; unicellular autotrophs

40. Members of the Sarcodina
a. move by pseudopods.
b. move by cilia.
c. move by flagella.
d. are sessile—unable to move.

* a. yes; these protozoans include the amoebas that move by pseudopods
b. no; these are the ciliates (*Celeophora*)
c. no; these are flagellates (*Mastigophora*)
d. no; these are nonmotile protozoa

41. Foraminifera are
a. amoebas with hard shells.
b. fossils of any protozoa.
c. the base of the food chain in many marine communities.
d. covered with needlelike spines.

* a. yes; with holes that allow the psuedopods to move
b. no; the Foraminifera belong to the Sarcodina
c. no; these protozoa are unable to produce food so that they would not be at the base of a food chain
d. no; the protozoans with the spines belong to the Radiolarians

42. The radiolarian shells are made of
a. calcium carbonate.
b. silica.
c. cobalt.
d. chitin.

a. no; the common ingredient in shells of most marine forms
* b. yes; siliceous compounds make up shells of the radiolarians and diatoms
c. no; not an ingredient in most shells
d. no; this chemical is found in the exoskeleton of arthropods and the cell walls of fungi

43. The heliozoans are members of the
a. Sporozoa.
b. Mastigophora.
c. Ciliates.
d. Sarcodina.

a. no; nonmotile parasitic forms
b. no; the Mastigophora include the flagellates
c. no; the needlelike structures radiating from the body are pseudopods
* d. yes; these protozoans possess pseudopods

44. Trichocysts are protective threads produced by
a. dinoflagellates.
b. Paramecium.
c. Trichomonas.
d. Euglena.

a. no; not produced by dinoflagellates
* b. yes; even though they are not very functional
c. no; this organism causes a sexually transmitted disease
d. no; a specialized protozoan that does not have trichocysts

45. The contractile vacuole eliminates
    a. excess water.
    b. nitrogenous waste.
    c. undigested food.
    d. all of the above

*   a. yes; water that enters the cell by osmosis is removed by this pulsing organ that could be compared to bailing out a boat as it fills with water
    b. no; removed via the anal pore
    c. no; removed through the anal pore
    d. no; a common distractor; but only one of the above is correct

46. Which of the following disease is *not* caused by a flagellate?
    a. African sleeping sickness
    b. chagas disease
    c. malaria
    d. intestinal infections caused by *Giardia*

    a. no; a flagellate
    b. no; a flagellate
*   c. yes; malaria is not caused by a flagellate, but by a sporozoan
    d. no; a flagellate

47. Which of the following groups is completely composed of parasitic protozoa?
    a. Sarcodina
    b. Mastigophora
    c. Ciliates
    d. Sporozoa

    a. no; this is the group that includes amoeba
    b. no; this is the group that contains the flagellates
    c. no; these are the protozoa that move by cilia
*   d. yes; all members of this group become encysted at some time during their life cycle and all members are parasitic

48. A pregnant woman should not be involved with cleaning up after cats because she may become infected with toxoplasmosis resulting in
    a. intestinal blockage.
    b. filling the lungs with fluid.
    c. muscular cramps and severe headaches.
    d. damage to the unborn fetus.

    a. no; not characteristic of the disease
    b. no; not characteristic of the disease
    c. no; not characteristic of the disease
*   d. yes; her fetus may become infected and die of brain damage

49. Which of the following statements is false about malaria?
    a. The Anopheles mosquito may infect humans or birds.
    b. The incidence of this disease is being reduced throughout the world.
    c. The characteristic changes in the life cycle produce regular changes in body temperature, resulting in cycles of chills and fever.
    d. Plasmodium reproduces sexually in the mosquito and asexually in the human body.

    a. no; this statement is true
*   b. yes; this statement is false; because of the rapid dispersal of the disease and the dispersal of humans throughout the world.
    c. no; this statement is true
    d. no; this statement is true

50. Which of the following statements is false?
    a. Most euglenoids are both heterotrophic and autotrophic.
    b. Most euglenoid have eyespots sensitive to light so that they will move to and stay in the light.
    c. Most euglenoids have a flagellum, contractile vacuole, pellicle, and a profusion of organelles.
    d. There are common marine phytoplankton.

    a. no; this statement is true
    b. no; this statement is true
    c. no; this statement is true
*   d. yes; this statement is false; the euglena are freshwater forms

51. The dinoflagellates are members of the
    a. Pyrrhophyta.
    b. Chlorophyta.
    c. Phaeophyta.
    d. Rhodophyta.

*   a. yes; these are the dinoflagellates
    b. no; these are the members of the green algae
    c. no; these are the members of the brown algae
    d. no; these are the members of the red algae

52. Which of the following is not a zooplankton?
    a. bacteria
    b. tiny crustaceans
    c. protozoans
    d. unicellular algae

a. no; these are zooplanktons
b. no; these are zooplanktons
c. no; these are zooplanktons
* d. yes; as a producer, it would be classified as a phytoplankton

53. The pigment fucoxanthin masks the presence of chlorophyll in
a. Chrysophyta.
b. Chlorophyta.
c. Rhodophyta.
d. Pyrrhophyta.

* a. yes; contains chlorophyll <u>a</u> and <u>c</u> and fucoxanthin
b. no; contains chlorophyll <u>a</u> and <u>b</u>
c. no; contains clorophyll and phycobilin
d. no; contains various pigments

54. Which of the following is matched incorrectly?
a. Pyrrhophyta–dinoflagellates, neurotoxin, and red tides
b. Chrysophyta–diatoms, golden algae
c. Rhodophyta–kelps, alternation of generations, Sargassum
d. Phaeophyta–brown algae, stipes, holdfasts, blades

a. no; correctly matched
b. no; correctly matched
* c. yes; incorrectly matched; the Rhodophyta are the red algae and the kelps and Sargassum are brown algae
d. no; correctly matched

55. Which of the following is not derived from the marine algae (*Rhodophyta* or *Phaeophyta*)?
a. algin
b. carrageenan
c. agar
d. starch

a. no; it is derived from the brown algae
b. no; it is derived from the red algae
c. no; it is derived from the red algae
* d. yes; it may be extracted from green algae but is more likely to be taken from plants

56. The large algae referred to as seaweed that are characteristically exposed on rocky coasts at low tide are
a. green algae.
b. brown algae.
c. red algae.
d. blue-green algae

a. no; not usually very large
* b. yes; very typical on rocky beaches
c. no; the red algae are usually small (less than four feet), finely branched delicate seaweeds
d. no; the blue-green algae are small microscopic filaments

57. The algae most closely related to the higher plants are the
a. red algae.
b. brown algae.
c. golden algae.
d. green algae.
a. no; another choice
b. no; another choice
c. no; another choice
* d. yes; similar to plants that have chlorophyll <u>a</u> and <u>b</u>, starch, cellulose, cell walls with pectin

58. Which of the following is *not* a representative of a group of true algae?
a. red algae
b. brown algae
c. blue-green algae
d. green algae

a. no; red algae include the delicate seaweeds
b. no; brown algae include the giant seaweeds such as the kelps
* c. yes; these are cyanobacteria and classified as monerans
d. no; marine, freshwater, and terrestrial algae

# CHAPTER 19

# PLANTS AND FUNGI

1. The land plants are descendants of
   a. red algae.
   b. fungi.
   c. green algae.
   d. cyanobacteria.

   a. no; the delicate seaweeds are advanced algae
   b. no; they invaded the land at the same time
 * c. yes; the land plants originated from the green algae
   d. no; perhaps the first organisms to adapt to the intertidal zones, but they were not the origin of the land plants

2. Sporophytes
   a. are the dominant phases in the life cycle of most terrestrial plants.
   b. are the haploid stage of the plant life cycle.
   c. reproduce sexually.
   d. develop from spores and produce gametes.

 * a. yes; these larger plants can release their spores to the wind for better dissemination
   b. no; sporophytes develop from the diploid zygote
   c. no; sporophytes reproduce asexually by spores
   d. no; develop from the zygote and reproduce by spores

3. Which of the following is *not* a vascular plant?
   a. bryophyte
   b. conifer
   c. angiosperm
   d. fern

 * a. correct; no vascular tissue in the nonvascular mosses and liverworts
   b incorrect; have vascular tissues
   c. incorrect; have vascular tissues
   d. incorrect; have vascular tissues

4. The sporophyte and gametophyte stages live independently in the following except
   a. lycophytes.
   b. bryophytes.
   c. horsetails.
   d. ferns.

   a. incorrect; both sporophyte and gametophyte are independent
 * b. correct; in the bryophytes the sporophyte is dependent on the gametophyte
   c. incorrect; both sporophyte and gametophyte are independent
   d. incorrect; both sporophyte and gametophyte are independent

5. A pine seed contains all but which one of the following?
   a. pollen grain
   b. seed coat
   c. female gametophyte
   d embryo

 * a. correct; only delivers the male gamete
   b. incorrect; covers the seed
   c. incorrect; contained within the seed
   d. incorrect; contained within the seed

6. Which of the following is a dicot?
   a. grasses
   b. lilies
   c. cacti
   d. orchids

   a. no; a typical monocot
   b. no; a typical monocot
 * c. yes; these are dicots
   d. no; a typical monocot

7. The endosperm
   a. is specialized tissue found only in the male reproductive system
   b. supplies food for the developing sporophyte
   c. becomes the young embryo
   d. is part of the zygote

   a. no; found surrounding the embryo in the female organ
 * b. yes; produces nourishment for the young embryo
   c. no; not a part that develops into the embryo
   d. no; a separate entity developed from the zygote

8. Which of the following was *not* one of the major evolutionary trends in the flowering plants?
   a. development of vascular tissue and increased independence from water
   b. shift of dominance from the haploid (gametophyte) generation to the diploid (sporophyte)
   c. reduction in the frequency of occurrence of sexual reproduction
   d. change to the development of two different types of spores

   a. incorrect; one of the important evolutionary developments
   b. incorrect; one of the trends is commonly described as the rise of the sporophyte and the decline of the gametophyte
   * c. correct; sexual reproduction increased with a corresponding decrease in asexual reproduction
   d. incorrect; two different spores called heterospores were produced (megaspores and microspores)

9. Which of the following are no longer dependent on water for reproduction?
   a. angiosperms
   b. bryophytes
   c. conifers
   d. both (a) and (c)

   a. no; a partial answer; flowering plants do not need water for reproduction
   b no; mosses, liverworts, and stoneworts require water
   c. no; a partial answer; conifers do not need water for reproduction
   * d. yes; both (a) and (c) are correct; both groups use pollen grains and nonmotile microspores

10. Which of the following statements is false?
    a. Nearly all plants are multicellular autotrophs.
    b. Nearly all plants are terrestrial, but their early ancestors were aquatic.
    c. All land plants have a waxy cuticle, root, shoot system, and internal vascular tissue to conduct water, minerals, and food.
    d. The seed-producing plants have been the most successful in invading land.

    a. no; this statement is true
    b. no; this statement is true
    * c. yes; this statement is false; all land plants do not have vascular tissue or even roots and shoot systems
    d. no; this statement is true

11. The bryophytes include the
    a. hornworts.
    b. liverworts.
    c. mosses.
    d. all of the above

    a. no; a partial answer; a more complete answer is available
    b. no; a partial answer; a more complete answer is available
    c. no; a partial answer; a more complete answer is available
    * d. yes; all of the above answers are correct

12. Which of the following bear seeds?
    a. lycophytes
    b. horsetails
    c. cycads
    d. ferns

    a. no; a seedless vascular plant
    b. no; a seedless vascular plant
    * c. yes; a seed-bearing gymnosperm
    d. no; a seedless vascular plant

13. The organic compound found in cells that supports the plant and enables it to grow upright and display leaves to the light is
    a. pectin.
    b. lignin.
    c. cutin.
    d. suberin.

    a. no; a chemical that tends to cement or bind cells together
    * b. yes; the strengthening chemical found in wood and other supporting tissue as sclerenchyma and colenchyma
    c. no; a waxy waterproofing chemical found on the epidermis
    d. no; a waxy waterproofing chemical found in cork cells

14. Sporophytes
    a. are the dominant phases in the life cycle of most terrestrial plants.
    b. are the haploid stages of the plant life cycle.
    c. reproduce sexually.
    d. develop from spores and produce gametes.

    * a. yes; these larger plants can release their spores to the wind for better dissemination
    b. no; sporophytes develop from the diploid zygote
    c. no; sporophytes reproduce asexually by spores
    d. no; sporophytes develop from the zygote and reproduce by spores

15. Which of the following are *not* vascular plants?
    a. bryophytes
    b. conifers
    c. angiosperms
    d. ferns

    * a. correct; no vascular tissues in the nonvascular mosses and liverworts
    b. incorrect; have vascular tissues
    c. incorrect; have vascular tissues
    d. incorrect; have vascular tissues

16. Which of the following contains the sperm?
    a. zygote
    b. antheridium
    c. archegonium
    d. sporangium

    a. no; the fertilized egg
    * b. yes; produces sperm
    c. no; produces eggs
    d. no; produces spores

17. The first land plants appeared in the
    a. Permian.
    b. Cambrian.
    c. Silurian.
    d. Devonian.

    a. no; too late
    b. no; too early
    * c. yes; the first land plants appeared in the Silurian
    d. no; too late

18. Coal-swamp forest with diverse fungi, lycopods, bryophytes, ferns, horsetails were characteristic of the
    a. Devonian.
    b. Carboniferous.
    c. Permian.
    d. Triassic.

    a. no; too early
    * b. yes; the time when the fossil fuels were formed
    c. no; too late
    d. no; too late

19. The rise of flowering plants to dominance occurred during the
    a. Permian.
    b. Triassic.
    c. Jurassic.
    d. Cretaceous.

    a. no; too late
    b. no; too late
    c. no; too late
    * d. yes; the flowering plants became the dominant plants in the Cretaceous

20. Which of the following features were ultimately responsible for the gymnosperms and angiosperms radiating into nearly all high and dry habitats?
    a. development of pollen
    b. dominance of the sporophyte generation
    c. the development of vascular tissue
    d. the development of alternation of generations

* a. yes; the development of pollen with its ability to deliver the sperm through the pollen tube eliminated the need for water for reproduction to occur
    b. no; the development of the sporophyte was essential for the establishment of plants on land, but there are many forms that had dominant sporophytes that have limited distribution
    c. no; vascular tissue was essential for terrestrial plants but was not the ultimate reason for success
    d. no; the bryophytes have alternation of generations but are restricted in habitat

21. Which of the following exhibits homospory?
    a. ferns
    b. Selaginella (a Lycophyte)
    c. conifers
    d. flowering plants

* a. yes; ferns produce only one type of spores
    b. no; Selaginella is a heterosporous club moss
    c. no; conifers are heterosporous
    d. no; flower plants produce two types of spores

22. The evolutionary development of heterospory led to
    a. male gametes that did not need water.
    b. sporophytes that could withstand drought conditions.
    c. female gametes that were retained until after fertilization, and then packaged with nutritive and protective tissue.
    d. both (a) and (c), but not (b)

    a. no; a partial answer; a more complete answer is available
    b. no; a partial answer; a more complete answer is available
    c. no; a partial answer; a more complete answer is available
    * d. yes; both (a) and (c) are correct, and (b) is wrong

23. Which of the following statements is false?
    a. The mosses are the most common type of Bryophytes.
    b. The gametophyte generation is dominant in the Bryophytes.
    c. The sporophytes are attached to the gametophyte and derive some mutation from it in the Bryophytes.
    d. The gametophyte produces spores in the Bryophytes.

    a. no; this statement is true
    b. no; this statement is true
    c. no; this statement is true
    * d. yes; this statement is false; gametophytes produce gametes and sporophytes produce spores

24. Which of the following is a vascular plant with seeds?
    a. cycads (*Cycadophyta*)
    b. whisk fern (*Psilophyta*)
    c. club moss (*Lycophyta*)
    d. horsetail (*Sphenophyta*)

  * a. yes; as a gymnosperm, it has evolved into a seed
    b. no; as a fern ally, it does not have seeds
    c. no; as a fern ally, it does not have seeds
    d. no; as a fern ally, it does not have seeds

25. Which of the following plants have sporophytes that do not have roots or leaves but do have photosynthetic stems with xylem and phloem?
    a. cycads (*Cycadophyta*)
    b. whisk fern (*Psilophyta*)
    c. club moss (*Lycophyta*)
    d. horsetail (*Sphenophyta*)

    a. no; has leaves, roots, and stems
  * b. yes; they lack roots and leaves
    c. no; has leaves, roots, and stems
    d. no; has roots, stems, and scalelike leaves

26. A strobilus is
    a. a cone-shaped cluster of leaves that produces spores.
    b. an underground storage and absorptive organ.
    c. an asexually reproducing structure found only in the nonvascular plants.
    d. a structure produced by a germinating spore.

  * a. yes; characteristic reproductive feature of the club mosses
    b. no; this structure is called a rhizome
    c. no; gemmae found in the liverworts have this function
    d. no; this structure is produced later in the life cycle and is produced by sporophytes

27. Which of the following is *not* one of the groups of plants that contributed to the formation of fossil fuels?
    a. ferns
    b. lycophytes
    c. cycads
    d. club mosses

    a. no; formed part of the flora found in the coal-swamp forest
    b. no; formed part of the flora found in the coal-swamp forest
  * c. yes; this group of plants did not arise until the Mesozoic
    d. no; formed part of the flora found in the coal-swamp forest

28. Which of the following was the first known vascular plant?
    a. Selaginella
    b. Cooksonia
    c. Gingko
    d. Equisetum

    a. no; a heterosporous club moss
  * b. yes; a small, branching plant with a cuticle
    c. no; the maidenhair tree is an isolated relative of the conifers
    d. no; the horsetails are extant plants that flourished in the swamp forests

29. Which of the following plants is suggested to belong to the oldest of all genera of plants and has scarcely changed over the last 300,000,000 years?
    a. cycads
    b. Equisetum
    c. Selaginella
    d. Lycopodium

    a. no; too modern
  * b. yes; present-day forms seem similar to fossils
    c. no; a common homosporous club moss
    d. no; the heterosporous club moss

30. A sorus is
    a. a cluster of sporangia.
    b. a sporophyll found in the club mosses.
    c. a photosynthetic stem characteristic of Equisetum.
    d. none of the above

  * a. yes; a cluster of sporangia found on the undersurface of a fern frond
    b. no; a sporophyll is a leaf that produces sporangia
    c. no; the stems of Equisetum carry on photosynthesis
    d. no; a common distractor; but one and only one of the above is correct

31. Which of the following plants could be said to have escaped its aquatic ancestry as far as reproduction is concerned?
    a. whisk ferns
    b. ferns
    c. gymnosperms
    d. horsetails

    a. no; their male gametes must swim to the egg
    b. no; their male gametes must swim to the egg
  * c. yes; the development of pollen grains eliminates the need to return to water for reproduction
    d. no; their male gametes must swim to the egg

32. The male gametophyte in the flowering plants is the
    a. stamen.
    b. anther.
    c. germinated pollen grain.
    d. generative nucleus.

a.  no; the male reproductive organ of a flower
b.  no; the sac where the pollen grain develops
* c.  yes; the microspore (pollen grain) germinates to form the microgametophyte (germinated pollen grain)
d.  no; the microgamete or male haploid sperm

33.  Which of the following structures produces the seed?
a.  zygote
b.  embryo sac
c.  ovule
d.  ovary

a.  no; results from the fusion of a generative nucleus and the egg
b.  no; the embryo sac is the female gametophyte and additional tissue is used to form a seed
* c.  yes; after fertilization the ovule develops into a seed
d.  no; the ovary will become the fruit, which may house many seeds

34.  An ovule contains one
a.  microspore.
b.  megaspore.
c.  pollen grain.
d.  both (a) and (c), but not (b)

a.  no; a male spore
* b.  yes; contains the megaspore that will develop into the female gametophyte
c.  no; contains the male gamete
d.  no; the correct answer is (b)

35.  The function of the seed is
a.  dispersal.
b.  survival of environmental extremes in a state of suspended animation.
c.  reproduction.
d.  all of the above

a.  no; a partial answer; a more complete answer is available
b.  no; a partial answer; a more complete answer is available
c.  no; a partial answer; a more complete answer is available
* d.  yes; all of the answers are correct

36.  Double fertilization produces the
a.  new sprorophyte.
b.  endosperm.
c.  zygote.
d.  embryo sac.

a.  no; the new sporophyte develops from the zygote
* b.  yes; one of the generative nuclei (1n) fuses with the polar nuclei (2n) to form the triploid endosperm (3n) that will provide food for the embryo
c.  no; the zygote is formed by the fusion of a generative nucleus and an egg
d.  no; the embryo sac is the female gametophyte developing after meiosis from the embryo sac (mother cell)

37.  Which of the following are dicots?
a.  grasses
b.  lilies
c.  cacti
d.  orchids

a.  no; a typical monocot
b.  no; a typical monocot
* c.  yes; these are dicots
d.  no; a typical monocot

38.  The endosperm
a.  is specialized tissue found only in the male reproductive system.
b.  supplies food for the developing sporophyte.
c.  becomes the young embryo.
d.  is part of the zygote.

a.  no; found surrounding the embryo in the seed
* b.  yes; the function of endosperm is to produce nourishment for the young embryo
c.  no; not a part that develops into the embryo
d.  no; an entity separate from the zygote

39.  The only plants that possess flowers belong to the
a.  angiosperms.
b.  gymnosperms.
c.  seed plants.
d.  all of the above

* a.  yes; the flowering plants
b.  no; there are no flowers in the gymnosperms
c.  no; there are no flowers in the gymnosperms, but they are found in the Angiosperms
d.  no; only one of the above is correct

40.  Which of the following statements is false?
a.  Fungi release enzymes outside their bodies and digest their food outside the body and then absorb it.
b.  A plant root may absorb the dissolved materials produced by fungal enzymes.
c.  Fungi are the world's premier decomposers.
d.  Fungi are not necessary in ecosystems; the autotrophs can supply all the food needed by the heterotrophs.

a.  no; this statement is true
b.  no; this statement is true
c.  no; this statement is true
* d.  yes; this statement is false; the minerals found in dead organisms have to be released by decomposition and then recycled

41.  Which of the following terms is inappropriate to use with fungi?
a.  producers
b.  decomposers
c.  recyclers
d.  saprobes

* 
   a. yes; fungi are incapable of producing food
   b. no; fungi decompose organic substances and make their chemical elements available
   c. no; they are responsible for nutrient cycling
   d. no; some fungi live on dead organic material

42. Which of the following is *not* considered to be one of the three major groups of fungi?
   a. zygomycetes
   b. imperfect fungi
   c. sac fungi
   d. club fungi

   a. no the Zygomycota is one of the major groups of fungi
* b. yes; these organisms do not have a recognizable sexual form, and therefore, they cannot be classified
   c. no; the sac fungi belong to the Ascomycota, one of the major groups of fungi
   d. no; the club fungi belong to the Basidiomycota, one of the major groups of fungi

43. Which of the following statements is false?
   a. Fungi are able to manufacture organic compounds from the inorganic nutrients they absorb.
   b. The majority of fungi are saprobes.
   c. Fungi exhibit extracellular digestion.
   d. Communities would not be able to survive with the contributions of decomposers.

* a. yes; this statement is false; they have to have an organic food source to supply energy that can be used to produce other organic compounds
   b. no; this statement is true
   c. no; this statement is true
   d. no; this statement is true

44. The cell walls of fungi are composed of
   a. cellulose.
   b. pectin.
   c. lignin.
   d. chitin

   a. no; not found in the cell walls of fungi
   b. no; not found in the cell walls of fungi
   c. no; not found in the cell walls of fungi
* d. yes; fungal cell walls have chitin

45. Which of the following parts of a typical fungal life cycle consist of diploid cells?
   a. hyphae
   b. spores
   c. gametes
   d. zygotes

   a. no; these are composed of haploid cells
   b. no; these are composed of haploid cells
   c. no; these are composed of haploid cells
* d. yes; the zygote is a diploid cell resulting from the fusion of two haploid gametes

46. Truffles are found by trained
   a. dogs and pigs.
   b. chickens.
   c. cats.
   d. goats.

* a. yes; trained dogs and pigs
   b. no; these animals are unable to find truffles
   c. no; these animals are unable to find truffles
   d. no; these animals are unable to find truffles

47. The specialized sacs that contain the characteristic spores produced by the sac fungi are called
   a. conidia.
   b. basidia.
   c. asci.
   d. gametangia.

   a. no; a general type of asexually reproducing spore in many different kinds of fungi
   b. no; a club-shaped sporangia characteristic of the basidiomycetes or club fungi
* c. yes; the word *ascus* means sac and is the stem for *Ascomycetes*
   d. no; gametangia are organs that produce gametes

48. Which of the following is(are) member(s) of the Basidiomycetes?
   a. chestnut blight
   b. ergot of rye
   c. Dutch elm disease
   d. smuts and rust

   a. no; this is an Ascomycetes
   b. no; this is an Ascomycetes
   c. no; this is an Ascomycetes
* d. yes; the smuts and rusts are major plant parasites belonging to the Basidiomycetes

49. Histoplasmosis is related to
   a. droppings of birds and bats.
   b. fertilizers used in yards for grass production.
   c. social insects such as bees and termites.
   d. farm animals and stockyards.

* a. yes; the droppings represent a place where the fungus can grow
   b. no; not a specialized habitat associated with histoplasmosis
   c. no; not a specialized habitat associated with histoplasmosis
   d. no; not a specialized habitat associated with histoplasmosis

50. *Claviceps purpurea* is a fungal parasite of rye and other grains that produces metabolic by-products that
    a. are used to treat migraine headaches.
    b. may produce hysteria, hallucinations, convulsions, vomiting, diarrhea, gangrene, and death.
    c. are used to shrink the uterus after childbirth.
    d. all of the above

    a. no; a partial answer; a more complete answer is available
    b. no; a partial answer; a more complete answer is available
    c. no; a partial answer; a more complete answer is available
 *  d. yes; all of the above answers are correct

51. A basidiocarp is
    a. a specialized underground hyphae.
    b. the fruiting body of a basidiomycete, the visible mushroom.
    c. a place where a fungus invades the host tissue.
    d. a specialized environmentally resistant spore.

    a. no; there is no specific name for these masses of hyphae that form the mycelium of a fungus
 *  b. yes; the structure commonly called the mushroom
    c. no; the specific name for this is the haustorium
    d. no; there are no specialized environmentally resistant spores for most fungi; they all are similar in their environmental tolerances

52. Mutualistic relationships include
    a. smuts and rusts with plants.
    b. mycorrhizae and plant roots.
    c. lichens.
    d. both (b) and (c), but not (a)

    a. no; smuts and rusts are plant parasites
    b. no; a partial answer; a more complete answer is available
    c. no; a partial answer; a more complete answer is available
 *  d. yes; both (b) and (c) are correct, but (a) is wrong

53. Mushrooms
    a. are composed of mycelia.
    b. are produced by basidiomycetes.
    c. are sexually reproducing structures.
    d. all of the above

    a. no; a partial answer; a more complete answer is available
    b. no; a partial answer; a more complete answer is available
    c. no; a partial answer; a more complete answer is available
 *  d. yes; all of the above are true

54. Yeasts are unicellular members of the ____ group.
    a. Ascomycetes
    b. Basidiomycetes
    c. fungi imperfecti
    d. chytridiomycetes

 *  a. yes
    b. no; club fungi
    c. no; a group of fungi that have no sexual reproduction
    d. no; water molds

55. Mycorrhizae are
    a. symbionts of trees.
    b. pathogens of animals.
    c. unicellular water molds.
    d. edible fungi.

 *  a. yes; increase the ability of trees to obtain water and minerals
    b. no; do not interact with animals
    c. no; are multicellular soil organisms
    d. no; are not edible

# CHAPTER 20

# ANIMALS:
# THE INVERTEBRATES

1. The Burgess Shale, a rich fossil deposit is found in
   a. Mexico.
   b. Bolivia.
   c. Greenland.
   d. Canada.

   a. no; another country
   b. no; another country
   c. no; another country
   * d. yes; located in British Columbia

2. The invertebrates differ from the vertebrates by the lack of
   a. a larval stage during their life cycle.
   b. a backbone.
   c. a coelomic cavity.
   d. radial symmetry.

   a. no; both vertebrates and invertebrates may have larval stages
   * b. yes; only vertebrates have a backbone
   c. no; both vertebrates and some invertebrates have coeloms
   d. no; both vertebrates and invertebrates may exhibit bilateral symmetry

3. Which of the following is *not* a characteristic of the Cnidarians?
   a. radial symmetry
   b. saclike gut
   c. only two primary tissue layers
   d. segmentation

   a. no; the Cnidarians exhibit this feature
   b. no; the Cnidarians exhibit this feature
   c. no; the Cnidarians exhibit this feature
   * d. yes; segmentation was an advanced feature, first developed in the Annelids

4. Which of the following statements is false?
   a. Radial symmetry is characteristic of terrestrial predators.
   b. The availability of a coelom enabled animals to grow larger by cushioning and protecting internal organs.
   c. Segments of segmented animals often appear similar on the outside but show considerable variation within.
   d. Animals with a pseudocoel (false coelom) lack a peritoneum.

   * a. yes; this statement is false; radial symmetrical forms are usually aquatic and filter feeders; they are not predators that need to be able to sense prey in the front (head) of their bodies and pursue, as is more typical of bilaterally symmetrical forms
   b. no; this statement is true
   c. no; this statement is true
   d. no; this statement is true

5. Which of the following is associated with survival and reproduction in the sponges?
   a. collar cells
   b. spicules
   c. gemmules
   d. osculum

   a. no; cells that make up the inner lining of sponges
   b. no; protective spines of silica or calcium carbonate
   * c. yes; clusters of cells that may survive extreme environments, germinate, and grow into new sponges
   d. no; the openings in a sponge through which water escapes

6. Which of the following is mismatched?
   a. osculum–Porifera
   b. nematocyst–Cnidaria
   c. mesoglea–Annelida
   d. organs–Platyhelminthes

   a. no; the osculum is an opening in the sponges
   b. no; the nematocyst is a stinging protective cell in the cnidarians
   * c. yes; the mesoglea is not characteristic of the annelids but found in the cnidaria
   d. no; the flatworms were the first organisms to have individual organs

7. A sea anemone forms a symbiotic relationship with
   a. earthworms.
   b. starfish.
   c. clown fish.
   d. octopus.

a. no; another organism
b. no; another organism
* c. yes; the anemone protects the clown fish from predators and obtains food from food scraps dropped by the clown fish
d. no; another organism

8. The corals belong to the phylum
   a. Cnidaria.
   b. Platyhelminthes.
   c. Mollusca.
   d. Arthropods.

* a. yes; members of the Anthozoa
b. no; corals are not flatworms
c. no; they do not have soft bodies like the mollusks
d. no; not related to the insects

9. Alternation of free-swimming generation with an immobile form is characteristic of some of the
   a. Ctenophora.
   b. Cnidarians.
   c. Nematodes.
   d. Platyhelminthes.

a. no; not a comb jelly
* b. yes; such as the medusae and polyps of the colonial hydrozoans
c. no; not a characteristic of roundworms
d. no; flatworms may often have complex life cycles, but they are not characterized by medusa and polyp stages

10. The Cestodes or tapeworms are unusual in that they do not possess
    a. sensory organs.
    b. digestive organs.
    c. segments necessary for larvae to find the host.
    d. reproductive tissues.

a. no; sensory organs are necessary for larvae to find host
* b. yes; they live in the digestive tract of their host and are surrounded by digested food, so they do not have to have their own system
c. no; the body of the tapeworm is composed of segments known as proglottids
d. no; the proglottids are filled with reproductive organs

11. Which of the following is mismatched?
    a. nephridia–Annelids
    b. scolex–Nematodes
    c. wheel organ–Rotifers
    d. proglottid–Flatworms

a. no; matched correctly
* b. no; the scolex is a holdfast attachment organ for the tapeworm
c. no; matched correctly
d. no; matched correctly

12. Elephantiasis is caused by a parasitic member of the
    a. trematodes.
    b. nematodes.
    c. cestodes.
    d. annelids.

a. no; the parasitic flukes
* b. yes; a roundworm that infects the lymph nodes
c. no; the tapeworms
d. no; not a segmented worm

13. Which of the following phyla do *not* have major parasitic forms?
    a. Annelids
    b. Mollusca
    c. Nematodes
    d. Platyhelminthes

a. no; the leaches are a parasitic class
* b. yes; no major parasites
c. no; the roundworms are major parasites of both plants and animals
d. no; contains the parasitic flukes and tapeworms

14. Which of the following are deuterostomes?
    a. Annelids
    b. Arthropods
    c. Mollusca
    d. Echinoderms

a. no; an example of a protostome
b. no; an example of a protostome
c. no; an example of a protostome
* d. yes; are deuterostomes

15. The mollusks are classified on the position and characteristics of their
    a. mantle.
    b. foot.
    c. shells.
    d. appendages.

a. no; another organ
* b. yes; such as cephalopods, gastropods, and pelecypods
c. no; another organ
d. no; another organ

16. Which is *not* a characteristic of Arthropods?
    a. exoskeleton
    b. jointed appendages
    c. metamorphosis
    d. radial symmetry

a. no; a hard, chitinous external skeleton is one of the reasons for their success
b. no; the word *arthropod* means jointed foot
c. no; the change in body form as an arthropod completes its life cycle is characteristic of many animals, including the arthropods
* d. yes; insects are bilaterally symmetrical

17. Book lungs are characteristic of
    a. the octopus.
    b. spiders and scorpions.
    c. terrestrial insects.
    d. crustaceans.

    a. no; they have gills
  * b. yes; book lungs are the respiratory organs of spiders and scorpions
    c. no; the terrestrial insects have a tracheal system
    d. no; the crustaceans have gills

18. Which phylum is found only in marine environments?
    a. annelids
    b. echinoderms
    c. chordata
    d. nematodes

    a. no; some are terrestrial or parasitic
  * b. yes; only found in salt water
    c. no; some freshwater and terrestrial forms
    d. no; terrestrial, parasitic, and free-living forms also exist

19. The flatworms belong to the phylum
    a. Cnidaria.
    b. Nematoda.
    c. Annelida.
    d. Platyhelminthes.

    a. no; includes the hydrozoans, jellyfish, corals, and sea anemones
    b. no; includes roundworms, such as hookworms and pinworms
    c. no; includes segmented worms, such as earthworms, sandworms, and leeches
  * d. yes; the turbellarians, flukes, and tapeworms are flatworms

20. The second largest phylum (second to Arthropoda) is
    a. Nematoda.
    b. Annelida.
    c. Chordata.
    d. Mollusca.

    a. no; 20,000 species
    b. no; 15,000 species
    c. no; 47,000 species
  * d. yes; 110,000 species

21. Which of the following exhibit cephalization?
    a. cnidarians
    b. arthropods
    c. roundworms
    d. sponges

    a. no; no head region
  * b. yes; in the insects the body is divided into the head, thorax, and abdomen
    c. no; no head region
    d. no; no head region

22. The peritoneum is
    a. the first part of the intestinal tract.
    b. the lining of the coelomic cavity.
    c. the membrane surrounding and protecting the heart.
    d. none of the above

    a. no; this is the duodenum
  * b. yes
    c. no; this is the pericardium
    d. no; a common distractor; one of the above is correct

23. Which of the following is characterized by the presence of a pseudocoelom?
    a. Annelida
    b. Mollusca
    c. Nematoda
    d. Platyhelminthes

    a. no; has a true coelom
    b. no; has a true coelom
  * c. yes; has a pseudocoelom
    d. no; no cavity between gut and body wall

24. Medusae are part of the life cycle of the
    a. Annelids.
    b. Poriferans.
    c. Platyhelminthes.
    d. Cnidarians.

    a. no; another phylum
    b. no; another phylum
    c. no; another phylum
  * d. yes; a free-floating, bell-shaped stage like a jellyfish

25. Which of the following is *not* characteristic of cnidarians?
    a. flame cells
    b. nerve net
    c. nematocysts
    d. mesoglea

  * a. correct; a specialized organ involved in excretion in turbellarians
    b. incorrect; pattern of nervous system of cnidarians
    c. incorrect; stinging devices characteristic of cnidarians
    d. incorrect; jellylike layer characteristic of cnidarians

26. Which of the following is *not* primarily parasitic?
    a. flukes
    b. rotifers
    c. tapeworms
    d. leeches

    a. no; parasitic
  * b. yes; free-living forms
    c. no; parasitic
    d. no; parasitic

27. A planula is
    a. a free-swimming larva of colonial hydrozoan.
    b. the head region of a tapeworm.
    c. the protective covering of a nematode.
    d. excretory organ of an earthworm.

  * a. yes
    b. no; the scolex
    c. no; the cuticle
    d. no; a nephridium

28. Humans are infected by the roundworm *Trichinella spiralis* by
    a. swimming in infected water.
    b. eating insufficiently cooked pork.
    c. eating contaminated vegetables.
    d. the bite of a female mosquito.

    a. no; may pick up other parasites this way
  * b. yes
    c. no; may pick up other parasites this way
    d. no; may pick up other parasites this way

29. Which of the following are protostomes?
    a. annelids
    b. echinoderms
    c. chordates
    d. both (a) and (c), but not (b)

  * a. yes
    b. no; a deuterostome
    c. no; a deuterostome
    d. no; chordates are deuterostomes

30. The name Mollusca literally means
    a. "spiny-skinned animal"
    b. "shelled animal"
    c. "soft-bodied animals"
    d. none of the above

    a. no; echinoderms
    b. no; mollusks have shells, but the name of the phylum refers to the soft inner body mass
  * c. yes; the names means "soft-bodied animals"
    d. no; one of the above is correct

31. Setae are
    a. the bristles of annelids that aid in locomotion.
    b. excretory organs of annelids.
    c. digestive organs of annelids.
    d. branches of an annelid nervous system.

  * a. yes
    b. no; the nephridia
    c. no; the crop gizzard and intestine
    d. no; called ganglia

32. The exoskeleton
    a. is made of protein and chitin to enable growth.
    b. restricts growth and must be shed if an insect outgrows it.
    c. prevents water loss and provides protection.
    d. all of the above

    a. yes; a partial answer; a better answer is available
    b. yes; a partial answer; a better answer is available
    c. yes; a partial answer; a better answer is available
  * d. yes; all of the above are correct

33. Tracheae are
    a. digestive organs.
    b. respiratory tubes.
    c. appendages.
    d. reproductive structures.

    a. no; another function
  * b. yes
    c. no; another function
    d. no; another function

34. ____ have ten legs (often with claws) and many segments with a covering (the carapace) over some or all of the segments.
    a. Crustaceans
    b. Chelicerates
    c. Insects
    d. Trilobites

  * a. yes; such as crayfish, lobsters, and shrimp
    b. no; eight legs
    c. no; six legs
    d. no; fossil forms with many pairs of legs

35. If reproductive capacity and habitat exploitation are important measures of success, the ___ would rank first.
    a. Mollusks
    b. Chordates
    c. Arthropods
    d. Echinoderms

    a. no; about 110,000 different species
    b. no; less than 50,00 different species
  * c. yes; most numerous and versatile group of animals
    d. no; only marine forms

36. Which of the following is *not* an echinoderm?
    a. sea urchin
    b. sea cucumber
    c. sea star
    d. sea anemone

a.   no; an echinoderm
b.   no; an echinoderm
c.   no; an echinoderm
*   d.   yes; a Cnidarian

37.   Which of the following is found in the
adult echinoderms?
a.   water vascular system
b.   bilateral symmetry
c.   a radula
d.   thorax

*   a.   yes; used for locomotion
b.   no; found only in larval echinoderms
c.   no; found is some mollusks
d.   no; a region of many animal bodies
with bilateral symmetry

# CHAPTER 21

# ANIMALS: THE VERTEBRATES

1.  Which of the following statements about the duck-billed platypus is false?
    a.   Its distribution is restricted to Australia and Tasmania.
    b.   It has fur and mammary glands.
    c.   Similar to birds and reptiles, it has a cloaca, a single opening that functions for excretion and reproduction.
    d.   It bears its young alive but maintains them in a pouch or marsupium.

    a.   no; this statement is true
    b.   no; this statement is true
    c.   no; this statement is true
    *   d.   yes; this statement is false; it is not a Marsupial but a Monotreme that lays eggs

2.  The invertebrate chordata include
    a.   tunicates or sea squirts.
    b.   monotremes.
    c.   marsupials.
    d.   both (a) and (b), but not (c)

    *   a.   yes; the tunicates do not have a vertebral column
    b.   no; an egg-laying mammal
    c.   no; a pouched mammal
    d.   no; only one choice is correct

3.  The most primitive of the vertebrates are the
    a.   chondrichthyes.
    b.   Agnatha.
    c.   osteichthyes.
    d.   placoderm.

    a.   no; even though they have cartilaginous bones, there are other features that make them more advanced
    *   b.   yes; they lacked paired jaws and fins
    c.   no; the most advanced of those listed
    d.   no; even though they are extinct, they had paired jaws and fins

4.  Which of the following statements is false?
    a.   The larva of a tunicate resembles a chordate more than the adult.
    b.   The adult tunicate is attached to a substrate and cannot move.
    c.   The tunicate is the more advanced invertebrate chordate.
    d.   The pharynx of the adult tunicate functions as a respiratory organ and a food-gathering organ.

    a.   no; this statement is true
    b.   no; this statement is true
    *   c.   yes; this statement is false; the lancelets or cephalochordates are more advanced than the tunicates or urochordates
    d.   no; this statement is true

5.  The notochord of the urochordates is located in the
    a.   abdomen.
    b.   pharynx.
    c.   head region.
    d.   tail region.

    a.   no; another site
    b.   no; another site
    c.   no; the head is the site for the notochord in the Cephalochordates
    *   d.   yes; the prefix *uro-*refers to tail; the notochord extends from the tail to the head in the larva of the tunicates

6.  The tunicates are
    a.   parasites.
    b.   filter feeders.
    c.   predators.
    d.   bottom scavengers.

    a.   no; not parasitic
    *   b.   yes; they create a current with the siphons and filter food out of the water into the pharynx
    c.   no; they are immobile and unable to pursue food
    d.   no; unable to move

7. Lancelets
   a. are filter feeders.
   b. have no internal respiratory system but a closed circulatory system.
   c. exhibit segmented muscles.
   d. all of the above

   a. no; a partial answer; a more complete answer is available
   b. no; a partial answer; a more complete answer is available
   c. no; a partial answer; a more complete answer is available
   * d. yes; all of the answers are correct

8. The vertebrates evolved from the
   a. urochordates.
   b. hemichordates.
   c. cephalochordates.
   d. all of the above

   a. no; on separate lines of evolution
   * b. yes; the acorn worms appear to be halfway between the echinoderms and the chordates
   c. no; on separate lines of evolution
   d. no; one of the above is correct

9. Which of the following statements is false?
   a. The ancestors of land vertebrates relied more on lungs and less on gills.
   b. The fish had a circulatory system composed of two circuits.
   c. In the four-chambered heart, the right ventricle pumps blood to the lungs.
   d. All vertebrates have closed circulatory systems.

   a. no; this statement is true
   * b. yes; this statement is false; the fish heart consists of two chambers, but only one circuit; two circuits, the pulmonary and the systemic, require at least three chambers in the heart
   c. no; this statement is true
   d. no; this statement is true

10. The swim bladder is a(n)
    a. adjustable flotation device.
    b. second respiratory organ.
    c. organ that collects nitrogenous waste.
    d. organ that helps maintain appropriate salt concentration in the blood.

    * a. yes; enables a fish to adjust to water density and remain motionless without using muscles
    b. no; does not participate in respiration
    c. no; not an organ that collects nitrogenous waste
    d. no; there are salt glands near the eyes of saltwater fish

11. The lampreys
    a. lack true jaws.
    b. are parasitic.
    c. do not have paired fins.
    d. all of the above

    a. no; a partial answer; a more complete answer is available
    b. no; a partial answer; a more complete answer is available
    c. no; a partial answer; a more complete answer is available
    * d. yes; all of the answers are correct

12. Which of the following is *not* a cartilaginous fish?
    a. skate
    b. ray
    c. chimaera (ratfish)
    d. lung fish

    a. no; a member of the chondrichthyes
    b. no; a member of the chondrichthyes
    c. no; a member of the chondrichthyes
    * d. yes; the lungfish are members of the osteichthyes or bony fish

13. Caecilians are
    a. fossil reptiles.
    b. wormlike amphibians with no limbs.
    c. primitive ray-finned fish.
    d. a group of lobe-finned fish that gave rise to the amphibia.

    a. no; not reptiles
    * b. yes; a wormlike amphibian
    c. no; not a fish
    d. no; not a fish

14. Which of the following is *not* a feature characteristic of the reptiles?
    a. slimy, slippery surface
    b. amniote egg
    c. a copulatory organ that allows internal fertilization
    d. kidneys secrete wastes as a semisolid rather than a liquid

    * a. yes; fish and amphibians have slippery, shiny skin, while reptiles have scales that make their surfaces dry
    b. no; reptiles have an amniote egg that may be deposited on land
    c. no; reptiles have a copulatory organ
    d. no; reptiles do excrete a semisolid uric acid for nitrogenous waste

15. Which of the following statements is false?
    a. A turtle shell consists of two layers, an inner bony layer and an outer horny layer of keratin.
    b. Turtles lack teeth but have a horny beak.
    c. Turtles are one of the more recently evolved reptiles.
    d. All turtles lay their eggs on land.

    a. no; this statement is true
    b. no; this statement is true
    * c. yes; this statement is false; the turtles arose during the Triassic period and are among the oldest of the extant reptiles
    d. no; this statement is true

16. Snakes evolved from the
    a. turtles.
    b. lizards.
    c. crocodiles.
    d. Tuataras.

    a. no; another ancestor
    * b. yes; apparently by regressive loss of legs
    c. no; another ancestor
    d. no; another ancestor

17. The birds are most closely related to the
    a. mammals.
    b. crocodilians.
    c. lizards.
    d. Tuataras.

    a. no; another animal is more closely related
    * b. yes; the crocodilians and birds share many similarities
    c. no; another animal is more closely related
    d. no; another animal is more closely related

18. The type of teeth that enables a person to bite into a sandwich or eat corn on the cob are the
    a. cuspids.
    b. bicuspids.
    c. molars.
    d. incisors.

    a. no; used to rip and tear flesh
    b. no; a tooth intermediate between a cuspid and a molar
    c. no; molars are grinding teeth
    * d. yes; the incisors are chisel-like teeth located in front of the mouth

19. Which of the following is the most highly evolved?
    a. sea squirt
    b. lancelet
    c. hagfish
    d. hemichordate

    a. no; least highly evolved protochordates (urochordate)
    b. no; a protochordate invertebrate (cephalochordate)
    * c. yes; a primitive vertebrate
    d. no; a nonchordate

20. Which of the following belongs to the most highly evolved group?
    a  skate or shark
    b. dinosaur
    c. caecilian
    d. duck-billed platypus

    a. no; the most primitive, a Chondrichthyes
    b. no; a reptile
    c. no; an amphibian
    * d. yes; a mammal

21. Which of the following are mismatched?
    a. sea squirt–siphon
    b. Osteichthyes–swim bladder
    c. lamprey eel–jaw
    d. ostracoderms–bony plates covering body

    a. no; matched correctly; siphon is used for flow of water for feeding
    b. no; matched correctly; swim bladder is a hydrostatic organ used for buoyancy
    * c. yes; these are mismatched; the lampreys lack jaws and paired fins
    d. no; matched correctly; the bony plates served as protection against giant sea scorpions

22. Which of the following gave rise to the first land vertebrates?
    a. ostracoderms
    b. placoderms
    c. lobed-finned fishes
    d. cephalochordates

    a. no; early agnathans that were bottom dwellers and filter feeders
    b. no; early jawed scavengers
    * c. yes; gave rise to the amphibians
    d. no; primitive chordates that gave rise to the vertebrates

23. The divergence and major expansion of the fishes took place during the
    a. Cambrian.
    b. Carboniferous.
    c. Cretaceous.
    d. Devonian.

    a. no; too early
    b. no; too late
    c. no; too late
    * d. yes

24. An axolotl is a sexually mature larval form of the
    a. salamander.
    b. frog.
    c. lizard.
    d. turtle.

    * a. yes; retains larval tail and gills and may never develop into an adult
    b. no; tadpoles do not breed
    c. no; reptiles do not undergo metamorphosis
    d. no; reptiles do not undergo metamorphosis

25. Reptiles underwent major adaptive radiation during the
    a. Carboniferous.
    b. Mesozoic.
    c. Cenozoic.
    d. Devonian.

    a. no; too early
    * b. yes
    c. no; too late
    d. no; too early

26. Which of the following dinosaurs were able to fly?
    a. plesiosaur
    b. ichthyosaurs
    c. therapsids
    d. pterosaurs

    a. no; large aquatic form resembling the "Loch Ness" monster
    b. no; a swimming dinosaur superficially resembling a shark
    c. no; synapsids that evolved into quadruped mammals
    * d. yes; a flying dinosaur

27. Tuataras
    a. do not have male copulatory organs.
    b. are found only on islands near New Zealand.
    c. are not lizards.
    d. all of the above

    a. no; a partial answer; a more complete answer is available
    b. no; a partial answer; a more complete answer is available
    c. no; a partial answer; a more complete answer is available
    * d. yes; all of the above are true

28. Which of the following is *not* characteristic of all chordates?
    a. a notochord
    b. a post-anal tail
    c. pharyngeal gill slits
    d. vertebrae

    a. incorrect; found in all chordates
    b. incorrect; found in all chordates
    c. incorrect; found in all chordates
    * d. correct; not found in the invertebrate chordates

29. Which of the following were the immediate ancestors of the land-dwelling vertebrates?
    a. cartilaginous fishes
    b. jawless fishes
    c. lobe-finned fishes
    d. ray-finned fishes

    a. no; more primitive than the bony fishes
    b. no; the most primitive group of fish
    * c. yes; the immediate ancestors of the amphibia
    d. no; they did not give rise to terrestrial forms

30. The part of the brain that underwent a major expansion during the evolution of the vertebrates was the
    a. medulla oblongata.
    b. cerebrum.
    c. cerebellum.
    d. reticular formation.

    a. no
    * b. yes
    c. no
    d. no

31. Placoderms were ancient
    a. fishes.
    b. reptiles.
    c. birds.
    d. mammals.

    * a. yes
    b. no; more primitive form
    c. no; more primitive form
    d. no; more primitive form

32. _____ are the most successful type of bony fish today.
    a. Ray-finned fish (teleosts)
    b. Bichirs
    c. Crossopterygians
    d. Lungfishes

    * a. yes; the ray-finned fishes
    b. no
    c. no; fossil forms now extinct
    d. no; marginally successful extant forms

33. The land egg is typical of all but which of the following?
    a. amphibians
    b. birds
    c. mammals
    d. reptiles

    * a. yes; do not possess an amniotic egg; must place eggs in a watery environment
    b. no; have an amniotic egg
    c. no; some have an amniotic egg; others modify it for internal development
    d. no; some have an amniotic egg; others modify it for internal develop

# CHAPTER 22

# PLANT TISSUES

1. Which of the following is *not* a ground tissue?
   a. parenchyma
   b. xylem
   c. sclerenchyma
   d. collenchyma

   a. incorrect; the most common ground tissue
   * b. correct; not a ground tissue, but a vascular tissue
   c. incorrect; a ground tissue
   d. incorrect; a ground tissue

2. Which of the following is specialized to conduct food?
   a. xylem
   b. parenchyma
   c. phloem
   d. sclerenchyma

   a. no; specialized to conduct water and minerals
   b. no; unspecialized cells used for various purposes such as food storage
   * c. yes
   d. no; dead strengthening fibers that function in support

3. Which of the following cells would be expected to have a thin cell wall surrounding them?
   a. parenchyma
   b. xylem
   c. sclerenchyma
   d. collenchyma

   * a. yes
   b. no; thick cells walls often with pits and recesses that are used as mechanical tissue to support the plant
   c. no; often very thick wall used in support
   d. no; irregularly thickened walls

4. Cutin is a waxy substance deposited on the outer surface of ____ cells.
   a. xylem
   b. collenchyma
   c. phloem
   d. epidermal

   a. no; lignin impregnates these cell walls
   b. no; lignin impregnates these cell walls
   c. no; cell walls not usually filled with any particular substance
   * d. yes; prevents excess water loss from plant surface

5. Which of the following is *not* considered to be one of the three types of tissue system in plants?
   a. meristematic tissue
   b. ground tissue
   c. vascular tissue
   d. dermal tissue

   * a. yes; these cells are embryonic and divide to form cells that differentiate into the three major plant tissues
   b. no; one of the three types of plant tissue
   c. no; one of the three types of plant tissue
   d. no; one of the three types of plant tissue

6. The chemical responsible for the strength of fibers, xylem, collenchyma, and sclerenchyma is
   a. lignin.
   b. cutin.
   c. suberin.
   d. pectin.

   * a. yes; strengthens and waterproofs cells.
   b. no; waterproofs epidermal cells
   c. no; waterproofs cork cells
   d. no; found in some fruits and in collenchyma cells

7. Secondary growth
   a. is responsible for the increase in the length of a stem.
   b. is the responsibility of lateral meristems.
   c. occurs at the root and stem tips.
   d. is found only in herbaceous annual plants.

   a. no; that would be the responsibility of apical meristem
   * b. yes; increases the width (girth) of a plant
   c. no; secondary growth occurs throughout the plant
   d. no; usually only primary growth found in herbaceous annuals

8. Wood is
   a. secondary xylem.
   b. produced by divisions of vascular cambium.
   c. tissue that conducts water and minerals.
   d. all of the above

   a. no; a partial answer; a more complete answer is available
   b. no; a partial answer; a more complete answer is available
   c. no; a partial answer; a more complete answer is available
   * d. yes; all of the answers are correct

9. The point where leaves arise from the stem is the
   a. stoma.
   b. cuticle.
   c. node.
   d. pith.

   a. no; a pore for gas exchange
   b. no; a layer composed of cutin that reduces water loss
   * c. yes
   d. no; central parenchyma in a stem

10. Roots
   a. absorb water and minerals.
   b. function in storage of materials.
   c. anchor the plant in the soil.
   d. all of the above

   a. no; a partial answer; a more complete answer is available
   b. no; a partial answer; a more complete answer is available
   c. no; a partial answer; a more complete answer is available
   * d. yes; all of the answers are correct

11. Which of the following are dicots?
   a. irises
   b. beech trees
   c. orchids
   d. grasses

   a. no; monocots
   * b. yes; trees are dicots (have a vascular cambium to produce secondary xylem)
   c. no; monocots
   d. no; monocots

12. The cells that give protection to seed coats and are found in the hard parts of seeds and fruits are ____ cells.
   a. collenchyma
   b. parenchyma
   c. sclerenchyma
   d. cork

   a. no; found in vascular bundle sheaths and in stems for support more than protection
   b. no; relatively undifferentiated cells that function in food production or food storage
   * c. yes; cells are filled with lignin that makes them hard and excellent for protection
   d. no; these are dead cells found on the outside of woody stems and roots

13. A cotyledon is a
   a. seed leaf.
   b. protective sheath.
   c. segment of the root system.
   d. part of a flower.

   * a. yes; monocots have one seed leaf, while dicots have two
   b. no; called the coleoptile
   c. no; part of a seed
   d. no; part of a seed

14. Which of the following tissues is *not* characterized by rapid cell division?
   a. cork cambium
   b. lateral meristem
   c. vascular cambium
   d. periderm

   a. incorrect; a type of embryonic tissue that produces the periderm
   b. incorrect; a group of embryonic cells that produces cells that cause the plant to thicken
   c. incorrect; a group of embryonic cells that produces vascular tissues
   * d. correct; secondary tissue produced by divisions of the cork cambium; does not divide itself

15. The periderm
   a. replaces the epidermis.
   b. is produced by the cork cambium.
   c. is a protective layer that surrounds older plant tissues (such as old stems or roots).
   d. all of the above

   a. no; a partial answer; a more complete answer is available
   b. no; a partial answer; a more complete answer is available
   c. no; a partial answer; a more complete answer is available
   * d. yes; all of the answers are correct

16. Which of the following is characteristic of dicots?
   a. pollen grains having one pore or furrow
   b. have a single seed leaf
   c. vascular bundles arranged in a ring surrounding a central pith
   d. have parallel veins in their leaves

    a.  no; a characteristic of monocots
    b.  no; a characteristic of monocots
\*  c.  yes; a characteristic of dicots
    d.  no; a characteristic of monocots

17.    The cortex is
    a.  a stem of a leaf.
    b.  tissue that directly surrounds the vascular bundles.
    c.  ground tissue found outside the ring of vascular tissues in stems.
    d.  a portion of a terminal bud.

    a.  no; the petiole
    b.  no; vascular bundle sheath
\*  c.  yes; cortex is located between the veins and epidermis
    d.  no; a region of the differentiated tissues in a stem or root

18.    The end walls of cells of ___ have perforations to allow the conduction of food.
    a.  vessels
    b.  tracheids
    c.  companion cells
    d.  sieve tubes

    a.  no; conducts water
    b.  no; conducts water
    c.  no; small cells that are associated with sieve tubes
\*  d.  yes; the sieve tubes, as their name implies, are long tubes with a sieve at both ends of the cells

19.    Companion cells are found in
    a.  phloem.
    b.  xylem.
    c.  cortex.
    d.  pith.

\*  a.  yes; a type of phloem cell that surrounds and supports sieve tubes
    b.  no; include tracheids and vessel elements
    c.  no; composed of parenchyma cells
    d.  no; composed of parenchyma cells

20.    Which of the following does *not* have deciduous leaves?
    a.  camellia or holly
    b.  hickory tree
    c.  maple tree
    d.  sweet gum tree

\*  a.  correct; evergreen, not deciduous
    b.  incorrect; sheds its leaves each year
    c.  incorrect; sheds its leaves each year
    d.  incorrect; sheds its leaves each year

21.    The monocots have flower parts in
    a.  twos or multiples of two.
    b.  threes or multiples of three.
    c.  four or multiple of four.
    d.  fives or multiples of five.

    a.  no; not an appropriate number
\*  b.  yes; monocots would be expected to have three sepals, three petals, six stamens, three carpels
    c.  no; not an appropriate number
    d.  no; not an appropriate number

22.    Photosynthesis primarily occurs in the ____ of a leaf.
    a.  upper epidermis
    b.  lower epidermis
    c.  mesophyll
    d.  all of the above

    a.  no; colorless cells with the exception of guard cells surrounding the stoma
    b.  no; colorless cells with the exception of guard cells surrounding the stoma
\*  c.  yes; the majority of the chloroplasts are found in the mesophyll cells
    d.  no; a common distractor, but one of the above choices is correct

23.    The monocots have
    a.  stems with scattered vascular bundles.
    b.  vascular cambium.
    c.  leaves with net venation.
    d.  two cotyledons.

\*  a.  yes; the vascular bundles are scattered
    b.  no; and therefore do not produce woody stems
    c.  no; monocots typically have parallel venation in their leaves
    d.  no; an embryo with a single food leaf

24.    Lateral roots arise from the
    a.  epidermis.
    b.  cortex.
    c.  endodermis.
    d.  pericycle.

    a.  no; another tissue
    b.  no; another tissue
    c.  no; another tissue
\*  d.  yes

25.    Which of the following statements is true?
    a.  It is not possible to determine which layer of cells is the upper epidermis and which is the lower epidermis.
    b.  The mesophyll tissue is the only tissue in the leaf with chloroplasts.
    c.  The stoma are openings that permit gas exchange.
    d.  The phloem is on top of the vascular bundle and the xylem is on the bottom.

    a.  no; this statement is false because the palisade mesophyll is adjacent to the upper epidermis
    b.  no; guard cells are epidermal cells with chloroplasts
\*  c.  yes; this statement is true
    d.  no; the positions are reversed, with xylem on top and phloem on the bottom

26. Grasses are primarily characterized by
    a. adventitious roots.
    b. fibrous root systems.
    c. taproot systems.
    d. both (a) and (b), but not (c)

    a. yes; a partial answer; the primary root dies and is replaced by adventitious roots
    b. yes; a partial answer; the adventitious roots form a fibrous root system
    c. no; although a few grasses may have a taproot
  * d. yes; both (a) and (b) are true, and (c) is false

27. Corn, marigolds, and beans are examples of
    a. annuals.
    b. biennials.
    c. perennials.
    d. both (a) and (b), but not (c)

  * a. yes; live for only one year
    b. no; live for less than two years
    c. no; live for less than many years
    d. no; only one of the above is correct

28. All the cells between the vascular cambium and the surface of a woody stem or root collectively make up the
    a. wood.
    b. bark.
    c. cork.
    d. cortex.

    a. no; inside the vascular cambium
  * b. yes
    c. no; only those cells produced by the vascular cambium
    d. no; only cells between vein and epidermis

# CHAPTER 23

# PLANT NUTRITION AND TRANSPORT

1. The concentration of carbon dioxide in the atmosphere is ____ parts per million.
   a. 35
   b. 350
   c. 3,500
   d. 35,000

   a. no; too little
   * b. yes
   c. no; too large
   d. no; too large

2. Which of the following is *not* one of the three major elements used in compounds that form the structural compounds of plants?
   a. carbon
   b. oxygen
   c. nitrogen
   d. hydrogen

   a. incorrect; is one of the three
   b. incorrect; is one of the three
   * c. correct; is not one of the three; but nitrogen is found in the proteins plants manufacture
   d. incorrect; is one of the three

3. Insectivorous plants developed the ability to capture insects to
   a. pollinate them.
   b. increase the available supply of certain elements.
   c. feed upon them, deriving organic materials for energy.
   d. eliminate herbivorous insects that feed upon them.

   a. no; use nectar and pollen as rewards for insects that pollinate them
   * b. yes; they derive supplies of a mineral that is usually in short supply in the boggy habitats where they live
   c. no; they do not derive energy from the process
   d. no; although some unwary insects may be killed by falling victim to the plant

4. Chlorosis is
   a. a yellowing of leaves due to a reduction in chlorophyll.
   b. a production of dead spots on leaves.
   c. the thickening and curling of leaves.
   d. the premature browning and shedding of leaves.

   * a. yes; chlorosis is the yellowing of leaves
   b. no; called necrosis
   c. no; called puckering
   d. no; a common deficiency symptom but is not chlorosis

5. Insectivorous plants derive the element ____ from the insects they eat.
   a. magnesium
   b. manganese
   c. phosphorus
   d. nitrogen

   a. no; another element
   b. no; another element
   c. no; another element
   * d. yes; the availability of nitrogen in their habitat is low, and this adaptation developed to partially solve the problem

6. Which of the following micronutrients has a role in electron transport and chlorophyll synthesis?
   a. zinc
   b. manganese
   c. chlorine
   d. iron

   a. no; in addition to formation of chlorophyll, zinc is involved in auxin and starch formation
   b. no; does involve chlorophyll, but not electron transport
   c. no; involved in root and shoot growth and in photolysis
   * d. yes; involved in both processes

7. Nitrogen-fixing bacteria
   a. take nitrogen out of the atmosphere and make it available to plants.
   b. are examples of symbiotic organisms.
   c. live in nodules on the roots of legumes.
   d. all of the above

   a. no; a partial answer; a more complete answer is available
   b. no; a partial answer; a more complete answer is available
   c. no; a partial answer; a more complete answer is available
   * d. yes; all of the above answers are correct

8. Although a deficiency of any one of the elements listed may result in chlorosis, only one of these elements is an element found in chlorophyll. Which is it?
   a. zinc
   b. iron
   c. magnesium
   d. chloride

   a. no; chlorosis induced by some other reason than occurring in the chlorophyll molecules (such as could be used in enzyme systems or needed for nitrogen metabolism)
   b. no; chlorosis induced by some other reason than occurring in the chlorophyll molecules (such as could be used in enzyme systems or needed for nitrogen metabolism)
 * c. yes; magnesium is the central atom of the porphyrin ring of chlorophyll
   d. no; chlorosis induced by some other reason than occurring in the chlorophyll molecules (such as could be used in enzyme systems or needed for nitrogen metabolism)

9. Which of the following elements is needed as a component in cell membranes, nucleic acids, and energy transfer?
   a. calcium
   b. potassium
   c. sulfur
   d. phosphorous

   a. no; not directly involved in any of the above
   b. no; not directly involved in any of the above
   c. no; not directly involved in any of the above
 * d. yes; phosphorous is found in phospholipids, phosphate groups in nucleotides, and ATP

10. Which of the following is classified as a micronutrient for plants?
   a. iron
   b. sulfur
   c. magnesium
   d. calcium

 * a. yes; needed in small amounts
   b. no; a macronutrient needed in proportionately greater amounts
   c. no; a macronutrient needed in proportionately greater amounts
   d. no; a macronutrient needed in proportionately greater amounts

11. The roots of members of the ____ plant family are well known for their symbiotic relationship with nitrogen-fixing bacteria.
   a. mint
   b. legume
   c. buttercup
   d. rose

   a. no; another plant family
 * b. yes; such plants as beans, peas, alfalfa, and clover
   c. no; another plant family
   d. no; another plant family

12. Root hairs are
   a. found on the root cap.
   b. branch roots.
   c. immature roots.
   d. extensions of epidermal cell.

   a. no; this is a protective cap and the root hairs would be destroyed if located here
   b. no; root hairs are too small to be called branch roots
   c. no; root hairs do not develop into roots
 * d. yes; each is an extension of a single epidermal cell

13. Mycorrhizae are
   a. symbiotic fungi that grow on roots.
   b. cytoplasmic extensions of root systems that increase their efficiency.
   c. parasites that cause root kill in certain breeds of trees.
   d. are sites where nitrogen fixation occurs.

 * a. yes; increase ability of plants to secure water and minerals
   b. no; mycorrhizae are living fungi
   c. no; not parasites
   d. no; fixation occurs in nodules filled with nitrogen-fixing bacteria

14. The Casparian strip
   a. is a layer of rapidly dividing cambium cells.
   b. is a tangential section of ring porous wood.
   c. prevents water from entering the vascular cylinder.
   d. funnels water destined for the vascular cylinder through the cytoplasm of endodermal cells.

   a. no; not a cellular layer
   b. no; not a section of wood or secondary xylem
   c. no; does prevent movement of water through itself, but water does reach the vascular cylinder.
 * d. yes

15. The Casparian strip is associated with the
   a. epidermis.
   b. endodermis.
   c. cortex.
   d. pericycle.

   a. no; the outer layer of the root
 * b. yes; serves as a barrier to control what reaches the stele
   c. no; the cortex serves as a storage area
   d. no; the pericycle gives rise to branch roots and cork cambium

16. Loss of water in a gaseous form from leaves, stems, and exposed plant parts is called
    a. guttation.
    b. transpiration.
    c. evaporation.
    d. cohesion.

    a. no; the loss of water in a liquid form
    * b. yes; the loss of water from plants in a gaseous state
    c. no; the correct answer is a special type of evaporation (a better answer is available)
    d. no; cohesion is the binding of water molecules to each other

17. Which of the following statements is part of Dixon's theory explaining movement of water through the plant?
    a. The air causes evaporation or transpiration from the parts of the plant exposed to air.
    b. Water in xylem is placed under a tension that allows pressure or continuous tension from the leaf tip throughout the entire plant.
    c. Unbroken columns of water show cohesion of water molecules held together by hydrogen bonds.
    d. all of the above

    a. no; a partial answer; a more complete answer is available
    b. no; a partial answer; a more complete answer is available
    c. no; a partial answer; a more complete answer is available
    * d. yes; all of the answers are correct

18. The major use of water in a plant (as measured by the amount used in each activity) is
    a. in photosynthesis.
    b. to promote growth.
    c. in transpiration.
    d. to maintain turgor and prevent wilting.

    a. no; only a small portion of water is incorporated into the organic compounds of a plant
    b. no; some small amount is used to supply the 70–90 percent of fresh body weight due to water found in protoplasm
    * c. yes; the amount of water that passes through the plant to supply the water lost through transpiration is astounding
    d. no; essentially the same as answer (b)

19. Transpiration *primarily* occurs through the
    a. stem.
    b. guard cells.
    c. cuticle.
    d. stomata.

    a. no; some small amount of water loss does occur through stomata and lenticels (spaces) in the stem
    b. no; a relatively small amount is lost through these cells that surround the stomata
    c. no; the waxy layer reduces water loss
    * d. yes; the water vapors simply move through these openings to the exterior of the leaf

20. Which of the following plants opens its stomata at night and closes during the day, using the carbon dioxide absorbed the night before for photosynthesis?
    a. $C_3$
    b. $C_4$
    c. CAM
    d. all of the above

    a. no; do not have this ability
    b. no; do not have this ability
    * c. yes; CAM plants use this approach to conserve water in the desert
    d. no; a common distractor, but only one of the above is correct

21. The stomata open
    a. when the guard cells are turgid.
    b. when active transport carries potassium out of a cell.
    c. at night when it is dark.
    d. none of the above

    * a. yes; the turgid condition forces the guard cells to open
    b. no; the stoma opens when potassium enters the guard cells
    c. no; the stomata usually close at night but may close at any time under stress
    d. no; one of the above is correct

22. The most universal source of ATP throughout the plant is
    a. anaerobic respiration.
    b. aerobic respiration.
    c. photosynthesis.
    d. cyclic photophosphorylation.

    a. no; not a major source of ATP
    * b. yes; throughout the plant ATP is made available in this way
    c. no; a source of ATP only in plant tissue with chloroplasts
    d. no; not a major source for most plants

23. In most plant cells, carbohydrates are stored as
    a. glucose.
    b. fructose.
    c. sucrose.
    d. starch.

    a. no; the primary form produced in photosynthesis
    b. no; combines with glucose to form sucrose
    c. no; is too mobile to be stored
    * d. yes; insoluble and easy to store

24. The main form of carbohydrates transported throughout a plant is
    a. glucose.
    b. fructose.
    c. sucrose.
    d. starch.

    a. no; this product of photosynthesis is modified before it moves
    b. no; combines with glucose before moving through the plant
    * c. yes; simple soluble, easy to move
    d. no; large insoluble molecules that cannot move from cell to cell

25. The honeydew of an aphid is
    a. a metabolic waste product of the sugar absorbed by aphids.
    b. the sugary contents of plant cells that is forced through the aphid by a pressure differential.
    c. pure fructose.
    d. none of the above

    a. no; it is sucrose excreted from the aphid's anus
    * b. yes; forced through the body of the insect by pressure
    c. no; contains sucrose
    d. no; one of the above is correct

26. The sink region of a plant for sucrose is
    a. the leaves.
    b. any green part of a plant.
    c. any place that needs sucrose.
    d. all of the above

    a. no; a source region
    b. no; a source region
    * c. yes; the sucrose flows to this part
    d. no; only one of the above answers is correct

27. The major cells responsible for translocation of food throughout the plant are the
    a. vessels.
    b. companion cells.
    c. tracheids.
    d. sieve tubes.

    a. no; xylem cells that transport water and minerals
    b. no; phloem cells that assist the sieve tubes in transport
    c. no; xylem cells that transport water and minerals
    * d. yes; continuous tubes responsible for the movement of food

28. Movement of material in the phloem is explained by
    a. gravity.
    b. pressure flow hypothesis.
    c. cohesion theory.
    d. transpiration pull.

    a. no; can move against the force of gravity
    * b. yes; pressure forces material to flow from source to sink region
    c. no; used to explain transpiration pull
    d. no; explains movements of water to the top of a plant

# CHAPTER 24

# PLANT REPRODUCTION AND DEVELOPMENT

1. Plants surpass humans in the capability to
   a. use color for sex.
   b. reproduce asexually.
   c. use aromas for sex.
   d. none of the above

   a. no; both use color for sexual attraction
   * b. yes; humans cannot reproduce asexually
   c. no; both use aromas for sex
   d. no; one of the above is correct

2. Sporophytes
   a. are exemplified by a radish plant, a cactus, and an elm tree.
   b. are produced through meiosis.
   c. give rise to cells that reproduce sexually.
   d. produce sexually reproducing gametes.

   * a. yes; these are all sporophytes
   b. no; sporophytes are produced through fertilization
   c. no; produce spores
   d. no; sporophytes reproduce asexually by spores

3. The name for the complete female part of a flower is the
   a. ovary.
   b. ovule.
   c. carpel.
   d. egg.

   a. no; a hollow chamber containing ovules; part of the female part of a flower
   b. no; a structure containing the female gametophyte
   * c. yes; consists of stigma, style, and ovary
   d. no; the female gamete

4. A part of the carpel where pollination occurs is the
   a. ovary.
   b. ovule.
   c. stigma.
   d. style.

   a. no; contains the ovules to which the pollen tube grows
   b. no; contains the embryo sac
   * c. yes; pollen is deposited here
   d. no; the neck through which the pollen tube grows

5. Imperfect flowers
   a. lack petals.
   b. may be either male or female.
   c. possess both sex organs.
   d. have stamens and carpels but lack petals or sepals.

   a. no; some flowers, such as wind-pollinated flowers, may lack petals
   * b. yes; they lack one sex, express the other
   c. no; one or the other is present, but not both
   d. no; lack either stamens or carpels

6. The outermost part of a flower is the
   a. corolla.
   b. stigma.
   c. sepal.
   d. stamen.

   a. no; formed by petals but still has structures outside of it
   b. no; part of the flower where pollination occurs
   * c. yes; the outermost part of a flower
   d. no; the male part inside the corolla

7. All of the ____ taken together compose a corolla.
   a. sepals
   b. petals
   c. anthers
   d. both (a) and (b), but not (c)

   a. no; are not part of the corolla
   * b. yes; all of the petals collectively are called the corolla
   c. no; are not part of the corolla
   d. no; (b) is the only correct answer

8. Microspores are produced by the
   a. embryo sacs.
   b. anther of the stamen.
   c. ovule.
   d. process of mitosis.

a. no; the tissue that produces the megaspore
* b. yes; the part of the stamen that produces pollen grains
c. no; contains the embryo sac or female gametophyte
d. no; by meiosis from the diploid microspore mother cells

9. The structure that will eventually develop into a seed is the
a. ovule.
b. ovary.
c. megaspore.
d. embryo.

* a. yes; develops into the seed
b. no; develops into the fruit
c. no; develops into the female gametophyte or embryo sac
d. no; is the young sporophyte which is contained in seeds

10. Bees are *not* attracted to flowers of ___ color because they cannot see them
a. yellow.
b. blue.
c. ultraviolet.
d. red.

a. incorrect; a common color of bee-pollinated flowers
b. incorrect; a common color of bee-pollinated flowers
c. incorrect; bees use this component to see flowers
* d. correct; bees cannot see this long wavelength of light (just as humans cannot see infrared radiation)

11. Which of the following pollinators would be attracted to large white flowers with strong sweet perfumes and long tubular corollas with large petals?
a. bees
b. butterflies
c. moths
d. beetles and flies

a. no; yellow or blue flowers preferred
b. no; usually day pollinators preferring red, flat, upright flowers
* c. yes; night fliers find flowers by the large white petals and strong aromas
d. no; usually strong, rancid or fetid odors

12. A germinated pollen grain with three nuclei, one tube nucleus, and two generative nuclei represents a
a. microspore.
b. microsporangium.
c. microgamete.
d. microgametophyte.

a. no; a microspore is a pollen grain
b. no; the microsporangium is the anther; the structure that produces microspores (pollen grains)
c. no; the microgamete is the generative nucleus (sperm) that fuses with the egg
* d. yes; the microspore (pollen grain) has germinated to form a microgametophyte (with three nuclei, two generative nuclei, and a tube nucleus)

13. Microspores are
a. produced in a carpel.
b. diploid cells.
c. produced by meiosis.
d. the male gametes.

a. no; produced in the anthers of the stamens.
b. no; haploid cells
* c. yes; meiosis forms spores
d. no; the gamete is contained in a microspore (the generative nucleus)

14. The seed coat develops from the
a. integument.
b. ovule.
c. placenta.
d. ovary.

* a. yes; develops into the seed coat
b. no; develops into a seed
c. no; leaves a scar, the hilium on a seed
d. no; the ovary develops into a fruit

15. The female gametophyte in the flowering plants is the
a. ovary.
b. carpel.
c. ovule.
d. embryo sac.

a. no; composed of diploid sporophyte tissue
b. no; composed of diploid sporophyte tissue
c. no; composed of diploid sporophyte tissue
* d. yes; consists of eight haploid nuclei produced by meiosis to produce a megaspore and three mitotic divisions to produce the female gametophyte

16. The larvae of Blister beetles feed upon
a. developing ovules.
b. bee eggs and pollen after they are transferred from flowers.
c. a variety of insect pollinators.
d. birds and bats as external parasites.

a. no; the larvae do not develop within a flower's ovary
* b. yes; the eggs are picked up by bees and hatch into larvae in the beehive where they feed on bee eggs and pollen
c. no; not a general predator of insects
d. no; does not parasitize bats or birds

17. Which of the following tissues would be triploid?
    a. anther
    b. embryo sac
    c. endosperm
    d. sporophyte

    a. no; the tissue would be diploid except for the haploid pollen it produces
    b. no; the tissue of the female gametophyte and is therefore haploid
  * c. yes; formed by the fusion of the generative tube nucleus with the two sets of female chromosomes found in the polar nuclei, thus producing triploid tissue with three sets of chromosomes
    d. no; the sporophyte is diploid throughout

18. Cotyledons are
    a. food for the developing seed.
    b. the embryonic seed leaves.
    c. part of the embryonic root system.
    d. a protective tissue surrounding the embryonic shoot system.

    a. no; the endosperm
  * b. yes; they may store excess food or become functional leaves
    c. no; the hypocotyl arises below the cotyledons on the embryo
    d. no; the coleoptile protects the embryonic shoot system of some monocot seeds

19. Which of the following statements is false?
    a. An unfertilized flower cannot produce fruits and seeds.
    b. Insect pollination requires less energy from a plant than wind pollination.
    c. Some plants produce more flowers than ever develop into fruits and may just produce excess pollen to export to other plants.
    d. If an animal eats a fruit, the seeds it contains will be destroyed by digestive enzymes in the animal's intestinal tract.

    a. no; this statement is true
    b. no; this statement is true
    c. no; this statement is true
  * d. yes; this statement is false; the digestive enzymes may rupture or scarify hard seed coat, enabling it to imbibe water and germinate

20. The function of a fruit is
    a. dispersal.
    b. reproduction and protection.
    c. dispersal and reproduction.
    d. dispersal and protection.

    a. no; a fruit is involved in more than just dispersal
    b. no; fruit is involved in dispersal, not included in this choice
    c. no; reproduction has already occurred
  * d. yes; the fruit performs both functions

21. Which of the following are examples of multiple fruits?
    a. pineapple, fig, mulberry
    b. strawberry, blackberry, raspberry
    c. rice, sunflower, maple, wheat
    d. grape, banana, cherry, lemon, orange

  * a. yes; multiple fruits include multiple ovaries plus accessory tissues
    b. no; these are aggregate fruits
    c. no; dry intact fruits
    d. no; fleshy fruits

22. The hypocotyl is
    a. a protective sheath that surrounds the first leaves.
    b. a seed leaf.
    c. the part of the embryo below the cotyledon that forms the root.
    d. the part of the embryo above the cotyledon that forms the root.

    a. no; the coleoptile
    b. no; a cotyledon
  * c. yes; the part of the seedling below the cotyledons (hypo-below)
    d. no; the part above the cotyledon that develops into the shoot system is the epicotyl (epi=above)

23. Which of the following statements is false?
    a. Asexual reproduction produces clones.
    b. Large flowering plants are sporophytes.
    c. Plants may be reproduced asexually.
    d. none of the above; all choices are true

    a. no; this statement is true
    b. no; this statement is true
    c. no; this statement is true
  * d. yes; none of the choices are false

24. Which chemical was the key to the successful invasion of land by plants?
    a. lignin
    b. pectin
    c. suberin
    d. cutin

    a. no; found in sclerenchyma and collechyma cells used for support and protection and in xylem cells specialized for conduction
    b. no; a cementing chemical found in cell walls
    c. no; a waxy chemical found in cork cells and as part of the Casparian strip in the endodermis
  * d. yes; a waterproofing agent that covers leaves and epidermal cells reducing water loss through transpiration

25. The easiest and fastest way to get copies of rare orchids is
    a. vegetative propagation by cutting.
    b. crossing two different varieties and collecting their seeds after they flower.
    c. cloning by tissue culture propagation.
    d. collect them from their natural habitat.

a. no; although orchids may be split and each half develop normally, it takes time for the plants to get large enough to divide
b. no; it takes seven years for some orchids to get from seed to seed
* c. yes; tissue culture propagation enables immediate replication of an orchid
d. no; in the natural habitat, the plants usually reproduce sexually so that it would be unlikely to be a source for clones

26. The foolish rice plants exhibit the effect of the plant hormone known as
   a. auxin.
   b. gibberellin.
   c. ethylene.
   d. abscisic acid

   a. no; the natural plant growth hormone associated with cell elongation
   * b. yes; a hormone secreted by a fungus that has infected rice plants
   c. no; a hormone responsible for ripening of fruits
   d. no; a hormone responsible for the dropping of plant parts, such as leaves or fruits

27. The plant hormone gibberellin
   a. controls flowering.
   b. promotes fruit ripening and abscission of leaves, flowers, and fruits.
   c. promotes closing of stomata and might trigger bud and seed dormancy.
   d. promotes stem elongation, stimulates the breakdown of starch, and might trigger bud dormancy.

   a. no; florigen
   b. no; ethylene
   c. no; abscisic acid
   * d. yes

28. The plant hormone cytokinin promotes
   a. cell elongation and is thought to be involved in phototropism and gravitropism.
   b. stem elongation and might control bud and seed dormancy.
   c. cell division, promotes leaf expansion, and retards leaf aging.
   d. fruit ripening and abscission of leaves, flowers, and fruits.

   a. no; auxin does this
   b. no; gibberellin does this
   * c. yes; cytokinin
   d. no; ethylene does this

29. ___ is the hormone associated with the following words: foolish rice, gigantic growth, fungus, seventy different kinds of chemicals.
   a. Auxin
   b. Gibberellin
   c. Ethylene
   d. Florigen

   a. no; the native growth hormone
   * b. yes
   c. no; a gaseous hormone
   d. no; the flowering hormone

30. Under which of the following conditions will a coleoptile grow?
   a. when it is decapitated
   b. when a decapitated coleoptile has a plain agar block on top
   c. when a decapitated coleoptile is covered with an agar block on which a coleoptile tip has been resting for some time
   d. when a decapitated coleoptile has light shining on it

   a. no; no source of auxin available
   b. no; no source of auxin available
   * c. yes; auxin from the tip moves to agar blocks and then to coleoptile to stimulate growth
   d. no; no source of auxin available

31. The growth response that enables a tendril to wrap around a support is known as
   a. gravitropism.
   b. phototropism.
   c. thigmotropism,
   d. none of the above

   a. no; the growth response to gravity
   b. no; the growth response to light
   * c. no; the growth response to touch
   d. no; one of the above is correct

32. Phytochrome far red controls
   a. flowering, fruiting, and setting of seeds.
   b. germination of seeds and leaf expansion.
   c. stem elongation and branching.
   d. all of the above

   a. yes; a partial answer
   b. yes; a partial answer
   c. yes; a partial answer
   * d. yes; all of the above are correct

33. Which of the following factors is usually more critical for the germination of seeds?
   a. availability of oxygen
   b. availability of water
   c. availability of minerals
   d. availability of light

   a. no; once the seed coat is ruptured, there is enough oxygen for aerobic respiration
   * b. yes; the availability of water allows imbibition, which initiates the process of germination
   c. no; not usually a critical factor and is eliminated when the primary roots start absorbing
   d. no; although this may be an absolute requirement for some small seeds with limited food reserves (thus preventing buried seeds from germination and being unable to grow enough to reach the light)

34. Germination is over when
    a. the seedling breaks through the soil surface and the epicotyl becomes visible.
    b. the primary root breaks through the seed coat.
    c. the cotyledons escape from the seed coat.
    d. both the root and shoot systems have emerged from the seed.

    a. no; germination does not have to be underground as this choice indicates
  * b. yes; the sign that germination has occurred
    c. no; in some seeds, the cotyledon may not escape or it may take a long time before the seed is shed
    d. no; only the hypocotyl needs to emerge

35. The chief explanation for the differentiation of cells in a plant is
    a. elongation.
    b. growth and maturity.
    c. selective gene expression.
    d. location in the developing plant.

    a. no; responsible for most of the growth in a plant
    b. no; there has to be an explanation for the differences in cells, other than just growth and maturity
  * c. yes; certain genes are active in some cells and inactive in others, resulting in differences
    d. no; although position may play a part because of proximity to certain regions or the existence of chemical gradients

36. The coleoptile is a(n)
    a. embryonic shoot system.
    b. protective sheath that protects the shoot system.
    c. covering for the cotyledons in dicot plants.
    d. protective sheath that covers the roots.

    a. no; this is known as the epicotyl
  * b. yes; a protective sheath for the growing tip of the shoot system that is used in research on plant growth and hormones
    c. no; the cotyledons do not have a specific covering other than the seed coat
    d. no; the protective covering for the roots is the coleorhizae

37. Plant hormones
    a. affect specific target cells.
    b. are general in their response, so that any cell may participate in the response.
    c. are collectively known as auxins.
    d. produce responses only through differential growth and elongation of cells.

  * a. yes; just as in animals, cells have to have appropriate receptors to respond to hormones
    b. no; response is restricted to cells with appropriate receptors
    c. no; auxins refer to only one of the five types of known plant hormones and include indolacetic acid and related growth hormones
    d. no; hormonal responses are quite variable and include such things as dormancy, opening and closing of stomata, fruit ripening, retarding aging, and others

38. Synthetic _____ are used as herbicides.
    a. auxins
    b. gibberellins
    c. cytokinins
    d. all of the above

    a. yes; 2, 4–D and 2, 4, 5–D are synthetic auxins used as herbicides
    b. no; these hormones cause stem lengthening and flowering
    c. no; stimulate cell division and leaf expansion
    d. no; only one of the above is correct

39. Which of the following was used as a defoliant in the Vietnam conflict?
    a. 2, 4–D
    b. 2, 4, 5–T
    c. dioxin
    d. abscisic acid

    a. no; a common herbicide
  * b. yes; another synthetic auxin used as a defoliant
    c. no; a contaminant of 2, 4, 5–T that is carcinogenic
    d. no; this hormone can be used to delay fruit drop until pickers arrive, thereby reducing the number of bruised fruits

40. Which of the following is a gaseous hormone that promotes development, ripening, and color of fruits?
    a. gibberellin
    b. abscisic acid
    c. ethylene
    d. cytokinin

    a. no; promotes growth and flowering
    b. no; promotes bud and seed dormancy
  * c. yes; produced by burning incense, kerosene, and by ripening fruit
    d. no; promotes cell division in the apical meristem

41. The shedding of plant parts is called
    a. photoperiodism.
    b. senescence.
    c. abscission.
    d. dormancy.

a. no; the response of an organism to duration of light and dark
b. no; the aging of a plant that leads to death
* c. yes
d. no; the decline in the physiological activities of a plant in dry seasons or before the onset of cold temperature

42. Which of the following statements is false?
    a. Only animals have biological clocks; there are none known in plants.
    b. Senescence is the sum total of all of the processes leading to the death of a plant.
    c. Plants adjust their patterns of growth in response to environmental rhythms and environmental conditions.
    d. Ethylene promotes fruit ripening and abscission.

    * a. correct; statement is false; photoperiodism is an example of a biological clock found in plants
    b. incorrect; statement is true
    c. incorrect; statement is true
    d. incorrect; statement is true

43. Which hormone has never been identified or isolated?
    a. cytokinin
    b. abscisic acid
    c. ethylene
    d. florigen

    a. no; this hormone has been identified and isolated
    b. no; this hormone has been identified and isolated
    c. no; this hormone has been identified and isolated
    * d. yes; although considerable evidence indicates that there is a hormone that induces flowering, it has never been isolated

44. Saponin are
    a. plant hormones.
    b. chemicals produced by insects that disrupt plant growth.
    c. chemicals produced by plants that kill or repel herbivores.
    d. chemicals that enable communication between plants.

    a. no; they are not hormones
    b. no; not produced by insects
    * c. yes; a plant defense mechanism
    d. no; do not have this function

45. Charles Darwin
    a. made the connection between the growth response of plants to light from one direction and growth-producing hormones.
    b. named the native plant growth hormone auxin.
    c. noticed that coleoptiles would turn and grow toward a single source of light.
    d. demonstrated that auxin moves from the coleoptile tip to cells found in the shade and stimulates them to grow faster.

    a. no; this was the work of Fritz Went
    b. no; this was the work of Fritz Went
    * c. yes; Darwin was aware of phototropism but did not discover the chemical basis for it
    d. no; this was the work of Fritz Went

46. Plants exposed to _____ light exhibit the greatest phototropic response.
    a. red
    b. blue
    c. white
    d. yellow

    a. no; a different color
    * b. yes; perhaps a yellow pigment, flavoprotein is responsible for the response
    c. no; a different color
    d. no; a different color

47. Which of the following statements is true?
    a. The cells on the shady side of stems elongate faster than those on the sunny side.
    b. The top of a horizontal stem grows faster than the bottom.
    c. The bottom of a horizontal root grows faster than the top.
    d. all of the above

    * a. yes; this is the appropriate explanation for the phototropic response
    b. no; this statement is false; the cells on the bottom of the stem grow faster, causing the stem to grow upwards
    c. no; this statement is false; the cells on the top of the root grow faster, causing the root to grow downwards
    d. no; a common distractor, but only one of the above is correct

48. The gravity-sensing part of a plant is located in
    a. the root tip.
    b. the apical meristems.
    c. starch grains known as statoliths found within modified plastids.
    d. small grains of sand incorporated in root cells.

    a. no; the site for the production of a growth inhibitor
    b. no; embryonic cells whose divisions produce primary growth
*   c. yes; statoliths collect on the lower part of a plastid
    d. no; there are no grains of sand found within roots

49. Phytochrome activation may stimulate plant cells to take up ___ ions or induce some plant organs to release them to initiate contact with a protein that produces some of the plant responses to light.
    a. phosphorus
    b. potassium
    c. cobalt
    d. calcium

    a. no; another element
    b. no; another element
    c. no; another element
*   d. yes; calcium seems to be the trigger

50. Which of the following statements is false?
    a. Plants will grow in the dark for a limited time.
    b. Plants grow toward the light because they need light.
    c. A single stem exposed to an appropriate environment will go ahead and break dormancy, even though the rest of the plant remains dormant.
    d. If a young peach tree was ordered from Georgia and planted in Colorado, it might start to grow too soon and be killed by a late frost.

    a. incorrect; they will grow for a limited time until their food supply is exhausted
*   b. correct; statement is teleological and therefore false because a plant doesn't have a purpose or needs as such. A plant simply responds to environmental stimuli.
    c. incorrect; statement is true
    d. incorrect; statement is true

51. Light is necessary for
    a. growth of plant cells.
    b. the production of carotenoids.
    c. the production of chlorophyll.
    d. inactive phytochrome (Pfr).

    a. no; plant cells can grow and elongate in the dark
    b. no; the carotenoids may be produced in the dark
*   c. yes; light is required for chlorophyll production
    d. no; light converts Pr into active Pfr

52. Long-day plants
    a. will not flower if their dark period is interrupted by light.
    b. will not grow in the tropics.
    c. will not reproduce in the tropics.
    d. flower in the early spring or late fall.

    a. no; interrupting the dark period interferes with short-day plants
    b. no; long-day plants will grow in the tropics where they get shorter than the number of critical daylight hours to flower
*   c. yes; they will grow but will not have appropriate long-day photoperiod in the tropics to bloom
    d. no; the long-day plants bloom during the long days of summer

53. Long-day plants
    a. actually respond to short dark periods, not to long light periods
    b. will not bloom if the dark period is interrupted by light
    c. include such plants as cocklebur, chrysanthemum, poinsettia
    d. all of the above

*   a. yes; more obvious in the short-day plants that will not bloom when the dark period is interrupted
    b. no; this is true of short-day plants, but long-day plants are induced by short dark periods
    c. no; these are all short-day plants blooming in the fall or winter
    d. no; one of the above is correct

54. Vernalization is a plant's environmental response to
    a. light.
    b. desiccation.
    c. cold temperature.
    d. warm temperature.

    a. no; another environmental factor
    b. no; another environmental factor
*   c. yes; for some seeds to germinate and some fruits to form, a plant must be exposed to a critical low temperature for a critical period of time
    d. no; another environmental factor

# CHAPTER 25

# TISSUES, ORGAN SYSTEMS, AND HOMEOSTASIS

1. A group of cells that have a similar structure and function are called
   a. cell complexes.
   b. organ systems.
   c. tissues.
   d. organs.

   a. no; a better term is listed
   b. no; too comprehensive
   * c. yes; this is the definition of a tissue
   d. no; too comprehensive

2. Which of the following is *not* one of the three "primary tissues"?
   a. ectoderm
   b. endoderm
   c. mesoderm
   d. zygoderm

   a. no; this is one of the "primary tissues"
   b. no; this is one of the "primary tissues"
   c. no; this is one of the "primary tissues"
   * d. yes; there is no term known as zygoderm

3. The lining of the digestive tract is formed by the
   a. ectoderm.
   b. endoderm.
   c. mesoderm.
   d. zygoderm.

   a. no; forms the integumentary and nervous system
   * b. yes; forms the lining of the digestive tract
   c. no; forms most of the body including muscles, kidneys, circulatory system, skeletal system, and more
   d. no; this is not one of the three primary tissues

4. Bones are examples of _____ tissue.
   a. muscular
   b. epithelial
   c. connective
   d. nervous

   a. no; enables bones to move
   b. no; covering of the body or lining of internal cavities
   * c. yes; one form of connective tissue
   d. no; forms the brain, spinal cord, and nerves

5. Cilia or microvilli are more likely to be found on the surface of _____ tissue.
   a. muscle
   b. epithelial
   c. connective
   d. nervous

   a. no; no external features
   * b. yes; these structures promote motion and allow absorption
   c. no; no external features
   d. no; external projections called axons and dendrites

6. Secretion and absorption are common functions of _____ epithelial tissues.
   a. cuboidal
   b. pseudostratified
   c. stratified
   d. squamous

   * a. yes; found lining the gut and respiratory tract
   b. no; possess cilia on their free surface for movement of mucus or to propel an egg through the oviduct
   c. no; function in protection of the skin
   d. no; form an impervious protective covering

7. Which of the following is *not* a characteristic of epithelial cells?
   a. have one free surface
   b. have an underlying basement membrane
   c. have specialized junctions with adjacent cells
   d. are held together by connective tissues

   a. no; a characteristic of epithelial cells
   b. no; a characteristic of epithelial cells
   c. no; a characteristic of epithelial cells
   * d. yes; epithelial cells do not have interspersed connective cells but are attached to the basement membrane that is attached to connective tissues

8. Which of the following is a shape of an epithelial tissue, not a type of epithelial cell?
   a. squamous
   b. simple
   c. stratified
   d. pseudostratified

\*     a. yes; squamous is a shape of epithelial cells
b. no; a type of epithelial tissue
c. no; a type of epithelial tissue
d. no; a type of epithelial tissue

9. Which of the following is *not* a product of an exocrine gland?
a. hormone
b. wax
c. mucus
d. milk

\*     a. yes; secreted by an endocrine, not an exocrine gland
b. no; secreted by an exocrine gland
c. no; secreted by an exocrine gland
d. no; secreted by an exocrine gland

10. Glands are classified
a. according to their products.
b. according to their locations.
c. by the kinds of cells they are composed of.
d. according to how their secretion reaches their site of activity.

    a. no; the secretion may be polypeptides or steroids
b. no; located all over the body
c. no; all have secretory epithelial cells
\*    d. yes; exocrine glands have ducts to carry their products while endocrine secretions are carried by the bloodstream

11. Which of the following types of cells is *not* classified as somatic tissue?
a. nerve cells
b. muscle cells
c. germ cells
d. epithelial cells

    a. incorrect; a type of body cell
b. incorrect; a type of body cell
\*    c. correct; reproductive cells are not body cells
d. incorrect; a type of body cell

12. Epithelial cells
a. line body cavities.
b. line body ducts and tubes.
c. are found in the skin covering the body.
d. all of the above and more

    a. no; a partial answer ; a more complete answer is available
b. no; a partial answer ; a more complete answer is available
c. no; a partial answer ; a more complete answer is available
\*    d. yes; all of the above are true

13. Tendons
a. are composed of connective tissue.
b. connect bone to bone.
c. are filled with collagen fibers.
d. both (a) and (c)

    a. no: a partial answer; a more complete answer is available
b. no; connects muscle to bone
c. no; a partial answer; collagen in the tissue resists being pulled apart under tension a better answer is available
\*    d. yes; both (a) and (c) are correct

14. Adipose tissue
a. serves as an energy reserve.
b. is a type of epithelial tissue that underlies the skin.
c. is a muscle tissue specialized to maintain body temperature.
d. is a specialized tissue found in the brain tissue of college students.

\*    a. yes; fat in these cells can be used as an energy source
b. no; may underlie the skin, but is not epithelial tissue
c. no; adipose does have an insulating characteristic, but it is not muscle tissue
d. no; not associated with nervous tissue

15. Adhesion junctions are comparable to
a. gasketlike seals.
b. spot welds between plasma membranes.
c. small channels between cells.
d. all of the above

    a. no; appropriate description for tight junctions
\*    b. yes; holds cells together
c. no; applies to gap junctions
d. no; only one of the above is correct

16. Ions and small molecules can pass through
a. tight junctions.
b. gap junctions.
c. adhesion junctions.
d. none of the above

    a. no; tight junctions prevent molecules from passing through epithelial cells
\*    b. yes; consist of small open channels for direct transport between cells
c. no; sites where cells that are subjected to stretching are bound together
d. no; one of the answers is correct

17. Which of the following connective tissues is specialized for storage?
a. adipose
b. loose connective tissue
c. cartilage
d. dense regular connective tissue

\*    a. yes; site for fat storage
b. no; fibrous tissue used for support and elasticity
c. no; strengthening tissue found in nose and ears
d. no; support and elastic tissues such as tendons

18. Which of the following is mismatched?
    a.   cartilage–lacunae
    b.   dense connective tissue–tendons
    c.   loose connective tissue–ligaments
    d.   bone–collagen fibers

    a.   no; correctly matched
    b.   no; correctly matched
    c.   no; correctly matched
*   d.   yes; no collagen fibers are found in supportive elastic tissue such as loose or dense connective tissues, not bone

19. Which of the following tissues is found lining the gut and respiratory tract?
    a.   simple squamous
    b.   simple columnar
    c.   simple cuboidal
    d.   stratified squamous

    a.   no; lines walls of blood vessels and air sacs
*   b.   yes
    c.   no; lines kidney tubules and ducts of some glands
    d.   no; lines mouth and throat and outer surface of skin

20. The most abundant and widely distributed tissue is
    a.   epithelial.
    b.   muscle tissue.
    c.   connective tissue.
    d.   nervous.

    a.   no; basically lining the cavities of the body and covering the surface of the body
    b.   no; large groups of muscles
*   c.   yes; includes bones, blood, cartilage, and adipose tissue
    d.   no; limited to individual nerves, spinal cord, and brain

21. Plastic surgeons utilize ___ to inject wrinkles and to create fuller lips.
    a.   collagen fibers
    b.   ground substance secreted by fibroblasts
    c.   extracellular matrix
    d.   elastin fibers

*   a.   yes; collagen forms protein fibers to serve as structural elements
    b.   no; fibroblast cells secrete a jellylike substance made out of proteins and polysaccharides that forms the matrix around connective tissue
    c.   no; the extracellular matrix shapes the organ where the connective tissue is located
    d.   no; elastin fibers allow some connective tissues to stretch

22. The macrophages found in loose connective tissue function
    a.   to hold the tissue together.
    b.   to allow the connective tissues to stretch.
    c.   to give connective tissue strength to withstand physical stress.
    d.   to protect the collagen tissue and the body from invasion.

    a.   no; collagen fibers hold loose connective tissue together
    b.   no; collagen and elastic fibers allow connective tissue to stretch
    c.   no; fibers and the extracellular matrix give strength to connective tissue
*   d.   yes; macrophages are marauding white blood cells that destroy invaders

23. Which of the following tissues stores mineral salts?
    a.   muscle
    b.   bone
    c.   epithelial
    d.   adipose

    a.   no; minerals are found here in connection with muscle action but not "stored"
*   b.   yes; may be extracted when needed
    c.   no; lines cavities and covers body
    d.   no; stores fat, serves as insulation

24. Cartilage is found
    a.   at the ends of many bones.
    b.   between vertebrae.
    c.   in the external ear and nose.
    d.   all of the above

    a.   yes; a partial answer; a better answer is available
    b.   yes; a partial answer; a better answer is available
    c.   yes; a partial answer; a better answer is available
*   d.   yes; all of the above are correct

25. Cartilage is characterized by
    a.   the presence of collagens and chondrocytes.
    b.   a liquid matrix.
    c.   osteocytes.
    d.   the presence of collagens and fibroblasts.

*   a.   yes; chondrocytes refer to cartilage cells
    b.   no; characteristic of blood
    c.   no; osteocytes are bone cells
    d.   no; describes loose connective tissue found under the skin

26. Cartilage cells are called
    a. osteocytes.
    b. chondrocytes.
    c. macrophages.
    d. adipose tissue.

    a. no; osteocytes are living bone cells
  * b. yes; chondrocytes are cartilage cells
    c. no; macrophages are white blood cells
    d. no; adipose tissue is composed of fat cells

27. Bone cells
    a. form the weight-bearing tissue of the skeleton.
    b. produce red blood cells.
    c. enable most movement to occur.
    d. all of the above

    a. no; the statement is correct, but only a partial answer
    b. no; the statement is correct, but only a partial answer
    c. no; the statement is correct, but only a partial answer
  * d. yes; all of the above are true

28. Bone is known as the major depository for the mineral
    a. manganese.
    b. sodium.
    c. calcium.
    d. potassium.

    a. no; although it may be stored in bone, it is not the major element stored
    b. no; although it may be stored in bone, it is not the major element stored
  * c. yes; the major depository for calcium
    d. no; although it may be stored in bone, it is not the major element stored

**29.** Compact bones are located
    a. in the skull.
    b. in the ends of long bones.
    c. in the center of long bones.
    d. in the shafts of long bones.

    a. no; characterized by spongy bone tissues
    b. no; characterized by spongy bone tissues
    c. no; characterized by spongy bone tissues
  * d. yes; compact bones are found in the shafts of the long bones

30. Blood is included under which of the following tissue types?
    a. epithelial
    b. muscle
    c. connective
    d. nervous

    a. no; forms protective covering
    b. no; enables body movement
  * c. yes; it is considered a "fluid" connective tissue
    d. no; brain, spinal cord, nerves

31. The muscle tissue(s) that is striated is the
    a. skeletal muscle.
    b. smooth muscle.
    c. cardiac muscle.
    d. both (a) and (c), but not (b)

    a. no; a partial answer; skeletal muscle is striated
    b. no; smooth muscle is not striated
    c. no; a partial answer; cardiac muscle is striated
  * d. yes; both skeletal and cardiac muscle are striated, but smooth muscle is not

32. Which of the following types of muscle cells is (are) striated, and branched?
    a. smooth
    b. skeletal
    c. cardiac
    d. both (b) and (c)

    a. no; neither striated or branched
    b. no; striated, but unbranched
  * c. yes; striated and branched
    d. no both (b) and (c) are striated, but only (c) is branched

33. Smooth muscle is found in all but which of the following places?
    a. circular muscles or sphincters such as the pupil of the eye, opening to stomach, and around arteries
    b. the walls of blood vessels
    c. the muscles that move the eye and tongue
    d. surrounding internal organs such as the stomach, bladder, and uterus

    a. no; they are found around these openings that change without voluntary control
    b. no; blood vessels are surrounded by smooth muscles that help to regulate blood flow
  * c. yes; these organs move under voluntary control by the action of skeletal muscles
    d. no; smooth muscles invest these organs to allow them to contract

34. Which of the following is a characteristic of skeletal muscles but not of smooth muscles?
    a. a banded pattern of actin and myosin
    b. contract slowly and maintain tension over longer periods of time
    c. are fusiform, tapered, individual fibers held together by cell junctions
    d. have a single nucleus rather than being multinucleate

\* a. yes; the skeletal muscles show the banding pattern known as striation that does not occur in smooth muscle
b. no; smooth muscles contract slowly for long periods of time
c. no; smooth muscles do not form fascicles or bundles as do the skeletal muscles
d. no; skeletal muscles have multinucleate cells because they are formed from fusion of many individual precursor cells

35. A muscle that is described as striated, uninuclear, involuntary, and possessing intercalated discs would be an example of
    a. skeletal muscle.
    b. cardiac muscle.
    c. smooth muscle.
    d. two of the above choices are correct

    a. no; skeletal muscle is striated but is multicellular and voluntary
\*  b. yes; cardiac muscle has all four features
    c. no; smooth muscle is nonstriated, uninuclear, involuntary and does not have intercalated discs
    d. no; only one of the above is correct

36. The bladder, rectum, and reproductive organs are found in the ___ cavity.
    a. cranial
    b. thoracic
    c. abdominal
    d. pelvic

    a. no; contains the brains
    b. no; location of heart and lungs
    c. no; location of stomach, liver, intestines, and other organs
\*  d. yes; this cavity is the area where these organs are found

37. Which organ system has the following functions: protection from injury, excretion, temperature control, reception of external stimuli, and defense against microbes?
    a. urinary system
    b. lymphatic system
    c. skeletal system
    d. integumentary system

    a. no; of those functions listed, involved in only secretion
    b. no; of those functions listed, involved only in defense
    c. no; of those functions listed, involved only in protection
\*  d. yes; carries out those functions listed

38. The integumentary system
    a. is the primary line of defense against invaders.
    b. is responsible for temperature control.
    c. excretes some wastes.
    d. all of the above

    a. no; only a partial answer; the integumentary system prevents invasion
    b. no; only a partial answer; controls temperature by blood flow through surface capillaries
    c. no; only a partial answer; eliminates some wastes through sweat glands
\*  d. yes; all of the above are correct

39. Homeostasis refers to the ability of an organism to
    a. rid its body of wastes.
    b. maintain a relatively constant internal environment.
    c. maintain a limited range of body temperature.
    d. control the pH of the body fluids within a narrow range.

    a. no; but a better more complete answer is available
\*  b. yes; the most complete therefore the best answer
    c. no; but a better more complete answer is available
    d. no; but a better more complete answer is available

40. Homeostatic mechanisms in an organism
    a. regulate changes that occur within certain limits.
    b. prevents any change from occurring and maintains a set point.
    c. encourages changes in response to changes in external environment.
    d. encourages changes in response to changes in internal environment.

\*  a. yes; prevents excess changes and maintains a relatively small range of internal conditions
    b. no; allows some change within limits and tend to bring conditions back toward a set point
    c. no; external changes (e.g., increased temperature) may provoke actions that lead to changes (e.g. response of sweating)
    d. no; encourages the reduction or limitation of changes in response to internal changes

41. Which of the following is *not* an example of homeostasis?
    a. secretion of buffers to keep the pH of the organ at a set point
    b. the use of sweating or shivering to maintain a body temperature
    c. contraction of leg muscles to maintain upright posture
    d. peristaltic contraction of the stomach to empty the contents into the small intestine

a. no; an example of homeostasis in which buffering maintains a given pH
b. no; a negative feedback system to either heat or cool the body to maintain a constant internal temperature
c. no; one set of leg muscles begins to contract whenever the body leans in one direction and contracts more and more until the leaning is corrected
* d. yes; the emptying of the stomach is a result of stomach muscle contraction, and the contractions may occur while the stomach is empty

42. Which of the following involves a positive feedback mechanism?
a. childbirth
b. temperature control
c. control of blood volume
d. gas content of blood

* a. yes; as oxytocin induces stronger contractions, more oxytocin is released
b. no; as sweating or shivering brings temperature back toward normal, signals reduce the amount of sweating or shivering
c. no; as the blood volume drops, the kidney reduces the volume of urine
d. no; as oxygen level in the bloodstream decreases, the rate of respiration increases

43. Negative feedback means
a. there is no activity occurring in response to an internal change.
b. that as the amount of one substance or action increases there is a decrease in the amount of another substance or action.
c. controls such physiological responses as sexual stimulation.
d. there is no nervous control over the physiological process involved.

a. no; negative feedback does result in some type of reaction or response
* b. yes; as the level of estrogen builds up in the bloodstream, the level of follicle stimulation hormone drops
c. no; an example of positive feedback control
d. no

44. Which of the following is an example of a negative feedback control?
a. continued sexual stimulation leads to a climax
b. the secretion of insulin controls the glucose level in the bloodstream
c. the emptying of the urinary bladder continues until it is essentially empty
d. the secretion of the hormone oxytocin leads to childbirth

a. no; an example of positive feedback control
* b. yes; an example of negative feedback control because as the level of insulin
c. no; an example of positive feedback
d. no; an example of positive feedback

45. Homeostasis requires the action of
a. integrators.
b. sensors or receptors.
c. effectors.
d. all of the above

a. no; a partial answer; the central nervous system has to interpret sensory information
b. no; a partial answer; sensors detect current conditions
c. no; a partial answer; effectors are glands or muscles that bring the body back forward to the set point
* d. yes; all three parts are essential for the body to be aware of internal conditions and to respond in an appropriate way to bring the body back to its set point

# CHAPTER 26

# PROTECTION, SUPPORT, AND MOVEMENT

1. Integumentary means
   a. integral.
   b. protective.
   c. covering.
   d. incumbent.

   a. no; another word
   b. no; another word
   * c. yes
   d. no; another word

2. Which of the following is *not* derived from the skin?
   a. hair and nails
   b. endocrine glands
   c. oil glands
   d. sweat glands

   a. incorrect; derived from the skin
   * b. correct; not derived from the skin
   c. incorrect; derived from the skin
   d. incorrect; derived from the skin

3. The skin produces vitamin
   a. A.
   b. E.
   c. C.
   d. D.

   a. no; another vitamin
   b. no; another vitamin
   c. no; another vitamin
   * d. yes; from ultraviolet radiation on the skin

4. Vitamin D is needed for ____ metabolism.
   a. potassium
   b. iron
   c. calcium
   d. phosphorus

   a. no; another element
   b. no; another element
   * c. yes; the lack of vitamin D produces rickets a bone deformity
   d. no; another element

5. The dermis
   a. anchors the epidermis to the rest of the body.
   b. is composed primarily of epithelial tissue.
   c. is primarily composed of dead cells.
   d. none of the above

   a. no; hypodermis attaches to the dermis and provides this anchoring
   b. no; composed of dense connective tissue
   c. no; epidermis is primarily dead because of keratinization in the mid-epidermis
   * d. yes; none of the above is correct

6. The pigment(s) responsible for skin color is (are)
   a. carotene.
   b. melanin.
   c. hemoglobin.
   d. all of the above

   a. no; a partial answer; abundant pigment in skin of most Asians/Orientals
   b. no; a partial answer; the pigment responsible for tanning
   c. no; a partial answer; the pigment found in capillaries that gives a pink cast to some skin
   * d. yes; all of the above answers are correct

7. Ultraviolet light
   a. ages the skin by destroying the elastin fibers, causing wrinkles and leathery appearance.
   b. could activate the herpes simplex virus and suppress the immune system.
   c. might activate proto-oncogenes and produce skin cancer.
   d. all of the above

   a. no; a partial answer; a more complete answer is available
   b. no; a partial answer; a more complete answer is available
   c. no; a partial answer; a more complete answer is available
   * d. yes; all of the answers are correct

8. The aging of the skin is increased by all but which of the following?
   a. cigarette smoke
   b. ultraviolet radiation
   c. exposure to cold winds
   d. exposure to infrared radiation

   a. incorrect; deepens wrinkles
   b. incorrect; reduces secretion of skin oil
   c. incorrect; stress causes skin to age
   * d. correct; no known effect

9. The tissue responsible for the production of red blood cells is
   a. other red blood cells.
   b. subcutaneous tissues.
   c. bone marrow.
   d. cartilaginous tissue at the ends of long bones.

   a. no; do not have a nucleus and cannot divide
   b. no; tissue located under the skin that does not have anything to do with production of blood cells
   * c. yes
   d. no; responsible for growth of the bone

10. A bone hardens as ____ salts are added to it.
    a. calcium
    b. iron
    c. phosphorus
    d. potassium

    * a. yes; the addition of calcium salts leads to ossification
    b. no; not a common ingredient in the bones
    c. no; not responsible for hardening of bone
    d. no; not responsible for hardening of bone

11. Bones function in
    a. mineral storage.
    b. blood production.
    c. protection and support.
    d. all of the above

    a. no; a partial answer; a more complete answer is available
    b. no; a partial answer; a more complete answer is available
    c. no; a partial answer; a more complete answer is available
    * d. yes; all of the above and more

12. The living cells of bones are the
    a. canaliculi.
    b. osteocytes.
    c. osteoblasts.
    d. lacunae.

    a. no; these are channels that connect osteocytes to each other
    * b. yes; the word means bone cells
    c. no; these are precursors of osteocytes
    d. no; these are spaces in the ground substance that surround the osteocytes

13. Which of the following substances hardens and gives a bone its strength?
    a. calcium salts
    b. collagen fibers
    c. carbohydrates
    d. proteins

    * a. yes; the calcium hardens and the bone is calcified
    b. no; gives strength to bone and some connective tissue
    c. no; gives strength to bone and some connective tissue
    d. no; gives strength to bone and some connective tissue

14. Osteocytes
    a. are cells that produce bone cells.
    b. are found in lacunae.
    c. are part of the Haversian canal system.
    d. secrete calcium and convert cartilage into bone.

    a. no; these cells are called osteoblasts
    * b. yes; these are openings where the osteocytes are found
    c. no; the Haversian system delivers food and gases to the osteocytes
    d. no; calcium is involved in the process; they are not involved in calcium secretion but produce enzymes that mobilize calcium

15. The appendicular skeleton includes the
    a. pelvic girdle.
    b. vertebral column.
    c. sternum.
    d. cranium or skull.

    * a. yes; appendages (feet) are attached
    b. no; part of the axial skeleton
    c. no; part of the axial skeleton
    d. no; part of the axial skeleton

16. The most frequently broken bone(s) is (are) the
    a. ribs.
    b. hip.
    c. collarbone.
    d. ulna.

    a. no; another bone
    b. no; another bone; although this bone often breaks in older people
    * c. yes
    d. no; another bone

17. The synovium is associated with
    a. the pelvic and pectoral girdle.
    b. bone marrow.
    c. the vertebral column.
    d. certain joints.

    a. no; the hip and shoulder do not have a protective pocket around them
    b. no; an internal part of long bones
    c. no; the backbone
    * d. yes; a protective capsule surrounding certain joints that contains a fluid to protect the joint

18. Which of the following statements is false?
    a. Skeletal muscle is the only type of muscle that contracts under voluntary control.
    b. Cardiac muscle contracts intrinsically.
    c. Smooth muscle cannot contract intrinsically.
    d. Cardiac muscle contracts under the stimulus of hormones and nerves.

    a. no; this statement is true
    b. no; this statement is true
    * c. yes; some smooth muscles may contract intrinsically
    d. no; this statement is true

19. Bones are joined to other bones by
    a. ligaments.
    b. collagen fibers.
    c. tendons.
    d. all of the above

    * a. yes; ligaments hold bones together
    b. no; collagen fibers are characteristic of some types
    c. no; tendons connect muscles to bones
    d. no; only one of the above is correct

20. Which of the following is not part of the axial skeleton?
    a. sternum
    b. tarsal
    c. scapula
    d. clavicle

    * a. yes; the breastbone is located at the juncture of the ribs
    b. no; part of the ankle bone
    c. no; the shoulder blade
    d. no; the collarbone

21. The hyoid bone
    a. encloses the frontal sinuses.
    b. supports the tongue and assists in swallowing.
    c. protects the knee joint.
    d. is part of the pectoral girdle.

    a. no; the frontal bone of the cranium surrounds the sinuses
    * b. yes; the hyoid bone is at the base of the tongue
    c. no; this bone is the patella
    d. no; the pectoral girdle is the shoulder that supports the arm, but it does not include the hyoid bone

22. Which of the following statements is false?
    a. The radius is located on the thumb side.
    b. The collarbone is the most commonly broken bone in the body.
    c. The tarsal bones are found in the ankle.
    d. The pectoral girdle refers to the hip.

    a. no; this statement is true
    b. no; this statement is true
    c. no; this statement is true
    * d. yes; this statement is false; the pectoral girdle is the shoulder and the pelvic girdle is the hip

23. Which of the following statements is true?
    a. Every muscle has an antagonistic muscle that works in opposition to it.
    b. The origin is the attachment to the bone that moves the most when it contracts.
    c. The human body has more different bones than muscles.
    d. Reciprocal innervation allows for coordinated movement.

    a. no; many act synergistically
    b. no; the insertion is on the bone that moves the most
    c. no; it has 206 bones and more than 600 muscles
    * d. yes; this statement is true

24. Which of the following includes the others?
    a. actin
    b. myofibril
    c. sarcomere
    d. myosin

    a. no; the thin muscle fibers
    * b. yes; includes the other three
    c. no; the functional unit of a muscle cell
    d. no; the thick filament

25. Which of the following statements is false?
    a. The striated appearance of cardiac and skeletal muscle is based upon the arrangement of actin and myosin filaments.
    b. The myosin forms beaded strands that are fitted together.
    c. A sarcomere extends from one Z-line to another.
    d. Cross-bridging between actin and myosin fibers is responsible for contraction.

    a. no; this statement is true
    * b. yes; this statement is false; actin fibers, not myosin, are beaded
    c. no; this statement is true
    d. no; this statement is true

26. Which of the following is the smallest unit?
    a. myofibril
    b. muscle fiber
    c. actin
    d. skeletal muscle

    a. no; composed of actin and myosin fibers
    b. no; composed of myofibril
    * c. yes; the thin fiber
    d. no; composed of muscle fiber

27. Which of the following statements about anabolic steroid is *not* true?
   a. They are variants of testosterone manufactured by pharmaceutical companies.
   b. They are useful in treating anemia and muscle-wasting disease.
   c. They are safe methods used to increase the size and strength and performance of athletes.
   d. They may be useful to prevent atrophy of muscles that are immobilized after surgery.

   a. incorrect; this statement is true
   b. incorrect; this statement is true
   * c. correct; this statement is false
   d. incorrect; this statement is true

28. According to the sliding-filament model,
   a. actin and myosin filaments slide by each other.
   b. one sarcomere glides by another.
   c. the dark portions of the striations shorten and the light portions lengthen.
   d. the myofilaments swell, resulting in the thickening of the entire muscle fiber.

   * a. yes; actin slides over myosin by forming cross-bridges
   b. no; the sarcomere is the basic unit of contraction
   c. no; this does not happen
   d. no; this happens but does not account for contraction

29. Which of the following statements is true?
   a. The head is on the actin, and the binding site is on the myosin.
   b. The head is on the myosin, and the binding site is on the myosin.
   c. The head is on the myosin, and the binding site is on the actin.
   d. The head is on the actin, and the binding site is on the actin.

   a. no; this statement is false
   b. no; this statement is false
   * c. yes; this statement is true
   d. no; this statement is false

30. ATP is necessary for muscle contraction
   a. to allow the heads to release from the binding sites.
   b. to allow the heads to bind to the binding sites.
   c. to prevent the formation of lactic acid that results in fatigue.
   d. none of the above

   * a. yes; if not available, the muscles will become rigid, as in rigor mortis
   b. no; allows cross-bridging to occur, but ATP must also be present to release the heads from the binding sites to allow ratchet action to move heads to new binding sites
   c. no; ATP will be produced under either aerobic or anaerobic respiration
   d. no; one of the above is correct

31. Cellular organelles that are especially abundant in muscle cells are
   a. mitochondria.
   b. Golgi bodies.
   c. ribosomes.
   d. centrioles.

   * a. yes; the organelle associated with ATP production
   b. no; muscle cells are not particularly involved in secretion
   c. no; not a type of cell that produces many proteins
   d. no; cells normally have only one until they start mitosis, and muscle cells do not divide often

32. Which of the following statements about sliding-filament theory is false?
   a. Myosin filaments physically bind to the actin filaments and pull them toward the center of the sarcomere.
   b. The myosin heads' attachment to actin filaments are called cross-bridges.
   c. The energy from ATP causes myosin to attach to actin.
   d. In rigor mortis, the cross-bridges become locked in place.

   a. no; this statement is true
   b. no; this statement is true
   * c. yes; this statement is false; the ATP allows the cross-bridges to detach
   d. no; this statement is true

33. The attachment of actin and myosin is dependent upon the action of ____ ions.
   a. potassium
   b. sodium
   c. calcium
   d. phosphorus

   a. no; not involved in attachment of actin and myosin
   b. no; not involved in attachment of actin and myosin
   * c. yes; calcium is used
   d. no; not involved in attachment of actin and myosin

34. Calcium ions bind to
   a. actin.
   b. myosin.
   c. troponin.
   d. tropomyosin.

   a. no; bound to another substance
   b. no; bound to another substance
   * c. yes; when the calcium ions bind to troponin, it changes its shape, the actin filament's conformation shifts, and the attachment site is cleared
   d. no; bound to another substance

35. The calcium used in muscle contraction is stored in the
   a. nerves.
   b. sarcoplasmic reticulum.
   c. T tubule.
   d. sarcomeres.

* a. no; the nerves supply the stimulus
* b. yes; the sarcoplasmic reticulum or plasma membrane for muscle fibers stores calcium
  c. no; T tubules speed the spread of action potentials
  d. no; these are the units of contraction

36. Anabolic steroids
    a. are used to lose weight.
    b. increase the size of muscle mass.
    c. enable the body to break down foods more efficiently.
    d. all of the above are true

    a. no; the use of anabolic steroids will increase weight
  * b. yes; used by athletes to "bulk up" and increase muscle mass
    c. no; *anabolism* means to build up
    d. no; only one of the above is true

37. Muscle makes up about ____ percent of body weight.
    a. 30
    b. 40
    c. 50
    d. 60

    a. no; a greater amount
  * b. yes; about 40 percent
    c. no; less than this percentage
    d. no; less than this percentage

38. Lifting weights will increase
    a. the number of muscle cells.
    b. the number of muscles.
    c. the size of individual muscle fibers.
    d. all of the above

    a. no; does not increase the number of muscle cells
    b. no; does not increase the number of muscles
  * c. yes; individual fibers increase in size
    d. no; only one of the above is correct

39. Motor units
    a. consist of an axon of a motor neuron, a neuromuscular junction, and muscle cells.
    b. are composed of different numbers of muscle cells, depending upon the precision of control involved in the muscles.
    c. are the units of muscle contraction; not all muscle cells in a muscle contract at the same time.
    d. all of the above

    a. no; a partial answer; a more complete answer is available
    b. no; a partial answer; a more complete answer is available
    c. no; a partial answer; a more complete answer is available
  * d. yes; all of the above are correct

40. The action of the twenty varieties of anabolic steroids mimics
    a. testosterone.
    b. estrogen.
    c. adrenalin.
    d. cortisone.

  * a. yes; a steroid hormone that increases muscle mass
    b. no; a female steroid hormone that does not affect muscle mass
    c. no; a hormone that stimulates the sympathetic nervous system to trigger the fight or flight response
    d. no; an adrenal steroid that does not affect muscle mass

41. The use of anabolic steroids leads to
    a. lethargy.
    b. docility.
    c. hyperactivity.
    d. aggressiveness.

    a. no; leads to another characteristic
    b. no; leads to another characteristic
    c. no; leads to another characteristic
  * d. yes; may be an artificial advantage in some types of athletic competition

42. Which of the following is defined improperly?
    a. a muscle twitch is the result of a single brief stimulus
    b. muscle fatigue occurs when a hardworking muscle exceeds its supply of ATP
    c. the all-or-none principle refers to the fact that when a muscle contracts, all of its fibers contract and when it relaxes, all of its fibers relax
    d. tetany is an example of maximum temporal summation

    a. no; correctly identified
    b. no; correctly identified
  * c. yes; the all-or-none principle states that a motor unit contracts fully or not at all and when a muscle relaxes, some of its fibers contract to produce muscle tone
    d. no; correctly identified

43. The storage form of energy in a muscle is
    a. glycogen.
    b. ATP.
    c. glucose.
    d. creatine phosphate.

    a. no; although some may be stored in the muscle and liver
    b. no; ATP is the energy currency of the cell and is used rapidly
    c. no; glucose is carried by the bloodstream to muscle where it is used
  * d. yes; creatine phosphate is the way that ATP may be stored in a muscle

44. The production of lactic acid or lactate
   a. is the result of aerobic respiration in muscle cells.
   b. will result in muscle fatigue.
   c. results in tetanus.
   d. does not produce enough ATP for a muscle to function

   a. no; lactate comes from anaerobic respiration
 * b. yes; the accumulation of lactate is toxic and eventually stops muscle contraction
   c. no; tetanus is also called lockjaw and is the result of a bacterial infection
   d. no; anaerobic respiration does produce a limited amount of energy, but enough to allow continued contractions

# CHAPTER 27

# CIRCULATION

1. In the textbook, there is a picture of Dr. Waller's pet bulldog, Jimmie, standing in four bowls of salt water. This photograph illustrates the experiments used to develop a(n)
   a. osmotic test for salt metabolism.
   b. electroencephalograph.
   c. electrocardiogram.
   d. sphygmomanometer.

   a. no; test was not designed to study salt movement
   b. no; did not involve brain waves
   * c. yes; measured the electrical impulse produced in heart contractions
   d. no; not involved in determining blood pressure

2. The circulatory system of humans does all but which one of the following?
   a. production and destruction of blood cells
   b. transport of gases
   c. maintaining body temperature
   d. providing a method of distributing hormones

   * a. yes; the blood cells are formed in the marrow and destroyed by the liver and spleen
   b. no; blood transports oxygen and carbon dioxide
   c. no; the capillaries' reservoirs enable blood to be shifted to the surface to cool the body or to be retained in the body core to retain heat
   d. no; hormones are chemical messengers that are transported by the bloodstream

3. Which of the following is an animal that does *not* have an open circulatory system?
   a. grasshopper
   b. octopus
   c. cat
   d. scorpion

   a. incorrect; has an open system
   b. incorrect; has an open system
   * c. correct; has a closed system
   d. incorrect; has an open system

4. In a bumblebee, the blood returns to the heart by the
   a. veins.
   b. sinuses.
   c. ostia.
   d. capillaries.

   a. no; does not have veins
   b. no; there may be spaces, but this is not the way that blood returns to the heart
   * c. yes; openings into the heart
   d. no; does not have capillaries

5. Blood flows through the ____ circuit(s).
   a. pulmonary
   b. coronary
   c. systemic
   d. both (a) and (c), but not (b)

   a. no; a partial answer; the pulmonary circuit transports gases to and from the lungs
   b. no; although there are coronary arteries and veins, they are not considered to be a separate circuit
   c. no; a partial answer; the systemic circuit involves all of the body other than the lungs
   * d. yes; there are two separate circuits: pulmonary and systemic

6. Blood flows slowest through
   a. the aorta.
   b. larger arteries.
   c. small arteries.
   d. capillaries.

   a. no; greatest rate of movement
   b. no; blood moves quickly
   c. no; blood moves slowly
   * d. yes; must flow slower to allow diffusion to occur

7. The amount of blood found in an average adult male is
   a. five pints.
   b. five liters.
   c. ten liters.
   d. five gallons.

a.　no; more
*　　b.　yes; or, in English measure, about five quarts
　　　c.　no; less
　　　d.　no; less

8.　Hemoglobin transports
　　　a.　oxygen.
　　　b.　carbon dioxide.
　　　c.　glucose.
　　　d.　both (a) and (b)

　　　a.　yes; a partial answer; a more complete answer is available
　　　b.　yes; a partial answer; a more complete answer is available
　　　c.　no; glucose is dissolved in blood plasma
*　　d.　yes; both (a) and (b) are correct

9.　Red blood cells have an average life span of
　　　a.　four days.
　　　b.　four weeks.
　　　c.　four months.
　　　d.　four years.

　　　a.　no; not long enough
　　　b.　no; not long enough
*　　c.　yes; has an average life span of 120 days
　　　d.　no; too long

10.　The heme group of hemoglobin contains a(n) ____ atom at its center.
　　　a.　iron
　　　b.　magnesium
　　　c.　calcium
　　　d.　manganese

*　　a.　yes; the central atom is iron
　　　b.　no; not associated with hemoglobin
　　　c.　no; not associated with hemoglobin
　　　d.　no; not associated with hemoglobin

11.　The color of oxyhemoglobin is
　　　a.　dull red.
　　　b.　bright red.
　　　c.　blue.
　　　d.　pink.

　　　a.　no; the color of hemoglobin
*　　b.　yes; oxyhemoglobin is bright red
　　　c.　no; the color of hemoglobin that is depleted of oxygen
　　　d.　no; not a normal color associated with hemoglobin

12.　Most of the oxygen in the blood is
　　　a.　dissolved in the plasma.
　　　b.　combined with the heme groups in hemoglobin.
　　　c.　combined with the globulin part of hemoglobin.
　　　d.　carried by the blood lipoproteins.

　　　a.　no; very little is found dissolved in the plasma
*　　b.　yes; the oxygen binds with the iron in the heme portion of hemoglobin
　　　c.　no; the globulin portion does not carry oxygen
　　　d.　no; lipoproteins do not carry oxygen

13.　The most common cells in the blood are
　　　a.　red blood cells.
　　　b.　lymphocytes.
　　　c.　leucocytes.
　　　d.　platelets.

*　　a.　yes; 4,500,000–5,000,000/microliter
　　　b.　no; 1,000–2,700/microliter
　　　c.　no; 4,275–10,620/microliter
　　　d.　no; –300,000/microliter

14.　Red blood cells arise from
　　　a.　other red blood cells.
　　　b.　cells in the red bone marrow.
　　　c.　white blood cells.
　　　d.　cells in the yellow bone marrow.

　　　a.　no; they do not have a nucleus
*　　b.　yes
　　　c.　no; may produce more white blood cells
　　　d.　no; yellow marrow enters into fat metabolism but is converted to red marrow under conditions of severe anemia

15.　The most common leukocytes are
　　　a.　neutrophils.
　　　b.　basophils.
　　　c.　monocytes.
　　　d.　eosinophils.

*　　a.　yes; 3,000–6,750/microliter
　　　b.　no; 1,000–2,750/microliter
　　　c.　no; 150–720/microliter
　　　d.　no;100-360/microliter

16.　The least common white blood cells are the
　　　a.　eosinophils.
　　　b.　basophils.
　　　c.　neutrophils.
　　　d.　lymphocytes.

　　　a.　no; 100–360 per ml
*　　b.　yes; 25–90 per ml
　　　c.　no; 3,000–6,750 per ml
　　　d.　no; 1,000–2,700 per ml

17.　Which of the white blood cells is sometimes called a macrophage?
　　　a.　eosinophils
　　　b.　neutrophils
　　　c.　lymphocytes
　　　d.　monocytes

a. no; have roles in inflammatory responses and immunity
b. no; although they do destroy invaders by phagocytosis
c. no; white blood cells involved in immunity
* d. yes; large marauding white blood cells that function through phagocytosis

18. Megakaryocytes produce
a. erythrocytes.
b. leucocytes.
c. platelets.
d. all of the above

a. no
b. no
* c. yes
d. no; only one of the above is correct

19. Megakaryocytes are
a. giant cells that break apart to form platelets.
b. preerythrocytes.
c. cells that divide to form agranulocytes.
d. macrophages that destroy invading bacteria.

* a. yes; small bits of cytoplasm surrounded by a plasma membrane and involved in blood clotting
b. no; preerythrocytes are the precursors of red blood cells
c. no; agranulocytes are white blood cells derived from stem cells in the bone marrow
d. no; macrophages are white blood cells derived from stem cells in the bone marrow

20. Which type of white blood cells are associated with parasitic infections?
a. neutrophils
b. monocytes
c. basophils
d. eosinophils

a. no; not related to parasitic infections
b. no; not related to parasitic infections
c. no; not related to parasitic infections
* d. yes; the number of eosinophils increases when a person is infected with parasites

21. Which of the following white blood cells has neither a lobed nucleus nor granules in the cytoplasm?
a. neutrophils
b. monocytes
c. basophils
d. eosinophils

a. no; have stained cytoplasmic granules and lobed nucleus, as do all granulocytes
* b. yes; white blood cells with an unlobed nucleus and no granules in the cytoplasm
c. no; the suffix-*phil* refers to cells that "love" or pick up stains to show cytoplasmic granules in addition to a lobed nucleus
d. no; the suffix-*phil* refers to cells that "love" or pick up stains to show cytoplasmic granules in addition to a lobed nucleus

22. Which of the following is *not* one of the formed elements of blood?
a. erythrocytes
b. platelets
c. leukocytes
d. plasma

a. no; one of the formed elements
b. no; one of the formed elements
c. no; one of the formed elements
* d. yes; plasma is the fluid portion of the blood, while the formed elements are restricted to the three types of cells

23. Which of the following statements is false?
a. Blood flows more rapidly through the capillaries than through the larger blood vessels.
b. Exchange with the interstitial fluid occurs in the capillaries.
c. Blood pressure forces water and some proteins out of the capillaries.
d. By dividing up the blood flow, capillaries handle the same total volume of flow as the large-diameter vessels.

* a. yes; this statement is false; the blood flow is slower in the capillaries
b. no; this statement is true
c. no; this statement is true
d. no; this statement is true

24. Which of the following is false?
a. Both the systemic and pulmonary circuits begin with arteries.
b. A given volume of blood making the systemic circuit often goes through two or more capillary beds.
c. The pulmonary circuit leaves the right side of the heart and returns to the left side.
d. The blood in the systemic circuit is high in oxygen at the beginning and high in carbon dioxide at its end.

a. incorrect; this statement is true
* b. correct; this statement is false
c. incorrect; this statement is true
d. incorrect; this statement is true

25. The elaborate network of drainage vessels that picks up excess interstitial fluid and returns it to the circulatory system is known as the _____ system.
   a. capillary
   b. venous
   c. interstitial
   d. lymphatic

   a. no; the capillaries supply tissues with material
   b. no; the venous system drains the body and returns blood to the heart
   c. no; there is no specific structure known as the interstitial system; the interstitial space lies between cells
 * d. yes; the lymphatic system picks up interstitial fluid and returns it to the venous system

26. The only artery in the body that carries deoxygenated blood is the
   a. coronary artery.
   b. aorta.
   c. carotid artery.
   d. pulmonary artery.

   a. no; the coronary artery carries oxygen to the heart
   b. no; the aorta is the major artery in the body
   c. no; supplies the head with blood and oxygen
 * d. yes; carries oxygen-poor blood back to the lungs for recharging

27. The largest artery in the body is the
   a. pulmonary artery.
   b. aorta.
   c. superior vena cava.
   d. carotid.

   a. no; a large blood vessel that goes to the lungs
 * b. yes; the largest artery in the body
   c. no; a vein, not an artery
   d. no; a large artery in the neck that supplies the head, but it is not the largest artery

28. The valve that closes when the blood leaves the right ventricle is the
   a. semilunar valve.
   b. tricuspid.
   c. mitral.
   d. bicuspid.

* a. yes; the semilunar valves are found between the ventricles and the arteries leaving the ventricles (aorta or pulmonary artery)
   b. no; the A-V valve called the tricuspid is found between the right atrium and ventricle
   c. no; the mitral valve is found between the left atrium and left ventricle
   d. no; the bicuspid is another name for the atrioventricular valve

29. The initiation of heart contraction begins at the
   a. semilunar valve.
   b. atrioventricular node.
   c. atrioventricular valve.
   d. sinoatrial node.

   a. no; valve at the exit from ventricles; not a site for excitation
   b. no; the second activating site
   c. no; a valve between the atrium and ventricle; not a site for excitation
 * d. yes; the initiator of heart contractions

30. The highest blood pressure outside the heart is found in the
   a. aorta.
   b. femoral arterioles.
   c. capillary beds.
   d. vena cava.

 * a. yes; highest blood pressure found closest to the heart
   b. no; blood pressure drops the farther away from the heart it is measured
   c. no; blood pressure drops the farther away from the heart it is measured
   d. no; blood pressure drops the farther away from the heart it is measured

31. Which of the following is the correct sequence of blood flow through the heart?
   a. left atrium, left ventricle, lungs, right atrium, right ventricle, aorta
   b. right atrium, right ventricle, lungs, left atrium, left ventricle, aorta
   c. right atrium, right ventricle, aorta, right atrium, left ventricle, lungs
   d. left atrium, right ventricle, aorta, right atrium, right ventricle, lungs

   a. no; another sequence is correct
 * b. yes; this is the right sequence
   c. no; another sequence is correct
   d. no; another sequence is correct

32. Another name for the pacemaker of the heart is the
   a. intercalated disc.
   b. sinoatrial node.
   c. atrioventricular node.
   d. Purkinje fibers.

a. no; the intercalated discs are found at junctions between adjoining cardiac muscle cells
* b. yes; initiates cardiac action potential
c. no; propagates the action potential to the ventricles
d. no; these conduct but do not initiate action potentials

33. The systole occurs when the
    a. ventricle relaxes.
    b. ventricle contracts.
    c. atrium contracts.
    d. atrium relaxes.

    a. no; the diastole
* b. yes; the time of maximum blood pressure
    c. no; the pressure from the atrium does not escape to the ventricle
    d. no; the pressure from the atrium does not escape to the ventricle

34. The inner lining of an artery or a vein is called the
    a. endothelium.
    b. basement membrane.
    c. layer of elastic fibers.
    d. smooth muscle layer.

* a. yes
    b. no; found between the endothelium and muscle/fiber layer
    c. no; found outside the basement membrane
    d. no; found outside the basement membrane

35. Which of the following blood vessels has a one-way valve?
    a. artery
    b. vein
    c. arteriole
    d. capillary

    a. no; there are no valves in arteries
* b. yes; veins have one-way valves to assist in moving blood back to the heart
    c. no; arterioles do not have valves
    d. no; capillaries do not have valves

36. The greatest resistance to blood flow occurs in the
    a. aorta.
    b. arterioles.
    c. capillaries.
    d. veins.

a. no; the aorta has the largest diameter and therefore produces little resistance to blood flow
* b. yes; the presence of smooth muscles allows the diameter to be reduced to control the flow of blood
c. no; the capillaries represent diffusion zones with thin walls and low resistance because the large number of capillaries have a large diameter when they are combined together
d. no; veins have thin walls and the ability to expand to accept more blood with very little resistance

37. The majority of the blood at any time would be expected to be located in the
    a. heart.
    b. arteries.
    c. capillaries.
    d. veins.

    a. no; there is another unit that serves as the major blood reservoir
    b. no; there is another unit that serves as the major blood reservoir
    c. no; there is another unit that serves as the major blood reservoir
* d. yes; the major reservoir is the venous system

38. A sphygmomanometer measures
    a. blood pH.
    b. blood volume.
    c. blood pressure.
    d. all of the above and other factors as well

    a. no
    b. no
* c. yes
    d. no; a common distractor, but only one of the above is correct

39. Which of the following statements is false?
    a. The tendency of fluid to leave the circulatory system is greater at the arterial end than the venous end.
    b. Edema is the condition in which fluid tends to accumulate in the interstitial spaces.
    c. Extracellular fluid tends to be taken up at the venous end of a capillary bed.
    d. There is no control over the amount of the blood that flows through a capillary bed.

    a. no; this statement is true
    b. no; this statement is true
    c. no; this statement is true
* d. yes; this statement is false because the smooth muscles in the arterioles control the volume of blood flow into a capillary bed

40. Veins differ from arteries in that they
    a. are reservoirs for blood and contain more blood than arteries.
    b lack valves that are found in arteries.
    c. have higher blood pressure to contend with than arteries.
    d. have a layer of smooth muscles that arteries lack.

  * a. yes; veins hold 50 to 60 percent of the blood
    b. no; veins have valves, arteries do not
    c. no; arteries have higher blood pressure
    d. no; both have smooth muscles

41. Which of the following would occur if there was an internal hemorrhage?
    a. There is a rise in blood pressure.
    b. The medulla sends signals to the heart to beat faster and more forcefully.
    c. The overall outcome is vasodilation.
    d. all of the above are true

    a. no; there would be a drop in blood pressure if there was a hemorrhage
  * b. yes; the increase in pulse rate and strength would increase blood pressure while vasoconstriction of capillaries would lead to funneling the limited blood to the important parts of the body
    c. no; hemorrhage would lead to vasoconstriction, not vasodilation
    d. no; only one of the above choices is true

42. Smoking
    a. increases blood pressure and carbon monoxide concentration in blood.
    b. causes adrenal gland to secrete adrenalin, which is a powerful vasoconstrictor.
    c. causes a more rapid pulse rate.
    d. all of the above

    a. yes; a partial answer
    b. yes; a partial answer
    c. yes; a partial answer
  * d. yes; all of the above are correct

43. Vasodilation of arterioles is triggered by
    a. angiotensin.
    b. sympathetic nervous stimulation.
    c. strenuous muscular exertion.
    d. lack of metabolic activity in the tissue supplied by the arterioles.

    a. no; angiotensin induces vasoconstriction
    b. no; sympathetic nervous stimulator leads to vasoconstriction
  * c. yes; changes in pH, levels of carbon dioxide, and different ions lead to vasodilation
    d. no; when the tissue supplied by the arterioles is inactive, there is no need to bring in blood to the area; therefore, vasoconstriction occurs

44. Which of the following forms of lipoproteins would be considered good for you?
    a. high-density lipoprotein (HDL)
    b. low-density lipoprotein (LDL)
    c. very low density lipoprotein (VLDL)
    d. no; none of the above; all forms of lipoprotein are dangerous

  * a. yes; HDL is known as the good lipoprotein and appears to attract cholesterol out of arterial walls and transport it to the liver
    b. no; high levels of this lipoprotein appear to be associated with heart trouble and appears to increase the amount of fat deposits in blood vessels
    c. no; high levels of this lipoprotein appear to be associated with heart trouble and appear to increase the amount of fat deposits in blood vessels
    d. no; HDL is good, the other two are bad

45. Which of the following statements is false?
    a. Balloon angioplasty is used to counteract plaque.
    b. Low density lipoprotein is the good form of lipoprotein.
    c. Bradycardia is a healthy condition.
    d. Proteins carry cholesterol in the bloodstream.

    a. incorrect; statement is true; balloons break loose or collapse plaque inside the walls of blood vessels
  * b. correct; this statement is false; LDL is bad and HDL is good because it seems to transport cholesterol
    c. incorrect; statement is true; athletes have bradycardia, or slow pulse rate
    d. incorrect; this statement is true

46. Which of the following is the first step in hemostasis?
    a. contraction leading to drawing ruptured blood vessels together
    b. clumping of platelets
    c. spasm of blood vessel
    d. coagulation of blood

    a. no; occurs fourth or last
    b. no; occurs second
  * c. yes; occurs first
    d. no; occurs third

47. The universal donors belong to blood type
    a. A.
    b. B.
    c. AB.
    d. O.

a  no; antigen A on the donor's blood cells would react with antibody A in the recipient's blood

b.  no; antigen B on the blood cells would react with antibody B in the recipient's blood

c.  no; antigen A and B on the donor's blood cells would react with antibody A or B in the recipient's blood

*  d.  yes; because blood type O has no antigens, it will not react with antibodies in any blood type, thereby allowing it to be used in transfusions with any blood

48.  A person with blood type ___ can tolerate a transfusion from all blood types.
a.  A
b.  B
c.  AB
d.  O

a.  no; has antibody B that will react with incoming blood

b.  no; has antibody A that will react with incoming blood

*  c.  yes; has no antibodies that will react with incoming blood

d.  no; has antibodies A and B, which will react with incoming blood

49.  A person who belongs to blood type A has antibodies against type ___ blood.
a.  A
b.  B
c.  both A and B
d.  neither A or B

a.  no; otherwise the person's own blood would clump

*  b.  yes; will have a transfusion reaction if given type B blood

c.  no; although the antibody B will clump red blood cells with B markers

d.  no; but type O has no antigens to trigger the type B antibody

50.  The only safe blood for a person with blood type O would be
a.  A.
b.  B.
c.  AB.
d.  O.

a.  no; the antibodies for A in type O blood would cause the incoming blood to clump

b.  no; the antibodies for B in type O blood would cause the incoming blood to clump

c.  no; the antibodies for both A and B in type O blood would cause the incoming blood to clump

*  d.  yes; there are no antigens in blood type O to react with the antibodies A and B

51.  The situation leading to erythroblastosis fetalis involves
a.  a Rh negative mother, Rh positive child.
b.  a Rh positive mother, Rh negative child.
c.  a Rh negative mother, Rh negative child.
d.  a Rh negative mother, Rh positive child.

a.  no; a positive mother does not become sensitized to produce positive antibodies

b.  no; a positive mother does not become sensitized to produce positive antibodies

c.  no; a negative child does not have positive blood to clump

*  d.  yes; a negative mother can be sensitized and produce positive antibodies that could affect the positive child

52.  The only way for a couple to have a child with the hemolytic disease of the newborn is if the
a.  man is positive and the woman is negative.
b.  man is positive and the woman is positive.
c.  man is negative and the woman is positive.
d.  man is negative and the woman is negative.

*  a.  yes; the negative woman produces positive antibodies if her child inherits the Rh+ from the father so that she becomes sensitive and her antibodies may react with any subsequent positive children

b.  no; the woman has to be negative to be able to produce positive antibodies

c.  no; the woman has to be negative to be able to produce positive antibodies

d.  no; there is no way for the child to inherit Rh+ if both parents are negative

53.  Which child is at risk to the hemolytic disease of the newborn?
a.  first positive child
b.  second positive child
c.  first negative child
d.  second negative child

a.  no; unless the mother was made sensitive by a transfusion with Rh− blood

*  b.  yes; if the mother was sensitized by the first positive child, but the disease is not always expressed

c.  no; negative children cannot express the disease

d.  no; negative children cannot express the disease

54. In atherosclerosis
    a. the blood vessels lose their elasticity.
    b. the blood vessels thicken.
    c. the blood vessels become clogged by fatty deposits.
    d. all of the above

    a. no; this statement is true, but it is only a partial answer
    b. no; this statement is true, but it is only a partial answer
    c. no; this statement is true, but it is only a partial answer
    * d. yes; all of the above are correct

55. Atherosclerotic plaque consists of
    a. increased smooth muscle cells and increased connective tissue components.
    b. lipids deposited within cells and in extracellular spaces.
    c. calcium salts that have been deposited.
    d. all of the above

    a. no; this statement is true, but it is only a partial answer
    b. no; this statement is true, but it is only a partial answer
    c. no; this statement is true, but it is only a partial answer
    * d. yes; all of the above are correct

56. Which of the following statements is false?
    a. The more body fat a person has, the more additional capillaries are required, and the harder the heart has to work.
    b. Nicotine in tobacco produces relaxation and enables a person to relax and reduce hypertension.
    c. Carbon monoxide found in cigarette smoke has a greater affinity for hemoglobin than oxygen.
    d. Until the age of 50 males are at a much greater risk for heart attacks than females.

    a. no; this statement is true
    * b. yes; this statement is false
    c. no; this statement is true
    d. no; this statement is true

57. Which of the following is *not* considered a lymphoid organ?
    a. liver
    b. thymus
    c. tonsil
    d. spleen

    * a. yes; not a tissue that produces infection-fighting cells
    b. no; an example of a lymphoid organ
    c. no; an example of a lymphoid organ
    d. no; an example of a lymphoid organ

# CHAPTER 28

# IMMUNITY

1. The person who developed an immunization procedure against smallpox was
   a. Jenner.
   b. Pasteur.
   c. Lister.
   d. Flemming.

   * a. yes; used injection of cowpox to develop immunity
   b. no; a noted bacteriologist, but not involved in this discovery
   c. no; developed aseptic surgical technique, but did not work on smallpox
   d. no; discovered penicillin, the first antibiotic, but did not work on smallpox

2. Edward Jenner developed the first vaccination in
   a. 1746.
   b. 1796.
   c. 1846.
   d. 1896.

   a. no; too early
   * b. yes
   c. no; too late
   d. no; too late

3. The first successful vaccination procedure used material from a person infected with
   a. smallpox.
   b. cowpox.
   c. chicken pox.
   d. influenza.

   a. no; although sometimes people would survive injection with material from a person infected with smallpox and develop an immunity
   * b. yes; the first vaccination used cowpox
   c. no; chicken pox will not confer immunity against smallpox
   d. no; influenza shots will not help against smallpox

4. The word *vaccination* is derived from the word for
   a. scratch.
   b. cow.
   c. injection.
   d. needle.

   a. no; although material is placed in a scratch
   * b. yes; the first vaccination involved cowpox
   c. no; smallpox vaccination does not use an injection, but a scratch
   d. no; unlike most vaccinations, smallpox does not use a needle for injection

5. Which of the following statements is false?
   a. The first response by the body after an invasion by a pathogen is specific against the invading pathogen.
   b. If the invasion of a pathogen persists, white blood cells initiate a specific response.
   c. One type of immunity involves the production of antibodies by white blood cells.
   d. Some white blood cells can recognize abnormal or foreign cells.

   * a. yes; this statement is false; the first response is the generalized inflammatory response
   b. no; this statement is true
   c. no; this statement is true
   d. no; this statement is true

6. Which of the following is *not* a phagocytic cell?
   a. neutrophil
   b. basophil
   c. eosinophil
   d. monocyte

   a. no; most abundant white blood cell
   * b. yes; secretes histamine and other substances that promote inflammation
   c. no; makes holes in parasitic worms
   d. no; immature macrophages

7. The complement system is composed of
   a. circulating plasma proteins.
   b. native antibodies.
   c. introduced antigens.
   d. phagocytic cells.

* a. yes
   b. no; antibodies are formed in response to exposure to antigen except in ABO blood typing
   c. no; introduced antigens come from outside the body
   d. no; the complement is not cellular

8. Which of the following is false?
   a. Gradients in complement proteins attract phagocytes to an area.
   b. Complement proteins help kill pathogens by promoting lysis.
   c. Complement proteins act antagonistically to phagocytes and antibodies.
   d. both (a) and (b), but not (c)

   a. no; this statement is true
   b. no; this statement is true
* c. yes; this statement is false
   d. no; only one of the above answers is false

9. Which of the following statements is false?
   a. The bacteria that characteristically inhabit the skin and mucus membranes keep pathogens in check by outcompeting them.
   b. The AIDS virus usually enters the body through cuts, lesions, or abrasions in the skin.
   c. The high pH of the skin is one of the most important features that prevents establishment of pathogens on the skin's surface.
   d. When a woman takes an antibiotic for a bacterial infection, she may change the flora (microorganisms) in her vagina and produce conditions that favor a yeast infection.

   a. no; this statement is true
   b. no; this statement is true
* c. yes; this statement is false; the low skin pH is one of the most important features that prevents establishment of pathogens on the skin's surface
   d. no; this statement is true

10. Which of the following is part of the specific response of the body to invasion?
   a. complement proteins, blood-clotting proteins, or infection-fighting substances
   b. interleukins 2
   c. fast-acting white blood cells such as neutrophils and eosinophils
   d. phagocytotic macrophages in the lymph nodes

   a. no; many of these proteins react the same way to all invasions
* b. yes; a chemical signal characteristic of specific infection
   c. no; these are active against all invaders
   d. no; these macrophages are active in the lymph nodes to clear them of any infection

11. Which of the following secrete histamine and prostaglandins?
   a. macrophages
   b. neutrophils
   c. eosinphils
   d. basophils and mast cells

   a. no; phagocytotic cells that take part in both specific and nonspecific responses and present antigens to helper T cells
   b. no; fast-acting phagocytes that participate in inflammation but not the specific response
   c. no; secrete enzymes, attack parasitic worms, and help reduce the inflammation of allergic responses
* d. yes; secrete histamine, prostaglandin, and other substances that act on small blood vessels

12. The chemical associated with rendering the capillaries "leaky" for the purpose of promoting the inflammatory response is which of these?
   a. antihistamine
   b. histamine
   c. histone
   d. immunoglobulins

   a. no; counteracts histamine
* b. yes
   c. no; used as a core in nucleosides, DNA is wound around this protein
   d. no; antibodies

13. Inflammation
   a. causes a localized increase in temperature, increasing the rate of reactions.
   b. results in the blood vessels near the infection site becoming "leaky."
   c. causes local swelling.
   d. all of the above

   a. no; a partial answer; a more complete answer is available
   b. no; a partial answer; a more complete answer is available
   c. no; a partial answer; a more complete answer is available
* d. yes; all of the above are correct

14. The only kinds of cells that produce antibodies are
   a. B cells.
   b. helper T cells.
   c. cytotoxic T cells.
   d. natural killer cells.

* a. yes; produce antibodies and after they are sensitized, they divide rapidly to form antibody secreting cells
b. no; recognize antigen-presenting cells and secrete interleukins that trigger division of B and T cells
c. no; kill abnormal or foreign cells and form a clonal population
d. no; kill infected abnormal or foreign cells

15. Which of the following is *not* an antigen and does *not* contain antigens?
a. "self" proteins
b. viruses and bacteria
c. bee venom
d. cells used in organ transplants

* a. yes; these contain the correct MHC markers, not antigens
b. no; the antigens found on these pathogens trigger the immune response
c. no; a common antigen
d. no; contains antigens; therefore; immunosuppresant drugs are used in conjunction with these procedures

16. Which of the following would *not* elicit an immune response?
a. self MHC marker only
b. any macromolecule recognized as foreign
c. antigen plus self MHC marker
d. damaged or mutant MHC marker

* a. yes; will not trigger the immune response
b. no; will trigger the immune response
c. no; will trigger the immune response
d. no; will trigger the immune response

17. Helper T cells secrete
a. histamines.
b. inteleukin-1.
c. lymphokine.
d. interferon.

a. no; secreted by basophils and mast cells
b. no; secreted by macrophages
* c. yes; secreted by helper T cells
d. no; secreted by cells infected with a virus

18. B cells, helper T cells, cytotoxic T cells, natural killer cells, and memory cells are all examples of
a. neutrophils.
b. eosinophils.
c. lymphocytes.
d. basophils.

a. no; fast-acting phagocytes that take part in inflammation but not sustained response
b. no; secrete enzymes that attack parasitic worms and help reduce inflammation of allergic response
* c. yes; these are all examples of lymphocytes
d. no; secrete histamine and prostaglandins

19. The mucus membranes contain ___ that destroy bacteria.
a. T cells
b. lysozymes
c. antibodies
d. all of the above

a. no; part of the specific response to invasion by specific pathogens
* b. yes; lysozymes are enzymes that are found in mucus, tears, saliva, gastric and intestinal juices
c. no; antibodies are part of the specific response to particular pathogens
d. no; only one of the above choices is correct

20. Nonspecific responses are usually triggered by
a. antigens.
b. tissue damage.
c. interleukins.
d. enzymes.

a. no; are highly specific
* b. yes; the substances released by injured cells turn on the nonspecific response
c. no; communication chemicals involved with the immune response
d. no; enzymes are specific, although lysozymes may function in the first line of defense against invasion

21. All white blood cells arise from division of stem cells located in the
a. thymus.
b. spleen.
c. bone marrow.
d. liver.

a. no; a site where some white blood cells mature
b. no; an organ where red and white blood cells are destroyed
* c. yes; the place where stem cells originate
d. no; an organ where red blood cells are destroyed

22. A virgin B cell
a. has membrane-bound antibodies and has not made contact with an antigen.
b. is an antibody-secreting descendant of an activated B cell.
c. is one of a clonal population of B cells set aside during a primary immune response.
d. modulates or turns off the immune response.

*     a. yes; no contact with antigen
    b. no; a plasma cell
    c. no; a memory cell that is responsible for the rapid secondary response
    d. no; a suppressor cell

23. An antibody is a receptor molecule shaped like the letter
    a. E.
    b. K.
    c. W.
    d. Y.

    a. no; a different shape
    b. no; a different shape
    c. no; a different shape
*     d. yes; with two antigen-binding sites

24. Pore complexes of complement proteins
    a. fuse with plasma membranes of pathogens causing them to lyse.
    b. are activated to produce a cascade of complement.
    c. bind to an antigen to mark them for destruction.
    d. interact with carbohydrates on the surface of a pathogen.

*     a. yes; the gross structural distortion of the plasma membrane leads to death of the virus
    b. no; the cascade of complement may lead to the development of pore complexes
    c. no; one of the ways to activate complement
    d. no; another way to activate complement

25. Mast cells are tissue-dwelling
    a. basophils.
    b. neutrophils.
    c. lymphocytes.
    d. macrophages.

*     a. yes; that are activated by tissue damage to secrete histamines
    b. no; fast-acting phagocytotic cells
    c. no; the B and T cells involved in the specific response
    d. no; larger white cells that eat debris and invade cells

26. Histamines cause
    a. localized edema.
    b. dilation of blood vessels.
    c. the capillary walls to become leaky.
    d. all of the above

    a. no; a partial answer; the accumulation of fluid causes swelling
    b. no; a partial answer; the dilation of blood vessels produces redness and increased temperature
    c. no; a partial answer; the cells separate and allow blood plasma to accumulate
*     d. yes; all of the above are features of the inflammation response

27. A cell with MHC (major histocompatibility complex) markers is said to be marked with a(n)
    a. antigen.
    b. antibody.
    c. self marker.
    d. non-self marker.

    a. no; a protein that marks the cell as foreign
    b. no; a gamma globulin compound that specifically reacts with an antigen
*     c. yes; an MHC marker identifies the cell as self
    d. no; non–self markers indicate that a cell is foreign

28. Which of the following events occurs first in the sequence of response of a B or T lymphocyte to an encounter with a cell with a foreign protein (non–self marker)?
    a. the rapid division of the lymphocyte
    b. the recognition of a non–self marker
    c. the differentiation of specialized effector cells
    d. the differentiation of a group of memory cells

    a. no; the foreign invader has to be recognized first before cell division starts
*     b. yes; the first step is the recognition that the cell has a non–self marker
    c. no; the production of mature effector cells comes after recognition and cell division occurs
    d. no; memory cells are formed concurrently with effector cells

29. Which of the following are the most efficient antibody factories?
    a. virgin B cells
    b. cloned B cells
    c. plasma cells
    d. memory cells

    a. no; have not contacted an antigen so they do not yet produce antibodies
    b. no; some produce antibodies and others divide to form more B cells
*     c. yes; 2,000 antibodies produced each second
    d. no; responsible for response to secondary invasion

30. Which of the following is considered to be the main switch to control the immune system?
    a. memory cells
    b. helper T cells
    c. killer T cells
    d. B cells

    a. no; not effective in the primary infection (have not been formed yet)
*     b. yes; major switch that turns on the production of killer T cells
    c. no; control only the cell-mediated immune response
    d. no; control only the antibody-mediated immune response

31. Which of the following cells produce antibodies?
    a. macrophages
    b. helper T cells
    c. cytotoxic T cells
    d. B cells

    a. no; these are large phagocytic cells
    b. no; these cells secrete chemicals that promote division of T lymphocytes—both effector and memory
    c. no; these cells kill foreign cells individually
    *  d. yes; these cells produce antibodies

32. When phagocytes begin attacking foreign cells, they
    a. destroy the entire cell.
    b. destroy the entire cell but save the antigens that are fragmented and placed on the surface of the phagocytes.
    c. destroy all markers or antibodies of the foreign cell so that it can no longer function.
    d. convert the dangerous foreign cells into harmless cells by removing their MHC markers.

    a. no; they use part of the cell to help the body fight other pathogens
    *  b. yes; then they display the markers to function as an antigen-presenting cell to increase the number of effective lymphocytes
    c. no; the markers are needed to increase the number of effective lymphocytes
    d. no; the markers are not the factors that do harm; they only label the invaders

33. Antibody diversity
    a. is the result of the action of memory cells.
    b. occurs because the plasma cells produce many different kinds of antibodies once they have been turned on.
    c. occurs because of DNA recombinations that occur in the development of B cells in the bone marrow.
    d. both (a) and (c)

    a. no; memory cells produce only one specific type of immune response
    b. no; clones of B cells called plasma cells produce the same kinds of antibodies
    *  c. yes; shuffling DNA
    d. no; only one of the above answers is correct

34. The primary immune response is ____ than the secondary immune response.
    a. slower
    b. of longer duration
    c. more intense
    d. both (b) and (c) are correct

    *  a. yes; it takes longer to produce defensive clones
    b. no; the secondary response lasts longer
    c. no; the secondary response is stronger because of the fast response of memory cells
    d. no; only one of the above answers is correct

35. The *purpose* of a vaccination is to provoke the production of
    a. killer and natural killer T cells.
    b. B cells.
    c. phagocytes.
    d. memory cells.

    a. no; an incidental effect
    b. no; an incidental effect
    c. no; an incidental effect
    *  d. yes; the purpose of vaccinations is to prepare the body to rapidly marshall the immune system defenses the next time the antigen is encountered—this is exactly what memory cells do

36. The trigger that causes the lymphocytes to divide and produce large numbers of effective lymphocytes is the
    a. presence of an antigen-MHC complex on a cell.
    b. presence of interleukin 1.
    c. exposure to an antigen.
    d. first contact with a secretion of histamine.

    *  a. yes; the presence of both antigen-MHC complex on antigen-presenting cells is necessary to start the development of effector and memory clones
    b. no; interleukin 1 is involved in the inflammatory response but interleukin 2 enhances division and differentiation of T cells
    c. no; some antigens may not induce a response
    d. no; only causes the capillaries to become "leaky"

37. T cells mature in the
    a. thyroid gland.
    b. thymus gland.
    c. spleen.
    d. kidney.

    a. no; an endocrine gland that controls basal metabolic rate
    *  b. yes; the thymus gland is part of the immunity system
    c. no; the spleen destroys blood cells
    d. no; does not play a part in the functioning of T cells

38. The difference between helper T cells and cytotoxic T cells is
    a. their origin.
    b. the antibodies they produce.
    c. the number and kind of antigens they display.
    d. that the cytotoxic T cells secrete suppressors that inhibit the action of helper T cells.

a. no; both types of T cells are formed in the bone marrow and develop in the thymus
b. no; B cells, not T cells, secrete antibodies
* c. yes; there is a difference in the number and kind of antigens
d. no; if there are suppressor cells, they would represent a third type of T cell

39. A T cell clone is
    a. produced by the divisions of a T cell once it has been presented by an antigen cell with an appropriate antigen-MHC complex.
    b. a group of genetically identical cells.
    c. differentiated into effector T cells or memory T cells with receptors for the antigen.
    d. all of the above

    a. no; only a partial answer
    b. no; only a partial answer
    c. no; only a partial answer
    * d. yes; all of the above are correct

40. Passive immunity
    a. fails to develop any response on the part of the body's immune system.
    b. utilizes antibodies from other sources to combat an exposure to a pathogen.
    c. is not lasting but is often an effective way to prevent a disease from striking a person.
    d. all of the above

    a. yes; a partial answer
    b. yes; a partial answer
    c. yes; a partial answer
    * d. yes; all of the above are correct

41. Allergies
    a. are supernormal or simple secondary immune responses to a normally harmless substance.
    b. are entirely environmental and have no genetic component.
    c. result in the production of all types of immunoglobulins except IgE antibodies.
    d. all of the above

    * a. yes
    b. no; tendency toward allergy is inherited, but allergies are strongly tied to the environment
    c. no; allergies elicit IgE antibodies
    d. no; only one of the above is correct

42. Passive immunity is accomplished by
    a. vaccination with attenuated or weakened disease-producing organisms.
    b. having a mild case of the disease.
    c. injection of antibodies purified from another source.
    d. injection of antigens purified from another source.

a. no; this procedure would result in active immunization because the person's own immune system has to develop its own antibodies and therefore develops memory cells
b. no; this procedure would result in active immunization because the person's own immune system has to develop its own antibodies and therefore develops memory cells
* c. yes; this procedure would not produce active immunity because the antibodies are not produced by the individual but come from another source
d. no; this procedure would result in active immunization because the person's own immune system has to develop its own antibodies and therefore develops memory cells

43. Active immunity can be developed by
    a. surviving the disease and learning to make the antibodies.
    b. having a vaccine of attenuated or weakened pathogens.
    c. being exposed to genetically engineered viruses.
    d. all of the above

    a. no; the statement is correct, but a more complete answer is available
    b. no; the statement is correct, but a more complete answer is available
    c. no; the statement is correct, but a more complete answer is available
    * d. yes; active immunity results from any procedure in which the ability to produce antibodies against a specific antigen is developed by the immune system

44. If a person were being considered to be a donor for a tissue or organ transplant, the donor's
    a. NK (natural killer) cells would be analyzed.
    b. cytotoxic T cells would be suppressed.
    c. antibodies would be catalyzed and compared to the recipient.
    d. MHC markers would be compared to the recipient.

    a. no; the donor's NK cells would not be a factor in the transplant
    b. no; the donor's cytotoxic T cells would not be a factor in the transplant
    c. no; the donor's antibodies would not affect the transplant
    * d. yes; the MHC would need to be a close match to the recipient to prevent rejection

45. Which of the following immunoglobulins is able to cross the placental barrier?
    a. IgA
    b. IgG
    c. IgM
    d. IgE

a. no; they neutralized ineffective agents
* b. yes; crosses the placental barrier and also transmitted via the mother's milk
c. no; IgM antibodies are the first to be secreted during immune responses
d. no; IgE antibodies bind to basophils and mast cells and release substances (such as histamine) that promote inflammation

46. The AIDS virus
    a. is a retrovirus containing RNA.
    b. does not elicit antibodies because it attacks and destroys the immune system.
    c. will have its RNA converted into DNA by the enzyme reverse transcriptase and then inserted into host chromosomes.
    d. both (a) and (c)

    a. yes; a partial answer
    b. no; antibodies to several HIV proteins are formed
    c. yes; a partial answer
    * d. yes; both (a) and (c) are correct

47. Early symptoms of AIDs include all but which of the following?
    a. weight loss and night sweats
    b. kaposi's sarcoma and a protozoan pneumonia
    c. brown or blue-violet spots on the legs and flu-like symptoms of fatigue and malaise
    d. body rash and itching, low grade fever, and hair loss

    a. no; common symptoms
    b. no; common symptoms
    c. no; common symptoms
    * d. yes; these are not symptoms of AIDS

48. Which of the following sites would be an unlikely place for a battle between invading microbes and the immune system?
    a. a large voluntary muscle such as the diaphragm
    b. a lymph node
    c. tonsils
    d. the adenoids

    * a. yes; the battles would most likely occur near the point of entry or in lymphoid tissue, not in a deep muscle tissue
    b. no; a lymphoid organ
    c. no; a lymphoid organ
    d. no; a lymphoid organ

49. Antigen-presenting cells in the lymphoid organs are
    a. arranged in clusters at the end of blind sacs surrounding lymph nodes.
    b. located near the place where antigens would enter the organ.
    c. dispersed evenly throughout the organ.
    d. found at the place where the blood and lymph leave the lymphoid organ.

a. no; they do not exhibit this distribution because it is not effective
* b. yes; they are located here to be most effective so that the antigen may be engulfed, then presented and allow the cloning of effector cells to begin
c. no; they do not exhibit this distribution because it is not effective
d. no; they do not exhibit this distribution because it is not effective

50. The immune response is halted when
    a. the antigen is removed.
    b. all virgin cells have been converted into effector or memory cells.
    c. the fever drops to normal.
    d. all of the above

    * a. yes; where there are no new antigens, the immune response declines and stops (inhibitory signals from suppressor T cells may also slow down antibody production)
    b. no; this strategy would allow the body to fight only one pathogen at a time
    c. no; there may still be some antibody production occurring as the fever drops
    d. no; only one of the above answers is correct

51. The explanation for the versatility of the immune system to combat the larger variety of antigens available is
    a. the B cells have a high mutation rate.
    b. all forms of antibodies can be produced by the genetic equipment available in any one generalized lymphocyte.
    c. different parts of the genetic information of a lymphocyte are active during its maturation and they are shuffled at random.
    d. generalized antibodies are modified to specifically fit new antigens when they come in contact with them.

    a. no; not a satisfactory explanation—the genetic code is more constant
    b. no; while it may be true that individual lymphocytes have great potential, each one will develop in only one direction so that a generalized lymphocyte cannot be modified to attach any antigen
    * c. yes; and this shuffling provides arrangements that are specific for only a given antigen
    d. no; antibodies are specific and do not change

52. The specificity of an antigen is based upon the ___ of antigen binding sites.
    a. shape
    b. chemical nature
    c. number
    d. constant portion of the heavy chain

* a. yes; the physical shape or configuration determines whether or not it fits an antigen
b. no; the variable portions of the antigen binding sites are different sequences of amino acids
c. no; there are two binding sites—one on each arm of the Y-shaped structure
d. no; if the constant portion were the code for the binding sites, then each antibody could only react with the same antigen

53. The explanation of how many antibodies are able to attack one specific type of antigen is
a. the clonal selection theory.
b. based upon DNA recombination.
c. due to the fact that only virgin lymphocytes with the same gene sequence (the one that codes for the antigen) are the ones that divide to produce the clone of effector cells.
d. all of the above

a. no; the statement is correct, but only a partial answer
b. no; the statement is correct, but only a partial answer
c. no; the statement is correct, but only a partial answer
* d. yes; all of the above are correct

54. Which of the following statements is *not* one of the steps involved in the production of monoclonal antibodies?
a. A mouse is immunized against a specific antigen.
b. Cells are extracted from an immunized mouse's spleen and fused with a cancer cell.
c. White blood cells from an immunized mouse are cloned and then injected into the patient.
d. A clonal population of antibody-producing hybridoma cells are maintained indefinitely, producing all the antibodies that are needed.

a. no; this is one of the steps in preparing monoclonal antibodies
b. no; this is one of the steps in preparing monoclonal antibodies
* c. yes; this is not one of the steps involved in producing monoclonal antibodies
d. no; this is one of the steps in preparing monoclonal antibodies

55. Which of the following statements is false?
a. Extreme allergic reactions may lead to anaphylactic shock.
b. Antihistamines are drugs that increase the body's inflammatory response.
c. Allergies are excessive responses of the immune system to a substance that is not life threatening.
d. Hybridoma cells used in manufacture of monoclonal antibodies are produced by the fusion of mouse spleen cells with cancer cells.

a. no; this statement is true
* b. yes; this statement is false; antihistamines are drugs that counteract histamines that trigger the inflammatory response
c. no; this statement is true
d. no; this statement is true

# CHAPTER 29

# RESPIRATION

1. Which of the following animals do not depend on integumentary exchange?
   a. earthworms
   b. humans
   c. flatworms
   d. nematodes

   a. no; depend on diffusion through integument to supply body with oxygen
*  b. yes; too large to depend on integumentary exchange; have lungs for gas exchange
   c. no; depend on diffusion through integument to supply body with oxygen
   d. no; depend on diffusion through integument to supply body with oxygen

2. All respiratory systems depend upon
   a. diffusion of dissolved gases.
   b. osmosis.
   c. bulk flow.
   d. active transport.

*  a. yes; the simple diffusion from a moist surface to a capillary system
   b. no; osmosis refers to the movement of a solvent
   c. no; responsible for movement of material from a source to a sink
   d. no; energy expenditure is not essential

3. Which gas has the highest concentration in the atmosphere?
   a. carbon dioxide
   b. oxygen
   c. nitrogen
   d. other gases

   a. no; less than 0.04 percent
   b. no; approximately 21 percent
*  c. yes; approximately 78 percent
   d. no; less than 1 percent

4. The barometric pressure at sea level is ____ mm of mercury.
   a. 340
   b. 570
   c. 620
   d. 760

   a. no; too low
   b. no; too low
   c. no; too low
*  d. yes; 760 mm or 29.92 inches

5. Which of the following is not a major factor controlling how fast oxygen or carbon dioxide diffuses across the respiratory surface?
   a. exposed surface area of the respiratory membrane
   b. thickness of the respiratory membrane
   c. the temperature of the air
   d. the partial pressure of gases across the respiratory membrane

   a. no; this factor does influence diffusion rates
   b. no; this factor does influence diffusion rates
*  c. yes; temperature is not a major factor controlling diffusion
   d. no; this factor does influence diffusion rates

6. Which of the following is false?
   a. Flatworms are small enough not to require a circulatory system.
   b. Humans would be unable to survive on the low concentrations of oxygen dissolved in water.
   c. In most large animals, the diffusion of oxygen at the body surface is fast enough to sustain the respiratory needs.
   d. Oxygen must dissolve in some fluid before it is able to move from the external environment to the interior of an organism.

    a.   no; this statement is true
    b.   no; this statement is true
\*   c.   yes; this statement is false
    d.   no; this statement is true

7.   External gills are characteristic of
    a.   some amphibians.
    b.   some fishes.
    c.   some insects.
    d.   both (a) and (c)

    a.   no; a partial answer
    b.   no; fish gills are covered by a flap of skin, the operculum
    c.   no; a partial answer
\*   d.   yes; both (a) and (c) are correct

8.   A spiracle associated with a trachea
    a.   allows the level of carbon dioxide to build up.
    b.   makes the gases flow in only one direction.
    c.   prevents excessive water loss through evaporation.
    d.   increases the efficiency of the respiratory system.

    a.   no; does not affect carbon dioxide concentration to any great extent
    b.   no; oxygen may enter and carbon dioxide may leave the trachea
\*   c.   yes; prevents excessive evaporation
    d.   no

9.   Bird respiratory systems are characterized by
    a.   tracheae.
    b.   air sacs.
    c.   gas exchange occurring in both inhale and exhale cycles.
    d.   both (b) and (c)

    a.   no; tubes found in insects for gas transport
    b.   no; a partial answer; a more complete answer is available
    c.   no; a partial answer; a more complete answer is available
\*   d.   yes; both (b) and (c) are correct

10.  Before entering the pharynx air is
    a.   filtered.
    b.   moistened.
    c.   warmed.
    d.   all of the above

    a.   no; a partial answer; a more complete answer is available
    b.   no; a partial answer; a more complete answer is available
    c.   no; a partial answer; a more complete answer is available
\*   d.   yes; all of the above are correct

11.  Which of the following is a cavity where air is warmed, moistened, and partially filtered?
    a.   oral cavity
    b.   nasal cavity
    c.   pharynx
    d.   larynx

    a.   no; a supplementary airway
\*   b.   yes; these activities take place in the nasal cavity
    c.   no; a connecting airway between the nasal and oral cavities and the larynx
    d.   no; the voice box containing the vocal cords

12.  The air that reaches the alveoli has been cleaned by the action of
    a.   nose hairs.
    b.   ciliated epithelium lining parts of the respiratory tree.
    c.   mucus secreted along the respiratory tract.
    d.   all of the above

    a.   no; a partial answer; a more complete answer is available
    b.   no; a partial answer; a more complete answer is available
    c.   no; a partial answer; a more complete answer is available
\*   d.   yes; all of the above are correct

13.  The epiglottis partially covers
    a.   the esophagus.
    b.   the food passage to prevent air from getting in the digestive tract.
    c.   the air passage to the larynx.
    d.   both (a) and (b), but not (c)

    a.   no; if this happened, food would not enter the digestive tract
    b.   no; not a problem for most eaters (except newborn infants that need to burp after taking a bottle)
\*   c.   yes; to prevent food from entering the lungs
    d.   no; both (a) and (b) are incorrect

14.  Which of the following statements is false?
    a.   The space between the vocal cords is the glottis.
    b.   The greater the air pressure on the vocal cords, the louder the sound.
    c.   The greater the tension on the vocal cords, the lower the pitch of the sound produced.
    d.   The epiglottis is usually in the position to leave the glottis open.

    a.   no; this statement is true
    b.   no; this statement is true
\*   c.   yes; this statement is false; the greater the tension, the higher the pitch of the sound produced
    d.   no; this statement is true

15. The tube leading to each individual lung is the
    a. trachea.
    b. larynx.
    c. pharynx.
    d. bronchus.

    a. no; leads to the two bronchi
    b. no; voice box
    c. no; the throat
    * d. yes; the bronchi lead to the lungs

16. Which of the following is mismatched?
    a. septum–partition separating nasal cavities
    b. sinuses–spaces
    c. pharynx–Adam's apple
    d. vocal cords–elastic ligaments

    a. no; matched correctly; the system separates the two nasal cavities
    b. no; matched correctly; sinuses are spaces
    * c. yes; mismatched; the pharynx is the throat and the Adam's apple is part of the larynx
    d. no; matched correctly; the elastic nature controls vibration frequency

17. The large muscle that separates the lungs from the abdominal cavity is the
    a. alveolus.
    b. bronchus.
    c. pleura.
    d. diaphragm.

    a. no; the air sac where gas exchange occurs
    b. no; the large tubes leading to the lungs
    c. no; the membrane surrounding the lungs
    * d. yes; its contraction increases space inside the lungs

18. The muscles found between the ribs are known as the
    a. diaphragm.
    b. pectoralis.
    c. intercostal.
    d. pleural.

    a. no; large muscle responsible for breathing
    b. no; large chest muscle external to the ribs
    * c. yes; these muscles are found between the ribs
    d. no; no muscles by this name

19. The goal of the Heimlich maneuver is
    a. to forcibly raise the diaphragm.
    b. to increase the space available in the lungs.
    c. to expand the volume in the chest cavity.
    d. none of the above

    * a. yes; and possibly the reduction in space will force any blockage out of the respiratory passage
    b. no; this would force the blocking object into the lungs
    c. no; actually want to increase internal pressure on the lungs to expel the foreign item
    d. no; one of the above is correct

20. When the diaphragm contracts,
    a. it moves upward.
    b. it moves downward.
    c. the other muscles lower and reduce the size of the pleural cavity.
    d. both (a) and (c), but not (b)

    a. no; must move downward to increase the size of the pleural cavity
    * b. yes; it moves downward into the abdominal cavity
    c. no; must raise and move the rib cage outward
    d. no; (a) and (c) are both incorrect

21. The diaphragm
    a. separates the thoracic and pleural cavities.
    b. separates the thoracic and abdominal cavities.
    c. is directly responsible for the expansion of the rib cage.
    d. is a membrane composed of connective tissue.

    a. no; the pleural cavities lie within the thoracic cavity and are separated from it by the pleura
    * b. yes; the muscular diaphragm separates the two major cavities of the body
    c. no; intercostal muscles raise and lower the rib cage
    d. no; the diaphragm is a muscle

22. Contraction of the diaphragm and intercostal muscles is under the control of the
    a. reticular formation.
    b. cerebral cortex.
    c. hypothalamus.
    d. thalamus.

    * a. yes; a system of neurons that run through the brainstem
    b. no; the cerebral cortex is in control of higher functions; a vital function such as breathing would be controlled by a center lower in the brain
    c. no; the area of the brain concerned with neural-endocrine control of visceral activities
    d. no; the switching station for the forebrain

23. The primary trigger for breathing is
   a. an increase in carbon dioxide in the blood.
   b. a decrease of oxygen in the blood.
   c. an increase in the pH of the blood.
   d. both (a) and (c), but not (b)

   * a. yes; the buildup of carbon dioxide triggers breathing
   b. no; the amount of oxygen in the blood is secondary and is usually triggered when the body is at high altitudes
   c. no; the increase in carbon dioxide decreases blood pH to trigger breathing
   d. no; (a) is correct but (c) is wrong; breathing occurs when blood pH drops

24. The movement of oxygen across the lungs to the capillaries involves
   a. active transport.
   b. bulk flow.
   c. osmosis.
   d. diffusion.

   a. no; no extra energy needs to be expended
   b. no
   c. no; does not involve movement of water
   * d. yes; simple diffusion is enough to account for the movement of oxygen

25. The majority of the carbon dioxide in the blood
   a. is carried by the hemoglobin molecule.
   b. is dissolved in the blood plasma.
   c. is carried by the bicarbonate ion.
   d. changes proportions depending on metabolic conditions.

   a. no; some carried by hemoglobin, but oxyhemoglobin is more common
   b. no; some simply carried as a dissolved gas
   * c. yes; the majority carried in bicarbonate ions
   d. no; the amount may change, but not greatly enough to change proportions

26. Each hemoglobin molecule binds with ____ oxygen molecule(s).
   a. one
   b. two
   c. four
   d. eight

   a. no; too few
   b. no; too few
   * c. yes; with four molecules
   d. no; too many

27. The majority of the oxygen in the blood
   a. is carried by the hemoglobin molecule.
   b. is dissolved in the blood plasma.
   c. is carried by the bicarbonate ion.
   d. changes proportions depending on metabolic conditions.

   * a. yes; majority of oxygen carried by oxyhemoglobin
   b. no; about one molecule in seventy
   c. no; not involved in oxygen transport
   d. no; not a major factor

28. Sensory receptors known as _____ monitor carbon dioxide levels.
   a. aortic bodies
   b. pulmonary bodies
   c. carotid bodies
   d. both (a) and (c), but not (b)

   a. no; a partial answer; a more complete answer is available
   b. no; the pulmonary blood vessels do not have monitoring sites
   c. no; a partial answer; a more complete answer is available
   * d. yes; both the aortic and carotid bodies monitor carbon dioxide concentration in the blood

29. Which of the following would tend to make hemoglobin release oxygen?
   a. a rise in the partial pressure of oxygen
   b. a rise in carbon dioxide
   c. a drop in temperature
   d. rise in blood pH

   a. no; this would increase the amount of oxygen picked up by hemoglobin
   * b. yes; as carbon dioxide level rises (as in metabolically active tissue), oxygen is released by hemoglobin
   c. no; as temperature drops, oxygen is retained and as temperature rises, oxygen is released
   d. no; as the blood becomes less acidic, hemoglobin retains oxygen

30. Carbon dioxide is transported from the metabolically active tissue to the lungs by
   a. being dissolved in the blood plasma.
   b. being carried in the form of bicarbonate.
   c. combining with hemoglobin to form carbaminohemoglobin.
   d. all of the above

a. no; a partial answer; a more complete answer is available
b. no; a partial answer; a more complete answer is available
c. no; a partial answer; a more complete answer is available
* d. yes; all of the above are correct

31. Which acid is associated with the movement of carbon dioxide?
   a. acetic acid
   b. hydrochloric acid
   c. carbonic acid
   d. citric acid

   a. no; an organic acid not involved with the movement of carbon dioxide
   b. no; an inorganic acid not involved with the movement of carbon dioxide
   * c. yes; formed when carbon dioxide combines with water
   d. no; an organic acid not involved with the movement of carbon dioxide

32. The enzyme carbonic anhydrase
   a. switches the respiration in a cell from the aerobic to the anaerobic pathway.
   b. mediates the reaction that enables carbon dioxide to enter red blood cells.
   c. splits the carbaminohemoglobin molecule, releasing oxygen.
   d. increases the affinity of hemoglobin for oxygen.

   a. no; this change occurs when all the hydrogen acceptors in the cell are in the reduced form
   * b. yes; speeds up the uptake of carbon dioxide by the red blood cells
   c. no; oxygen is not released from carbaminohemoglobin
   d. no; does not affect the affinity of hemoglobin for oxygen

33. Which of the following function in the buffering of the blood?
   a. hemoglobin
   b. carbonic acid/bicarbonate
   c. some plasma proteins
   d. all of the above

   a. no; a partial answer; a more complete answer is available
   b. no; a partial answer; a more complete answer is available
   c. no; a partial answer; a more complete answer is available
   * d. yes; all of the above function in the buffering of the blood

34. Which of the following statements is false?
   a. Asthma usually affects the upper reaches of the respiratory tree, particularly the windpipe.
   b. Asthma is a chronic incurable disease.
   c. Allergens can set off an asthma attack.
   d. The contraction of smooth muscles in the respiratory tree is responsible for the symptoms of asthma.

   * a. yes; this statement is false; the rings of the cartilage in the upper respiratory tract keep the airway open and prevent the smooth muscles from collapsing the windpipe
   b. no; this statement is true
   c. no; this statement is true
   d. no; this statement is true

35. Which of the following conditions shows the greatest improvement after a person stops smoking?
   a. risk of lung cancer
   b. risk of heart attacks
   c. cancers of other body organs such as esophagus, mouth, pancreas, larynx, and bladder
   d. none of the above; there is a slow change in risks that may take eight to fifteen years to reach the risk levels of someone who never smoked

   a. no; it takes ten to fifteen years to lower risk to the level of nonsmokers
   * b. yes; there is a very sharp drop in the first year
   c. no; it takes ten to fifteen years to lower risk to the level of nonsmokers
   d. no; there is one factor in which there is an immediate improvement

36. Pleurisy results from
   a. fluid filling the interpleural cavity.
   b. inflammation of the alveoli.
   c. filling of the alveoli with fluid.
   d. the inability to fully expel residual air in the lungs.

   * a. yes; the normal lubricating fluid interferes with the expansion of the alveoli
   b. no; pleurisy occurs outside the alveoli
   c. no; pleurisy occurs outside the alveoli
   d. no; there is a small volume of residual air that cannot be forced out of the lungs

37. Which of the following statements is false?
    a. Ventilation includes both inspiration and expiration.
    b. The diaphragm contracts when you exhale.
    c. As the chest cavity expands, the pressure of the interpleural space drops below atmospheric pressure.
    d. Exhalation is a passive activity.

    a. no; this statement is true.
  * b. yes; this statement is false
    c. no; this statement is true
    d. no; this statement is true

38. Which of the following statements is true?
    a. Ventilation and respiration are synonyms.
    b. In external respiration, air is brought into the lungs.
    c. Respiration is the muscular activity leading to gas exchange.
    d. In internal respiration, oxygen is moved from the blood to the tissue and carbon dioxide leaves tissues and moves into the blood.

    a. no; this statement is false; ventilation involves muscular activity to move gases while respiration involves diffusion of gases
    b. no; this statement is false; the description fits inhalation
    c. no; this statement is false; respiration involves gaseous diffusion
  * d. yes; this statement is true

39. Air pollution may
    a. cause bronchitis.
    b. interfere with the ciliary action of the ciliated epithelium in the lungs.
    c. increase the secretion of mucus and increase the number of mucus producing cells.
    d. all of the above

    a. no; a partial answer; a more complete answer is available
    b. no; a partial answer; a more complete answer is available
    c. no; a partial answer; a more complete answer is available
  * d. yes; all of the above may lead to an inflammation of the bronchi

40. In emphysema
    a. there is a reduction in the number of capillaries surrounding the alveoli.
    b. the elastic tissue of the alveoli breaks down and the alveoli become surrounded by thick, stiff fibrous tissue.
    c. there is difficulty in inhaling air, but no trouble expelling air.
    d. all of the above

    a. no; the number of capillaries around the alveoli are not the prime feature of emphysema
  * b. yes; the lack of elastic tissue makes it hard to empty the lungs
    c. no; the difficulty is in exhaling, not inhaling
    d. no; only one of the above answers is correct

41. In emphysema
    a. the bronchioles become clogged.
    b. the alveoli become enlarged.
    c. the alveoli fill with fluid.
    d. the spaces around the alveoli become filled with fluid.

    a. no; a number of conditions could produce this
  * b. yes; the lungs enlarge and lose flexibility
    c. no; characteristic of some pneumonia
    d. no; characteristic of pleurisy

42. The enzyme antitrypsin may prevent
    a. bronchitis.
    b. emphysema.
    c. lung cancer.
    d. all of the above

    a. no; it is not effective in bronchitis
  * b. yes; the enzyme inhibits tissue-destroying enzymes produced by bacteria
    c. no; not effective against cancer
    d. no; only one of the above is correct

43. Cigarette smoking
    a. inhibits ciliary action.
    b. stimulates mucus production.
    c. kills infection-fighting phagocytes.
    d. all of the above

    a. no; a partial answer; a more complete answer is available
    b. no; a partial answer; a more complete answer is available
    c. no; a partial answer; a more complete answer is available
  * d. yes; all of the above are reactions to cigarette smoke

44. It has been recently shown that smoking dramatically increases the chances that the smoker will develop
    a. cataracts.
    b. glaucoma.
    c. astigmatism.
    d. night blindness.

  * a. yes; somehow it causes the lens to cloud
    b. no; smoking has not been implicated in this condition
    c. no; smoking has not been implicated in this condition
    d. no; smoking has not been implicated in this condition

45. Deep sea divers have to be careful of the accumulation of _____ in the tissues to avoid the occurrence of the bends.
    a. hydrogen
    b. oxygen
    c. carbon dioxide
    d. nitrogen

    a. no; not the gas involved in bends
    b. no; not the gas involved in bends
    c. no; not the gas involved in bends
    * d. yes; can accumulate in the body at high pressure and produces severe pain known as the bends when the body returns to normal air pressure

46. Nitrogen gas may accumulate in ___ tissue of a deep sea diver.
    a. adipose
    b. brain
    c. connective
    d. muscle

    * a. yes; nitrogen tends to accumulate in this tissue
    b. no; although nitrogen may reach this tissue, it is not a storage site
    c. no; although nitrogen may reach this tissue, it is not a storage site
    d. no; although nitrogen may reach this tissue, it is not a storage site

47. The pain of the bends occurs in the
    a. stomach.
    b. muscles.
    c. blood vessels.
    d. joints.

    a. no; not the site of most pain
    b. no; not the site of most pain
    c. no; not the site of most pain
    * d. yes; the nitrogen gas causes pain at the joints

48. At depths of more than 150 meters, the accumulation of ___ induces a euphoria or narcosis.
    a. oxygen
    b. carbon dioxide
    c. nitrogen
    d. helium

    a. no; not the gas
    b. no; not the gas
    * c. yes; the condition is referred to as nitrogen narcosis
    d. no; not the gas

49. Hypoxia occurs
    a. at high altitudes.
    b. when carbon monoxide competes with oxygen for the hemoglobin molecule.
    c. during hyperventilation before compensation for lack of oxygen has been reached.
    d. all of the above

    a. yes; a better answer is available
    b. yes; a better answer is available
    c. yes; a better answer is available
    * d. yes; under all of the above conditions there is a lack of oxygen in the bloodstream

50. A disease that was very rare in the United States but has dramatically increased in recent years, perhaps because of AIDS and drug resistant strains, is
    a. influenza.
    b. tuberculosis.
    c. pneumonia.
    d. bronchitis.

    a. no; there are flu epidemics almost every year
    * b. yes; a very dramatic recent rise in this disease
    c. no; not a noticeable increase, although many AIDS patients may eventually succumb to a form of pneumonia
    d. no; bronchitis is an inflammation of the bronchi that may have many causes

# CHAPTER 30

# DIGESTION AND HUMAN NUTRITION

1.  In which of the following organs does no digestion actually take place?
    a.  mouth
    b.  esophagus
    c.  stomach
    d.  small intestine

    a.  no; the enzyme amylase in saliva begins the process of digestion by splitting starch
    * b.  yes; simply a muscular tube connecting the pharynx with the stomach
    c.  no; protein digestion begins here
    d.  no; the majority of digestion occurs here

2.  In addition to digestion, the digestive system is characterized by
    a.  movement.
    b.  secretion.
    c.  absorption.
    d.  all of the above

    a.  yes; a partial answer; to allow mixing and passage of food through the system
    b.  yes; partial answer
    c.  yes; a partial answer; to make food available to the rest of the body
    * d.  yes; all of the above are correct

3.  Which of the following are classified as ruminant animals?
    a.  parasitic flatworms
    b.  birds
    c.  cattle
    d.  humans

    a.  no; have an incomplete digestive system
    b.  no; have a standard complete digestive tract
    * c.  yes; have four stomachlike chambers
    d.  no; have a standard complete digestive tract

4.  Peristalsis
    a.  refers to the contraction of smooth muscles in the digestive tract.
    b.  is independent of neural or hormonal control.
    c.  involves chewing food in the mouth.
    d.  refers only to the contraction of the sphincter that allows food to enter and leave the stomach.

    * a.  yes; involved in mixing food with enzymes in digestive organs
    b.  no; the smell of food can initiate stomach contractions
    c.  no; called mastication, a voluntary muscular action
    d.  no; involves the smooth muscles in the walls of digestive organs

5.  Peristalsis and segmentation are involved in
    a.  increasing efficiency of digestive enzymes.
    b.  the process of secretion of hormones and enzymes.
    c.  providing motility to food materials.
    d.  both (a) and (c), but not (b)

    a.  no; a partial answer; by increasing the contact of enzymes with their substrate, digestion occurs more rapidly
    b.  no; muscular movement is not thought to stimulate secretion
    c.  no; partial answer; these two muscular contractions mix food and force it through the digestive tract
    * d.  yes; see answers (a) and (c)

6.  Saliva
    a.  contains no digestive enzymes, only mucus.
    b.  initiates the digestion of starch.
    c.  initiates the digestion of fats.
    d.  initiates the digestion of proteins.

a. no; amylase is present
* b. yes; amylase begins the digestion of starch
c. no; no fat-digesting enzymes are available in saliva
d. no; no protein-digesting enzymes are available in saliva

7. The hardest substance in the body is
a. tooth enamel.
b. tooth dentine.
c. bone.
d. dental pulp.

* a. yes; the hardest material
b. no; this is bonelike material underneath the enamel
c. no; bones are not necessarily very hard
d. no; this is the soft tissue underlying the crown and surrounded by the root

8. Emulsification
a. breaks down cholesterol.
b. produces gallstones.
c. causes cholecystitis.
d. increases surface area of fat droplets in the small intestine.

a. no; does not contain enzymes
b. no; gallstones are mineral deposits
c. no; inflammation of the gallbladder results from gallstones
* d. yes; when the fat droplets remain separated, the lipase are able to digest fats more rapidly

9. Protein digestion begins in the
a. mouth.
b. stomach.
c. small intestine.
d. esophagus.

a. no; polysaccharide digestion (starch specifically) starts here
* b. yes; protein digestion begins in the acid environment here
c. no; most of digestion is completed here
d. no; no digestion occurs here; simply a connection between mouth and stomach

10. The speed at which food moves through the stomach is influenced by
a. the size of the meal just eaten.
b. the influence of hormones.
c. fear, depression, and emotional condition.
d. all of the above

a. yes; a partial answer; a more complete answer is available
b. yes; a partial answer; a more complete answer is available
c. yes; a partial answer; a more complete answer is available
* d. yes; all of the above are correct

11. Which of the following statements is false?
a. The epiglottis covers the trachea when you swallow.
b. The pharynx and esophagus are not involved in digestion.
c. The stomach often begins its secretion before food is put in the mouth.
d. Gastrin is an enzyme that digests proteins.

a. incorrect; this statement is true
b. incorrect; this statement is true
c. incorrect; this statement is true
* d. correct; this statement is false; gastrin is a hormone, not an enzyme

12. Gastric juice includes all but
a. hydrochloric acid.
b. gastrin.
c. pepsinogen.
d. mucus.

a. no; part of gastric juice
* b. yes; this hormone is secreted into the blood in response to the presence of gastric juice
c. no; part of gastric juice
d. no; part of gastric juice

13. Bicarbonate is secreted by the
a. small intestine.
b. gallbladder.
c. pancreas.
d. stomach.

a. no; although its the site of bicarbonate action
b. no
* c. yes
d. no

14. The innermost layer of the wall that surrounds the organs of the digestive tract is the
a. serosa.
b. mucosa.
c. muscle layer.
d. lumen.

a. no; the serosa is the outer layer of a digestive organ
* b. yes; the mucosa lies under the submucosa and surrounds the lumen
c. no; the muscle layer lies between the serosa and the submucosa
d. no; the lumen is the cavity of the internal organs of the digestive tract

15. Excess undigested food may be stored in the
a. liver.
b. stomach.
c. small intestine.
d. large intestine.

a. no; undigested food never reaches the liver
* b. yes; some excess food may be stored in the stomach waiting for the opportunity to pass through the pyloric sphincter to the small intestine
c. no; food is digested and absorbed in the small intestine
d. no; almost all food that can be digested has been digested by the time it reaches the large intestine

16. Fecal material is stored in the
    a. appendix.
    b. anus.
    c. rectum.
    d. colon.

    a. no; a vestigial structure that does not have a function
    b. no; the terminal opening of the digestive tract
    * c. yes; the rectum refers to the lower end of the digestive tract where feces are stored prior to elimination
    d. no; another name for the large intestine were undigested material is concentrated; the storage is limited to the posterior end of the colon

17. Bile is stored and concentrated by the
    a. liver.
    b. gallbladder.
    c. small intestine.
    d. common bile duct.

    a. no; the liver is the site of the bile production
    * b. yes; the bile is collected in this organ
    c. no; the small intestine is the site where bile is released to emulsify fats
    d. no; the common bile duct drains the gallbladder, while the bile is transported to the gallbladder by the cystic duct

18. Bile contains all but which of the following?
    a. digestive enzymes
    b. bile salts and pigments
    c. cholesterol
    d. lecithin (a phospholipid)

    * a. yes; contains no digestive enzymes
    b. no; bile salts aid in the emulsification (making small droplets) and digestion of fats in the small intestine
    c. no; one of the ways cholesterol is removed from the body
    d. no

19. The teeth that are essential for eating corn on the cob or biting into an apple or sandwich are the
    a. premolars or bicuspids.
    b. cuspids or canines.
    c. molars.
    d. incisors.

a. no; these are grinding teeth
b. no; these are teeth for tearing flesh or ripping prey
c. no; these are the grinding teeth characteristic of herbivorous animals
* d. yes; these eight chisel-like teeth are necessary for humans to be able to bite through food

20. Which of the following statements is false?
    a. The epiglottis covers the trachea when you swallow.
    b. The pharynx and esophagus are not involved in digestion.
    c. The stomach often begins its secretion before food is put in the mouth.
    d. Gastrin is an enzyme that digests proteins.

    a. incorrect; this statement is true
    b. incorrect; this statement is true
    c. incorrect; this statement is true
    * d. correct; this statement is false; gastrin is a hormone, not an enzyme

21. Gingivitis is a disease of
    a. liver.
    b. gums and periodontal tissue.
    c. stomach.
    d. the pharynx and larynx.

    a. no; try another choice
    * b. yes; serious disease that may eventually result in tooth loss
    c. no; try another choice
    d. no; try another choice

22. The glottis is
    a. a flaplike fold of skin that directs the food when it is swallowed.
    b. the opening of the trachea at the base of the larynx.
    c. the opening of the esophagus at the base of the larynx.
    d. a small, isolated portion of the palate and pharynx.

    a. no; the name for the flap is the epiglottis; the glottis is an opening
    * b. yes; when it is covered by the epiglottis, food particles will be directed to the esophagus and will not go down the windpipe
    c. no; there is no need for a covering of the esophagus
    d. no; an actual opening into the trachea

23. The region of the small intestine located closest to the stomach is the
    a. appendix.
    b. duodenum.
    c. jejunum.
    d. ileum.

a. no; located near the caecum, a blind pouch near the juncture of the small and large intestine

* b. yes; the first fifteen inches of the small intestine

c. no; the second portion of the small intestine

d. no; the last part of the small intestine

24. There must be more than two different organs involved in the digestive process because
    a. the structure of one organ would be insufficient space to allow digestion to occur.
    b. there are too many enzymes and hormones for one organ to be sufficient.
    c. some proteolytic enzymes require acid conditions while others require an alkaline environment to function.
    d. the digestive process must be compartmentalized to allow enough time for digestion of complex compounds to occur and for their products to be absorbed.

    a. no; space is not the factor
    b. no; the majority of the digestive secretions all function in the small intestine
* c. yes; the pH requirements for enzymes force there to be two or more organs
    d. no; time is not a major factor in the digestive process, even though some foods are digested faster than others

25. The primary function of the stomach is
    a. absorption of alcohol and other toxins.
    b. digestion in an acidic environment.
    c. detoxification.
    d. production of digestive enzymes and hormones.

    a. no; although absorption of alcohol and other substances occur in the stomach, this is not the primary function
* b. yes; early digestion of some proteins requires an acidic environment such as is found in the stomach
    c. no; although the acid environment may reduce toxicity of some compounds, most detoxification occurs in the liver
    d. no; although the stomach does produce proteases and hormones, the majority are produced by other organs

26. Villi are structures found in the
    a. esophagus.
    b. stomach.
    c. small intestine.
    d. large intestine.

    a. no; there are no accessory structures associated with the esophagus
    b. no; the rugae are internal ridges lining the stomach
* c. yes; to increase the surface area available for absorption
    d. no; there are no additional structures associated with the large intestine

27. The lymphatic vessels will absorb and transport
    a. triglycerides and fats.
    b. nucleotides and their components.
    c. monosaccharides.
    d. amino acids.

* a. yes; carried by lymph vessels that eventually drain into general circulation
    b. no; carried by capillaries and veins that eventually drain the intestines
    c. no; carried by capillaries and veins that eventually drain the intestines
    d. no; carried by capillaries and veins that eventually drain the intestines

28. Which of the following is *not* a final product of the digestion in the small intestine?
    a. fatty acids and monoglycerides
    b. disaccharides
    c. amino acids
    d. glucose, fructose, and other monosaccharides

    a. incorrect; produced in the breakdown of fats and lipids
* b. correct; produced by action of the disaccharides but broken down further to monosaccharides
    c. incorrect; produced in the breakdown of proteins
    d. incorrect; final product of polysaccharide digestion

29. The human appendix is located
    a. on the left side of the body.
    b. at the end of the small intestine, beginning of large intestine.
    c. at the beginning of the small intestine.
    d. both (a) and (b), but not (c)

    a. no; the appendix is on the right side of the body
* b. yes; at the beginning of large intestine
    c. no; at the beginning of the large intestine
    d. no; only (b) is correct

30. Which of the following is *false*?
    a. We may be able to prevent appendicitis and colon cancer by our diet.
    b. Our diets are too high in bulk or fiber.
    c. Diet may affect the incidence of kidney stones, breast cancer, and circulatory disorders.
    d. Body weight varies because of differences in physical activity, basic rate of metabolism, age, sex, hormonal activity, and emotional state.

    a. incorrect; this statement is true
*   b. correct; this statement is false; our diets are generally deficient in fiber
    c. incorrect; this statement is true
    d. incorrect; this statement is true

31. Micelles contain all but which of the following?
    a. cholesterol and lecithin
    b. monoglycerides
    c. fatty acids
    d. water and minerals

    a. no; are part of the nonpolar micelles
    b. no; are part of the nonpolar micelles
    c. no; are part of the nonpolar micelles
*   d. yes; not found in micelles because of the nonpolar nature of the micelles

32. Chylomicrons are
    a. absorbed by the lacteals.
    b. a combination of protein and triglycerides.
    c. transported by the lymphatic system.
    d. all of the above

    a. no; a partial answer; a more complete answer is available
    b. no; a partial answer; a more complete answer is available
    c. no; a partial answer; a more complete answer is available
*   d. yes; all of the above answers are correct

33. The storage form for glucose in the human body is
    a. glycogen.
    b. starch.
    c. fat.
    d. complex glycoproteins.

*   a. yes; a supply is maintained in the liver
    b. no; the storage form for glucose is in plants
    c. no; the most efficient form to store excess food energy
    d. no; glycoproteins have particular functions, but storage of excess glucose is not one of them

34. If you were a physician and had a patient who complained of having colorless or ash gray feces, which of the following is a likely explanation?
    a. extreme anemia
    b. a parasitic infection
    c. a problem with the gallbladder
    d. either cirrhosis of the liver or hepatitis

    a. no; although part of the color of feces is supplied by the heme pigment from hemoglobin, the total lack of color would have other causes
    b. no; parasitic infections are identified by finding the eggs of the parasites in the feces
*   c. yes; bile pigments give the brown color to feces and if the color is lacking, there may be a blockage of the bile duct
    d. these conditions are diagnosed by other symptoms than the characteristics of the feces

35. Diarrhea may result from
    a. a deficiency of soluble fibers such as pectin.
    b. a deficiency of insoluble fibers usually found in bulk foods.
    c. the secretion of excess water and sodium into the large intestine.
    d. a delay in the passage of food through the intestine.

    a. no; lack of fiber may lead to constipation
    b. no; lack of fiber may lead to constipation
*   c. yes; bacterial toxins may cause more fluid to be added to the feces, thereby producing loose and liquid stools
    d. no; the longer the feces remain in the rectum, the more water is extracted

36. Which of the following hormones triggers the release of bile from the gallbladder?
    a. gastrin
    b. gastric inhibitory
    c. cholecystokinin
    d. secretin

    a. no; controls secretion in the stomach
    b. no; slows release of gastric juice and rate of emptying the stomach
*   c. yes; causes gallbladder to release bile
    d. no; secretin triggers the release of pancreatic juices

37. The lymphatic vessels will absorb and transport
    a. triglycerides and fats.
    b. nucleotides and their components.
    c. monosaccharides.
    d. amino acids.

&ast; a. yes; carried by lymph vessels that eventually drain into general circulation
b. no; carried by capillaries and veins that eventually drain the intestines
c. no; carried by capillaries and veins that eventually drain the intestines
d. no; carried by capillaries and veins that eventually drain the intestines

38. A person's ideal weight is based on
a. height.
b. frame or bone size.
c. sex.
d. all of the above

a. no; a partial answer; a more complete answer is available
b. no; a partial answer; a more complete answer is available
c. no; a partial answer; a more complete answer is available
&ast; d. yes; all of the above are correct

39. The body's main source of energy is
a. fat.
b. protein.
c. simple carbohydrates.
d. complex carbohydrates.

a. no; fats contribute energy but are not a major source
b. no; very minor contribution to energy yield
c. no; not a large component of most diets
&ast; d. yes

40. Which of the following statements is (are) true?
a. Eight of the twenty amino acids can be synthesized by the human body.
b. Proteins should be the second most common food in the diet, after carbohydrate.
c. Plant proteins are often incomplete, and animals provide complete proteins.
d. both (b) and (c) are true, (a) is false

a. no; twelve amino acids that must be synthesized by the body
b. no; fats should be the second most common food in the diet, proteins third
&ast; c. yes; this statement is true
d. no; only one of the above is true

41. Which of the following enzymes does *not* digest proteins or long chains of amino acids?
a. pepsin
b. carboxypeptidase
c. trypsin and chymotrypsin
d. lipase

a. no; digests proteins in the stomach
b. no; digests peptide fragments in the small intestine
c. no; digests proteins and polypeptides in the small intestine
&ast; d. yes; digests triglycerides in the small intestine

42. Which of the following is a fat-soluble vitamin?
a. A (retinol)
b. $B_1$ (thiamine)
c. C (ascorbic acid)
d. all of the above

&ast; a. fat; yes; a fat-soluble vitamin
b. no; a water-soluble vitamin
c. no; a water-soluble vitamin
d. no; only one is a fat-soluble vitamin

43. Which of the following sources of protein is highest in net protein utilization (NPU) value?
a. milk
b. eggs
c. cheese
d. meats

a. no; ranked second
&ast; b. yes; ranked first
c. no; ranked fourth
d. no; ranked fifth

44. Which mineral is used in thyroid hormone formation?
a. iron
b. zinc
c. iodine
d. potassium

a. no; used in hemoglobin and cytochrome formation
b. no; digestive hormone ingredient, sperm formation
&ast; c. yes; thyroid hormone formation
d. no; used in muscle and nerve function, pH balance and protein synthesis

45. If the body's supply of glucose decreases, blood levels of glucose are maintained by
a. glycerol breakdown to glucose.
b. breakdown of proteins, conversion of amino acids to glucose.
c. fats breaking down to form fatty acids and glycerol, and then glycerol is converted to glucose.
d. all of the above

a. yes; a partial answer; a more complete answer is available
b. yes; a partial answer; a more complete answer is available
c. yes; a partial answer; a more complete answer is available
* d. yes; all of the above are correct

46. If you are an average person, to determine the number of daily kilocalories needed to maintain current weight multiple your current weight by
    a. 10.
    b. 15.
    c. 20.
    d. 25.

    a. no; 10 should be used for a very sedentary life-style
    * b. yes; the appropriate value for the average person
    c. no; 20 should be used if the person is very active
    d. no; 25 is excessive except for those with extremely high caloric demands

47. A well-balanced diet consists of
    a. 60–80 percent carbohydrates, 10–30 percent fat, and 10 percent protein.
    b. 60–80 percent carbohydrates, 10–30 percent protein, and 10 percent fat.
    c. 40–60 percent carbohydrates, 30–50 percent protein, and 10 percent fat.
    d. 30–50 percent carbohydrates, 30–50 percent protein, and 20 percent fat.

    a. no; too much fat, not enough protein
    * b. yes; this is the right ratio
    c. no; too much fat and protein
    d. no; too much fat and protein

48. Which of the following is a water-soluble vitamin and cannot be stored in the body?
    a. vitamin A
    b. vitamin K
    c. vitamin C
    d. vitamin D

    a. no; fat soluble
    b. no; fat soluble
    * c. yes; water soluble
    d. no; fat soluble

49. A deficiency of ___ leads to scurvy.
    a. vitamin A
    b. niacin
    c. vitamin C
    d. vitamin D

    a. no; lack of vitamin A leads to night blindness
    b. no; lack of niacin leads to pellagra
    * c. yes; lack of vitamin C leads to scurvy
    d. no; lack of vitamin D leads to rickets

50. Which of the following is mismatched?
    a. calcium–osteoporosis
    b. iodine–metabolic disorders
    c. sulfur–diarrhea
    d. sodium–muscle cramps

    a. no; matched correctly
    b. no; matched correctly
    * c. yes; there are no known problems with lack of sulfur
    d. no; matched correctly

51. Excess intake of water-soluble vitamins
    a. may induce cardiovascular disease.
    b. may initiate cancer.
    c. may lead to severe digestive upsets.
    d. does not pose serious health threats.

    a. no; usually excess water-soluble
    b. no; vitamins are eliminated in the urine but massive doses may cause chemical imbalances
    c. no; not generally an effect
    * d. yes; excess water-soluble vitamins are eliminated in the urine

52. Authorities state that the lack of dietary ___ is a major factor contributing to high death rates from intestinal and respiratory infections in many countries.
    a. vitamins
    b. iron
    c. essential amino acids
    d. fiber

    a. no; lack of individual vitamins produce recognizable vitamin-deficiency diseases such as rickets, night blindness, and scurvy
    * b. yes; lack of iron leads to anemia and other illnesses and is particularly debilitating in intestinal and respiratory disorders
    c. no; lack of essential amino acids (the body cannot synthesize these amino acids) leads to kwashiokor
    d. no; fiber in the diet is generally not a major problem in most of the undeveloped world

# CHAPTER 31

# THE INTERNAL ENVIRONMENT

1. Water is lost through
   a. feces.
   b. sweat.
   c. vapor in exhaled breath.
   d. all of the above

   a. no; a partial answer; a more complete answer is available
   b. no; a partial answer; a more complete answer is available
   c. no; a partial answer; a more complete answer is available
   * d. yes; all of the above are sources of water loss

2. Which of the following is a major example of unnoticed water loss?
   a. urination
   b. respiration
   c. sweating
   d. defecation

   a. no; an obvious form of liquid loss
   * b. yes; lost as a gas and therefore not noticed
   c. no; liquid forms on the skin and is noticeable
   d. no; not as noticeable as some other ways because most water is absorbed by the large intestine. The consistency of the feces is controlled by the amount of water

3. Potentially toxic nitrogen-containing wastes are the result of the metabolism of
   a. fats.
   b. proteins.
   c. carbohydrates.
   d. steroids.

   a. no; fats do not contain nitrogen
   * b. yes; the nitrogen-containing amino acids are broken down to produce the nitrogenous waste product of urea and sometimes ammonia
   c. no; this organic compound does not have nitrogen and is broken down into carbon dioxide and water
   d. no; steroids do not contain nitrogen and are broken down into carbon dioxide and water

4. The purpose of sweating is to
   a. get rid of excess salt.
   b. get rid of excess water.
   c. dissipate heat.
   d. get rid of wastes.

   a. no; excess salt is managed by the kidneys
   b. no; excess water is eliminated through the kidneys
   * c. yes; the heat is dissipated by evaporation of water
   d. no; although some waste are eliminated in sweat, the most common exit is through the kidneys

5. The most abundant waste product of metabolism is
   a. urea.
   b. uric acid.
   c. ammonia.
   d. carbon dioxide.

   a. no; urea is a nitrogenous waste product of protein metabolism
   b. no; uric acid is a nitrogenous waste product of nucleic acid metabolism
   c. no; ammonia is a nitrogenous waste product of protein metabolism
   * d. yes; carbon dioxide is the waste product of respiration throughout the body and is the most abundant waste

6. Which of the following is *not* considered to be a metabolic waste?
   a. water
   b. ammonia
   c. urea
   d. uric acid

   * a. correct; a byproduct of metabolism, but because it can be used again it is not considered a waste substance
   b. incorrect; a waste product of primitive forms
   c. incorrect; a waste product of humans
   d. incorrect; a waste product of birds and reptiles

7. Urine is first formed in the
   a. nephron.
   b. urethra.
   c. ureter.
   d. urinary bladder.

   * a. yes; the site where urea is collected
   b. no; the last place where urine is found in the body
   c. no; the tube between the kidney and the bladder
   d. no; the place where urine is stored

8. Urea is formed in
   a. all cells of the body as a waste product of metabolism.
   b. liver cells.
   c. the kidneys.
   d. all of the above

   a. no; nitrogen wastes are formed in all cells of the body, but urea is not formed in them
   * b. yes; two ammonia molecules are joined together with carbon dioxide in the liver to form urea
   c. no; urea is concentrated by the kidney
   d. no; only one of the above is correct

9. Urea is
   a. produced in the liver.
   b. the major nitrogenous waste produced from protein breakdown.
   c. produced by fusing carbon dioxide with two molecules of ammonia.
   d. all of the above

   a. no; a partial answer; a more complete one is available
   b. no; a partial answer; a more complete one is available
   c. no; a partial answer; a more complete one is available
   * d. yes; all of the above are correct

10. The kidneys
   a. continuously filter water, mineral ions, organic wastes, and other substances from the blood.
   b. regulate the volume of the extracellular fluid.
   c. regulate the solute concentration of the extracellular fluid.
   d. all of the above

   a. no; a partial answer; there is a more complete answer available
   b. no; a partial answer; there is a more complete answer available
   c. no; a partial answer; there is a more complete answer available
   * d. yes; all of the above are correct

11. Urine is stored in the
   a. renal pelvis.
   b. ureter.
   c. bladder.
   d. urethra.

   a. no; the collecting central cavity of the kidney
   b. no; the passageway from the kidney to the bladder
   * c. yes; a muscular sac that stores urine
   d. no; the external opening that carries urine away from the body

12. The removal of nitrogen from amino acids is called
   a. ammonification.
   b. deamination.
   c. denitrification.
   d. nitrogen metabolism.

   a. no; although ammonia may be formed
   * b. yes; the removal of nitrogen from amino acids is called deamination
   c. no; denitrification is one of the steps in the nitrogen cycle
   d. no; the removal of nitrogen from amino acids is just one type of nitrogen metabolism

13. The outer portion of the kidney is the renal
   a. pelvis.
   b. cortex.
   c. capsule.
   d. medulla.

   a. no; the pelvis is the central cavity of the kidney where collection of urine takes place
   * b. yes; the cortex is the outer region of the kidney
   c. no; the outer coat of connective tissue that encloses and protects the kidney but not considered part of the kidney proper
   d. no; the inner portion of the kidney

14. The functioning unit of the kidney is the
   a. nephron.
   b. Bowman's capsule.
   c. glomerulus.
   d. loop of Henle.

   * a. yes; the kidney is made up of millions of individual nephrons
   b. no; a cup-like structure in a nephron where filtration takes place
   c. no; a tuft of capillaries that fits in Bowman's capsule
   d. no; a portion of the nephron that controls reabsorption of water

15. Which of the following activities is characteristic of the renal corpuscle?
   a. filtration
   b. reabsorption
   c. secretion
   d. active transport

    *     a.   yes; the blood in the glomerulus is filtered into Bowman's capsule
        b.   no; materials are entering the nephron, not leaving it
        c.   no; secretion occurs in the tubules
        d.   no; active transport is not involved, because there is a concentration gradient favoring the filtration of waste products

16.   Filtration starts in the
    a.   loop of Henle.
    b.   glomerulus.
    c.   proximal tubule.
    d.   distal tubule.

        a.   no; another site
    *     b.   yes; the filtration occurs in the glomerular capillaries surrounded by the Bowman's capsule
        c.   no; another site
        d.   no; another site

17.   Water, nutrients, and salts are selectively returned to the blood by
    a.   filtration.
    b.   excretion.
    c.   reabsorption.
    d.   secretion.

        a.   no; these substances are removed from the blood in the glomerulus/ Bowman's capsule
        b.   no; the removal of these substances from the nephron to the bladder
    *     c.   yes; the substances are reabsorbed rather than lost with the urine
        d.   no; the movement of substances by active transport from the peritubular capillaries to the tubules of the nephrons

18.   The movement of excess hydrogen and potassium ions from the capillaries to the tubular parts of the nephrons is known as
    a.   filtration.
    b.   secretion.
    c.   reabsorption.
    d.   excretion.

        a.   no; water and small solutes removed from blood
    *     b.   yes; involves active transport
        c.   no; water and solutes which entered the interstitial fluid earlier, move into the peritubular capillaries
        d.   no; water and solutes that were not reclaimed by the capillaries flow through the collecting duct to the renal pelvis

19.   Secretion refers to the movement of
    a.   water out of the tubules.
    b.   ions and other substances out of the tubules.
    c.   ions and other substances into the tubules from the peritubular capillaries (capillaries around the tubules).
    d.   water into the proximal and distal tubules.

        a.   no; would result in retention of water
        b.   no; would result in retention of ions
    *     c.   yes; movement of material into the nephron for later excretion
        d.   no; would result in a more copious flow of urine

20.   Which of the following is removed from the blood during filtration?
    a.   water
    b.   proteins
    c.   blood cells
    d.   large solutes

    *     a.   yes; removed from the blood and into Bowman's capsule
        b.   no; too large to be removed during filtration
        c.   no; the cells remain behind in the blood
        d.   no; too large to be removed during filtration

21.   Which of the following structures is the last structure that urine passes through in the nephron?
    a.   Bowman's capsule
    b.   loop of Henle
    c.   distal tubule
    d.   proximal tubule

        a.   no; Bowman's capsule is the first part of the nephron
        b.   no; the loop of Henle is situated between the proximal tubule and the distal tubule
    *     c.   yes; *distal* means distant or furthest away
        d.   no; *proximal* means proximate or close

22.   Which of the following structures lies mainly in the medulla region of the kidney?
    a.   glomerulus
    b.   loop of Henle
    c.   proximal tubule
    d.   distal tubule

        a.   no; the first part of a nephron found in the cortex
    *     b.   yes; the loop of Henle extends mainly through the renal medulla
        c.   no; the proximal tubule is primarily in the cortex
        d.   no; the distal tubule is primarily in the cortex

23.   Which of the following substances is reabsorbed to the least extent in the tubules?
    a.   glucose
    b.   sodium ions
    c.   water
    d.   urea

a. no; glucose is reabsorbed into the bloodstream to be used again
b. no; sodium ions are reabsorbed to participate in water balance of the intracellular fluids
c. no; most is reabsorbed through increasing the concentration of urine
* d. yes; although about 44 percent is reabsorbed, the process is designed for this material to be concentrated and eliminated by micturition

24. The blood vessels involved in reabsorption are the
   a. capillaries of the glomerulus.
   b. peritubular capillaries.
   c. afferent arterioles.
   d. venules leading to the renal vein.

   a. no; the site for filtration
   b. no; the blood vessel that delivers blood to each nephron
* c. yes; these blood vessels surround the tubules and reabsorb vital substances before they are lost in the urine
   d. no; the renal venules and veins take the purified blood away from the kidneys

25. Which of the following is reabsorbed in greatest quantity?
   a. glucose
   b. water
   c. sodium ions
   d. urea

* a. yes; glucose does not usually occur in the urine unless diabetes or some other abnormality is involved
   b. no; the amount of water is controlled by the volume of urine
   c. no; some is lost; may affect blood volume
   d. no; the function of the kidney is to eliminate urea in the urine, but the organ is not completely efficient, so that some is reabsorbed

26. Which of the following statements is false?
   a. As the solute concentration increases, the loop of Henle extends deeper into the renal medulla.
   b. The permeability of the tubules to water and solute is constant throughout the loop of Henle.
   c. Water moves out of the loop of Henle by osmosis, thereby increasing the concentration of urine.
   d. Sodium ions are actively transported out of the distal and proximal tubules.

   a. no; this statement is true
* b. yes; the statement is false; the permeability of the tubules and loop of Henle is variable
   c. no; this statement is true
   d. no; this statement is true

27. The solute concentration is highest
   a. in Bowman's capsule.
   b. in the proximal tubule.
   c. in the deepest part of the inner medulla.
   d. as it leaves the distal tubule for the collecting ducts.

   a. no; there is a place in the nephron where the concentration of solute is greater
   b. no; there is a place in the nephron where the concentration of solute is greater
* c. yes; the concentration is greatest because of the reabsorption of water
   d. no; there is a place in the nephron where the concentration of solute is greater

28. Water is conserved by the kidney under the influence of ADH because this hormone
   a. makes the end regions of the distal tubules and collecting ducts more permeable to water.
   b. makes the end regions of the distal tubules and collecting ducts less permeable to water.
   c. makes the loop of Henle more permeable to minerals, thereby increasing water uptake.
   d. none of the above

* a. yes; more water is absorbed from the urine, making it more concentrated
   b. no; if this were to happen, more water would be lost through copious flow of urine
   c. no; this would also increase the flow of urine
   d. no; one of the above is correct

29. The antidiuretic hormone is produced by the
   a. adrenal cortex.
   b. anterior pituitary.
   c. posterior pituitary.
   d. kidney.

   a. no; not the site of production
   b. no; not the site of production
* c. yes; the posterior pituitary produces ADH
   d. no; not the site of production

30. Sodium reabsorption is controlled by
   a. aldosterone.
   b. cortisol.
   c. ADH.
   d. oxytocin.

* a. yes; aldosterone controls the reabsorption and retention of sodium
   b. no; affects amino acid metabolism
   c. no; increases the retention of water
   d. no; involved in contraction of the uterus during childbirth

31. ADH is secreted
    a. when the blood pressure falls.
    b. after the consumption of large amounts of beer.
    c. when the solute concentration of the extracellular fluid falls below a set point.
    d. all of the above

    * a. yes; when blood pressure falls, ADH helps to retain water and to restore water balance
    b. no; large amounts of beer add fluid, but the alcohol in the beer acts as a diuretic
    c. no; ADH is secreted when solute concentration rises above a set point
    d. no; only one of the choices is correct

32. The antidiuretic hormone is produced by the
    a. kidneys.
    b. adrenal medulla.
    c. adrenal cortex.
    d. none of the above

    a. no; does not produce this hormone
    b. no; does not produce this hormone
    c. no; does not produce this hormone
    * d. yes; none of the above is correct; ADH is secreted by the posterior pituitary

33. Thirst is controlled by the
    a. thyroid gland.
    b. parathyroid.
    c. hypothalamus.
    d. cerebrum.

    a. no; a different site
    b. no; a different site
    * c. yes; the saiety center, where major drives are located
    d. no; a different site

34. Of the following minerals, which is found in greatest quantity in the interstitial fluid?
    a. calcium
    b. phosphorus
    c. sodium
    d. magnesium

    a. no; another ion
    b. no; another ion
    * c. yes
    d. no; another ion

35. Aldosterone
    a. triggers active transport of sodium by the distal tubules and collecting ducts to reabsorb sodium faster.
    b. stimulates active transport of sodium in the proximal tubule to increase sodium excretion.
    c. is secreted when the extracellular fluid contains too much sodium.
    d. directly controls the water/salt balance in the body by controlling water excretion in the urine.

    * a. yes; aldosterone causes reabsorption of sodium
    b. no; reduces sodium excretion
    c. no; aldosterone is secreted when the salt concentration in the extracellular fluid drops
    d. no; water excretion is directly under control of the pituitary hormone, the antidiuretic hormone

36. Renin is a(n)
    a. hormone that controls kidney function.
    b. enzyme that prods the adrenal cortex to secrete aldosterone.
    c. enzyme that digest steroids, such as cholesterol and aldosterone.
    d. activator for the enzyme aldosterone.

    a. no; not a hormone
    * b. yes; triggers aldosterone secretion
    c. no; does not digest aldosterone
    d. no; not a coenzyme

37. High salt concentration in the diet may
    a. lead to increased water retention.
    b. lead to hypertension.
    c. cause increased urine flow.
    d. both (a) and (b)

    a. no; a partial answer; a more complete one is available
    b. no; a partial answer; a more complete one is available
    c. no; a partial answer; a more complete one is available
    * d. yes; both (a) and (b) are correct

38. The body controls pH by
    a. kidney excretion.
    b. respiration.
    c. buffer systems.
    d. all of the above

    a. yes; a partial answer
    b. yes; a partial answer
    c. yes; a partial answer
    * d. yes; all of the above are correct

39. The normal range of pH for extracellular fluid is
    a. 5.8–5.9.
    b. 6.54–6.84.
    c. 7.34–7.45.
    d. 8.0–8.2.

    a. no; too acidic
    b. no; too acidic
    * c. yes; this is the normal pH range of the blood
    d. no; too alkalinic

40. Peritoneal dialysis
    a. is characterized by an external membrane that is used to remove toxic wastes.
    b. involves the flow of blood from an artery through a kidney machine.
    c. places a fluid with proper concentration in the abdominal cavity and then drains it.
    d. is another name for hemodialysis.

    a. no; characteristic of hemodialysis
    b. no; characteristic of hemodialysis
    * c. yes; the peritoneum serves as the dialysis membrane
    d. no; the peritoneal dialysis is the other choice in dialysis

41. The kidney acts to control body pH by
    a. secretion of hydrogen ions into the filtrate.
    b. extraction of sodium and other ions from the extracellular fluids.
    c. increasing the flow of urine through the kidneys.
    d. extraction of bicarbonate from the extracellular fluid.

    * a. yes; one way to reduce pH is simply to remove hydrogen ions
    b. no; the removal of sodium and other ions primarily affects water balance, not pH balance
    c. no; increased urine flow reduces the amount of fluid in the extracellular fluid
    d. no; removal of bicarbonate reduces the available buffering and would tend to reduce the body's control over pH

42. Which of the following statements is false?
    a. At temperatures above 41°C some proteins become denatured.
    b. If the temperature of the body drops below 95°F (35°C), the heart will stop beating.
    c. For a drop of 10°C, the rate of enzyme activity is cut in half.
    d. At 35°C, (95°F), heat-generating mechanisms such as shivering fail.

    a. no; this statement is true
    * b. yes; this statement is false; the temperature must drop below 80°F for this to happen
    c. no; this statement is true
    d. no; this statement is true

43. Which of the following is the last action to occur as the body temperature drops?
    a. Ventricular fibrillation occurs.
    b. Heartbeat becomes irregular.
    c. Voluntary motion is curtailed.
    d. Consciousness is lost.

    * a. yes; occurs at 24–26°C
    b. no; this response occurs at 30–31°C
    c. no; this response occurs at 30–31°C
    d. no; this response occurs at 30–31°C

44. Hypothermia
    a. refers to the fact that mammals are warm-blooded and generate their own heat.
    b. is another name for the dive reflex.
    c. occurs when the core temperature drops a few degrees below normal.
    d. is the name given to the condition that occurs when the external temperature falls below 37°C (98.6°F).

    a. no; this adaptation is called endothermy
    b. no; the dive reflex enables small children to survive low temperatures in the water by slowing the heart rate and restricting blood circulation to the core
    * c. yes; by definition, hypothermia occurs when the core body temperature drops
    d. no; the external environment is usually below this temperature and endothermic processes (muscle contraction, metabolic heat, behavior, and so on) result in raising the body temperature to normal

# CHAPTER 32

# NEURAL CONTROL AND THE SENSES

1.  In the experiment described in the beginning of this chapter, the microchip described in reality was
    a.  anabolic steroids.
    b.  illegal drugs.
    c.  a placebo.
    d.  an understanding of biological processes.

    a.  no; although this would be an appropriate analogy for some athletes
    *   b.  yes; the behavior of the microchip is the same as some kinds of addictive drugs
    c.  no; the microchip had more than a psychological effect
    d.  no; this would be a nice option if it were available, but it was not the equivalent of the microchip

2.  Crack cocaine
    a.  can be addictive to babies who are born to addicted mothers.
    b.  reduces sexual appetite and produces a short euphoric high.
    c.  causes periods of severe depression that can only be alleviated by time or another exposure to it.
    d.  all of the above

    a.  no; a partial answer; a more complete answer is available
    b.  no; a partial answer; a more complete answer is available
    c.  no; a partial answer; a more complete answer is available
    *   d.  yes; all of the above are correct

3.  The passage of a nerve impulse from one neuron to another is from
    a.  axon to axon.
    b.  axon to dendrite.
    c.  cell body to axon.
    d.  dendrite to axon.

    a.  no; axons do not connect to each other but to dendrites
    *   b.  yes; the movement of an impulse is from an axon across a synapse to the dendrite to the cell body to the axon to another synapse
    c.  no; movement of an impulse is away from the cell body out the axon
    d.  no; the impulse moves in the opposite direction

4.  The output zone of a neuron includes the
    a.  axon.
    b.  axon endings.
    c.  cell body.
    d.  dendrite.

    a.  no; the conducting zone
    *   b.  yes; the signals leave the nerve at the end of an axon
    c.  no; part of the input zone
    d.  no; part of the input zone

5.  Which of the following statements is false?
    a.  Nerve impulses may travel in both directions in a neuron.
    b.  In the motor neurons, the axon is usually the longest cell process of a neuron.
    c.  The normal sequence of neurons starts in the sense receptor, travels to a sensory neuron through an interneuron, and through a motor neuron to an effector.
    d.  Dendrites carry impulses toward the cell body.

    *   a.  yes; this statement is false; movement is from synapse to dendrite to cell body to axon; the refractory condition prevents an impulse from moving backward
    b.  no; this statement is true
    c.  no; this statement is true
    d.  no; this statement is true

6.  The most common cells in the nervous system are
    a.  sensory neurons.
    b.  interneurons.
    c.  neuroglia cells.
    d.  motor neurons.

    a.  no; receive and transmit sensory information
    b.  no; integrate sensory perception and response
    *   c.  yes; cells that physically support and protect neurons
    d.  no; neurons that transmit information to effectors

7. Which of the following statements is false?
   a. Action potential generated in one neuron will transfer to adjacent neurons.
   b. An action potential is a brief reversal in polarity of charge across the plasma membrane.
   c. When an action potential originates, the cytoplasmic side of a small patch of a membrane will be positive for a short period of time.
   d. Once an action potential is initiated, a wave of excitation is actively propagated down the membrane of the neuron.

   * a. yes; the statement is false; neurotransmitters are needed to bridge the gap (synapse) between neurons
   b. no; this statement is true
   c. no; this statement is true
   d. no; this statement is true

8. Which of the following is matched correctly?
   a. thoracic and lumbar–sympathetic nervous system
   b. thoracic and cervical–sympathetic nervous system
   c. thoracic and sacral–parasympathetic nervous system
   d. cervical and sacral–sympathetic nervous system

   * a. yes; the thoracic and lumbar regions of the spinal column give rise to the sympathetic nervous system
   b. no; the thoracic and cervical regions give off part of both the sympathetic and parasympathetic systems
   c. no; the thoracic and sacral regions give off part of both the sympathetic and parasympathetic systems
   d. no; the cervical and sacral regions of the spinal column give rise to the parasympathetic systems

9. The greatest proportionate difference between the inside and outside of a nerve at rest involves _____ ions.
   a. sodium
   b. potassium
   c. chloride
   d. calcium

   a. no; for every 15 sodium ions inside there are 150 outside
   * b. yes; for every 5 potassium ions outside there are 150 inside
   c. no; ratio indefinite
   d. no; ratio indefinite

10. *Clostridium botulinum*
    a. produces a neurotoxin.
    b. may cause death.
    c. is an anaerobic bacteria.
    d. all of the above

   a. yes; a partial answer; a more complete answer is available
   b. yes; a partial answer; a more complete answer is available
   c. yes; a partial answer; a more complete answer is available
   * d. yes; all of the above are true

11. Which of the following depicts the concentration of sodium and potassium when a neuron is at resting potential?
    a. high potassium and high sodium outside the neurons
    b. high potassium and low sodium outside the neurons
    c. low potassium and low sodium outside the neurons
    d. low potassium and high sodium outside the neurons

   a. no; not the appropriate concentration at resting potential
   b. no; not the appropriate concentration at resting potential
   c. no; not the appropriate concentration at resting potential
   * d. yes; this concentration gradient is maintained by the expenditure of energy and keeps the neuron's membrane ready to transmit an action potential

12. Which of the following values would be greater?
    a. the amount of sodium that leaks into the membrane
    b. the amount of sodium that is pumped out of the membrane
    c. the amount of potassium that leaks out of the membrane
    d. the amount of potassium that is pumped into the membrane

   a. no; the amount of sodium that leaks in is equal to the amount pumped out
   b. no; the amount of sodium pumped out is equal to the amount leaked in
   * c. yes; the amount of potassium that leaks out must equal the amount of potassium that leaks in and is pumped in
   d. no; some channels remain open to potassium all the time so that the sodium-potassium pump has to compensate for the free movement of potassium

13. An action potential
    a. is triggered by a voltage disturbance of a minimal level called a threshold.
    b. will move down the neuron whenever any stimulus that exceeds the threshold is applied.
    c. causes the sodium channels to open in an accelerating way, as in a positive feedback mechanism.
    d. all of the above

a. yes; a better answer is available; a more complete answer is available
b. yes; a better answer is available; a more complete answer is available
c. yes; a better answer is available; a more complete answer is available
* d. yes; all of the above are true

14. After an action potential passes,
a. the sodium gates are open.
b. the potassium gates are shut.
c. the original voltage difference across the membrane is restored by the sodium-potassium pump.
d. all of the above

a. no; the sodium gates are shut
b. no; the potassium gates are open
* c. yes
d. no; only one of the above is correct

15. The refractory period
a. refers to the neuron during its resting potential.
b. refers to the propagation of an action potential.
c. prevents an action potential from moving backward.
d. is the time at which a nerve is most sensitive to an action potential.

a. no; the resting potential is the general condition of a neuron when there is no action potential being transmitted
b. no; the term that refers to the propagation of an impulse is the action potential
* c. yes; during this recovery period, the neuron cannot transmit a second impulse
d. no; unless the neuron is receiving a series of graded stimuli below the threshold level, a neuron at resting potential is as ready to "fire" as it will ever be

16. The significance of the sheath surrounding some neurons is that it is
a. composed of fat cells.
b. composed of Schwann cells, which completely isolate the neuron.
c. able to transmit impulses faster because they jump from node to node.
d. a means to overcome the limitation on response of nerves imposed by the threshold effect.

a. no; the statement is true; but not significant by itself
b. no; there are gaps in the coverings at the nodes
* c. yes; the significant feature is the speed of transmission
d. no; the limitation is still there

17. An oscilloscope can be used to
a. block nerve transmission.
b. provide a graphic display of electrical changes in a neuron over time.
c. demonstrate how the sodium gates work.
d. illustrate the action of the sodium-potassium pumps.

a. no; an oscilloscope cannot be used to block nerve transmissions
* b. yes; the oscilloscope is like a television tube and can display the passage of an action potential along a nerve
c. no; the sodium gates are too small to be visualized on the oscilloscope
d. no; the sodium-potassium pump is too small to be visualized on the oscilloscope

18. The nodes of Ranvier
a. represent areas of myelinated neurons that lack the myelin sheath.
b. are located between Schwann cells.
c. enable an action potential to jump down the myelinated nerve and thus allow for more rapid transmission of impulses.
d. all of the above

a. no; a partial answer; a more complete answer is available
b. no; a partial answer; a more complete answer is available
c. no; a partial answer; a more complete answer is available
* d. yes; all of the above are correct

19. Saltatory conduction
a. occurs only in the sympathetic and parasympathetic nervous system.
b. involves the jumping of an impulse between nodes of myelinated nerve fibers.
c. is much slower than the regular propagation of nerve impulses.
d. is restricted to the central nervous system.

a. no; characteristic of myelinated neurons in the peripheral and central nervous system
* b. yes; saltatory conduction jumps from node to node
c. no; saltatory conduction may be up to 100 times faster (270 miles per hour)
d. no; occurs in myelinated fibers throughout the body

20. Patches of myelin sheath are destroyed by
a. polio.
b. multiple sclerosis.
c. meningitis.
d. muscular dystrophy.

a. no; nerve injury may occur, but the myelin sheath is not a target
* b. yes; a slow destruction of the myelin sheath occurs with this disease
c. no; an inflammation of the membrane surrounding the brain
d. no; a disease of muscles

21. Action potentials
a. simply travel directly from one neuron to the next because neurons overlap each other.
b. are able to move from one neuron to another via chemical transmitter substances released at the synapse.
c. travel across synapses that occur only between two neurons.
d. are propagated by simple diffusion of chemical transmitter substances across the synapse.

a. no; there is no physical connection between neurons; a physical gap called the synaptic cleft exists
* b. yes
c. no; may also occur between a neuron and an effector (muscle or gland)
d. no; not fast enough; involves active transport

22. Which of the following statements is false?
a. Concentration and electrical gradients exist across the plasma membrane of a neuron.
b. Transport proteins in the plasma membrane expend energy continually to move potassium into the neuron and sodium out of the neuron.
c. Both ionic and electrical gradients exist across a membrane at resting potential.
d. Protein channels that permit ions to cross the plasma membrane are voltage gates and only respond to changes in voltage.

a. no; this statement is true
b. no; this statement is true
c. no; this statement is true
* d. yes; this statement is false; some of these protein channels are also activated by chemical signals as occurs in transfers of signals between neurons

23. An action potential is
a. a rapid polarization of a region of a neuron membrane.
b. a brief reversal of a charge across a neuron membrane.
c. the result of the closing of voltage-gated sodium channels.
d. an example of negative feedback.

a. no; it is a rapid depolarization of the membrane; polarization reestablishes the resting potential after the action potential passes
* b. yes; as the sodium gates open, the flood of positively charged sodium ions makes the interior of the nerve change from negative to positive
c. no; the action potential is the result of opening voltage-gated sodium channels
d. no; the movement of sodium triggers the opening of more sodium channels, as occurs in positive feedback

24. Synaptic integration
a. is the moment-by-moment combining of excitatory and inhibitory signals acting on adjacent membrane regions of a neuron.
b. involves the release of acetylcholine into the synaptic cleft.
c. involves the transmission of impulses to the brain and central nervous system.
d. is the response characteristic of myelinated neural fibers.

* a. yes; by definition
b. no; only one aspect, that dealing with the transmission of information from the presynaptic fiber
c. no; also involves nerve transmission among neurons throughout the body
d. no; not restricted to myelinated fibers

25. Which of the following statements is false?
a. Trigger zones are regions of a neuron that are only capable of receiving, but not propagating, an action potential.
b. During an action potential the flow of sodium into the membrane reduces the negative charge in the cytoplasm.
c. A threshold is reached when enough sodium has moved across the membrane, entered the neuron, and reversed the voltage difference.
d. Immediately after the passage of an active potential the voltage difference is restored by the movement of potassium out of the neuron.

* a. yes; this statement is true of input zones but trigger zones have many voltage-gated channels for sodium ions so that an action potential can be initiated
b. no; this statement is true
c. no; this statement is true
d. no; this statement is true

26. Which of the following statements is false?
    a. All action potentials reach the same energy levels.
    b. Once a threshold is reached, the nerve follows the all-or-none law.
    c. After the propagation of an action potential, the continued opening of sodium channels to propagate an action potential is based upon the strength of the stimulus.
    d. Active transport by sodium potassium pumps helps restore the original ion gradients of a resting potential.

    a. no; this statement is true
    b. no; this statement is true
    * c. yes; this statement is false; after an action potential has been generated, the nerve follows the all-or-none law and the strength of the stimulus no longer matters
    d. no; this statement is true

27. Which of the following is responsible for control over circadian rhythms?
    a. pons
    b. pineal gland
    c. hypothalamus
    d. thalamus

    a. no; bridge connecting both sides of the cerebellum and the spinal cord with the cerebrum
    * b. yes; controls circadian rhythms
    c. no; responsible for neural-endocrine coordination of visceral function
    d. no; major coordinating center for sensory signals

28. Through synaptic integration, signals arriving at any given neuron can be
    a. dampened.
    b. reinforced.
    c. suppressed or sent on.
    d. all of the above

    a. yes; a partial answer
    b. yes; a partial answer
    c. yes; a partial answer
    * d. yes; all of the above are correct

29. The release of neurotransmitters from the presynaptic vesicles is by
    a. osmosis.
    b. diffusion.
    c. exocytosis.
    d. facilitated diffusion.

    a. no; osmosis involves the movement of water molecules
    b. no; movement along a concentration gradient would eventually result in emptying the vesicle and make it ineffective in propagating a nerve impulse
    * c. yes; a type of active transport
    d. no; there are no specific protein channels connecting the vesicles with the cell's exterior

30. Which statement is false?
    a. An action potential is an all-or-nothing event.
    b. An action potential continues indefinitely until a quenching signal is released.
    c. An action potential is self-propagating.
    d. An action potential transmission depends on activities at the membrane.

    a. no; this statement is true
    * b. yes; this statement is false; the impulse terminates at the synapse without a quenching signal required
    c. no; this statement is true
    d. no; this statement is true

31. A reflex arc consists of
    a. motor neurons.
    b. sensory neurons.
    c. brain.
    d. both (a) and (b)

    a. yes; a partial answer; a more complete answer is available
    b. yes; a partial answer; a more complete answer is available
    c. no; not involved in the reflex response to a stimulus
    * d. yes; both (a) and (b) are required

32. The stretch reflex
    a. is activated by stretch-sensitive receptors inside the muscle spindles.
    b. is a simple, stereotyped, and repeatable motor action.
    c. is elicited by a sensory stimulus.
    d. all of the above

    a. no; a partial answer; a more complete answer is available
    b. no; a partial answer; a more complete answer is available
    c. no; a partial answer; a more complete answer is available
    * d. yes; all of the above are correct

33. The nerves that supply skeletal muscles are more specifically part of the ____ nervous system.
    a. somatic
    b. central
    c. autonomic
    d. sympathetic

    * a. yes; the most specific response
    b. no; includes spinal cord and brain
    c. no; includes parasympathetic and sympathetic nervous system
    d. no; a division of the autonomic nervous system

34. Nerves that supply the glands and smooth muscles are part of the _____ nervous system.
    a. autonomic
    b. somatic
    c. central
    d. afferent

* a. yes; supplies smooth muscles and glands
b. no; supplies skeletal muscles
c. no; nerves to and from brain and spinal cord
d. no; carries sensory messages to the central nervous system

35. The element responsible for the release of neurotransmitters from the presynaptic vesicle is
a. sodium.
b. potassium.
c. chlorine.
d. calcium.

a. no; another element is responsible
b. no; another element is responsible
c. no; another element is responsible
* d. yes; when calcium enters the presynaptic neuron, it causes the vesicles to fuse with the plasma membrane and release the neurotransmitter

36. At any chemical synapse
a. the postsynaptic cell releases neurotransmitter molecules.
b. the signal given may have an excitatory or inhibitory effect on the postsynaptic cell.
c. the outcome of a chemical signal at a synapse depends on which presynaptic cell releases the neurotransmitters.
d. excitatory and inhibitory signals operate independently of the threshold effect.

a. no; neurotransmitters are released by the presynaptic neurons
* b. yes; both stimulatory or inhibitor signals may occur
c. no; the result is dependent on which postsynaptic neurons are activated
d. no; the excitatory signal can decrease the stimulus needed, and the inhibitory signal can raise the stimulus needed

37. Signals from ____ nerves tend to slow down "housekeeping" chores and speed up parts of the body that would be involved in "fight-flight" response.
a. peripheral
b. somatic
c. parasympathetic
d. sympathetic

a. no; nerves to and from the central nervous system include some of these nerves
b. no; nerves to skeletal muscles
c. no; antagonistic to the sympathetic system
* d. yes; slows down housekeeping, speeds up defense

38. The parasympathetic nervous system
a. originates in the thoracic-lumbar region of the spinal column.
b. stimulates peristalsis.
c. contracts the sphincter muscles.
d. none of the above

a. no; originates in the cranial and sacral vertebrae
* b. yes; increases the digestive process
c. no; relaxes the sphincter muscles
d. no; one of the above is correct

39. Which of the following statements is false?
a. The white matter of the spinal cord contains the ascending and descending tracts to and from the brain.
b. The gray matter of the spinal cord deals with reflex actions.
c. "Biofeedback" refers to conscious efforts to enhance or dampen autonomic and physiological responses.
d. The gray matter is composed of nerves surrounded by myelin sheaths.

a. incorrect; this statement is true
b. incorrect; this statement is true
c. incorrect; this statement is true
* d. correct; this statement is false; the myelin sheath is found in the white matter

40. The hindbrain includes all but which one of the following?
a. pons
b. medulla oblongata
c. tectum
d. cerebellum

a. no; part of the hindbrain
b. no; part of the hindbrain
* c. yes; part of the midbrain
d. no; part of the hindbrain

41. The emotional part of the brain is the
a. cerebellum.
b. pons.
c. limbic system.
d. reticular activating system.

a. no; center for coordination
b. no; bridge for nerve tracks between brain centers
* c. yes; regions the of thalamus, hypothalamus, amygdala, hippocampus
d. no; region of the brain controlling levels of consciousness

42. Which of the following is *not* a substance occurring naturally in the body?
a. serotonin
b. dopamine
c. norepinephrine
d. dexedrine

a. incorrect; occurs in the body
b. incorrect; occurs in the body
c. incorrect; occurs in the body
* d. correct; an artificial stimulant

43. Which of the following is a natural internal analgesic produced by humans in response to stress?
   a. endorphin
   b. enkephalin
   c. serotonin
   d. both (a) and (b)

   a. no; a partial answer
   b. no; a partial answer
   c. no; induces sleep
   * d. yes; both (a) and (b) are correct

44. The reason we perceive different sensations from identical action potentials is
   a. some parts of the brain can interpret incoming signals in certain limited ways.
   b. there is a difference in frequency of action potentials.
   c. there are differences in the number of action potentials.
   d. all of the above

   a. no; a partial answer; a more complete answer is available
   b. no; a partial answer; a more complete answer is available
   c. no; a partial answer; a more complete answer is available
   * d. yes; all of the above

45. Pheromones are detected by
   a. chemoreceptors.
   b. mechanoreceptors.
   c. photoreceptors.
   d. thermoreceptors.

   * a. yes; the pheromones are chemicals detected by the sense of smell and occasionally taste
   b. no; no hair cells or mechanical deformation is involved
   c. no; does not involve light
   d. no; does not involve temperature

46. Hair cells are part of the sense receptor for
   a. sight.
   b. taste.
   c. olfaction.
   d. none of the above

   a. no
   b. no
   c. no
   * d. yes; none of the above is correct; hair cells are found in mechanoreceptors (sense of hearing, motion, and balance)

47. The outer coat of the vertebrate eye is the
   a. choroid.
   b. retina.
   c. sclera.
   d. none of the above

a. no; the dark pigmented material in the middle layers
b. no; the inner visual tissue
* c. yes; the outer coat
d. no; one of the above is correct

48. Which of the following statements is false?
   a. Sensory nerves are afferent.
   b. The autonomic nervous system deals with involuntary responses.
   c. Some peripheral nerves are mixed and carry both sensory and motor impulses.
   d. Ganglia of the autonomic nervous system are located within the central nervous system.

   a. no; this statement is true; *afferent* means to bring to and sensory information is brought to the central nervous system
   b. no; this statement is true; hence the name *autonomie*, which means without conscious thought
   c. no; this statement is true; many peripheral nerves have both motor and sensory neurons within the nerve
   * d. yes; this statement is false; the ganglia for the autonomic nervous system are located outside the central nervous system

49. A disease characterized by lower than normal levels of acetylcholine in the brain is
   a. Alzheimer disease.
   b. meningitis.
   c. encephalitis.
   d. epilepsy.

   * a. yes; there is a reduction in acetylcholine in this disease
   b. no; an inflammation of the covering of the brain and spinal cord
   c. no; an inflammation of the brain
   d. no; abnormal electrical activity in the brain that alters brain function

50. Alzheimer disease is the responsibility of the buildup of
   a. serotonin.
   b. endorphins.
   c. amyloid protein.
   d. norepinephrine.

   a. no; serotonin acts on brain cells that govern sleeping, sensory perception, temperature regulation, and emotional conditions
   b. no; these are neuromodulators that function as painkillers
   * c. yes; there is an abnormal buildup of masses of amyloid protein
   d. no; norepinephrine affects brain regions concerned with emotional states

51. Which of the following statements is false?
    a. The parasympathetic nervous system handles "housekeeping" chores and tends to slow down the body overall.
    b. The parasympathetic nervous system is antagonistic or opposite in action to the sympathetic nervous system.
    c. The gray matter of the spinal column forms the nerve tracts with myelinated nerve fibers for rapid conduction.
    d. The meninges are three protective coverings surrounding both the brain and spinal cord.

    a. no; this statement is true
    b. no; this statement is true
*   c. yes; this statement is false; the tracts are white because of the presence of myelinated sheaths
    d. no; this statement is true

# CHAPTER 33

# INTEGRATION AND CONTROL: ENDOCRINE SYSTEMS

1.  The first hormone discovered was
    a.  insulin.
    b.  testosterone.
    c.  secretin.
    d.  thyroxin.

    a.  no; the first synthesized
    b.  no; although its affects were probably the first observed
    *   c.  yes; discovered by Bayliss and Starling in the early 1900s
    d.  no; not the first hormone discovered

2.  The first hormone to be discovered was one secreted by the
    a.  anterior pituitary gland.
    b.  pancreas.
    c.  thyroid.
    d.  adrenal cortex.

    a.  no; a different gland
    *   b.  yes; secretin
    c.  no; a different gland
    d.  no; a different gland

3.  Bayliss and Starling discovered the hormone secretin by
    a.  severing the nerves leading to the small intestine.
    b.  testing cells lining the small intestine.
    c.  isolating the small intestine from its normal blood supply.
    d.  both (a) and (b), but not (c)

    a.  yes; a better answer is available
    b.  yes; a better answer is available
    c.  no; it is not possible to isolate the organs from their blood supply and expect them to continue functioning
    *   d.  yes; both (a) and (b) are correct

4.  Hormones
    a.  are secreted by glands having ducts.
    b.  are carried by the bloodstream to all cells but only affect certain target cells that have appropriate receptors.
    c.  only affect glands and internal organs.
    d.  all of the above

    a.  no; hormones are secreted by endocrine glands that have no ducts but deliver their hormones directly to the bloodstream
    *   b.  yes; only cells with appropriate receptors respond to hormones
    c.  no; all parts of the body may be affected by hormones, such as hair production or uptake of glucose
    d.  no; only one of the above choices is correct

5.  The "master" endocrine gland is the
    a.  pituitary.
    b.  thyroid.
    c.  adrenal.
    d.  pancreas.

    *   a.  yes; secretes the greatest variety of hormones that control the other glands
    b.  no; controls metabolic rate primarily
    c.  no; produces several hormones but still not considered "master"
    d.  no; produces three hormones

6.  Signaling molecules include
    a.  transmitting substances.
    b.  local signaling molecules.
    c.  pheromones.
    d.  all of the above

    a.  no; one of the signaling molecules; a better answer is available
    b.  no; one of the signaling molecules; a better answer is available
    c.  no; one of the signaling molecules; a better answer is available
    *   d.  yes; all of the above are signaling molecules

7.  Which of the following hormones is *not* a steroid?
    a.  cortisol
    b.  insulin
    c.  testosterone
    d.  estrogen

    a.  no; cortisol is a steroid
    *   b.  yes; insulin is a protein
    c.  no; testosterone is a steroid
    d.  no; estrogen is a steroid

8. The posterior lobe of the pituitary gland secretes
   a. prolactin.
   b. somatotropin.
   c. oxytocin.
   d. luteinizing hormone.

   a. no; an anterior pituitary secretion
   b. no; an anterior pituitary secretion
 * c. yes; a posterior pituitary secretion
   d. no; an anterior pituitary secretion

9. The releasing hormones of the pituitary would eventually lead to stimulation of all but which one of the following?
   a. gonads (sex organs)
   b. adrenal medulla
   c. thyroid gland
   d. adrenal cortex

   a. no; leads to effects via luteinizing and follicle-stimulating hormones
 * b. yes; activated by stimulation from the autonomic nervous system
   c. no; effects via thyrotropin-stimulating hormones
   d. no; effects via corticotropin-stimulating hormones

10. Which of the following hormones from the anterior pituitary gland would not be classified as a trophic hormone?
   a. luteinizing hormone
   b. follicle-stimulating hormone
   c. growth hormone
   d. ACTH

   a. no; stimulates the corpus luteum to develop and release progesterone in females
   b. no; stimulates the follicle to develop and release estrogen
 * c. yes; a general hormone that stimulates cell division and growth, protein synthesis, and metabolism
   d. no; ACTH means adrenocorticotrophic hormone, which stimulates the adrenal cortex to release glucocorticoids and mineralocorticoids

11. Which of the following is *not* one of the organs affected by hormones secreted by the posterior pituitary?
   a. adrenal gland
   b. breast
   c. kidney
   d. uterus

 * a. yes; the adrenal gland is not affected by hormones from the posterior pituitary
   b. no; oxytocin stimulates milk release from the breast
   c. no; the antidiuretic hormone controls water retention in the kidney
   d. no; oxytocin controls contraction of the uterine wall in labor

12. Lack of ____ in early childhood results in pituitary dwarfism.
   a. oxytocin
   b. somatotropin
   c. prolactin
   d. luteinizing hormone

   a. no; secrete by the posterior pituitary but does not influence growth
 * b. yes; the growth hormone
   c. no; secreted by the posterior pituitary to stimulate and sustain milk production
   d. no; secreted by the anterior pituitary to stimulate the gonads

13. Acromegaly is a disease resulting from excessive secretion of the ___ gland.
   a. pituitary
   b. pancreas
   c. thyroid
   d. parathyroid

 * a. yes; due to excessive secretion of somatotropin in an adult
   b. no; does not contribute to excessive growth
   c. no; the thyroid gland can be responsible for cretinism, a dwarfing disorder
   d. no; affects calcium metabolism

14. The ____ gland is the site where white blood cells grow and differentiate.
   a. adrenal
   b. parathyroid
   c. thyroid
   d. thymus

   a. no; medulla controls fight/flight response, cortex controls glucose, sodium reabsorption and salt-water balance
   b. no; increases calcium level in blood
   c. no; controls basal metabolic rate
 * d. yes; important in body defense

15. Melatonin is secreted by the
   a. pineal body.
   b. pancreas.
   c. parathyroid.
   d. placenta.

 * a. yes; that influences sexual activity and biorhythms
   b. no; secretes glucagon, insulin, and somatostatin
   c. no; secretes parathyroid hormone
   d. no; secretes progesterone and chorionic gonadotrophin

16. The adrenal medulla secretes
   a. cortisol.
   b. corticotropin hormone.
   c. epinephrine.
   d. thyroxine.

a. no; secreted by adrenal cortex
b. no; secreted by the pituitary
&ast; c. yes; secreted by the adrenal medulla
d. no; secreted by the thyroid gland

17. The adrenal medulla
a. secretes hormones that increase blood pressure.
b. secretes hormones that dilate the air passages in the lungs.
c. secretes hormones that trigger the sympathetic nervous system.
d. all of the above

a. no; a partial answer; a better answer is available
b. no; a partial answer; a better answer is available
c. no; a partial answer; a better answer is available
&ast; d. yes; all of the above are correct

18. Which of the following hormones is antagonistic to calcitonin?
a. thyroxine
b. parathyroid hormone
c. somatostatin
d. mineralocorticoid

a. no; although both are secreted by the same gland, thyroxine controls basal metabolic rate
&ast; b. yes; calcitonin lowers calcium while parathyroid hormone elevates calcium in the bloodstream
c. no; a general growth hormone
d. no; primarily influences the metabolism of minerals throughout the body

19. The thyroid gland
a. controls basal metabolic rate.
b. stimulates the sympathetic nervous system.
c. influences secondary sexual characteristics.
d. all of the above

&ast; a. yes
b. no; the adrenal medulla does this
c. no; the adrenal cortex and gonads do this
d. no; a common distractor, but only one is correct

20. The following symptoms (overweight, sluggishness, dry skin, and intolerance of cold) are characteristic of an insufficient secretion from the
a. thyroid.
b. pancreas.
c. adrenal cortex.
d. adrenal medulla.

&ast; a. yes; hypothyroidism
b. no; primary control over glucose metabolism
c. no; protein breakdown and conversion to glucose
d. no; promotes sodium reabsorption and controls saltwater balance

21. Thyroid hormones require the element
a. sodium.
b. iodine.
c. chlorine.
d. cobalt.

a. no; not involved with thyroid gland
&ast; b. yes; majority of iodine in the body is metabolized by thyroid gland
c. no; not involved with the thyroid gland
d. no; not involved with the thyroid gland

22. The ____ gland secretes its hormone when the level of calcium in the blood drops.
a. thyroid
b. thymus
c. parathyroid
d. pancreas

a. no; calcitonin is secreted to lower calcium levels
b. no; thymosin is involved in the immune response
&ast; c. yes; parathyroid hormone is secreted to raise calcium level
d. no; pancreatic hormones control glucose levels in blood

23. The lack of vitamin D leads to
a. scurvy.
b. night blindness.
c. rickets.
d. goiter.

a. no; lack of vitamin C
b. no; lack of vitamin A
&ast; c. yes; affects bone structure
d. no; a condition resulting from lack of thyroid hormone due to lack of iodine

24. Glucagon
a. raises the glucose level in the bloodstream.
b. raises the level of calcium and phosphorus in the blood.
c. regulates growth rate.
d. controls basal metabolic rate.

&ast; a. yes; causes glycogen to be broken down into glucose
b. no; the parathyroid gland
c. no; the pituitary gland
d. no; the thyroid gland

25. The cells that secrete glucagon in the pancreas are the ____ cells.
a. alpha
b. beta
c. delta
d. sigma

&ast; a. yes; the alpha cells secrete glucagon
b. no; the beta cells secrete insulin
c. no; the delta cells secrete somatostatin
d. no; there are no sigma cells in the pancreas

26. Insulin promotes the production of all but which one of the following?
    a. glucose
    b. proteins
    c. fats
    d. glycogen

  * a. yes; glucose production is inhibited by insulin
    b. no; insulin promotes protein synthesis
    c. no; insulin promotes synthesis of fats
    d. no; insulin promotes glycogen synthesis

27. Which of the following does not affect the glucose level in the bloodstream?
    a. aldosterone
    b. insulin
    c. glucagon
    d. cortisol

  * a. yes; affects sodium balance, not glucose
    b. no; causes fat cells, muscle cells, and other cells to take up glucose and use it as an energy source or convert it to glycogen
    c. no; stops the liver from producing glycogen and converts glycogen to glucose, which enters the bloodstream
    d. no; cortisol raises the glucose in the bloodstream when it falls below a set point

28. Glucagon is secreted by _____ cells of the pancreas.
    a. alpha
    b. beta
    c. gamma
    d. delta

  * a. yes
    b. no; secretes insulin
    c. no; no such cells involved in hormone production
    d. no; secretes somatostatin

29. Ketones are
    a. normal products of the breakdown of fats.
    b. produced in diabetes mellitus.
    c. secreted by the pineal gland.
    d. both (a) and (b), but not (c)

    a. yes; a better answer is available
    b. yes; a better answer is available
    c. no; the pineal gland secretes melatonin
  * d. yes; (a) and (b) are correct, but (c) is incorrect

30. Type I diabetes
    a. is characterized by normal or near normal levels of insulin in the blood.
    b. is the less common but the more serious form of diabetes.
    c. is called adult onset diabetes.
    d. all of the above

    a. no; characteristic of type II diabetes
  * b. yes; characteristic of type I diabetes
    c. no; characteristic of type II diabetes
    d. no; both (a) and (c) refer to type II diabetes

31. The pineal gland is primarily influenced by
    a. other hormones.
    b. nerves.
    c. internal chemical changes.
    d. environment.

    a. no; acts independently
    b. no; only as conduits of information about light intensity and duration
    c. no; produces changes in biorhythms and body temperature
  * d. yes; responds to the photoperiod

32. Second messengers are
    a. ancillaries that trigger a response in target cells.
    b. characteristic of steroid hormones.
    c. exemplified by cyclic adenosine monophosphate.
    d. both (a) and (c), but not (b)

    a. yes; a better answer is available
    b. no; characteristic of nonsteroid hormones
    c. yes; a better answer is available
  * d. yes; both (a) and (c) are correct, but (b) is incorrect

33. In testicular feminization syndrome
    a. the individual has functional testes but develops phenotypically as a female.
    b. the individual fails to produce testosterone.
    c. the secondary sexual characteristics are male even though he is sterile with defective testes.
    d. both (a) and (b) are correct

  * a. yes
    b. no; testosterone is produced, but the defective receptor prevents its uptake by the target cell
    c. no; phenotypically a female even though the testes are normal
    d. no; only one of the above is correct

34. Which of the of following is mismatched?
    a. thymus–immunity
    b. adrenal medulla–aldosterone and cortisone
    c. parathyroid glands–calcium metabolism
    d. pineal gland–biological clock

a. no; matched correctly; the hormone thymosin has significant roles in immunity
* b. yes; this is mismatched; the adrenal cortex produces these two hormones
c. no; not mismatched; parathyroid hormone and calcitonin from the thyroid gland control calcium metabolism
d. no; correctly matched; the pineal gland secretes melatonin that controls biological clocks

35. The chronic lack of _____ can lead to hypoglycemia.
a. thyroxine
b. cortisol
c. mineralocorticoids
d. glucagon

a. no; might decrease metabolic activity
* b. yes; the mechanisms in the liver that spare glucose and generate new glucose fail to function so that glucose levels in the blood sugar may fall
c. no; does not affect glucose management
d. no; raises blood sugar level

36. President Kennedy suffered from
a. Addison disease.
b. acromegaly.
c. Graves disease.
d. diabetes, type II.

* a. yes; a glandular disease due to the lack of hormone production from the adrenal cortex
b. no; a continuation of growth after adulthood
c. no; did not have a thyroid disorder
d. no; did not have maturity onset diabetes

37. The endocrine gland with the greatest connection to the nervous system is the
a. adrenal cortex.
b. anterior pituitary.
c. posterior pituitary.
d. gonads.

a. no; no connection with the nervous system.
b. no; although located on the floor of the brain, it is mostly glandular tissue
* c. yes; basically nervous tissue that is an extension of the hypothalamus
d. no; even though adrenaline and noradrenaline interact with the autonomic nervous system

38. Which of the following organs or tissues secretes a hormone?
a. gall bladder
b. urinary bladder
c. spleen
d. heart

a. no; stores bile
b. no; stores urine
c. no; destroys blood cells
* d. yes; secretes the atrial natriuretic peptide

39. Which of the following is mismatched?
a. erythropoietin–kidney
b. thymosin–thyroid
c. angiotensin–kidney
d. somatostatin–pancreas

a. no; this is matched correctly
* b. yes; thymosin is secreted by the thymus gland
c. no; this is matched correctly
d. no; this is matched correctly

40. Which of the following hormones does not act on the kidney?
a. mineralocorticoids
b. glucagon
c. atrial natriuretic peptide
d. parathyroid hormone

a. no; acts on the kidney to promote sodium reabsorption and controls salt and water balance
* b. yes; acts on the liver to raise blood sugar level
c. no; acts on kidney to increase sodium excretion and lower blood pressure
d. no; acts on the kidney and bone to raise calcium levels in the blood

41. The target for melatonin is the
a. skin where pigment is produced.
b. internal organs of the body.
c. part of the brain that controls sleep.
d. adrenal gland.

a. no; melanin is the pigment found in the skin
b. no; does not directly affect the internal organs
* c. yes; melatonin partially controls the pattern of waking and sleeping
d. no; melatonin does not affect the adrenal gland

42. The pineal gland senses
a. changes in atmospheric pressure.
b. changes in light intensity.
c. the concentration of glucose in the bloodstream.
d. the external temperature.

a. no; in general, the body is unaware of changes in atmospheric pressure
* b. yes; the pineal gland responds to changes in light intensity by changing the amount of melatonin it produces
c. no; the pineal gland does not monitor blood sugar levels
d. no; the sensing of external temperature occurs in thermoreceptors in the skin

43. A disorder of the pineal gland and the improper secretion of melatonin
a. is characterized by depression and a need to sleep.
b. is a symptom of an upset in the biological clock.
c. occurs during the winter season.
d. all of the above

a. no; a partial answer; a more complete
answer is available
b. no; a partial answer; a more complete
answer is available
c. no; a partial answer; a more complete
answer is available
* d. yes; all of the above are characteristic
of seasonal affective disorder, a
disease of the pineal gland

# CHAPTER 34

# REPRODUCTION AND DEVELOPMENT

1. Which of the following statements is false?
   a. Development begins with the development of gametes in the parents.
   b. Development ends with the birth of a baby.
   c. Cleavage is the first event that follows fertilization.
   d. Every tissue in an adult originates from ectoderm, endoderm, or mesoderm.

   a. no; this statement is true
 * b. yes; this statement is false; development continues after birth
   c. no; this statement is true
   d. no; this statement is true

2. The chief value of sexual reproduction is
   a. its efficiency.
   b. the number of offspring produced.
   c. the variation found among the offspring.
   d. the conservation of the energy needed for reproduction.

   a. no; asexual reproduction is more efficient
   b. no; asexual reproduction often produces more offspring than does sexual reproduction
 * c. yes; called sexual recombination
   d. no; more energy is released in sexually reproducing forms

3. Which of the following statements is false?
   a. Asexual reproduction is more efficient than sexual reproduction.
   b. Sexual reproduction is more energy demanding and requires more of the animals that use it than asexual reproduction.
   c. The timing of reproduction is more critical in asexual reproduction than sexual reproduction.
   d. The major advantage of sexual reproduction over asexual reproduction is the amount of variation produced.

   a. no; this statement is true
   b. no; this statement is true
 * c. yes; this statement is false; in sexual reproduction, both sexes must mature at the same time and must be found together so that courtship can occur
   d. no; this statement is true

4. Which is formed first?
   a. blastula
   b. morula
   c. gastrula
   d. germ layers

   a. no; a hollow ball of cells that develops after the morula
 * b. yes; a solid ball of cells that precedes the others mentioned
   c. no; the structure that follows the blastula
   d. no; the germ layers are formed in the gastrula

5. Yolk
   a. is a protein-rich, lipid-rich food source for the egg.
   b. is more concentrated in the vegetal pole.
   c. controls the plane of cleavage in the early embryo.
   d. all of the above

   a. no; a partial answer; a more complete answer is available
   b. no; a partial answer; a more complete answer is available
   c. no; a partial answer; a more complete answer is available
 * d. yes; all of the answers are correct

6. The germ layers form during
   a. gastrulation.
   b. cleavage.
   c. organ formation.
   d. growth and tissue specialization.

 * a. yes
   b. no; too early
   c. no; too late
   d. no; too late

7. Which is formed last?
   a. gastrula
   b. ectoderm
   c. endoderm
   d. mesoderm

   a. no; this structure formed by rearrangement of embryonic tissue that eventually leads to the three germ layers
   b. no; formed at the same time as the endoderm
   c. no; formed at the same time as the ectoderm
   * d. yes; formed between the ectoderm and endoderm

8. In the adult, the endoderm gives rise to the
   a. circulatory system.
   b. muscular system.
   c. digestive system.
   d. skeletal system.

   a. no; produced by the mesoderm
   b. no; produced by the mesoderm
   * c. yes; produced by the endoderm
   d. no; produced by the mesoderm

9. The mesoderm gives rise to all but which of the following?
   a. circulatory system
   b. digestive system
   c. skeletal system
   d. reproductive and excretory systems

   a. incorrect; produced by the mesoderm
   * b. correct; produced by the endoderm
   c. incorrect; produced by the mesoderm
   d. incorrect; produced by the mesoderm

10. Which of the following is responsible for the development of the nervous system and brain?
    a. ectoderm
    b. endoderm
    c. mesoderm
    d. gastroderm

    * a. yes; and the external covering of the body
    b. no; produces the digestive tract
    c. no; produces most of the adult tissues of the body
    d. no; not one of the germ layers of the embryo

11. The ectoderm gives rise to the
    a. integumentary system.
    b. nervous system.
    c. excretory system.
    d. both (a) and (b), but not (c)

    a. no; a partial answer; a more complete answer is available
    b. no; a partial answer; a more complete answer is available
    c. no; produced by the mesoderm
    * d. yes; both (a) and (b) are correct, and (c) is incorrect

12. Cell differentiation
    a. is the gene-directed process by which cells in different parts of the embryo become specialized in form and function.
    b. is the result of the loss of certain genes as cleavage occurs.
    c. is limited to between 40 and 50 cell types.
    d. is not a part of organogenesis.

    * a. yes; by definition, cells become different or specialized
    b. no; the number of genes remains the same; the differences are due to which genes are active
    c. no; there are more than 150 differentiated cell types
    d. no; differentiation is a vital part of the formation of organs

13. In cleavage
    a. the two daughter cells represent the same total volume as the cell that produced them.
    b. a zygote is converted into a blastula.
    c. the daughter cells do not increase in size.
    d. all of the above

    a. no; a partial answer; a more complete answer is available
    b. no; a partial answer; a more complete answer is available
    c. no; a partial answer; a more complete answer is available
    * d. yes; all of the above answers are correct

14. Which stage of embryonic development is a hollow ball of cells one cell thick?
    a. morula
    b. blastula
    c. gastrula
    d. early cleavage

    a. no; a solid cluster of cells that resembles a mulberry without a central cavity
    * b. yes; a hollow ball of cells one layer thick
    c. no; invagination has taken place so there are two or three layers of cells
    d. no; too early in embryonic development to be a hollow sphere

15. The gray crescent
    a. controls the body axis of a frog embryo.
    b. is the site for the beginning of gastrulation.
    c. is an area with less yolk and pigmentation, resulting from reorganization of the frog after fertilization.
    d. all of the above

a. no; a partial answer; a more complete answer is available
b. no; a partial answer; a more complete answer is available
c. no; a partial answer; a more complete answer is available
* d. yes; all of the answers are correct

16. Morphogenesis
    a. leads to the development of form and structure of the embryo.
    b. results from cell migration and recognition of surface characteristics of neighboring cells.
    c. is exemplified by cell death.
    d. all of the above

    a. no; a partial answer; a more complete answer is available
    b. no; a partial answer; a more complete answer is available
    c. no; a partial answer; a more complete answer is available
    * d. yes; all of the above answers are correct

17. Cell migration
    a. is characteristic of the developmental stage called morphogenesis.
    b. is a response to chemical gradients established in the embryo.
    c. stops when the cells encounter adhesion clues on cells with which they come in contact.
    d. all of the above

    a. no; a partial answer; a more complete answer is available
    b. no; a partial answer; a more complete answer is available
    c. no; a partial answer; a more complete answer is available
    * d. yes; all of the answers are correct

18. Morphogenesis involves
    a. massive tissue migration.
    b. death of cells.
    c. localized cell division and growth.
    d. all of the above are correct

    a. no; a partial answer; a more complete answer is available
    b. no; a partial answer; a more complete answer is available
    c. no; a partial answer; a more complete answer is available
    * d. yes; all of the above are correct

19. Selective gene expression during embryonic development is specifically called
    a. morphogenesis.
    b. pattern formation.
    c. differentiation.
    d. embryonic induction.

a. no; the development of shape or form
b. no; the specialization of tissues and their positioning in the embryo
c. no; the name given to the development of differences between cells and tissues
* d. yes; embryonic induction specifically refers to the induction or turning on of specific genes in specific cells

20. Gastrulation
    a. establishes a lengthwise axis for development.
    b. is initiated by the formation of the primitive streak.
    c. results in dramatically rearranging the embryo and changing its appearance.
    d. all of the above

    a. no; a partial answer; a more complete answer is available
    b. no; a partial answer; a more complete answer is available
    c. no; a partial answer; a more complete answer is available
    * d. yes; all of the above are correct

21. The neural tube
    a. is derived from ectoderm tissue.
    b. is a modification of the neural plate resulting from changes in cell shape.
    c. will eventually form the brain and spinal cord.
    d. all of the above

    a. no; a partial answer; a more complete answer is available
    b. no; a partial answer; a more complete answer is available
    c. no; a partial answer; a more complete answer is available
    * d. yes; all of the above are correct

22. Which of the following takes place last?
    a. formation of embryonic disc
    b. gastrulation
    c. organogenesis
    d. formation of three germ layers

    a. no; occurs first about one week after conception
    b. no; occurs after the embryonic disc and before the formation of germ layers
    * c. yes; organogenesis is last of those listed and occurs after the formation of the three germ layers
    d. no; the formation of the three germ layers occurs prior to organogenesis and after gastrulation

23. A mutation of homeobox genes will result in
    a. the failure of a chicken wing to fully develop.
    b. the growth of a lens on the belly.
    c. development of legs on an insect where the antennae should be located.
    d. the production of extra body parts.

a. no; an example of what happens when certain ectodermal cells are removed

b. no; a result of a signal from a morphogen from retinal cells that alters the development of ectodermal cells

* c. yes; homeobox genes control development of sequential groups of cells along the body's anterior-posterior axis

d. no; the result of the duplication of development patterns

24. Rising estrogen levels in the bloodstream trigger the pituitary to
   a. release FSH.
   b. release LH.
   c. stop secreting FSH.
   d. stop secreting LH.

   a. no; FSH initiates follicle development and subsequent release of estrogen
   * b. yes; the rise in estrogen triggers a surge in LH, which triggers the rupture of the follicle
   c. no; turned off by progesterone
   d. no; turned off by progesterone

25. High levels of progesterone are secreted during
   a. the follicular phase.
   b. ovulation.
   c. the luteal phase.
   d. all of the above

   a. no; characterized by rising levels of estrogen
   b. no; triggered by a surge of LH
   * c. yes; the corpus luteum secretes both estrogen and progesterone
   d. no; only one of the above is correct, even though there is some progesterone produced by the zona pellucida just before ovulation

26. Which of the following is most critical to the completion of meiosis II in the female reproductive cycle?
   a. puberty
   b. ovulation
   c. menstruation
   d. fertilization

   a. no; the beginning of reproductive maturity
   b. no; in ovulation, eggs are released from the follicle in meiosis I
   c. no; in menstruation, the endometrial lining is sloughed along with the unfertilized egg
   * d. yes; meiosis is completed only after fertilization by a sperm occurs

27. The male gonad is the
   a. testis.
   b. penis.
   c. scrotal sac.
   d. prostate gland.

* a. yes; produces both sperm and the male hormones responsible for secondary sexual characteristics
   b. no; the male copulatory organ
   c. no; the sac that houses the testes
   d. no; one of the glands that secretes seminal fluid

28. Which of the following statements is false?
   a. The scrotal sac is equipped with muscles that help to control the temperature of the testis.
   b. The sperm have to develop in an environment with a temperature around ninety–five degrees.
   c. It only takes two or three days for a sperm to mature.
   d. Sperm formation begins in the seminiferous tubules.

   a. no; this statement is true
   b. no; this statement is true
   * c. yes; this statement is false; the process takes nine to ten weeks
   d. no; this statement is true

29. The development and maturation of sperm takes place in the
   a. seminiferous tubules.
   b. vas deferens.
   c. epididymis.
   d. urethra.

   a. no; site where sperm are first formed
   b. no; tube leading to urethra for sperm delivery
   * c. yes; sperm are stored and complete development happens here
   d. no; the common urogenital duct leaving the body

30. In the development of male gametes, ___ are formed after meiosis I.
   a. primary spermatocytes
   b. secondary spermatocytes
   c. spermatogonial cells
   d. spermatids

   a. no; after mitosis of spermatogonial cells
   * b. yes; after meiosis I
   c. no; the diploid stem cells from which sperm are derived
   d. no; after meiosis II

31. The last structure the sperm travel through before they leave the male body is the
   a. vas deferens.
   b. urethra.
   c. ejaculatory duct.
   d. vas efferens.

   a. no; leads from the epididymis to the ejaculatory duct
   * b. yes; the common tube for the male urogenital tract through which the sperm leave the penis
   c. no; connects the vas deferens and the urethra
   d. no; the vas efferens lies between the seminiferous tubules and the epididymis

32. Seminal fluid is produced by the
    a. prostate gland.
    b. bulbourethral glands.
    c. seminal vesicles.
    d. all of the above

    a. yes; a partial answer; a more complete answer is available
    b. yes; a partial answer; a more complete answer is available
    c. yes; a partial answer; a more complete answer is available
  * d. yes; all of the above

33. The acrosome
    a. is filled with mitochondria.
    b. contains enzymes that digest away the membrane around the egg.
    c. consists of a core of microtubules.
    d. is the name for the package of male chromosomes.

    a. no; the mitochondria are found in the midpiece and supply energy for the sperm to swim
  * b. yes; there must be enough cooperating sperm to furnish enough enzyme to weaken the membrane to allow penetration by only one sperm
    c. no; found in the tail to help contract the flagella
    d. no; the male genome is found in the nucleus in the head of the sperm

34. During the process of spermatogenesis which of the following cells is the first to be a haploid cell?
    a. spermatid
    b. spermatogonia cell
    c. primary spermatocytes
    d. secondary spermatocyte

    a. no; there is a cell before this stage that is haploid
    b. no; a diploid cell
    c. no; a diploid cell
  * d. yes; even though it contains duplicated sister chromatids there is only one centromere, which is considered to be haploid

35. The Leydig cells
    a. secrete follicle-stimulating hormone.
    b. secrete testosterone.
    c. nourish developing sperm.
    d. respond to follicle-stimulating hormone.

    a. no; follicle-stimulating hormone. is secreted by the anterior pituitary
  * b. yes; the site for male hormone production
    c. no; this is the responsibility of the Sertoli cells
    d. no; the Leydig cells respond to luteinizing hormone

36. Which of the following is *not* part of the vulva?
    a. labia minora
    b. labia majora
    c. clitoris
    d. uterus

    a. incorrect; part of the external genitalia
    b. incorrect; part of the external genitalia
    c. incorrect; part of the external genitalia
  * d. correct; part of the internal female reproductive organs

37. After ovulation, the follicle becomes transformed into the
    a. primary oocyte.
    b. endometrium.
    c. corpus luteum.
    d. cervix.

    a. no; the primary oocyte is the egg that is released
    b. no; this is the lining of the uterus
  * c. yes; the yellow body that fills the follicle
    d. no; the neck of the uterus

38. Oocytes are stored in the
    a. follicles.
    b. oviducts.
    c. uterus.
    d. cervix.

  * a. yes; pockets in the ovary where oocytes are stored
    b. no; a channel between ovary and uterus
    c. no; the site where the embryo develops
    d. no; the neck of the uterus

39. The surge of ____ in the blood triggers ovulation.
    a. progesterone
    b. estrogen
    c. follicle-stimulating hormone
    d. luteinizing hormone

    a. no; stimulates growth of endometrium and maintains pregnancy
    b. no; rising estrogen levels in bloodstream triggers pituitary to release a surge of LH
    c. no; stimulates follicle to grow as indicated by its name
  * d. yes; causes rupture of follicle, ovulation, and development of corpus luteum

40. In endometriosis
    a. endometrial tissue anywhere in the body reacts to estrogen.
    b. sterility may result.
    c. displaced cells can grow, resulting in pain during urination, menstruation, and/or sexual relations.
    d. all of the above

a. yes; a partial answer; a more complete answer is available
b. yes; a partial answer; a more complete answer is available
c. yes; a partial answer; a more complete answer is available
* d. yes; all of the above answers are correct

41. In the development of the female gamete in humans, meiosis I is completed
    a. before birth.
    b. eight to ten hours before ovulation.
    c. on the trip down the oviducts.
    d. after the sperm has penetrated the egg.

    a. no; all of the primary oocytes a female will ever have will be found in her ovaries before birth, but meiosis I is not complete
    * b. yes; meiosis I and the formation of the first polar body occur just prior to ovulation
    c. no; too late, meiosis I has already been completed
    d. no; meiosis I has been completed and penetration by the sperm triggers the second meiotic division

42. A soft, fuzzy hair that covers the embryo is called
    a. lanugo.
    b. zona pellucida.
    c. thalidomide.
    d. estrus.

    * a. yes
    b. no; membrane surrounding an unfertilized egg
    c. no; a chemical teratogen that disturbs limb bud formation
    d. no; the reproductive cycle of female mammals

43. Fertilization most commonly occurs in the
    a. vagina.
    b. oviduct.
    c. uterus.
    d. ovary.

    a. no; another site
    * b. yes; in the upper portion of the oviducts
    c. no; another site
    d. no; another site

44. Which of the following statement is false?
    a. One or both sexes must achieve orgasm for the female to become pregnant.
    b. Only one sperm will ever penetrate the egg.
    c. The egg does not complete meiosis II until after a sperm penetrates the egg.
    d. After an egg has been fertilized, there will be three visible polar bodies.

* a. yes; this statement is false; neither sex has to achieve a climax as may often occur in the withdrawal method of contraception
b. no; this statement is true
c. no; this statement is true
d. no; this statement is true

45. The newly conceived offspring implants on the uterine wall as a
    a. zygote.
    b. morula.
    c. blastocyst.
    d. fetus.

    a. no; the fertilized egg; too early
    b. no; a solid ball of cells; too immature to implant
    * c. yes
    d. no; an embryo recognizable as human; occurs much later

46. In eggs with a shell suitable for deposition on land, the ____ stores waste.
    a. allantois
    b. amnion
    c. chorion
    d. yolk sac

    * a. yes; a structure in humans that is involved in the formation of blood and the urinary bladder
    b. no; a fluid-filled sac
    c. no; the outer membrane that interacts with the endometrial lining to form the placenta
    d. no; a vestigial structure

47. Which of the following is a fluid-filled sac?
    a. allantois
    b. amnion
    c. chorion
    d. yolk sac

    a. no; a structure in humans that is involved in the formation of blood and the urinary bladder
    * b. yes; a fluid-filled sac that protects the embryo
    c. no; the outer membrane that interacts with the endometrial lining to form the placenta
    d. no; a vestigial structure

48. Which of the following membranes is most closely associated with the placenta?
    a. allantois
    b. amnion
    c. chorion
    d. yolk sac

    a. yes; a structure in humans that is involved in the formation of blood and the urinary bladder
    b. no; a fluid-filled sac
    * c. yes; the outer membrane that interacts with the endometrial lining to form the placenta
    d. no; a vestigial structure

49. The chemical that is tested for in home pregnancy tests is
    a. estrogen.
    b. progesterone.
    c. oxytocin.
    d. human chorionic gonadotropin.

    a. no; secreted by the ovaries during normal menstrual cycles when the woman is not pregnant
    b. no; secreted by the corpus luteum during normal menstrual cycles when the woman is not pregnant
    c. no; a hormone involved in labor
    * d. yes; produced by the placenta and only found when the woman is pregnant

50. A fetus cannot survive if it is born prematurely before ___ weeks after conception.
    a. twenty-two
    b. twenty-four
    c. twenty-six
    d. twenty-eight

    * a. yes; chances of survival very remote
    b. no; a baby that has developed for this long has a chance to survive but still is at risk
    c. no; a baby that has developed for this long has a chance to survive but still is at risk
    d. no; a baby that has developed for this long has a chance to survive but still is at risk

51. The organ(s) that is (are) not well developed and places most premature babies at greatest risk is (are) the
    a. kidneys.
    b. lungs.
    c. heart.
    d. brain and nervous system.

    a. no; not usually a major concern
    * b. yes; the baby has trouble breathing often due to the lack of surfactants needed to reduce surface tension in the alveoli
    c. no; another organ; the heart usually does well or can be stimulated to beat
    d. no; not mature for some time, but sufficiently developed to maintain most body functions

52. During pregnancy, the average mother gains ___ pounds.
    a. 10–15
    b. 15–20
    c. 20–25
    d. 25–30

    a. no; too little, places the baby at risk
    b. no; too little, places the baby at risk
    * c. yes; the average weight gain
    d. no; somewhat excessive and may lead to birth complications

53. Which drug caused malformation of human embryos, resulting in babies born without arms or legs?
    a. thalidomide
    b. tetracycline
    c. streptomycin
    d. anti-acne drugs

    * a. yes; this problem occurred in Europe but had not been cleared for use in the United States
    b. no; causes teeth to yellow
    c. no; may cause problems with hearing or development of the nervous system
    d. no; anti-acne drugs may produce abnormal facial and cranial development

54. Identical twins
    a. occur when two secondary oocytes are released and fertilized in the same menstrual cycle.
    b. may be of either sex.
    c. are genetically identical.
    d. two of the above answers are correct

    a. no; the eggs are fertilized by different sperm; they are just like any sibling, but they share the same birthday
    b. no; must be of the same sex
    * c. yes; identical in all genetically controlled characteristics
    d. no; (a) and (b) are incorrect, and (c) is correct

55. Milk production is stimulated by
    a. estrogen.
    b. progesterone.
    c. oxytocin.
    d. prolactin.

    a. no; stimulates the growth of the mammary glands and ducts in the breast
    b. no
    c. no; causes breast tissue to contract and force milk into the milk ducts
    * d. yes; prolactin stimulates milk production

# CHAPTER 35

# POPULATION ECOLOGY

1. The study of the interaction of organisms with one another and their environment is
   a. evolution.
   b. physiology.
   c. demographics.
   d. ecology.

   a. no; evolution is the change in organisms over time
   b. no; physiology is the study of functions
   c. no; demographics is the study of population
   * d. yes; ecology is the study of the relationship of organisms with themselves and their environment

2. Which of the following statements is false?
   a. According to Hindu tradition, a son must conduct the last rites for his father so that he may rest in peace.
   b. Enforced sterilization of males led to the downfall of Indira Ghandi.
   c. There are more people alive in India than in North and South America.
   d. none of the above statements are true

   a. no; this statement is true
   b. no; this statement is true
   c. no; this statement is true
   * d. yes; this choice is false because all of the above statements are true

3. The place where an organism lives is called its
   a. niche.
   b. habitat.
   c. community.
   d. ecosystem.

   a. no; what an organism does in the environment
   * b. yes; where the organism could be found
   c. no; a group of interacting populations
   d. no; the functional unit in nature consisting of both biotic and abiotic factors

4. The most common distribution pattern of a population is
   a. random.
   b. uniform.
   c. clumped.
   d. dispersed.

   a. no; if the resources the population uses are uniformly dispersed, the population distribution may be random
   b. no; occurs under artificial conditions such as a farm
   * c. yes; because resources are often clumped
   d. no; individuals tend to congregate because of resource availability

5. Zero population growth occurs when
   a. immigration and emigration are equal.
   b. the biotic potential is reached.
   c. natality and mortality are equal.
   d. both (a) and (c), but not (b)

   a. no; a partial answer; a more complete answer is available
   b. no; would probably result in rapid growth
   * c. no; a partial answer; a more complete answer is available
   d. yes; both (a) and (c) must occur for population to remain level

6. The graph of exponential growth forms a ____ curve.
   a. J-shaped
   b. L-shaped
   c. M-shaped
   d. S-shaped

   * a. yes; will continue to expand indefinitely until something slows growth down
   b. no; not a letter that refers to growth rates
   c. no; not a letter that refers to growth rates
   d. no; characteristic of a growth curve in which exponential growth has been limited

7. When organisms neither attract nor repel each other, they are most likely to exhibit
   a. uniform distribution.
   b. clumped distribution.
   c. random distribution.
   d. all of the above

a. no; not the type of distribution characteristic of organisms that do not interact
b. no; characteristic of environments in which the resources are not evenly distributed

* c. yes; since there are no specific factors influencing the distribution of organisms, they exhibit random distribution
d. no; a common distractor; only one of the above is correct

8. To experience exponential growth, a population must
a. increase.
b. increase at a constant rate.
c. not have immigration or emigration.
d. have a birth rate higher than its death rate.

a. no; population will grow, but not necessarily exponentially

* b. yes; will produce a J-shaped curve of exponential growth
c. no; both factors may affect population growth, but only if population growth occurs at a steady rate will it grow exponentially
d. no; this condition will result in growth, but not necessarily exponential growth

9. Competition and aggressive interaction lead to
a. uniform distribution.
b. clumped distribution.
c. random distribution.
d. all of the above

* a. yes; organisms tend to repel one another to reach maximum dispersal resulting in uniform dispersal
b. no; clumped resources lead to clumped distribution
c. no; random is very uncommon in nature and indicates that there is nothing in the environment that will affect distribution of individuals
d. no; one of the above is correct

10. The biotic potential of a population
a. refers to its maximum reproductive rate.
b. could theoretically be achieved under ideal conditions for a limited time.
c. is influenced by the age at which reproduction starts and the number of offspring that are produced.
d. all of the above

a. no; a partial answer; a more complete answer is available
b. no; a partial answer; a more complete answer is available
c. no; a partial answer; a more complete answer is available

* d. yes; all of the above answers are correct

11. When a population experiencing exponential growth stops growing and levels off, it has reached
a. its biotic potential.
b. its maximum density.
c. the carrying capacity of the environment.
d. competitive exclusion.

a. no; refers to the maximum offspring an organism can produce
b. no; maximum density varies, based upon the age and size of the individuals as well as the quality of the environment

* c. yes; the more appropriate answer because the population has reached the limits of the environment, and various factors in the environment begin to dampen population growth until it stops
d. no; refers to the interaction of two species in competition

12. A population may not reach its full biotic potential because
a. some limiting factor is present.
b. predation, pollution, or competition may influence survival and/or reproduction.
c. environmental resistance prevents the population from reaching its carrying capacity.
d. all of the above

a. no; a partial answer; a more complete answer is available
b. no; a partial answer; a more complete answer is available
c. no; a partial answer; a more complete answer is available

* d. yes; all of the above answers are correct

13. Which of the following is constant?
a. reproductive potential
b. carrying capacity
c. environmental resistance
d. none of the above

a. no; many factors affect reproductive rates
b. no; the number of individuals that can be sustained in a given area varies from time to time depending on environmental conditions
c. no; the interaction of all of the limiting factors would be expected to vary over time

* d. yes; none of the above are constant

14. Which of the following leads to an increase in population size?
a. emigration
b. immigration
c. natality
d both (b) and (c), but not (a)

a. no; organisms leave the population
b. no; a partial answer; a more complete answer is available
c. no; a partial answer; a more complete answer is available
* d. yes; both (b) and (c) are correct, and (a) is incorrect

15. Which of the following is *not* a density-dependent factor controlling population growth?
a. predation
b. parasitism
c. competition
d. drought

a. incorrect; is a density-dependent factor; a large number of predators will reduce a population and if the number dropped, the pressure on the prey population will relax
b. incorrect; is a density-dependent factor; the more organisms are forced together by a large population, the greater the chance that parasitism will occur
c. incorrect; is a density-dependent factor; the denser the population, the greater the competition among organisms
* d. correct; the number of organisms in a population does not affect the intensity of a drought

16. A cohort is a group of individuals in a population that
a. are the same age.
b. belong to the same phenotypic group.
c. are of the same sex.
d. die of the same cause.

* a. yes; all members of the same age
b. no; would be described as those that had a particular trait
c. no; they would simply be described as male or female
d. no; they would simply be described as those that died of a particular cause

17. The bubonic plague is transmitted by
a. fleas.
b. flies.
c. mosquitoes.
d. cockroaches.

* a. yes; living on infected rodents
b. no; another arthropod vector transmits the disease
c. no; another arthropod vector transmits the disease
d. no; another arthropod vector transmits the disease

18. A type III survivorship curve is characteristic of all but which of the following?
a. marine invertebrates
b. songbirds or lizards
c. most insects
d. plants

a. no; large number of deaths immediately after hatching and then chances of death are low throughout life
* b. yes; songbirds and lizards have about equal chance of dying throughout their entire life
c. no; large mortality early in life
d. no; large mortality early in life

19. Which of the following is the closest approximation of current birth rates?
a. 10,000/hour
b. 1,700,000/week
c. 90,000,000/year
d. all of the above

a. yes; a partial answer; a more complete answer is available
b. yes; a partial answer; a more complete answer is available
c. yes; a partial answer; a more complete answer is available
* d. yes; all of the above answers are correct

20. Which of the following led to dramatic increases in human population?
a. domestication of plants and animals leading to agriculturally based urban societies
b. the end of the bubonic plague
c. the start of the industrial revolution
d. all of the above

a. no; a partial answer; a more complete answer is available
b. no; a partial answer; a more complete answer is available; a temporary drop of 25 million people during the plague
c. no; a partial answer; a more complete answer is available
* d. yes; all of the above answers are correct

21. The current exponential growth
a. will double the world's population in about fifteen years.
b. will add one billion new people in about twenty-five years.
c. is not sustainable.
d. all of the above

a. no; it will take about forty years
b. no; it may take less than ten years
* c. yes
d. no; a common distractor; but only one is correct

22. Which of the following is *not* a country characterized by large numbers of immigrants?
a. Australia
b. United States
c. Canada
d. Japan

a. incorrect; many immigrants
b. incorrect; many immigrant
c. incorrect; many immigrants
* d. correct; few immigrants

23. The greatest annual population growth occurs in
    a. Africa.
    b. South America.
    c. Europe.
    d. Asia.

    * a. yes; greatest
    b. no; second greatest growth
    c. no; least growth
    d. no; intermediate growth

24. Population growth rate is greatest during the
    a. preindustrial stage.
    b. transitional stage.
    c. industrial stage.
    d. postindustrial stage.

    a. no; high birth and death rates with little population growth
    b. no; high birth rates and low death rates with much population growth
    * c. yes; both birth and death rates decline
    d. no; zero population growth is reached

25. Mexico would be classified as a country belonging to
    a. preindustrial stage.
    b. transitional stage.
    c. industrial stage.
    d. postindustrial stage.

    a. no; underdeveloped countries belong to this stage
    * b. yes
    c. no; not that far advanced
    d. no; not that far advanced

26. If family planning programs were fully successful,
    a. the replacement level in less developed countries would be 2.5/woman.
    b. the replacement level in more developed countries would be 2.1/woman.
    c. it would take sixty years for zero population growth to occur.
    d. all of the above

    a. no; a partial answer; a more complete answer is available
    b. no; a partial answer; a more complete answer is available
    c. no; a partial answer; a more complete answer is available
    * d. yes; all of the above answers are correct

27. The reason that the human population has increased to such a high level is
    a. we have expanded into new habitats and climatic zones.
    b. we have increased the carrying capacity of existing habitats.
    c. we have sidestepped several limiting factors.
    d. all of the above

    a. no; a partial answer; a more complete answer is available
    b. no; a partial answer; a more complete answer is available
    c. no; a partial answer; a more complete answer is available
    * d. yes; all of the above answers are correct

28. The deadly disease that has had seven major epidemics this century and whose current strain is not affected by vaccines is
    a. the bubonic plague.
    b. the flu.
    c. cholera.
    d. tuberculosis.

    a. no; only one major epidemic
    b. no; numerous epidemics, but is not generally described as deadly
    * c. yes; a serious and deadly epidemic of cholera frequently occur in Asia and Africa
    d. no; although tuberculosis is making a comeback as a serious disease

29. An age-structure population graph of a rapidly growing country
    a. resembles a pyramid with a broad base rather than a diagram with all age classes about the same dimensions.
    b. shows a disproportionate number of males.
    c. shows a relatively small number of people in prereproduction categories and major increase in the number of those in the reproductive category.
    d. all of the above

    * a. yes
    b. no; usually almost the same sex ratio
    c. no; large number of prereproductive stage
    d. no; only one choice is correct

30. Which of the following statements is false?
    a. Even if every couple only had two offspring, it would take sixty years to reach population stability.
    b. Once the birth rate and death rate matches, zero population growth has been reached.
    c. To reach zero population growth, the number of children a couple would need to have would be slightly less than two.
    d. More than a third of the world's population is fifteen or younger.

    a. no; this statement is true
    b. no; this statement is true
    * c. yes; this statement is false; couples would need to have slightly more than two children on the average to insure replacement level
    d. no; this statement is true

# CHAPTER 36

# COMMUNITY INTERACTIONS

1. In the rain forests of New Guinea, there are nine different species of pigeons because there are at least nine different ___ in the rain forest.
   a. habitats
   b. nesting sites
   c. niches
   d. fruits or food sources

   a. no; habitats control number of organisms, not number of different species
   b. no; these control amount of reproduction and density of population
   * c. yes; each species has its own distinct niche
   d. yes; although fruits and food sources would control population size and pigeons could feed on more than one food source; a better answer is available

2. The structure of a community is influenced by
   a. climate and topography that dictates the physical features of the community.
   b. the number and type of resources in a community that determines the species that live there.
   c. the individuals in a community that have similar adaptive traits.
   d. all of the above

   a. no; a partial answer; a more complete answer is available
   b. no; a partial answer; a more complete answer is available
   c. no; a partial answer; a more complete answer is available
   * d. all of the above

3. From a community standpoint, diversity refers to the number of different
   a. genotypes.
   b. individuals.
   c. habitats.
   d. species.

   a. no; would be most likely referred to as genetic diversity to avoid confusion
   b. no; would be most likely referred to by the term *density*
   c. no; diversity is a biological feature, not a physical feature, of a community
   * d. yes

4. The full range of environmental and biological conditions an organism can live is its
   a. niche.
   b. habitat.
   c. community.
   d. adaptation.

   * a. yes; a niche involves the response of an organism to its complete environment
   b. no; the habitat is the physical space where an organism is found
   c. no; the community involves the biological aspect of an organism
   d. no; adaptations are features that enable an organism to fit into its niche

5. In which of the following reactions is one species benefited while the other species is not harmed?
   a. predation
   b. commensalism
   c. parasitism
   d. competition

   a. no; one species is benefited, the other is harmed
   * b. yes; one species is benefited, the other is not harmed or helped
   c. no; one species is benefited, the other is harmed
   d. no; both species are harmed

6. The decline in the hare population is produced by
   a. increase in the number of lynx.
   b. lack of food for the lynx/hare populations.
   c. stresses to the hares from feeding on toxic plants coupled with increased predation by the lynx.
   d. changes in physical factors that are completely independent of biotic considerations.

   a. no; not the critical factor
   b. no; not the critical factor
   * c. yes; toxic plants allow for lynx predation to reduce population size of the hares
   d. no; sometimes may reduce both populations but would not give the oscillation pattern produced by the interaction of the lynx and hare

7. A yucca moth and a yucca plant exhibit
   a. commensalism.
   b. parasitism.
   c. mutualism.
   d. symbiosis.

   a. no; in commensalism, only one species is benefited, but both are benefited in this relationship
   b. no; neither is parasitic; the yucca moth is a pollinator and a predator
   * c. yes; both are benefited
   d. no; in symbiosis, the organisms are associated for life, but in the yucca plant and yucca moth the relationship is temporary

8. In a commensal relationship
   a. both species benefit.
   b. one species gains while the second loses.
   c. one species gains while the second is essentially unaffected.
   d. both species are negatively affected.

   a. no; mutualism
   b. no; parasitism or predation
   * c. yes; by definition
   d. no; competition

9. If the yucca moth were to become extinct, then
   a. some other insect would fill its niche.
   b. the yucca plant would become extinct.
   c. the seeds of the yucca plant would develop without interference from the moth.
   d. nothing else would happen, and there would simply be one less species on earth.

   a. no; no candidates are immediately available; it is unlikely that enough time would be available for another insect to fill the niche
   * b. yes; no way for pollination to occur, and therefore reproduction could not be accomplished
   c. no; if the yucca moth were extinct, there would be no seeds
   d. no; the yucca plant depends upon the yucca moth for survival

10. Mycorrhizae and plants are
    a. symbiotic.
    b. parasites/hosts.
    c. commensal.
    d. mutualistic.

    * a. yes; they are permanently associated and benefit by the relationship
    b. no; the fungus is not parasitic because it provides an advantage to the plant
    c. no; both benefit
    d. no; because both are permanently associated; there is a better answer

11. When two niches overlap, ____ occurs.
    a. symbiosis
    b. commensalism
    c. mutualism
    d. competition

    a. no; the two organisms supply what each other needs
    b. no; only one benefits, and the other is unaffected
    c. no; requires that the organisms be permanently associated
    * d. yes; the organisms have the same needs and whenever there is a shortage of a resource, they compete for it

12. Resource partitioning
    a. is the reason for competition.
    b. explains the competitive exclusion principle.
    c. tends to reduce competition.
    d. leads to a lower carrying capacity.

    a. no; it reduces competition
    b. no; it tends to reduce the overlap of niches
    * c. yes; the organisms use different resources so they do not compete as often
    d. no; it increases carrying capacity and allows more organisms to survive in a habitat

13. The interaction of predator and prey is an example of
    a. disruptive selection.
    b. coevolution.
    c. stabilizing selection.
    d. directional selection.

    a. no; disruptive selection results in two forms of a species, such as occurs in sexual dimorphism
    * b. yes; the interaction between species A and species B results in changes in each, resulting in evolution of both
    c. no; stabilizing selection results in reduced variability
    d. no; directional selection involves changes in one population, not an interaction between both populations

14. Which of the following is *not* an example of coevolution?
    a. development of sexual dimorphism in a species
    b. the interaction of pollinator and flower
    c. the development of parasitism
    d. development of mimicry

    * a. correct; may result from disruptive or differential selection
    b. incorrect; both interact to result in coevolution of both organisms
    c. incorrect; another example of coevolution in which the longer the two are together, the less severe is the reaction between them
    d. incorrect; in coevolution, the more noxious the model, the more successful the mimic

15. From an evolutionary perspective, the longer a parasite has been associated with a particular host species,
    a. the greater number of offspring it will produce.
    b. the more likely it is that the host will develop a defense against the parasite and severe reactions would develop in the host as soon as the parasite enters the host.
    c. the less likely it is that the host will develop any symptoms that would indicate the presence of the parasite.
    d. no relationship can be drawn, for the interactions between parasites and hosts are too variable to enable generalizations.

    a. no; there is no relationship between length of host/parasite association and the number of offspring; number of offspring is more likely to be related to the difficulty of the parasite of completing its life cycle
    b. no; it would be a disadvantage to the parasite if the host reacted adversely to its presence
    * c. yes; through coevolution, the longer the two species are together, the less likely that symptoms will develop when host is infected
    d. no; the longer the association, the less violent the interaction

16. A brightly colored organism is likely to be
    a. toxic, dangerous, or bad tasting.
    b. a slow-moving defenseless form.
    c. found in habitats such as caves where its color would not be noticed.
    d. a form of aggressive coloration typical of many predators.

    * a. yes; a predator will quickly learn to associate the color pattern with negative results, thereby increasing survival chances for the brightly colored forms
    b. no; these defenseless forms would quickly become extinct under unrestricted predation pressure
    c. no; in such habitats, the colors would go unnoticed and not be effective; cave forms are often drab in color or albino
    d. no; warning coloration is a defense, not an offense; most predators are cryptic (hidden) so they may get close to their prey

17. Moment-of-truth defenses involve
    a. warning coloration.
    b. startle display behavior.
    c. mimicry.
    d. none of the above

    a. no; a continuous feature of their appearance
    * b. yes; a pattern of visual display or other defense that enables the organisms to escape
    c. no; a continuous feature of their appearance
    d. no; one of the above is a moment-of-truth defense

18. Moths and butterflies in Hawaii are being killed by
    a. wasps imported to control other organisms.
    b. DDT.
    c. excessive competition.
    d. habitat destruction.

    * a. yes; the biotic control organism also attacked moths and butterflies
    b. no; no longer used in Hawaii
    c. no; no evidence that the competition is more severe than usual
    d. no; although this is one of the most common reasons for decline in natural populations

19. The reason that water hyacinths became a pest in the southeastern United States in the twentieth century was
    a. the introduction of the manatee, which destroyed the hyacinth competitors.
    b. the completion of the intercoastal waterway, which gave the hyacinth access to the entire Southeast.
    c. the lack of any native competitors to keep it in check once it was introduced into this country.
    d. the development of many man-made impoundments that provided a new habitat that enabled them to flourish.

    a. no; the manatee is actually one animal that reduces the hyacinth population
    b. no; no correlation whatsoever
    * c. yes; typical of exotics that have no natural controls once they become established
    d. no; water hyacinths can become established in any waterway

20. In a community of annual plants, mallow plants
    a. grew where their shallow fibrous roots could extract moisture quickly.
    b. became established early in deep soil where their taproots were effective.
    c. were found in shady areas away from excess heat and drying sunlight.
    d. grew only in areas where the soil was continually wet.

a. no; mallow plants have taproots
* b. yes; the structure of the root system allowed them to dominate areas where early moisture allowed the taproot to become established
c. no; no information that would support the idea that light was a critical factor controlling distribution or survival
d. no; not supported by the information given; smartweed was characteristic of the wet areas

21. According to the definition used by the book, which of the following is *not* a predator?
a. goat
b. tapeworm
c. mosquito
d. leopard

a. no; considered a predator on thistle or whatever plant it feeds upon
* b. yes; considered a parasite because it stays with its host for a long period of time
c. no; a predator
d. no; a classic predator

22. Parasitoids
a. are true parasites.
b. are nonliving viruses that infect and kill their host.
c. are parasites that are restricted to human hosts.
d. can be an effective biotic control for some type of pests.

a. no; they are insect larvae that usually kill their hosts, whereas parasites seldom kill their hosts
b. no; parasitoids are not viruses, but insect larvae
c. no; parasitoids seldom infect humans
* d. yes; more effective than pesticides, and pests do not develop resistance to them

23. Which of the following is *not* characteristic of organisms that are camouflaged?
a. an irregular color pattern that masks the shape or characteristic of an organism
b. a pattern that startles or gives warning, such as a large eyespot
c. a color pattern that resembles the background of the area where the organism is found
d. a modification in behavior that enables an organism to pass undetected

a. incorrect; typical camouflage such as patterns painted on warships
* b. correct; an example of warning coloration
c. incorrect; typical of well-known animals such as chameleons, anoles, and bottom fish that change to resemble their background
d. incorrect; behavior has to be modified or camouflage will not be successful; for example, an insect that resembles a twig must be motionless or it will be eaten

24. Pioneer species are characterized by all but which of the following?
a. small plants with numerous seeds that are easily dispersed
b. often symbiotic with nitrogen-fixing soil microbes
c. perennial plants that can store energy to gain advantage in competition early in the growing season
d. small low-growing plants that often start from scratch at the beginning of the growing season

a. incorrect; need to be able to reach areas where succession is beginning
b. incorrect; there is little or no nitrogen in a bare area where succession starts
* c. correct; not characteristic of pioneers, but of later stages in succession; these features would enable these plants to outcompete early successional species in a mature community
d. incorrect; typical of plant in early successional stages

25. Which of the following is an example of primary succession?
a. an area where a glacier retreats
b. an abandoned farm
c. a shallow pond
d. an area that has been burned

* a. yes; a newly exposed area subject to invasion for the first time
b. no; an example of a disturbed system that is subjected to secondary succession
c. no; the pond life fills in during succession
d. no; the recovery from fire is an example of secondary succession

26. A keystone species can be identified by
a. an introduction of a competitor into an ecosystem.
b. its ability to survive environmental stress.
c. removal experiments.
d. population studies.

a. no; there can be a number of responses to competition
b. no; some very hardy species may be able to withstand extreme physical conditions but be threatened by biotic factors
* c. yes; as different species are removed, the greatest effect develops after the removal of a keystone species
d. no; population changes can respond to any biotic or environmental factors

27. Fire tends to favor the growth of
a. sequoia trees.
b. cedar trees.
c. oak trees.
d. dogwoods.

* a. yes; their seeds germinate only in the absence of shade-tolerant plants with little litter on the forest floor
b. no; although fire tends to remove competition, there is no evidence that this plant survives fire better or grows better after a fire
c. no; although fire tends to remove competition, there is no evidence that this plant survives fire better or grows better after a fire
d. no; although fire tends to remove competition, there is no evidence that this plant survives fire better or grows better after a fire

28. Which of the following exotic organism came from Argentina?
a. chestnut blight
b. carp
c. starling
d. fire ant

a. no; from Asia
b. no; from Germany
c. no; from Europe
* d. yes; from Argentina

29. The classic example of the upset of the balance of nature is exemplified by the introduction of _____ into Australia.
a. ostriches
b. rabbits
c. parrots
d. sea lamprey

a. no; these are native to Australia
* b. yes; underwent a population explosion
c. no; not a problem in Australia
d. no; a problem in the Great Lakes, not Australia

30. Sursey Island
a. is a new volcanic island off the coast of Iceland.
b. is an area where the dispersal of organisms is being actively studied in natural experiments.
c. demonstrates both the distance and area effected for island distribution.
d. all of the above

a. no; a partial answer; a more complete answer is available
b. no; a partial answer; a more complete answer is available
c. no; a partial answer; a more complete answer is available
* d. yes; all of the above

31. Which of the following are considered specialists?
a. humans
b. houseflies
c. crows
d. body lice

a. no; an omnivore with wide latitude of tolerance
b. no; a common versatile insect
c. no; an omnivore with a wide range of activities
* d. yes; a highly specialized parasite

32. The final organisms in ecological succession are the
a. climax species.
b. pioneer species.
c. dominants.
d. invaders.

* a. yes; the organisms best adapted to this particular environment
b. no; the first organisms to enter an environment
c. no; refers to the most common organism in the community that will change with time
d. no; there can be many kinds of invaders at different times in a given area

33. The orderly change in the species composition of a community is known as
a. succession.
b. progression.
c. colonization.
d. all of the above

* a. yes; *succession* is the ecological term for progressive change
b. no; the word implies orderly succession but is not used to describe the sequence of biological organisms
c. no; might be an appropriate term for early changes in a community
d. no; a common distractor; only one of the above is correct

34. Which of the following is an example of secondary succession?
a. the development of a community on a lava flow
b. the revegetation of an area after a fire
c. the development of vegetation on bare granite rock
d. the development of plants on new sand dunes

a.   no; an example of primary succession

*   b.   yes; the process of succession is interrupted by fire and the succession process is set back and has to start over

c.   no; an example of primary succession

d.   no; an example of primary succession

# CHAPTER 37

# ECOSYSTEMS

1. Krill are
   a. small crustaceans that are food for baleen whales.
   b. the waste materials discarded by tourists in Antarctica.
   c. birds that migrate from the equator to breed in Antarctica.
   d. small rabbitlike mammals that live in Antarctica.

   * a. yes; a small aquatic form that is an essential food for many of the marine animals in Antarctica
   b. no; there has been considerable waste discarded by tourists in Antarctica, but krill is a living organism
   c. no; krill are not migrating birds
   d. no; krill are not small mammals

2. Krill are
   a. shrimplike aquatic animals.
   b. the sole food for the Adelie penguins.
   c. food for baleen whales.
   d. all of the above

   a. no; a partial answer; a more complete answer is available
   b. no; a partial answer; a more complete answer is available
   c. no; a partial answer; a more complete answer is available
   * d. yes; all of the above are correct

3. An ecosystem is a
   a. complex of organisms and their physical environment.
   b. group of interacting organisms sharing the same habitat.
   c. group of interbreeding organisms sharing the same gene pool.
   d. group of interacting physical factors found in an environment surrounding a community.

   * a. yes; by definition
   b. no; a community
   c. no; a species
   d. no; leaves out the biotic component and not broad enough

4. Which of the following statements is false?
   a. Biogeochemical cycles are global in scale.
   b. The flow of energy in a ecosystem is one-way.
   c. Ecosystems are open systems with inputs and outputs of energy and nutrients.
   d. Nutrients flow through the ecosystem from producers to consumers, but not in the other direction.

   a. no; this statement is true
   b. no; this statement is true
   c. no; this statement is true
   * d. yes; this statement is false; nutrients from consumers can be picked up by producers

5. The origin of energy in an ecosystem is (are) the
   a. carnivores.
   b. sun.
   c. herbivores.
   d. all of the above

   a. no; they derive their energy from herbivores
   * b. yes; the sun's energy is captured in photosynthesis by plants
   c. no; they derive their energy from the sun
   d. no; a common distractor; only one of the above is correct

6. Which of the following groups gets energy from partly decomposed organic material?
   a. decomposers
   b. detritivores
   c. parasites
   d. omnivores

   a. no; extract energy from the remains or products of organisms
   * b. yes
   c. no; the food source for parasites is definitely living organisms
   d. no; this group feeds on anything

7.   Which of the following statements is false?
     a.   All organisms other than the primary producers are heterotrophs.
     b.   Herbivores belong to the second trophic level.
     c.   Decomposers are assigned to the fourth trophic level.
     d.   Carnivores are found in the third and upper trophic level.

     a.   no; this statement is true
     b.   no; this statement is true
*    c.   yes; this statement is false; the decomposers may fit in any trophic level other than the first
     d.   no; this statement is true

8.   Which of the following statements is false?
     a.   Biogeochemical cycles occur on a global scale.
     b.   Human activities tend to support the stability of ecosystems.
     c.   Producer organisms supply energy for others in the ecosystem.
     d.   Energy flows in only one direction in an ecosystem.

     a.   no; this statement is true
*    b.   yes; this statement is false; human activities tend to disrupt stability
     c.   no; this statement is true
     d.   no; this statement is true

9.   Which of the following includes earthworms, crabs, and nematodes?
     a.   decomposers
     b.   detritivores
     c.   parasites
     d.   omnivores

     a.   no; fungi and bacteria
*    b.   yes; extract energy from partially decomposed material
     c.   no; includes tapeworms, flukes, and ectoparasites
     d.   no; includes humans, primates, and some birds

10.  The living world encompasses
     a.   an ecosystem.
     b.   a biome.
     c.   a habitat.
     d.   the biosphere.

     a.   no; involves a larger limit
     b.   no; involves a larger limit
     c.   no; involves a larger limit
*    d.   yes; the biosphere is that portion of the earth's crust, water, and atmosphere where life is found

11.  Which group secures nutrients and energy for the ecosystem?
     a.   producers
     b.   decomposers
     c.   consumers
     d.   detritivores

*    a.   yes; plants store food energy through photosynthesis and supply minerals
     b.   no; function in the cycling of elements but don't supply food
     c.   no; use both nutrients and energy but don't supply food
     d.   no; use fragments and partially decomposed materials

12.  Which of the following statements is true?
     a.   Ecosystems are closed systems.
     b.   Nutrient input equals nutrient output in all ecosystems.
     c.   Ecosystems are self-sustaining.
     d.   Energy output from an ecosystem occurs as low-grade energy (heat).

     a.   no; energy is externally supplied
     b.   no; for example, eutrophic lakes have an excess input of nutrients
     c.   no; require input of energy
*    d.   yes; an increase in entropy as governed by the laws of thermodynamics

13.  Which of the following statements is false?
     a.   The amount of energy moving through food webs differs from one ecosystem to another.
     b.   The organisms in grazing food webs and detrital food webs do not interact.
     c.   More energy passes through the detrital food web than the grazing food web.
     d.   both (b) and (c) are false, but (a) is true

     a.   no; this statement is true
*    b.   yes; this statement is false
     c.   no; this statement is true
     d.   no; only one choice is false

14.  Organisms that derive their food from partially decomposed organic material are called
     a.   omnivores.
     b.   carnivores.
     c.   herbivores.
     d.   detritivores.

     a.   no; feed on both plants and animals
     b.   no; feed on animals
     c.   no; feed on plants
*    d.   yes; feed on partially decomposed organic material

15.  A snail is an example of a
     a.   producer.
     b.   primary consumer.
     c.   secondary consumer.
     d.   tertiary consumer.

     a.   no; producers are autotrophs
*    b.   yes; snails feed on plants
     c.   no; does not feed on animals
     d.   no; found earlier on the food chain

16. A wolf is an example of a
    a. producer.
    b. primary consumer.
    c. secondary consumer.
    d. none of the above

    a. no; a wolf is not a producer
    b. no; wolves are not primary consumers or herbivores
  * c. yes; wolves are secondary consumers or carnivores
    d. no; one of the above is correct

17. Producers
    a. are the members of the ecosystem closest to the energy source.
    b. include photosynthetic autotrophs.
    c. form the base of any food chain or pyramid.
    d. all of the above

    a. no; a partial answer; a more complete answer is available
    b. no; a partial answer; a more complete answer is available
    c. no; a partial answer; a more complete answer is available
  * d. yes; all of the above are correct

18. The stem of the word *trophic* means
    a. turn.
    b. level or group.
    c. food.
    d. none of the above

    a. no; *tropism* means a growth toward or away from a stimulus but it does not have the h of *troph-*
    b. no; a word used with trophic
  * c. yes; food
    d. no; a common distractor, but one of the above is correct

19. Net primary productivity is controlled by
    a. gross primary productivity.
    b. rate of respiration by the autotrophs.
    c. activity of consumers and decomposers.
    d. all of the above

    a. no; a better choice is available; gross primary productivity determines the amount of energy fixed
    b. no; a better choice is available; the rate of respiration of autotrophs reduces the amount of energy that can be stored
    c. no; a better choice is available; the feeding of consumers and decomposers determines the amount of energy available to be stored
  * d. yes; all of the above

20. Gross primary productivity is controlled by
    a. the activity of living organisms, other than plants.
    b. the amount of sunlight received.
    c. other physical environmental factors.
    d. (b) and (c), but not (a)

    a. no; other organisms may affect net primary productivity but not gross (which is controlled by the plant)
    b. no; a better choice is available; the energy source determines how much is available for photosynthesis
    c. no; a better choice is available; other physical factors such as rainfall or temperature could affect the rate of photosynthesis
  * d. yes

21. Which of the following statements is true?
    a. Heat loss represents a one-way flow of energy out of an ecosystem.
    b. In grazing food webs, the energy flows from plants through decomposers and detritivores.
    c. In detrital food webs, energy flows from plants to herbivores and then to carnivores.
    d. all of the above

  * a. yes; there is no way available to capture this loss
    b. no; refers to detrital food webs
    c. no; refers to grazing food webs
    d. no; a common distractor; but only one is true

22. The most accurate representation of the trophic structure of an ecosystem is a pyramid
    a. with four trophic levels.
    b. of numbers.
    c. of biomass.
    d. of energy.

    a. no; the number of trophic levels varies for different ecosystems
    b. no; this pyramid could be inverted if large trees were considered
    c. no; this pyramid could be inverted if large trees were considered
  * d. yes; a better choice; indicates the amount of energy available in each trophic level

23. In discussing energy flow, energy inputs are measured in terms of energy per unit of
    a. weight.
    b. time.
    c. space.
    d. both (b) and (c), but not (a)

    a. no; amount of energy varies from one organism to another, depending on factors such as type of tissue or metabolic rate
    b. yes; a better choice is available
    c. yes; a better choice is available
  * d. yes; for example, kilocalories per square meter per year

24. About ___ percent of the energy available at one tropic level is transferred to the next.
    a. 1–5
    b. 6–16
    c. 15–23
    d. 25 or more

a. no; too little
* b. yes; the rule of 10
c. no; too much
d. no; too much

25. In nutrient cycling in an ecosystem
   a. the nutrients being recycled are organic compounds such as fats, carbohydrates, and so on.
   b. the amount of nutrient being recycled is usually less than the amount entering or leaving an ecosystem in a year's time.
   c. environmental inputs include rainfall, snowfall, sedimentation, metabolism, and the physical and chemical weathering of rocks.
   d. are primarily controlled by the producers and consumers found in the ecosystem.

   a. no; nutrients are mineral ions
   b. no; correctly stated would be the opposite of this statement
* c. yes
   d. no; primarily through decomposers and detritivores

26. The nutrient that influences the growth of land plants that is in shortest supply is
   a. carbon.
   b. nitrogen.
   c. phosphorus.
   d. potassium.

   a. no; sometimes a limiting factor
* b. yes
   c. no; sometimes a limiting factor
   d. no; sometimes a limiting factor

27. Carbon dioxide enters the atmosphere from
   a. volcanic eruption.
   b. respiration.
   c. combustion.
   d. all of the above

   a. no; a partial answer; a more complete answer is available
   b. no; a partial answer; a more complete answer is available
   c. no; a partial answer, a more complete answer is available
* d. yes; all of the above are correct

28. Nitrogen is lost to the atmosphere during
   a. ammonification.
   b. nitrification.
   c. denitrification.
   d. nitrogen fixation.

   a. no; nitrogen compounds broken down into ammonia
   b. no; ammonia is converted into nitrite or nitrate
* c. yes; nitrate converted into nitrogen gas that may be lost
   d. no; nitrogen gas converted into ammonia

29. Nitrogen scarcity may be attributed to
   a. denitrification.
   b. leaching from soil.
   c. water logging the soil causing decomposers to convert fixed nitrogen to nitrogen gas.
   d. all of the above

   a. yes; a partial answer; a better choice is available
   b. yes; a partial answer; a better choice is available
   c. yes; a partial answer; a better choice is available
* d. yes; all of the above

30. Plants that are symbiotic participants in nitrogen fixation with nitrogen bacteria belong to the ____ family.
   a. mint
   b. rose
   c. legume
   d. all of the above

   a. no
   b. no
* c. yes; only legumes seem to have this ability
   d. no; a common distractor; but only one is correct

31. DDT
   a. is insoluble in water and soluble in fat.
   b. builds up in concentration as it moves through a food chain.
   c. is a target-specific insecticide.
   d. both (a) and (b), but not (c)

   a. no; a partial answer; a better choice is available
   b. no; a partial answer; a better choice is available; known as biological magnification
   c. no; not target-specific and may affect any organism that comes in contact with it
* d. yes; (a) and (b) are correct, and (c) is incorrect

32. Which of the following statements is false?
   a. The pyramid of energy may be upside down.
   b. The pyramid of biomass may be upside down.
   c. The pyramid of numbers may be upside down.
   d. both (b) and (c) are false, and (a) is true

* a. yes; the pyramid of energy cannot be turned upside down
   b. no; this statement is true
   c. no; this statement is true
   d. no; this statement is true

33. The reservoir that has the greatest amount of carbon is
   a. plants.
   b. animals.
   c. oceans.
   d. atmosphere.

   a. no; another storage compartment
   b. no; another storage compartment
   * c. yes; the carbon dioxide fixed by the phytoplankton plus dissolved carbon dioxide and carbon in calcium carbonate shells of marine organisms
   d. no; another storage compartment

34. Which of the following statements is false?
   a. In sedimentary cycles, an element moves from land to seafloor and only returns to land by geological uplifting.
   b. The earth's crust is the main storehouse for the sedimentary cycle.
   c. Nitrogen and carbon are elements that have sedimentary cycles.
   d. There is no gaseous phase in the sedimentary cycle.

   a. no; this statement is true
   b. no; this statement is true
   * c. yes; the statement is false; they have atmospheric cycles
   d. no; this statement is true

35. Which of the following has the lowest amount of carbon?
   a. atmosphere
   b. animal life
   c. ocean
   d. plant biomass

   a. no; the major reservoir for carbon is the carbon dioxide in the atmosphere
   * b. yes; there is less carbon in animals than other sites
   c. no; there is about the same amount in the ocean as in plants
   d. no; there is about the same amount in the ocean as in plants

36. Which of the following gases is *not* one of the ones that contributes to the greenhouse effect?
   a. chlorofluorocarbons
   b. sulfur dioxide
   c. nitrous oxide
   d. ozone

   a. no; these gases contribute to the greenhouse effect
   * b. yes; this gas is not involved in the greenhouse effect but contributes to acid rain
   c. no; this gas contributes to the greenhouse effect
   d. no; this gas contributes to the greenhouse effect

37. The greenhouse gases increase the temperature of the earth because they
   a. reduce the amount of infrared radiation leaving the earth.
   b. reduce the amount of infrared radiation penetrating the earth's atmosphere.
   c. block the passage of visible light.
   d. prevent penetration by ultraviolet radiation.

   * a. yes; acts as a blanket to prevent long wave or heat energy from leaving the atmosphere
   b. no; if the infrared radiation in the incoming radiation from the sun were blocked, the temperature of earth would decrease
   c. no; they are transparent to visible light
   d. no; the ozone layer in the stratosphere is the ultraviolet shield

38. Which of the following greenhouse gases has not been increasing?
   a. ozone
   b. water vapor
   c. carbon dioxide
   d. chlorofluorocarbons

   a. no; the ozone in the stratosphere has been decreasing, but ozone in the troposphere (lower atmosphere) is a pollutant and has been increasing
   * b. yes; although water vapor is the most variable of the atmospheric gases, its overall concentration has remained relatively constant
   c. no; carbon dioxide has been gradually increasing since the beginning of the industrial revolution
   d. no; these relatively new compounds of chlorine have been increasing dramatically in the past few decades

39. The greenhouse effect is accentuated by
   a. deforestation and desertification.
   b. a decrease in photosynthetic activity and the declining biomass of the world.
   c. slash and burn destruction of the tropical rain forests.
   d. all of the above

   a. no; a partial answer; a more complete answer is available
   b. no; a partial answer; a more complete answer is available; less carbon is fixed in the biomass
   c. no; a partial answer; a more complete answer is available
   * d. yes; all of the above answers are correct

40. Which of the following statements is false?
    a. Some bacteria, volcanic action, and lightning can fix nitrogen into forms that can be used in ecosystems.
    b. Plants are the ultimate source of nitrogen for animals.
    c. Because nitrogen is one of the most common gases in the atmosphere, the availability of nitrogen is unlikely to ever develop into a limiting factor in plant growth.
    d. The action of decomposers makes nitrogen available to plants.

    a. no; this statement is true
    b. no; this statement is true
*   c. no; nitrogen does compose about 80 percent of the atmosphere, but it is unavailable until it is fixed in a form that can be absorbed by plants
    d. no; this statement is true

41. In ammonification
    a. decomposers break down the nitrogen-containing compounds in dead plants and animals.
    b. bacteria produce nitrite from ammonia or ammonium.
    c. the conversion of nitrite into nitrate is involved.
    d. all of the above

*   a. yes; the nitrogen compounds are broken down into nitrogen gas
    b. no; called nitrification
    c. no; called nitrification
    d. no; a common distractor; only one of the above is correct

42. Agriculture really became a major activity of man ____ years ago.
    a. 10,000
    b. 25,000
    c. 40,000
    d. 60,000

*   a. yes; man changed from a hunting-gathering society about this long ago
    b. no; too early
    c. no; too early
    d. no; too early

43. Which of the following statements is false?
    a. Energy exhibits a one-way flow through an ecosystem.
    b. Nutrients cycle in an ecosystem.
    c. Toxic substances concentrate as they pass through a food chain.
    d. The solution to pollution is dilution.

    a. no; this statement is true; energy only passes to the organisms that are lower on the food chain
    b. no; this statement is true; chemical elements follow biogeochemical cycles in nature
    c. no; because of the factor of biological accumulation, pollutants are reconcentrated in the food chain
*   d. yes; this statement is false because of biological magnification

44. Trophic level refers to the
    a. amount of nutrients stored in an ecosystem.
    b. reservoirs of nutrients that organisms may draw upon.
    c. the different feeding levels in a food pyramid.
    d. biogeochemical cycles in an ecosystem.

    a. no; but if all the energy or nutrients in all the trophic levels were added together, it would equal the amount stored
    b. no; there are many storage compartments for nutrients in an ecosystem
*   c. yes; the different feeding levels represent the different trophic levels
    d. no; trophic levels represent temporary deposits of nutrients in part of the ecosystem

45. Most of the water vapor in the earth's atmosphere comes from
    a. evaporation from the oceans.
    b. transpiration by vegetation.
    c. evaporation from freshwater sources.
    d. evaporation from land surface.

*   a. yes; the greatest surface area where water is available
    b. no; although much water is returned to the atmosphere in this way
    c. no; a relatively small amount of water available
    d. no; there is much more surface available in the ocean

46. Methane is produced by
    a. anaerobic bacteria in swamps and is sometimes called swamp gas.
    b. landfills.
    c. bacteria in the digestive tracts of cattle.
    d. all of the above

    a. no; a partial answer; a more complete answer is available
    b. no; a partial answer; a more complete answer is available
    c. no; a partial answer; a more complete answer is available
*   d. yes; all of the above are correct

# CHAPTER 38

# THE BIOSPHERE

1. The similarity of the desert plants of the southwest and the desert plants of Africa as well as the similarity between shrubs on the Mediterranean coast and in the chaparral is explained by
   a. evolutionary similarity.
   b. continental drift.
   c. man's intervention.
   d. peculiar distributions that have no natural explanations.

   a. no; evolutionarily different although they show similar adaptations to similar environments
   * b. yes; the plants were carried to different locations after Pangea broke up and drifted apart
   c. no; although man has substantially altered distribution patterns
   d. no; there is a satisfactory explanation given

2. Climate is influenced by
   a. topography and distribution of land and water.
   b. variations in the amount of incoming solar radiation.
   c. the earth's daily rotation and its yearly path around the sun.
   d. all of the above

   a. no; a partial answer; a more complete answer is available
   b. no; a partial answer; a more complete answer is available
   c. no; a partial answer; a more complete answer is available
   * d. yes; all of the above answers are correct

3. The sun
   a. provides energy to run ecosystems.
   b. is responsible for the different climates.
   c. controls or influences the amount of rainfall and characteristics of the soil.
   d. all of the above

   a. no; a partial answer; a more complete answer is available
   b. no; a partial answer; a more complete answer is available
   c. no; a partial answer; a more complete answer is available
   * d. yes; all of the above answers are correct

4. The global air circulation that influences weather occurs in the
   a. troposphere.
   b. stratosphere.
   c. ionosphere.
   d. mesosphere

   * a. yes; name means "turning sphere" the movement of atmosphere in this layer is responsible for our weather
   b. no; some circulation and mixing do occur here but do not produce major effects on weather
   c. no; variations here may affect communications, but generally not the weather
   d. no; movement here does not affect the weather

5. The desert and chaparral biomes are located close to ___ degrees north and south latitudes.
   a. 10–20
   b. 20–30
   c. 30–40
   d. 40–50

   a. no; too close to the equator
   b. no; too close to the equator
   * c. yes; usually on the leeward side of mountain ranges
   d. no; too far from the equator

6. Deserts occur at about 30 degrees north and south of the equator because
   a. of the prevailing easterly and westerly winds.
   b. of the subsidence (falling) of dry air that had risen over the tropics.
   c. a belt of high temperature persists in these two regions of the world.
   d. none of the above

   a. no; the east-west movement of air is not the major contributing factor
   * b. yes; the global circulation pattern brings dry air down to the earth's surface at these latitudes
   c. no; the lack of moisture, not the high temperatures, produces the deserts
   d. no; a common distractor; but one of the above statements is correct

7. Which of the following includes the other three?
    a. biosphere
    b. atmosphere
    c. lithosphere
    d. hydrosphere

* a. yes; the biosphere includes all areas where organisms live
    b. no; too limited
    c. no; too limited
    d. no; too limited

8. The Northern Hemisphere is warmer in the summer for all but which of the following reasons?
    a. The angle at which the light strikes the earth is more direct during the summer.
    b. The amount of atmosphere that the light must travel through is less in the summer.
    c. The length of the day is longer.
    d. The sun is closer to the earth.

    a. incorrect; the more direct or perpendicular the sun, the warmer the temperature; thus the earth warms up at noon, but highest temperatures come later in the day
    b. incorrect; the light is more direct so there is less atmosphere to absorb the energy
    c. incorrect; the longer the sun is up, the more energy strikes the earth and can be absorbed
* d. correct; even though the text does not point this out, the sun is actually closer to the earth in the winter, but the difference is negligible

9. Warm ocean currents are found on the
    a. western coast of the United States.
    b. western coast of Africa.
    c. eastern coast of the United States.
    d. western coast of South America.

    a. no; a cold current, the California current
    b. no: a cold current, the Benguela current
* c. yes; the Gulf Stream
    d. no; a cold current, the Humboldt current

10. Which of the following statements is false?
    a. The incoming solar radiation has different heating effects at different latitudes.
    b. Because of the earth's rotation the prevailing winds are from the west at all latitudes.
    c. The earth loses heat by evaporation or radiation.
    d. Warm air holds more moisture than cool air.

    a. no; this statement is true
* b. yes; this statement is false; it is westerly in the midlatitudes, but easterly from 0 to 30 degrees and 60 to 90 degrees
    c. no; this statement is true
    d. no; this statement is true

11. Which of the following statements is true?
    a. The rain shadow appears on the leeward side of the mountain.
    b. The vegetation at the top of the mountain is likely to consist of drought-adapted plants.
    c. Drought is characteristic of the windward side of the mountain.
    d. all of the above

* a. yes; this statement is true; the descending air warms and can hold more moisture so that rain is less likely
    b. no; this statement is false; orographic precipitation provides water, as the wet air rises it cools and releases water
    c. no; this statement is false; the windward side is the side of the mountain closest to the water source (even though there may be water on the leeward side of the mountain, the prevailing winds would carry it away from the mountain)
    d. no; only one of the above is correct

12. Which of the following statements is false?
    a. Air pressure increases as warm air rises.
    b. It takes longer for water to heat up than soil.
    c. Solar radiation tends to be less focused or concentrated at the poles than at the equator.
    d. Air tends to rise at 0 and 60 degrees and descend at 30 and 90 degrees of latitude.

* a. yes; this statement is false; low pressure is produced by rising air
    b. no; this statement is true
    c. no; this statement is true
    d. no; this statement is true

13. Which of the following statements is false?
    a. Seasonal changes are greater close to the equator.
    b. There is an annual variation in the amount of incoming solar radiation.
    c. The annual rotation of the earth around the sun produces seasonal changes in weather patterns.
    d. none of the above are true

* a. yes; this statement is false; the seasonal variation is greater toward the poles
    b. no; this statement is true
    c. no; this statement is true
    d. no; one of the above statements is false

14. Short, stunted plant species tend to be found in
    a. cold, dry latitudes at high elevations.
    b. lowlands with moderate temperature and moisture.
    c. tropical areas.
    d. wetlands with warm temperatures.

  * a. yes; of the choices given, this type of plant would be expected to be found in such a habitat
    b. no; more likely intermediate-sized plants
    c. no; usually characterized by luxuriant growth
    d. no; usually characterized by luxuriant growth

15. Which of the following statements is true?
    a. Clay soils are often characterized by excessive leaching.
    b. Clay soils have rapid percolation.
    c. Loam is a mixture of sand, silt, clay, and humus.
    d. The soil of tropical rain forests is characterized by a rich nutrient load.

    a. no; more likely to be waterlogged
    b. no; high percolation characteristic of sand and loose soils
  * c. yes
    d. no; very low nutrient content because rainwater promotes much leaching

16. Which of the following statements is true?
    a. Cold currents are found on the east side of the continents.
    b. The sea level is higher at the poles than the equator.
    c. Even though the latitude of London and Ontario is the same, London is colder.
    d. The rotation of ocean currents in the northern hemisphere is counterclockwise.

    a. no; this statement is false
    b. no; this statement is false
    c. no; this statement is false
  * d. yes; this statement is true

17. Which of the following statements is false?
    a. Only plants that are adapted to dry conditions grow on the leeward side of mountains.
    b. Monsoons are seasonal rains.
    c. Only dwarf plants, such as those found in the arctic, are found growing on the top of very tall mountains at the equator.
    d. As air descends from the top of a mountain, it can hold more water.

    a. no; this statement is true
  * b. yes; this statement is false; monsoons refer to seasonal wind patterns that may bring seasonal rainfall
    c. no; this statement is true
    d. no; this statement is true

18. The biome characterized by spectacularly flowering annuals and perennials, prickly pear, ocotillo, mesquite, and creosote bush is the
    a. desert.
    b. dry shrubland and woodlands.
    c. prairie.
    d. deciduous forest.

  * a. yes
    b. no; characteristic of the chaparral
    c. no; characterized by grasses
    d. no; characterized by trees that shed their leaves

19. The biome characterized by winter rains and fire during dry periods is the
    a. shortgrass prairie.
    b. chaparral.
    c. desert.
    d. deciduous forest.

    a. no; although fire may be a very important factor
  * b. yes; often followed by mudslides after the rains
    c. no; rainfall limited
    d. no; rainfall general

20. Distantly related species may look alike as a result of ____ evolution.
    a. divergent
    b. parallel
    c. convergent
    d. regressive

    a. no; divergent evolution results in producing differences in closely related species so that they diverge or become different
    b. no; related organisms retain similarities
  * c. yes; distantly related forms have the same adaptations to enable them to live in a particular environment
    d. no; regressive evolution refers to the loss of an advanced feature

21. Most tallgrass prairies
    a. have scattered trees.
    b. were destroyed by the Dust Bowl.
    c. have been converted to farmland.
    d. exhibit a monsoon climate.

    a. no; scattered trees occur in wet, tropical grasslands; there may be trees along stream banks in tallgrass prairies
    b. no; Dust Bowl occurred in the shortgrass prairie
  * c. yes
    d. no; characteristic of tropical grasslands

22. Short plants would *not* be the characteristic plant found
    a. in a swamp.
    b. at the top of a tall mountain.
    c. at the poles.
    d. in a desert.

* a. yes; there is no advantage for plants to be short in a swamp
   b. no; the top of a tall mountain is characterized by alpine tundra
   c. no; tundra consisting of dwarf plants and lichens is found at the poles
   d. no; small dwarf plants are less likely to be stressed by drought than tall plants

23. Which type of soil has the smallest soil particles?
    a. clay
    b. silt
    c. loam
    d. sand

* a. yes; has the smallest particles
   b. no; silt has intermediate-sized particles
   c. no; a mixture of all three soil particles
   d. no; has the largest soil particles

24. Evergreen broadleaf forests are found in all but which of the following locations?
    a. South and Central America
    b. Australia
    c. Africa
    d. East Indies and Malay Archipelago

   a. no; found there
* b. yes; not found in Australia
   c. no; found there
   d. no; found there

25. The biome characterized by bromeliads, vines, mosses, lichens, orchids, and aerial plants is the
    a. desert.
    b. tropical rain forest.
    c. temperate deciduous forest.
    d. savanna.

   a. no; requires drought-resistant plants
* b. yes; covers the upper strata of the tropical rain forest
   c. no; not warm enough or moist enough to support such plants
   d. no; a grassland with scattered trees

26. Which of the following soils is poorly aerated and may become waterlogged?
    a. clay
    b. silt
    c. loam
    d. sand

* a. yes; even though it has more pore space, water does not percolate through it easily
   b. no; intermediate in pore space and particle size
   c. no; a combination of all three soil particles
   d. no; sand allows water to percolate through the soil rapidly

27. If you wanted to convert a natural ecosystem into farmland, the one with the richest soil would be the
    a. temperate deciduous forest.
    b. grassland.
    c. tropical rain forest.
    d. evergreen coniferous forest.

   a. no; although it would have the chance to be a rich soil under some circumstances
* b. yes; has the richest soil
   c. no; the high rainfall leaches away most of the nutrients
   d. no; the soil is too acidic and the environment too cool

28. The biome that occupies much of southern and mid Canada is
    a. temperate deciduous forests.
    b. tundra.
    c. evergreen coniferous forest.
    d. chaparral.

   a. no; broad-leaved trees do not do as well in the snow as conifers
   b. no; found in the northern part of Canada
* c. yes; also called the taiga
   d. no; found primarily in California in North America

29. The tundra is
    a. characterized by evergreen trees.
    b. dominated by spruce and fir.
    c. found above the Arctic circle and above the tree line of tall mountains.
    d. is one of the most productive biomes.

   a. no; trees in the tundra are dwarf spruce and willow (tundra means treeless plain)
   b. no; dominant plants are lichens
* c. yes; the Arctic and alpine tundra, respectively
   d. no; very low productivity due to poor growing conditions

30. Which biome has the greatest daily range in temperature?
    a. tundra
    b. tropical rain forest
    c. temperate deciduous forest
    d. desert

   a. no; the coldest of the biomes, but not the greatest range in temperature
   b. no; the most uniform temperature of all the biomes
   c. no; there may be a great range of temperature in a day, but one of the other biomes has a greater range
* d. yes; the lack of moisture allows high temperature during the day from high insolation and lack of clouds allows loss of heat through radiation at night

31. Which of the following ecosystems is characterized by frequent fires?
    a. grasslands
    b. coniferous forest
    c. chaparral
    d. tropical rain forest

    a. no; grasslands are favored by fire, but there is an ecosystem where fire is more characteristic
    b. no; there are some fires, but not an essential feature as long as there are occasional fires
*   c. yes; fires are characteristic of this ecosystem, often followed by mudslides
    d. no; slash and burn is destroying this ecosystem

32. The lake zone close to shore is the
    a. limnetic.
    b. profundal.
    c. thermocline.
    d. littoral.

    a. no; open sunlit areas beyond the littoral zone
    b. no; the deep portion of the lake where it is too dark for photosynthesis
    c. no; the zone of temperature change in a thermally stratified lake
*   d. yes; the correct answer is the littoral zone

33. Overturns occur in a lake during
    a. spring and fall.
    b. summer.
    c. winter.
    d. both (b) and (c), but not (a)

*   a. yes; when the lake reaches 4° C, the water on the bottom exchanges places with water on top
    b. no; a thermocline has been established
    c. no; no change until sufficient heat has been added
    d. no; overturn occurs in spring and fall, but not in winter or summer

34. Eutrophication
    a. is characterized by a dense bloom of algae.
    b. occurs naturally as lakes age.
    c. can result from pollution of water with sewage or wastes containing nitrogen and/or phosphorus.
    d. all of the above

    a. no; a partial answer; a more complete answer is available
    b. no; a partial answer; a more complete answer is available
    c. no; a partial answer; a more complete answer is available
*   d. yes; all of the above answers are correct

35. An estuary
    a. is part fresh water and part marine.
    b. is an area of low productivity and of little value.
    c. often contains *Spartina*, a salt-tolerant marsh grass that is the base of detrital food webs.
    d. both (a) and (c), but not (b)

    a. no; a partial answer; the mixing place for fresh water from rivers with salt water from oceans
    b. no; highly productive area, often the area that forms the cradle and breadbasket for marine life
    c. no; a partial answer; often *Spartina* forms large marshes in the estuaries
*   d. yes; both (a) and (c) are correct, and (b) is incorrect

36. Diversity is greatest in
    a. upper littoral zone of a rocky shore.
    b. mid littoral zone of a rocky shore.
    c. lower littoral zone of a rocky shore.
    d. all of the above; no variation in life found in the three zones.

    a. no; environment harsh, and many animals die of desiccation or become baked by the sun
    b. no; not the highest diversity
*   c. yes; most protected and only exposed at the lowest tide
    d. no; only one of the above is correct

37. The relatively shallow waters overlying the continental shelf form the
    a. neritic zone.
    b. pelagic province.
    c. oceanic zone.
    d. benthic province.

*   a. yes
    b. no; includes the entire volume of ocean water
    c. no; water over the ocean basins
    d. no; all of the above material on the ocean bottom

38. In the neritic and oceanic zones, the photosynthetic organisms form a suspended pasture of food that provides food directly for
    a. fish.
    b. zooplankton.
    c. detrivores.
    d. carnivores.

    a. no; do not feed directly on phytoplankton
*   b. yes; zooplankton represent the trophic level next to the phytoplankton
    c. no; usually these are found on the ocean floor
    d. no; feed on herbivores, the zooplankton in this case

39. The producers in the hydrothermal vent community
   a. use sunlight as their primary energy source.
   b. use energy from chemical reactions involving hydrogen sulfide.
   c. lack any significant carnivore predators.
   d. are similar to species found in the phytoplankton at the surface.

   a. no; too deep and dark to depend upon this energy source
   * b. yes
   c. no; carnivores include clams, mussels, tubeworms
   d. no; these are chemosynthetic forms while the surface forms are photosynthetic

40. Which of the following statements is false?
   a. There are two overturns of lakes in the spring and fall.
   b. Water reaches its maximum density at 32°F or 0°C.
   c. Human activities may lead to eutrophication.
   d. Glaciers may form natural lakes.

   a. no; this statement is true
   * b. yes; this statement is false; water reaches its maximum density at approximately 40°F or 4°C
   c. no; this statement is true
   d. no; this statement is true

41. Upwelling
   a. occurs in the oceans along the margin of continents as a result of wind patterns.
   b. brings colder nutrient-rich water to the surface.
   c. supports a rich phytoplankton population that in turn supports a rich fish population.
   d. all of the above

   a. no; a partial answer; a more complete answer is available
   b. no; a partial answer; a more complete answer is available
   c. no; a partial answer; a more complete answer is available
   * d. yes; all of the above answers are correct

# CHAPTER 39

# HUMAN IMPACT ON THE BIOSPHERE

1. The problems discussed in this chapter will be resolved
   a. only by stabilizing population.
   b. by realizing that reversing current damaging trends outweighs the personal benefits of ignoring them.
   c. only through individual efforts and sacrifices, not by group activity.
   d. very quickly, once education makes enough people realize the magnitude of the problem.

   a. no; not necessarily the solution because some affluent societies expend many resources more than the LDCs (less developed countries)
   * b. yes; a philosophical change in viewpoint is necessary to resolve the problems
   c. no; only if enough individuals are involved; much more likely to accomplish goals by appealing to groups, leading to changes in popular opinion and individual support
   d. no; it's not enough to make them aware of the problem; they must be motivated to change their habits

2. The most general definition of pollutants includes the concept that pollutants are
   a. substances with which ecosystems have no prior experience.
   b. any artificial substances released into the ecosystem.
   c. fat-soluble chemicals that build up in food chains.
   d. inorganic chemicals such as toxic heavy metals.

   * a. yes; there has not been sufficient time for ecosystems to develop a way to degrade or destroy these substances
   b. no; some artificial substances such as inorganic fertilizers can cycle through an ecosystem
   c. no; this is characteristic of chlorinated hydrocarbons such as DDT
   d. no; these are often pollutants, but this definition is too limited

3. Which of the following is *not* an organic pollutant?
   a. methane
   b. peroxyacyl nitrate
   c. benzene
   d. chlorofluorocarbon

   a. incorrect; an organic hydrocarbon
   * b. correct; does not contain carbon
   c. incorrect; a six-carbon hydrocarbon that is usually one of the first compounds considered in an organic chemistry course
   d. incorrect; an organic compound

4. The major cause for photochemical smog is
   a. nitrous oxides from cars and trucks.
   b. carbon monoxide and carbon dioxide from combustion.
   c. sulfur dioxide from coal-fired power plants.
   d. chlorofluorocarbons.

   * a. yes; react with sunlight and hydrocarbons to form photochemical smog
   b. no; do not react with sunlight to form photochemical smog
   c. no; involved more in acid deposition than in photochemical smog
   d. no; involved in ozone destruction

5. The 1952 air pollution disaster that killed 4,000 people occurred in
   a. Pittsburgh.
   b. London.
   c. Chicago.
   d. New York.

   a. no; a polluted area, but has not had an air pollution disaster
   * b. yes; caused by industrial smog (use of high sulfur coal)
   c. no; a polluted area, but has not had an air pollution disaster
   d. no; a polluted area, but has not had an air pollution disaster

6. Which of the following is true about acid deposition?
   a. It is produced by coal-fired power plants, industrial plants, and metal smelters.
   b. It reaches the ground only when the sulfur and nitrous oxides combine with water in the atmosphere to form acid rain.
   c. It is equally damaging no matter where it occurs.
   d. It affects only living organisms.

* a. correct; this statement is true; these are the major sources
b. incorrect; this statement is false; dry acid deposition is common
c. incorrect; this statement is false; some areas are very sensitive, whereas others have alkaline soils that will help buffer against acids
d. incorrect; this statement is false; a common cause in the destruction of statutes, metals, mortars, rubber, plastic, and nylon stockings

7. Acid rain is a major problem in the ____ part of North America.
a. northwestern
b. southwestern
c. northeastern
d. southeastern

a. no; the wind patterns in this part of the continent do not concentrate acid rain in this area
b. no; the wind patterns in this part of the continent do not concentrate acid rain in this area
* c. yes; because of the concentration of industries and the prevailing winds
d. no; the wind patterns in this part of the continent do not concentrate acid rain in this area

8. Chlorofluorocarbons are released from
a. aerosol propellants.
b. coolants in refrigeration and air conditioning units.
c. the process involved in the formation of styrofoam and packaging material.
d. all of the above

a. yes; a partial answer; a more complete answer is available
b. yes; a partial answer; a more complete answer is available
c. yes; a partial answer; a more complete answer is available
* d. yes; all of the above are correct

9. In primary treatment of sewage,
a. sludge is filtered from the water and is treated with chlorine.
b. microbial populations break down organic matter.
c. waste water is trickled through gravel or aerated.
d. reverse osmosis, stripping nitrogen from ammonia, and use of ultrasonic energy vibration may be used.

* a. yes; primary treatment
b. no; secondary treatment
c. no; secondary treatment
d. no; tertiary treatment

10. The major component of solid waste is
a. plastic.
b. garbage.
c. paper products.
d. glass.

a. no; another substance
b. no; another substance
* c. yes; over 50 percent of solid waste
d. no; another substance

11. Modern agriculture employs massive use of
a. pesticides.
b. fossil fuels.
c. fertilizers.
d. all of the above

a. yes; a partial answer; a more complete answer is available
b. yes; a partial answer; a more complete answer is available
c. yes; a partial answer; a more complete answer is available
* d. yes; all of the above are correct

12. Tropical rain forests are characterized by all but which one of the following?
a. rich source of nutrients in the understory and soil
b. slash-and-burn agriculture/shifting cultivation
c. the richest and most diverse flora and fauna in the world
d. an extremely rapid rate of extinction

* a. correct; not characteristic of tropical rain forests; very little nutrients available anywhere in this ecosystem
b. incorrect; this is a characteristic; efforts to provide more food leads to cutting and burning the ecosystem
c. incorrect; this is a characteristic ; there are more species here than in the rest of the world
d. incorrect; this is a characteristic; more and more species go extinct each day as the ecosystem is exploited

# CHAPTER 40

# ANIMAL BEHAVIOR

1.  Animal behavior involves the
    a.  nervous system.
    b.  skeletal-muscular system.
    c.  endocrine system.
    d.  all of the above

    a.  no; a partial answer; a more complete answer is available
    b.  no; a partial answer; a more complete answer is available
    c.  no; a partial answer; a more complete answer is available
    *   d.  yes; all of the above answers are correct

2.  Which of the following is false?
    a.  Behavior differences may be controlled by one gene.
    b.  There is a genetic component to behavior.
    c.  For a bird to learn its song, it must hear the song during development.
    d.  Hormones affect the internal environment of an organism but do not have an effect on its behavior.

    a.  incorrect: this statement is true; textbook gives the example of sparrow songs that could be affected by one gene
    b.  incorrect; this statement is true; to be able to respond to certain signals, organisms must be capable of recognizing signals.
    c.  incorrect; this statement is true; in the textbook example, the white-crowned birds were unable to sing their songs because they did not hear them during development
    *   d   correct; this statement is false; hormones are responsible for sexual maturation and animals are not aware of sex signals until they mature

3.  Melatonin
    a.  is secreted by the parathyroid gland.
    b.  suppresses the growth and function of the gonads.
    c.  increase and the lack of sunlight in the winter triggers the migration of birds.
    d.  levels increase in the spring and initiate sexual reproduction.

    a.  no; secreted by the pineal gland
    *   b.  yes; for reproduction to occur, the levels of melatonin must drop
    c.  no; migration not controlled in this manner
    d.  no; melatonin level drops in the spring, allowing gonads to develop

4.  The ability (not the trigger) of the male to sing is controlled by
    a.  melatonin.
    b.  estrogen.
    c.  testosterone.
    d.  insulin.

    a.  no; sexual maturity
    *   b.  yes; for the development of brain and sound system
    c.  no; testosterone is a triggering mechanism
    d.  no; does not have any responsibility in singing

5.  Which of the following statements is false?
    a.  Humans do not exhibit instinctive behavior.
    b.  Male birds must hear their song during a critical period after birth to be able to sing it when mature.
    c.  Young cuckoo birds will push other eggs out of a nest.
    d.  Human infants will smile at any mask with dark eyespots.

    a.  correct; this statement is false because humans do exhibit instinctive behavior
    b.  incorrect; this statement is true; an example of imprinting, a time-dependent form of learning
    c.  incorrect; this statement is true; cuckoos lay eggs in other birds' nest and the young cuckoos simply get rid of potential competition by eliminating eggs
    *   d.  incorrect; this statement is true; an example of human instinctive behavior

6.  Imprinting involves
    a.  failure to respond to unimportant stimuli; for example, a dog learns to ignore its master banging his pipe as he cleans it.
    b.  young birds adopting large moving inanimate objects as their parents.
    c.  reflex actions.
    d.  development of an internal clock.

    a.  no; this is known as habituation
    *   b.  yes; the object may be another species; or young birds may even imprint on humans
    c.  no; imprinting is learned behavior not reflex,
    d.  no; the internal clock is independent of imprinting

7. Altruistic behavior is best defined as
   a. innate behavior.
   b. selfish behavior.
   c. self-sacrificing behavior.
   d. learned behavior.

   a. no; though some altruistic behavior may be innate
   b. no; just the opposite
 * c. yes; similar to the golden rule
   d. no; perhaps partially learned, partially instinctive

8. Newborn garter snakes from the interior of California
   a. preferred banana slugs to tadpoles.
   b. rejected banana slugs because they tasted similar to leeches.
   c. were the offspring of snakes that were not killed by eating leeches.
   d. both (b) and (c) are correct

   a. no; those from the coastal area preferred banana slugs
   b. yes; a partial answer; a more complete answer is available
   c. yes; a partial answer; a more complete answer is available
 * d. yes; both (b) and (c) are correct

9. For birds, singing
   a. is a way for a male to attract a female.
   b. is a method of establishing a territory.
   c. reduces the number of conflicts between male birds.
   d. all of the above

   a. no; a partial answer; a more complete answer is available
   b. no; a partial answer; a more complete answer is available
   c. no; a partial answer; a more complete answer is available
 * d. yes; all of the above answers are complete

10. Which of the following species does *not* produce female defense behavior?
   a. lions
   b. elks
   c. red-winged blackbirds
   d. sage grouse

   a. incorrect; exhibit clustering behavior
   b. incorrect; exhibit clustering behavior
   c. incorrect; exhibit clustering behavior
 * d. correct; no harem involved

11. Which of the following organisms are strongly cued by tactile signals?
   a. majority of birds
   b. honeybees
   c. bats
   d. wolves

   a. no; seldom come in direct contact with other birds
 * b. yes; the round and tail wagging dances are examples
   c. no; seldom come in direct contact with other bats
   d. no; wolves mark their territories with scent pheromones

12. Altruism leads to
   a. natural selection.
   b. kin selection.
   c. disruptive selection.
   d. none of the above

   a. no; natural selection may favor altruism, but altruism does not necessarily lead to natural selection (the less alert may also be saved by altruistic behavior)
 * b. yes: altruistic behavior may save close relatives thereby allowing related genes to be passed on to the next generation
   c. no; there is no specific altruistic behavior that would result in developing disruptive selection
   d. no; one of the above is correct

13. Which of the following does *not* commit suicide in defending other members of its species?
   a. soldier termites
   b. bees
   c. spiders
   d. ants

   a. incorrect; commit suicide in defending others
   b. incorrect; commit suicide in defending others
 * c. correct; most are nonsocial and do not defend other spiders
   d. incorrect; commit suicide in defending others

14. In insects
   a. suicidal behavior is adaptive.
   b. sterility is adaptive.
   c. close relatives benefit from kin selection.
   d. all of the above

   a. yes; a partial answer; a more complete answer is available
   b. yes; a partial answer: a more complete answer is available
   c. yes; a partial answer; a more complete answer is available
 * d. yes; all of the above are correct